CAD/CAM TECHNIQUES

Michael F. Hordeski

Reston Publishing Company, Inc.
A Prentice-Hall Company
Reston, Virginia

Library of Congress Cataloging in Publication Data

Hordeski, Michael F.
  CAD/CAM techniques.

  Bibliography: p.
  Includes index.
  1. CAD/CAM systems. I. Title. II. Title:
C.A.D./C.A.M. Techniques.
TS155.6.H67 1985   670'.28'54   84-24965
ISBN 0-8359-0620-5

To my mother, who allowed me to pursue the study of the technical world.

CAD/CAM has more potential to radically increase productivity than any development since electricity.
                    The National Science Foundation of the United States

Production supervision/interior design:
Tally Morgan

© 1986 by
Reston Publishing Company, Inc.
A Prentice-Hall Company
Reston, Virginia

10 9 8 7 6 5 4 3 2 1

Printed in the United States of America

CONTENTS

PREFACE

This book on *Computer-Aided Design and Manufacturing Techniques* provides a complete overview of modern design and manufacturing methods which employ computers.

CAD/CAM will play an ever increasing role in design and production circles. It is likely to become one of the major growth areas of the 80s and 90s. International competition, inflation and price factors, the high cost of capital due to rising interest rates, the decreased availability of skilled labor, and the increased emphasis on quality are forcing manufacturers to automate much of their design and production. Service firms that support or supply these manufacturers must also automate many of their functions in order to compete.

The dramatic changes in computing power allow lower costs for equipment that does more. This provides an increased capacity for CAD/CAM techniques at all levels. It also makes a knowledge of CAD/CAM equipment and technology more critical. Manufacturers who do not utilize CAD/CAM techniques are expected to find it difficult to survive in the late 80s and almost impossible to compete in the 90s.

Business will continue to improve in many markets that had been depressed, but the companies that will do best are those that utilize automated design and manufacturing equipment and CAD/CAM techniques. CAD/CAM techniques are of interest to those who are involved in manufacturing or use automated equipment. This includes the users and suppliers of data-processing equipment, software, and services on both the domestic and international fronts.

Parts of the book are written in nontechnical language; these sections will be particularly useful to those involved in the overall management of systems and plants. Other sections, such as Chapters 5 and 6, give details of design in enough depth for practicing enginers and engineering faculty.

Chapter 1 introduces the complete field of CAD/CAM. It covers the major topics of the book.

Chapter 2 continues the topic of interactive graphics with an emphasis on the user interface. Chapter 3 approaches the same subject in terms of the technology and hardware used in present-day systems.

The topic of modeling is the subject of Chapter 4. Electronic circuits are one of the more mature areas in modeling, since a great deal of effort has gone into analytical techniques for computer-aided circuit analysis. Much of this work can be extended into the other areas of modeling and simulation which are discussed in this book.

Chapters 5 and 6 continue the treatment of computer-aided circuit analysis with a discussion of modern analysis techniques and the methods currently available for their application.

Chapter 7 is concerned with a different area of modeling—the geometric models that are used in mechanical design. Chapter 8 goes on to discuss the many mechanical design techniques that are available as tools.

Manufacturing applications are the subject of Chapter 9. Here we are concerned with such subjects as data processing and communications, factory-related software, the use of microcomputers in the factory, industrial networks, machine mobility, robots, unconventional materials, automated handling systems, vision systems, object recognition, interactive systems for plant modernization, and plant floor layout.

Chapter 10 explores the entire future realm of CAD/CAM technology and includes such topics as flexible manufacturing systems (FMS), computer-integrated manufacturing (CIM), automated test and inspection systems, automated storage and the new environment, automated factories, and the new technologies that may be used for interactive systems.

The first three chapters are common to any curriculum that treats the subject of CAD/CAM. The next three chapters are of particular interest in electrical engineering, and Chapters 7 through 9 contain material of interest in mechanical engineering and related disciplines. The final chapter offers material relating to the future which should be of interest to all groups. The exercise and review questions are designed to draw the reader into many of the basic topics and in many cases will require an extension of the material presented. The references listed in the bibliography allow additional research and study of many topics.

This book would not have been possible without the help of a number of others. For their support and assistance on this project I wish to thank Karen Bashara of Adage, Robert Duncan and Terence Binion of Catronix, Kevin Ryan, Joyce Anderson, and Paul Murphy of Lexidata, Bruce Gladstone of FutureNet, Dan Bowman and Ray Barger of Spectragraphics, Douglas Bombay of Engineering Automation Systems, William Ewer of Lasergraphics, Ralph Manildi of Nicolet Computer Graphics, Tom Lazear of T & W Systems, and a special thanks to the red-haired lady who helped in so many ways throughout the preparation of this book.

The present trends in computer automation are aimed at developing unified systems for directing the activities of interconnected groups of robots and other automatic machines. This is expected to pave the way for totally automated factories and offices. Total automation does not mean a factory or office without people but rather one automated to the fullest practical extent.

Most factory and office systems in the future will be made up of workers teamed up with robots and other automated machines. How well these systems operate will depend to a large extent upon the expertise that went into the selection and implementation of the technology. Thus, there is a great need for technical information and expertise in this area, for if computer-aided systems are to be successfully implemented in any situation, they must be fully understood.

We know that the face of business is changing quickly, and so must the management strategies that we have kept, in many instances, far too long. Management must understand the new technologies in order to beneficially employ them without serious disruption of business operations.

MICHAEL HORDESKI, P.E.
Atascadero, California

INTRODUCTION TO CAD/CAM

1

Computer-aided design and computer-aided manufacturing, or CAD/CAM, can encompass the entire range of engineering activity. The use of computer aids may be also called computer-aided engineering, or CAE. Manufacturers can use many of these activities in an integrated process for the entire range of product design and development. In this process, product development time and cost are reduced substantially by a heavier reliance on computer simulation methods rather than prototype development and testing.

CAD/CAM systems allow most routine engineering tasks to be performed quickly, since they automate the repetitive functions, performing these tasks more quickly and accurately than would ever be possible by manual methods. Since the information is stored in computer memory instead of hard copy, the transfer of data tends to be quicker, more reliable, and less redundant.

CAD/CAM systems free one from these tedious, time-consuming chores that have little to do with ingenuity. Experience has shown that CAD/CAM speeds the design and manufacturing process, while reducing much of the paperwork and repetition that hampers one's productivity and creativity.

In a typical CAD/CAM system, the user interacts with the computer using a graphics terminal, designing and manufacturing a part with information stored in the computer database. With CAD the user constructs a geometric model, analyzes the structure, performs kinematic studies, and produces engineering drawings. Using a CAM system, the user can create instructions for machine tools, produce process plans for fabricating an assembly, program robots to handle tools and workpieces, and coordinate plant operation using a factory management system (Figure 1-1).

More realistic displays make it easier to generate truer representations. Programs allow one to change views, perspectives, and shadow placements. Displays can be animated or highlighted for instructional, promotional, or simulation purposes.

Complex products can be observed as they will appear in final form. Geometric flaws are revealed before the design is transformed into hardware.

CAD/CAM EVOLUTION

Design engineers have been using computers for many decades, but the use of CAD/CAM techniques has increased greatly in the last few years, owing to several related trends. One of the most important of these is the drastic reduction in the cost of computing. This cost reduction makes it practical to solve complex problems and to perform elaborate simulations that previously were beyond the reach and scope of many organizations.

Mass-produced microprocessors have played an important role in this dramatic cost reduction. They evolved from the interaction of technology and the market. Semiconductor manufacturing advanced to the point where a

3

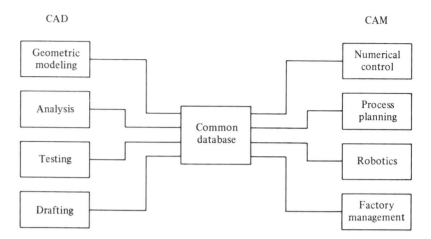

Figure 1-1 CAD/CAM functions.

computer could be fabricated on a chip (Figure 1-2). At the same time the volume of semiconductor products being sold became great enough to support the investment necessary to build and test microprocessors. As the market made microprocessors an attractive product, many quickly appeared. The *micro* part of the name evolved from the fact that the processor is fabricated on one chip, or a small number of chips. The name now has little to do with its capabilities.

The number of transistors that can be included on a 200-mil square chip of silicon provides microprocessors with instruction sets larger than those available in many early minicomputers. Microprocessors are now used in products ranging from simple entertainment devices to sophisticated instruments.

Consumer applications have been important to the industrial marketplace, since they make up a large part of the total market for microprocessors, which helps reduce prices and stimulates development. The effects of volume pricing and product competition are illustrated in the case of the hand-held calculator, which originally cost hundreds of dollars when introduced and today is sometimes given away as an advertising gift.

Microprocessors function in consumer and industrial applications both as controllers and as computers. When used as controllers, they are embedded in the equipment in such a way that their existence is not obvious to a user. The user of a high-speed printer, for example, is not aware that pushing the control buttons initiates the execution of a program in a microprocessor. The justification for the microprocessor in these applications is the equal or greater functional capability it provides at lower costs than the alternatives.

The low cost of mass-produced, general-purpose microprocessors affords flexible components which may be adapted through programming to

Figure 1-2 Intelligent peripheral controllers. Microprocessor devices such as these have made CAD/CAM hardware more affordable. (Courtesy: Rockwell International)

provide the different functions required by a wide variety of products.

The machine-language instructions required by any computer are a limiting factor in productivity. Higher-level languages, along with improved system software, have made the computer easier and simpler to use. Many high-level languages are currently available. The limitations of available software have been due in large measure to the recent emergence of microcomputers. As software developers can expect more satisfactory means of recovering their program-development investments, more substantial software support for microcomputers will be offered.

The other components of a computer, the peripherals, particularly those with electromechanical parts, initially provided a sharp contrast to the processors. But mass production has brought the price of peripherals down to the point that these devices represent costs similar to those of the processor. In recent years, less-expensive peripheral equipment has been designed specifically for use with microcomputers. The level of performance of these peripherals is such that it integrates well with the performance of most microcomputers currently on the market.

Microcomputers differ from larger computers in application and experience. The biggest difference is in philosophy: the microprocessor is an inexpensive device that can be customized to perform a specialized task. The existence of this inexpensive device has changed the way in which computer solutions are designed and implemented. Computer systems can now use microcomputers as components for system solutions. As a basic building block of these systems, a microprocessor can be defined as a component that is capable of performing arithmetical and logical operations under program control.

Microprocessors date from about 1971, and since that time the term microprocessor has generally referred to the computer-on-a-chip concept as defined above. Prior to 1971, and in isolated cases afterward, the term had a different meaning. Before 1971, a microprocessor was a processor that executed microinstructions; thus it was a processor that was micropro-grammed. This use of the term appeared particularly in the academic literature. Since about 1971, the term has referred to a computer-on-a-chip device. All of the world's leading general-purpose computer manufacturers have products which contain microprocessors. These microprocessors include advanced large-scale-integrated devices with speeds and computing power equivalent to or better than that of most minicomputers of past years.

SOFTWARE CHARACTERISTICS

Another key to the emergence of the CAD/CAM industry was the creation of software which made it possible to perform the required analysis and simulations on this new generation of affordable computers. A *program* consists of the series of instructions which, when operated on by the computer, result in the performance of the required function. These instructions, when present in the processor, consist of patterns of digits which represent combinations of numbers or symbols. At this level the instructions are known as *machine code*. Programs can be written directly in this code, but the process is very tedious and difficult. Thus most programming is done using a language which can be converted into machine code by means of another program, such as a compiler.

The *low-level languages* are the simplest form of language. They consist of instructions which have an exact equivalent in machine code. This simplification of programming is achieved by making the instructions mnemonic, such as using the letters ADD for an addition instruction. The areas of storage are given labels, which are referred to within the program, both for addressing the data-storage areas and for the program instructions. The actual numerical addresses of the storage areas are inserted when the program is converted into machine code.

Low-level languages may also incorporate certain software facilities, such as the ability to call into the program standard subroutines and housekeeping packages for input and output operations. Since low-level languages have a one-to-one relationship with the processor's machine code, they can usually be converted only into the machine code for a particular computer.

High-level languages are more powerful than low-level languages, since they enable the programmer to use single instructions which involve large numbers of machine-code instructions. This has the effect of simplifying the programming, since fewer instructions need to be coded in order to produce the required result. Various kinds of programs are used on computer systems. The programs written to do some kind of useful task, such as plotting data or making calculations, are called *application programs* or *source programs*. These are generally written in a high-level language such as FORTRAN or BASIC. The FORTRAN or BASIC programs must be translated into machine language to actually control the computer circuits. This translation takes place using either an interpreter or a compiler.

The *compiler* or *interpreter* operates on the high-level language and produces the version of the program called the *object program*. The object program is constructed of machine code so that it will run directly on the computer.

FORTRAN

As a computer language, FORTRAN has had a great influence as well as staying power. FORTRAN's basic form and style have changed little in thirty years. The language has acquired new features and capabilities. It has been standardized twice, in 1966 and 1977, and we can expect to see other standardizations in the future.

Besides winning its own popularity, FORTRAN inspired BASIC, which is essentially a streamlined and simplified version of the FORTRAN language. Although it can be used as a general-purpose programming language, FORTRAN's main use is in scientific and engineering applications, and this is the area where it is used today.

Its special capabilities for scientific calculations along with the thousands of subroutines that have been developed in FORTRAN are primarily responsible for its continued use. The existence of many FORTRAN programs that can be used and adapted for scientific or technical purposes means that the language is still very useful, no matter how elegant and efficient the newer languages become.

FORTRAN has provisions for the standard programming constructs such as looping, branching, subroutines, functions, and the assignment of values to variable names. It supports a number of data types, including:

1. Integer.

2. Single- and double-precision floating-point (real) numbers.

3. Complex numbers.

4. Logical (Boolean) expressions.

5. Strings.

The only structure available for organizing data is the *array*. The variables in FORTRAN may have names of up to six characters, beginning with a letter. Variable names beginning with the letters I through N usually represent integers.

The FORTRAN program or subroutine consists of the following:

1. A header statement in which the program is named.

2. A series of specification statements in which data types may be specified and array dimensions declared.

3. A list of executable statements that makes up the body of the program.

FORTRAN programs use a rigid format that dates back to the earlier years when programs were entered statement by statement on 80-column punched cards. Spaces were reserved for labels in the first five columns, and a character in the sixth column indicated that a statement was continued from the line above. The actual program statements were in columns 7 through 72. Blanks are ignored, so B OD is the same as the variable BOD. The letter C or an asterisk in column 1 indicates a comment to be ignored by the compiler.

The line numbers in FORTRAN programs are used only where required to control loops, conditionals, or GOTO statements. Line numbers are used as shown below:

```
DO    50 I = 1,20
         .
         .
         .
         .

50     CONTINUE
       GOTO 200
200    IF (A) 10,20,30
```

The arithmetic IF statement in FORTRAN branches to:

1. The first line number if the value of A is negative.

2. The second line number if it is zero.

3. The third line number if it is positive.

FORTRAN also allows a logical IF statement that executes a command based on the true or false value of a logical expression. FORTRAN's input and output statements require a specific format for the reading, writing, and printing of data. Subroutines can be called from within a program or from another subroutine using a CALL statement. Functions which return values can be used directly within an algebraic expression, such as the function $E(C)$ as used in $(A+B*E(C))$.

The major strength of the language in scientific and technical programs is its algebraic formulas, which are written in almost the same format as conventional mathematical formulas.

A sample FORTRAN program follows, in which we compute the mean of real numbers which are in an array A. The number of elements in A is NUM. The computed mean is returned in the argument Mean.

```
        Calculating Subroutine;
        Integer Num A        ; Defines variables
        Real A(Num A), Mean
            Sum = 0.0
            Do 100 I = 1, Num A
              Sum = Sum + A(I)
    100  Continue
            Mean = Sum/Num A
            End
        Calling Subroutine;
          Program Test
          Dimension R (5)
          R (1) = 1
          R (2) = 2
          R (3) = 3
          R (4) = 4
          R (5) = 5
          Call Rmean (R, 5, Answer)
          Write (*, 200) Answer
    200  Format ('The mean is:', F5.2)
          End
```

BASIC

BASIC was written to allow students to learn programming easily by trial and error. The immediate error messages are simple, and program changes are easy to make and test. A SYNTAX ERROR IN LINE 10 means just that. In order to provide the rapid interaction, BASIC is *interpreted*: the program is converted line by line into machine language. This conversion occurs each time the program is run, so BASIC programs can be up to 50 times slower than similar programs written in FORTRAN. FORTRAN programs are always compiled; the entire program is converted at once to machine language. A compiled program can be inconvenient to debug, because you work with the source program and then recompile it. An interpreted program is more convenient to debug but runs slower.

Since it is relatively easy to write, run, and modify programs in BASIC, the language encourages a trial-and-error approach to programming. One can start with simple statements and extend or expand them in a number of directions. We could start with a program that calculates and prints the squares of the numbers from 1 to 10:

```
10   FOR I = 1 to 10
20   PRINT I, I*I
30   NEXT I
```

The comma on line 20 instructs the computer to print the numbers I and I*I in separate columns. Then for the results, we type RUN.

```
RUN
1      1
2      4
.      .
.      .
.      .
10     324
```

Suppose we want a program to print the sum of the squares. We can define two new variables, SUM and SQ, and write

```
 5   LET SUM = 0
10   FOR I = 1 TO 10
15   LET SQ = I*I
20   PRINT I,SQ
25   LET SUM = SUM + SQ
30   NEXT I
40   PRINT SUM
```

This program will print the numbers and their squares along with the sum of the squares at the end of the list. The number of squares can also be listed as an option for the user, as shown below:

```
 2   PRINT "HOW MANY SQUARES DO YOU WANT?"
 4   INPUT N
 5   LET SUM = 0
10   FOR I = 1 TO N
15   LET SQ = I*I
```

```
20   PRINT I,SQ
25   LET SUM = SUM + SQ
30   NEXT I
40   PRINT SUM
```

The fact that the program was easily modified illustrates one of the key aspects of BASIC. The program can start with a simple idea that the programmer extends and expands. Since the final program is not part of the original plan, as the program evolves and new variable names are added and new lines squeezed in, the clarity of the original program can become lost. This approach permits many small patches and changes, and the modifications made to each section eventually become obscure to the programmer. One can design BASIC programs that are well structured and relatively easy to read. But it's easy to learn BASIC in a way that fosters bad programming habits. An example is the frequent use of the GOTO command, which transfers control from a line in the program to another line. This can cause the sequence of command execution in a complex BASIC program to overlap and interweave.

It is also possible to write a convoluted program in a language such as FORTRAN, but it is less likely. The fact that the language is compiled rather than interpreted encourages planning, since the entire program must be recompiled after even minor changes. Structured languages like Pascal make it even harder to write badly organized programs, because they don't allow one to jump from one line to another at will. The cost of this structure is a loss of flexibility.

The following program illustrates how to manipulate string variables. The purpose is to determine if a particular string, sometimes called a *search string*, is contained within another string called the *text string*. This program might be a subroutine in a larger program used to store and manipulate text or data strings in a CAD system.

```
10    INPUT "ENTER TEXT" SA$
20    INPUT "ENTER STRING TO FIND" SB$
30    INPUT "ENTER STARTING POSITION" SP
40    GOSUB 100
50    IFSF = 0 THEN 80
60    PRINT "FOUND AT POSITION" SF
70    GOTO 10
80    PRINT "NOT FOUND"
90    GOTO 10
100   SF = 0:REM START OF SUBROUTINE
110   FORSJ = J = SP TO LEN(SA$) − LEN(SB$) + 1
120   IFSB$ MID$(SA$, SJ, LEN(SB$)) THEN 150
130   SF = SJ
140   SJ = LEN(SA$) − LEN(SB$) + 1
```

```
150  NEXT SJ
160  RETURN
```

A string variable is indicated by a $ at the end of the variable name. SA$ is the name of the text string and SB$ is the name of the search string. SP is the number of the position in the text string at which the search starts. SF is the position at which the search string is found. If the string is not found, SF will be 0.

The program has two parts. The first part identifies a text string, search string, and the starting position and prints the result of the search. This part tests the subroutine and would not be used if the routine were used in a larger program.

The routine itself begins in line 100 and ends with a RETURN command at line 160, which returns control of the program to line 50, which is the line after the subroutine call. The value of SF is initially set to 0. If the string is never found, this value never changes. Lines 110 to 150 form a FOR-NEXT loop in which the loop variable SJ increases from the value of the starting position of SP to a number that is one more than the difference between the lengths of the two data strings.

Line 120 checks to see if the search string is equal to the part of the text string that starts at the present value of SJ. If it is not equal, the condition on line 120 is true and control is transferred to line 150, where SJ is increased by one and the loop is repeated. If it is equal, the condition is false and lines 130 and 140 are executed, setting the values of SF to the present value of SJ and then setting SJ to the value that ends the loop.

The original Dartmouth BASIC was limited in its capabilities, and many newer versions have been produced. Nearly every BASIC used on today's computers has enhanced options tailored to the particular machine. Most versions of BASIC are capable of string manipulations, single- and double-precision arithmetic, and transcendental functions. The more sophisticated versions for engineers can do matrix manipulation. The need for versions tailored to various machines has made it difficult to transfer programs from one machine to another.

Pascal

As a result of the design of newer computer languages that make large programs easy to create, understand, and maintain, Pascal emerged. It is a structured programming language created by Niklaus Wirth and named for the seventeenth-century French mathematician Blaise Pascal. It has proved successful in the creation of large programs and has become a significant commercial programming language in the era of modern computers. Being a *structured language* means that a Pascal program is made up of smaller programs, each of which is a structured program. Since variables and names can have a high degree of flexibility, the programs are easy to read. Pascal variables must be specified at the beginning of the program, which avoids errors. The large variety of data types, together with a capability for defining new data types, makes the language suitable for a range of applications.

All variables and their types are declared in a special section at the beginning of the program. The fact that each programmer-defined symbol and its uses must be declared is a major reason why Pascal programs tend to be free of errors and easy to modify.

Pascal is compiled rather than being interactively interpreted like BASIC. Thus, program preparation is separate from testing and execution. In Pascal a text editor is normally used in program preparation. Then the prepared text, or *source program*, is submitted to a compiler to translate the source code into object code. Changes in the source code require the programmer to go back and recompile the program. Because they are not interpreted, Pascal programs run much faster than BASIC programs.

A Pascal program has three major sections:

1. The header.
2. The declaration.
3. The body.

This is illustrated below:

```
Header        PROGRAM TEST
Declaration   VAR
                 data: String;
Body          BEGIN
                 data: = 'max',
                 writeln (data);
              END.
```

The header is made up of the keyword PROGRAM and the name of the program. The declaration section is a listing of the variables, data, and subprograms used. Only one variable is declared in the example; this is the string called data. The body of the program is made up of statements or commands in Pascal. The statements in the body of this example give the value 'max' to the variable and display it on the screen.

Pascal encourages the programmer to combine different primitive data objects to form new higher-level ones. It offers all the simple data types commonly found in other languages: Boolean character, integer, and real. Pascal's Boolean logic does not include bit manipulations. The original Pascal did not include strings, but strings are now found in most versions.

In addition, Pascal includes:

1. Sets (structured collections of data objects).
2. Records (hierarchical data structures).
3. Arrays (tables of identical kinds of data objects).
4. Pointers (indirect references to data).
5. Files (external aggregates of records).
6. Programmer-defined data types.

The programmer's ability to define data types is a powerful feature in CAD/CAM applications. As an illustration of this capability, we write

```
TYPE
  color = (red, yellow, green);
```

This defines the data type "color" that can be given to variables. Then we write

```
VAR
  pipe : color;
```

This declares a variable named pipe whose permissible values are the symbols red, yellow, and green. Then a statement like

```
pipe : = red;
```

assigns pipe the value red.

The *set* is a data type which allows one to define variables whose values are collections of other values. The set serves to collect the values so we can define a variable called liquids as shown below:

```
VAR
  liquids : SET OF color;
```

This assigns the variable *liquids* values that are collections of colors. We may have sets of characters, sets of integers, or, as illustrated, sets of programmer-defined types.

The following Pascal program asks the user for two numbers, prints the sum of those numbers, and asks if the job is done. If the user types YES, the process stops. Otherwise, a REPEAT-UNTIL loop repeats the entire process.

```
PROGRAM add numbers until done;
VAR
```

```
   a, b, t :REAL;
PROCEDURE get number (VAR X  :  REAL);
BEGIN
   write ('Enter a number: ');
   readln (x);
END;
PROCEDURE do_total (x, y  :  REAL; VAR sum  :  REAL);
BEGIN
   sum := x + y;
END;
PROCEDURE report_total (z  :  REAL);
BEGIN
   writeln ('TOTAL = ', z);
END;
FUNCTION done  :  BOOLEAN;
VAR
   ch  :  CHAR;
BEGIN
   write ('Done?');
   read (ch);
   writeln;
   IF (ch IN ['YES', 'y']) THEN done := TRUE
   ELSE done := FALSE;
END;
BEGIN
   REPEAT
   get number (a);
   get number (b);
   do_total (a, b, t);
   report_total (t);
   UNTIL done;
END.
```

Note that each part of the process uses a separate procedure or function, as shown in the body of the program, which starts with BEGIN. At the top of the listing are the program name and the variable declaration. The procedure and function definitions make up most of the program, each with its own heading, declaration, and body.

Procedures can be nested within programs and may also be nested within each other, further increasing the modular structure of the program. Procedures can also contain parameters which apply the same action to a number of inputs and produce different outcomes. Thus, the procedure with parameters is not unlike a recipe.

Many simple programs are designed for quick solutions to particular problems. Here the use of Pascal may not be required. The characteristics of Pascal that tend to make it unsuited for small programs are a result of its strengths as a programming language. The discipline required by the language makes large programs easier to understand, but it may be used for small programs also. For the development of large programs or for the creation of tools that will be used over and over again, such as operating systems, Pascal is very useful. Pascal is now the required language for advanced-placement courses in computer science for high school students.

An experienced programmer can write structured programs in any language, but learning the principles of structured programming can be easier using Pascal. Pascal's utility is relative and may depend on which language you learn first. We can become accustomed to the first language we learn, making it the standard by which others are judged. Even the poorer features of the more familiar language become necessities, and any new language can seem inferior.

The memory labels used in any high-level language are translated into the actual physical memory locations by the compiler or interpreter program. A compiler translates the entire source program into a complete object program, which then runs on the computer. An interpreter does not operate on the entire source program at once. It translates each program statement into object code and then executes the object code of the statement. The interpreter operates on each source program statement, one at a time. The advantage is that changes can be made to the source program easily. BASIC programs that run on interactive terminals will generally operate on interpreters.

Interpreters require that the interpreter program itself reside within the computer memory while the application program is executed. With compilers, only the translated object code needs to reside in memory during the execution. Since the compiler does not operate while the program is running, more memory space is freed for the application programs. The difference in translation methods used by compilers and interpreters results in different system implementation. Compilers and interpreters must be designed for individual computers because these programs are intimately tied to individual characteristics of the computer, such as the instruction mix and how the computer is physically laid out (the architecture).

We are also concerned with how much memory it contains. A Fortran application program will run on any computer for which a Fortran compiler is available. But the Fortran object code compiled on a computer with 48K of main memory will not run on a computer containing only 24K of memory, even if the two computers are the same in every other way.

The computer operating system (OS) is the program that supervises other programs running on the computer. When several users at different terminals all use a CAD computer system, the OS prevents one program from interfering with others. The speed at which a CAD system can interact with users at terminals depends on how efficiently the OS handles its tasks. A multiprogramming OS allows the computer to work with several programs, although only one program executes at any given time. The OS runs one portion of the program, then switches to another program in the queue while the first program waits for data from a peripheral device or some other slower process. A program runs until it signals the computer that it can no longer run, either because it is waiting for another operation to occur or because it has finished processing.

The OS will start running the highest-priority program ready to execute. A disadvantage in multiprogramming is that the computer requires time to switch between the program portions while it keeps track of what part of the program was executing when it stopped. This housekeeping can cause delays when many terminals are working simultaneously.

A multitasking OS does not run portions of programs in a queue. It runs programs in response to the requests or interrupts coming from terminals or other equipment. An interrupt initiates another program. When it is finished, the computer switches to a background program that runs until another interrupt occurs. The peripheral equipment generates interrupts when it needs to transmit or receive data. This OS can operate at high speeds without being burdened with the slow response found in multiprogramming systems.

Operating systems which use both multiprogramming and multitasking are available for most computers. The disadvantage with using such an OS is that it may require a larger mass memory and more main memory. Some CAD system vendors write their own OS software and supply it with their systems. OS software from computer manufacturers may be preferable because an OS from a computer manufacturer is more widely used and therefore is more likely to have had most of the flaws removed.

A program frequently used on computer systems is the loader program. All computer systems use loaders, but only some users will have any contact with these programs because many systems have built-in loaders. In many computers the loaders are a part of the read-only memories in the machine, and the loader program automatically runs as soon as the power is turned on.

The most common type of loader is known as a *bootstrap* loader. It brings programs into the main memory to run them. This type of loader allows the computer to recognize data from input devices and put the incoming data into the memory. The bootstrap loader is also used to load the operating system into the memory. Other basic loaders operate in a similar fashion. They place data into main memory without interpreting it.

Another type of loader is the *relocating* loader. This program will operate on object programs produced by interpreters or compilers, which have no specific memory locations assigned. The relocating loader is loaded before the object program, and it places the object-program segment at the locations in memory which are assigned to them.

CAD Software Characteristics

Many CAD systems may not be fully ready to run when they arrive from the manufacturer. These systems may lack some of the software necessary to perform the complete range of functions that the user needs.

Although the manufacturers of CAD equipment will supply a considerable amount of software, most systems will still require some programming to be done onsite. This programming is generally done by the user and concerns specific design practices or needs peculiar to the installation.

The drawings of a particular class of parts may require a certain type of dimensioning, or one may need a number of parts having a similar outline. If stored in a special program, the part outline can be called every time it is needed. Then the other characteristics, such as dimensions and details, can be modified for the design.

As an aid in creating drawings interactively, CAD systems may use special CAD programming languages. One such language is similar in appearance and structure to FORTRAN and is designed to allow the creation of any part within a family of parts by specifying the geometric parameters. These characteristics are used for entering a specific geometry into a database from which the user builds a library of repetitively used parts. Alternate designs can be created, or existing designs can be modified and combined into the database from which a bill of materials is generated.

Other design languages also use Fortranlike statements and can be used with FORTRAN routines. The language statements can be assigned unique names and permanently filed in a database for future use. The part definitions which are created can also be filed for future use.

These languages save terminal time, since they allow the operator to define parts much more quickly. The time savings can be significant with complicated parts.

These interactive languages use routines that create and alter graphics on the CRT screen immediately, in real time, once the routine is called. Most CAD systems that use CRTs operate interactively.

Another operating mode, called the *batch mode*, may also be used to run CAD programs. Batch-mode programs run completely at one time, with no interactions occurring between the programmer and the program while the program is running. CAD programs which run on time-sharing service are often run in a batch mode.

Special features may be included in the CAD system language to aid in the definition of part characteristics that can later be used in the database. The information in the database can then be used as a basis for manufacturing. As an example, the language can be used to generate numerical-control tool paths. These tool paths can be translated automatically into the part programming, which can then be sent to a processor for a machine-tool link. This eliminates the need for manually generating the geometry and tool-motion program.

Other software features may define the characteristics in the drawings that can be extracted for wiring lists, bills of materials, and other manufacturing functions. This type of feature is called an *attribute function*.

The designer assigns descriptive data to symbols on the drawings. These attributes can be in the form of text fields or mathematical expressions, and they provide a method of linking to the programs for extracting data. Typical attributes can be part numbers, part names, material, or pipe or hold size.

Some CAD systems can be classified as turnkey systems. The term *turnkey* arises because the CAD system is ready to run with complete hardware and software. A high-level language structure is commonly used in turnkey CAD systems. This short routine is designed to draw concentric circles on a CRT screen. It accepts typed-in commands for the circle radius, line increments, and number of concentric circles. The circle is entered using a lightpen. Once defined, the routine can be called up by touching a digitizing pen to an area on a digitizing pad. To associate the routine with the pad area, an editor routine prompts for the name of the routine to be put on the pad. The user then types in the routine name, which for this example is TOP, then a carriage return. Whenever the defined pad is stroked with the digitizing pen, the concentric circle routine begins as follows:

CRT terminal	Comment
PROGRAM TOP	Program name.
PROMPT "USER CODE"	
PROMPT "ENTER STARTING RADIUS"	Write the information in quotes on the CRT screen.
INPUT RADIUS	Accept a number typed in the keyboard.
PROMPT "ENTER INCREMENT"	
INPUT INCREMENT	
PROMPT "HOW MANY:"	
INPUT NUMBER	
PROMPT "DIGITIZE FOR CENTER"	
P = PDG DIG	Note the point on the CRT screen that the digitizer touches.
RAD R	Make R a radius.
FOR 1 = 1 TO NUMB	Make R a radius.
C = CRC	Make point the center of circle C.
PERM C	Draw circle C on the screen.
R = R + INC	Define a new R equal to R + INC.
RAD R	Make point the center of circle C.
CONTINUE	Continue the process until all circles are drawn.
END	

The CAD equipment for a turnkey system may come from various manufacturers. The system vendor makes these hardware components operate correctly as a single unit, then writes and installs software to perform the CAD functions. The resulting system allows the user to plug in the equipment turnkey and immediately operate the keyboard. In the turnkey approach to CAD the user depends on the turnkey vendor to keep the system running, to implement the software modifications, and to change peripherals such as plotters or terminals.

Users having computer expertise may not wish to obtain all the system components from a single vendor. Buying equipment and integrating it into a CAD system can be less costly than obtaining everything from a single vendor. The system may even offer higher performance.

GRAPHIC TECHNIQUES

The other element which was important in the development in this triad of CAD/CAM technologies was interactive graphics. This provided a window through which the computer could be reached and observed. Graphic terminals provide a means of communication so natural to humans now that graphics-based systems are evaluated on the basis of how friendly they are to the users operating them.

Computers formerly required operators who were thoroughly familiar with programming and computer technology. Training was so specialized that a mystique and following developed for certain machines and operations. The newer systems can be operated through graphic displays and require no knowledge of programming or detailed computer technology. This new generation of equipment now puts powerful computers within the reach of a larger range of users.

In the 40s, users were required to communicate with computers directly in machine language, consisting of sequences of zeros and ones. A single number or letter of the alphabet would be represented by a code such as

I 0010001

Writing the codes for even a simple routine was tedious and time-consuming and required considerable experience in machine-language programming.

These low-level languages gave programmers direct control over details of computer hardware such as memory locations, registers, and input/output ports. High-level languages distance programmers from these details, forcing them instead to work with abstractions such as files, arrays, and variables. The lowest level is machine language, and the highest level tends to imitate a natural language such as English.

Assembly language is one step above machine language. It uses alphabetic abbreviations for instructions and symbolic names for memory circuits and data. Compare a machine-language command

```
I 00100001
1 0001111
00001000 I
```

with an assembly-language command

```
I LD
HL
MEMLOC
```

and its meaning:

```
I load
register HL
with the value of the variable MEMLOC
```

By the mid-50s, programming was simplified with symbolic coding in which sets of English-language-like statements stood for specific standard computer commands. Programming languages such as FORTRAN used compilers to convert the statements automatically into machine-language equivalents.

These high-level languages took care of the hardware details automatically and allowed the programmer to think in terms of the application at hand. A single BASIC command such as

```
PRINT USING
"###.##"
I /100 I
```

replaced many machine-level instructions. This convenience entails some loss of efficiency and flexibility. A few languages such as C and FORTH offer some of the efficiency of machine language together with the power of high-level languages. However, these languages are not widely used.

Many languages are created to serve specific purposes such as teaching, controlling industrial robots, or creating graphics. Many languages are flexible, and their uses far exceed the original plans of their designers.

General-purpose languages include BASIC, FORTRAN, COBOL, LISP, ALGOL, Pascal, APL, and PL/I. The majority of applications were written in BASIC, FORTRAN, or COBOL. These languages greatly increased the speed with which instructions and data could be entered. But programming skills and a familiarity with computer operation were still required. The computer outputs were in the form of lengthy printouts that could be difficult to interpret.

In the 60s, interactive graphics developed as a smoother, more efficient way to communicate with the computer. In these systems, cathode-ray tubes display the data entered using a lightpen. These pencillike devices have a photocell detector attached to one end. The computer senses the position of the lightpen, which can be placed anywhere on the screen surface, and it responds by lighting up that point on the screen. It also stores the coordinates for the point in its memory. Today, a number of different methods are used to interact with the CRT display, including lightpens, digitizer tablets, touch-sensitive screens, joysticks, pushbuttons, and thumbwheels.

Specifying points and line segments in this manner can quickly produce an entire drawing on the screen. The database of coordinates which are stored in the memory can be used to manipulate the display image or to produce hard-copy drawings on a plotter or can be used for analysis by the computer.

The interactive graphics systems which emerged in the 60s were mostly in-house systems which were developed at several automotive and aerospace companies. These large companies could justify the high development costs, and they already had the large, powerful mainframe computers required to operate the systems.

In the 70s interactive graphics became available on the less-expensive minicomputers. This made interactive graphics systems more practical for a wide range of industrial companies. With the use of even cheaper and more powerful microcomputers, what was considered exotic and expensive a few years ago has now become cost-effective and commonplace.

By specifying the required points and lines on the interactive graphics display screen, the user constructs an outline representation, commonly known as a wire-frame image or model. The actual model is a mathematical representation of the screen image which is stored in the computer database. But today the use of computer graphics to represent the data has become so common that the term *model* is now used to describe the graphical image on the screen. The basic concepts of creating the computer model are essentially the same, regardless of the particular graphics system used. However, these systems may use a variety of input, display, and data-handling techniques. Almost all systems enter commands and data through a typewriterlike keyboard.

There are many ways to manipulate points and lines and select specific menu commands. Some systems may use an electronic stylus and digitizing tablet. Others use lightpens touched to the CRT or incorporate touch-sensitive screens which are activated by the contact from a finger or pencil. Some systems use mechanical cursors or joysticks connected to the CRT terminal.

A computer model constructed with wire frames is the simplest approach to modeling and can be adequate for most engineering applications. In the sequence of pictures in Figure 1-3 a typical wire-frame model is created using the terminal of an interactive graphics system.

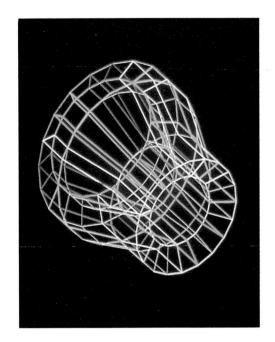

Plate 1 A 3D wire-frame model. (Courtesy: Adage, Inc.)

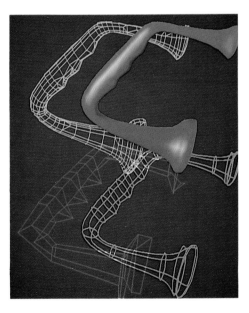

Plate 2 Bicubic surface control points, 8-spline patches, polygon subdivisions, and shaded display created on a color master display system in less than 3 seconds. (Courtesy: Adage, Inc.)

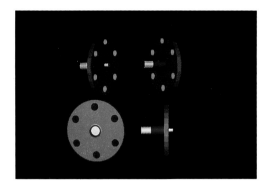

Plate 3 Solid modeling views of flanged wheel. (Courtesy: T. R. Binion/ Catronix Corporation)

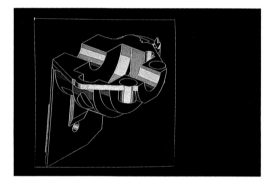

Plate 4 Solid modeling display of a chainsaw crankcase. (Courtesy: T. R. Binion/Catronix Corporation)

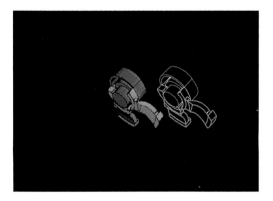

Plate 5 Solid modeling display of a casting core. (Courtesy: T. R. Binion/ Catronix Corporation)

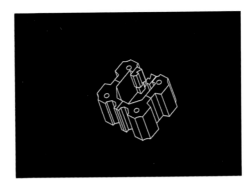

Plate 6 Solid modeling display of a styrofoam molded part. (Courtesy: T. R. Binion/Catronix Corporation)

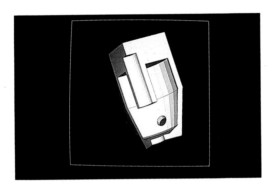

Plate 7 Solid modeling display—quarter section of a pressure vessel. (Courtesy: T. R. Binion/Catronix Corporation)

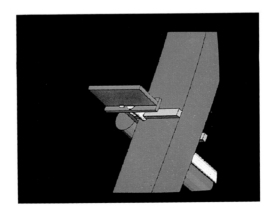

Plate 8 Solid modeling display of power plant piping. (Courtesy: T. R. Binion/Catronix Corporation)

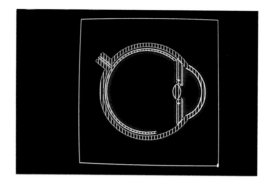

Plate 9 Solid modeling display—two-dimensional view of the eye. (Courtesy: T. R. Binion/Catronix Corporation)

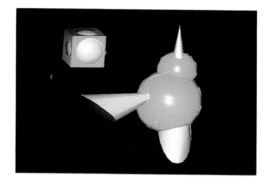

Plate 10 Solid modeling display of piercing objects. (Courtesy: Lexidata Corporation)

Plate 11 Solid modeling display of a brake cylinder. (Courtesy: Lexidata Corporation; software by Manufacturing and Consulting Services)

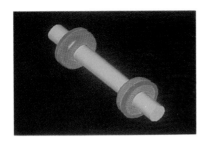

Plate 12 Incremental construction of a bicycle hub using a solid modeling system. (Courtesy: Lexidata Corporation)

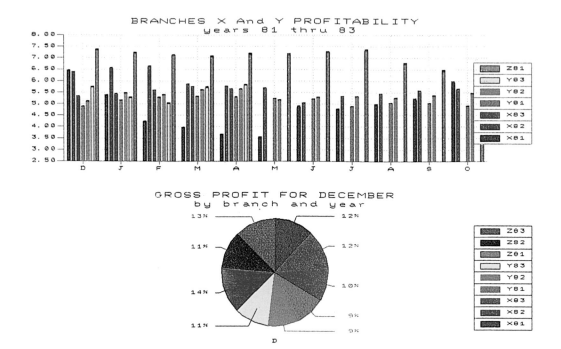

Plate 13 Conversion of display graphics into multiple-color hard copy using thermal ink transfer. (Courtesy: Lasergraphics, Inc.)

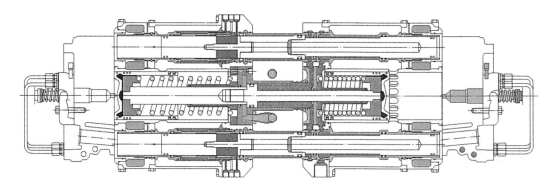

Plate 14 Example of a multicolor cross-sectional view that can be produced on an ink-jet copier. (Courtesy: Lasergraphics, Inc.)

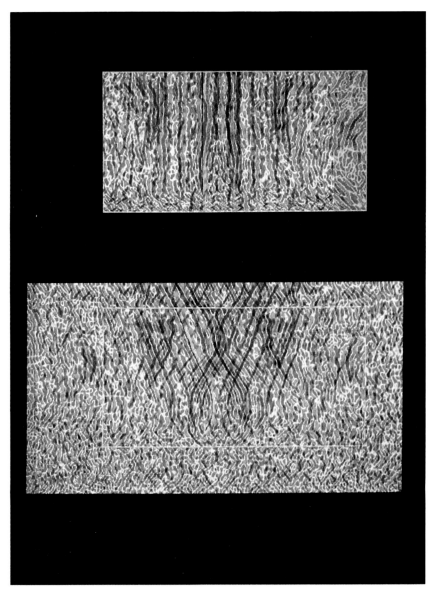

Plate 15 Seismic data section display with subsurface horizon flattening created on a color raster display system in less than 2 seconds. (Courtesy: Adage, Inc.)

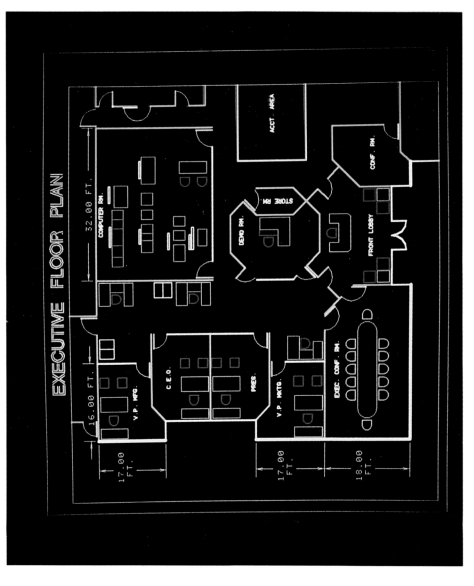

Plate 16 Example of a color-coded floor plan that allows the placement of furniture and the location of non-load-bearing walls for maximum space utilization. (Courtesy: Spectragraphics Corporation)

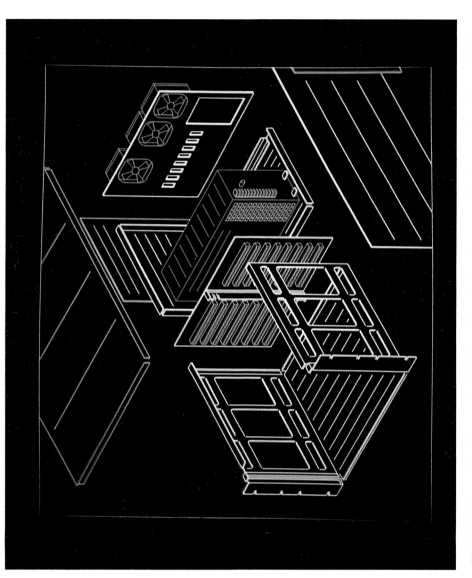

Plate 17 Example of an exploded view of an electronics assembly that can be color-coded to identify the parts and optimize the design. (Courtesy: Spectragraphics Corporation)

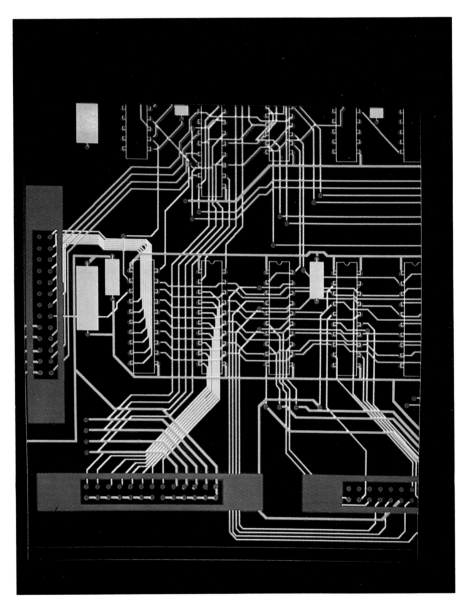

Plate 18 A display of individual printed-circuit layers that allows the checking of the design tolerances. (Courtesy: Spectragraphics Corporation)

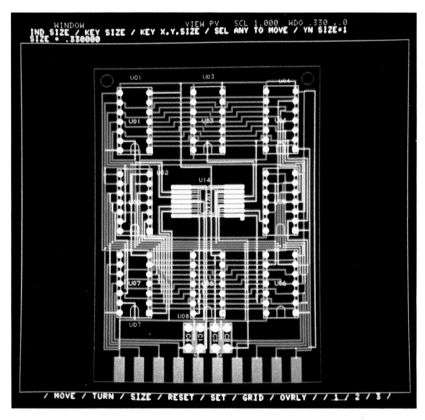

Plate 19 A display of a small circuit board along with the menu, which allows the operator to choose a particular operation by pointing with a lightpen. (Courtesy: Spectragraphics Corporation)

Plate 20 An engineering workstation for printed circuit-board design. The user's menu is shown on the right side of the display. (Courtesy: Engineering Automation Systems)

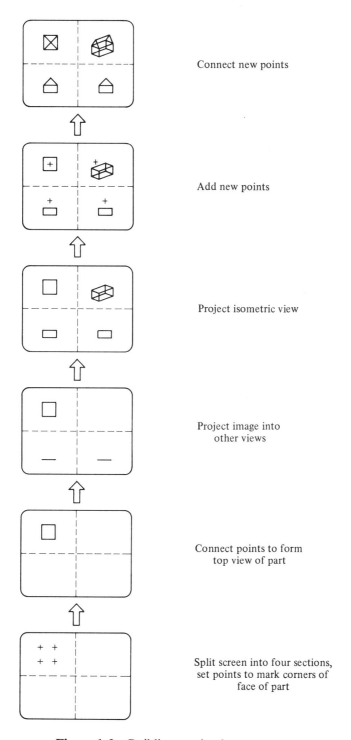

Connect new points

Add new points

Project isometric view

Project image into
other views

Connect points to form
top view of part

Split screen into four sections,
set points to mark corners of
face of part

Figure 1-3   Building a wire-frame model.

The procedures for creating models may differ depending on system capabilities and the individual technique of the user. Many turnkey systems use a split-screen approach, as shown in Figure 1-3, in which multiple views can be displayed and manipulated simultaneously.

The operator uses the screen in a similar fashion as a drawing board to create top, bottom, side, isometric, and other views of the model. Unlike mechanical drafting methods, interactive graphics provides the automatic features which speed design. The designer does not need to draw each line in a wire-frame model. The CAD/CAM computer system automatically constructs the lines based on the specified points and commands.

For many applications, wire-frame line drawings contain the required engineering information and have sufficient accuracy (see Plate 1). But they lack some realism and require interpretation for many complex shapes (Figure 1-4).

Automated drafting systems generally draw parts in the outline representations known as wire-frame drawings. The wire-frame technique is useful for part drawings and detail work. There are problems when it is used for mathematical models of parts.

For modeling purposes, parts need to be represented in the computer in a way that allows mass properties, such as the center of gravity or weight, to be associated with the parts. Models with mass properties are required in the calculation of the properties of finished products, such as weight, stability, moments of inertia, and volume. These properties can be obtained when solid models of parts are used. The solid models are stored in the computer as volumes which are enclosed by surfaces rather than frames, as shown in Plates 2 through 12.

In addition to providing weight and mass properties of parts, solid models are used in kinematic analysis to provide interference checks with other moving parts in three dimensions. Wire-frame representations can be checked only for interferences in a single plane at a time.

The properties of solid models allow them to be used as inputs in finite-element analysis. The main reason that the mass characteristics of solid models can be calculated by a computer while those of wire-frame models cannot lies in the way the models are mathematically defined. A wire-frame

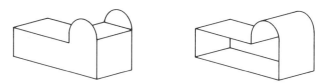

Figure 1-4 Wire-frame models can be interpreted several ways as three-dimensional solids.

model of a cylinder and a solid model of a cylinder might look the same when displayed on the screen, but within the computer memory the wire-frame cylinder is stored as two ellipses connected by two line segments whereas the solid model of the cylinder is stored as a three-dimensional solid which encloses a volume.

The computer must calculate the volume of the wire-frame cylinder by using the formula for cylinder volume. This formula is valid only for cylinders, so the computer must be programmed with a different formula for each shape that it deals with. Having the computer calculate volumes in this manner for complex shapes is impractical, because each volume would have a unique algorithm. The computer would also have to know the shape of the part in advance so that it could produce the proper volume formula.

When the computer calculates the volume of a solid model, it can use general numerical integration methods that can be applied to any kind of solid. The computer could calculate the volume by dividing one face of the solid into a rectangular grid, then projecting the rectangular shapes back through the solid to the back edges of the model. The sum of the volumes enclosed by the parallelepipeds created then equals the volume. This procedure is used in many solid-modeling programs. It is called *approximating sum integration.*

One can construct solid models in one of two ways. (1) In *primitive* or *building-block modeling*, parts are modeled by combining primitive solids. (2) In *boundary* or *perimeter modeling*, elastic lines are stretched to form part outlines. Each method has its strengths and weaknesses, and some modeling programs may combine the two methods.

Both of the methods develop complex geometries from successive combinations of simple geometric operations. In the primitive method (Figure 1-5) elementary shapes such as blocks and cylinders are combined using a building-block approach. The user positions these primitives as required and then creates a new shape with a Boolean logic command, such as a union, difference, or intersection.

The boundary-definition method uses two-dimensional surfaces which are swept through space to trace out the volumes, as shown in Figure 1-6. A linear sweep will translate the surface in a straight line to produce an extruded volume. A rotational sweep will produce a part with axial symmetry, and a compound sweep can move a surface through a curve to generate a complex solid.

Another boundary-construction technique called *gluing* can join two solids with a common surface. One then makes changes to mold the overall shape.

Each construction method is best suited for a particular class of shapes. Industrial parts that consist of planar, cylindrical, or other simple shapes are easily modeled with primitives. But parts with complex contours, such as exhaust manifolds on turbine blades, are more easily modeled with the boundary-definition method. Because the two methods have specific limita-

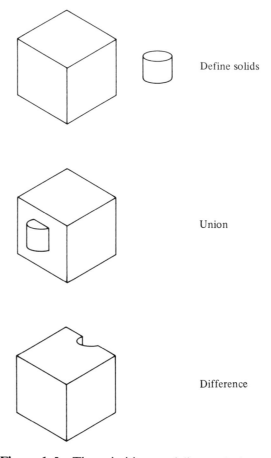

Define solids

Union

Difference

Figure 1-5 The primitive modeling technique.

tions, CAD/CAM programs combine the primitive and boundary-definition technique into unified software packages.

The basis of any computer-aided design is the mathematical representation within the computer describing the part or process being designed. In some cases the mathematical model is relatively simple, such as in automated drafting where mechanical parts can be represented in the computer by the use of simple outlines. The models can be more complex in other cases, such as in geometric modeling, where parts are represented in three dimensions as discussed above.

Models may take different forms depending on the application. Different applications can require varying kinds of CAD equipment to translate the model into the proper format.

In the modeling of integrated circuits the color graphic capability is

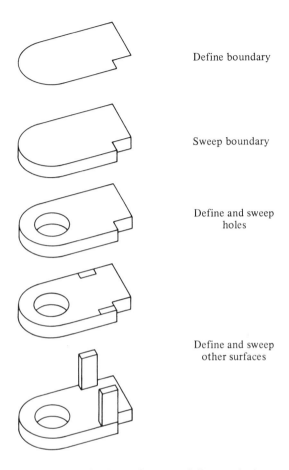

Define boundary

Sweep boundary

Define and sweep
holes

Define and sweep
other surfaces

Figure 1-6   The boundary modeling technique.

important, since each layer of the circuit must be represented by a different color for visual clarity. High resolution is important in displays of complex mechanical parts, because low resolution can produce distortion in the curves and surfaces.

Other characteristics of computer-aided design equipment can affect the speed with which the models can be constructed. Some graphic display terminals can manipulate displays using various operations such as rotations, stretching, zooming, and panning. Other terminals without these features may be slower in design but less costly to purchase. The digitizers and digitizing systems which are used for entering the data can have a wide range of features. High-accuracy, high-resolution digitizers can be used for entering data. Smaller or less accurate devices may be used as CAD-terminal menu pads.

Output devices also offer a range of features. Plotters and printers may do multiple color plotting (Plates 13 and 14) or use built-in memory to reduce the load on the CAD computer. These developments tend to keep the amount of interaction between the computer and peripheral equipment to a minimum. This allows the use of smaller, less-expensive computers.

Usually the computer models are analyzed in some way and then the data is put through further graphics processing. In this way the computer can condense large amounts of data into a visual format for quick evaluation.

For complex models these graphical displays are essential to convey a volume of data that is difficult to interpret in tabular form. An image on the screen conveys the information much more quickly than a hard-copy printout.

Computer graphics is used in a wide range of applications to take advantage of the data-manipulation power of the computer and the rapid interpretation of information through visual techniques. Factors such as profit trends and geographic sales distributions can be retrieved and compared quickly.

Interactive graphics can also be used to diagnose diseases, analyze tennis swings, generate art, control traffic, and forecast weather. The most dynamic use of interactive graphics has been in engineering applications. Contour plots can indicate lines or patterns of constant stress, strain, or temperature. Color-coded diagrams can also show the same parameters in vivid detail with critical levels highlighted (see Plate 15).

Deformed plots can show displacements exaggerated for clarity in dynamic analysis. These deformed shapes can be animated in slow motion to show how a structure will bend and twist.

EXERCISES

1. Diagram a typical CAD/CAM system and list its advantages.

2. Discuss the effect of low-cost microprocessors and microcomputers on the CAD/CAM industry.

3. Discuss the differences in the use of an interpreter and a compiler.

4. What are the characteristics and disadvantages of the FORTRAN language?

5. Why is BASIC used in many home computers?

6. Write a program in BASIC to sum the cube of a number.

7. Why do many experts consider Pascal an important language for people who are planning to study computer science or who are about to learn programming?

8. Discuss the functions of the basic parts of a Pascal program.

9. Discuss the use of a multitasking operating system in a CAD/CAM system.

10. Why is the database a critical part of the CAD/CAM system?

11. How is the attribute function used in a typical CAD/CAM system?

12. Use a series of diagrams to illustrate the interactions involved in drawing a series of circles with a digitizing pen.

13. Discuss the features and disadvantages of a wire-frame model.

14. What are the differences between primitive and boundary modeling?

15. Discuss some applications of contour plots that have potential commercial value.

INTERACTIVE
GRAPHICS

2

Interactive computer graphics greatly increases design and drafting productivity. The users of computer graphics systems can perform routine tasks much more quickly and accurately than possible with pencil and paper. Using a keyboard or electronic tablet, they can make changes quickly and inexpensively. Numerical printout was once the only way to provide computer output. Now interactive computer graphics can display large amounts in more readily understood form. This capability is used in a broad range of applications in many areas.

Oil and chemical companies have used computer graphics to design piping layouts for refineries and petrochemical plants. Civil engineers use it to design highways, bridges, dams, and other construction projects. Cities use this technology for locating facilities such as water mains, telephone lines, electric cables, and natural gas pipelines. Some cities also use computer graphics to monitor and control traffic flow. In mapping applications, computer graphics is used to define the location of mineral and oil deposits (Plate 15). Computer graphics can display data and equipment for strategic planning and expansion in manufacturing (Plate 16).

In this chapter we define the general form of the set of capabilities of interactive graphics to be provided to the user. This includes the types of interactions the user must know about and the kinds of actions which need to be performed. A typical interactive drafting system might be designed to:

1. Mimic the tools and techniques used in drafting.
2. Extend these tools and techniques to three dimensions.
3. Depart from traditional drafting and allow the user to manipulate or position volumes.
4. Depart from traditional drafting and provide capabilities which allow procedures using programs to draw or construct objects in three dimensions.

Important also, besides the input and output techniques, is the conversation protocol, which defines the user-to-computer and computer-to-user conversations. Input commands either can be executed immediately and their results displayed, or they can be batched into groups for execution.

Systems may have a type-ahead ability to enter new commands while the old ones are still being executed, but without batching. The response times are also a part of the protocol, as is the feedback the computer provides in response to the input.

What constitutes a good design for an interactive graphics system's user-computer interface? Is it a good conceptual model? How do the components of the input and output and of the conversation protocol fit in? We need to examine some of the considerations which add to the quality of the user-computer interface in an interactive graphics system.

This chapter will describe some of the design principles which contribute to the human interaction in an interactive design application. These concepts tend to also improve the success of the graphics system design. Their application is considered necessary for a successful human interface.

INTERACTIVE COMMUNICATION

Language Communications

In the user-computer interface, there are two basic languages. The user must communicate to the computer and the computer must communicate to the user. The user-to-machine language is expressed using actions which are applied to the input devices, and the machine-to-user language is expressed graphically using the lines, points, characters, and colors which form the displayed images and messages.

The language used has four major features:

1. Concept.
2. Semantic.
3. Syntax.
4. Lexical meaning.

There are always some key application concepts which must be mastered by the user. These can be grouped into a user model of the application. This model will define:

1. The objects or classes of objects to be used in relationships between these objects or their classes.
2. The objects or classes.
3. The operations allowed on these objects or classes.

In a text editor, the objects are made up of lines and files; the relationship between objects is that the files are sequences of lines. The operations on the lines and the files can include the following:

Add	Add lines entered from the terminal into the text file.
Delete	Delete lines from the text file.
List	List lines on the terminal.
Find	Find a character string or line.
Replace	Replace a character string with a new character string.

Modify   Modify character strings with subcommands.

Copy   Copy lines or a block of lines.

Text   Read a block of text from memory.

Keep   Store a block of text.

The editor may assign line numbers to the stored text so the individual lines can be identified and accessed. Some editors renumber the lines each time new ones are added or deleted. Others may use incremental line numbers. For example, a line added between lines 102 and 103 could be numbered 102.1.

The *conceptual* part of the model defines the objects and the class of objects. The relationship between objects is also a part of the concept.

The *semantic* part specifies the detailed functionality. It tells what information is needed for each operation on an object, what semantic errors may occur and how they are handled, and the results of each operation. The semantic design defines the meanings.

The *syntactic* part defines the sequence of the inputs and outputs. The sequence or grammar sets the rules by which the words in the language are formed into sentences. The types of words or tokens in an input sentence are commands and quantities. In most natural and artificial languages the words or tokens are basic units of meaning and cannot be decomposed without losing their meaning.

The output words include the space and time locators for the display. These may include 2D and 3D organizations as well as any time variations in the form. These tokens are often expressed graphically as symbols or drawings rather than as sequences of characters. These symbols may have no meaning if broken up into individual lines or characters. A resistor symbol has a meaning in a circuit layout, but the individual lines of the symbol do not.

The *lexical* part of the language model determines how input and output words are formed from the available hardware primitives, called *lexemes*. The input lexemes are the input devices that are available, and the output lexemes are the primitive shapes, such as the lines and characters, and their attributes, such as color and font, provided by the graphics software. The lexical part involves an interaction technique for each input word. For the outputs, the lexical structure is the combining of the output primitives and attributes to form the output words.

In a typical layout the input-language semantics are CREATE, DELETE, and MOVE. The ADD operation, for example, might involve the following sequence of actions:

1. Enter ADD command for a new symbol.

2. Select symbol to be added.

3. Move symbol to new position.

4. Terminate operation.

The lexical components of the input language for layout programming serve the functions of:

1. Picking commands from the menu.
2. Picking templates to be deleted.
3. Providing locations.

If a keyboard-oriented language is used, one of the lexical components of the language would be the definition of the string of characters for the command to place symbol.

The semantic part of the application's output language is the state of the layout, plus any prompt and control information such as the menu. The syntax of the output language defines the screen arrangement, including the partition into different areas and the exact placement of menus, prompts, and error messages. The lexical part of the output language includes the font of the text, the line thickness and color, the color of filled regions, and the way in which the output primitives are combined to create the output language's primitive symbols, such as those that represent the objects being manipulated by the user. An alternate output syntax would be a tabular presentation of the position, orientation, and type of each object. Then the lexical component becomes the character sizes, fonts, and spacings used to make up the table.

The conceptual model can be documented as shown below for a simple line graphics application:

The objects include:
1. Pages
2. Lines
3. Points

The relations between objects are:
1. A page is a collection of zero or more lines and points.
2. A line connects two points.

The actions on objects include:
   For pages:
1. EMPTY

   For lines:
1. CREATE
2. DELETE
3. MOVE

For points:
1. CREATE
2. DELETE
3. MOVE

The semantic model includes:
1. The action.
2. The information needed by the action.
3. The results of the action.
4. The potential errors and their consequences. The actions are given in a procedure-like syntax.

The semantic model for adding a symbol is shown below:

Function:	ADD SYMBOL.
Parameters:	Symbol identifier. Symbol position.
Description:	The symbol is created and added to the figure at the designated position. This symbol becomes the currently selected object, and succeeding operations apply to it. The previous selected object is no longer current.
Feedback:	The symbol is seen on the display and is highlighted to show it is the currently selected object. The previous selected object is not.
Potential errors:	1. The symbol identifier must be known; this implies the use of a menu for selecting the symbol. 2. The symbol position is outside the viewing area. We must constrain the positioning device to the viewing area.

The other possible models for the interactive text editor discussed earlier are:

1. A string-oriented editor, with operations performed on strings of text.
2. A window editor, with operations performed on strings in certain areas of the screen.

The semantics of an application are highly dependent on the conceptual model. It may be desirable that the conceptual model be similar to concepts with which the user is already familiar. But then another model may be more powerful and efficient. The more adaptable the user, the more the system power can be.

The task along with the conceptual model defines the application's semantics. Each necessary operation is identified, and the information needed to carry out the operation is detailed. The *entities* are the symbols and titles. *Actions* on the symbols are commands such as ADD and DELETE. Adding a symbol requires that the symbol and its desired location be designated. Replacing a title requires a character-string input.

The user must understand the conceptual model and its semantics. Both should be structured so that beginners can use the system without first understanding all the semantics and thus can grow into the system.

In the syntactic design, a number of command sequences are possible. Even a simple command such as adding a symbol can use at least six syntaxes, as shown here:

1. ADD,　　　　ENTITY,　　　POSITION.
2. ADD,　　　　POSITION,　　ENTITY.
3. ENTITY,　　　ADD,　　　　POSITION.
4. ENTITY,　　　POSITION,　　ADD.
5. POSITION,　　ADD,　　　　ENTITY.
6. POSITION,　　ENTITY,　　　ADD.

The command sequences 1 and 2 allow complete prompting. The prefix forms such as used in 1 and 2 allow the command to be easily changed if it was chosen incorrectly. The postfix forms used in the other sequences allow the operands to be changed if incorrectly selected.

A syntactic consideration involves the use of open-ended commands which allow multiple symbols to be added to the drawing, one after the other, until another command is selected. A typical input sequence would be

ADD
　　ENTITY, POSITION
　　ENTITY, POSITION
DELETE
　　ENTITY
　　ENTITY

This technique reduces the number of actions needed for a required task. Another way to reduce the number of user actions at the cost of more commands is to have a different ADD command for each symbol. Rather than selecting the ADD command and then the symbol, the user just selects one command, perhaps by picking the symbol from a menu.

Menus are an important interaction technique, since memorization is replaced by recognition. Icons can be recognized more quickly than text.

Some computers now use symbolic representations of in and out baskets, desktops, file folders, and other common objects. To print a report, the user might select the report symbol and move it on top of a printer symbol. A simple menu for a window-oriented system is shown below:

Page Layout Arrangement
   Show Standard Rulers
   Show Custom Rulers
   Hide Rulers
   Show Distance
   Hide Distance
   Plain Paper
   Grid Paper
   Auto-Grid Paper
   Scale of Ruler
   Drawing Size

This menu shows all the options available for starting a graph or chart page.

The menu uses a graph or chart page. The most common type of menu contains character strings, while a symbolic menu uses icons, or symbols, to represent the various objects. Command menus can use icons, where a straight arrow can indicate translation and a curved arrow can indicate rotation.

If menus contain too many selections, the entire screen may be taken up to show the menu. The effect on visual continuity is great, and there is a loss in the interaction dialogue, since the visual portion is lost each time the menu is shown.

An abbreviated menu is generally used, although the entries can be harder to understand. A *static* menu is always displayed in the same position on the screen and it may or may not appear at all times. A *dynamic* or *pop-up* menu will appear on the screen in different locations, usually where the screen cursor happens to be. The operator's eyes will be on the screen cursor, so the dynamic menu is displayed at this point to minimize hand and eye movements.

Dynamic menus are normally used with raster displays, since the menu replaces a rectangular section of the display. In a vector display, the menu may overlie the image, causing confusion. Static menus don't cause drastic changes in the display, while dynamic menus are displayed where the operator is looking, and visual searching is minimized.

In interactive graphic systems, ease of use, not ease of implementation, is the crucial consideration. In the past, human factors have not been a traditional concern in the use of computers. The emphasis has been on optimizing the use of resources like computer time and memory. Program efficiency had the highest priority. Now hardware costs are lower, and the increasingly powerful computing environments require that we optimize user efficiency rather than computer efficiency. This philosophy requires additional computer resources in both time and memory. The increases in user productivity are more important than the additional cost of these resources.

The proper design of the user-computer interface involves the elements of perceptual psychology (how we see) and cognitive psychology (how we acquire knowledge). The human factors—how we interact with the equipment—must also be taken into account. The system should be easily understandable to the user and readily invoked. The basic approach is to apply concepts and insights from human communication and language theory to the interface.

An important point is that the answers we get depend totally on the questions we ask, especially where the fundamental characteristics or properties of the information are concerned. For example, suppose the display contains a shape that is round and uniformly black. We cannot tell if it is hard or soft, spherical or flat, because we have no way to ask such questions. We can, however, decide if it is really circular. We ordinarily know things only in terms of their interactions with the particular measuring device we are using.

One basic task for pattern recognition is the production of computer-compatible descriptions of the objects we wish to identify. How do we describe to a computer what something looks like? When we look at something, we recognize it primarily by the amount of agreement between our visual image of it and our memory of things similar to it.

We can either prepare property lists or let the computer build its own lists. Is there a suitable theory of perception or cognition that can be drawn upon? Similarly, is there a concise set of procedures that can be made into a computer program?

We can write codes that work for limited applications. The approach is to let the computer do the digitizing, while a human does the pattern recognizing through the display terminal.

Another problem is that on occasion the machine might lie to us. This can occur when noise influences the data. In general the digitizing will always contain some extraneous data. Anything that is not exactly the current data is extracted as noise. Dirt can cause noise and so can intermittent component failures, scratches, dust, low-contrast images, and so on.

If two or more of the objects being examined touch or overlap, they act as sources of noise for each other. The recognition procedure must be able to decide that some particular array of spots is a B even if it is smudged or touching a neighboring character.

A certain amount of noise filtering can be applied to the data as it is produced, but the pattern-recognition scheme must be able to correctly function with some noise. It must be independent of data conditions such as size, position, orientation, and perspective variations. The recognition of an object must depend on the object, not on its apparent size or the direction it is facing.

A practical solution must be expressible in a comparatively small number of steps, require a finite amount of time and memory for execution, and be iterative, so that the reapplication of the algorithms improves the results.

Despite the scope and number of difficulties confronting us in the area of pattern recognition, it would be erroneous to conclude that little or no progress can be made. The situation is much brighter in the area of character recognition. Several commercially available machines recognize characters quite well. A few general-purpose designs are on the market and more are coming. Many of these are examples of research projects that successfully evolved into production applications. So, while not wanting to minimize the difficulties in this field, we can expect eventually a greater measure of success.

Pattern Recognition

One of the more basic questions that we face is, "How can or should pictures be described in a computer?" The answer will influence that part of graphic processing known as *pattern recognition*. The overall scope of graphics covers more than the display. A large part of graphics is the inputting of pictorial data, and here the role of pattern recognition is fundamental. Whether the data is an architectural drawing or an electronic circuit, we need to identify what the various shapes and lines mean. We need to be able to reconstruct shapes, including the hidden lines, from pictures or sketches.

Whichever language evolves for the graphic output, ideally it should work for the graphic input as well. From the user's point of view it should make no logical difference where the graphic data came from or where it is going. Any graphic structure must be described in terms of the operations that a display generator can produce.

The language should be precise, as well as expressive enough for easy use by people. A higher-level language allows us to express more than operations. Once there is enough structure, we find that we can describe:

1. Certain kinds of interrelationships (A is a part of B).
2. Qualities (A is green).
3. Concepts (find all the square parts).

FORTRAN and others are good examples, in that people actually communicate ideas using them.

The human world is made up of at least three levels of perception: everyday (life-size), macrocosmic (telescopic), and microcosmic (microscopic). Of these, we are able to experience with our unaided senses only one level.

Visually, the level we do see appears to be made up of radiant light and its reflection from the edges and surfaces of things, which appear to us as patches and patterns of colors. What we see is the emission of light or the reflection of it.

We tend to select those parts of the world of emitted and reflected light that we want to experience at any one time. If we choose to stay in instead of going out, we select one field of experience and cut ourselves off from the rest. And if we have a CRT screen with four windows, we narrow the field of our vision when we choose which window we want to look through. The direction in which we choose to look decides the experiences we are going to have.

Since no two people can be in exactly the same spot at exactly the same time, all of our experiences, to that extent, tend to be different. Many problems in communication arise when we forget that individual experiences are never identical.

Can we discover what is similar in our individual experiences of the same event? While any one experience is unique for an individual, a series of individual experiences can be nearly identical to another series. If we study a chair, its shape will change as we change the angle at which we view it. If someone else studies the chair and views it in the same angles, he or she will have different individual experiences, but the overall effect of the series will be much the same. Thus a succession of individual experiences enables us to agree upon what we have experienced, even though the individual experiences may differ.

Symbols

Most failures in interactive communications can be traced either to misunderstandings of the role of symbols or to inadequacies in the way that we create, transfer, and perceive symbols.

If we tend to define symbols, not as things, but as *events* which we create and experience, we can find it easier to reduce and eliminate the errors we make that lead to misunderstandings. We communicate by visible movements. Much of our daily communication occurs by:

1. A finger pointing.
2. A wink of an eye.
3. A nod of the head.
4. A shrug.
5. A smile . . . or a scowl.

These are all *visible* symbols. Visible symbols are created by manipulating lines and colors to create patterns. These patterns reflect visible light in unique ways and can thus be distinguished from each other. To the person who sees them, they are real events that are to be experienced and can be interpreted internally, just like any other real event. Thus, we communicate by symbols, which stand for something we have experienced internally.

We also use *audible* symbols, such as alarms, buzzers, and bells. *Spoken* symbols are events we create by directing our vocal muscles to vibrate a pulsed code, setting into motion similarly pulsed vibrations in the air. These are picked up as events by the person we are talking to.

As visual (rather than spoken) symbols, words and combinations of words give us more trouble in communication than other types of visual symbols. Consider what a word appears to be if we view it as a pattern that reflects wavelengths of visible light. Let us look at the word STAR. The four letters that make up the word have 24 possible combinations:

STAR	TSAR	ASTR	RSTA
SATR	TASR	ATSR	RTSA
SART	TRSA	ARTS	RATS
SRAT	TARS	ASRT	RTAS
STRA	TSRA	ATRS	RSAT
SRTA	TRAS	ARST	RAST

Only one of these configurations reflects the wavelength pattern we call STAR. In the patterns we create in our nervous system and transmit to our muscles, which move a lightpen or push keys, we are instructing our muscles to arrange something outside ourselves in a unique code.

It does not matter if the image we create is large or small. It is still recognizable as the word STAR and as nothing else, because of the relationship of each letter, from left to right, or even from top to bottom. If we were to program instructions for writing the word, we could say,

1. S is always first whether the word is written from left or right or from top to bottom.
2. T always appears immediately to the right of or just below S.
3. A always appears to the right of or below T.
4. R always appears to the right of or below A.

We have to be taught to recognize these unique patterns, in the same way we are taught to recognize other symbols or patterns, no matter at what angle we view them, or in what colors or under what conditions, providing only that the edges remain visible. Thus in the following array one can recognize STAR a number of times in both horizontal and vertical orientations:

ARSTARSTARS

RSTARSTARST

STARSTARSTA

TARSTARSTAR
ARSTARSTARS
RSTARSTARST

In the use of words for written communication, it is the spelling—the adherence to a positional notation—that is of the most importance. The spelling is more important than the meaning, because the meaning is not in the word, but in the way the word is used. Spellings change only slowly over a period of time, and even when they do, the uniqueness of the pattern remains much the same. The meanings change with regions, contexts, and time.

Thus, in summary, the visible that we experience directly is made up of patterns, colors, and edges. It is the effect these have on us that causes us to react.

LANGUAGE CONSIDERATIONS

The user-computer dialogue or user-machine dialogue is critical in interactive systems, because an interactive graphics program is a graphical user-computer dialogue. There is an important analogy between the user-computer dialogue and communications.

The language of computer graphics seldom uses spoken or written words. Instead, pictures and actions (such as keyboard button pushes and locator movements) serve as the input and output for the language. The desirable attributes of personal conversations can help to convey those of a successful graphic user-computer dialogue.

One of these desirable attributes is the *language* of the human conversation. The user-computer dialogue should be in the language of the user and not that of the computer. The language should be natural to the user.

An analogy exists in learning a foreign language. At first sentences come slowly, as one learns the vocabulary and grammatical rules. As the rules become more natural through practice, one goes on to build vocabulary. A new user of an interactive system goes through a similar learning process. This process can be more difficult than learning a foreign language, since the user must learn not only new grammar rules and vocabulary, but new concepts as well. It is desirable, then, to keep the rules and vocabulary simple and to use concepts which the user already knows or can easily learn. The user should not have to know such concepts as linked lists, iteration, and segmentation. To the typical CAD user these are not familiar concepts; they may be foreign concepts which the user has neither the time nor the inclination to learn.

The language of the user-computer dialogue should be efficient, complete, and have a natural grammar. The user must be able to command the computer effectively and concisely. A complete language will allow the expression of any idea relevant to the task.

The rules of a natural grammar tend to be minimal in number, simple, and easy to learn. This helps to minimize the user training required, and it allows the user to concentrate on the problem. Complex grammatical rules tend to introduce discontinuities and distractions to the user's thought processes.

A complete language can be concise. A language for logic design needs only a single building block, a NOR or a NAND, from which any logic circuit can be built.

The language may also have a facility for building up commands from a few basic definitions. *Extensibility* is the technique which allows new terms to be defined by combinations of existing terms. Extensibility is used in operating systems as catalogued procedures and in some programming as macro programming. Beyond these considerations there are some useful characteristics that we can examine in personal conversations. For example, when one person asks a question or makes a statement, the other responds. If a reply is not given, the speaker usually sees some reaction to the statement. These forms of feedback are an important component of interactive systems. If we make a mistake, we must be able to adjust accordingly.

Correcting mistakes is important in a user-computer dialogue. In personal conversations we can always ask the listener for help to explain the various points. These capabilities should be in the user-computer dialogues. A trait of personal conversation which has been difficult to implement in the user-computer dialogue is the use of previous statements to resolve ambiguities. Some of these problems are beginning to be solved by artificial-intelligence methods and some of the newer languages, which we now consider.

Smalltalk

Computational metaphors are ways of thinking about programming. The basic computational metaphor is a simple one: a program is a sequence of instructions that operate on data contained in memory locations. This has been a way of thinking about programming for the past three decades. It is closely tied to the physical makeup of most computers; a single processor executes instructions one by one using a single memory. The use of the word "sequence" doesn't suggest programs that run in parallel, with different computations going on at once.

In 1969, at the University of Utah, Alan Kay proposed a metaphor in which we view computation as the sending of messages between objects. Thus, instead of viewing 6 + 3 as "Run the sequence of instructions for addition, using 6 and 3 as data," we send a message to the object 6 asking it to add itself to 3. This idea is more general about the physical structure of the computer being used. It is much more general than the instruction-data metaphor, since nothing prevents many objects from sending many messages at one time. In order to send many messages at one time, Smalltalk uses a system of *classes*. We can simplify it by summarizing the essential points:

1. Classes inherit the attributes of their superclasses.
2. We can add to or change what they've inherited.

This system helps to gather commonalities in one place so they needn't be duplicated, and it allows the programmer to delegate some jobs to classes that have already been written, provided that the job is placed in the class it belongs to. Smalltalk classes are hierarchically ordered. Thus, one object is a subclass of another object. Smalltalk also uses *instance variables* of a class, which are pieces of information that the instances of that class can possess. For example, every point or area will have some location, some characteristics, and may have points or areas intersect it.

For every class we have to specify how instances of that class will react when they receive messages. The list of instructions that describes reactions to a message is called the *method* for that message. We can have messages that let other objects examine the location, tell objects how to move, and so on.

These features of the Smalltalk language are important, but the designers of Smalltalk realized that the environment in which you program is just as important as the language itself. The Smalltalk environment is regarded as the state of the art. A key aspect is that it is integrated. All the different parts—the text editor, the file system, and the compiler—are written in Smalltalk and are available to the user for inspection or change.

The other important aspect of the environment is the user interface, which is window-oriented. In most systems, when you want to switch tasks, you have to leave the program you are working with and start up another. In Smalltalk, each of the things you are working with is contained in a rectangular window on the screen. For example, one window might contain a plan or drawing you are writing, another might have the data output of an analysis program, and so on. To switch tasks you select the window you want, typically by using a pointing device like a mouse. This is a convenient way of working, because you can see at the same time all the different tasks you're involved with, which are represented on the screen as a group of overlapping windows. Thus one can easily switch between tasks in a matter of seconds. This technique is used in Apple's Lisa computer.

Smalltalk was originally designed for children, but it has grown into a far more complicated programming language. The pleasant user interface and the pervasive message-passing metaphor make it easy to learn, but it is powerful enough to rival LISP in artificial-intelligence areas.

LISP

LISP (the name stands for LISt Processor) is one of the oldest computer languages that is not considered obsolete. The other languages that were invented in the late 50s or early 60s, such as ALGOL, FORTRAN, and COBOL, although still widely used, are not considered viable for artificial intelligence. LISP, however, is popular for artificial-intelligence research.

In 1960, John McCarthy brought together a branch of mathematics called the lambda-calculus and the programming concept of list processing. The *lambda-calculus* is a mathematical system for dealing with functions, and McCarthy drew on some of these ideas to design a programming language that uses lists as the only data structure.

In LISP a list is just a group of elements in a particular order. Lists are useful for representing all sorts of objects, ranging from members of a physical structure to numbers or commands. Among the things you can represent with LISP lists are LISP programs. For example, a LISP program to find the cube of a number follows.

```
(DEF CUBE (LAMBDA (N)
   (*N(*NN))))
```

The program itself is nothing but a list. In LISP, programs and data are represented in the same way. Thus, one can easily write programs that write and run other programs.

The CUBE program uses a function called CUBE, which takes one argument called N. The LAMBDA indicates the beginning of a function. Most modern versions of LISP do away with LAMBDA in the definition, using instead the syntax

```
(DEFUN CUBE (N) ... )
```

where DEFUN stands for "define function."

In the body of the function, (*NN) signifies "multiply N by itself." It is the same as N*N in Pascal or BASIC. But in LISP, all functions are written as lists, with the name of the function first, followed by the arguments to the function;

```
(*N (*N N N))
```

means "multiply N by N times N," which yields N cubed. Most of the modern versions of LISP let us write

```
(*N N N)
```

because functions such as * and + can take any number of arguments. LISP's strange syntax can be a bother in the beginning, but it all depends on what languages one is familiar with.

While defining the functions, we can use a COUNT function to count the number of individual words in a given list. Using the COUNT function, we can easily make programs into a much more general algebraic simplification. The distinction between program and data is not made. We can use

(+ X X X)

as data, but it is also a valid LISP expression, just as

(* N N N)

is.

A most important characteristic is that LISP is ideal for manipulating symbols. In artificial intelligence one does a lot of this type of manipulation, since the human thoughts which artificial intelligence tries to imitate involve far more symbol manipulation than number manipulation.

Another feature of LISP is its extensibility. You'll recall from our discussion that an extensible language lets you add features that are indistinguishable from those of the original language. In LISP, user-defined functions are written and used in exactly the same way as built-in functions.

PROLOG

PROLOG is a newer language which appeared around 1970. It is just beginning to be recognized as a useful language for artificial intelligence. One result is that the Japanese have chosen PROLOG to be the standard language for their fifth-generation computer project. Like LISP, PROLOG has a mathematical foundation. LISP is based on the lambda-calculus. PROLOG is based on logic.

PROLOG is short for PROgramming in LOGic. As an example of how PROLOG works, consider the following:

A circle is a closed form.

All closed forms have an area.

Therefore, circles have area.

The first two statements are nothing more than facts or assertions. The third statement, as its first word suggests, is the conclusion we can draw from those assertions. Here are the first two statements written in PROLOG:

closed form (circle)

area (Something):–closed form (Something)

The first line corresponds to the first line of English, asserting that a circle is a closed form. In PROLOG, it is common to write the attribute of an object first, then the object itself in parentheses. Notice that we don't capitalize "circle." That is because "circle" is a *constant*—a particular combination of letters that always refers to the same unique shape. PROLOG uses names that start with capital letters only to indicate variables.

The second statement also corresponds to its English counterpart. One way to read this line is: "Something has area if that same something is a closed form." In more mathematical terms: that something has area is implied by its being a closed form.

This particular statement is saying, "If you're trying to show that a particular thing has an area, you can do that by showing that it is a closed form." PROLOG statements of this form are called *rules*.

The word "Something" in the second PROLOG statement is a variable. It doesn't refer to a specific thing, although in PROLOG we may give it a value at certain times. A PROLOG word that starts with a capital letter is always a variable.

Now assume that PROLOG has the two facts we have programmed above. We can then ask

area (What)

Here we are asking PROLOG, "What is an area?" Notice that What is a variable. PROLOG will look up the answers to these questions.

As another example, if we define the rules for addition correctly and then ask

plus (8, 4, X)

(meaning "What is 8 + 4?"), PROLOG responds with

X = 12

But we could also ask

plus (X, Y, 12)

and PROLOG should give all pairs of numbers that add up to 12, depending on our prior program.

Programming in logic can be a powerful tool, but there are some problems. It couldn't answer "plus (X, Y, 12)" correctly without some limiting definitions, because there are infinite answers to the solution.

You can program in logic, but keep in mind that an ordinary computer is only an approximation of logic, and sometimes its approximations can be strange. The order in which you enter rules and assertions will change the answers you get. This makes the language difficult to learn.

Another problem is the rigid control mechanism. The language is classified as nonprocedural, since one doesn't have to write an exact procedure to solve something. One has only to describe the problem, and PROLOG will do the rest. But PROLOG has its own built-in way of solving problems, and sometimes it can be difficult to do things differently.

One other problem with PROLOG focuses on artificial intelligence and just how good logic is for solving the real-world problems that artificial-intelligence researchers explore. In ordinary logic (the kind PROLOG is based on), there is no real way to say, "Okay, I don't care, since anything that can't be true is automatically false." Thus, is logic really a solution to these types of problems?

Modula-2

The major feature of Modula-2 over Pascal is the module. A *module* is a collection of type declarations, variables, and procedures. Users of UCSD Pascal will recognize the module as being similar to a *unit*. Modules can be complete programs or just provide data and procedures to be used by other modules. For example, in a CAD database system, there would be many parts, some involved with the user interface and others with storing and updating information.

Consider the part of the program that actually stores and retrieves the information. Using Modula-2, we can write this as a module, since it is self-contained and independent of the rest of the system. The thing we need to provide for the other parts of the system is the ability to add, delete, and retrieve information. It isn't necessary that the other parts of the system know about the actual way we store and retrieve information.

Using Modula-2, we can write the following description of what we are providing other parts of the CAD system.

```
DEFINITION MODULE Database;
  From DataObject IMPORT key, datum;
  EXPORT QUALIFIED add, delete, retrieve;
  PROCEDURE add(k:key, d:datum);
  (* adds a piece of data to the database, stored under a function key *)
  PROCEDURE delete (k:key);
  (* deletes the piece of data associated with a function key *)
  PROCEDURE retrieve (k:key):datum;
  (* finds the piece of data associated with a function key *)
  END Database;
```

This is the definition part of the module called Database. It says nothing about how the module works. It just provides a list of things the module is expected to give to the other modules.

The definition gives a procedure called "add" that takes as arguments a key and a datum. Then there is a comment about this procedure. The procedures for deleting and finding a datum are also described. Just writing these specifications is not enough. They must be visible to other modules. This is what the line beginning with EXPORT does; it makes the needed procedures available to the other modules. The word QUALIFIED is also required to do this.

The modules use these procedures by importing them, just as we have imported from a module called DataObject the definitions for key and datum. To actually write the three procedures we described above, we can use a list of all things that have been entered. To implement this we write

```
IMPLEMENTATION MODULE Database;
FROM DataObject IMPORT key, datum;
const maxrecords = 4000;
type
  datarecord = record
    key: key;
    d: datum;
    end;
var dbase: array (1..maxrecords) of datarecord;
  nsofar: integer;
procedure add(k:key; d:datum);
begin
  nsofar: = nsofar + 1;
  dbase(nsofar).k: = k;
  dbase(nsofar).d: = d;
end;
procedure delete (k:key);
begin
  .
  .
end;
procedure retrieve(k:key):datum;
begin
  .
  .
end;
begin (* initialization *)
  nsofar := 0
END Database;
```

One would add the bodies of the delete and retrieve procedures to complete the program module. This is an IMPLEMENTATION module, since it contains the program statements. No EXPORT statement is used here, so any other module cannot know about any of the declared constants, types, or variables. Other modules can know only what they are told in the EXPORT statements.

This approach differs from Pascal, where the same constants, types, variables, and procedures may be defined as part of a bigger Pascal program. The main result is one of security. In Modula-2 it is impossible for any part of the program except the add, delete, and retrieve procedures to use the actual data in the database. Using Pascal, nothing would prevent any part of the program from using the contents of the database array or changing the value of variables. In Modula-2, the structure of the data is controlled; in Pascal, it's available.

When would one want to hide some parts of a program from others? One of the best ways to write a successful human-interface program is to hide the detail. Everything that anyone would want to do with a database can be done with the procedures in the module shown above: no other part of the program needs access to the internal representation of the database, and with Modula-2 no other part of the program can get access to it. Thus, with Modula-2 one can write programs consisting of groups of modules that will never interfere with data in another part. A module is an independent entity that communicates with the rest of the world only through the data and procedures allowed in the IMPORT and EXPORT statements.

Also, changes in the implementation tend to introduce bugs into program, but the Modula-2 program above makes it easy to insert something but difficult to delete or retrieve it. To make the database system more efficient, we would rewrite the three procedures, add some variables, delete others, declare new types, and so on. But even with all these changes, we can be confident the program will work, as long as we make sure that the three procedures operate per the definition module.

Since no other part of the program knows about the module except the three procedures, then whatever changes are made have no influence on anything else as long as the procedures have the same effects as they did before. The ability to hide detail is useful for any complex task, and it becomes more useful as the task gets bigger. Complex tasks can have many parts that interact in complicated ways. Different parts are written to interact in different ways. Thus, it's important to be able to guarantee that certain parts are visible and other parts are hidden.

DESIGN OF THE USER-COMPUTER INTERFACE

How should a user-computer interface for an interactive graphics system be designed? The first step is to understand the problem; then a prospective model or system can be evaluated. This can be accomplished by studying the ways in which the problem can be treated. To provide a starting point: a mathematician does not prefer to manipulate equations at a keyboard, nor does a circuit or structural designer. This does not imply that a computer graphics system should operate the way in which the user works manually or with nongraphics computer equipment. Computer graphics provides the means for making major improvements in the methods by which a problem is solved, and any increase in efficiency from changing methods must be balanced against the training and adaptation costs of switching users over to the new methods. A typical approach has been to first computerize the current design methods and then utilize better, more efficient methods to help the users become familiar with the computer system.

The process of understanding the application and users has been called *task analysis*. It uses a set of functional requirements, or *capabilities*, which are made available through the user-computer interface.

The analysis can also provide insights into how the capabilities of the system should be presented. In order to evaluate a system we need to analyze the following:

1. The conceptual design of the system.
2. The semantics: those operations performed on objects in the conceptual model, the changes caused to the objects, and the information to be displayed on the screen.
3. The syntax: how the user's action sequences affect each operation and its organization on the display.
4. The lexical design: how each word is bound to the physical action of the interaction devices, and how the visual encodings are bound to the capabilities of the display device.

The Structure of the Display

In many cases a great deal of information must be displayed to the user. If it is presented in an unstructured form, it can be difficult to understand. To help structure the information, the view surface can be divided into different areas for specific types of information. Prompts, error messages, system status, and the graphical representation of information should each have its own area. An uncluttered and organized display allows the user to quickly locate information. Some systems allow the user to arrange different feedback areas on the display screen.

The way in which we use space affects the way that we communicate. The distance between areas on the screen may determine the nature of this communication. The communication will tend to have its tone and nature changed. The change is greater if there is a large amount of information. Here the nature of the message may also determine the communication.

Space speaks also in the way that we distribute the information in the views. As long as there is optional space, most people will tend to concentrate on one section at a time. The distance used to separate one section from others on the screen is in itself a form of communication. In rigidized constructions the distance to be maintained between data of different rank may even be a requirement of regulation.

There are cultural differences in the way we distribute ourselves in formal space, such as in an office. Europeans are most likely to put their desks in the center of the room, since they believe that authority flows outward from the center, and proximity to the center is important. Americans tend to distribute their working space around the edges of an office. Americans tend to see the edges of things and the intersection points of crossing lines, and to attach importance to them. Thus American streets are normally laid out in a grid pattern, and Americans identify places by their proximity to intersections. Europeans and Orientals attach more importance to an area. A French street or avenue may change its name every few blocks, and houses in Japan may not have street numbers but be identified by name and area or the time at which they were built. While some areas might overlap, borders can be effectively used to set one off from another and provide logical groups.

Visual continuity can be achieved with fixed display areas, but the perception of the structure of the display can be enhanced by using some type of visual coding such as color, line style, or intensity. Structural displays may contain details that are hard to observe. If one uses color to display the same structure, then the details of the structure can be easily distinguished. Following are some ways to encode information, listed in decreasing order of effectiveness.

1. Color.
2. Geometric shapes.
3. Line width.
4. Line type.
5. Intensity.

Color is the most widely used method of distinction between items (although it cannot be used for those who are color-blind). It is readily available in raster display devices.

These coding methods can be combined to increase the discrimination using redundant coding or to increase the number of discernible items. For instance, the boxes and triangles can be easier to discriminate from other shapes using the following pairs:

1. Red box, red triangle.
2. Green box, green triangle.

3. Red box, green box.
4. Red triangle, green triangle.

Here the shape codings and colors are redundant, since either coding 1 or 3 can be used to find a red box or 1 or 4 to find a red triangle. They allow the user to use either one or both coding methods in an interactive graphics system.

The structure of 3D objects can be enhanced by the use of depth cues. The user's attention can be directed to a specific part of the display by:

1. Displaying objects in that area in a different color.
2. Blinking the object two to three times per second with an on-time of at least 50 milliseconds.
3. Pointing with a colored or blinking overlay.

These methods can help the user locate and track objects which are moving or must be modified.

Other aspects of the structuring of displays to aid perception and understanding involve selective graphic principles and their application. A common means of creating a more readily apparent structure is to reduce the visual clutter by using a selective display. If one is interested in the gross overall structure of a design, a full view is preferred. For detailed information, however, a zoom capability permits one to decrease the visual clutter on the screen by enlarging a small area of the display to expose more detail.

Whenever an enlarged part of a larger drawing is being shown, some way must be provided to place it in the overall drawing. One way is to use an overall spatial relationship. A small square inside a larger square area indicates which part of the overall drawing is being shown. This can also be done with separate displays—one for the overall view and the other for the close-up. Pairing of display views for close-ups has been used effectively in LSI chip design, where high resolution can be required to display the chip.

Different highlighting techniques can be combined. We can also assign properties to them, such as color, size, rotation, translation rates, and so on. The total description can be kept in a nesting of files and directories such that the user can, with a minimum of distraction, produce graphical presentations and alter them at any depth desired. Listed below are examples of properties that we might use:

Function	Characteristic
Turn	Three-axis rotation
Pan, Zoom	Three-axis translation
Perspective-Projective	Geometric transformation

Function	Characteristic
Blink	Attention direction
Shade	Optical density variation or texturing
Color	Associate a color with the image parts
Name	Associate a name with an image
Attach	Join line segments
Connect	Object linking
Draw	Follow the light pen or locator
Smooth	Apply a relaxation operator to the display data
Modify	Change a display listing
Dimension	Assign lengths—areas, volumes, masses
Erase	Remove image parts
Write	Prepare text

For user convenience one can combine several of these elementary functions into defined or derived functions and do this in a fairly general way. Thus, the user need not think of a three-line segment, but rather can call for the triangle function. One can also combine the triangle function with others of these higher functions to any desired level.

One of the properties of these artificial functions is that they can be any combination of elementary or higher functions to which a unique name might be given. It is important that such functions imply a precise, reproducible description of a picture or an actual thing in a form suited to automatic processing. They must be alterable, retrievable, and communicable. Thus, they are clear statements of ideas or procedures in terms of a fixed, known set of primitives. The user guides the kind of processing done with these lists by requesting a visual operation on the screen.

Learning to Operate the System

An interactive graphics system may be used by a wide spectrum of personnel—from inexperienced beginner to those who have worked with the system for many hours. The users can be broken into classes on the basis of experience level:

1. Novice users, who are learning the basic concepts and mechanics of the system.

2. Intermediate users, who have learned how to do some productive work and are now gaining proficiency.

3. Experienced users, who are proficient in most system aspects and capabilities.

Some systems may have so many capabilities that most users will be experienced only in certain areas of the most frequently used capabilities.

An interactive system that meets the needs of all these users must be flexible. The novice user's first requirements are:

1. A guided tour of the system with examples of what the system does.
2. Guided instruction in the use of the basic command set.

In a computer-aided instruction scheme the most common form of interaction uses a series of yes-no or multiple-choice questions corresponding to the points mentioned earlier. Although the only answers possible may be "yes" or "no", most machines are built so that an edited answer is also possible.

The successful use of this device implies that we ask the right questions. The first problem then is to decide which points belong to the information we seek, given that we are limited in what we can ask. It also turns out that if we aren't careful about the way we ask, the machine can lie to us. For example, probing the same point too frequently may give contradictory results. In any event, we end up with a mosaic of yes-no responses, and the computer program, by suitably combining these elementary responses, produces the desired learning data.

Thus, to a certain extent, we are taught what to see. The event which has not been experienced before does not make sense. Successive experiences enable us finally to recognize the sameness of the sequence of experiences, even though individually they are different. For instance, in a number of views, pictures of common items like a cup and saucer will almost always be recognized. Yet, considered as separate experiences, each image we form of the cup and saucer is different.

Somewhat the same thing applies to the learning of sounds. The interpretation of sounds as intelligible experience depends on our ability to recognize a sequence of patterned sound waves moving through time. Thus, we have to be taught to see what we see and to hear what we hear.

Since we may each be taught differently, the very basis of our understanding of what we see or hear differs to some extent from what others see or hear. This is one reason why verbal communications often are less satisfactory than written ones, because the spoken language allows so many different intonations, pitches, and variations.

Two or more people, hearing the same sounds, may not experience or interpret them the same way. When we assume that everyone sees or hears the same thing, then we base our communication on a false and misleading premise.

To aid us in this area, the two basic tools are the use of *prompting* and *help*. Unlike feedbacks, which acknowledge specific user actions, prompts suggest to the user what to do next. The more experienced the user is, the less prompting is required.

The prompting should not be done in a way which can slow the pace of the interaction. Many systems use several levels of prompting which are controllable by the user. Those who are inexperienced can be led slowly with many prompts, while those who are experienced can proceed more quickly without many of the distracting prompts.

Prompting may take many forms. The most direct form is a displayed message explaining what to do next, such as

SPECIFY LOCATION

One can also give the user verbal instructions. Other forms of prompting are available:

1. Buttons eligible for selection can be illuminated.
2. A tracking cursor can be displayed when a selection must be input.
3. A blinking cursor can indicate that text is required.
4. A scale or dial can be displayed when a value is desired.

Some unobtrusive prompts may be appropriate for intermediate and advanced users, but not for beginning users.

A user-computer dialogue which employs menus and promptings is a *computer-initiated* dialogue, since the computer takes the initiative in guiding the user through the steps of specifying the inputs. These techniques are popular for novice users, and menus are appropriate for experienced users if the menus are presented quickly. Dialogues in which the user has control and initiates one of several alternatives are called *user-initiated* dialogues and are more suitable for experienced users. Most time-sharing systems use this style of dialogue, since it is easily implemented using keyboard input. The more effective forms of menu selection use high-resolution displays and pointing devices.

From the user's point of view there may be other problems. To get started one may have to first get involved with details that one feels, rightly or wrongly, are nonproductive relative to what one wants to do. If one tries to use one of these systems too quickly, one may have to contend with the following situations:

1. The software system is not complete enough, so progress is slow to the point where one will not achieve what was desired.
2. The software system imposes what appear to be disabling constraints or unreasonable work habits.

3. The software system is so large that one cannot really utilize it for the size of the problem intended.

4. The software system is too slow for the user with its many prompts.

5. The system is implemented on a computer that in some aspect is inadequate for the application.

There are cures for these difficulties, and in a large number of cases it turns out that a carefully chosen set of primitives is enough to allow really useful work to be done. If this were not true, effective communication would be almost impossible. When we talk to someone, we establish communication best by discovering what is common in the succession of our experiences, while keeping in mind that we may differ in our interpretation of any individual experience. Although we experience things in bits and pieces, the sequence in which we experience them flows together, and we feel them as a continuous panorama. When we try to communicate about this panorama, we have to break it down into bits and pieces—and perhaps a large part of our trouble starts there.

A good way to show that we have to learn to see is the inkblot test. Looking at one, different people will see different things in it. The internal experience of it will tend to differ from person to person. You will also find that if you look away from it, and then look back again, you can discover new shapes that you had not seen before that give you new experiences. When you are talking to other people, it is sometimes useful to keep in mind that if the experience you are talking about is new to them, they will have trouble making sense out of it, just as you perhaps had trouble making sense out of an inkblot symbol when you first saw it. Much of our difficulty in introducing new ideas and much of the human resistance to change arises from the fact that we have to *learn what to experience* in the events we experience.

Some of the things different people have reported seeing in the inkblot test show us that they have been taught by other people what to see. When you are communicating to someone, remember that they may have been taught to experience things differently than you have, and perhaps the reason you have difficulty understanding them is that you are not allowing for this.

A HELP facility can allow the user to obtain additional information about the commands and how to request them. The user typically does this by keying in the HELP command. It should be possible to request HELP at any point in the user-computer dialogue, and the request should always use the same mechanism. The return from HELP should leave the system at exactly the same state as it was when HELP was invoked. If HELP is requested while the system is awaiting a command, a list of commands which can be used in this state should be shown.

Entering HELP and then a command name can give more information about what the command does. If a command has been specified and HELP is then requested, details of how to enter the command's initial parameter should be given to the user.

A second request for HELP can produce more detailed information on the same subject and perhaps more general browsing through instructional documentation. A HELP capability can be used even if prompts and menus are typically displayed, since the user is provided with an opportunity to receive more detailed information than can be provided in a prompt. Even experienced users can forget detail, especially in a large and complex application. They should be able to turn to HELP as a quick way to get the required information.

The need for HELP reminds us that the world we live in is built up of the different experiences that people have had, some aspects of which they have managed to communicate to each other. Consider also that if people exchanged places, and individually experienced those aspects of the world that they had not felt previously, they ultimately would be able to agree upon much more than they do. As we read, and listen, and experience, we establish the basis for a closer understanding of what others experience, and thus we can, in the end, find that we have much more to agree on than to disagree about. It is when we stop learning that we begin to build the barrier that keeps us from understanding other people.

Table 2-1 summarizes these and other considerations for various types of users.

Table 2-1   Interface characteristics appropriate for various users

Class of user	Characteristics of the user-computer interface
Casual—uses system irregularly.	Prompting and menus are especially appropriate.
Regular—uses system often, does not forget the details.	A terse command language or fast menu selection is required with only a few steps to complete a task.
Motivated—desires to use the system.	This user will invest sufficient time in learning how to use system, even if difficult.
Unmotivated—does not really want to use the system.	Flaws in the interface design will give this user an excuse to criticize or stop using the system.
Stressed—is under pressure to get the task completed quickly.	Simplicity is especially important, so that work can proceed by instinct or reflex. Characteristics should depend heavily on typical outside experiences.

The Requirement of Memorization

Learning to use a system always involves some memorization of information. An important consideration is to make the memorization as simple as possible and, where possible, avoid it. Consistency is a way to do this, as are the use of menus and prompting. There are other ways also.

The keyboard can use full-word commands which express their meaning, such as DELETE. The short forms of such commands can also be used. The need to remember the order of positional parameters can also be avoided. Unnecessary memorization, as where objects are referred to by numeric rather than by alphanumeric names, should be avoided. This means that names must not be numeric. If mnemonic names are available to the user, productivity will surely improve.

The explicit picking of displayed objects or icons eliminates the need for memorization. Here the user's recognition rather than the memory recall is used.

In an interactive graphic system, a command such as PLOT NET may produce a trend chart of net income. The style of line might be controlled using a command such as LINESTYLE DASH. The plot would use a dashed line. The command could also be LINESTYLE 2. The "2" refers to the third variable named in the most recent PLOT command—in this case, NET. Since the most recent PLOT command is not generally left on the screen, the user must remember the order of the parameters. In some text editors, two steps are required to change a text string, since the CHANGE command operates on the current text line. First SEARCH command is used to locate the line containing the text string to be deleted, and then a CHANGE command is required to replace the text.

One must remember the old string from one command to the next. An editor can remove the need for this remembering by searching forward from the current line until a matching string is found and then performing the change in one step.

Memorization can be required when the HELP facilities on many systems are used. Obtaining the HELP information causes large changes in the display area, which can cause the user to lose track of the context for which the help was asked. The user may remember characteristics of the situation, such as the error message or display layout which led to the seeking of help. After the help information is understood, the user must retain in memory while returning to the previous task in which the problem occurred.

A user interface based on window managers, such as used in Smalltalk, eliminates much memorization.

A Smalltalk Example

We now take a detailed look at what *window managers* are and look at an example of what they do. Suppose you want to prepare a chart to illustrate a certain point. With a few movements of the pointing device, you "tear off" a sheet of graph paper, displaying an empty grid on the screen. Then you type the numbers onto the grid, name the graph and the x and y axes, and request a bar graph. You get the bar graph superimposed on top of the data.

At this point, you can print the graph or save it. If you are not satisfied with the way it looks, then use the pointing device to cut the graph from the graph paper and put it in temporary storage. You can now throw away the graph paper you were using. Next you can tear off a new sheet of paper and paste on the bar chart. If you want to make a bar darker, you move the cursor onto that rectangle, which tells the computer that you want to work on that bar.

In most systems, you select what you want to work on, then you select the action you want performed. Small black squares which appear on the edge of the object are called *handles*; not only do they show which object has been selected, they also serve as handles by which the cursor can move or change a shape.

After the bar is selected, you move the cursor to one of the menu titles at the top of the screen as shown here:

File/Print
Edit
Type Style
Page Layout
Arrangement
Lines Shades

You will see a menu of possible actions and point the cursor at the desired menu.

Close Everything
Close "Sales Report"
Put Back
Save This Version & Continue
Revert to Previous Version
Intended for Printer
Print . . .
Printing in Progress . . .

A typical menu is a grid of the varieties of shading that could be used to fill the selected area. When you move the cursor to the desired shade box and select a shade, this menu disappears and the shading fills the desired box. One can also change the size, type style, and position of the title using the cursor. We might also select an area of text to be put in reverse video. An option from the "Type Style" menu causes the text to be displayed in a new size and style. We might modify the title to an italic font and pick up the title with the cursor and drag it to a new location. Other alterations are possible. When we are satisfied with the graph, we can print it or save it in memory.

Usually several windows are displayed at the same time, and each window shows a different context, such as a HELP facility in one and an interactive application in another. Switching between the application and the obtaining of HELP in using the application can be as simple as moving the screen cursor from one window to another.

Copying part of one document into another can also be accomplished easily with multiple windows. One window can show part of the document being copied and the other the part of the document being copied into. Scrolling and other positioning commands can be issued to either window. When the text to be copied and the insertion point have been located in the windows, the copy is invoked. There is no need to remember one context when switching to another, since they are both visible.

The Smalltalk environment provides a great utility in its use of metaphor. When you turn on the system, the screen may be empty except for several icons. The computer may depend on the metaphor that the display is a desktop and the icons are objects on the desktop. Each peripheral connected to the computer can be represented on the desktop by an icon if it is not in use or a window if it is available for use.

One can also replace the conventional file directory with a collection of objects displayed in the window of the associated mass-storage device. Each file is represented by an object, and objects can be grouped together in folders, which are also treated as objects. Actually, the window is just an opening into whatever the folder contains. Symbols on the margin of each window are points from which the cursor can direct operations on the window. For example, when the cursor points to a folder icon in the window, the folder closes and the display reverts to the image it had before the folder was opened.

If the folder contains more than the window can show, you can do one of two things to see the additional contents:

1. Scroll the window either horizontally or vertically.
2. Put the cursor on an expand/contract icon in the corner of the window. An outline of the new window will follow the cursor action, and the window will grow to its new size.

Once you have been shown the mechanics of manipulating objects and windows, you have a working knowledge of the essential operations of the file system. The use of a metaphor does two things:

1. It helps one to remember the operations, because they are in the context of the object-related icons.
2. It draws on your general knowledge and how it is used.

These elements help to create a system that people can learn to use some aspect of within 30 minutes. This "data-as-concrete-object" metaphor is the foundation of the system design.

The file system makes you feel as if you are actually moving and changing objects, not merely manipulating abstract data. The system creates this illusion through its application programs. The success of the "data-as-concrete-object" metaphor depends on the condition that reasonable operations can be performed on objects at any time.

Many programs use modes that restrict activities at any given time. For example, word-processing programs may not let you do numerical calculations and then incorporate them into the document or specification. With the Smalltalk application programs, you can switch back with no problem, just as you could if they were two sheets of paper on your desk. Also, because you deal with recognizable objects, you feel secure in the knowledge that the data will not disappear.

The use of dynamic window management is not without some costs. A high-performance computer is needed to do an effective job, and much more memory as well as software complexity is required than in a more traditional environment. One can expect window managers to increase as part of the basic support software on graphics systems. CAD applications will routinely use them, just as graphics packages have been used in the past. When several programs must run in parallel on a system, the operating system must handle multitasking. The software must provide the switching from one task to another. The operating system assigns the various tasks different priorities. A line printer would normally get a high priority, because a line printer is relatively slow and in high demand. The high priority keeps the line printer busy as much as possible.

Several techniques are used to decide when a task is to run next. In the slice procedure, each task runs for a small fraction of CPU time. It is then suspended and the next task is started up.

Event-driven systems change over when a significant event such as a completion flag or interrupt from a peripheral occurs. Some event-driven systems are interactive, allowing a user to send data to the program from the terminal during execution. As a prompt appears on the terminal and one enters a command and receives a response, some software interprets the command and processes a response. In a window-driven system, because of the level of information and the choices available, the software overhead is much greater.

RESPONSE-TIME AND ERROR CONSIDERATIONS

The response time of a system is of critical importance to the system's overall utility. In time-sharing systems it usually cannot be directly controlled.

When response times can be controlled, what they should be may have no single answer.

If we think in terms of personal communications, when you ask someone for the time, you tend to expect an answer in a matter of seconds, and after about 30 seconds you become annoyed. But 30 seconds is not long to wait for the answer to a problem requiring complex computations. If we consider the machines we use, when we strike a typewriter key, we expect to hear the sound of the type on the paper relatively quickly, and if we sense any delay, we question the operation of the machine.

When we are ahead of time, on time, or behind time, and when we are early or late, our timing has a meaning in our culture. Failure to keep this in mind can lead us into situations in which communication becomes difficult, if not impossible. The mere fact of being late can create an aura of hostility in which we are forced to perform.

Another aspect of time, as it relates to communication, is the difference between points in space and duration. *Points in space* are intersections on a three-dimensional grid. The grid is an x, y, z matrix plus a specified time track or match for an event. Failure to match these up in an interactive system can result in a communications failure.

Time *duration* appears to us as a beginning and an end with an unsegmented middle. It is a psychological area which is unmapped with no events, as the time we spend in the doctor's waiting room or in waiting for someone else.

Duration is experienced differently by different people. When you are talking to someone else, their area of duration may be different from your own. They may not be at the same x, y, z' but at some indeterminate part of the spectrum. It is almost as if you had agreed to meet at a certain place at a certain time, but only one of you showed up.

These differences in experience of duration can cause communications problems and breakdowns. The response-time requirements tend to relate to the user's expectations. There is a hierarchy of required response times, which corresponds to the level of psychological closure or the feeling of completing a task. The larger or more substantial the task, the greater the response time that will be tolerated.

Two problems are caused when system response times are noticeable to the user:

1. The time the user spends waiting for the computer to respond is wasted.

2. The user also wastes time regaining the train of thought, once the system does respond. This delays the work at hand that needs to be continued.

Response-time requirements can be broken down into two areas of response: that to reflex actions and that to simple processing interactions.

Reflex actions entail either a learned or a natural reflex, such as typing a character or moving a display cursor. In these cases the system response must appear to be almost immediate—which means a lag of no more than 100 milliseconds between typing or moving a stylus and viewing the result.

Simple processing interactions are those which the user believes the system should be able to do without any substantial processing time. The user is not willing to wait. How long the response time can be before the user realizes a delay is occurring depends on the problem. About two seconds is considered to be appropriate for much syntactic-level feedback and for the simple semantics such as deleting a line when using an edit feature. Part of the reason for this two-second response time is found in present expectations. As small computers and dedicated graphics systems become more common, increasing expectations will occur, forcing these systems to be capable of faster responses to user actions, with the possible exception of requests requiring extensive numeric calculations or file searches. Thus one can expect more interactions to occur within 100 or 200 milliseconds of initiation.

Another response-time consideration is *consistency*. Some experience shows that users tend to be more productive with a slower system having a smaller response-time variance than with faster systems having higher response-time variance. Predictability is preferred rather than occasional faster responses in these cases.

A consistent system tends to use a conceptual model, semantics, command-language syntax, and display format that are uniform and lack exceptions or special conditions. Some examples of consistency in an output language are:

1. The same codings should always be used. This means that all circle centerlines have the same intensity and dot-dash structure, and colors always code information in the same way.

2. The system status messages are shown at a logically but not necessarily physically fixed place on the display. Thus the user always knows where to look.

3. Items are always displayed in the same relative position in a menu.

Consistency in the input-language system means that:

1. The keyboard characters, such as carriage return, line feed, and backspace, always have the same function and can be used whenever text is the input.

2. Global commands, such as HELP, STATUS, and CANCEL, can be used any time.

3. Keywords in a character-string-oriented language are abbreviated using a constant-length string.

An important application of consistency is in the syntactic and lexical definition of the input language. Many of these languages are regular and can be represented by transaction or transition graphs. The input events can be user actions, and the outputs may be the computations and resulting changes to the display. Each branch of a graph is labeled with the user action which causes the transition and the resulting system action.

The Use of Feedback

It is hard to imagine conversing with someone who never smiles or nods and who responds only when forced to. It is frustrating because there is little or no indication that the listener is really hearing what is being said.

Feedback is as essential in conversation with a computer system as it is in human conversation. In normal conversations with another person the sources of feedback include:

1. Physical gestures.
2. Facial expressions.
3. Eye contact.

These are usually provided without any conscious action by either of the participants in the conversation. A graphics terminal gives little automatic feedback except for the feedback that is planned and programmed into the system.

Even a personal conversation may be meaningless without feedback. Here is just one example (you can find dozens of others every day, if you listen or look for them). People actually believe that they communicate when they use words in the following way: "Too much government is bad for business!"

This statement may mean something to the person who used it. But it can be without effective meaning to the person who hears or reads it. You can clarify the statement by asking a few questions:

1. What government do you mean? Federal, state, county, city? Executive, legislative or judicial? Elective or appointed?
2. Where is the government you mean?
3. What time are you talking about?

The speaker might then rephrase the statement: "The policies of the Committee of Ten in Carthage in the fourth century B.C. were destructive to the growth of commercial competition."

You can now either agree or disagree with the speaker. But at least you know what it is you agree or disagree with. At this point, one might be tempted to ask, "Why didn't you say so in the first place?"

It is sometimes useful to think of human communications as transactions. We mean here, a *transaction* involves the interaction of the observer and what is observed. This transaction can take place between ourselves and a computer system. Or it can take place between two or more humans.

The transaction can be an exchange of visual events, such as written words, art, charts, or equations, or of spoken symbols, as in ordinary conversation, speeches, songs, and music. Whatever the symbolization, the basic ingredients of the transactions are the same.

These transactions can include:

1. Something taken in.	These may be light waves, sound waves, tactile impressions, odors, tastes, from outside ourselves.
2. Something transformed.	These light and sound waves are transformed into electrical codes for transmission to the muscles.
3. Something retained.	Memory patterns are stored in the nervous system as electrochemical codes.
4. Something created.	The internal electrical impulse codes are changed into muscular reactions.
5. Something transmitted.	Muscular movements move objects in such a way that they emit or reflect unique patterns of visible light waves or create pulsed sound waves, which are then received by others as events seen or heard.

When we communicate with each other, it is useful to keep in mind that our common words may not evoke the same image in someone else's mind as they do in ours. Knowing this, we can help improve our communications by being as specific as possible. If we are on the receiving end, it often helps to ask questions. Assuming that everyone knows what we are talking about and assuming that we know what others are talking about without asking questions are two common causes of communications failure.

In our daily operations, many interlocking communications loops may have to be used in order to perform even quite simple communications. In the simplified cases diagrammed in Figure 2-1 we see the interlocking loops that

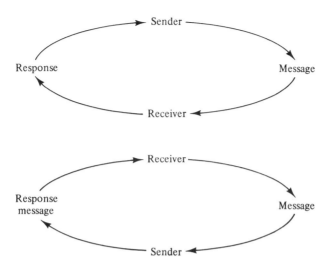

Figure 2-1   Interlocking loops in effective human communications.

might be required. This communication might get a new product specification started, prepared, submitted, and returned for corrections. We note how many minds the information has to pass and remember that each mind will see the problem somewhat differently.

In an interactive system there are three possible levels of feedback corresponding to the levels of the language: lexical, syntactic, and semantic. The lowest level of feedback is lexical. Each physical action in the input language can be provided with a lexical response in the output language—for example, echoing characters typed in on a keyboard or moving a cursor as the user changes the position of a locator.

Feedback to a syntactic input will occur as each word of the input language, such as a command, position, or picked object, is accepted by the system. A command picked from a menu or an object to be moved can be highlighted, so the user will know that the actions have been accepted.

Other forms of feedback to syntactic inputs are prompting for the new input, lighting the key button which has just been depressed, and echoing a verbal input with a verbal output. Another form of feedback on the syntactic level can occur not as each word is input, but as a complete syntactic sequence (a sentence in the command language) has been input and has been found to be well formed. This acknowledgement of a proper sentence is generally used only if performing the semantics of the sentence (the actions specified by the command) takes more than a second or two.

Semantic feedback can also take the form of partial results which appear slowly on the screen. When the results appear in some logical order, the effect this produces can help the user to understand the final graphical presentation

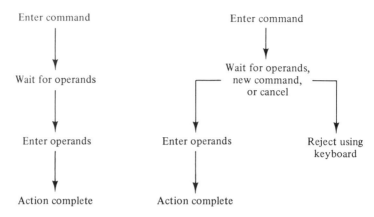

Figure 2-2 A graphics system that does not use consistency in its command structure.

better than if the entire graphical form were to appear all at once, after all the processing is done.

The positioning of feedback is also important. The tendency to use a fixed area of the screen for feedback and error messages can affect the visual continuity. The reason is that the user's eyes must move between the working area and the message area. Audio feedback can be used to eliminate this problem, but a better technique is to place the feedback where the user is working.

In a system where a tablet and cursor comprise the interaction tool, the user's eyes will normally be at or near the cursor. One can place the error messages at the current text insertion point on the screen. Some layout systems use the form of the cursor itself for feedback: one symbol means the user has made an error, another tells the user the system is carrying out a task.

The command continuity is also important from the viewpoint of the user. Figure 2-2 shows a system with a command language which is not consistent. In the initial starting state, any command can be entered. This causes a transition to an await-for-operands state, in which the user is prompted to input the appropriate information. There are different sentence structures. Commands can also use the concept of explicit acceptance or rejection of a command's effect, while here we show only explicit rejection and implicit acceptance.

A particularly troublesome problem exists when there is a difference on how the effect of a command can be canceled. Users who wish to cancel commands must then remember how to do so. This greatly increases the possibility of errors and detracts from the creative utility of the graphics system.

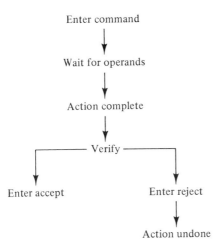

Figure 2-3   A command structure that uses explicit rejection and acceptance.

Representing all the command structures of an inconsistent system can result in a large number of complex graphs. Consider instead the simple case of explicit versus implicit acceptance. Figure 2-3 represents a one-operand command with explicit acceptance and rejection. Figure 2-4 shows implicit acceptance and explicit rejection.

In the first case, three steps are required to carry out all commands, while in the case shown in Figure 2-4 only two steps are required. Minimizing the steps per task is important to the interface, especially for experienced users, since the speed with which experienced users can input the commands is closely related to the number of steps required.

We can also expect that in functionally equivalent systems, the one with the simpler syntactic structures will produce fewer errors and be more quickly learned. One should always minimize the number of different sentence structures required. At the semantic level, a good design also requires that operations which can be applied to one class of objects be equally applicable

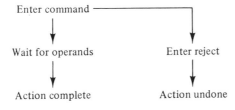

Figure 2-4   A command structure that uses explicit rejection and implicit acceptance.

to other similar objects without requiring changes or restrictions on the part of the user.

After a command has been requested, the more useful form of semantic feedback indicates to the user that the requested operation has been completed. This is usually done with a new or modified display which shows the results. Some programs use only type of semantic feedback, since each command can be carried out quickly. In cases where the user asks that a drawing be filed for later use, explicit graphical feedback may not be appropriate, and prompts or completion messages of either text or icons are used instead.

Another form of semantic feedback, which is used only if completion of the semantics takes more than a few seconds, is some indication that the computer is at least working on the problem. In the absence of such feedback, some users will express their frustration physically on the graphics terminal.

This type of feedback can take many forms; one is a 360-degree dial with a rotating indicator that completes one revolution by the time the problem is solved. The user can extrapolate from the dial when the data will be ready.

Another type of semantic feedback, which is given before any of the semantics are carried out, is to echo a definitive statement of what the interactive system believes has been requested. This type of feedback is not as good as showing the actual results, and it should be used only if performing the semantics consumes an unacceptable amount of time or other resources or if several commands must be grouped together before they are performed. This type of feedback is helpful to new users if context dependencies are possible. Figure 2-5 shows an example: the command language accepts keywords, such as TITLE, X, Y, AXIS, and BAR, in a logical way to produce the graph indicated from this sequence.

If the feedback detects that the system has misunderstood the input, the incorrect commands can be changed before the chart being requested is drawn. Changes can be requested to the original graph to produce a new graph. Only those parts of the chart which need to be changed should need to be modified by the user.

A picking or pointing device has no inherent motion to provide levels of hierarchy, yet the user's intent should somehow be available to the graphics application. Some systems have the interaction commands such that the level of object to be operated on can be inferred without any explicit user action. This can be done using a structured hierarchy. For example, in a task having to do with placing parts in an assembly, the assembly would be designated, while in a phase for designing individual parts, the part components would be selected for the part subassemblies. When the intent is not implicit, then the command language must provide the user with an explicit way for conveying it. Commands such as MOVE SUBASSEMBLY illustrate this. When the hierarchical level at which the user operates changes infrequently, it may be more convenient to have a separate command which sets the level for the next

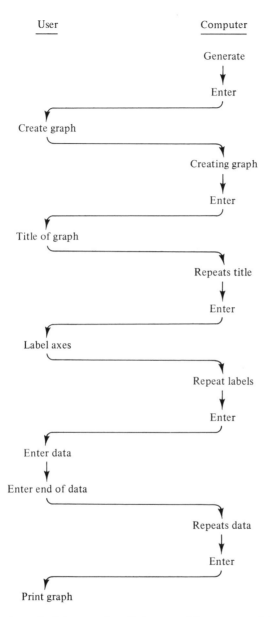

Figure 2-5   A typical interactive dialogue with command feedback.

sequence of operator actions. In this scheme the user respecifies the level when required.

Another approach is required if the number of hierarchical levels of objects is large, as it might be in a drafting system where templates may be defined to contain both other templates and basic objects such as lines, points, and arcs. Commands are required that tell the system to *travel up the hierarchy* and *come back down*. When we as users select something, the system can highlight the lowest-level object seen. If this is what is desired, we can proceed. If not, we issue a command to *travel up the hierarchy*. The entire first-level object of which the detected object is a part can be highlighted. If this is not what we want, we travel up again so that still more of the view is highlighted. If we accidentally travel too far up the hierarchy, we reverse the direction with the command *come back down*.

Some text editors use a hierarchy of:

1. Character.
2. Word.
3. Sentence.
4. Paragraph.

In using the editor, one selects a character by positioning the cursor on the character and pushing a select button on a mouse. To choose a word, one pushes twice. Further moves in the hierarchy are accomplished by further pushes.

Error Accommodation

Since, when working, we make mistakes, we need simple and convenient ways to correct these mistakes quickly in order to prevent them from creating other, more critical errors. Most interactive systems use a backspace key to delete the last character entered. The system can also allow the entire current input line to be deleted, and there may be a way to abort the execution of a command before it is completed.

The system is usually restored to the stage before the abort was entered, unless changes to files have been made. Some systems even have the ability to revert back to the previous state before the effects of the most recent command, even when file changes have been made. Some of these systems use multiple versions of files. Another strategy is to record all the user inputs for an entire session and then allow the session to play back up to the point where the error was made. Thus, we can have error accommodation at three levels: lexical, syntactic, and semantic.

The cost of semantic recovery is high, since the program must continually save either the system state or changes made to system state and must provide the logic to restore the previous state. But the cost of not accommodating errors is frustration and less productivity. The availability of semantic recovery frees the user to explore new system facilities, since the recovery is so simple and easy to use.

Many dynamic interaction techniques allow some backup. The trial position of an object being moved into place is simple to change; thus many positions can be tried. This is syntactic-level backup, since many different values of one syntactic unit (the position) in the overall command can be easily changed. Semantic backup would have the system return the object to its starting position by undoing the effect of the positioning command. Another form of backup is involved when we use a locator in picking. When the picking is done with a lightpen, the item being sensed by the pen is usually highlighted. The user moves the lightpen until the item desired is highlighted and then presses the button. This sequence of positioning the lightpen and pushing a button forms the syntactic unit, which is a picked item. When an item has been picked, the designating of another item in its place can require additional backup capabilities, which this time are at the semantic level.

Some systems provide the ability to cancel the effect of a complete command by requiring the user to explicitly verify the command by accepting or rejecting the results of the operation. This adds to the number of user actions needed to accomplish a task. An alternative requires explicit action only to reject the results of a command. The command can be implicitly accepted as the next command is entered.

Cancellation is most easily understood when the interaction language uses a clear sentence structure which states the start and the end of commands. Then the unit to which cancellation applies is clear. Providing for the cancellation of commands requires extra programming, especially for the commands which involve major changes to data structures.

An alternative to cancellation is to require the user to confirm those commands which might require a large effort to undo. File deletion is the most common example of this. Deletion confirmation is standard in many interactive systems. But some systems may use an erase button to both erase the trace off the screen and erase it from the computer memory. A slightly better scheme is to require that this button be hit twice before an erase action is taken. Erasure can cause files to mysteriously disappear, whereas objects such as reports and tools do not. If a file disappears, there should be a logical explanation: either you erased it or you let its usefulness expire and it was automatically erased.

EXERCISES

1. Describe the basic principles involving interactive graphics which need to be applied in each step of the design process. Why is it necessary to iterate through the process several times before a completely satisfactory design is achieved?

2. Diagram an example of effective language communications in an editing session.

3. Describe the conceptual, semantic, syntactic, and lexical component language analogy. What are some ways to expand these concepts in future products?

4. Give some text-editing recommendations based on the use of strings or windows. Although one of these may not be appropriate for every situation, tentative guidelines can be suggested along with the areas for detailed studies.

5. Discuss the use of static and dynamic menus.

6. Discuss the importance of pattern recognition in computer graphics.

7. We have seen that one purpose of consistency is to allow the user to generalize knowledge about one aspect of the system to other aspects. Consistency is also important in the use of symbols. Discuss the use of symbols in an interactive design program.

8. Use of the consistency principle can help avoid the user frustration which occurs if a system does not behave in an understandable and logical way. How can we achieve this consistency through top-down design?

9. What does it mean when a language has a natural grammar?

10. Why is the principle of extensibility important in a language?

11. What are the basic characteristics of the Smalltalk language?

12. Write a program for finding the square of a number in LISP.

13. Write a PROLOG statement that finds the possible surface dimensions for a single-story building of 25,000 square feet.

14. How does Modula-2 differ from UCSD Pascal?

15. Discuss five ways in which we can structure information in a display.

16. Discuss the use of consistency in the graphic command structure.

17. How should prompting and HELP facilities be structured in order to be of greatest benefit to the user?

DISPLAY
TECHNIQUES

3

The terminals used to display graphics are generally referred to as *graphics-display terminals* or *graphics-display processors*. These terminals are often classified by their display type. They use a raster scan which is similar to a common television, a direct-view storage tube similar to the displays in analog storage oscilloscopes, and random-scan vector displays.

Video-display terminals, or video terminals, are sometimes used in CAD/CAM systems. These terminals generally display only text, although some can provide simple line drawings.

In a typical CAD application a small video terminal might handle the text or engineering data, with the drawing being displayed on large graphics display. Desktop computers can also be used as terminals in CAD/CAM systems. A desktop computer is sometimes used in small to medium-sized CAD/CAM systems to control plotters and printers. These computers generally contain some form of mass-memory storage that can be used to store the files for the drawings.

TECHNOLOGIES FOR DISPLAY

CRT Displays

Interactive computer graphics requires display devices whose images, unlike those shown on plotters, can be changed quickly. A nonpermanent image display allows an image to be changed by the user, making possible the dynamic movement of portions of the image. The cathode-ray tube (CRT) display is the most common display device and will remain so for many years in the future: however, solid-state technologies are being developed which may, over the long term, have an impact on the use of CRT technology.

Refresh cathode-ray tubes are those used in black-and-white home television sets. These are similar in most respects to the tubes used in many monochrome graphics displays. Figure 3-1 shows a sectional view of a CRT. The electron gun emits a stream of electrons which are ejected from the cathode located at the small end of the vacuum tube. These electrons are accelerated by establishing a difference in voltage levels between the cathode and the screen. Using other controlled electrostatic or magnetic fields, the electrons are focused and deflected in a manner analogous to ordinary light beams. There are electrical and magnetic equivalents to the lenses, prisms, and filters involved. In any case, the main reason for using CRTs under computer control is their ability to transduce electrical signals into light, which we can then see or photograph. The electron beam can be switched on or off and deflected both rapidly and precisely. Table 3-1 shows some elementary comparisons between light optics and electron optics. It should be emphasized, however, that this tabulation is for analogical illustration only.

The light-emitting compounds used as CRT screens are luminescent

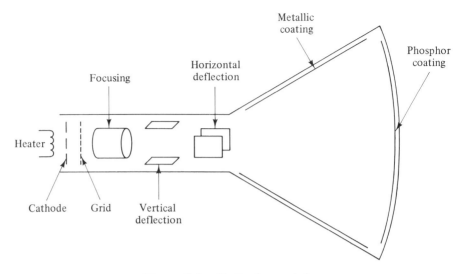

Figure 3-1 Cathode-ray tube.

phosphors. They contain compositions which radiate visible electromagnetic radiation when stimulated by the electron beam. Chemically, the phosphors are composed of various salts of zinc, cadmium, magnesium silicates and sulfides, or other alkali metal tungstates. To these a small amount of some other metal such as silver, copper, or cerium is added. These impurities help to determine spectral characteristics, and they also function as activators to increase the luminous efficiency, or as killers to reduce the phosphoresence time.

Important characteristics of phosphors A phosphor's *fluorescence* is the light emitted as the unstable electrons lose their excess energy while the phosphor is being struck by the electron.

Table 3-1 An illustrative comparison between electron and light optics

CRT	Photograph
Electron gun	Light source
Control elements for regulating electron current	Lens diaphragm, shutter
Accelerating elements	Filters
Focus elements	Focus ring
Deflection elements	Image-positioning prisms
Screen or faceplate	Photographic emulsion

Phosphorescence is the light taken off by more stable excited electrons as they return to their unexcited state, once the electron beam is removed. This light decays exponentially with time.

There are many different phosphors, each with its own characteristics. The phosphors known as P1 and P4 are used in black-and-white TV while P7 and P31 are used in graphics-display terminals.

A phosphor's *persistence* is the time from the removal of excitation to the time when the phosphorescence has decayed to 10% of the initial light output. The persistence of some phosphors can reach several seconds, but for most phosphors used in graphic terminals it ranges from 10 to 70 microseconds.

The persistence determines the *refresh rate*, which is the number of times per second a picture is redrawn. Refreshing is required to produce a flicker-free picture. The longer the persistence is, the lower the refresh rate can be. A flicker-free picture tends to appear constant to the viewer, even though at any given time it is off longer than it is present on the screen.

The human visual faculty can be an extremely sensitive "data channel." If good visual data is badly presented in part, the average viewer tends to reject the entire picture. For most, a flickering picture is bad. For others, a lack of contrast can be the most annoying factor. The usual procedure is to provide manual adjustments to control such things as picture size, focus, and brightness. Many screens can also be tilted to reduce glare and improve contrast in lighted rooms.

Beyond reducing the number of things to be displayed, a user cannot directly do very much to solve the problem of flicker. Most viewers do not accept it, although some of the early radar display operators found that flicker actually helped them to notice new blips quicker.

The rate of flicker is a function of the time needed to display the entire picture once. The other factors, besides the type of phosphor used, are the brightness and contrast of the picture parts, the level of background illumination, and the sensitivity of the viewer's eyes. The average persistence time for human vision is about $\frac{1}{40}$ sec. This means that in order for our eyes to see some point of light on the screen as a constant-intensity source, it must be refreshed at least once every $\frac{1}{30}$ to $\frac{1}{60}$ sec.

Some phosphors have such short decay times that the illusion of constant brightness depends mostly on the persistence of vision. For example, a P31 phosphor emits strongly in the green portion of the visible spectrum, and it has a decay time of about 38 microseconds. Refresh cycles as low as 35 per second could be used with this phosphor, but the flicker becomes obvious and may be annoying. Most manufacturers use a refresh rate of 40–60 per second. Based on the persistence time, if the picture content changes rapidly, a cleaner picture is obtained from a fast-decay phosphor. However, many special effects can be produced when a long-persistence phosphor such as P7 (400 milliseconds) is used to show rapidly changing pictures.

The electron beam   As the electrons are accelerated toward the phosphor-coated screen, they are forced into a narrow beam by the focusing mechanism and are directed toward a particular point on the screen by an electrostatic or magnetic field provided by a deflection system. When the electrons hit the screen, the phosphor emits visible light.

Character and vector generators trace a picture on the screen by detecting the beam along the desired path. Since the phosphor's light output decays exponentially with time, the picture must be redrawn so that the viewer sees what appears to be a constant unflickering picture.

This stream of electrons is generated by thermionic emission, while in a vacuum a heated metal or metal oxide surface bubbles off the electrons. A high voltage of thousands of volts is applied to a metallic coating on the interior of the sides of the tube to drive the electrons toward the screen. The final velocity the electrons attain depends on this voltage; thus it is called the *accelerating voltage*.

A control-grid voltage determines how many electrons actually reach the screen. As this voltage becomes more negative, fewer electrons get through to the screen, and the beam current becomes smaller. This provides a way to control the picture's intensity, since a phosphor's light output follows the number of electrons striking it. If the grid's voltage is made negative enough, no electrons can pass by it, and the screen is blank.

There are two general methods, electrostatic and electromagnetic, for directing the light-producing beam of electrons. The electromagnetic or magnetic scheme is ordinarily held to be capable of higher positioning accuracy. Alternatively, the electrostatic method is faster. Some CRTs have used a combination of the two, but this is not now common. We will note that both methods have their proper uses.

The focusing system can use either electric or magnetic fields to focus the beam so it converges to a small point on the screen's surface. In electrostatic focusing the elements are mounted inside the tube's neck, as shown in Figure 3-1, while in magnetic focusing electromagnetic coils are placed around the outside of the neck. A fine parallel beam of electrons tends to diverge because of electron repulsion, so the focusing must force the electrons to converge.

Except for this tendency to diverge, focusing an electron beam is analogous to focusing light. An optical lens and electron lens both have a *focal distance*. In the CRT this length is such that the beam converges as it hits the screen surface. Figure 3-2 illustrates a focusing problem that occurs with CRTs. The beam is shown deflected in two positions. In one position the beam converges at the point where it touches the screen. In the second case, the convergence point is not on the screen and the image is blurred. Most CRTs have a radius of curvature far greater than the distance from the lens to the screen, and not all the points on the screen are the same distance from the lens. If the beam is in focus at the center of the screen, it will not be in focus anywhere else on the screen. The further the beam is deflected from the center

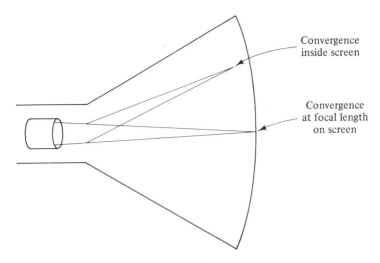

Figure 3-2   The deflection problem.

of the screen, the more out of focus it will be. Most precision displays solve this problem by changing the focus as a function of the beam's position, rather than by using a fixed focus.

The deflection system in a computer graphics terminal is one of the most critical parts of the CRT. The deflection system is used to trace the picture on the screen. Either electrostatic or magnetic methods can be used. With electrostatic deflection, two sets of plates are used in the CRT neck, as shown in Figure 3-1. The electron beam must pass between the vertical deflection plates, which lie in a horizontal plane. The beam will be bent toward the plate with the higher voltage. The magnitude of the deflection is controlled by changing the difference in the voltage between the two plates. A second set of plates is used to control the horizontal component.

Electromagnetic deflection systems use two coils around the tube's neck. The field from one coil deflects the electron beam horizontally, while the field from the other deflects it vertically. The magnitude of the deflection is related to the current in the corresponding coil.

Deflection compensation circuitry or permanent magnets placed around the tube's neck are used to correct for the nonlinearities. Without any correction, a square grid tends to have a curvature, as shown in Figure 3-3. Two separate distortion effects are shown in the figure. Along the horizontal and vertical centerlines the grid points are not equally spaced, and the deflections away from the centerlines are greater than at the centerlines.

In a magnetic deflection system the tube construction is simpler because of the external coils. The intensity control is simpler, and the higher acceleration voltages that can be used in magnetic systems make brighter images possible, since the brightness is a function of electron velocity.

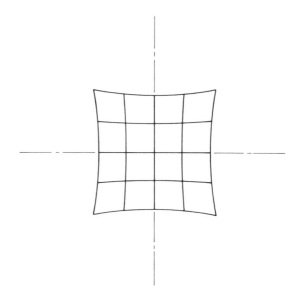

Figure 3-3 Magnetic-deflection distortion.

Higher acceleration voltages are possible with magnetic deflection, since the power needed to produce a given deflection is linearly proportional to the acceleration voltage, while in electrostatic systems it is proportional to the square of the acceleration voltage. This also allows magnetic deflection tubes to be shorter than electrostatic tubes.

Raster-Scan Terminals

Raster-scan terminals operate in much the same way as television tubes. The image is formed by controlling the intensity of the electron beam that scans left to right across the tube surface for a fixed number of horizontal lines. The intensity of the beam is timed so that the beam is at highest intensity when passing over a bright spot, and lowest when passing over a dark area.

In a raster-scan system, the drawing is divided into horizontal lines. All parts of the drawing appearing in the first line are reproduced in left-to-right order, then all parts of the drawing in the second line, and so on. Some hardcopy devices operate in either a random or raster scan. The printer is a raster-scan hard-copy device, since the print head moves from left to right and top to bottom. The pen plotter, in which the pen can be moved in any direction over the paper, is a random-scan device.

In a raster-scan terminal, after all scan lines have been drawn, the beam

Figure 3-4 A raster-scan outline, composed of a series of circular spots.

returns to the upper corner. Broadcast TV in the United States operates with 525 scan lines, but raster graphic terminals can use from 256 to 1024 lines. The more lines, the better the picture quality. A raster display outline would be drawn as illustrated in Figure 3-4, which shows the scan lines and the points at which they are intensified.

Figure 3-5 shows the basic raster-scan pattern starting at the upper left of the screen. Using a left-to-right sweep, the beam intensity is modulated to create different shades. At the right edge the beam is turned off, then repositioned back to the left edge, one unit down from the previous scan line.

The images which are to be displayed by a random-scan system are encoded as commands for each output primitive by using the endpoints of lines as coordinate data values. The encoding for raster-scan systems is easier, since the output primitives are broken down into their constituent points for the display. The major difference between simple point-plotting random-scan displays that store the sequences of points and raster-scan displays is in the organization of the stored points. In point-plotting display systems the

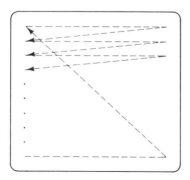

Figure 3-5 A raster-scan pattern.

component points of each output primitive are stored sequentially in memory, and these are plotted in order, one picture element at a time. In a raster display system, the refresh memory is arranged in a two-dimensional array.

The location at a particular row and column stores the brightness or color of the corresponding (x, y) position on the screen as shown in Figure 3-6. Each screen location and memory location is referenced by an x coordinate which ranges from 0 to $M - 1$ and a y coordinate which ranges from 0 to $N - 1$. The rows of memory correspond to the screen lines, and the image refreshing is done by a sequential raster scan through the memory by scan line rather than by an output primitive, as done in the random scan.

Each memory location defines one point-sized element of the image. This screen location and its corresponding memory location are called a *pixel* or *pel*, which is short for the image-processing term of *picture element*. It is common in computer graphics to use the term *pixel* for the points on a raster display and the terms *picture elements* and *output primitives* for the higher-level primitives such as lines, points, and characters.

The most basic *refresh buffer* has a one-bit *pixel* which defines two colors, usually black and white, for the image. Modern refresh buffers, also called *frame buffers* or *bit maps*, use solid-state random-access memories (RAM). Earlier raster displays have used mechanical drums, delay lines, or shift registers to store images.

The image-refresh system shown in Figure 3-7 cycles through the refresh memory row by row for each scan line at 30 to 60 times per second. The memory reference addresses are generated along with the raster scan as the contents of the memory are used to control the CRT beam's intensity.

An image-refresh system has the general structure shown in Figure 3-8.

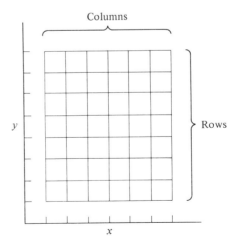

Figure 3-6 Refresh memory.

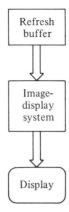

Figure 3-7   Image-refresh system.

The raster-scan generator produces the deflection signals which are used to generate the raster scan. It also controls the address registers which control the location of the image to be fetched next. At the beginning of a refresh cycle, the x-axis address register is set to zero and the y-axis register is set to $N - 1$ for the top scan line. The first scan line is generated as the x address is incremented up through $M - 1$.

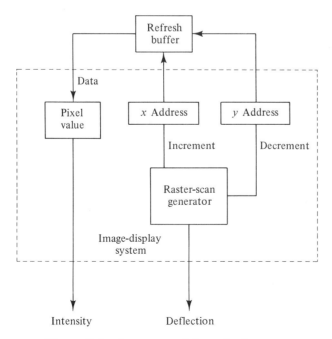

Figure 3-8   Structure of the refresh system.

As each pixel value is fetched, it controls the intensity of the CRT beam. When the first scan line is complete, the x address is reset to zero and the y address is decremented by one. This process continues until the last scan line at $y = 0$ is completed.

The image refresh is sometimes used to interrupt the computer when the raster scan is completed. The computer can then make changes in the image during the 1.3-millisecond flyback time in which the beam is moved from the lower right to the upper left of the screen. The image refresh can be stopped if the changes take longer than the flyback time. The changes can also be implemented while the image refresh is in progress, but this can be distracting to the viewer, and a partially updated display may not be preferred to a blanked display.

The refresh system may use an interlaced scan of two fields, which is done in commercial TV. Here, the refresh cycle is broken into two phases of $\frac{1}{60}$ second each. The full refresh takes $\frac{1}{30}$ second. The first phase displays the odd-numbered scan lines and the second phase the even-numbered ones.

The interlaced scan can update the screen in $\frac{1}{60}$ second, eliminating the tendency of a raster-scan image to flicker at the $\frac{1}{30}$-second refresh rate. This technique produces a picture with an effective refresh rate closer to 60 than to 30 Hz. This scheme works well, as long as the adjacent scan lines tend to display similar information.

Another technique for a raster display is to use a repeat-field scan with the entire image displayed 60 times a second. This is easily done at 512×512 resolution, but it becomes more difficult at higher resolutions with 30-Hz refresh for a 512×512 display; each scan line must be displayed in about 60 microseconds, or about 100 nanoseconds per pixel. Using a repeat-field, this is halved to about 50 nanoseconds per pixel. A high-resolution image of 1280×1024 must be displayed about 30 microseconds per scan line, or about 25 nanoseconds per pixel. Halving this pixel time for a repeat-field refresh requires the display of one pixel each 12 nanoseconds. This requires the deflection amplifiers and intensity-control amplifier to have very high bandwidth, and the refresh buffer must transfer to support these rates also.

Two-intensity images may not be satisfactory for all applications. Additional control over the intensity of each pixel can be gained by storing multiple bits for each pixel. These bits can be used to control not only intensity, but color as well. The number of bits per pixel needed for an image which appears to have continuous shades of grey is about five or six. But up to eight bits may be needed. For a color display three times as many bits are needed—eight bits for each of the three additive primary colors (red, blue, and green).

Most advanced raster graphics systems use 24-bit color because it allows the use of a virtually unlimited number of colors. By combining the three primary colors—red, green, and blue—and using them in varying intensities, an infinite variety of colors throughout the spectrum can be generated by a computer graphics display. The varying intensities of each primary color are determined by separate intensity settings. The color orange, for example, might have the following scale settings:

Red   .35
Green   .15
Blue   .35

By assigning a numerical scale, we can express the color intensities as numbers. Using eight bits for each value provides 256 (2^8) gradations of intensity for each primary color. In a computer graphics system, each displayable color becomes defined as three numbers, representing an intensity for each component primary color. The color orange thus requires three groups of values:

10101101   for red
00011011   for green
10100110   for blue

In a system with 24 bits of output, eight bits are assigned to each color, and 16.7 million color combinations are available.

Systems with 24 bits per pixel are relatively expensive in spite of the dramatic decreases in the cost of random-access memory. Many applications don't require up to 2^{24} different colors in a single picture, which may have only 2^{14} to 2^{20} pixels. What may be needed is a smaller number of colors in any one picture together with an ability to change colors between pictures or applications.

It may also be desirable to change the appearance of an image without changing the data defining the image. One might want to display pixels with values below some threshold to create a pseudodisplay of the image. For these reasons the image-refresh system of most raster displays uses a *look-up table* (also called a *color table* or *color map*). The pixel's value is used as an index for this look-up table, and the table entry's value is then used to control the intensity or color of the image. A pixel value of 89 causes the contents of table location 89 to be accessed.

Since the look-up operation must be done for each pixel for each display cycle, the table memory must access data quickly. A 512×512 image allows only about 100 nanoseconds to process each pixel. The look-up table has as many entries as there are pixel values.

Many systems have traditionally used less than 24 bits of color definition because of high image-memory costs. A typical system might use four bits to define each pixel with 24 bits of color output. Look-up tables are then used to define the relationship between the pixel value and the actual color output.

Each pixel displayed on the screen has a value defined by the image memory. The number of bit planes of memory determines the number of bits per pixel. For example, 24 bit planes provide 24 bits per pixel. The number of bit planes determines the number of simultanously displayed colors.

In many systems, the number of possible colors is larger than the number of simultaneously displayable colors. This is shown below:

Image memory	Simultaneous colors used	Possible colors available
4 bits in, 24 bits out	16 (2^4)	16.7 million (2^{24})
24 bits in/out	16.7 million (2^{24})	16.7 million (2^{24})

Graphics display systems with 24 bits in and 24 bits out are sometimes called *direct-definition* systems, since the 24-bit value in the image memory corresponds directly to the 24-bit value that is sent to the digital-to-analog converters that control the pixels on the screen. These systems provide full-color imaging, since so many colors are available. In systems with less than 24 bit planes, the value in the image memory is used for indexing into the look-up table.

A 4-bit-in/24-bit-out system has 16 entries in the table, and each entry can be thought of as an index to one of 2^{24} possible values. The user can then set the value of the index as required out of the 16 look-up table entries as shown below:

0	8
1	9
2	10
3	11
4	12
5	13
6	14
7	15

Using this scheme, 16 simultaneous colors are available from a palette of 16.7 million.

A block diagram of a system with a look-up table of m bits is shown in Figure 3-9. For a monochromatic system, 2^m intensity levels are defined. With color, the available bits are divided into three equal groups for the red, blue, and green electron guns of the shadow-mask CRT.

The color representations which are to be used in the application program are stored in the refresh buffer. Each command for a representation is converted into red, green, and blue control signals by an intensity/

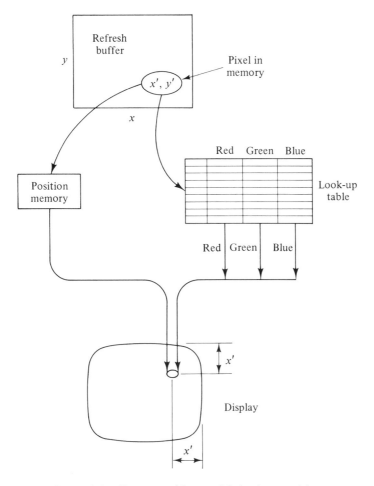

Figure 3-9 System with a *m*-bit look-up table.

chrominance to red/green/blue look-up table. As the user specifies an address in the look-up table, the contents of the address then specify the color. Thus, the operator builds the look-up table during programming with the addresses of the colors to be used. Some typical programming commands might be:

1. Draw circle radius 6 center (A,B) (Color 1) (Comment: Green)
2. Draw line from (A,B) to (C,D) (Color 2) (Comment: Purple)
3. Draw circle radius 3 center (C,D) (Color 3) (Comment: Orange)

Programming with a look-up table requires that a new entry be made to the table for each new color. When the operator exhausts the number of color entries, it is time to delete color entries or reorganize the entire list, which also changes the colors already displayed.

During the program execution, a list of values is entered in the look-up table. The graphics system then looks up the intensities of red, green, and blue to be used for each color identification in image memory, as discussed above.

Since only those colors defined in the table appear on the display, the number of colors used is a function of the size of the look-up table. The number of entries that can be made to the table is determined by how many bits can be used. If 12 bits are used, the table may hold up to 2^{12} or 4096 entries, and the system is called a 12-bit system.

Some of the limitations in using look-up tables to specify colors are inherent in the method, which takes a finite amount of time in addition to the memory requirement. Restrictions can arise from the needs of newer graphics applications, such as those requiring the fine shading of many colors.

The programming for the look-up table can be complicated in these cases, since each entry must be defined as a separate number or address. Existing programs for look-up table systems can also be difficult to modify because of complexities due to the use of tables. Not only must programmers know the colors to be displayed before the program execution, but they must remember what colors have been used and how much space remains in the table. The efficient use of the look-up table requires that the programmer use existing color definitions whenever possible and allocate the table space for the application.

Image Considerations

The images of real objects come directly or indirectly from a scanning device of some sort of a film scanner or TV scanner. But we are concerned instead with the creation of images. These images of objects exist as abstract collections of lines, points, and curves in the computer's memory. This is the realm of interactive computer graphics.

Since there is a fundamental difference between the two-dimensional array of values used to drive a raster system and the line, point, and curve representations of the objects stored and manipulated by the application program, we require the image memory and a program to match in these sets of data in raster-scan devices.

The act of converting a line, point, and area representation to the pixel array in the image storage is called *scan conversion*. Scan-converting algorithms are normally used in actual systems. These algorithms must be executed each time that even some of the displayed image changes. The scan conversion can be a major bottleneck in updating the picture in a timely manner.

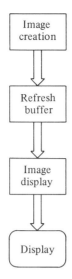

Figure 3-10   Raster display system.

time that even some of the displayed image changes. The scan conversion can be a major bottleneck in updating the picture in a timely manner.

Since the scan-conversion algorithms are needed in raster interactive graphics, they are often incorporated into the system as a functional unit called the *image-creation system*, as shown in Figure 3-10. The entire raster system accepts a program having the general task of the one discussed above. Instead of driving the CRT directly, the instructions are sent to the refresh buffer.

A raster-display instruction set usually includes points, lines, conic sections, solid areas, and text. The various attributes of these output primitives can be controlled, such as color or intensity, line style, text spacing, orientation, font, and size. The coordinates are usually kept in the coordinate system of the refresh buffer itself. For example, if the buffer is a 512×512, then the coordinates will range from 0 to 511 in each dimension.

The image-creation system usually accepts images which are in pixel form. These may be images of real or synthetic objects which have been scan-converted. Note that a rectangular area of the image storage can be easily moved around in the buffer. The image-creation system will usually load the look-up table, start and stop the image refresh, and process the input devices.

We have noted that a given image can use only a limited number of colors, with the result that there may not be enough tones or colors to do gradual shading or display enough information. This can result in striping or moire effects on areas of the shaded color. In addition to this artificial look, there may not be enough colors available to display small variations in data, such as those needed in some seismic applications and detailed parts drawings.

In the direct-definition system, the image memory contains the information to generate each color directly from the intensity values for red, green, and blue that are stored in memory. If the intensity for each primary color is stored as an eight-bit number, the total number of bits stored for each pixel is 24. Thus, there are 2^{24} possible colors available for each pixel.

While eight-bit systems with look-up tables can be limited to only ten intermediate tones between blue and red, a direct definition system of 24 bits allows a great many more tones than there are pixels on the screen.

A direct definition of 24-bit system provides graphics with more complete information content, simpler but extensive programming capabilities. A 24-bit direct-definition system of color graphics has several advantages over look-up table systems:

1. There is no limit to the availability of colors, tones, shades, or gradations in a program or image.

2. There is no need to keep track of what colors have been used, predict what colors are needed, or eliminate any colors. A 24-bit look-up table is usually available; normally it is changed only if a photographic color correction is needed.

3. Blends and overlays are generated without first determining the color availability, since the colors can be defined and specified as needed.

4. Colors are used and manipulated more easily in the program execution.

Many 24-bit systems are available in 512×512 resolutions with video synchronization, so video recorders can be used for animated sequences. Eight-bit systems can also record images, but only 24-bit systems can produce the color ranges found in recorded video. This allows special effects to be tailored to images along with the generation of smooth-shaded synthetic images.

Antialiasing is a technique used to blend two colors smoothly, or to make a slanted line appear smooth instead of jagged. Pixels of an intermediate color between the line and the background are placed around the edge of the line. Antialiasing of edges can also be used when shades overlap, and when shaded images need to be blended. Because there is no limit to the number of shades or colors available with 24 bits, antialiasing can be done more accurately. Programming tends to be simpler, because the next closest color is easily determined without referring to a look-up table.

Shading is important in generating images of three-dimensional objects. Graduated shifts in color are needed to provide the necessary perspectives which clue the eye. The proper shading can require very fine gradations of color and may use large numbers of these gradations for each shading.

Without this type of capability, displays of smooth 3D objects can have stripes or waves on their surfaces, and even the colors can appear to be textured.

Large-scale integrated-circuit memory chips are making direct definition more cost-effective. A typical $512 \times 512 \times 8$-bit display contains 256K bytes, or ¼ megabytes, of image memory. A $512 \times 512 \times 24$-bit system contains ¾ megabytes or 375,000 16-bit words. When 16K RAMs were the largest memory chips available, 24-bit systems were costly. Look-up table systems with one-sixth the image memory were more cost-effective, despite their limitations in color. With the introduction of 64K RAMs, memory became relatively inexpensive, and the benefits of 24-bit systems may outweigh the decreasing cost difference of an eight-bit system.

Many CAD applications can benefit from the 24-bit direct-definition approach. In solid-modeling applications smooth shading and color freedom are especially important. The quality of the image produced by a 24-bit system lets the user see and identify surface details that otherwise may not be apparent, such as wrinkles or flaws on solid models.

The reason for the decreasing costs of raster displays should now be apparent. The basic components are semiconductor memory, logic circuits, a scan generator, and a CRT monitor. There is no need for fast, linear, accurate vector generators or high-current deflection amplifiers. The well-developed and inexpensive deflection and beam-control technology of commercial TV can easily be used for medium-quality systems with 256×256 resolution. A raster display also allows solid areas for continuous grey scale or color, with video mixing with standard TV signals from video cameras, video recorders, and video disks. There is no flicker problem regardless of the picture complexity. Except for those applications requiring quick motion, very rapid update, and a very high resolution, raster technology is the best choice for price and performance.

Many CAD/CAM systems use raster displays because of their full color capability. Integrated circuits and printed-circuit-board design, as well as architectural design, commonly use overlays or layers of drawings with different colors which are generated on raster terminals.

Raster graphic terminals can range from low-cost systems where nearly all the graphics processing is done by the host computer to the more sophisticated terminals which contain a small computer and solid-state memory for a bit-map or refresh buffer. This memory is used to refresh the screen image so that the main processing computer does not need to spend a great deal of time maintaining the displayed images. As discussed above, each memory location in memory corresponds to a picture element on the display screen, and each location in the bit map holds a digital number that represents the color of a corresponding picture element.

The computer accesses the memory to alter the screen image. Some terminals may use a zoom feature that enlarges the image. This function is performed by replicating the picture elements to provide the enlarging effect. Other terminals can have more bits in memory than picture elements on the screen; thus the memory holds more graphics than can be displayed on the screen at any one time. Here features for scrolling and panning allow the display to show selected portions of the image in a manner analogous to having a TV camera move over a drawing.

The memory is generally treated as a set of memory planes, with each plane containing one bit for every picture element. These memory planes are often used to provide the color mixing in integrated circuit and printed-circuit layout. The images stored on separate memory planes appear as layers printed on separate sheets of color cellophane. Each image depicts a layer of the circuit board or chip. When two images overlap, the colors blend to form a different hue. Often this hue is programmed to be some distinctive color that easily stands out and alerts the operator to this condition.

Directed-Beam Displays

Another type of CAD/CAM display is the directed-beam display. It also uses an electron beam, but the beam does not scan across the tube periodically. Instead, it moves from point to point on the screen to produce the desired image. The beam skips those areas where there is no image. The electron beam completely redraws the image on the screen many times each second at the frequency referred to as the *refresh rate*.

These displays are also known as *beam-penetration CRTs*, and they are sometimes used with random-scan systems to obtain color. The inside of the tube's viewing surface is coated with layers of different phosphors, usually red and green. Each of these phosphors has a different excitation-energy level. The acceleration voltage of the electron beam can select the phosphor to be excited. Several colors are obtained with mixtures of red and green and by using acceleration voltages which are in between those of the individual phosphors.

The processor in these systems can be viewed as a special-purpose CPU, with its own set of commands and data formats. It executes a sequence of display instructions to create a drawing on the display screen. The individual DPU instructions typically draw a point or line or create character strings. The interaction devices, with which the user inputs the commands as well as other information, are connected to the processor. The system may be programmed to create a drawing by either random scan or raster scan.

The random-scan system is also called a vector, stroke, or calligraphic system. The parts of the drawing can be depicted on the display in any order. A rectangular object might be traced by deflecting the beam to the starting point, turning it on, and continuously deflecting it between successive line endpoints to trace the outline.

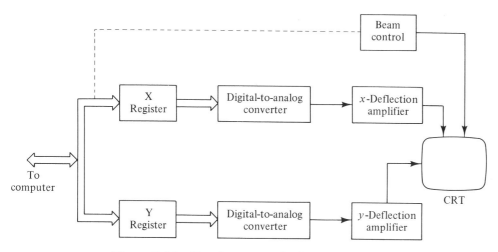

Figure 3-11   Random-scan display system.

The simplest random-scan plots use individual discrete points under processor control. We can think of the display surface as a grid of positions, with the original in the screen's lower left corner. To draw a point at any grid position requires that ten bits of x and y values be available over a 1024×1024 grid. An organization like that in Figure 3-11 can be used to achieve this.

The computer can use I/O commands to load the X and Y registers with the coordinate values. The analog equivalents of the coordinate values are used by the deflection system. The current amplifiers for the magnetic deflection coils or the voltage amplifiers for the deflection plates produce the desired current or voltage.

The electron beam is turned on for a few microseconds and then blanked so that it can move to a new point to be drawn. The process can take from about 5 microseconds per point in a fast system to as much as 50 microseconds per point in a slow system.

The time between the display of successive points is roughly proportional to the distance between them. A simple program to plot points using the coordinate pairs in the x and y arrays might take the following form in Pascal:

```
PROGRAM REPEAT UC            : Refresh loop.
    WAIT (.0333);            : Wait for the next  1/30  second.
PROCEDURE FOR i: = 1 to n do
BEGIN UC
    REPEAT UC                : Wait until refresh is complete.
```

```
UC UNTIL dpu ready;
    DPU XREG (x[i])                    : Procedure to load DPU
                                         X-register.
    DPU YREG (y[i])                    : Procedure to load DPU
                                         Y-register.
END UC                                 : One refresh cycle.
UC UNTIL terminate flag                : Flag set by operating system
                                         when refresh is to stop.
```

This program segment displays points stored in arrays x and y with lengths of n. If n is less than the number of points which can be displayed without flicker, the CPU will have time to do other work. If n is close to the flicker limit, however, the CPU must spend most of its time refreshing the display. Now if a request is made for some other service by the computer, the CPU must abandon the refresh task, leaving the user with a blank screen. This can become unacceptable.

We can expand our simple program for displaying lines. We wish to display a line from (x_1, y_1) to (x_2, y_2). To do this we must fill in the x and y arrays with the coordinates of points that lie approximately on the line. The reason is that an integer value of x for corresponding value of y on the line may not be an integer. Thus rounding or truncating is required. A basic line-drawing algorithm like the one below:

1. Assumes that $x_1 < x_2$.
2. Steps along the x axis from x_1 to x_2.
3. Calculates the y coordinate.
4. Rounds this to the nearest integer value.

The expression for y is based on the slope-intercept form of the line equation $y = mx + b$. A rounding operation is used so that the points which do not fall exactly on a grid point appear sometimes above the line and sometimes below it.

```
PROGRAM,
UC PROCEDURE DRAW LINE
  x1, y1,                        : starting point of line
  x2, y2:  INTEGER;              : ending point of line
VAR m, b, dx, x, y:  REAL;
  inty:  INTEGER UC
BEGIN UC
  compute coefficients m and b of y = mx + b
  dx:  = FLOW(x2 − x1);
  dy:  = FLOW(y2 − y1);
  IF dx <> 0, THEN               : avoid division by zero
    BEGIN UC
```

```
m:    = dy/dx;
b:    = FLOW(y1) − m*FLOW(x1); :y-intercept
x:    = x1
REPEAT UC
  y:   = m * FLOW(x) + b;
  inty:  = ROUND(y);
  PLOT(x,y);               : fill in output array with (x,Y)
  x:   = x + 1
UC UNTIL x > x2
UC END
UC END DRAW LINE
```

This simple program to calculate the points on a line works for lines with an absolute value of 1 or less, but not for other lines. This occurs because the calculated points will be separated in y by more than one unit. It is often desirable to have a program that is computationally faster. The slope m of a line is

$$m = \frac{dy}{dx}$$

or

$$dy = m * dx$$

where dy is the change in y that corresponds to the change of dx in x. Now if

$$dx = 1, \quad \text{then} \quad dy = m$$

This is the change in y for a unit change in x. When incrementing along the x-axis, each unit change in x causes an incremental change of m in y. We can use

$$x = x + 1$$

and

$$y = y + m$$

If we increment along the y axis, then

$$dy = 1$$

and

$$dx = \frac{1}{m}$$

and

$$x = x + \frac{1}{m}$$

and

$$y = y + 1$$

can be used as the scan-conversion algorithm.

While these are all examples of things that a random-scan display might perform, we might pause a moment and reconsider the mechanics of display-address generation. When we wish to plot an image, we also have to say where to plot it.

The addressing scheme chosen is obtained by imagining a two-dimensional Cartesian coordinate system superimposed on the screen of the CRT. In both the horizontal (x) and vertical (y) directions we assign integers for each point to which the electron beam can be digitally deflected. Most CRTs provide at least 1024 x and 1024 y addresses, and any x may be associated with any y value.

There is a time-constraint problem when displaying lines as points in a random-scan system display. Since only so many points can be displayed without flicker, then only so many inches of flicker-free lines can be displayed. The number of points displayable can have an effect on the number of lines that can be drawn on the screen.

The displaying of curves requires that the line-drawing procedure be generalized to plot the function $y = f(x)$. The units of $f(x)$ must be the same units as the display coordinates, so we can increment along the x axis, evaluating $f(x)$ at each point. The resulting values must be rounded or truncated, since each point may not be an integer.

Displaying characters can be done by defining a pattern of dots on a grid, as shown in Figure 3-12. At the minimum a 5 × 7 grid is needed for each character. The grid then contains 35 points, and each character can be represented with 35 bits. A character-generating algorithm uses the 35-bit representation of the characters to fill in the x and y arrays, which in turn are used by the refresh memory. We use the character code of the symbol to be displayed, and the coordinates of the screen position at which character is to be displayed. The character definition is the two-dimensional array of bits which indicate which points in the 5 × 7 grid are to be intensified.

In a line-drawing random-scan display we use a pair of registers in which to hold the line's endpoint, and a vector generator, which moves the CRT

Figure 3-12   Character generation using a 5 × 7 matrix.

beam from one point to another. The vector generator must move the CRT beam in a straight line—or what appears to the viewer to be a straight line. It must also draw all lines with the same brightness. As the beam moves slower, more electrons hit a given area of the phosphor, making the area appear brighter. A constant brightness is obtained by moving the beam with a constant velocity or by adjusting the beam intensity. The vector generator must also turn on the beam as it leaves the start point and turn it off at the endpoint and not cause smearing.

The vector generator produces outputs for the x and y deflections and the intensity. If intensity compensation is not needed, then the intensity signal can be an on-off switch. Figure 3-13 shows the signals required to draw several different lines on the display. We note that the actual time required to draw a vector is proportional to the change in x or y, whichever is greater.

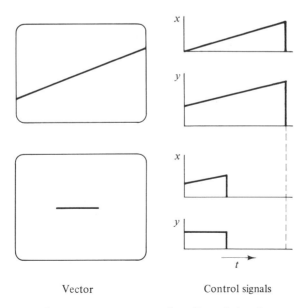

Vector   Control signals

Figure 3-13   Drawing a vector: proportionality of the time required to the change in x or y.

Two methods can be used to generate the deflection signals. Analog vector generators use an analog integrator to produce a reference voltage which varies linearly from 0 to some maximum. The x and y deflection signals are generated by multiplying the reference ramp by signals derived from the desired changes in x and y. This produces the signal to drive the deflection amplifiers, and a straight line results. High-performance systems using this technique can draw a short vector in 1 microsecond and full-screen vector in 10 microseconds.

The other method is to use digital techniques to increment or decrement the coordinate registers at a rate proportional to the change in x and y. The registers are sent to digital-to-analog converters, and these are used to control the deflection amplifiers. These signals are not smooth and appear as staircase inputs to the deflection amplifiers. This effect is not found in analog vector generators. Digital vector-generator technology allows a line to be drawn anywhere across the screen in 30 microseconds. Depending on the speed of the vector generator, short vectors can be drawn in as little as 0.1 microsecond of the line. Digital generators require fewer adjustments and tend to cost less than analog generators. The addition of a vector generator means that more instructions must be added to the graphics system. The functions that must be performed have expanded beyond drawing a point and jumping and now include moving the beam's position without drawing as well as drawing a line.

In the beam-manipulation instructions, the position is loaded into the x and y registers, and, after the beam has been moved, the system logic updates the registers. The most common instructions fall into five required groups:

1. Load x coordinate.
2. Load y coordinate and move beam to new position.
3. Load y coordinate and move new beam to drawing point.
4. Load y coordinate and draw line to new point from old point.
5. Jump without drawing.

These instructions are used in combination to draw points, connected line segments, and disconnected line segments. A vector generator can also be used to draw straight-line parts of characters and piecewise linear approximations to curves. This provides an improvement over drawing these with individual dots.

A major disadvantage of the random-scan directed-beam type of CRT is that the time needed to change the acceleration voltage can be as long as 200 microseconds. Making many color changes through acceleration voltage changes in the $\frac{1}{30}$-second refresh-time space limits the amount of information that can be displayed without flicker and overstresses the acceleration power supply. It may be necessary to limit the use of color, such that lines, points, and characters of one color are displayed in sequence. The quality and range of colors (usually red, orange, yellow, and green) which is available with these CRTs is limited, but this is an expensive way to obtain color in a random-display system.

Direct-View Storage Tubes

Another type of a CAD/CAM display is the *direct-view storage tube* (DVST). It, too, draws images from point to point on a screen with an electron beam, much as the directed-beam display does. However, the DVST system draws each image only once, with no periodic rescanning. The image is stored using a phosphor that coats the screen surface, and periodic refreshing is unnecessary, since the image is held there. The direct-view storage tube is similar to a standard CRT, except that the image is stored inside the DVST as a distribution of charges on the inside surface of the screen. Figure 3-14 shows the basics of the tube.

The electron gun, focusing system, and deflection system are functionally identical to those in the conventional CRT system. The function of the focused electron gun is the creation of the stored image, while the flood beam allows the stored image to be visible. Initially the tube surface has a uniform negative charge. As the high-energy electron beam strikes this surface, electrons are dislodged and are attracted to the more positively charged collector grid. This decrease in the number of electrons creates a positive charge. The storage surface is nonconducting, so the electrons cannot migrate, and the created charge pattern is stored as an image on the display.

Some commercial displays use the *direct-view bistable storage tube*. Here, the number of electrons lost over a unit area is constant, so that only two intensities, on and off, are possible. Continuous tubes have also been built, but they are not as widely used in commercial intensity. Writing systems up to 8000 inches per second are available to create a stored image.

Besides writing onto the storage screen, the flood gun emits low-velocity electrons, which are also attracted to the screen. This flood beam is not

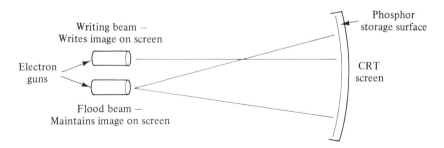

Figure 3-14   The direct-view storage tube.

focused. It floods or covers the entire screen with electrons. A constant voltage is applied to collimating plates, which force flood-beam electrons to reach the storage surface at right angles. As they approach a positively charged part of the storage surface, they strike the phosphor and cause light emission. The electrons approaching other areas of the surface are repelled away. The charge pattern on the surface thus produces a visible image.

The image is erased in two steps. First a positive voltage is applied to the storage surface. This attracts flood electrons and causes the entire surface to be written with a flash of light as the storage tube is erased.

The storage surface has lost some of its electrons, so a negative voltage is applied to the surface. The new electrons are retained on the surface. The operating voltage is returned to normal, and a new image can be formed.

Decreasing the energy of the writing beam allows a write-through function. The writing beam will create an image on the screen, but it does not affect the stored charge distribution on the screen. This feature is useful to display cursors or to allow characters to be refreshed from a buffer so that parts of the picture can change while other parts are stored as a charge distribution.

Some newer kinds of direct-view storage-tube terminals display images in two colors. Some images are stored on the screen in green, while other images are refreshed from a solid-state memory to be displayed in yellow-orange. The second color is used for interactive prompts and user responses. These disappear when no longer required, without altering the graphics in the picture.

DVSTs have several disadvantages, but they also have some major advantages. Erasing just some parts of the picture is not normally possible, and the contrast between the dark and bright picture areas is low. On the other hand, the relative cost of DVST display systems is lower than that of random-scan and many raster-scan systems, since no refresh buffer is needed and the deflection circuits need not be as fast.

Complex pictures with sharp lines and characters can be displayed without flicker problems. A typical 19-inch diagonal DVST can display over 40,000 characters.

CRT Display Characteristics

The speed of a display can be measured in a number of ways. In general terms we define it to be the average time required to move the beam to a given point on the screen and display a spot there. The amount of flicker-free information that can normally be displayed is inversely proportional to this time. The refresh rate above which a picture stops flickering and fuses into a steady image is sometimes called the *fusion frequency*. As we have seen, the refresh rate for a raster-scan system is fixed at 30 or 60 per second, and it is independent of the picture complexity. The refresh rate for a vector system depends directly on the picture complexity, which includes the number of lines, points, and characters. The complexity of the image increases the time for a single refresh cycle and decreases the refresh rate.

The relation between fusion frequency and persistence tends to be nonlinear, since doubling the persistence from 10 to 20 microseconds does not halve the fusion frequency. As the persistence increases into several seconds, the fusion becomes very small.

Phosphors with very low or no persistence can be used, since the eye can detect light for a short period of time if it is repeated at a frequency above the fusion frequency. In most phosphors, a large amount of the light is caused by phosphorescence. If a zero-persistence material is used, the electron beam must remain longer on each point, and this reduces the number of points the beam can reach during a refresh cycle.

Fusion frequency also increases with the image intensity and ambient room lighting and can vary with different colors. It depends on the user, since it is a physiological phenomenon. Specified fusion frequencies are usually average for a number of observers.

Other evaluation criteria for a CRT include the quality of the display's focusing system. These can be measured in terms of resolution, spot size, repeatability, linearity, and speed. Resolution and spot size (the latter being a function of the diameter of the focusing beam) are reciprocals. A resolution of 100 lines per inch implies a spot size of 0.01.

Resolution is usually measured with a *shrinking raster*. Here, a number of equally spaced parallel lines are displayed; then line spacing is uniformly decreased until the lines begin to merge together. The *resolution* is the distance between the two outer lines, divided by the number of lines in the raster. As the intensity of the beam increases, the resolution appears to decrease, since the line will be wider. This is caused by *blooming*, which is a tendency of the phosphor's excitation to spread over the area being hit by the electrons. The resolution for raster displays is usually given in terms of the total number of scan lines rather than in lines per inch.

Since the refresh rate can be decreased with a long persistence, a very long-persistence phosphor would appear to be a solution to this problem. But consider what would happen to the screen upon changing images. The moving image would leave a smear of the previous images. Dynamic CAD/CAM applications need low-persistence phosphors, but some computer-aided design applications may trade off dynamic capabilities for a larger number of flicker-free picture elements to produce complex, relatively static drawings.

The *shadow-mask CRT* employs multiple electron guns for random displays. Compared to the directed-beam CRT, its line width is greater and its resolution is less.

Shadow-mask color CRTs are used in most color TV sets. The shadow-mask tube is surface-covered with phosphor dots arranged in triangular patterns, as shown in Figure 3-15. Every group of three dots is called a *triad*. Each of these has one dot of phosphor for emitting red light, one for blue, and one for green. These triads are small, so that when viewed from a distance, the light from the individual dots mixes and appears to the viewer as a mixture of the three colors. A wide range of colors can be provided by using different intensities of the components of the color mixture.

The individual phosphor dots are excited by three different electron guns, arranged in a triangular pattern like the triads shown in Figure 3-15. The guns operate synchronously, as they are focused at the same point on the screen. Behind the viewing surface is a shadow mask. It has a small hole for each triad, and holes are aligned such that each dot in the triad receives electrons from only its gun. In this way the number of electrons from each gun can control the amounts of red, green, and blue light in the color mixture.

The use of the shadow-mask concept imposes limits on the resolution of these CRTs that are not present in monochrome CRTs. In high-resolution tubes the triads are placed on centers of about 0.30 mm, while in home TV tubes 0.50-mm centers are used.

Repeatability is a measure of the deflection system's ability to move the beam to the same spot on the screen for a given deflection signal. The measured distance can be as low as 0.01 inch in high-quality systems. Repeatability applies primarily to random graphic systems.

A display's *linearity* is a measure of how straight the lines are. It can be specified in either absolute or relative terms. The *absolute linearity* is the maximum pendicular distance between the displayed line and a truly straight line connected with the same endpoints. The *relative linearity* is the ratio between the absolute linearity and the line's length, expressed as a percentage. A 1% linearity for a full-screen line can be achieved in many CAD/CAM systems.

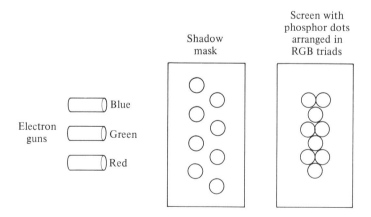

Figure 3-15   The shadow-mask color technique.

The raster-scan directed-beam and direct-view storage tubes used in CAD/CAM terminals have advantages and limitations which can affect the display resolution, the user effectiveness, and the amount of information the terminal can display.

Full-color images are most common in the raster-scan displays. Some directed-beam systems provide a limited number of colors through the use of special screen phosphors. Here the voltage on the beam controls the depth of beam penetration into the screen phosphor which produces the different colors. Directed-beam systems usually produce four colors using this technique, although one such system generates over 400 different colors this way.

Most DVST displays generate only green images, but there are some two-color DVST displays. This type of display can show parts of a drawing stored in a display memory in green, while objects currently being redrawn or manipulated appear in a yellow-orange. The technique uses a mixture of red and green screen phosphors. The yellow-orange lines on the screen can be changed to green by retracing them with a more intense electron beam.

Each display technology provides some features that are suited for certain CAD/CAM applications. The raster-scan terminals provide more colors than the other technologies. CAD terminals for the design of integrated circuits and circuit boards use these terminals, since each layer in a chip or circuit board can be represented by a different color. The raster-scan displays can also produce solid filled-in areas in displayed images more easily than the directed-beam or storage-tube displays.

The raster-scan terminals often do not provide as much picture resolution as do the directed-beam tubes. A typical raster screen might contain 512×512 picture elements, but directed-beam tubes often provide 1024×1024 locations and sometimes as many as 4096×4096.

The low resolution in raster terminals also causes the problem of aliasing. Aliasing occurs because straight lines on many raster terminals appear to have a stair-step effect as the line extends from the picture elements on one scan line to the next.

High-resolution can be critical where the accuracy of the relationship between drawn lines is high. Raster-scan terminals are available with 4096×4096 resolution, but at high cost.

Directed-beam displays have some limitations, the major one concerning the amount of information that can be displayed. Because each point on a directed-beam image must be refreshed periodically, the more information there is on the screen, the longer the time period required for each refresh of the screen images. When the screen display contains a great deal of information, the image may not be refreshed fast enough to prevent flicker. In contrast, raster terminals use a fixed frame rate so that flicker never appears to the user, regardless of the amount of information on the screen.

Storage-tube displays may cost less than either directed-beam or raster-scan terminals. The reason is that storage-tube displays hold graphical information on the face of the CRT itself. The other display technologies may cost more because they require built-in memory to hold the image. Storage-tube terminals, however, tend to construct images on the screen much more slowly than do other CRTs, because the entire drawing must be erased and redrawn when only a small part of the image is to be altered or changed.

Other differences in CRT display technologies become important when the terminals are interfaced with peripheral CAD/CAM equipment. Lightpens are often used on the display screens to create or change the display information. Changing drawings with lightpens can be slower on the directed-beam and storage-tube terminals than on raster terminals. As the user triggers a lightpen on a raster system, the pen can pick up light from the display quickly, since the electron beam scans the entire display surface a number of times each second. The electron beam in the directed-beam or DVST display does not scan the entire screen. These displays must sequence through the other parts of the screen until they reach the portion under the lightpen to indicate the lightpen position. This takes some additional time and can decrease the effectiveness of the design process.

Other Interactive Display Technologies

The *plasma panel* display is an interactive display that is not based on CRT technology. A plasma panel is an array of small neon bulbs. Each bulb can be switched on or off. A typical plasma panel has 64 cells or bulbs per inch and is 8 inches square with a quarter of a million cells. Panels up to 40 inches square have been fabricated.

The plasma panel provides medium-resolution in a storage display that does not need a refresh buffer. The bulbs are not separate units. They are fabricated as an integrated panel made of three layers of glass, as seen in Figure 3-16. One layer has thin vertical strips for electrical conductors. The center layer has holes which form the bulbs, and the inside surface of the other layer has thin horizontal strips for electrical conductors.

To turn on a bulb, the voltages on the lines are adjusted so their difference is large enough to fire the neon in the cell and make it glow. Once the glow starts, a lower voltage can be used to sustain the glow. To turn off a bulb the voltages on the lines are made less than the sustaining neon voltage. The bulbs can be switched on or off in about 20 microseconds. In some designs individual cells are replaced with an open cavity, since the neon glow can be contained in a localized area between the front and back glass layers.

The plasma display panel provides a digitally controlled display using neon gas for producing light. It has some storage-tube features, median resolution, long persistence, and microsecond erase times. Digital addressing structures can be used, and the panel is flat, transparent, and rugged. It needs

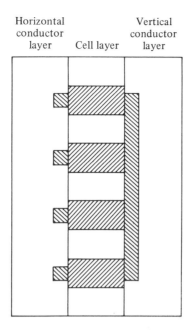

Figure 3-16   The plasma-panel display.

no refresh buffer. Plasma display panels have been used in rear-projection systems to mix photographic slides for computer-generated dynamic graphics. The cost of this system is relatively high for its limited resolution.

Two other display techniques using solid-state technology show promise for use in CAD/CAM displays in the future. Light-emitting diodes (LEDs) and liquid-crystal displays (LCDs) are used in many numerical readout panels. One can use either LED or LCD arrays of closely spaced dots and turn each dot on or off using digital drivers without refresh buffers. An array of a million cells in an area 10 inches square would provide the display. The LCD is attractive for portable displays, since it is not a light source but reflects ambient light in the desired pattern. Its power requirements are very low. Color filters could be used in LCD systems to provide color. LEDs are available in several basic colors, so color mixing could be used as in CRT color tubes.

Lasers comprise another technology that has been used in several types of displays. The laser beams are deflected by mirrors or by passing the beam through a material whose index of refraction can be controlled by an electrical signal. The problem has been that only limited amounts of graphics can be refreshed by these methods.

One type of system avoids the refresh problem by using the laser beam to trace an image in a film. The film material darkens when exposed to the laser's wavelength. Another wavelength of light is then used to project this image onto a larger screen. A complex image can be drawn in a few seconds. The film material is not partially selective, so making changes requires redrawing the entire image, just as is done with a DVST system.

Some useful display features apply in general to all technologies, as described below.

For point plotting and line generation some current displays produce lines by sequential point plotting. Instead of this, using any two points on the screen, a straight line should be drawn between them by the graphics processing.

Edge-fault detection is useful when the display screen is taken to be a window through which we are seeing a partial section of an arbitrarily large drawing. Then we want to know when the program that is producing the drawing tries to draw beyond the field of view.

Producing characters by dot plotting is time-consuming, so the tendency has been to use the faster method of wired generators. These produce characters that are usually oriented along a horizontal line. By using rotation, we should be able to produce characters along any slanted line.

Utility features are useful for any display with buffer memory. It should be possible to send codes that cause it to do something other than display, such as set or sense flags and transfer control. Asynchronous deflection and unblank controls can eliminate the need to penalize the user by designing in a fixed time delay based on a maximum deflection requirement. If the beam is moved only a small distance, the time required is shorter, and the user ought to be able to benefit from this.

Coordinate registers are useful, since after a lightpen signal while in the display mode, we normally do not know the beam position (x, y) explicitly. If we want to subscript or superscript a character, then the display tells where the beam is.

Multilevel and independent gain controls can allow one to change the raster size for each axis. Usually CRT rasters are inscribed squares. This can waste portions of the screen, since they are not addressable. Sometimes it would be better to circumscribe the raster, even if some of the x, y addresses would then be illegal. Flat-face tubes of variable-persistence phosphors would allow somewhat more convenience for lightpen work and allow some applications to use the storage-tube principle while permitting conventional raster-scan techniques for others.

Hard-Copy Display

Computers were used for drawing before the development of interactive graphics. In this section we discuss the printers and plotters that are the principal graphic output devices. Most hard-copy drawings or diagrams produced by CAD systems are drawn with pen plotters. These plotters use a fiber-tip or similar type of pen to draw each line under the control of the computer. Faster technologies such as electrostatic printing and ink-set printing may become more dominant, but pen plotters can produce accurate multicolor drawings at low cost.

Pen plotters can be of either the drum or the flatbed type, and some plotters combine some features of each. The drawing material in a flat-bed plotter rests on a flat plate or bed and does not move during the drawing process. Such plotters range from page-sized units costing a few hundred dollars to large table-sized units.

Drum plotters rotate the drawing surface over a drum past the drawing pens. The drum eliminates the need for a large, flat drawing surface, and drum plotters can be less expensive than equivalent flat-bed plotters.

Many early drum plotters were less accurate than the flat-bed units, because their drawing surfaces were not stable and they moved back and forth slightly. These problems have largely disappeared in the more recent drum plotters.

Several pen plotters designed for use in CAD systems incorporate microprocessors and solid-state memories. The built-in computers allow the CAD system to minimize the amount of information the host computer must use to control the plotter functions. For example, the drawing size and line thickness might be specified using single commands issued through the host computer. The computer in the plotter then takes this command and processes the details.

These built-in computers allow the plotters to print text in different fonts, change the length of dashed lines, or provide other variations. Other programmed characteristics can include the drawing speed, acceleration, and pen force. These characteristics could be changed using through commands from the main computer or manually using pushbuttons on the plotter.

Some plotter units can also be programmed to write coarse characters that can be printed faster or higher-quality characters that take longer to generate but appear more perfect. Units can have the capability to print special graphics such as foreign-language characters or mapping symbols. These features may be provided using plug-in memory modules that can be changed as required.

Another plotter option is the capability to be down-loaded with data from the main computer. These plotters must contain enough solid-state memory to hold a complete drawing. The advantage of down-loading is that it allows the plotter to produce the drawing without requiring the computer to intervene. This additional memory makes these plotters cost more than less sophisticated types.

Multiple-color capability is also available in pen plotters. Some units automatically select pens from a multiple pen turret. These devices are also equipped with an 8K-byte memory buffer to reduce the communication time between the plotter and the host computer.

One of the characteristics of pen-plotter quality is repeatability—the ability to return to a predefined point. Drum plotters can attain 0.000-inch repeatability.

The maximum writing speed is also important. Quality units generally inscribe lines at 60 cm/s and accelerate to this speed from stop within a few tenths of a second. The pen plotters may draw with a variety of writing implements, including roller-ball, fiber-tip, and standard liquid-ink pens. Drawing mediums can include paper, vellum, or polyester film, and the media size ranges from $8 \times 10\frac{1}{2}$ inches to $24\frac{1}{2} \times 47\frac{1}{2}$ inches.

All random plotters accept a number of general commands, such as lower pen, raise pen, move to the left or right, and move up or down. A feedback system consisting of position sensors and servomotors implements the commands. The pen is raised and lowered using an electromagnet. Some plotters can move in any of 16 directions.

Those plotters that incorporate microprocessors can accept commands to draw circles and arcs as well as characters, since the microprocessor generates the low-level command sequences.

The most common type of raster plotter—the electrostatic plotter—uses a deposit with a negative charge on those parts of the paper that are to be black. The plotter then flows a positively charged black liquid over the paper, as shown in Figure 3-17. The paper can be up to 72 inches wide and can move at a speed of 3 inches per second. A row of electrical contacts is spaced 100 to 250 to the inch, and each contact that is ON imparts a negative charge. From 100 to 250 vertical dots per inch are produced as the paper moves. Each dot is an electrostatic plot of either black or white, although some units allow shading levels to be obtained by defining texture patterns with different numbered codes.

Electrostatic plotters can generate drawings more quickly than pen plotters, especially drawings containing large filled-in areas. Electrostatic

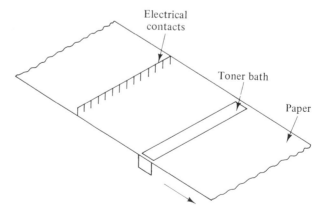

Figure 3-17   Electrostatic plotter operation.

plotters require special conductive paper coated with a thin dielectric film. This paper is necessary to retain the electric charge when a high voltage is impressed on it. Once the paper has been charged, the developing liquid (the *toner*, which is typically carbon particles in suspension) deposits the black material on the charged areas. Resins in the toner fix the particles after the charge is neutralized, and the paper is then air- or vacuum-dried.

Pen plotters can produce sharp-contrast images and can use pens of different colors and thicknesses. Electrostatic plotter images have a lower contrast, since a slight toner residue adheres to the charged part of the paper, and they may be limited to black and white images. The electrostatic plotter can be 10 to 20 times faster than a pen plotter. Electrostatic plotters can also be used as medium-speed line printers.

Electrostatic plotters can produce 22×34-inch drawings with 100-lines/inch resolution in 30 seconds or in under 60 seconds at 200 lines/inch. Electrostatic plotters make little noise and have good reliability characteristics, because they have few moving parts.

One can also use printers for graphical output. The major areas in which line printers are practical for graphical output are flowcharts, block diagrams, plottings of functions of a single variable such as bar graphs, and plottings of functions of two variables, with one function being indicated by the darkness of the characters.

A major factor in determining if a graphical output device is useful for a particular application is the resolution, which is the number of distinguishable units per unit of distance. The low resolution of some printers, which may be 10 units per inch horizontally and 6 units per inch vertically, tends to limit their utility.

The line printer's speed and low cost per page of output may outweigh the resolution factor, since it costs much less to produce graphs and charts on printers than on plotters. Some printers use a dot matrix technique to print discrete dots at resolutions of up to 100 points per inch. When equipped with multicolor ribbons, these printers can also produce colored hard copy.

Most electrostatic printers use a logic section that controls the printing and accepts the incoming information, generally in the form of ASCII characters. These devices accept incoming characters and plot at the same time.

Electrostatic printers are raster devices rather than vector devices. Pen plotters draw one line or vector in a drawing at a time. Electrostatic printers print one horizontal section or raster of the image at a time in the same way a CRT image is displayed.

Electrostatic printers are normally used to provide a hard copy of CRT displays only after the drawings have been completed. Electrostatic printers, unlike pen plotters, plot at a constant speed, regardless of the density of the information on the drawing.

Electrostatic printer resolution is usually given in terms of dots/inch and is determined by the spacing of the electrodes in the print head. Resolution is of the order of 250 horizontal dots/inch and 150 vertical dots/inch. Units with 400 dots/inch are also available.

A number of other technologies can also be used to provide hard-copy output. Most of these have limited graphics capabilities and are used mostly in applications requiring text only.

Other Hard-Copy Technologies

Another hard-copy technology is the *xerographic* technique. This type of copier reproduces a page by creating an electrostatic charge of electrons where there is black. A dry toner is attracted to a drum where there is a charge, and this toner is transferred to the paper to complete the copy. Color xerography repeats the process three times. Powdered pigments in each primary color mix on the paper to form the colors to be copied.

This basic technique has been extended to computer-controlled image creation, in which a laser beam is scanned across the rotating selenium drum, creating a charge distribution based on the original document. After the charge pattern is set up, the process continues as in the conventional copies. A resolution of several hundred points per inch is possible this way.

Ink-jet plotters spray jets of ink at paper moving on a rotating drum (Figure 3-18). The ink jets move on a track between the ends of the drum. The three colors are deposited at the same time as the drum rotates.

A camera can be used to photograph an image displayed on a cathode-ray tube to produce hard copy. Simple systems use a standard TV or movie camera aimed at a display in a darkened room. Commercial systems that use the same idea are available with precision CRTs and color filters. Figure 3-19 shows the basic concept.

The displayed image can be color-sorted to avoid many color-filter changes. Color mixtures can be created by double exposure of parts of the

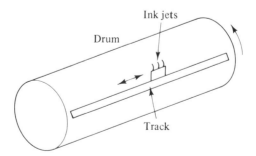

Figure 3-18   Ink-jet plotter operation.

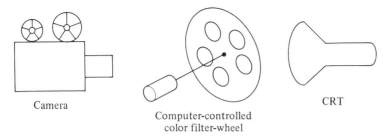

Camera

Computer-controlled
color filter-wheel

CRT

Figure 3-19   The basic camera recording concept.

image through several filters with different color intensities. Some systems use the signals which drive the CRT to drive a dedicated high-quality monitor; then the photography is performed through color filters to eliminate any degradation caused by the use of the shadow-mask in the tube.

Motion picture equipment can also be used to produce special motion sequences or effects. For good results, the following rules should be observed:

1. Accurate film registration in the camera is necessary in order to minimize jitter effects when projecting the film.
2. The time for the CRT phosphor light to decay below the film-sensitivity threshold should be short compared to the frame-advance time.
3. The frame-advance time should be as short as possible, consistent with the two previous items.
4. The CRT deflection and brightness control circuits must be stable and show good repeatability.

The power to convey information and stimulate our intuition is strong in motion sequences. Beyond the use of motion, it is possible to employ color and stereoscopic views to add even more content to the filmed output. Such techniques are relatively easy to employ using computer control.

We can consider motion in the context of sensing changes in the position of one body relative to another at particular times. A standard motion picture camera photographs these positional relationships every $\frac{1}{24}$ of a second. This time can be taken as an independent variable, called *real time*, in contrast to the *computer time* used to do a calculation. A model might require only a few minutes to run while the real time implied is several years. Some programs use computers to control a procedure in real time. In this case the real time is the same as the computer time. The real-time interval (t) between two consecutive frames can be under computer control to either compress or expand time as desired.

The method used to add color to the picture should give the best and most consistent quality. In filmed displays, the total picture can be organized in the computer as a number of separate picture parts according to the colors that the finished picture should have. When these parts are plotted and photographed, each frame of the film contains only those picture parts that are to appear in one color. Using this procedure of color separation, any number of hues can be produced for each final frame of film. In practice eight separate colors give satisfactory results. The separated picture parts are merged using the appropriate color filters.

INTERACTION DEVICES

No discussion of interactive displays would be complete without consideration of the associated input devices. While we must attach values to the visual presentation, it is equally important to be able to conveniently and quickly interact with the CAD/CAM process. Several types of input devices are used for this activity. An ordinary keyboard suitably connected to the computer is one example. Arrays of switches, buttons and control knobs are others.

By using the program, we can assign various special functions to any key or button. Striking the R key on a typewriter, for example, ordinarily causes an R to be typed. The program, however, might be set up to change the view or the perspective of the image on the CRT when the R key is activated. How such programmable devices are used depends on the programmer, and their utility derives from the fact that they are programmable. At one instant we can be using the keyboard to type in a new program, and immediately thereafter we can use it to move keyboards and buttons around on the CRT screen.

Keyboards can be divided into two basic types. The *alphanumeric keyboard* can be used to enter commands, text, and parameter values. Each key causes a seven-bit code to be stored in a character register. The interpretation of the code is determined by the CPU program.

We might also accumulate consecutive characters into a buffer until a termination character is typed, thereby producing a character-string input.

The *programmed-function keyboard* (PFK) is a keyboard with 16 to 32 pushbuttons. The depression of each button generates a unique code, which is stored in a register. Some PFKs may have, in each button, lights which are controlled by the CPU. These lights are used for operator feedback or to indicate which functions are available for use.

The *alphanumeric keyboard* is a text-only device. Several technologies are used to detect a key depression. These include mechanical contact closures, a change in capacitance, and a change in magnetic coupling. The basic functional characteristic of any keyboard device is that it creates a code for a letter or number uniquely corresponding to the depressed key. Many factors tend to make one keyboard preferable to another. These include:

1. The key spacing.
2. The slope of the keyboard.
3. The shape of the key caps.
4. The pressure needed to depress a key.
5. The feeling of contact when a key is depressed.

Other considerations deal with the design layout, such as making frequently used correction keys easily reachable and eliminating the need to simultaneously depress the control or shift keys, and separating such keys as line delete from other frequently used keys such as that for the return function.

The *programmed-function keyboard* (PFK) is the most common button device. It is sometimes designed as a separate unit, but more often the buttons are integrated with the main keyboard. Button devices are also used on many tablet cursor systems.

Button devices differ from text devices in that the latter are always prelabeled. Button-device keys may have no predefined character meanings, and the number of keys may vary.

Button devices can report pressure releases as well as depressions. This makes it easy to start an activity such as the rotation of a displayed object when a button is depressed and then to terminate the activity when the button is released. One can view the text device as a special type of button device, but since text devices are so common they are given a separate identity.

Buttons are generally used to enter commands or menu options. Dedicated systems use buttons with permanent labels. To allow the changing of soft labels, some systems use coded overlays on which the command names are printed. Tabs are used on the overlay so the system knows which overlay is in place. The operator inserts the overlay containing the command and then depresses a key. Some keyboards also use mirrors to superimpose labels from a CRT to an unlabeled keyboard.

An unusual button device is the *chord keyboard* which has five keys shaped like piano keys. It is operated by depressing several keys at the same time, as in playing a chord. The five keys allow 31 chords to be generated. Learning the chords takes time, but skilled users can operate the device rapidly, and it allows fast touch typing. But it is not suitable as a substitute for the standard alphanumeric keyboard.

The *touch panel* is a device which allows the user to give full attention to the screen and to indicate items on it using a finger rather than by moving a screen cursor to the item. The touch panel is mounted across the face of the CRT. When the user's finger touches the panel, this position is detected using one of several different technologies.

Panels with from 10 to 50 resolvable positions in each direction may use a series of light-emitting diodes and photodiodes or phototransistors to form a grid over the display area. Touching the screen breaks a set of vertical and horizontal light beams which are used to determine relative position.

Another type of panel with about 500 positions in each direction uses bursts of high-frequency shock waves which travel alternately in the horizontal and vertical directions within a flat glass plate. A finger on the glass causes part of the wave to be reflected back to its source. The distance to the touched point can be calculated from the time interval between the start of the wave burst and its arrival back to the source.

Another type of high-resolution panel uses two layers of transparent material; one is coated with a thin conductor and the other is resistive. Finger pressure causes a voltage drop on the resistive substrate, which is measured to calculate the coordinates of the pressure point.

Digitizing Tablets

Many CAD systems are designed to receive input data through *graphic pad digitizers*. These devices consist of a flat tablet and a cursor. One of the most commonly used locators, the *tablet*, is a flat surface over which a stylus pencil or cursor is moved. The position of the cursor or stylus is monitored by the computer.

The stylus usually incorporates a pressure-sensitive switch which closes when the user pushes down on the stylus. This indicates the stylus is at a position of interest. Most cursors have one or more buttons, which are used by the operator to input commands. The stylus switch and the cursor buttons are really separate input devices which are integrated into the system design.

Most tablets use some electrical sensing scheme to measure the stylus or cursor position. In one design, a grid of wires is embedded in the tablet surface. The electromagnetic coupling between the electrical signals in the grid and in a wire coil in the stylus or cursor induces an electrical signal in the stylus or cursor. The strength of the electromagnetic coupling can be used to determine how far the stylus or cursor is from the tablet. A screen cursor is usually displayed to track the position being read from the tablet and to provide visual feedback to the operation.

A drawing placed on the tablet is digitized by positioning the cursor over each point or line to be recorded. The digitizer senses the position of a pen, cursor, or some other pointer and electronically relays this information to the computer as an x,y coordinate on the pad. The cursors in these systems usually contain a set of cross-hairs for lining up the point on the pad to be digitized. Some cursors also contain pushbuttons which can start predefined computer routines or other operations to simplify the graphic data entry. Digitizers can generally resolve lines to within 0.025 mm.

The most common digitizer technologies are electrostatic, magneto-strictive, and electromagnetic. *Electrostatic tablets* radiate an electric field which is sensed by the pen. The system changes the frequency of the radiated field as a function of where the pen touches the surface. This frequency changes for each tablet position. The digitizer circuits translate the frequency changes into x,y coordinates, which are then sent to the computer.

Electrostatic digitizers can sense the pen position through most media that have a low dielectric constant, such as paper, plastic, or glass. Electrostatic systems cannot digitize accurately in close proximity to metal or to partially conductive material such as pencil lead or some felt-tip inks.

Magnetostrictive tablets use magnetostrictive wires laid beneath the table to keep track of pen position. A magnetic pulse on one end of the wires produces a small strain wave which propagates across the tablet. The wave is detected using a pick-up coil in the pen or cursor. The time elapsed from the start of the pulse to the probe's sensing of it is then related to the position of the pen.

Magnetostrictive tablets are not sensitive to conductive materials. However, magnetic objects which are near the tablet surface can disturb the magnetic properties and degrade the accuracy. These tablets must also be periodically remagnetized with large magnets.

Electromagnetic tablets sense position using the magnetic coupling between the pen and the tablet surface. The electromagnetic tablets also contain a grid of wires under the tablet surface. Either the table or the pen transmits a small ac signal which is then detected by receiver circuits, which produce a digital signal defining the pen location. Electromagnetic digitizers are not affected by conductive or magnetic materials on their surface and generally require no periodic recalibration.

Digitizer pad sizes can range from 10×11 to 44×60 inches. The smaller pads are often used to select commands from a menu.

On the tablet an overlay is placed which has blocked-off areas labeled with the graphic commands, such as Draw Line; Circle; or Arc. Pointing the cursor at the labeled block causes the action to be carried out. This method of entering commands is much faster than typing in commands on an alphanumeric keyboard.

The larger pad sizes are generally used to digitize drawings and schematics. Table surfaces include formica, epoxy, laminated glass, and plastic. Many digitizers use glass or epoxy surfaces for their mechanical stability. The less expensive systems generally use plastic surfaces. Some systems utilize back-lighted or rear-projected images, which are then projected on the tablet.

The information can be obtained from the tablet controller in one of three ways:

1. Each demand when the computer makes a request.

2. At intervals of time.

3. Each time the cursor or stylus is moved more than some specified distance.

The time-interval technique is more helpful if a screen cursor is being displayed to reflect the position of the tablet cursor or stylus. The distance technique is useful for digitizing drawings, since it avoids recording an excessive number of points.

Some specialized CAD systems are built around a digitizing table and are called *digitizing systems*. Generally this hardware is designed specifically to digitize and plot drawings. Most of these systems consist of a digitizing table and cursor, video terminal, microcomputer, and mass memory in the form of magnetic tape or floppy or hard disc.

These systems accept input either in the form of drawings digitized with the cursor or from points entered through a keyboard. The system stores drawing information in mass memory and generally produces a serial digital output that can be used directly by plotters or line printers or can be sent to a larger computer for further processing.

The keypad type of cursor on many systems, besides recording points for digitizing, can also enter commands. The cursor commands can invoke responses on the display terminal. This terminal may do the following:

1. Give coordinates of the current digitized position.

2. Prompt the user with requests for information needed by the system.

3. Display the results of computations.

4. Identify errors in the entered information.

The cursor functions are determined by the digitizing system software. A number of programmed routines can speed the digitizing process. Some common routines include:

1. Length calculations. The line length and sums of line lengths are calculated, accumulated, and displayed.

2. Area calculations. The sums and differences of areas are calculated, accumulated, and displayed. Automatic closure is included on some systems, eliminating the need to close an area boundary with the cursor.

3. Volume calculation. The space volume is computed with slices digitized in the x,y, y,z, or z,x planes.

4. Label insertions. Identifying labels are assigned to the digitized data.

5. Event counting. The operator selects events, such as End-of-coordinate or End-of-data, and starts an event counter. The event-counter contents can be displayed or sent out as a part of the digitized output data.

6. Orientation conditions. A number of operations are performed before entering data to indicate how the digitized data will be scaled, formatted, and processed. Rectangular or polar coordinates may be selected. Polar coordinates are used in many mapping applications. The coordinates can also be measured in an absolute mode, as an absolute displacement from a fixed point, or in a delta (Δ) mode where each point is output as the difference (or delta) between it and the last digitized point.

7. Scaling. Here the number of units being represented by each unit on the digitizing table is selected. Different axes can be scaled independently, and one can digitize a point to which all other points will be related.

8. Translation and rotation. Here the orientation of the drawing is described with respect to the axis of the digitizing table. Each axis may be rotated with respect to table coordinates. This can be used to correct orthogonal-based errors inherent in some media, such as photographs.

Digitizers are usually equipped with several operating modes. In the *point mode*, single coordinate points are entered one at a time. In the *run mode* the digitizer sends a stream of x,y coordinates to the computer as the pen moves along the surface. This mode can be used to position a cursor on a CRT or a pen on a plotter. The *track mode* is similar, except that data is sent only when the pen is activated. The *true increment mode* also uses a stream of data, but the data stream stops when the pen stops moving.

These digitizing modes often can be selected from the cursor through software. The point mode enters a coordinate every time the user presses an output key with the cursor centered over a point to be digitized. Modes are also available to enter data as the cursor moves continuously.

In the *rate-digitizing mode*, the rate of entered points can be selected so that data is entered at 1 to 100 points per second as the cursor moves. This allows the user to enter curves accurately. The cursor movement is slowed or accelerated to adjust the number of points representing the curve.

Some digitizing tablets are available with built-in computers. These digitizers with microcomputers may perform some calculations, such as area and volume of figures. The coordinate origins can be relocated using rotation and translation functions, and scale factors can be called for the x and y directions separately.

A number of digitizer specifications can be used for the purposes of evaluation. The *resolution* is the number of points that can be digitized per inch. For example, 100-lines/inch resolution provides an identifiable x,y coordinate every 0.010 inch. Most industrial systems provide between 400 and 1000 lines/inch.

Repeatability indicates how consistently a digitizer identifies the same position on the tablet surface with the same set of x,y coordinates. Factors that can degrade repeatability include thermal expansion of the tablet surface, humidity, and variations in electrical characteristics.

Potentiometric Devices

A number of devices which provide scalar values use a potentiometer. A set of rotary potentiometers can be mounted in a group as pictured in Figure 3-20. *Rotary potentiometers* are more appropriate for controlling object rotation. *Slide potentiometers*, in which a linear movement replaces the rotation, are more appropriate for specifying values with no angular movement. The setting of a slide potentiometer is much easier for the user to gauge than that of a rotary potentiometer. However, most graphics systems use rotary potentiometers. The use of both types of potentiometers can help the operator remember what functions are associated with each unit. In systems involving potentiometers, one must be sure to use a consistent interpretation for increasing and decreasing values. Clockwise movements normally increase a value.

Potentiometers are sampled by devices whose analog values are converted and stored in registers to be read by the computer. The values read from the registers are then converted to equivalent numbers to be used in the

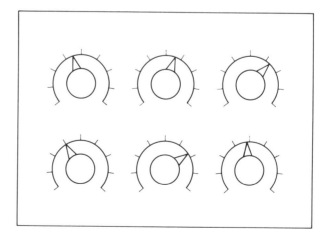

Figure 3-20   A set of controls used for screen positioning.

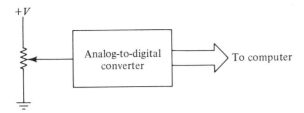

Figure 3-21 Potentiometer interface.

program. An analog-to-digital converter and a power supply can be used to determine the potentiometer's position by measuring the voltage, as shown in Figure 3-21. The voltage is proportional to the amount of shaft rotation about the axis. With the converter properly adjusted, a zero position will correspond to a digital reading of all zeros, while a full position will correspond to all ones.

In some systems, the graphics package will poll the pointing device to see if it has been changed more than some small amount. If it has, the computer will then generate an event, which is placed in an event queue.

Trackball controls are large plastic balls mounted with some fraction of the ball surface protruding from the top of the enclosing unit. Rotating the ball moves the screen cursor.

Trackballs are often used to select commands displayed on the display screen. The ball positions the cursor in the area of a menu. Pushing a keyboard key (usually Return) makes the selection. The computer reads the cursor position at the time when the key is pressed and executes the procedure listed in the menu.

Trackballs are sometimes called *crystal balls*. They have the form shown in Figure 3-22. The ball's motion turns potentiometers, whose output is converted into digital data. The ball rotates freely within its mount and typically is moved by drawing the palm of the hand over it. Large and rapid position changes can be difficult to make with a trackball.

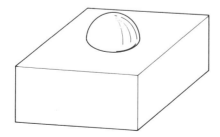

Figure 3-22 A trackball control. A large plastic ball is moved with the palm of the hand.

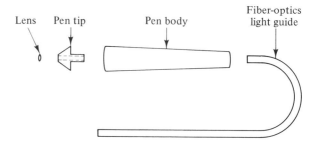

Figure 3-23   Basic lightpen design.

Interactive Pointing Techniques

A number of methods are available to interact with graphics displayed on CRT terminals. Lightpens are the most common input device for CAD systems, but joysticks and trackballs are also used.

Lightpens   *Lightpens*, as shown in Figure 3-23, are element-indicating or picking devices. The lightpen does not emit light to draw a picture; it senses or detects light from the picture elements on the screen. Some lightpens do have a narrowly focused light source called the *finder beam* which is directed at the screen to indicate what picture elements are in the pen's field of view.

A hand-held lightpen consists of a pencil-sized cylinder with a light sensor in one end. The other end is connected to the computer by a cable. As the user positions the light-sensitive pen tip to select a point on the screen, the lightpen sends a pulse when this screen area is bright. The pulse produced by the lightpen is then used to calculate the screen position that the pen was at. Most lightpens also produce a second signal, which the user generates by pushing a button on the pen to signal to the computer the user's selection of a point, as shown in Figure 3-24.

The pen senses the burst of fluorescent light emitted when the electron beam is bombarding the phosphor. This is the light emitted during the period the computer is drawing the picture element. It is not sensitive to the more prolonged phosphorescence or to ambient room light. The pen's output is usually connected to the system's control logic in such a way that the computer stops executing commands when the pen senses the light.

The existence of this signal can be correlated with the program display list to deduce which particular item was being displayed at the instant that the light from the pen was encountered. This synchronous input makes it possible for the computer program to find out where or at what the user is pointing.

We can distinguish two programmed styles of using the lightpen. First, we may wish to follow or track the lightpen as the user moves it around on the

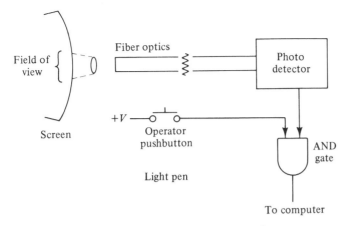

Figure 3-24 Lightpen operation.

screen, drawing lines or paths. Second, we may wish to designate or activate a new procedure or mark some particular picture part.

A common procedure is to program a series of bright points at the lower portion of the screen. These can be treated as programmable pushbuttons. By selectively touching these buttons with the lightpen, the user can tell the program what needs to be done. Some common functions include enlarging or zooming, rotating, erasing, and tracking. One lightpen design is shown in Figure 3-23. A large number of different designs are currently in use.

When the computer is stopped by the lightpen signal, its instruction counter will contain the address of the next instruction after the one that drew the detected element. This address can be used by the graphics program to give the application program the location of the segment containing the detected element. One can then operate on the segment. Note that in order for the graphics program to actually use the lightpen, it must be able to read the computer's instruction counter. In this way the lightpen can act as a locator for a raster display, stopping the raster scan at the detected pixel. The x,y-coordinate/address of this point provides the location.

A number of factors can affect lightpen performance. Most CRT display screens use bonded implosion shields over the display tube, leaving a gap between the outer glass surface and the phosphor. This gap can cause difficulties in positioning the lightpen accurately.

In display systems other than raster types, pens cannot detect blank portions on the screen. In this system some means of sensing the lightpen position over blank portions of the screen must be provided. One can flash the entire screen for one frame to allow the system to get the pen position. Some systems fill the entire screen with characters line by line, until a character is generated under the lightpen.

Lightpens were developed very early in the history of interactive computer graphics. They were originally used in air defense systems to point at targets on a screen. Unless properly adjusted, lightpens can detect false points, such as adjacent characters, or fail to detect the desired points. When used for a period of hours, a pen can be tiring to the user, who must pick it up, point it, and set it down for each use. As a result, more systems now use a tablet or mouse to simulate the picking function. The popularity of lightpens is expected to decrease even further in the future.

In one sense the lightpen is the simplest and the most general or flexible input device. But often its function must be supplemented with one or more pushbuttons. A major limitation is that it cannot be used where no image is being displayed. In order to know where the lightpen is, the computer must find it. Other devices, such as the trackball, volunteer their position coordinates. The procedure for correlating the position with the display list can become complicated, because the input is not synchronized with the display list.

Joysticks In the console of some graphics terminals a *joystick* acts as a control stick. The user controls the motion of a cursor on the screen by pushing the joystick in the direction of desired motion. In the displacement-type joystick, the joystick actually moves. In the force-actuated joystick, the stick is fixed and the force from the user's hand causes the cursor motion. Joysticks can sometimes be rotated or pushed on the end to control other variables besides position. Display color content is sometimes controlled this way.

The joystick can be moved left or right or forward or backward (Figure 3-25). Potentiometers sense these movements. Often springs are used to return the joystick to its center position. Some joysticks have a third degree of freedom, since the stick can be twisted clockwise and counterclockwise. The force-actuated or isometric joystick has strain gauges on the shaft to measure the slight deflections caused by the force applied to the shaft.

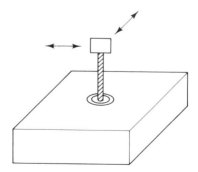

Figure 3-25 Displacement joystick.

There are also two kinds of displacement joysticks available: the absolute and the rate. The travel of the *absolute joystick* corresponds directly to the screen position. Moving the absolute joystick to its upper position places the cursor at the top of the display. Moving it to its lower left position places the cursor at the lower left corner of the display.

The travel of the *rate joystick* imparts a direction of motion to the cursor. If you move the rate joystick to the left, the cursor will move from its present position. Push it to the lower left, and the cursor will move diagonally in that direction. If you return the joystick to center, then the cursor comes to a halt. In most designs, by varying how far in any direction the rate joystick is moved, one controls the speed at which the cursor will move.

An *absolute/rate joystick* is a hybrid that combines both designs. A switch on the joystick handle is depressed to select the absolute mode. In this position, a motion to the upper left corner of the joystick corresponds to the movement of the cursor to the upper left corner of the computer display. Once the target area is reached, the switch is released, and the cursor can be positioned using the rate mode.

It is sometimes difficult to use a joystick to control the absolute position of a screen cursor accurately, since a slight hand movement is amplified in the position of the cursor. The cursor's movements can become erratic, since the joystick doesn't allow fine positioning.

The joystick is sometimes used to control the velocity of the screen cursor's movement instead of its absolute position. This changes the position

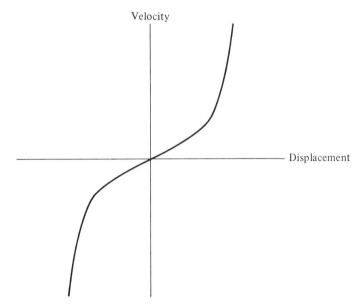

Figure 3-26 Nonlinear joystick characteristic.

of the cursor over a time rate determined by the joystick. A small dead zone is used to allow for drift in the joystick's center position. The relation of cursor velocity to joystick displacement is usually nonlinear, as shown in Figure 3-26. This curve is used to make the final positioning occur faster.

The *joy switch* is a variation of the joystick. It may be moved in any of eight directions: up, down, left, right, and in the four diagonal directions. The joy switch has nine states, and in each of the eight ON states, the position of the screen cursor is changed at a constant rate, in that direction.

The joystick can also be used for 3D orientation, especially when the shaft rotates for a third degree of freedom. The three values from the joystick can then be used to control the rate of rotation about each of the three axes. When the joystick does not have a spring return to zero, its values can be used as absolute rotations rather than rates of rotation.

The mouse   Another device is the *mouse* shown in Figure 3-27. This is a hand-held unit with rollers. Moving the unit across a flat surface causes the rollers to turn the internal potentiometers. These sense the relative movements of the mouse in two directions. The motion is converted to digital values and used by the computer to determine the direction and magnitude of the mouse's movement.

The mouse can be moved on the screen and then put down without any change in the position of the cursor. The computer maintains a current mouse position which is incremented or decremented by the mouse's movements. The mouse usually has one or more pushbuttons which are used to input commands.

The accuracy of the mouse is not that of a tablet, and drawing is more difficult than with a tablet and stylus, since control is more difficult. On the

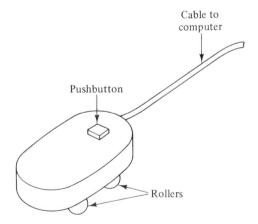

Figure 3-27   A mouse: a hand-held unit with rollers on the bottom.

other hand, a mouse requires only a small flat surface to use and is less costly. These devices are moved with the user's hands, while the cursor is watched with the eyes.

Other interaction devices   There are other interaction devices that are useful for graphics systems, but they do not enjoy the popularity of the devices we have discussed. For instance, *speech recognizers* can accept verbal commands and values as input and are available in versions recognizing over 1000 words. In some units the words are defined as discrete utterances preceded and followed by fixed millisecond pauses. Continuous speech recognition is available in a few commercial systems. Most of these word recognizers must be trained to the characteristics of an individual's speech. A word is filtered into several frequency bands, and patterns based on the relative loudness or pitch of the sound are matched against a dictionary of recorded patterns. Training the recognizer unit requires establishing a dictionary of patterns, during which the user must speak the word several times.

Speech output from digitized patterns can be used for prompts, feedback, and error messages. Synthesizers can be inexpensive and are used in some home computers. As more units become available, the use of speech input-output will increase, since it is natural, easy, quick, and requires no manual dexterity.

Another sound device is the *sonic tablet*. It uses sound to couple a stylus with microphones along the sides of the tablet. A spark is generated at the tip of the stylus, and the time from the occurrence of the spark to the arrival of its

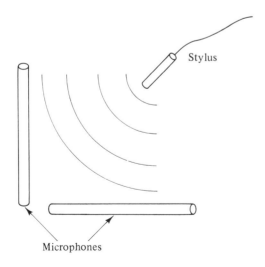

Figure 3-28   Sonic tablet.

sound at each microphone is used to calculate the distance of the stylus from each microphone, as shown in Figure 3-28.

These devices that we have discussed are all 2D units. Two-dimensional devices can always be used in sequence to specify three dimensions.

The sound-coupling technique can be extended to create a 3D sonic enclosure. In one scheme, three microphones are used, as shown in Figure 3-29. Here each microphone senses the position of the stylus on a cylinder of known radius. This is determined by the time of the sound to the microphone. The intersection of the three cylinders is used to determine the position of the stylus. Another technique is to use strip microphones and to arrange four of them in a square. One can also use four point microphones at the corners of the display area. The time of sound arrival is measured, with the times now determining the radii of four spheres, since each sphere is centered on a microphone. Only three spheres are required to determine a position. The fourth sphere can be used for error checking or a backup in case the path to one microphone is blocked.

Mechanically coupled 3D devices can also be used. These take the form of a box with slides to allow the control knob to be moved anywhere in the cube. Long slide potentiometers are used to record the position along each axis.

These devices all work in relatively small volumes of several cubic feet. One can also sense the motion of the operator's hands and fingers and use these to define positions and shapes in 3D. This is done using optical or electromagnetic coupling. Active light sources are moved by the user, and the sensors are mounted in the corners of a small room. The sensor can be

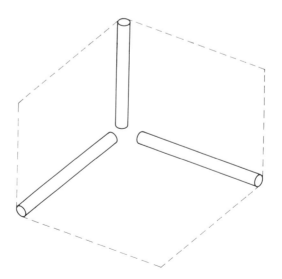

Figure 3-29   Sonic enclosure using microphones.

organized to provide the parameters of a plane in which the source is located. Three sensors, which define three planes, are enough to determine the position of the light source. A fourth sensor can be used for error checking and for backup when one of the other light sources becomes obscured from a sensor. Sound- and light-coupling methods are susceptible to noise and obstructions. To avoid this, one can generate electromagnetic fields which are detected by a small sensor on the hand or other part of the body. The position and orientation of the sensor can be determined very precisely, but the technology is expensive.

In this section we have described how some interaction devices actually work. Many types are in use; we have focused on those which are more common or more innovative. The devices can be grouped in categories according to their inherent ease of implementation—that is, the ability to implement them with a minimum of support software. The ease of implementation may not be equivalent to ease of use.

We consider next how the physical devices are best used to implement the functions which are required. We will seek comparisons and contrasts among the different devices, which are meant to help in the process of selecting the appropriate interaction technique.

The input devices described include the sampled locators and the event-causing alphanumeric and button keyboards. These devices require that the computer contain a number of registers in which we can input and store appropriate values. Event- or interrupt-generating devices load these registers and interrupt the CPU. The CPU will then read the registers. The sampled devices load these registers with data whenever they are polled by the computer. Many devices require analog-to-digital converters to load the registers with digital data.

Pointing-Device Considerations

A pointing device must be compatible with the requirements of both humans and machines. Attention must be paid to the joints and muscles that have to operate the device. We must focus not only on the required positioning precision (Figure 3-30) for the specific task, but also on the duration of the task for the muscle group and its particular fatigue factor.

The two main muscle groups involved in pointing devices are the forearm/wrist and the thumb/finger/wrist. The relationships between these two groups and the various pointing devices are important to their basic designs. The movement of the forearm/wrist group generally requires more energy and is more fatiguing than the movement of the thumb/finger/wrist group.

The digitizing tablet, by making use of forearm and wrist motions, nearly approximates the activity of writing and drawing. With the high lineal

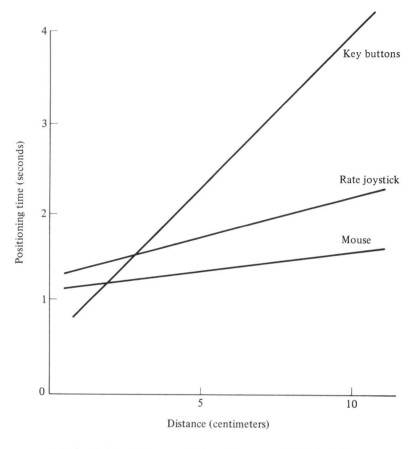

Figure 3-30 Characteristics of some pointing devices.

resolution of the tablet the thumb/index-finger motions are captured as well. The tablet is the only drawing device that represents both the thumb/finger/wrist and forearm/wrist motions.

A mouse requires forearm/wrist motion except for switch activation, while the joystick uses only the motion of thumb/finger/wrist group. The operation of a keyboard requires the repeated striking motion of the finger and wrist. The key is either up or down, and there is no way to control and modulate movements.

It is common to use pointing devices for text or related editing. A keyboard-mounting pointing device is particularly advantageous, since it always leaves the wrist and forearm in a known relationship to the keyboard. The return hand motion is then minimal and direct. In contrast, the return hand motion from either a tablet or mouse may vary and is not automatically repeatable. Thus the editing process can be interrupted and delayed. For text editing, the joystick may position faster and with fewer errors than the mouse. Once the joystick has placed the cursor in the region of a text line or character column, the rate mode can be used to move it in a horizontal or vertical direction. This can allow the selection of a character within a line, or a line within a paragraph. When moving the cursor along a line of text in the rate mode, inadvertent upward deviations will not necessarily push the cursor off the text line of interest.

The cursor movements should tend to adhere to the lines and columns of the text. Without the rate mode, however, an inadvertent motion can place the cursor too far, resulting in a positioning error.

These suggested guidelines are based primarily on the resolution and positioning speed required, as well as cost. Factors such as space requirements and fatigue should also be taken into account, as shown in Table 3-2.

For high-resolution applications where cost is not a primary consideration, the digitizing tablet is usually best.

The tablet is the most convenient way for the user to enter x and y positions, since the tablet stylus is held like a pencil and moved over the tablet face. With most tablets, the position may be determined whenever the stylus is within a half inch or so of the tablet surface.

The relevant parameters of tablets and other locator devices are their resolution, repeatability, and size or range. These parameters are particularly crucial in maps and drawings but are of less concern when the device is used to position a screen cursor, since the user has the feedback of the screen cursor to guide the hand movements.

The tablet offers a natural, absolute mapping of the user's motions onto the display space, with a resolution as high as 500 to 1000 points per inch. An area must be provided for the tablet, and the fatigue factor is low.

For applications that are more cost-sensitive, however, either a mouse or a joystick can be used. The mouse offers good speed and resolution with 100–

Table 3-2 Considerations for inaction devices

Pointing device	Resolution	Positioning speed	Cost	Fatigue factor
Digitizing tablet	High	High	High	Low
Absolute joystick	Medium	High	Low	Low
Rate joystick	High	Medium	Low	Low
Mouse	Medium	High	Low	Medium
Keys	Digital	Low	Low	Medium
Lightpen	Low	High	Low	High

300 points per inch, but it does not offer a natural, absolute mapping, and the fatigue factor is higher.

The joystick offers high speed and a medium resolution of 100–400 points per inch in the absolute mode and 1000–10,000 points per inch in rate mode. The joystick provides a natural, absolute mapping in the absolute mode, and the fatigue factor is low.

For medium-resolution applications that are cost-sensitive, either a mouse or an absolute joystick can be used. For this degree of resolution, a joystick with a rate mode can be adjusted to operate more coarsely.

For lower-resolution applications, either a mouse or an absolute joystick is appropriate. The absolute joystick is recommended, since it offers high speed, it provides natural, absolute mapping, and the fatigue factor is low.

By high resolution we mean the operator will have the ability to resolve over one part in 2000—usually 2048×2048 picture elements. Medium resolution corresponds to a 512×512 display, and low resolution to 256×256 pixels.

For extremely low-cost applications, *step keys* can be used. The step keys, which function much like a rate joystick, provide an ultralow-cost pointing device, and the fatigue factor is moderate.

The cost of a pointing device depends in large measure on the degree of resolution required. For comparable applications, however, a joystick can be typically 50% less expensive than a mouse implementation.

GRAPHICS IMAGING

A general trend in CAD technology is to allow each terminal to take over many of the graphic-generating functions that previously were done by the main computer. This reduces the amount of calculations required from the main computer in generating graphics. This approach makes each graphics terminal more expensive. The trend toward generating graphics at the terminal itself has resulted in sophisticated terminals that contain small computers.

Some of these displays are referred to as *graphics-imaging displays*. These displays provide the same functions as conventional graphics-display terminals, but they also have the capability to provide complex imaging features. Often, for example, they provide real-time animated displays. Such systems are also used in generating CAT scanner images and images for other scientific and medical applications.

Graphics-imaging display terminals generally can manipulate images using processes such as zooming and panning. *Zooming* allows the user to enlarge certain portions of the displayed image to provide more detail. *Panning* allows one to shift a specific displayed area across a larger stored image. Some systems also provide split screens or segmented images, where the user can display several images simultaneously. This can be used for the orthographic projections of a given part drawing.

Even more powerful than graphics-imaging displays are the *image-processing displays*. These displays generally provide all the features of graphics-imaging displays while performing high-speed calculations on the image data, often using a separate computer. This computer reduces even further the amount of image data that must be transferred between the main computer and the display. This is an advantage, because even relatively simple images require a large memory. Raster-scan full-color images can easily use a million words. It is possible to transfer this much information between computers and terminals without substantial delays.

Graphics and image-processing displays typically are used only in those applications which justify the additional cost. One such application is finite-element modeling. Here the display can provide image-intensity distribution analysis. The terminal tracks the intensity levels of each picture element in the image. The intensity distributions are corrected at the terminal to some normalized curve. The finite elements are then displayed in colors corresponding to the particular stress levels in the parts.

Techniques for Simulating Interactions

Many graphics programs have a need for a specific pick, keyboard, or button devices, but in many graphics systems not all these physical devices may be available. It is possible, however, to provide the function of any of these devices with a device from any other class, although some simulations may be awkward.

Many interactive systems have only one positioning device (usually a mouse or a tablet), a keyboard, and sometimes a few special-purpose function buttons on the keyboard. These three physical devices are used to implement all the commands. In the sections that follow we describe some of the more common input simulation techniques. These implementations are a part of the graphics software package.

We have considered the use of menus and programmed function keyboards for command entry. Many applications can have dozens or even hundreds of different commands—more than can be displayed in a single menu or assigned to 16 or 32 special function buttons. This many commands must be dealt with by grouping them into menus or selection modes. Each menu can contain a group of related commands. If a programmed-function keyboard is used for commands, then the commands can be grouped using separate overlays. If the application employs a small nucleus of often-used commands, these should be made available in each menu. The name of the current menu phase should be well displayed, so that the operator can easily remember the context in which the commands will be performed. The method of changing from one mode to another should be simple and obvious to the user.

Several levels of menus can be used. In some applications there may be as many as four or five levels in the command hierarchy. This means that four or five successive menu selections must be made in order to actually specify a command. For constant users the menu selection can appear slow and tedious unless the menus are displayed almost instantaneously.

An alternative is to allow any command name to be typed at the keyboard, even if it is not in the currently displayed menu. This allows newer users to pick from the menu while more experienced operators can use the keyboard.

When the command names must be typed on a keyboard, a shorthand method is useful to minimize input. In order to display a command, only the number need be typed. Abbreviations can also be used, but they should be easy to remember and of uniform length. The shortest unambiguous abbreviations—with a fixed length, if possible—should be used.

Interaction techniques are the higher-level functions which are implemented through the devices that we have already discussed. These techniques are in general application-independent in the ways they represent the interacting with the computer. They are used in many graphics programs as the basic building blocks from which the complete human-machine dialogues are constructed.

Interactive Construction

We can think of drawing construction as the process of creating and modifying a model of a process or object. The common operations are drawing points and lines and moving, rotating, or scaling the displayed objects. We manipulate these objects by indirectly manipulating their physical appearance on the display screen.

Dragging is a technique of moving an object around with a locating device. We can use it to position objects or symbols. The locating device is read at least once each refresh cycle, and the position is used to move the displayed object.

In a random or vector display, the new position is found by modifications in the scan program. The task is not easy in a raster display, but it can be and is done in many systems. Dragging an image in a direct-view tube requires the use of a write-through mode and a refresh buffer.

An extension of dragging is the *dynamic scaling and rotation* of objects. In two dimensions this requires that two locating devices be continually read and their values used to control the size and rotation angle.

The orientation of many complex 3D objects is difficult to interpret in

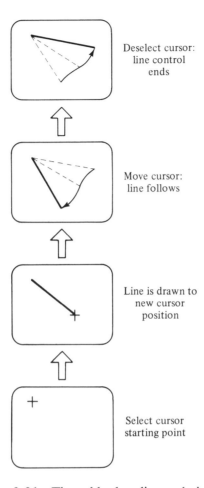

Deselect cursor:
line control
ends

Move cursor:
line follows

Line is drawn to
new cursor
position

Select cursor
starting point

Figure 3-31   The rubberbanding technique.

two dimensions, so we can use an axis view or a *gnomon* to show the orientation of the principal axes. The gnomon facilitates the rotation tasks in three dimensions.

Lines are usually constructed with *rubberbanding*. The push of a button marks the starting point of the line, which is read from the locating device. The line is drawn from this point to wherever the cursor is positioned. As the cursor moves, the line endpoint moves. Another push of the button, or the release of the button, and the locating device is no longer connected to the endpoint. A tablet which uses a stylus may have a tip switch. Then starting and ending button pushes are done at the stylus. Figure 3-31 shows a rubberband sequence.

We can apply a number of formal conditions called *constraints* to a line

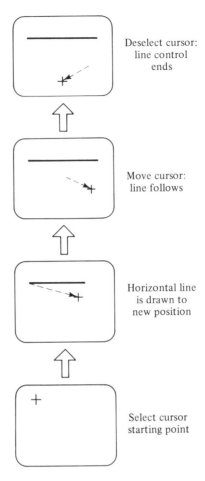

Deselect cursor:
line control
ends

Move cursor:
line follows

Horizontal line
is drawn to
new position

Select cursor
starting point

Figure 3-32 Rubberbanding with a horizontal constraint.

resulting from rubberbanding. Figure 3-32 shows a sequence of lines drawn from the cursor positions, where now a horizontal constraint is in effect.

Vertical lines or lines in some other orientation can be drawn in this same way, as well as parts of circles, ellipses, or other curves. The curve is initialized at some position; then the cursor movements control how much of the curve is displayed.

Another type of constraint is *gridding*. Here the endpoints of lines are required to fall on a grid of points or lines. Gridding generates borders. The program rounds the coordinates to the nearest grid point.

In the construction of drawings, one frequently wants a new line to begin on or at the endpoint of an existing line. Positioning the cursor at the exact point can be difficult unless gridding is used.

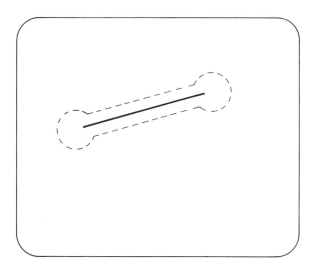

Figure 3-33   A gravity field around a line.

We can also use a *gravity field* around the line, so that the cursor is attracted to the line as it enters this gravity field. Figure 3-33 shows how a line with a gravity field operates. The field is larger around the line's endpoints to make the matching of endpoints less difficult. A very complex and cluttered display can make the use of this technique difficult to implement. The approach taken is similar to allowing the tolerance factor to be larger for the endpoints than for the lines.

If we need to trace or draw a freehand curve or contour, we can use the sketch technique. Here lines are drawn along the path of a cursor, much like the drawing of a line with a pencil. *Discrete sketching* requires the user to push a button each time one line is to end and the next is to start. This is shown in Figure 3-34. The specific points are connected by straight lines. Smooth curves require that we use continuous sketching. This technique does not require any explicit user action to terminate one line and start another. A series of short lines approximating a smooth curve is displayed along the path of the cursor, as shown in Figure 3-35. More short lines are used where the radius of curvature is small in order to give a smoother appearance.

From a user's point of view we are interested in these elementary abilities that a display can have. It is easy to see that whatever the display produces must, in the final analysis, be combinations of its elementary functions. Thus, plotting a point seems to be one of the most basic functions in the sense that lines, arcs, and characters can be made with plotted points. All the other features described above are time-savers and of great importance for effective CAD/CAM interactions.

Depending on factors such as frequency of use, execution times, and sometimes costs, some parts of these functions will be expressed as software

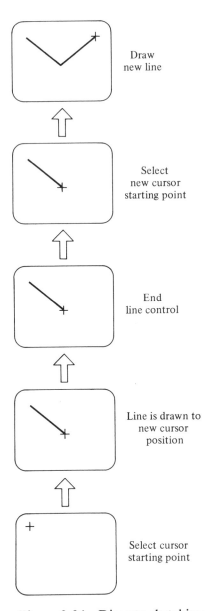

Figure 3-34   Discrete sketching.

while others can be built into the display. In most cases the wired-in functions are chosen on the basis of speed of interaction, but these can make the equipment more complicated and expensive. A circle generator is an example of a built-in function that might be justified, although when time is not so critical, algorithms exist for producing equivalent results. There are also

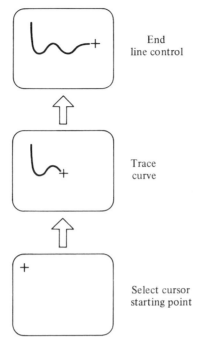

End
line control

Trace
curve

Select cursor
starting point

Figure 3-35   Continuous sketching.

systems that use algorithms to recognize command motions, as shown in Figure 3-36. Some of the meanings in this example are specialized; others are more general. The technique is especially useful when the motion is performed on top of the object to be operated upon. This allows several parts of a complete image to be input to the system at once. A number of commercially available intelligent tablets have the capability to recognize patterns and characters.

We have seen how dragging dynamically moves a selected object or symbol from one position to another, as shown in Figure 3-37. Typically a button is pushed to start the dragging, and in some cases the button push can also do the selecting. Then either another button push or the release of the button freezes the object in place, so that further movements of the locating device have no effect on the object.

All these construction techniques use an immediate form of dynamic feedback, which can be provided only if the computer gives rapid and regular service. This requires the computer to have sufficient computation capability to provide the feedback required. This can be done using a dedicated computer, but it is more difficult with a time-shared computer. Without this dynamic feedback, slower and more cumbersome interaction techniques must be used. If we replace rubberbanding by the capability to specify the line's endpoints, then we have to adjust the endpoints until the line is satisfactory.

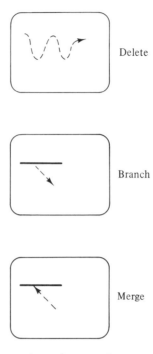

Figure 3-36   Cursor motions that can be recognized as commands.

This process can continue until the results are satisfactory. Thus we have replaced the dynamic feedback of rubberbanding by a much slower and less satisfactory type of static feedback. This requires the user either to take more time to complete the required construction tasks or to produce less satisfactory drawings.

Object-Selection or Picking Techniques

An important part of graphics interaction is selecting the object to be operated upon. We can use a hierarchical object structure which allows the operator to pick a basic object, a collection of basic objects, and a collection of collections. We have discussed the various devices that can be used in addition to the keyboard. Any of these devices can be simulated by any other device, using the interaction techniques we will now discuss. Such simulations require the concept of a logical input device. This is rather like the concept of a logical file in an operating system. A sequential input file may be implemented physically by a number of different units—a magnetic tape drive, a disk drive, or a keyboard. The user doesn't care which one it is, since the operating system makes them all look alike functionally, despite their physical differences.

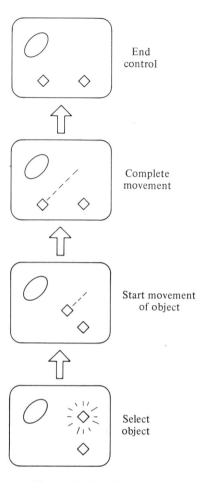

Figure 3-37   Dragging.

Similar differences can exist in the use of the various selection devices. For example, a direct-view storage tube cannot be used with a lightpen. The cross-hair cursor can be used; here the cursor is placed on top of the item to be picked. Then the user depresses a key, and its character code and the cursor position are sent to the computer.

Some software graphics packages define up to five types of devices to be available and imply that a reasonable input implementation will be provided by the software if the corresponding physical device is not available. This means that the interface may be less user-friendly and more time-consuming.

In order to realize as much of the predicted benefits as possible, a great amount of sophisticated system development must be done. But for the most part these things are just not ready yet, so in order to get started in CAD/CAM, a number of decisions have to be made.

One of these is to face up to the fact that some graphics processing jobs need to be done on a large computer. No one denies that small computers can control and recycle a display device. But displaying a picture is normally a small part of graphics processing.

Actually, what troubles people is not the use of a large computer; it is the user's sitting in front of the display thinking, while the large computer sits idle. Time sharing can help to resolve this dilemma, but we have noted that the user interactive dialog may be impaired.

If we require control from the keyboard, the locating device can be simulated by four keys which move the cursor up, down, left, and right. Some keys may have other purposes. Holding a key down could cause rapid continuous motions of the cursor, while a quick key depression might cause only a single-unit move, with a unit being a little more than the display's resolution. Rapid positioning is allowed, with the cursor's speed to increase as the key is held down. Then, as the key is released, the cursor stops.

A basic way to simulate a locating device is by typing in the position coordinates on a keyboard. In this approach the desired visual results must be translated into numbers. The immediate feedback that is present in a smooth dynamic position or rotation is delayed by the long interaction cycles, and each one ends in a static presentation. If the storage display lacks local refreshing, this is what one can expect. Unless the precise coordinates are already known, the method is painfully slow.

Many locating actions start with a physical action in which the user moves the cursor to the object of interest and then pushes a button. The graphics software then searches through its files for the element closest to the cursor position. There may be several buttons on a mouse, and each can have a different meaning, such as select, delete, or move. Too many buttons can quickly become confusing, so a single button may be best for menu selection.

The search may take place in a number of ways. We can use a correlation table which holds a screen-extension segment. This area is a rectangular surface surrounding the image segment. We use the correlation table to find the required device position. The table is searched for all segments that meet the x- and y-coordinate positions.

In some cases only one segment satisfies the conditions and the processing is done. But, where segments overlap, several segments might satisfy the test conditions.

The next step is to consider the elements that make up each of the segments which overlap. Again the use of extension elements is called for, this time for individual primitives. Consider a point defined by x_1, y_1. Then define a rectangle around these points. This rectangle could be stored in a correlation table or could be computed each time it is needed. The size of the rectangle is chosen to allow for inaccuracies in positioning the cursor. The greater the rectangle, the less precise the user needs to be, but the greater the possibility that several points might be within the enclosed area.

If we define a line from x_1, y_1 to x_2, y_2, the rectangle is defined by:

$$(x_1, x_2) - d, \qquad (x_1, x_2) + d$$
$$(y_1, y_2) - d, \qquad (y_1, y_2) + d$$

where d is the distance from the endpoints of the lines to the sides of the rectangle.

The program needs to know if an endpoint of the line itself has been selected. Therefore, it must compare the areas surrounding the points. If there are overlapping elements, then the next step is to determine the relative distances to find which of the sections is actually closest to the points. One can take the squares of the distances involved, and then the squared distances can be compared to find a minimum.

The calculation of the shortest distance from a line to a point will take several multiplications and divisions. An approximation is to use the minimum of the horizontal and vertical distances from the locating-device position to the line. This is easier to calculate, but it can be incorrect by the square root of 2. Forming the sum of squares itself can be time-consuming and approximations are available which allow an error of about 3% to 5%. The maximum error can be acceptable, since only comparisons between distances need to be made. The calculation of these approximations is faster, but whatever method is used, we compute the distances from each element to the simulated position. The first element found to be within the area of the position is reported as having been selected. If no such element is found, no selection is reported.

A stepped screening process can be used to avoid detailed examination of elements which are far from the simulated position by first examining elements and then actual distances. The basic idea is to clip each element's distance to a small window. The first element which passes through the window is detected. Systems with hardware windowing use this approach.

We have noted that locating devices can appear identical, so that the application program is unaware of their physical differences. This removes control of some of the more detailed, low-level interaction techniques that are available. Some implementations can require considerable CPU overhead. This can occur when interrupting devices are simulated by the use of polling loops.

Device Simulation

An example of a simulation is now considered for a lightpen. The lightpen is frequently used on a random display with a tracking cross. The cross is initially displayed somewhere on the CRT screen. To locate a new position, the lightpen is first pointed at the cross and is then used to move it to the desired position. This is done with a feedback loop which operates each

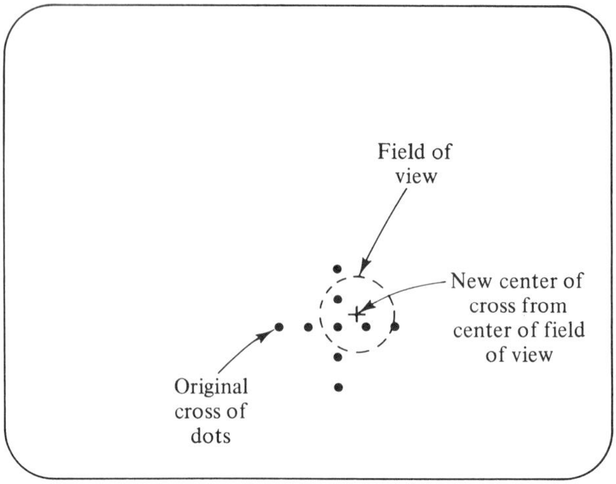

Figure 3-38 Lightpen tracking.

refresh cycle and moves the cross so that it is always under the lightpen. The pen's new position, where the tracking cross is displayed, is calculated by determining those dots from the previous tracking cross that were just within the field of view, as shown in Figure 3-38. The new center position can be found by averaging the coordinates of each point detected by the pen. When no points on the cross are detected, tracking is lost. This can happen when the user moves the pen faster than the tracking algorithm can move the cross or when the user moves the pen away from the CRT screen.

If the tracking is lost, the system may attempt to obtain tracking again to determine if the loss was intentional. It will thus try to find the lightpen. If the pen has been moved away from the screen, it cannot be found, and the system knows that the loss of tracking was intentional. One way to attempt tracking again is to draw points around the last known pen position, until either the entire screen has been covered or the pen is found. Another way is to perform a complete raster scan of the screen. The scan-line spacing must be less than the diameter of the pen's field of view. If the pen is still on the screen, this scan line can be detected, and if the vectors are in digital format, the coordinates are easily available. If analog vector generation is used, then a search along the scan line must be done to find the pen's horizontal position. A character fill of the screen with characters, points, or short lines can be used until the pen is detected. These techniques can be used independently of tracking to determine where the pen currently is on the screen.

The tracking algorithm must be able to move the cross at such a speed that the tracking will not be lost. The maximum distance the cross can move for each iteration of the algorithm is the length of an arm on the cross.

To decrease the probability of loss of tracking we can increase the speed at which the cross can move. We do this by predicting where the pen will be during the next cycle based on where it has been during the last few cycles. The cross is placed at this position rather than at a position calculated by averaging.

Many physical devices can be used to move the screen cursor to a desired target. Some experiments have found that a mouse can be faster than an isometric joystick or cursor control keys. In selecting characters and character groups from a page display, it has been demonstrated that the time to move the cursor corresponds to Fitts' law. This law predicts that the time is proportional to the log of the ratio of the distance moved to the size of the target.

This shows that the targets should be as large as possible. Other tests have found the mouse superior to lightpens and joysticks, and still others have found the trackball superior to joysticks with and without spring returns and to isometric joysticks. As the technology evolves, there are sure to be many other device tests and comparisons.

Whether we can obtain accurate drawings and pictures as the result of program interactions is not really an issue. The questions are how to do this and whether there is a best way. These questions will no doubt continue to be explored for some time. We still need to find the most efficient ways to use computers to help us achieve the goals we desire.

EXERCISES

1. Describe the analogy between electron and light optics.
2. Compare magnetic and electrostatic deflection systems.
3. Discuss the use of look-up tables in raster display systems.
4. Diagram and discuss how an image display system cycles through the refresh buffer and displays its contents on the CRT screen. How does a row in the refresh buffer correspond to a scan line on the CRT? How does the buffer map a dot on the screen?
5. What is a direct-definition system and how many colors can it provide?
6. A refresh buffer that is 256×256 will provide how many coordinate intersections?
7. Draw the typical components of a graphics-display terminal with bit-map memory in a simplified block diagram, and discuss their operation.
8. Compare the three major display technologies.

9. A kind of input device is the lightpen or lightpencil. Discuss how, when held at or near the CRT screen, it can sense the presence of a brightening spot of light and signal the computer as to the location of this spot.

10. Compare the two major plotter technologies.

11. What are the soft buttons and how should they be utilized?

12. Many other devices that provide functions similar to those of the lightpen are available. Report at length on each of these input devices separately.

13. Why should the study of the muscle groups be helpful to establish evaluation criteria for future pointing-device development? What devices make the best use of these muscle groups?

14. Show how the generation of the color orange by control of the primary colors can be accomplished in a raster system.

15. Compare the three major digitizing-tablet technologies, and discuss the various operating modes.

16. What is the difference between a rate joystick and an absolute joystick?

17. Discuss the techniques of dragging and rubberbanding.

18. How can we use extension elements as an aid in pointing?

19. Discuss Fitts' law and its implications for pointing-device technology in the future.

MODELING OF ELECTRONIC DEVICES

4

The accuracy of the computer analysis for any system is a direct function of the accuracy of the models used. Some circuit-analysis programs may require the user to generate models for active elements. In many cases the models used are developed using methods such as piecewise-linear approximations.

A computer can rapidly and accurately solve large systems of equations, either linear or nonlinear, whose solution would not be feasible otherwise. Thus, is is possible to use accurate, nonlinear, complex models to account for first- and second-order physical effects. Using these models we can effectively utilize the computer's capabilities to accurately predict circuit performance.

MODEL TYPES AND CONSIDERATIONS

System models, in general, are of three basic types:

1. Physical.
2. Analytical.
3. Descriptive.

Physical models have some obvious advantages, since experiments can be conducted on them. However, such models are not usually economical, since they may be time-consuming to construct and difficult to experiment with. *Analytical models* are the mathematical expression of the characteristics of the system, usually in the form of sets of simultaneous equations. *Descriptive models* may bridge the entire scale of abstraction. They can begin as the basic word pictures of the processes that make up the system. These descriptions can include:

1. The interactions between the variables.
2. The attributes of the variables.
3. The constraints that tend to limit the performance.

These models can sometimes be prepared quickly and at relatively low cost, but their development requires a few special skills. Descriptive models can be applied to a wide variety of problems requiring decisions. Many models of business systems can be easily expressed in the descriptive format.

The need for a variety of model types results from the detailed description of an electronic circuit with each specified function of the resistors, capacitors, transistors, and integrated circuits. The modeling is quite different in a chemical processing plant with its oxidation reactors, heat exchangers, distillation columns, and compressors. Again this model would be described differently from that of a highway network with its exits, access points, interchanges, and the random flow of vehicles. In spite of these differences, the

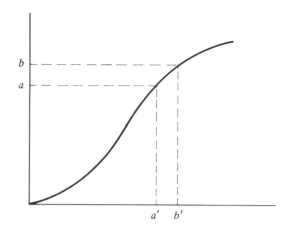

Figure 4-1 Incremental or small-signal operation.

analytic study of these systems requires that some convenient model be developed. It is not possible to fully represent all quantitative aspects of the system under study, and the validity of the analysis can be no more accurate than the model that is used.

The modeling process may consider a limited range such as a–b, as shown in Figure 4-1. This is referred to as *incremental operation* and is an important operating range for transistors and vacuum tubes. The assumption of linear response over the range a'–b' is reasonably valid under these conditions.

A small-signal model can be developed by finding an operating point and assuming that all responses are linear about that point. These models are valid over only a limited operating range, where the response characteristic is linear. An example of a static V-I characteristic for a diode is shown in Figure 4-2.

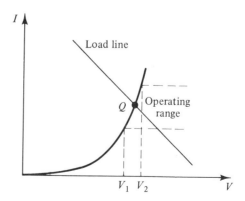

Figure 4-2 The small-signal operating range for a diode.

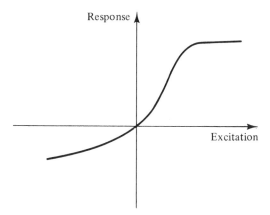

Figure 4-3   A nonbilateral characteristic.

The foregoing discussion implies that if the sense of the excitation is reversed, the response-excitation relation will remain the same. Mathematically this means that the excitation-response characteristic is an odd function. These elements are bilateral. There are a wide range of physical elements that are not bilateral. Figure 4-3 shows a nonbilateral characteristic.

In the case when there is a zero response for any reversal of excitation, the element is known to be unilateral. Figure 4-4 shows a diode characteristic that is unilateral.

Since exact description of all elements of a system is not always possible, approximate representation becomes necessary. It is possible to provide more than one model that is appropriate for a given element, particularly if the element is a complicated device. The different models may have equivalent forms that model the element over some restricted operating range, and different models may be used for different ranges.

Often the model to be used must be in a form that is most convenient to

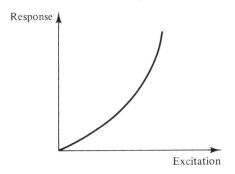

Figure 4-4   A unilateral characteristic.

the method of computer analysis to be employed. If the analysis is to be numerical, a tabular numerical description may be used.

Several steps are involved in developing a model for any family of semiconductor devices. Some of these steps involve the use of existing diode and transistor models. An outline of these conceptual models will be given, and some of them will be discussed in more detail in the subsequent sections on integrated circuits. An understanding of the physical processes which produce the external electrical characteristics is usually required. Although it is possible to use a pure black-box approach, it is usually necessary to know which phenomenon can be the result of tunneling, avalanche of a junction, stored charges, conductivity modulation, or other physical actions.

The manufacturing process used in making a given device can be pertinent to the model. A power transistor of planar construction will exhibit different transient characteristics than a transistor having the same structure but constructed using the annular method. This results in the need to use two different models or two different sets of model parameters, one for each manufacturer or manufacturing process.

A major portion of any model is derived from the set of mathematical equations which describe the physical operation. These may be derived in a number of ways, but two major criteria which must be met are (1) an adequate description of the device behavior and (2) a compatability with the language of the computer used. The model topology is made up of the interconnection of the discrete lumped components for the circuit which approximates the device. It is usually desirable to have one element or set of elements to represent each physical phenomenon. One resistor might be used for bulk resistance and another for leakage resistance. One capacitor could be used to represent the transition capacitance and another for the diffusion capacitance. One current source would characterize tunnel current, another the minority carrier current, while a third could represent the conductivity modulation flow.

The development of a model involves the determination of a number of defining parameters. These parameters can be obtained from the device physics or from the operating characteristics. If these operating characteristics are not supplied by the manufacturer, measurements must be made. It can be more difficult to determine what measurements to make and how to make them than to formulate the equations and the model topology. Once a model has been formulated, the device parameters must be obtained. If it is necessary to extract these parameters from measured data, the data reduction can involve the curve-fitting of data points and other analytical manipulations to get the desired parameters in the proper form.

One basic type of model is concerned primarily with the device physics. These are the equations describing the device in such quantities as base width, junction contact area, doping levels, and carrier mobilities. These models are usually constructed as sets of simultaneous partial differential equations which attempt to solve, for example, the charge distribution or the continuity equation in the junction region for one or two spatial dimensions. This microscopic approach can rapidly exhaust the capabilities of even the largest and fastest computers. The analysis of circuits with more than a few devices is usually not feasible when using models of this type.

Another type of model is not concerned primarily with the device physics, yet it depends on the physical interactions. The quantities of interest are electrical characteristics which can be observed at the external terminals using a black-box approach. The modeling of this type of behavior consists mainly of finding the mathematical expressions to represent the electrical characteristics.

We will approach device modeling using both of the above methods, with the emphasis on the latter. Physical constants will be used whenever possible, but if a characteristic cannot be related physically, empirical descriptions will be used.

The mathematical equations of a physical semiconductor model are based on the assumptions of current flow in semiconductor material (consisting of the drift and diffusion components), the continuity equations of holes and electrons, and the relationships between net space charge and electric field. The basic equations for the hole and electron current densities due to drift and diffusion are:

$$j_p = e\mu_p p E - e D_p \nabla p$$
$$j_n = e\mu_n n E + e D_n \nabla n$$

where e = electronic charge
   μ = mobility
   D = diffusion constant
   E = electric field
   p = density of holes
   n = density of electrons
   ∇p = hole density gradient
   ∇n = electron density gradient

The continuity equation for the hole minority carriers in an n-type semiconductor is:

$$\frac{\partial p}{\partial t} = \frac{p_n - p}{\tau p} - \frac{1}{e} \nabla j_p$$

and for the electron minority carriers in a p-type semiconductor:

$$\frac{\partial n}{\partial t} = \frac{n_p - n}{\tau_n} + \frac{1}{e} \nabla j_n$$

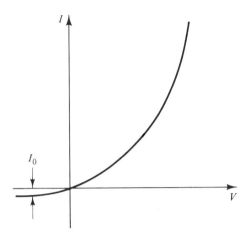

Figure 4-5 Diode characteristic.

These equations can be used to describe the internal behavior of the device. It is also possible, by using certain simplifying assumptions, to solve these equations and relate the external voltages and currents of a model to the internal parameters.

For the computer-aided analysis it is instructive to relate external behavior to measurable quantities. For example, the terminal current and voltage of p-n junction diodes are related by the equation that describes the characteristic (Figure 4-5) of a silicon diode. This diode characteristic is based on semiconductor carrier theory and is called the *diode equation*:

$$I = I_0 \left[\exp\left(\frac{qV}{kT} \right) - 1 \right]$$

where q, V, k, T are the electron charge, diode voltage, Boltzmann's constant, and the absolute temperature. This equation is not particularly convenient for numerical calculations. For numerical calculations it may be more convenient to prepare a table giving the currents appropriate to the selected values of voltage over the presumed operating range. In some cases it may be more convenient to approximate the curve by a number of linear segments. A simple piecewise-linear approximation for a smooth characteristic will be of the form shown in Figure 4-6. The same advantages and disadvantages apply for the piecewise-linear model as for a small-signal representation, although operation of the device is defined for a wider range of values. By the use of several regions, a piecewise-linear model can usually be made to approximate the actual behavior quite accurately. As more regions are added, however, more constants must be provided, and the awkwardness involved in determining the correct region of operation and the correct set of constants can prove to be time-consuming.

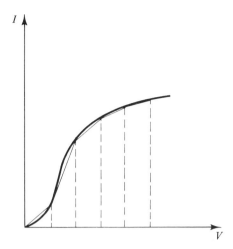

Figure 4-6   Piecewise-linear approximation.

Large-Signal Models

For use in computer circuit analysis and design, the models discussed thus far tend to be rather specialized and limited. Ideally, a model should be frequency-independent, be valid for any current or voltage excitation within the device ratings, and have a fixed topology which provides a one-to-one correspondence with physical processes. It should consist of passive elements (preferably of a fixed value) and current and voltage sources, and the mathematical equations should be well behaved.

A *large-signal model* is one which can be used over a wide range of operation. By its nature, it is one of the models best suited for use in computer circuit analysis.

Two common semiconductor structures which occur in circuit analysis are the p-n junction diode and the junction-diode pair which form a transistor. The models which are commonly used to represent these two structures in circuit analysis are based on the low-level-injection theories introduced by Shockley. Three large-signal models have been commonly used: the Ebers-Moll model, the charge-control mode of Beaufoy and Sparkes, and the Linvill lumped model. The first two lead to the same ac and transient results.

Although a number of such models have been proposed, these three are most widely known and used. We shall compare the three models and use the conclusions in discussing the advantages and disadvantages of large-signal models for computer circuit analysis and design.

The *Ebers-Moll model* describes the device behavior in terms of simple measured terminal quantities. This black-box type of mode is expressed by relatively simple mathematical equations. Although the model topology is such that each element represents a physical feature of the actual device, the Ebers-Moll model provides little insight into the actual physical device.

The *charge-control model* is similar in a topological sense to the Ebers-Moll model. However, some relation is established with the physical interactions by describing the generated currents in terms of the minority carrier charge. The charge-control model is somewhat more complex, but the model parameters can still be extracted from terminal measurements, and there is a one-to-one correspondence with the Ebers-Moll parameters.

The *Linvill model* is more general. It uses lumped elements called diffusance, storance, and combinance which relate to the physical processes of the device. Here, a one-to-one correspondence exists between each element and a physical action. The values of the lumped elements are not directly measurable and are not expressed in terms of terminal parameters.

In computer programs for circuit analysis and design, the first two models are more suitable. One of the primary objectives is to aid in the design of better circuits. Thus, the designer is more interested in obtaining a desired response, so the terminal behavior of a device becomes more important than the internal physical actions.

The basic semiconductor equations which are either explicitly or implicitly solved to determine the electrical characteristics of semiconductor devices are:

1. The continuity equations for both electrons and holes.
2. The drift and diffusion equations for holes and electrons.
3. Poisson's equation.

Any model depends on the accuracy with which it models these equations. If the doping profile is known, the equations can be solved for the device as a whole. But solutions are obtainable this way only in a small number of cases. The solutions can be obtained numerically, and this approach lends itself to computer data processing.

The more typical way that the problem is solved is by considering the different parts of the device separately and matching the boundary conditions for the adjacent parts. One assumption is that the currents are low enough so that the field distribution within the device is affected by current distribution. This allows the excess carriers injected into the device in regions other than junction regions to be proportional to the current, making the problem in that sense linear.

Most models are derived this way. They are, to an extent, linear, and thus can be treated using the techniques of linear circuit analysis. The relationship between the junction voltage and current is highly nonlinear, but the boundary-condition approach allows us to treat the whole device as linear.

It is beyond our scope to consider the complete theory of diode and transistor models. Instead, we describe the underlying assumptions, examine their range of validity, and discuss some of the important high-level injection effects and the circumstances under which they occur in practice. The junction diode includes all these effects, although they are of more concern in transistors. Their origin can be traced more simply in the analysis of the diode model. They will be considered in more detail in the case of the diode, and then attention will be given to their effects in the case of the transistor models.

Low-Level-Injection Diode Considerations

The junction diode can be considered as consisting of uniformly doped, field-free p and n layers separated by a high-field layer in the vicinity of the junction. The semiconductor parameters, such as lifetime, diffusion constant, and mobility, are assumed to be constant within the p and n regions, while the values will differ for the two regions. In the high-field region, the ratio of the diffusion constant to the mobility is assumed to be constant.

The drift and diffusion equations for holes and electrons in the high-field region are then solved. This gives us the density of excess carriers injected into the boundaries of the p and n regions as a specific voltage is applied to the high-field region. The solution results in the junction-diode characteristics, with its exponential character.

The only assumption required is that the actual currents are negligible in comparison to the larger drift and diffusion currents. This assumption was rarely violated in older devices, but with the trends toward higher current density the assumption may not be valid for all present devices.

In solving the equations for the p and n regions, we treat Poisson's equation using the assumption that the regions are essentially field-free. This assumption implies that the carrier flow occurs only by diffusion.

The diffusion and continuity equations then simplify to ordinary second-order differential equations with constant coefficients, since the lifetime and the diffusion constants are assumed to be fixed. The solution gives a linear relationship between injected-carrier density and current, which, along with the solution for the high-field region, gives the complete junction characteristic. The approach can be used for the other types of diodes, such as the diffused-junction and epitaxially grown units, in which large fields occur in the p and n regions.

The basic equations for these regions are also linear under low-level-injection conditions, but they have nonconstant coefficients. The diode characteristic still applies, but a closed-form solution for I_0 cannot be obtained in all cases. The solutions become nonlinear when the injected-carrier densities are high enough to affect the semiconductor parameters or the field distribution of the diode.

The field distribution is usually the first to be affected, and then the solution of the basic equations for the p and n regions is much more complicated. The solution for the high-field region is not affected, but its boundaries tend to move as the current changes, which causes the boundary conditions for the p and n regions to be nonlinear. In most cases where the diodes and transistors are designed to operate at low or moderate frequencies the current levels will be low enough for the low-level-injection theories to apply. In devices designed for high-frequency or high-switching-speed applications, the bias currents will be higher to minimize the effect of the junction capacitances. The currents will then be restricted high-level-injection effects, and these effects become fundamental to the behavior of the high-frequency devices.

High-Level-Injection Considerations

The bulk p and n regions can easily contribute a significant amount of series resistance which can cause the field distribution within the device to vary with a varying current. At low current levels these can be represented by a linear resistance, but at higher current levels the injected carriers can have an effect on the conductivity of these regions, and the resistance in the diode equivalent circuit must become nonlinear.

In some planar diodes, the bulk resistance effects vary from the center to the edge of the junctions, and the current distribution can vary as the voltage drops in these resistors increase owing to the increasing current. The other diode parameters will also vary. This effect is not large in diodes, but in transistors it produces current-crowding, which can cause major variations in the device parameters.

A number of other effects can occur when the injected currents become high enough so that the excess-carrier densities become comparable with the doping levels.

The minority carriers that are injected into the p and n regions cause a build-up of majority carriers. A net space charge results which causes significant field and voltage drops to occur in these regions. The voltage drops cause the total voltage which must be applied to the junction to maintain a given current to be higher than that given by the normal diode characteristic. The carrier lifetimes increase with increasing carrier density, which also requires a higher applied voltage.

The boundaries of the high-field region tend to move in the direction of the more highly doped side of the junction. This effect is not important in dc analysis, but the excess charge it causes will greatly affect the transient performance of the diode.

The basic diode equation changes under these conditions to:

$$I = I_0 \left[\exp\left(\frac{qV}{nkT} \right) \right]$$

Here n is a function of the current and has integer values according to the current level.

A typical epitaxial diode used at only a few milliamps will reach the current levels at which high-level-injection conditions set in. It can be assumed to be a p-n junction formed with uniformly doped 0.1 ohm-cm n-type epitaxial layer 3 μm thick and having a lifetime of 3 ns. The junction area is about one square mil. These high-level effects occur in transistors also where they are of major importance.

Transistor Models

The transistor is generally modeled as a current-controlled device. The analysis of the transistor is usually based on a set of relations which include continuity equations. These, along with the Poisson equation, provide the boundary conditions for the minority-carrier concentrations at the edges of the junctions. These equations are used with a space-charge neutrality assumption and then solved for specified conditions of operation, yielding a description of the electrical behavior of the device.

Because of the physical configuration of the transistor, we will usually find it most convenient to begin with the common-base connection. In the basic volt-ampere characteristics shown in Figure 4-7, V_E and I_E appear as the input quantities and V_C and I_C are the output quantities, with the base common to the input and output. The reverse-biased collector diode collects almost all the minority carriers injected by the forward-biased emitter diode, so I_E appears as the controlled quantity in the output characteristics. In the absence of emitter current, $I_C = I_{CO}$ (where the subscript O indicates that the collector is open-circuited). For any $I_E > 0$, the collector current is increased in magnitude by an amount nearly equal to I_E. The collector characteristic has essentially the same shape as when $I_E = 0$, but it is shifted along the I_C axis by an amount αI_E. The coefficient α is one of the more important transistor parameters, typically having a value slightly less than, but close to, unity. The following equation approximately describes the collector characteristics in the active region:

$$I_C = -I_{CO} - \alpha I_E$$

This approximation is derived from the assumption that the collector current does not depend on the collector voltage. I_{CO} is the small leakage current, which is extremely temperature-sensitive. At low frequencies, α can be assumed to be a constant. Actually, α is a function of V_C, and it also depends on I_E. Using the transistor characteristics, a first approximation to a small-signal equivalent circuit can be derived. We note that a small-signal variation in I_E will result in a small-signal collector current $I_C = -\alpha I_E$, since I_{CO} is a constant. This collector current does not depend on the collector voltage

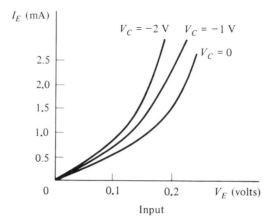

Input

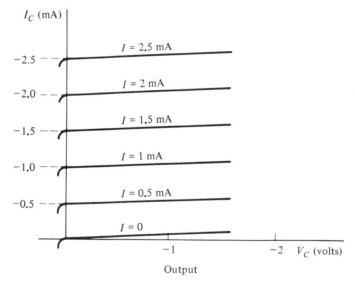

Output

Figure 4-7 Typical transistor volt-ampere characteristics.

according to our approximation. So the output circuit can be represented by a current generator of magnitude αI_E. Neglecting any interaction between I_E and V_C, the equivalent input circuit appears to be a forward-biased junction diode with a dynamic resistance of

$$r'_E = \frac{kT}{qI_E}$$

The approximate equivalent circuit is shown in Figure 4-8. Although it

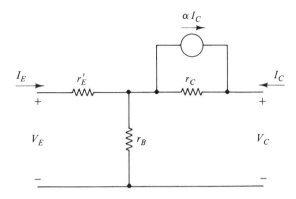

Figure 4-8   T-equivalent circuit for common-base configuration.

may be simplified for many circuit-analysis applications, this equivalent circuit illustrates the essential transistor characteristic properties in the common-base connection. This includes a small input impedance and a current which is almost completely transferred to a high-impedance output.

We have developed the T-equivalent circuit for the common-base connection. Its elements bear only an approximate relation to the physics of the transistor. Typical values which we might encounter in a high-frequency transistor are shown below:

r_C (2 megohms)	high impedance of reverse-biased collector junction
α (0.98)	transport factor of minority carriers across the base
r_B (100 ohms)	total effect of output-input interaction
r_E' (25 ohms)	low impedance of forward-biased emitter junction

A common-emitter T-equivalent can be developed in a similar manner, as shown in Figure 4-9. The two transistor equivalent circuits discussed thus far are valid only at relatively low frequencies. When we include one high-frequency transistor operation, the transit-time and capacitance effects must be considered in the models.

High-Frequency Effects

Accurate models for high-frequency, high-speed diodes and transistors are complicated by the inherent nonlinearities due to high-level-injection effects. The narrow layers used in these devices, and the boundaries which may move over distances sometimes greater than the layer widths themselves,

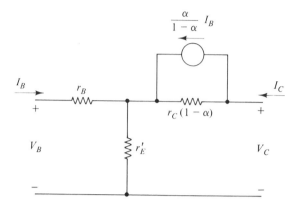

Figure 4-9 T-equivalent circuit for common-emitter configuration.

complicate the separation of the devices into the conventional emitter, base, and collector regions.

An approach which gives a more accurate representation regards them as a single entity for which the basic semiconductor equations are solved as a whole. To be successful, this approach requires detailed knowledge of the actual transistor doping profiles. The one-dimensional approach also needs to be extended to include the two-dimensional effects such as current-crowding.

The best frequency responses or switching speeds are obtained from diodes and transistors only if they are operated under high-level-injection conditions. At low current levels, the frequency cutoff of a transistor is low because of the depletion-layer capacitances. The frequency cutoff increases as the current level increases, until high-level-injection effects cause the cutoff frequency to decrease with further increases of current level. In high-frequency operation the bias currents should be set to give the maximum cutoff frequency, ensuring high-level-injection conditions.

Although transistor operation is affected by all the high-level-injection effects described here, for the ac and transient performance of a transistor the two dominant effects are:

1. The space-charge effects, which lead to a widening of the collector-depletion layer and the base.
2. The current-crowding toward the edge of the emitter, which is worse under high-frequency or transient conditions because the base-current densities are higher.

Because the current densities are higher, base and collector widening can occur at much lower current levels than under dc conditions. This behavior requires a two-dimensional analysis. Reduced frequency response is caused by these effects owing to the increased transit-time delays under high-level-injection conditions. The space-charge effects cause an increased delay owing to the widening of the base and collector layers. Current-crowding also leads to longer transit delays, since the base is wider around the edges of the emitter than in the center.

A high-level-injection effect which can be an important consideration in determining the collector resistivity for a switching transistor is shown in Figure 4-10. The collector current will follow in the collector-epitaxial layer only in the vicinity of the emitter, and a significant spreading resistance will occur here. This may exceed a few hundred ohms, and the transistor will begin to saturate in the vicinity of the emitter. Lower saturation voltages can occur, since the minority carriers injected into the epitaxial layer owing to saturation effects will reduce the spreading resistance. If the lifetime is high enough, the conductivity modulation can be large while the effects on the dc characteristics are small.

The frequency response of the transistor at low collector voltages will be decreased, owing to the excess stored charge in the collector layer. This can be critical, since switching transistors must have low saturation voltages for the highest possible noise immunity. In these cases, a low-resistivity epitaxial layer must be used.

From the physical theory of transistors, we can derive an expression for the frequency dependence for most models. This expression can be simplified to

$$\alpha = \frac{\alpha_0}{1 + \dfrac{j\omega}{\omega_\alpha}}$$

This relationship shows that if α has the value of α_0 at low frequencies, then at

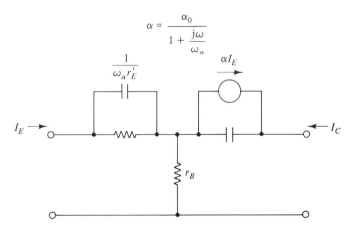

Figure 4-10   High-frequency T-equivalent circuit.

a radian frequency of ω_a its amplitude is 3 dB down from α_0, and from then on it decreases at a rate of 6 dB/octave. The quantity ω_a, called the *alpha cutoff frequency*, is considered the most fundamental high-frequency parameter for transistors.

Another effect of major importance in transistor frequency response is due to the space-charge region existing at the reverse-biased collector-base junction. This region acts as a dipole layer of charged acceptor and donor ions which constitutes a displacement current. The effect on the circuit is that of a capacitance C_C, as shown in the high-frequency T-equivalent circuit of Figure 4-10.

Along with the diffusion mechanism we have noted that charge storage occurs in the base region. The larger the emitter current becomes, the more minority carriers will exist in the base region. If the emitter current is suddenly increased, the initial increment must be a displacement current to supply the required increase in charge.

In general a more useful model in high-frequency computer-aided circuit analysis and design is the common-emitter pi-equivalent circuit shown in Figure 4-11. The entire frequency dependence of this circuit is due to the two capacitances. Figure 4-12 shows another pi-equivalent model, which includes the header and overlap diode capacitances.

Computer optimization techniques for matching experimental data to these models will be described later in this chapter. Many of these models have a limited frequency range, and it may be necessary to use a number of models over a frequency range or resort to nonlinear models.

Nonlinear Models

Transistor operation in the small-signal active region is that in which the emitter is forward-biased and the collector is reverse-biased. In a switching application, the transistor is driven beyond the active region either by reverse-biasing the emitter or by allowing the collector voltage to go to zero. In order

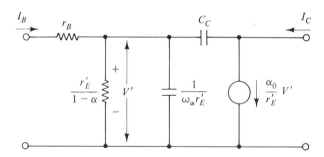

Figure 4-11 Hybrid pi-equivalent circuit.

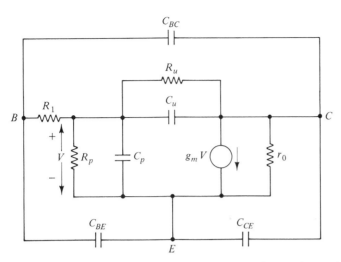

Figure 4-12   Hybrid pi-equivalent circuit with header and overlap diode capacitances.

to characterize the transistor's terminal behavior under such conditions, it is necessary to model the behavior of the transistor in all regions of operation.

One way we can do this is by using a piecewise-linear approximation, where the overall range of operation is broken into a number of smaller ranges and each one of these is approximated by a linear model. This technique is commonly used with nonlinear devices. Piecewise-linear approximation is essentially a graphical technique where the characteristics are linearized. When the operational characteristics of the device are in piecewise-linear approximated sections, then the operation of the device is represented using a different model for each region, and attention must be given to matching the device descriptions at the boundaries between these regions.

For the transistor there exist four regions of operation:

1. Both the emitter and collector junctions reverse-biased: the cutoff region.
2. The emitter forward- and the collector reverse-biased: the active region.
3. Both junctions forward-biased: the saturation region.
4. The emitter reverse-biased and the collector forward-biased: the inverted active region.

These regions are shown in the carrier density distribution for the base region of Figure 4-13.

One advantage of the Ebers-Moll model is that one can consider two separate excitations to represent the result of any excitation of the transistor

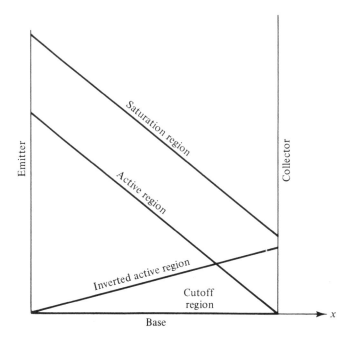

Figure 4-13   Carrier density in the base region.

when they are applied in combination. The emitter and collector junction voltages will determine the minority-carrier densities at the edges of the transition region. They will set the boundary conditions for the carrier densities in the base region. The same total carrier diffusion currents can exist with the application of the required emitter voltage and zero collector voltage and the required collector voltage and zero emitter voltage as when both voltages are applied together.

The validity of the use of superposition of carrier current densities occurs when linear density profiles are obtained in the base. This occurs when the base width is much smaller than the minority-carrier diffusion length. Then the minority-carrier flow mechanisms are linear in the diffusion model of the transistor. The linearity of the carrier flow processes allows us to write the emitter and collector currents I_E and I_C in terms of their components under both forward- and reverse-voltage conditions:

$$I_E = I_{EF} + I_{ER}$$
$$I_C = I_{CF} + I_{CR}$$

We can also write the currents into the terminals of the model of Figure 1-14 in terms of the emitter and collector junction voltages V_E and V_C from the diode characteristic equation:

$$I_E = I_{EO}\left[\exp\left(\frac{qV_E}{kT}\right) - 1\right] - \alpha_I I_C$$

$$I_C = I_{CO}\left[\exp\left(\frac{qV_C}{kT}\right) - 1\right] - \alpha_N I_E$$

where

α_N = common-base current gain in the active region

α_I = common-base current gain in the inverted active region

I_{EO} = emitter current under a large reverse bias with the collector open-circuited

I_{CO} = collector current under a large reverse bias with the emitter open-circuited

The Ebers-Moll model has been used for nonlinear circuit analysis with several circuit-analysis programs. The Beaufoy and Sparkes model takes another point of view by viewing the transistor as a charge-controlled current source. This model requires the definition of a number of fundamental time constants which are related to the model circuit quantities.

This model relates the terminal currents and the total stored minority charge. The total based-stored minority charge is regarded as a dependent variable. It does not depend on spatial coordinates, but on time, so ordinary differential equations can be used.

Basically, we are interested in modeling transistors for large-signal transient analysis and, in particular, characterizing transistors for the efficient analysis by computer programs. Although there are many large-signal models that can be used, the three that have been more commonly used are those named earlier in the chapter:

1. Ebers-Moll large-signal model.
2. Beaufoy-Sparkes charge-control model.
3. Linvill lumped model.

All three can be used to predict the large-signal behavior of transistors, but they differ in their representation of the physical processes, as we have seen for some of the conditions that exist. The Linvill model can be used to represent built-in fields, such as in the base region of transistors. In this case the field is assumed to be independent of current, which is true only under low-level injection conditions.

The charge-control model assumes that the base, emitter, and collector regions are short compared to the diffusion length, so significant transport delays do not occur within these layers. The Ebers-Moll model uses a similar assumption. This is true for the base and emitter layers, if the transistor is

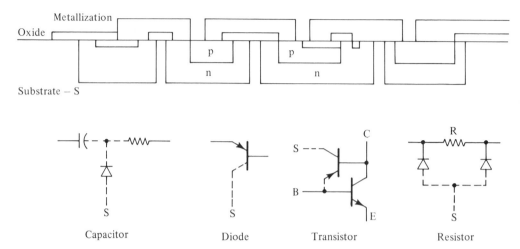

Figure 4-14 Planar-diffused integrated-circuit structure.

operated at frequencies greatly below the cutoff frequency, but not for the collector layer. This condition can lead to difficulties in modeling the transistor in saturation.

Integrated-Circuit Modeling

The models for the computer analysis and design of integrated circuits are based upon the physical equations for semiconductor and thin-film materials. The metal oxide semiconductor (MOS) and hybrid integrated-circuit structures incorporate a combination of these technologies and therefore tend to be dependent on the same physical conditions. The device and circuit models can be derived from the application of these equations, using the appropriate boundary conditions imposed by the structure and geometry. The models used in computing the device and circuit responses can then be developed from an approximation of these equations.

In the basic planar-diffused integrated circuit, as partially shown in Figure 4-14, the intrinsic transistor is shown in solid lines, while the parasitic transistor is represented with dashed lines. Each device is modeled according to its discrete equivalent circuit, depending on the signal amplitude and frequency of operation, using one of the models described earlier.

Diodes, resistors, and capacitors can be modeled in a similar fashion with their parasitic elements. The equivalent circuit of an IC gate modeled in this way is shown in Figure 4-15.

For greater accuracy over a wider frequency range of operations, a distributed model can be used. Consider a diffused resistor as shown in Figure

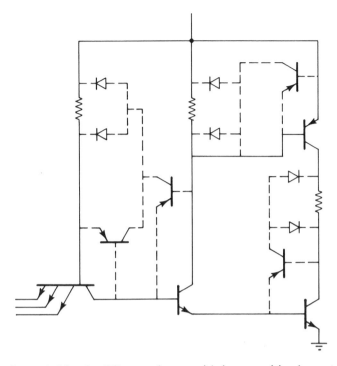

Figure 4-15 An IC gate shown with its parasitic elements.

4-16. In the model of Figure 4-17, p is the resistance per unit length. The isolation junction between the p and n regions can be modeled by a parallel combination of ideal diodes, with their associated capacitances distributed along the junction. The parallel combination of capacitance C_S with the ideal diode models the isolation junction between the n and the substrate regions. The number of elements required for the distributed model will depend on the desired accuracy. In some cases, the distributed resistance can be represented by a T-section, as shown in Figure 4-18.

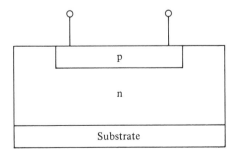

Figure 4-16 Diffused resistor.

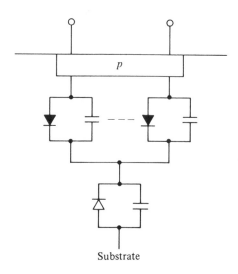

Figure 4-17   Diffused resistor distributed model.

A simplified distributed model for a bipolar n-p-n transistor is shown in Figure 4-19 along with the schematic model. In each region of the model the structure is uniformly distributed. Each region of the model then relates to its physical counterpart.

A more complex approach, such as the lumped-parameter method used in the Linvill model, is desirable for circuits that must operate over a wider range of conditions. It is based directly on the physics of the structure and can be used to model thermal gradients and electromagnetic, nuclear, and cosmic radiation effects.

The Linvill model method differs from the basic distributed technique in the way the physical structure is partitioned for modeling. Rather than being

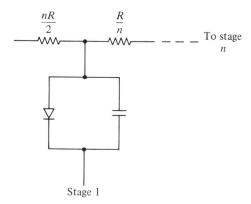

Figure 4-18   Diffused resistor T-section model.

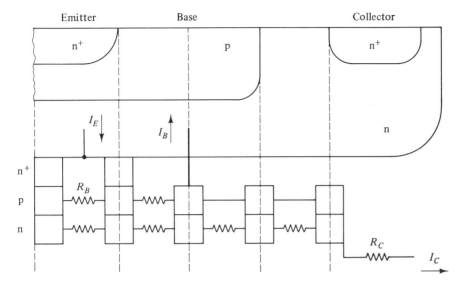

Figure 4-19   Transistor distributed model.

divided into equivalent diodes and associated capacitances, the integrated circuit is separated into nonuniform lumps, with each one representing a portion of the structure.

Film components deposited on passive substrates are well isolated from each other and can be considered as closely placed discrete components with only a few interactions. The only exception is a distributed RC network. One model for this structure is shown in Figure 4-20. This model uses a finite transmission line with distributed resistance and capacitance. The parameters for a distributed RC structure are transcendental functions.

Thick or thin films on active substrates which contain active devices may exhibit interactions between the components and the substrate. The interactions are small, and the passive components may be represented by discrete model representations.

Much information is available concerning the operation and models of discrete MOS devices. The major difference between discrete MOS-FET

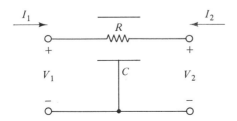

Figure 4-20   Distributed RC network model.

operation and its characteristics in large ICs is the interaction through the common substrate between devices. The MOS-FET transfer curves tend to shift with respect to the gate voltage as the substrate is back-biased.

Integrated-circuit field-effect transistor models which account for the substrate interaction between devices have been developed. A typical model, which is valid for any combination of terminal voltages, is shown in Figure 4-21. The model capacitances appear as lumped elements, since the metallization and other parasitic capacitances are much larger than the intrinsic capacitance from the relatively small channel region of the integrated field-effect transistor.

MODEL SELECTION AND CHARACTERIZATION

Since the arrival of integrated circuits an important part of electronics has been the emphasis on thorough and accurate analysis of circuit designs. Much of the design work with circuits that used discrete components was based on rule-of-thumb calculations, followed by developmental work on breadboard circuits. This approach does not work for integrated circuits, and the design problem is compounded by the length of time by which circuit

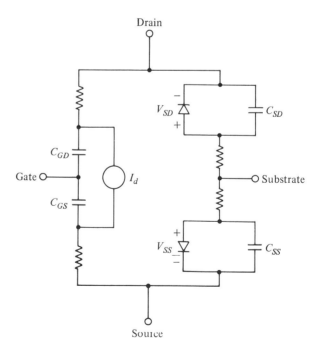

Figure 4-21 Field-effect transistor model.

realization lags the completion of the design. The development of both computers and circuit-design programs has allowed a large part of the burden of the design to be transferred to machines.

These machine designs may still be expensive, particularly if one must optimize a design. The proper development involves more complete representation of integrated circuits and the automatic generation of masks from circuit performance specifications. Circuit program development has followed the lines of classical network theory. Integrated circuits have been regarded as linear passive networks with models of nonlinear active elements embedded in them, and the models have been linearized as much as possible. Actually, only the resistors in integrated circuits appear linear, and the economic rule of integrated circuits is to replace passive elements with active elements wherever possible. If classical network theory is used as the basis for circuit design, then the importance of the models used for the active devices must be emphasized. One purpose of this section is to outline the underlying assumptions of the models used for bipolar devices and to examine how well they correspond with reality.

A fundamental investigative technique that has been discussed is the representation of physical structures or phenomena by idealized, but mathematically relatable, models. Extensive use has been made of this modeling technique in the design and fabrication of many physical components and circuits.

High-frequency circuits are particularly intolerant of partial component or device characteristics. The models are generally required to be as simple as possible, subject to model errors within prescribed bounds. Extremely accurate models are generally more complicated and can reduce the maximum allowable size of the network which may be analyzed.

A particular device or phenomenon can usually be described by a number of models, and the selection of one model over another represents a compromise between simplicity and the accuracy with which the device under consideration can be described. Another important criterion for the model choice is the ease with which the physical properties internal to the model can be described.

The first criterion should be used when the device, object, process, or phenomenon being modeled is a part of a larger system, and the major interest is confined to the influence of its external properties on the system performance. The elements of the model need not have any particular relation to the internal processes, since the terminal characteristic simulation is the real concern.

The second criterion is used when the phenomena within the device are to be studied. In these cases, the model must be selected with great care so that maximum correlation is obtained between the internal phenomenon and the model.

A type of two-port model which is used in much active-circuit work consists of a number of circuit elements arranged in such a way that the network, by using the proper element values, realizes the two-port parameters of the device over as wide a frequency range as possible.

This approach requires the proper derivation of element values for the selected model. The difficulty here depends directly on the model. The derivation may be simple, or it may be complicated enough to make the calculations unreasonably difficult.

In this case, the derivation of the element values for the model can be programmed and completed using a computer. The modeling problem can then be treated as the process of finding the values which best simulate the measurements made on the object being modeled. Note that only the terminal or external performance need be simulated. A modeling procedure is shown in Figure 4-22 in which the initial steps consist of:

1. The required model performance.
2. The weighting factors which are used to emphasize and determine the desired features.
3. The initial estimate of the parameter values.

The model performance for the initial element values is computed and compared with the required performance using a predetermined error

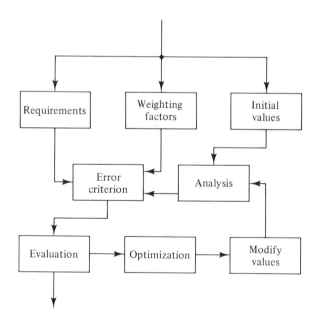

Figure 4-22 The modeling procedure.

criterion. A satisfactory model performance at this point leads to termination of the modeling program. An unsatisfactory-modeling error leads to a reinitialing of the element values and a repeat of the process until the model performance falls within the desired values. Many available optimization programs meet these criteria.

The program might reinitialize the element values using two slope-following techniques such as the method of steepest descent and the Newton-Raphson technique. These could be used consecutively or either technique can be used alone. The steepest-descent method is preferred initially, since it tends to converge rapidly when the parameter values are displaced far from optimum.

The error function is evaluated at two more points along the descent line. The parabola fitting these points is evaluated, and its minimum can be the next starting point, since it corresponds to the minimum value of error. When an overall minimum is near approximately less than 5% reduction in the error function per iteration, the second slope-following technique can be used. The Newton-Raphson method is substituted then because it converges quickly when reasonable parameter values are used.

This optimization can continue until the improvement in error from the successive approximations is acceptable. The function minimized becomes the normalized error and can be expressed as

$$E = \frac{\sum_i W_i(f_i - R_i)^2}{\sum_i W_i}$$

where
F_i = the computed value of the function at some frequency f_i
R_i = the required value of the function at some frequency f_i
W_i = the weighting factor at the frequency of f_i
f_i = the frequency at which the normalized error is evaluated

The expression implies that a single frequency-dependent function is being matched, but the technique can easily include more than a single curve. The partial derivatives can be approximated by computing the difference in the function at each frequency due to a 0.01% change in each individual parameter. These approximated partial derivatives can also be used as an aid in evaluating the sensitivity of the required function to each parameter value. The application of this type of modeling program includes many problems in electronic circuit design, such as the modeling of passive components and transistors and their application to high-frequency amplifier design, which will be considered next.

High-Frequency Model Development

High-frequency models are those that are affected by the electrical length of the lines and connections. Lumped elements such as resistors, inductors, or capacitors may be characterized using analytical expressions of R, Ls, or Cs, where $s = j\omega$. Multiterminal lumped networks might be characterized at the terminals in ratios of complex polynomials. Elements such as bandpass filters with linear phase shifts may be characterized by analytical phase and magnitude expressions. When these analytical expressions are available and are accurate enough, they are preferable because of their convenience. Sometimes analytical expressions are not available but discrete data is. The discrete data might have been measured or calculated.

The general shape of the curve from which the discrete data points were sampled sometimes allows the discrete data to be replaced by standard functions using a process of curve fitting. The choice of functions is determined primarily by the application, but some considerations include:

1. When the range of frequencies and the range of the values of the functions are small, low-order polynomials can be adequate for the slowly varying functions.

2. When the range of frequencies is large and the range of values is small, low-order polynomials in the logarithm of the frequency can be used.

3. When both the range of values and the range of frequencies tend to be large, the logarithms of the values versus the logarithms of the frequencies can be used with low-order polynomials.

In cases where the data varies erratically, different curves can be fitted for each frequency range. These methods tend to be among the simplest that can be used, and a library of routines can be made available to implement them. The user should select functional form and adjust the parameters with the optimization routines. With several subroutines available, the user, depending on the problem, must control what types of standard functions are used for the interpolation. In cases where the discrete data is spaced sufficiently close, analysis can be done only at the frequency values of the data. This assumes that the components are all characterized at the same frequencies. In this case curve fitting is not required.

When we attempt to approximate a curve with a linear combination of functions, one problem is that calculations performed by computer carry a limited number of significant figures. Subtraction of large numbers to obtain small numbers can cause considerable errors due to truncation. This problem will not occur if orthogonal functions are used.

The powers of x are not orthogonal. The higher the order of the polynomials, the less the projection of one upon another, as shown by their inner products. Thus, when one fits a curve with a high-order polynomial, it is generally necessary to carry a significant number of digits, especially for the higher powers.

Although the experimental data may be accurate to two significant figures, we may need to provide polynomial coefficients which are accurate to seven figures. If one rounds off the polynomial coefficients to the same significant figures as the data, this can result in inaccurate results.

This problem is eliminated if we use functions other than powers of x. There are several families of orthogonal polynomials which can be normalized over different intervals. Some examples include:

1. Legendre, orthogonal in $(-1, 1)$.
2. Chebyshev, first kind, orthogonal in $(-1, 1)$.
3. Chebyshev, second kind, orthogonal in $(-1, 1)$.
4. Jacobi, orthogonal in $(-1, 1)$.
5. Generalized Laguerre, orthogonal in $(0, \infty)$.
6. Hermite, orthogonal in $(-\infty, \infty)$.

These polynomials represent the solutions to certain sets of differential equations with designated boundary conditions. One can also generate orthogonal polynomials for any interval using the Gram-Schmidt process. The choice is a compromise between the availability of subroutines to do the curve fitting and the size, efficiency, and accuracy of the subroutines. We must also be willing to work with analytical tools to which we may not be accustomed.

Another technique, which we have discussed before, that has been found to be quite effective is the piecewise fitting of curves over the intervals. Different curves can be fitted over the intervals. We might fit a quadratic polynomial to the first three points and fit other quadratics through each additional point, matching the previous curve both in value and derivative at the last common point.

The subroutine can decide what quadratic to use depending on the interval. A continuous curve with a continuous derivative passing through the data points can be obtained. Another version of this approach is a linear interpolation between the data points. This produces a continuous curve between the data points, although the derivative will be discontinuous. Linear interpolation can be effective, and it is simple to use. It is most suitable in the characterization of curves which will not become part of a library. When a subcircuit or module is used often or is part of a library, then one can fit the curves with computations from an optimization program. With an optimization program we write an expression of some variable parameters, and the program will automatically determine the best parameters for the fit. This can provide the analytical model for such cases when we need to fit lumped circuits to many frequency curves.

This can occur in some transformers when describing the details of some complex electrical devices. Independent of the internal construction of a device, if the circuit tends to be linear and time-invariant, then the frequency response in the complex plane will describe the device accurately.

In some cases the frequency response must be obtained experimentally without knowledge of the internal structure. In other cases the circuits will be analyzed first and the network then characterized by elements which are functions of frequency. The circuit's internal structure is then ignored. This technique, known as the *black-box approach*, can have a number of advantages for integrated circuits.

1. The model can accept experimental as well as analytical data.
2. Complete integrated circuits can be modeled. This can be extremely advantageous if the same circuits are used many times in the model.
3. There is no basic difference between lumped, distributed, or ideal networks.
4. The solution can be done in pieces quite well.

Conventional models are still valuable for giving insights into the interaction of the device with the rest of the circuit. But tools, such as the computer, should be used in ways appropriate to themselves. Certain intuitive tools such as circuit schematics and Bode diagrams may also be appropriate. A computer, though, handles polynomials well, and it can fit experimental curves to these polynomials.

Conventional models are fine for insight, but the black-box modeling approach can be more appropriate for handling interconnections involving linear integrated circuits, since the only available points for connection, measurement, and characterization are the external terminals.

The central ideas to keep in mind are:

1. In analyzing linear stationary networks one should always be able to handle them as black boxes.
2. The modeling of a circuit with two or more terminals should be flexible enough to allow not only ratios of complex polynomials but also curves in the frequency domain.
3. One can always preanalyze pieces of a circuit and eventually interconnect the pieces.

Another method of using transistors and other elements in computer analysis is to use measured terminal immittances directly without any attempt to fit them to circuit model. The measured terminal immittances on a three-terminal device such as a transistor can be numerically converted into the two-port impedance parameters known as the Z-parameters. The self- and mutual impedance terms in the loop equations can be easily identified. As an aid in visualizing how this is done, we can use the circuit model in Figure 4-23. The Z-parameters can be identified as the values of the self-impedances and transimpedances in the generalized circuit shown.

Active Filters

The trend of events in filters with integrated-circuit realization has developed techniques which require no inductors. Because of the requirements in the volume storage of magnetic energy and the available ranges of magnetic permeability and conductivity of the materials, thin-film inductors have been limited both in the total inductance and in inductance/resistance ratio, which is proportional to the Q.

The general approach to linear filter synthesis is to first approximate the requirements of a given filter description by some realizable immittance function and then to construct a circuit which realizes this function. For communications applications the most widely used filters fall into one of the following classes. There is the bandpass filter, which is used for separation of channels in telephone carriers. There is the equalizer, which has a magnitude and phase characteristic which approximates the inverse characteristic of the transmission channel over some bandwidth. These bandwidths are restricted, and the equalizer is usually required to have only a slowly varying magnitude-vs.-frequency function, in contrast to the sharp characteristics of the bandpass filter. The channels in which equalizers are used are those in which the preservation of the waveshape is important.

There is another class of filters used in pulse-amplitude modulation or pulse-code modulation systems. This type of filter is also called an equalizer,

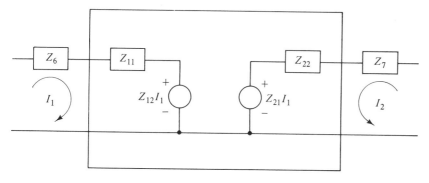

Figure 4-23 Z-parameters.

but it is used in nonlinear time-varying systems with gating circuits. These systems require only that the response of this equalizer have the correct value at a certain point in time.

Using a combination of resistance, capacitance, and active elements such as transistors, virtually any network function can be realized by means of RC networks in inductorless form.

In order to realize the same function, an active LC filter must have at least as many components as, and sometimes more than, a passive RC filter. The mounting and interconnection of these parts can be a large portion of the fabrication cost, and the number of parts can have a large cost significance. Integration of the circuits along with automatic assembly and interconnection techniques can reduce the cost. Thus the trend of development has been to reduce the cost of the parts count. Another problem is the variation in circuit properties due to changes in the element values of the circuits from such causes as temperature and aging. The selection of parts to meet initial tolerances is not as great a problem in integrated circuits because of the physical proximity and available trimming techniques. Once the fabrication of the circuit is complete, other variations due to environmental conditions may prove to have an effect on the behavior of the circuit. There are two factors to consider when attacking these problems:

1. The tolerances in component values which are fixed by the fabrication technology.
2. The sensitivity of the circuit performance to changes in the element values.

The latter problem can be aided by modifications in the circuit design based on computer analysis of the deviations in the element values. These studies can be extended to find the worst-case deviations due to the worst possible variations of simultaneous changes in all elements of the circuit, with each element remaining within its allowable limits.

The natural frequencies of an active network, which are usually inversely proportional to the resistance-capacitance products or time constants of the network, can be compensated for large changes by using resistance and capacitance elements which have opposite changes in value due to temperature or aging.

Many lower-order circuit functions can be synthesized by a standard active RC configuration and then analyzed for its sensitivity. Many such elementary circuits may need to be combined into a complicated filter along with the related changes in element values which are to be used for compensation.

Resistor modeling is normally initiated by the measurement of the terminal characteristics of the component over the desired frequency range. From the nature of the data one then postulates a circuit model consisting of idealized elements. The impedance of the components being characterized, the accuracy desired, and the capabilities of the measuring instruments usually dictate the band of frequencies over which the characterization may be done.

Wideband measurements are usually made with instruments that use transmission-line techniques. The instruments for measuring wide ranges of impedance magnitudes typically use balanced-bridge techniques and provide data over limited frequency ranges. The transmission-line type of instrument may be capable of providing measurements through the UHF frequency range within accuracies of a few percent. These instruments may employ a combination of transmission-line and balanced-bridge techniques. They are able to provide data for limited ranges of element values and typically use transmission lines with a characteristic impedance Z_0 of 50 ohms.

If the component impedance Z_c differs substantially from Z_0, the accuracy of measurements decreases drastically, since the reflection coefficient becomes less sensitive to additional changes in Z_c, according to the following ratio:

$$\frac{\left(\dfrac{Z_c}{Z_0}\right) - 1}{\left(\dfrac{Z_c}{Z_0}\right) + 1}$$

Some balanced-bridge techniques which use discrete components for standards are limited in frequency to several hundred megacycles.

Thin-film resistors can be characterized using this technique in order to determine uniformity, evaluate the parasitics, and establish a model which allows these effects to be taken into account. In this case the resistance is characterized and represented by the circuit model. This is shown in Figure 4-24. The measured data is taken so the model characteristics closely simulate the component characteristics over the frequency range. Since resistor lead lengths and the corresponding lead inductance would vary and cause errors, the measurements should be made with zero lead length.

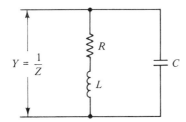

Figure 4-24   Thin-film resistor model.

The admittance of the model is

$$Y = G + jB$$

where

$$G = \frac{1}{R}\left(1 + \frac{1}{Q^2}\right)$$

$$B = \omega C\left(1 - \frac{\dfrac{L}{R^2 C}}{1 + Q^2}\right)$$

and

$$Q = \frac{\omega L}{R}$$

The requirements for this model are the measured values of $G(\omega)$. The initial parameter values can be found by relating the asymptotic behavior of G and B to the data.

The optimum element values for the circuit model can be found by matching the model curves to the $G(\omega)$ and $B(\omega)$ data. A higher priority requiring a larger weighting factor can be assigned to the $B(\omega)$ data match to allow the parasitic effects to be simulated with a higher accuracy.

A more complex circuit model can be used, in which case the final element values and model predictions are compared with the measured data. The agreement is considered satisfactory over a range of frequencies which indicates the nature of the limitations of the measurement technology. If the modeling were required over a wider range of frequencies, a modified measurement technique would also be needed.

The characterization of the resistors should be initiated by first considering the uniformity of nominally identical units, since this can influence the mode parameters. If the resistors are identical within the instrument resolution, this indicates a high degree of uniformity in materials and fabrication processes. This can also allow simplification of the characterization program, since detailed frequency data can be taken for a single small representative of the total group.

The modeling procedure for a thin-film capacitor differs from the above example primarily in the choice of circuit model and the measurement technique. In the characterization of a thin-film capacitor, we are dealing with small values of capacitance, usually tens of picofarads. The nature of the parasitic effects and the frequency range over which they are important also need to be evaluated. The circuit model to be developed must provide an accurate simulation of the terminal characteristics over as wide a frequency range as possible, thereby permitting the parasitic effects which are very likely to be present in integrated circuits to be studied.

Distributed *RC* Circuits

An analysis of any electrical circuit will show that the voltage-current terminal relation depends on both time and space. The wave speed in most lumped networks is so fast that changes in the terminal current or voltage reach all parts of the element quickly. Except in the case of extremely fast transients, or very high frequencies, most circuit elements act as lumped components. In a distributed *RC* structure the transmission effects qualitatively act like a very slow wave, and these networks may not be accurately represented by a few lumped elements, even for slow transients or low frequencies. We define a distributed element as one whose terminal current-voltage relations must be described by a partial differential equation which depends on both time and space. Figure 4-25 shows two distributed circuits. The transmission line has the properties of inductance, resistance, capacitance, and leakage conductance distributed along its length. The *RC* distributed circuit is generally not applicable to general transmission purposes because of its limited size. The *RC* circuit might be in the form of a tantalum resistive film, where the conversion of the resistive film into the dielectric allows the adjustment of the resistive values. We might ask how these distributed structures might be used, and which geometries might be most useful. Generally, three- and four-terminal transmission networks are of greatest use, and the rectangular geometries are most easily analyzed. Distributed-resistance networks which act as pads and attenuators can use a rectangular geometry with conducting tabs, as shown in Figure 4-26. Distributed-*RC* networks with uniform rectangular cross sections can be designed using conformal mapping implemented by a computer.

Essentially we work with the resistance in squares between two terminals placed on the perimeter of the rectangular structure. This can be extended to the determination of distributed structures with more than two terminals.

The integrated resistive-film network offers several advantages when compared to the lumped element equivalents. The power is dissipated more uniformly over a larger area, rather than being generated in a line-resistor pattern which may contain local hot spots. The reliability is also improved by allowing multiple current paths between the terminals. Thus, local film or substrate defects may have little effect on the network's overall performance. There are fewer interconnections, since all nodes except the external terminal contacts are eliminated. Simpler photolithography and fabrication processes are also gained by the distributed geometry.

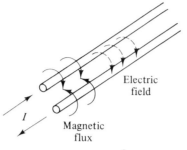

Electric
field

I

Magnetic
flux

Long
transmission line

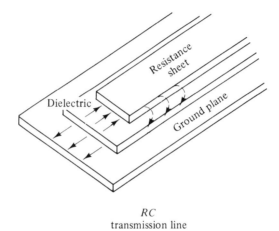

Resistance
sheet

Dielectric

Ground plane

RC
transmission line

Figure 4-25   Transmission lines.

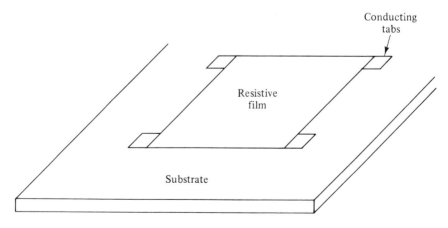

Conducting
tabs

Resistive
film

Substrate

Figure 4-26   Rectangular distributed-resistance network.

A major problem that can occur in microwave integrated circuits is the effect of the electrical lengths of the interconnecting transmission lines. This effect can be used to advantage by deliberately choosing the proper lengths and letting them perform useful functions in the circuit. A necessary condition is the understanding and knowledge of the electrical properties of these lines. This includes the characteristic impedance and phase velocity for the various geometrical and electrical combinations.

Consider the design of a transmission line for the TEM mode of propagation for an integrated circuit. One approach is shown in Figure 4-27. The space between the parallel ground planes contains two dielectric sheets of equal thickness with the center conductor printed on one of these sheets.

A soft substrate such as irradiated polyethlyene could be used in this type of configuration. But the expansion coefficient of polyethylene is an order of magnitude higher than that of most metals, and after a number of temperature variations, fatigue in the conductor material can cause a crack in the printed circuit. Harder substrates such as quartz, glass, and ceramic will not cause the problem. Mainly because of its low cost, ceramic has generally been favored.

A number of configurations using ceramic substrates can be used. One is to fill the space between the two ground planes and the center conductor with ceramic. Because of the high dielectric constant, a 50-ohm line would have the same strip width as a 150-ohm line in air, and higher-impedance lines would have very narrow linewidths. Precise grinding of the ceramic surface may be necessary to prevent air gaps between the ceramic boards and the conductor.

Another design is the microstrip configuration of Figure 4-28. The high dielectric constant and the difficulty in obtaining the proper quality of ceramic material may again create problems in certain applications.

Another configuration might use a center conductor on each side of a ceramic board. Since air is used as the main dielectric, 50-ohm and higher impedance lines tend to be wider. Grinding of the ceramic is usually not

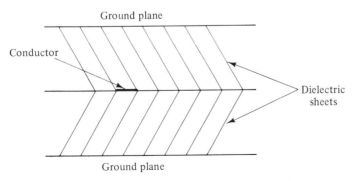

Figure 4-27   A microwave line configuration.

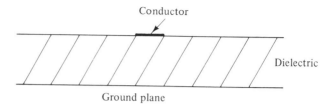

Figure 4-28   Single-ground-plane configuration.

necessary. But the medium between the conductors is not homogeneous, so the line supports the TEM mode only in an approximation.

The phase velocity in the dielectric part of the medium is different from that where there is no dielectric. This produces an axial component of the field. In many cases this component can be neglected, and an average phase velocity can be found from the effective dielectric constant.

One more simplification is to replace the two center conductors by a single one. This increases the effective dielectric constant slightly, but it simplifies the structure for mechanical mounting. No holes are required in the ceramic to interconnect the two center conductors electrically.

In microwave circuits the number of components per unit area is usually less important than cost. Therefore we seek an optimum design with high performance and reliability when operating all components within their limits. Usually these circuits are shielded by enclosing them within a coaxial-type metal housing to keep the distortion and interference low and to protect the circuits from outside radiation. The integrated circuit is placed on a glazed ceramic substrate, which is mounted halfway between two parallel ground planes. Metal springs may be used to provide the ground connections.

Microwave integrated circuits use relatively large passive elements which are deposited directly on the ceramic substrate with thin- and thick-film techniques. Resistors, capacitors, and conductors can be formed by the deposition of a thin film. To keep losses and noise down, the conductors are about 10 microns thick, which is equal to several skin depths at the lower microwave frequencies. The conductor width for a 50-ohm line is about 0.10. The resistors can be trimmed to the desired value by electrolytic anodization or laser trimming. The active circuits are formed on single-crystal semiconductor substrates. Before the use of beam-lead technology these devices were encapsulated and connected to the thin-film circuit using external leads. By keeping the lead lengths to a minimum, these circuits offer good performance up to several GHz.

For better performance, especially at higher frequencies, the active device must be closer to the thin-film circuit than is possible with encapsulation. This can be done with beam-lead technology.

To model the characteristic impedance and phase velocity of microstrip configurations, we start by solving the Laplace equation. We can then divide the cross section of the configuration into a number of squares and apply the necessary boundary conditions. The characteristic impedance and the phase velocity can then be found and plotted for the various conditions of interest. The active circuits can be modeled as discussed before for high-frequency circuits, with attention given to the characterization of all parasitics.

General Model Characteristics

We have seen that a device or circuit model used in a computer program may be linear, piecewise-linear, or nonlinear. It may be limited to dc, small-signal steady-state ac, or transient operation. It may be composed of lumped electrical network elements or based upon elements which relate directly to the physics of the device, such as the high-level-injection effects that have been discussed.

We have noted that the approximate behavior of transistors and the approximate current levels at which the maximum frequency response occurs can be obtained from the physical analysis. But for more accurate results, empirical data for transistors and other semiconductor devices, which is valid for the ranges which the devices are to operate, is best used for the purpose of network analysis.

One difficulty obstructing the development of models which are valid over wide current ranges is the use of very narrow emitter, base, and collector layers in transistors. The depletion layers and the transition regions from depletion layer to base, emitter, or collector layer are no longer narrow in comparison with these layers. In this case, the only approach that provides any accuracy is to regard the device as a single structure within which the basic semiconductor equations are solved.

A number of factors should be considered when representing any active device by an equivalent circuit:

1. Operating region. When the device performs only over a small range in voltages and currents, the parameters in the model may be regarded as approximately linear. Otherwise the device model can require a nonlinear representation.

2. Frequency range. If the analysis is over a limited frequency range, additional simplification may be made in representing the device.

3. Accuracy. The degree of accuracy required will normally affect the complexity of the model.

4. The measurement of parameters. The numerical values for the circuit elements in the model must be determined, and their dependency on electrical and physical conditions must be considered as well.

The equivalent-circuit model may include factors for the environmental conditions, such as temperature-dependence, electromagnetic, or radiation effects. The models presently used in most computer programs can be divided into the following categories:

1. Linear dc models.
2. Linear steady-state ac models.
3. Nonlinear dc models.
   (a) Piecewise-linear.
   (b) Exponential nonlinear.
4. Nonlinear transient models.
   (a) Piecewise-linear.
   (b) General nonlinear.

We have seen that the emitter and collector static characteristics are represented by the curves on device specification sheets, and these curves may be used directly, or the parameters for the model representation may be found from the curves. A parameter like the extrinsic base resistance changes with current level, so to represent the transient response accurately, we must represent it as a nonlinear element in the analysis. Similar requirements are necessary for other parameters such as the collector saturation resistance.

There are a number of ways to describe the electrical behavior of any element. In most computer programs, the representations fall into four classifications:

1. A numerical constant.
2. A table.
3. An analytical expression.
4. Or some combination of the above.

In performing the analysis, not all of these representations are equivalent in terms of efficiency. A table look-up may require more time than extracting a single constant value for an unknown, and evaluating an analytical expression may require many more program operations compared to a table-look-up procedure.

Besides electrical circuits we may also perform a more general system study by developing an equivalent model of the system and then studying the model. This procedure is especially useful in carrying out a new design, since no actual system may exist which is equivalent to the one to be developed.

The system can be represented by the interconnection of a collection of components, each of which is individually modeled. For a mathematical study a mathematical model is usually necessary, although physical models may also be used. The suspension of an automobile could be modeled by electrical circuitry whose voltage-time behavior approximates the solution of the differential equations that describe the behavior of the suspension system. In practice a pilot plant is often employed as a physical model for a chemical manufacturing process. In a similar way, a detailed scale model in a wind tunnel can be used to simulate the performance of a full-sized aircraft. We have noted that the modeling procedure may be analytical and is obtained from the basic physical laws that describe the components. This is often the case for some physical devices, but in other cases the components are so involved that the models must be approximations that involve empirical data. In some cases it is necessary to develop a mathematical model of the system, and the modeling process becomes a problem in statistical description. We have considered both the mathematical and the descriptive modeling process.

Some of these models have been concerned with lumped elements, while others have involved distributed physical elements. The lumped physical elements are those that can be isolated and treated as possessing the features of idealized elements.

In many cases real elements are not lumped, but this is still a valid approximation. It might appear unreasonable to consider that a long transmission line is lumped or that a compact microwave circuit is distributed, and yet these approximations may be valid for the range of interest.

In the simplest case we assume that the elements are linear. This assumes a linear relation between the cause and effect or excitation and response. This is because most system studies are carried out for groups of interconnected linear elements and numerical methods are usually required for systems that involve nonlinear elements. When we assume linearity for a nonlinear system, such an assumption may completely negate some particular feature that can be achieved only by the presence of the nonlinear element. The use of the computer makes these linear approximations unnecessary.

Many elements that are considered linear are actually nonlinear, but the range over which their response-excitation characteristic is required may be linear to a reasonable approximation. If the approximation is not valid, then the resulting behavior will probably not agree with the analysis. But over a small range the assumption of linearity may be valid, and we can use a stepwise or staircase approximation for the various increments.

We have discussed the case of a general nonlinear nonbilateral characteristic for which an exact theoretical description is not possible and how these single-valued nonlinear curves of this type can be approximated by a polynomial of the form

$$i = a_0 + a_1 v + \cdots + a_n v^n$$

Some of the techniques for fitting a polynomial to a given characteristic have been discussed. Often this response-excitation characteristic which one may seek to describe by an analytic form is obtained experimentally. The device or process may be quite complicated, having a number of ports and internal nonlinear elements.

Experimental methods may have to be used to provide an applicable mathematical model. This could be true even if one were modeling a traffic interchange for a highway system. The form of an acceptable model depends not only on the system being modeled but also on the subsequent uses to which the model is to be put.

For the more general classes of models that can exist, most physical two-terminal or one-port elements can be described in terms of two variables. For electrical elements these are the current and the voltage, and for thermal elements these are heat flow per unit time and temperature difference. If the elements are linear, they may fall into one of three control-system classes: proportional, derivative, and integral. Descriptions of some general physical elements are shown in Table 4-1.

Table 4-1 Linear system elements

System parameters	Dependent variables	
Mechanical (translational)	v = velocity	f = force
Mass M	$v = \dfrac{1}{M}\displaystyle\int f\,dt$	$f = M\dfrac{dv}{dt}$
Damping D	$v = \dfrac{1}{D}f$	$f = Dv$
Compliance K	$v = \dfrac{1}{K}\dfrac{df}{dt}$	$f = K\displaystyle\int v\,dt$
Mechanical (rotational)	ω = angular velocity	T = torque
Inertia J	$\omega = \dfrac{1}{J}\displaystyle\int T\,dt$	$T = J\dfrac{d\omega}{dt}$
Damping D	$\omega = \dfrac{1}{D}T$	$T = D\omega$
Compliance K	$\omega = \dfrac{1}{K}\dfrac{dT}{dt}$	$T = K\displaystyle\int \omega\,dt$
Electrical	v = voltage	i = current
Capacitance C	$v = \dfrac{1}{C}\displaystyle\int i\,dt$	$i = C\dfrac{dv}{dt}$
Resistance R	$v = Ri$	$i = \dfrac{v}{R}$

Table 4-1   *(continued)*

System parameters		Dependent variables	
Inductance	L	$v = L \dfrac{di}{dt}$	$i = \dfrac{1}{L} \displaystyle\int v \; dt$
Fluid (liquid form)		$h = \text{head}$	$Q = \text{flow}$
Capacitance	C	$h = \dfrac{1}{C} \displaystyle\int Q \; dt$	$Q = C \dfrac{dh}{dt}$
Resistance	R	$h = RQ$	$Q = \dfrac{h}{R}$
Inertance	L	$h = L \dfrac{dQ}{dt}$	$Q = \dfrac{1}{L} \displaystyle\int h \; dt$
Fluid (gas)		$p = \text{pressure}$	$w = \text{flow}$
Capacitance	C	$p = \dfrac{1}{C} \displaystyle\int w \; dt$	$w = C \dfrac{dp}{dt}$
Resistance	R	$p = Rw$	$w = \dfrac{p}{R}$
Inertance	L	$p = L \dfrac{dw}{dt}$	$w = \dfrac{1}{L} \displaystyle\int p \; dt$
Thermal			
Capacitance	C		$q = C \dfrac{d\theta}{dt}$
Resistance	R		$q = \dfrac{\theta}{R}$

EXERCISES

1. Given a *V-I* characteristic, *V* is the voltage across an ideal p-n junction and is less than the terminal voltage of a practical diode by a voltage drop IR_b, where R_b is the bulk resistance of the semiconductor material. Show how to include this effect in a model.

2. Discuss why the low-level-injection models of diode and transistors are satisfactory for low to moderately high frequency or switching-speed operation.

3. Diagram and discuss a high-frequency T-equivalent model for common-emitter connections.

4. Compare the following approaches for the analysis of inter-connected black boxes.

   a. Analytical expressions which give the terminal characteristics of the boxes.

   b. Standard functions fitted to discrete data which was either measured or calculated.

   c. Calculations performed only at the frequencies for which discrete data is available through either measurement or calculations.

5. Discuss the use of model computation based on device performance from the basic semiconductor equations and its application in circuit programs.

6. Draw a general nonlinear, nonbilateral characteristic for a semiconductor device.

7. Compare the Ebers-Moll and the charge-control models for general use in computer analysis programs.

8. Describe a model of the type that can be used to compute the ac and dc characteristics of double-diffused junction transistors in terms of the basic device parameters.

9. Describe how piecewise-linear and piecewise-constant approximations can be used to obtain a smooth model characteristic for a problem like that of Exercise 8.

10. Show how a three-terminal area-resistance network might replace an arbitrary pi or T of three resistors.

11. Diagram and discuss a distributed model of a diffused resistor.

12. Why are the dc equations characterizing the dependence of threshold voltage and drain current on the terminal voltages of a field-effect device important?

13. What are some devices which could be described accurately enough with analytical expressions over a limited frequency range for many applications?

14. Under what conditions could a smooth uniform transmission line be described with matrices whose entries contain hyperbolic functions?

15. Most equations that we have used describe the terminal behavior in terms of physical constants. Another type of equation is empirical, such as approximating the common-emitter current gain of a transistor by a polynomial of degree n. Write a fourth-order equation of this type.

ELECTRONIC CIRCUIT ANALYSIS

5

The computer provides circuit designers with an analytical tool of power and versatility. The computer can produce reliable solutions to network problems except where the solution involves pathological related or numerical difficulties or where the method of analysis is poorly chosen.

It is the user's responsibility to accurately represent the circuit under consideration, since the computer will do only what is explicitly instructed. Accurate models for diodes, transistors, and other devices are essential to the successful solution of almost every network-analysis problem. The area of device modeling has evolved in response to the increasing use of computers in circuit design, as we have seen in the last chapter. The computer has also had an influence on network methods. Since matrix notation is convenient in programming, many network-analysis programs are based on a matrix formulation of the network problem. This is related to the inherent elegance of the matrix approach, which has promoted its acceptance among network programmers.

In a more general sense, there has also been an increasing recognition that the inherently broad scope of network theory allows much more than the solution of electrical networks. Many analysis programs are theoretically capable of solving a large array of problems.

While it may not also be practical to write a single program for this, programs have been written for solving nonelectrical problems by network analytical methods. Some can handle either electrical or mechanical engineering problems, based on a network approach to structural analysis.

Computers have also influenced network theory by requiring methods of analysis better adapted to the solution of large-sized circuit problems. The solution to these larger network problems requires a method which properly matches the computer to the problem.

The traditional methods for the solution of networks are not necessarily useful on a computer with networks of any size. Laplace transform techniques are in this category, while numerical methods are better adapted to a computer. In general these methods can give essentially all the information obtained by Laplace transforms.

METHODS FOR THE SOLUTION OF NETWORKS

Circuit Equations

For the simple circuit of Figure 5-1, we can write the loop equations using Kirchhoff's voltage law (KVL) and separate the impedance terms as shown below:

$$z_{11} = L_1 + \left(\frac{1}{C_1} + \frac{1}{C_2} \right) + R_1$$

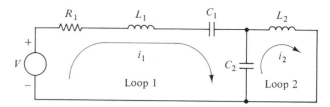

Figure 5-1   Illustrative circuit used for the development of loop equations.

$$z_{12} = z_{21} = \frac{1}{C_2}$$

$$z_{22} = L_2 + \frac{1}{C_2}$$

where

 z_{11} = sum of all impedances around loop 1
 $z_{12} = z_{21}$ = negative of the sum of all impedances common to loops 1
  and 2
 z_{22} = sum of all impedances around loop 2
 v = algebraic sum of all voltages in loop 1

Then we can express the loop equations in matrix form:

$$\begin{bmatrix} z_{11} & z_{12} \\ z_{21} & z_{22} \end{bmatrix} \begin{bmatrix} i_1 \\ i_2 \end{bmatrix} = \begin{bmatrix} v \\ 0 \end{bmatrix}$$

which can be written simply as

$$[ZI] = [V]$$

These are known also as the *loop equilibrium equations.* The loop currents i_1 and i_2 may be found using these equations, which are a general form of Ohm's law. Because of the matrix form they apply to the entire system. We could also use similar describing equations for mechanical systems, and we would observe that the equations are identical in form, although the through variable might be interchanged with the across variable as the independent variable for a nodal network. These systems are thus duals.

  If the electrical network shown were a nodal network with the same topology, then the systems would be analogs of each other, because the through variables of one correspond to the through variables of the other, with a similar correspondence among the across variables. This correspondence of the through variables with the across variables makes them dually related.

  The more general case of a single branch of a network is shown in Figure

5-2. Here, the branch consists of an impedance (or admittance) element Z_u (or Y_u) in series with a voltage source E_i and in parallel with a current source I_i. There are three voltage and current variables to identify in this branch. The branch current i_i enters the branch at its initial node, and the element current J_i passing through Z_u is

$$J_i = I_i + i_i$$

The branch voltage as measured from the initial to the final node is e_{in}, and the element voltage across Z_{ii} is

$$V_i = E_i + e_i$$

Since E_i and I_i may be nonzero, Ohm's law for this branch must be written in terms of the element voltage and the element current variables V_i and J_i. Ohm's law for the entire network is expressed as the matrix equations

$$[V] = [ZJ]$$

or

$$[J] = [YV]$$

Here the vectors V and J will contain the entire set of element-voltage and element-current variables for the network, and the admittance matrix Y is the inverse of the impedance matrix Z. The diagonal terms of the Z or Y matrix are the self-impedances or self-admittances of each branch. The off-diagonal terms are called the *transimpedances* or *transadmittances* of the branches.

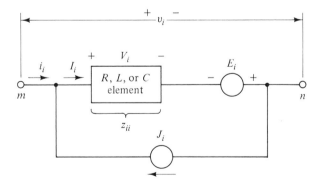

Figure 5-2   The general case of a branch in a network.

Linear Differential Equations

When one combines the integrodifferential equations of any system with the input-output relationship of interest, the result can be described by a general differential equation of the form

$$a_n \frac{d_n y}{dt^n} + a_{n-1} \frac{d_{n-1} y}{dt^{n-1}} + \cdots + a_0 y = b_m \frac{d^m u}{dt^m} + b_{m-1} \frac{d^{m-1} u}{dt^{m-1}} + \cdots + b_0 u$$

where the a and b coefficients are real constants which are defined in terms of the system parameters. An important feature of linear differential equations of this type is that the pth order of response of the system is the solution of the system to the pth order of the initial excitation function. We can replace this equation by the reduced equation

$$a_n \frac{d^n x}{dt_n} + a_{n-1} \frac{d^{n-1}}{dt^{n-1}} + \cdots + a_0 x = u(t)$$

and then carry out differentiations to the pth order. We can use this equation plus

$$y(t) = b_m \frac{d_m x}{dt^m} + b_{m-1} \frac{d^{m-1}}{dt^{m-1}} + \cdots + b_0 x$$

The general solution to these equations consists of two parts. One is due to the nature of the system in the absence of the excitation; the other is a function of the applied excitation function.

The part of the solution that is due to the system or the network alone is obtained from the original integrodifferential equation with the right-hand terms set to zero:

$$a_n \frac{d^n y}{dt^n} + a_{n-1} \frac{d^{n-1} y}{dt^{n-1}} + \cdots + a_0 y = 0$$

The solution to this equation is called the *complementary function*, and this is the transient portion of the total solution. The portion due to the applied excitation is called the *particular solution*. Finding the particular solution can be a difficult task except for a few special functions. One important function is the case specified by $n = 2$ and $m = 0$. The general equation is reduced to

$$a_2 \frac{d^2 y}{dt^2} + a_1 \frac{dy}{dt} + a_0 y = b_0 u$$

A trial solution to the complementary equation is an exponential function of the form e^{st}, since the form of this function does not change with repeated differentiations or integrations. The trial solution is then taken as

$$y_t = Ce^{st}$$

We find that a solution is possible if

$$a_2 s^2 + a_1 s + a_0 = 0$$

Then we define the characteristic time ratio as

$$\tau = \sqrt{\frac{a_2}{a_0}}$$

and the damping ratio as

$$\zeta = \sqrt{\frac{a_i^2}{4a_2}}$$

and the solution becomes

$$\tau^2 s^2 + 2\zeta\tau s + 1 = 0$$

The two roots to this equation are

$$s_1 = -\frac{\zeta}{\tau} + \frac{1}{\tau}\sqrt{\zeta^2 - 1}$$

$$s_2 = -\frac{\zeta}{\tau} - \frac{1}{\tau}\sqrt{\zeta - 1}$$

These roots are called the *normal modes, eigenvalues,* or *characteristic values* of the system. Since $e^{s_1 t}$ and $e^{s_2 t}$ are solutions to this equation, the sum is also a solution, and the total complementary solution is

$$y_t = C_1 e^{s_1 t} + C_2 e^{s_2 t}$$

This solution satisfies the requirement that there be as many arbitrary constants in the solution as the highest order of the derivative appearing in the equation. The detailed form of the complementary solution can have a number of forms, depending on the particular value of ζ. Three cases are possible:

$$\zeta > 1: \quad y_t = e^{-\zeta t/\tau}\left(C_3 \cosh \sqrt{\zeta - 1} \ \frac{t}{\tau} + C_4 \sinh \sqrt{\zeta - 1} \ \frac{t}{\tau} \right)$$

$$\zeta = 1: \quad y_t = (C_5 + C_6 t)e^{-t/\tau}$$

$$\zeta < 1: \quad y_t = e^{-\zeta t/\tau}\left(C_7 \cos \sqrt{1 - \zeta^2}\frac{t}{\tau} + C_8 \sin \sqrt{1 - \zeta^2}\frac{t}{\tau} \right)$$

These are the *overdamped, critically damped*, and *underdamped* cases.

The particular solution depends on the excitation function and is not obtainable by general methods. Standard techniques exist when $u(t)$ is a constant, an exponential, a power series, or a sinusoid. In order to solve higher-order differential equations the procedure in finding the complementary function becomes an extension of that for the second-order equation that we discussed above. One complication is to factor the polynomial in s. For higher-order polynomials this can be a chore, but a number of computer programs are now available for this. The problem of finding the particular solution is the more difficult task.

The complete solution of the linear nth-order differential equation takes the form:

$$y = C_1 e^{s_1 t} + C_2 e^{s_2 t} + \ \cdot \ \cdot \ \cdot \ + C_n e^{s_n t} + y_s$$

For the case of nonrepeated eigenvalues y_s is the *steady-state* or *particular* solution. To completely describe the response of a given system or network the constants of integration C_i must be evaluated. Since there are n constants, n initial conditions must be used. In an electrical system these might include the initial voltages across capacitors and the initial currents through inductors at some initial time, usually $= 0$. If the initial voltages and currents are zero, the system is said to be in an *initially relaxed state*. The initial conditions must be combined with the total solution. When the initial conditions change owing to instantaneous changes in the system configuration, these changes must be translated into new initial conditions.

We have considered how the fundamental formulation of system equations for continuous systems can be expressed by Kirchhoffian methods into sets of integrodifferential equations. For discrete time systems or for sampled time systems the equations can be given in difference-equation form or in terms of discrete time-state equations.

First the dynamic equations of the interconnected system are written. The next step is to find the response of the system to the excitation or driving functions that can be introduced at one or more points in the system.

The analysis usually assumes that the system elements can be represented as linear, generally lumped, bilateral devices. These may not always be valid assumptions, but they yield equations that are mathematically tractable. First-order differential equations can be handled without much difficulty, and second-order differential equations can be tolerable, but higher-order differential equations rapidly become very time-consuming. Because of this, transformation techniques such as the Laplace transform, Fourier transform, and others are used to aid in the solution process.

These methods allow certain steps in the solution to be accomplished by algebraic manipulation instead of by the manipulation of differential equations. Finding the time response of a dynamic system by any analytic method is greatly aided by computing.

The computer is a powerful tool for carrying out response calculations. Both linear and nonlinear problems can be solved, although the numerical integration of a nonlinear system can be a long procedure. For linear systems, if there is a wide spread in eigenvalues, the solution may take many calculations.

The forms of the system description for hand computations are not the best for machine computations. For linear systems the Kirchhoffian integro-differential equation description, when used with the Laplace transformation, provided the most common technique for hand calculations. The state-variable formulation in the time domain provides a much better approach for a machine solution. We will now cover some of these considerations.

The State-Variable Approach

The state description of a system differs in several areas from the Kirchhoffian description. Besides the input and output variables we introduce a set of variables called the *state variables*. These state variables account for the fact that the behavior of any dynamic system depends not only on the presently applied forces but also on those that had been applied in the past. These state variables thus account for a memory of state that is spread over many elements in which the effects of past forces have been stored.

One important feature of state variables is that a knowledge of the state of the system at any time t_0, without regard to the past history in reaching this state, plus a knowledge of the forces that are to be applied, will permit a determination of the solution of the system at any time greater than t_0. Another important feature of the state method is that it can be accomplished using a set of n first-order differential equations instead of n/2 second-order differential equations as in the Kirchhoffian formulation. This set of first-order differential equations describes an n-dimensional state space and has the form

$$\frac{d(x)}{dt} = x_i(x_1, x_2, \ldots, x_n, t) + u_i(t)$$

for $t > 0$, $i = 1, 2, \ldots, n$

The variables x_1, x_2, ..., x_n are the dynamic state variables, while $u_i(t)$ represents the inputs. We can also write this system of simultaneous first-order differential equations in the more compact vector or matrix form:

$$\frac{d(x)}{dt} = x(x, t) + u(t), \qquad t > 0$$

where x, u, X are $n \times 1$ column vectors. A linear system of matrix equations can be described as

$$\frac{d(x)}{dt} = Ax + Bu + G\frac{d(u)}{dt}$$

where $x(t)$ is the state vector that describes the system at any time t and A is an $n \times n$ square matrix that is specified by the topology or the connections of the system as well as the terminal properties of the elements of the system. In the most general case A, B, G can be time-dependent, but they are usually considered time-independent. To change the state variable we can write

$$\bar{x} = x - Gu$$

Then the matrix differential equation becomes

$$\bar{x} = A\bar{x} + (B + AG)u$$

which in the most general form becomes

$$\bar{x} = A\bar{x} + Bu$$

The selection of the node-pair and loop variables in the Kirchhoffian description is not a unique process, nor is the selection of the state variables. Many acceptable state variables can be used for any given system. The *state vector* $x(t)$ can be defined as the minimal set of state variables that uniquely determines the future state of the system, so any minimum set of through and across variables that completely describe the system can be a suitable state vector, provided that the present values are known. Since the state variables account for the essential memory characteristics of the elements, this suggests we use the following for the selection of the state variables:

1. The through variables associated with the inductive elements (L, K).
2. The across variables associated with the capacitive elements.
3. The constraint considerations imposed by the closed loops of capacitive elements and the junctions of inductive elements must be

accounted for, since with these constraints not all of the state variables are independent.

We illustrate the technique using the circuit of Figure 5-3. The state-variable form requires that we label the voltage across the capacitors.

The state variables are v_3, v_4, and i_1, i_2. We then write the following equations for the state variables:

$$C_1 \frac{dv_3}{dt} = i_1$$

$$C_2 \frac{dv_4}{dt} = i_1 - i_2$$

$$L_1 \frac{di_1}{dt} = -v_2 - v_3 - R_1 i_1 + v_1$$

$$L_2 \frac{di_2}{dt} = v_2$$

Then these place in matrix form as shown below:

$$\frac{d}{dt}
\begin{bmatrix} v_2 \\ v_3 \\ i_1 \\ i_2 \end{bmatrix}
=
\begin{bmatrix}
0 & 0 & \dfrac{1}{C_1} & 0 \\
0 & 0 & \dfrac{1}{C_2} & \dfrac{1}{C_2} \\
-\dfrac{1}{L_3} & -\dfrac{1}{L_3} & -\dfrac{R_1}{L_1} & 0 \\
0 & \dfrac{1}{L_2} & 0 & 0
\end{bmatrix}
\begin{bmatrix} v_2 \\ v_3 \\ i_1 \\ i_2 \end{bmatrix}
+
\begin{bmatrix} 0 \\ 0 \\ v_1 \\ 0 \end{bmatrix}$$

The system description is now given by four first-order differential equations in accordance with the feature of state equations already discussed.

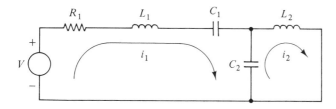

Figure 5-3   Illustrative circuit used for the development of the state-variable equations.

This suggests that higher-order differential equations can be replaced by an appropriate number of first-order differential equations. This is shown below, where we convert a set of differential equations into a set of first-order differential equations. Given:

$$\frac{d^2y}{dt^2} + 8\frac{dy}{dt} + 4(y - x) = f_1(t)$$

$$\frac{d^2x}{dt^2} - 4\frac{dx}{dt} - 8\frac{dy}{dt} + 2x = f_2(t)$$

To obtain the solution we define the quantities

$$\frac{dx}{dt} = w$$

$$\frac{dy}{dt} = z$$

Combine these with the given set of differential equations to find

$$\frac{dz}{dt} + 8z + 4(y - x) = f_1(t)$$

$$\frac{dw}{dt} - 4w - 8z + 2x = f_2(t)$$

In matrix form this set is written:

$$\frac{d}{dt}\begin{bmatrix} x \\ y \\ w \\ y \end{bmatrix} = \begin{bmatrix} 0 & 0 & 1 & 0 \\ 0 & 0 & 0 & 1 \\ -2 & 0 & 4 & 8 \\ 4 & -4 & 0 & -8 \end{bmatrix}\begin{bmatrix} x \\ y \\ w \\ z \end{bmatrix} + \begin{bmatrix} 0 \\ 0 \\ f_2 \\ f_1 \end{bmatrix}$$

This technique for replacing an nth-order differential equation by a set of n first-order differential equations is called the *normal form reduction*. As another example, suppose we wish to reduce the following differential equation to normal form and express the result in matrix form:

$$\frac{d^4x}{dt^4} + 8\frac{d^3x}{dt^3} + 7\frac{d^2x}{dt^2} + 5\frac{dx}{dt} - 6x = 0$$

Then, again, we

$$\frac{dx}{dt} = w_1$$

$$\frac{d^2x}{dt^2} = \frac{dw_1}{dt} = w_2$$

$$\frac{d^3x}{dt^3} = \frac{dw_2}{dt} = w_3$$

Then, combine these with the original differential equation

$$\frac{dw_3}{dt} = -8w_3 - 7w_2 - 5w_1 + 6x$$

Then express this in matrix form

$$\frac{d}{dt}\begin{bmatrix} x \\ w_1 \\ w_2 \\ w_3 \end{bmatrix} = \begin{bmatrix} 0 & 1 & 0 & 0 \\ 0 & 0 & 1 & 0 \\ 0 & 0 & 0 & 1 \\ 6 & -5 & -7 & -8 \end{bmatrix}\begin{bmatrix} x \\ w_1 \\ w_2 \\ w_3 \end{bmatrix}$$

Solution of the State Equations

When the solution of the state equations is obtained in matrix form, it produces the results for all the state variables at the same time. For the force-free case,

$$\frac{d(x)}{dt} = Ax$$

with initial conditions $x(0)$. Now consider the following matrix function:

$$\Phi(t) = e^{At} = I + At + \frac{A^2t^2}{2!} + \cdots = \sum_0^\infty \frac{A^k t^k}{k!}$$

where I is the identity matrix. $\Phi(t)$ is called the *fundamental matrix* or the *state-transition matrix* of the system. Note that

$$\frac{d}{dt}(e^{At}) = Ae^{At} = e^{At}A$$

A solution to the force-free case is

$$x(t) = e^{At}x(0)$$

or, expressed another way:

$$x(t) = \Phi(t)x(0)$$

Now for an initial time of t_0 instead of $t = 0$ the solution has the form:

$$x(t) = \Phi(t - t_0)x(t_0)$$

or

$$x(t) = e^{A(t-t_0)}x(t_0)$$

This shows that the fundamental matrix relates the state at any time t with that at time t_0.

Now the general state equation is

$$\frac{d(x)}{dt}(t) = Ax(t) + Bu(t)$$

If we multiply each term by e^{-At}, we get

$$e^{-At}\frac{d(x)}{dt} = e^{-At}Ax + e^{-At}Bu$$

This simplifies to

$$\frac{d}{dt}(e^{-At}x) = e^{-At}Bu$$

Now we multiply by dt, integrate over the interval of t_0 to t, and change the variable to v:

$$\int_{t_0}^{t}\frac{d}{dv}(e^{-Av}x)\,dv = \int_{t_0}^{t}e^{-Ax}Bu\,dv$$

This simplifies to

$$e^{-At}x(t) - e^{-At_0}x(t_0) = \int_{t_0}^{t}e^{-Av}Bu\,dv$$

Now multiply all terms in this equation by e^{At}, and we get

$$x(t) = e^{A(t-t_0)}x(t_0) + \int_{t_0}^{t}e^{A(t-v)}Bu(v)\,dv$$

In terms of the fundamental matrix, this becomes

$$x(t) = \Phi(t - t_0)\,x(t_0) + \int_{t_0}^{t}\Phi(t - v)\,Bu(v)\,dv$$

The first term represents the part of the total system response that occurs from the free or natural response of the system due to the initial conditions. The second term is the part of the solution due to the applied drivers or forcing functions. This is the particular solution, and it appears in a matrix convolution integral. The sum of these two parts is a closed-form solution of the state equations. To seek a solution to this equation we write $t + h$ for t:

$$x(t + h) = e^{Ah}e^{A(t-t_0)}x(t_0) + \int_{t_0}^{t+h} e^{A(h+t-v)}Bu(v)\ dv$$

This solution can also be expressed as

$$x(t + h) = e^{Ah}x(t) + \int_{t}^{t+h} e^{A(h+t-v)}Bu(v)\ dv$$

Then by a change of variable, $\tau = v - t$, we obtain

$$x(t + h) = e^{Ah}x(t) + \int_{0}^{h} e^{A(h-\tau)}Bu(t + \tau)\ d\tau$$

This solution is exact, but its utility depends on the computation of e^{Ah}. We can use a finite number of terms in the series expansion of e^{Ah}. This method avoids eigenvalue problems, in that it does not require the calculation of eigenvalues, but there is another kind of eigenvalue problem which tends to limit its usefulness.

When the matrix A has a large eigenvalue, the integration step size h must be kept small, somewhat less than the reciprocal of $|\tau_{\max}(A)|$, in order to permit a rapid convergence of the series. The same limitation occurs in numerical integration using a method like Runge-Kutta, where h must remain small to avoid numerical instability problems.

We can diagonalize e^{Ah} from the series relationship, yielding

$$X^{-1}e^{Ah}X = e^{\Lambda h}$$

where $e^{\Lambda h}$ is a diagonal matrix with terms $e^{\lambda_i h}$ that are simple to compute. Solving this expression for e^{Ah}, we obtain

$$x(t + h) = xe^{\Lambda h}x^{-1}x(t) + \int_{0}^{h} xe^{\Lambda(h-\tau)}x^{-1}g^{(t+\tau)d\tau}$$

and the computational problem reduces to the evaluating of an integral expression. If the driving function $g(t + \tau)$ is approximated as a polynomial in τ, the integration can be carried out exactly, term by term. This provides a way of evaluating the integral on a computer.

If $g(t) = 0$ and we apply the initial conditions to the network which correspond to the ith eigenvector X_i, then the solution becomes

$$x(t) = Xe^{\Lambda t}X^{-1}\chi_i$$

But since $X^{-1}X$ is a unit matrix, $X^{-1}\chi_i$ is equal to the ith column of a unit matrix. The columns of X are the eigenvectors χ_i. Thus, the solution reduces to

$$x(t) = x_i e^{\lambda_i t}$$

The ith eigenvector has those particular initial conditions required to excite the ith characteristic mode or eigenmode of response and suppress all the others. For the case of arbitrary initial conditions, all the eigenmodes may be excited.

We have noted that using a finite number of terms for the series expansion of e^{Ah} requires a criterion for the selection of the number of terms in the series, since when the matrix A has a large eigenvalue, the integration step size h must be kept small in order to ensure the rapid convergency of the series expansion for e^{Ah}. There is also a quasi-analytic approach to the solution of the general state equation. Here the diagonal terms and the off-diagonal terms of A are separated, the off-diagonal terms being lumped together with $Bu(t)$ as a part of the driving function. The general state equation is written as

$$\frac{dx}{dt} = Ax + Bu = Dx + (Ex + Bu)$$

here $A = D + E$, with D containing all the diagonal terms and E all the off-diagonal terms of A. $Ex + Bu$ acts as an equivalent driving function. The solution to this equation is

$$x(t + h) = e^{Dh}x(t) + \int_0^h e^{D(h-\lambda)}[Ex(t + \lambda) + Bu(t + \lambda)] \, d\lambda$$

The quantity e^{Dh} is easy to calculate, since D is a diagonal matrix. The second term can be carried out using a polynomial approximation to the desired degree for $(Ex + Bu)$.

When the A matrix diagonal terms exceed the sum of the magnitudes of the off-diagonal terms in the same row or column, then a much larger integration step size h may be used in solving this solution than that allowed with the usual methods.

Discrete-Time Increments

We have so far discussed systems with components that can be represented by ordinary differential equations, algebraic equations, or both. If some or all of the components in the system are characterized by ordinary difference equations, the system becomes a *discrete-state system*. If the system assumes instantaneous changes at regular intervals of time, the system becomes a *discrete-time system*. A digital computer is an example of a discrete-time system, since the output may remain quiescent during the time intervals established by the clock signals. Then there are state transitions at the end of these intervals.

When a computer is used to compute the solution of a differential equation, we must approximate the differential equation by a difference equation. The difference equation is a recursive relation, and the computer can handle such relations directly.

In the difference-equation approximation the derivatives are replaced by differences, and the time increments are chosen small enough to allow a good approximation. We can write the derivative dx/dt as the difference expression

$$\frac{dx}{dt} \simeq \frac{x(t + T) - x(t)}{T}$$

Time is divided into equal increments T sec long, and we are concerned only with the values of x at the times specified by $t = 0, T, 2T, \ldots, nT$. For values of x between a pair of values of T, interpolation can be used. Using a difference-equation approximation, the differential equation given by

$$\frac{dx}{dt} = f[x(t), u(t), t]$$

becomes

$$x(t + T) = Tf[x(t), u(t), t] + x(t)$$

which can also be written as

$$x(n + 1) = Tf[x(n), u(n), n] + x(n)$$

This is a recursion relation which allows the calculation of the increments of $x(t_0 + mT)$, given the initial state $x(t_0)$. The system output in the continuous-time case is given by

$$y = g[x(t), u(t), t]$$

In discrete time this becomes

$$y(n) = g[x(n), u(n), n]$$

A discrete-time system is one that can be represented by these two equations. The system is linear if the functions f and g are linear in x and u. For the discrete-time system the equations take on the form:

$$x(n + 1) = A(n)x(n) + B(n)u(n)$$

$$y(n) = C(n)x(n) + D(n)u(n)$$

Here the matrixes A, B, C, D depend on the discrete-time variable n. When these matrixes are constant, the system is time-invariant.

For a differential equation of order higher than the first, then finite-difference approximations to these higher-order derivatives are used. For the second-order derivative the approximation becomes

$$\frac{d^2y}{dt^2} = \frac{d}{dt}\frac{dy}{dt} \simeq \frac{1}{T}\left[\frac{y_{n+2} - y_{n+1}}{T} - \frac{y_{n+1} - y_n}{T}\right]$$

and the approximation for the third-order case is

$$\frac{d^3y}{dt^3} \simeq \frac{y_{n+3} - 3y_{n+2} + 3y_{n+1} - y_n}{T^3}$$

The finite-difference approximation can be solved recursively. We can also write the finite-difference approximation in state form.

A technique for the solution of the state equations is to develop a set of difference equations and find the solution recursively. For the linear state without driving sources we can consider the general solution, for two successive integration times. For $t = nT$, we get

$$x(nT) = e^{A_n T}x(0)$$

and for $t = (n + 1)T$

$$x(n + 1)T = e^{A(n+1)T}x(0)$$

From these the recursive formula becomes

$$x(n + 1)T = e^{At}x(nT)$$

For the more general case that includes drivers we begin with the more general solution. With $t = nT$ this becomes

$$x(nT) = e^{A_n T}x(0) + e^{A_n T}\int_0^{nT} e^{-Av}Bu(v)\,dv$$

Now for $t = (n + 1)T$

$$x(n + 1)T = e^{A(n+1)T}x(0) + e^{A(n+1)T}\int_0^{(n+1)T} e^{-Av}Bu(v)\,dv$$

Combining these two equations, we get

$$x(n + 1)T = e^{At}x(nT) + e^{A(n+1)T} \int_{nT}^{(n+1)T} e^{-Av}Bu(v)\, dv$$

We can use a recursive procedure to complete the evaluation for a specified source function $u(t)$. In this type of sampled system the driving function can be approximated using a staircase function with $u(t)$ constant during the time interval $nT \leq t \leq (n + 1)T$. The integration can be carried out under these conditions. The final result is

$$x(n + 1)T = e^{AT}x(nT) + (e^{AT} - 1)A^{-1}Bu(nT)$$

which can be simplified to

$$x(n + 1)T = Fx(nT) + Gu(nT)$$

This equation describes a system with a discrete-time base.

Numerical Integration

Most numerical methods of integration are based on the use of finite-difference approximations. For the general differential equation of the form

$$dx = f(x, t)$$

a solution may be found by the general finite-difference expression

$$x_n = \sum_{i=1}^{M} a_i x_{n-i} + h \sum_{j=0}^{N} b_j f_{n-j}$$

where h is the integration interval, $x_n = x(nh)$, and $f_{n-j} = (x_{n-j}, (n - j)h)$. The number and values of the coefficients a_i and b_i are determined by the number of terms of the Taylor expansion of $s(nh)$ to be used. These are matched by the integration formula. In the case where $b_0 = 0$, the integration formula is called a *predictor*, since the new value of x_n is predicted in terms of previous values (x_{n-i}) and derivatives (f_{n-j}).

If $b_0 \neq 0$, the formula is called a *corrector*, since it is generally used with a predictor formula to produce a corrected value of x_n. This is done by using the predicted value of x_n to compute an approximate value of the new derivative f_n, which is then used in the corrector formula.

In the case of a homogeneous linear differential equation with constant coefficients we assume at least one coefficient is nonzero and all other coefficients of higher index are zero. If we assume a particular solution of the form $x_n = p^n$, then this equation can be reduced to a polynomial equation, and any value of p which is a root of the characteristic equation is a suitable candidate for a particular solution $x_n = p^n$. The general solution has the form of a linear combination of particular solutions:

$$x_n = \sum_{k=1}^{r} C_r p_k^n$$

Here the p_k are all the roots of the polynomial.

The root lying near the point $1 + j0$ in the complex plane becomes the principal root, since it will determine the approximation to the solution of the differential equation. The other roots are parasitic roots, and when a parasitic root lies outside the unit circle, x_n eventually diverges. This condition is called a *numerical instability* and it negates the solution. In order to prevent numerical instability, the integration step h must be small enough such that all the parasitic roots are inside the unit circle. In the case of a system of linear differential equations with constant coefficients, the condition for h in most integration formulas becomes

$$h \, | \lambda_{\max}(A) | \leq c$$

Here $\lambda_{\max}(A)$ is the largest eigenvalue of the coefficient matrix A. The constant c is usually between 1 or 2, depending on the integration method used.

In the case of nonlinear differential equations, an equivalent restriction, involving the largest eigenvalue of the Jacobian matrix, must be used to prevent numerical instability.

This constraint on the integration interval tends to slow most integration techniques if the network has a wide value of eigenvalues. The largest eigenvalue or its reciprocal, the smallest time constant, controls the permissible size of the integration step h. But the smallest eigenvalues which contain the largest time constants control the network response, and these determine the total length of time over which the integration must be carried out to characterize the response. In the case of a network with a 100-to-1 ratio of largest to smallest eigenvalue, it can be necessary to take 100 times as many integration steps as required by the Runge-Kutta method or some other method that is free of the integration-step restriction.

Some integration formulas for which this constraint of h does not apply include

$$x_n = x_{n-1} + hf_n$$

and

$$x_n = x_{n-1} + \frac{h}{2}(f_n + f_{n-1})$$

These have characteristic equations of the first degree and have no parasitic roots. They also have a lower accuracy, and the integration interval must be short for them to be useful. Another disadvantage is that f_n must be computed before x_n is known.

GRAPHICAL NETWORK TECHNIQUES

A computer program which is based on signal-flow graphs can compute the calculation of gains in symbolic form as well as the sensitivity and the worst-case circuit conditions. Flow-graph methods, as compared to classic matrix methods, can be particularly economical in both memory space and operating time for symbolic analysis.

Mason's signal-flow graph is a useful tool for the circuit designer. It provides a picture of the relationships between the circuit variables and the physical structure. Signal-flow graphs are most useful in linear systems for determining single input/output functions. If there is more than one input, superposition can be used to obtain the combined output.

There are two basic techniques for finding the relationship between the output variable and the input variable. One method is to use internal node removal, which is continued until the Mason graph is of the form shown in Figure 5-4. There are a number of specific rules and techniques for accomplishing this reduction. The procedure is similar to the systematic elimination of a set of variables from simultaneous linear equations.

The other technique is sometimes referred to as a topological formula, since the gain G is found by inspection of the Mason graph. It is an enumerative procedure, and its application can be the basis for a computer program to determine the gain sensitivities and worst-case conditions for linear circuits.

We can define a set of linear simultaneous equations which are arranged in a cause-effect relationship. To do this we write the equations in terms of an effect which is due to the transmission of a cause. We must also assume we have a consistent and a linearly independent set of equations. To formulate a graph we designate the nodes as $x_1, x_2, \ldots, x_n$ and do likewise for y_i. Now if in the equation there is an α connecting an x node to a y node, then we can draw a directed line segment from x to y with weight α. This is done for all rows in the set. Proceeding in this manner, a graphical representation can be achieved for the system of simultaneous equations. The signal-flow graph as formulated by the above rules contains the same information as the simultaneous equations from which it was developed. The x node can be thought of as a summing amplifier, where the output voltages are equal to the sum of the incoming weighted input voltages.

Figure 5-4 Final Mason graph.

As an illustration of the signal-flow graph technique we write the equations:

$$x_1 + ax_a = y_1$$
$$bx_1 + x_2 = 0$$

We can rewrite these as

$$x_1 = -ax_2 + y_1$$
$$x_2 = -bx_1$$

The signal-flow graph for these equations is shown in Figure 5-5.

A node which has only incoming edges is called a *sink node*, while a node that has only outgoing edges is a *source node*. A node with one or more incoming edges is defined as a *dependent node*. The weight of the edge connecting node x_i to x is known as the *edge transmittance*, and each node is weighted by either x_i or y_i. Self-loops will not occur if the equations are formulated as shown above. This restriction is not critical since a graph with self-loops can always be modified to be a graph without self-loops.

We would like a systematic method for obtaining a set of simultaneous equations which can be represented by a signal-flow graph and then applied to computer analysis. We would also like the formulation based on the topology of the network. Initially assume that the network consists only of reciprocal passive elements and independent current and voltage sources. This restriction can be removed later. The fundamental principles involve the following, which are independent:

1. Kirchhoff's current law (KCL).
2. Kirchhoff's voltage law (KVL).
3. The voltage-current (V-I) relationships for each passive element.

The KCL and KVL relationships are both determined by the same tree, where a *tree* is a set of connected edges touching all the nodes in the network but not forming any circuits.

The tree is fundamental in formulating the independent network equations. If we replace each edge in a tree by a voltage source, then by

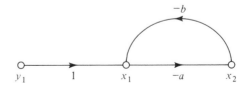

Figure 5-5 Illustrative signal-flow graph.

shorting the voltage sources all the edge voltages will be reduced to zero. Thus the edge voltage for each tree edge, which is called a *branch*, will form an independent set of voltage variables from which all the other voltage and current quantities can be found. If we replace each edge in the complement of the tree, called a *cotree*, by a current source, then by opening all of the current sources all the edge currents will be reduced to zero. Thus the edge currents associated with each cotree, called *links*, form an independent set of current variables from which all the other current and voltage variables can be found.

After a tree has been chosen, the formulation proceeds as indicated below:

1. The tree will define a unique set of voltage variables (the tree branches) and current variables (the cotree links).

2. Express the link voltages as a linear combination of the branch voltages.

3. Express the branch currents as a linear combination of the link currents.

Steps 2 and 3 yield the KVL and KCL equations for the set of voltage and current variables.

4. Complete the description by specifying the link admittances and branch impedances.

It should always be possible to choose a tree which contains all the specified independent voltage sources. Then the associated cotree contains all the independent current sources. Otherwise, the voltage and current sources would not be independent. The signal-flow graph which illustrates this is called *Mason's primitive graph*. Figure 5-6 shows this graph.

The signal-flow graph is associated with a set of simultaneous equations, $2e$ in number, where e is the number of edges in the network. The functional

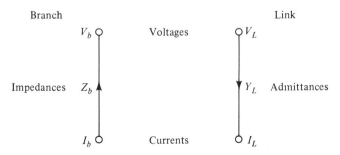

Figure 5-6   Mason's primitive graph.

relationships between the link and branch currents and branch and link voltages are based upon linear graph theory. The dependent sources are treated as either independent current sources or voltage sources. This requires inserting them into cotree links or tree branches. The signal-flow graph can then be generated using the following procedures:

1. First choose a tree; this will establish a set of independent voltage and current variables.
2. Then find the link voltages as a linear combination of the branch voltages.
3. Find the branch currents as a linear combination of the link currents.
4. Find the link admittances and the branch impedances.
5. Draw the signal-flow graph.

Four major topological matrices can be derived by the linear graph of a network. Using the graph of Figure 5-7 we can write the branch-node connections as follows:

Branches	Initial node connection	Final node connection
1	A	B
2	B	C
3	B	E
4	D	E
5	D	B
6	E	C
7	C	C

These connections are from the network configuration, which is a convenient starting point for compiling the network equations.

Another alternative way of stating this information is to use a matrix display as shown below:

$\bar{A}$-Matrix

Branches	Nodes				
	A	B	C	D	E
1	1	-1	0	0	0
2	0	1	-1	0	0
3	0	1	0	0	-1
4	0	0	0	1	-1
5	0	-1	0	1	0
6	0	0	-1	0	1
7	0	0	0	0	0

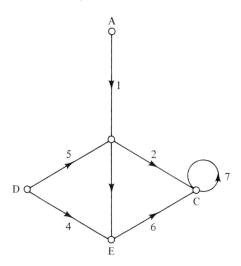

Figure 5-7   Network graph.

Here the columns show which branches are connected to which node and the sign of these connections. This matrix can be obtained from the connections. For example, branch 7 is short-circuited; it has both a +1 and a −1 in column C, and both these entries cancel. Since each row of this matrix contains both a +1 and a −1 in all nonzero rows, its columns are linearly dependent. Thus the sum of any column is equal to the negative sum of all the other columns. This means that any one column may be deleted, since it contains redundant information. If we delete the column for node E, then this node becomes the *reference* or *ground node*. The resulting matrix, sometimes called the *branch-node matrix*, is shown below:

A Matrix

Branches	Nodes				
	A	B	C	D	
1	1	−1	0	0	
2	0	1	−1	0	Trees
3	0	1	0	0	
4	0	0	0	1	
5	0	−1	0	1	
6	0	0	−1	0	Links
7	0	0	0	0	

Each link along with its tree branches can define a *basic mesh*. Then each basic mesh will contain only one link, with a positive orientation as shown in Figure 5-8. The link submatrix is then a unit matrix, and it does not need to be calculated and stored in the computer. Only the other submatrix, which gives the path-in-tree for each basic mesh, is needed, and this can be obtained in the following way. In a linear graph, the branch-node and branch-mesh matrices will have the following relationship:

$$A'C = 0$$

and

$$C'A = 0$$

Here the product is a null matrix. We can write the first of these in the partitioned form as

$$[A'_T A'_L]\begin{bmatrix} C_T \\ U_L \end{bmatrix} = A'_T C_T + A'_L = 0$$

Here the unit matrix U_L replaces C_L. This equation can be solved for C_T by inverting A'_T and using the inverse relationship discussed earlier:

$$C_T = -B_T A'_L$$

Another important topological matrix is the cutset matrix D. We have seen that each link, along with a certain set of tree branches, defines a basic mesh. Each tree branch, along with a certain set of links, defines a *basic cutset*.

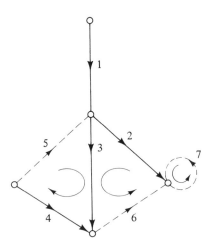

Figure 5-8 Mesh or circuit graph.

This is shown in Figure 5-9. The cutset matrix for this graph is shown below:

D Matrix

	Cutset				
Branch	1	2	3	4	
1	1	0	0	0	
2	0	1	0	0	D_b
3	0	0	1	0	
4	0	0	0	1	
5	0	0	-1	1	
6	0	1	-1	0	D_L
7	0	0	0	0	

The columns of this matrix show which branches are related to each cutset. If each tree branch is positively oriented in its cutset, the submatrix D_b contains the tree branches and it is a unit matrix. The other submatrix contains the links and it is the negative transpose of C_t. Thus we can write

$$D = \begin{bmatrix} D_T \\ D_L \end{bmatrix} = \begin{bmatrix} U_T \\ -C_T^t \end{bmatrix} = \begin{bmatrix} A_T \\ A_L \end{bmatrix} B_T^t = A B_T^t$$

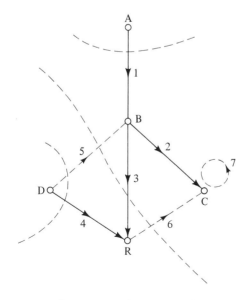

Figure 5-9   Cutset graph.

Thus the cutset matrix can be computed in terms of A, B_T, and C_T. It is also useful to note that

$$D'C = 0$$

and

$$C'D = 0$$

If we now choose a tree in the graph made up of branches 1, 2, 3, and 4 shown in Figure 5-10, then the remaining branches become links. This partitions the matrix into two submatrices of tree branches and links. We could use an algorithm for performing a tree-link sort on the computer.

The tree submatrix is square, and its inverse can be determined from the graph of the tree in terms of the node-to-reference path matrix B_T for the tree. Using the tree shown, the columns of B_T are given below:

B_T Matrix

	Node			
Branch	A	B	C	D
1	1	0	0	0
2	0	0	−1	0
3	1	1	1	0
4	0	0	0	1

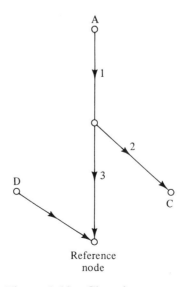

Figure 5-10   Choosing a tree.

They indicate which branches are included in the paths from each node and reference node. The relationship between B_T and the inverse of A_T, the branch-node matrix, is

$$A_T^{-1} = B_T^t$$

Here B_T^t is the transpose of the B_T matrix. We could also use an algorithm for determining the B_T matrix from the $\bar{A}$ matrix.

The matrix called the branch-mesh or circuit matrix is shown below. The columns of this matrix show which branches belong to each mesh.

C Matrix

Branch	Mesh			
	5	6	7	
1	0	0	0	
2	0	-1	0	C_T
3	1	1	0	
4	-1	0	0	
5	1	0	0	
6	0	1	0	C_L
7	0	0	1	

The Topological Approach to Circuit Analysis

The topological technique bypasses the numerical matrix inversion required in the solution of the node voltage equations. The problem of solving the node voltage equations using either determinant or matrix methods is transformed by the Binet-Cauchy theorem to the topological and combinatorial problem of finding the trees and associated n-tree products of a linear graph.

The tree-finding problem becomes somewhat more difficult in the case of the active network, since the tree-finding routine now must select the trees common to both the voltage and current graph of the network. The correct sign for the n-tree products must also be determined by this routine.

The tree-finding problem is the critical task in the topological approach to circuit analysis. The concern is primarily in the amount of computer time required to solve a particular circuit's unknowns. The advantage over the usual determinant solution of either loop or node equations is that the topological technique does eliminate the terms in the evaluation of a determinant that ultimately cancel out, but this computational advantage is counterbalanced by the disadvantage of having to learn a different approach.

The topological approach is conveniently programmed. Increasing the use of topological techniques are the artificial two-terminal elements which extend topological analysis to active and mutually coupled networks.

The topological properties of the linear circuit shown in Figure 5-11 can be illustrated by replacing the schematic of this electrical network by the linear graph shown in Figure 5-12. The basic theory relating to such a linear graph has been introduced; Table 5-1 provides a more complete definition of linear graph theory.

Topological analysis concepts are based on the node-voltage equations and the reduced incidence matrix A. A dual path can be taken using mesh-current equations and the circuit matrix B. The second technique is similar but introduces an additional task, since the process requires the determination of the chords of a tree. This presents an extra step beyond the determination of the tree branches which is required in the node-voltage approach. For this reason the second approach is not often used. We have seen how a passive RLC network can be represented as a linear graph. Each edge of the linear graph is weighted by an admittance, and each admittance satisfies the following:

$$Y_{ab} V_{ab} = i_{ab}$$

Here v_{ab} is the edge voltage with the positive reference at a, and i_{ab} is the edge current from a to b.

In matrix form the complete network with the graph equations becomes

$$Y_b V = I$$

Here Y_b is a $b \times b$ diagonal matrix, V is the $b \times 1$ branch-voltage column matrix, and I is the $b \times 1$ branch-current matrix.

Kirchhoff's current law takes the form:

$$AI = J$$

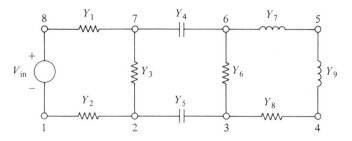

Figure 5-11   Network schematic.

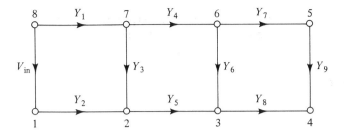

Figure 5-12 Network graph.

Table 5-1 Basis of linear graph theory

1. An edge or element is a line segment with two endpoints.
2. The end points are called nodes.
3. A node and an edge are incident with each other if the node is an endpoint of the edge.
4. The edge is self-looped if its nodes are identical.
5. A linear graph is a collection of edges with no self-looped edges.
6. An oriented graph is a graph in which the direction of each edge is specified. Otherwise, the graph is nonoriented.
7. The degree of a node is the number of edges incident at that node.
8. A path between nodes i and j in a graph is an ordered sequence of edges in the graph in which every node is of degree two, except nodes i and j, which are of degree one.
9. A connected graph has a path between every pair of nodes in the graph. It cannot contain any isolated edges or nodes.
10. A circuit is a connected graph of nodes, all of which are of degree two.
11. A tree is a connected graph or subgraph containing all nodes of the graph but no circuits.
12. A tree branch is an edge of a tree.
13. A chord is an edge of the complement of a tree.
14. The incidence matrix, $A_a = [a_{ij}]$, of an oriented graph with n nodes and b edges is a matrix with n rows and b columns. Each row corresponds to a node, and each column corresponds to an edge, such that
    $a_{ij} = 1$, if edge j is incident at node i and directed away from node i;
    $a_{ij} = -1$, if edge j is incident at node i and directed toward node i;
    $a_{ij} = 0$, if edge i is not incident at node i.
15. The matrix obtained by deleting any row from A_a is called the reduced incidence matrix A.
16. The rank of the incidence matrix A_a of n rows and b columns is $(n-1)$.
17. The rank of A is $n-1$ for n rows and b columns.
18. A square submatrix of A of order $n-1$ is nonsingular if, and only if, the columns of this submatrix correspond to the branches of a tree.
19. In the formulation of the A matrix each edge of the graph determines a column of the A matrix.
20. The determinant of a nonsingular submatrix of A is always equal to $+1$ or -1.

Here J is the column matrix of current sources, I is the column matrix of edge currents, and A is the reduced incidence matrix.

Combining these equations gives

$$A Y_b V = J$$

or

$$V = A' V_n$$

where V_n is the column matrix of node voltages measured with respect to the reference node. The basic node-voltage equation is obtained from combining these equations to give

$$A Y_b A' V_n = Y_m V_n = J$$

The solution for this equation requires the inversion of the matrix Y_m. This can be difficult to implement except in some special cases. In general the members of the matrix Y_m consist of polynomials in s, and these must be carried in literal form until the matrix inversion is complete.

The determination of a system function may require only the partial solution of the node-voltage equation. The driving-point impedance requires the voltage across a pair of terminals to be expressed in terms of a current source applied to the terminals. Other system functions, such as the driving-point or transfer functions, require only a partial solution of the node-voltage equation.

Instead of matrix inversion we can use Cramer's rule to find the required variables. We define the driving-point function

$$Z_{ij}$$

as the ratio of V_{ij} to J_{ij} where j is the reference node and J_{if} is a current source connected between nodes i and j.

To solve for V_{if} we apply Cramer's rule and set all other current sources except J_{if} to zero; then

$$V_{if} = \frac{J_{ij} \Delta_{11}}{\Delta}$$

Here $\Delta = |Y_m| = |A Y_b A'|$, and Δ_{11} is the 1, 1 cofactor of Y_m. We can determine Δ and Δ_{11} using conventional determinant techniques.

An alternate approach is the Binet-Cauchy theorem. This theorem provides a method for evaluating the determinant of the product of two matrices. The Binet-Cauchy theorem says that: *If* P *or order* (m, n) *and* Q *of order* (n, m) *are matrices of elements with* m < n, *then the determinant of the product PQ is the sum of the products of corresponding majors of* P *and* Q. Here the summation is over all such majors.

A *major*, which is also called a *major determinant*, is the determinant of the largest square submatrix. In this case it is of order m. The *corresponding major* means that if columns $i_1, i_2, \ldots, i_m$ of P are the major, then rows $i_1, i_2, \ldots, i_m$ of Q are chosen to form the corresponding major.

To use the Binet-Cauchy theorem to calculate the determinant of AY_bA^t we note that AY_b is related to the matrix P and A^t by the matrix Q. Since Y_b is a diagonal matrix, the product of AY_b has the same structure as A except that column j is multiplied by Y_j for $j = 1, 2, \ldots, b$. Thus the nonsingular submatrices of AY_b still correspond to the trees of the network, but the value of the determinant of each nonsingular submatrix, instead of being $\pm$, is now

$$(\pm 1) \; (Y_{i1}) \; (Y_{i2}) \; \cdots \; (Y_{ik})$$

where $k = n$ and $i_1, i_2, \ldots, i_k$ are the branches of the tree.

The corresponding submatrix of A^t is the transpose of the submatrix of A; thus it is also nonsingular, and it has the same determinant (± 1) as the submatrix of A. The product of the determinant of the two submatrices is $(Y_{i_1}) \; (Y_{i_2}) \; \ldots \; (Y_{i_k})$, and this is defined as the *tree-admittance product*.

In a passive network the tree-admittance product always has a positive sign. The other majors do not correspond to trees. These are all zero and do not contribute to the solution of AY_bA^t. Using the above analysis and the Binet-Cauchy theorem, then

$$\Delta = |AY_bT^t| = \sum_{\substack{\text{all} \\ \text{trees}}} \text{tree-admittance products}$$

This is called Maxwell's rule or formula. In order to calculate the node-admittance determinant, each tree of the network is found, then the tree-admittance product is found for each tree, and finally all the tree-admittance products are summed.

The use of Maxwell's rule can produce a computational advantage, since a partial calculation of terms occurs in the determinant evaluation. In a computer, literal matrix inversion can be achieved by basic orientation operations.

A network function can also be determined in several different forms. It can be expressed in terms of its poles and zeros in the s domain. This operation can be difficult if one attempts to invert the matrix Y_m directly. A network function could also be obtained in terms of the individual admittances of the network, or one could express the network function as a function of a single element. One can also extend this approach for evaluating Δ to cofactors Δ_{ij}.

The Evaluation of Cofactors Using the *n*-Tree Concept

A *symmetrical cofactor* is one having the form Δ_{jj}. To obtain a cofactor *jj*, both row *j* and column *j* of the node-admittance matrix Y_m are deleted. Now

$$A Y_b A^t = Y_m$$

so the same result can be obtained by deleting row *j* of the first matrix and column *j* of the last matrix. But column *j* of A^t is row *j* of *A*, so let A_j be defined as the matrix *A* with row *j* deleted, so

$$\Delta_{jj} = \det (A_j Y_b A_j')$$

We now need to define the relation of A_j to the original network *N*. If node *j* is shorted to the reference node, then the incidence matrix of this new network N_1 is written. None of the other nodes are affected, so the reduced incidence matrix of N_1 is A_j. Thus

$$\Delta_{jj} = \sum \text{ tree-admittance products of } N_1.$$

We also know that Δ_{jj} is related to the original network *N*. Network N_1 has $n-1$ nodes, so the trees of N_1 cannot be trees of *N*. The node *j* and the reference node are in two different pieces. This structure is sometimes called a *2-tree*, and in this case we have a 2-tree (*j, r*), where *r* is the reference node.

The network shown in Figure 5-13 corresponds to the cofactor Δ_{11} network shown in Figure 5-14. Node 5 is the reference node.

Figure 5-15 shows some 2-trees of *N* where node 1 and node 5 are in different parts. Each of these terms will contribute to Δ_{jj}. Maxwell's formula for a symmetrical cofactor now becomes

$$\Delta_{jj} = \sum_{\substack{\text{all} \\ \text{2-trees}}} \text{2-tree } (j, r) \text{ admittance products}$$

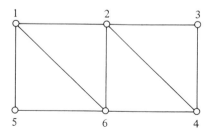

Figure 5-13   Basic network.

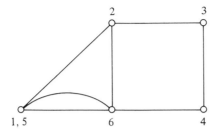

Figure 5-14   Cofactor Δ_{11} network.

Here r is the reference node.

If we define $W_{i,j}$

$$W_{i,j} = \sum_{\substack{\text{all} \\ \text{2-trees}}} \text{2-tree } (i, j) \text{ admittance products}$$

Here the subscripts in W_{ij} indicate the nodes that are in different parts of the network.

Asymmetrical cofactors occur if row i and column j are deleted, and we obtain

$$\Delta_{ij} = \det (A_i Y_b A_j^t)$$

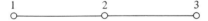

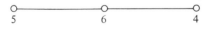

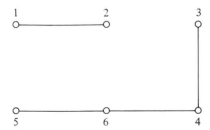

Figure 5-15   2-Trees.

If we use the Binet-Cauchy theorem, we get

$$\Delta_{ij} = \text{products of the corresponding majors of } A_i Y_b \text{ and } A'_j$$

The nonzero majors of $A_i Y_b$ again correspond to 2-trees (i, r), where r is the reference node. The nonzero majors of A'_j correspond to 2-trees (j, r). The terms that contribute to Δ_{ij} then must be both 2-trees of (j, r) and (i, r), and these occur at the intersection of $W_{i,r}$ and $W_{j,r}$. Since a 2-tree has only two parts, r must be in one part and both i and j must be in the other. Thus

$$\Delta_{ij} = W_{ij,r} = W_{i,r} \, \Omega \, W_j, \, r$$

We now have formulas for Δ, Δ_{jj}, and Δ_{ij} of the node-admittance matrix. Transfer functions of network parameters originally expressed in terms of the node-admittance matrix can now be expressed in terms of tree or n-tree products. The open-circuit voltage transfer function for the network shown in Figure 5-16 is

$$H = \frac{V_2}{V_1} = \frac{\Delta_{12}}{\Delta_{11}} = \frac{W_{12,3}}{W_{1,3}}$$

Some network functions will require more than the values of the determinant and the first cofactors. Second and higher cofactors will lead to 3-tree and n-tree products, which can be regarded as an extension of the methods discussed here.

Using the Topological Method for Active Networks

Many linear networks contain some active device. One strategy that has been developed uses two-terminal elements which combine current and voltage elements. These make it possible for the theory of linear graphs to be extended to the analysis of active networks.

Assume that we have a linear network as shown in Figure 5-17 with node-pairs (pq) and (mn); then

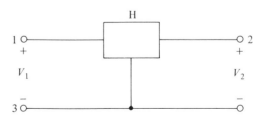

Figure 5-16 Open-circuit voltage transfer function.

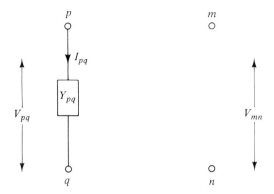

Figure 5-17   Network with node-pairs.

$$Y_{pq}V_{pq} + Y_{pq,mn}V_{mn} = I_{pq}$$

Here the Y's act as proportionality factors

$$I = \mathcal{L}(i(t))$$
$$V = \mathcal{L}(v(t))$$

The self-admittance is Y_{pq} and the mutual admittance term is $Y_{pq,mn}$. I_{pq} is a function of both V_{pq} and V_{mn}.

If we break I_{pq} into two components, the one due to V_{pq} is called I'_{pq}, and the one due to V_{mn}, I''_{pq}. Then

$$Y_{pq}V_{pq} = I'_{pq}$$
$$Y_{pq,mn}V_{mn} = I''_{pq}$$
$$I'_{pq} + I''_{pq} = I_{pq}$$

By adding a voltage element between nodes m and n we can sense a voltage difference in the node-pair. The element introduced in the node-pair (pq) is a current element that produces a current of magnitude I''_{pq} flowing from node p to node q owing to the voltage difference in the node-pair m. The voltage and current elements are related by the mutual admittance $Y_{pq,mn}$. The voltage and current elements are always used in pairs, but between different node-pairs. If they are used in the same node-pair, then $p = m$ and $q = n$, and the mutual admittance $Y_{pq,mn}$ becomes the self-admittance Y_{pq}.

The representation of voltage and current elements for dependent node-pairs (pq) and (mn) is shown in Figure 5-18(a). These are two-terminal elements, so they are represented by the edges of a linear graph as current and voltage edges. The weight of these edges is the mutual admittance.

The orientation of a current edge is determined by the direction of the

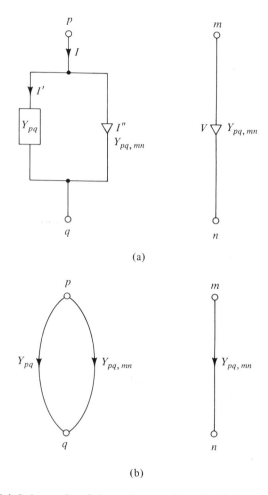

(a)

(b)

Figure 5-18 (a) Schematic of dependent node-pairs. (b) Graph of dependent node-pairs.

current flow in the current element and the orientation of a voltage edge is given by the polarity of the voltage element. The graph for the network N discussed above is shown in Figure 5-18(b). The current edge appears as open arrows and the voltage edge is shown as a closed arrow. The dashed arrow represents a passive element.

Next we need to express the node-voltage equations in terms of the current and voltage graph. Let A_v and A_i be the incidence matrixes. Kirchhoff's current law gives

$$A_{iI} = J$$

Here I is the column matrix of edge currents and J is the column matrix of current sources.

The node transformation for the voltage graph is

$$V = A_v^t V_n$$

Here V is the column matrix of edge voltages and V_n is the column matrix of node voltages with respect to the reference. We also know that

$$Y_{pq} V_{pq} = I'_{pq}$$

can be expressed in matrix form as

$$Y_b V = I$$

Here Y_b is a diagonal matrix in which each diagonal entry gives an admittance in the network.

From the above we get

$$Y_n V_n = J$$

where

$$Y_n = A_i Y_b A_v^t$$

As in the case of a passive network, the Binet-Cauchy theorem is used to solve for the determinant and cofactors of Y_n:

$$\Delta = |A_i Y_b A_v^t| = \sum \text{ corresponding majors of } A_i Y \text{ and } A_v^t$$

We note that:

1. A major of $A_i Y_b$ is a nonsingular if, and only if, the columns of A_i correspond to a tree of the current graph.
2. A nonsingular major of $A_i Y_b$ has the value $+(Y_{i1}), (Y_{i2}), \ldots, (Y_{ik})$, where $k = n - 1$ and $i_1, i_2, \ldots, i_k$ are the branches of the tree.
3. The corresponding major A_v^t has the value of $\pm$ if the columns of A_v correspond to a tree of the voltage graph.
4. The term common tree is used to denote a tree that is common to both the current and the voltage graph.

Now Δ can be given in terms of the tree products of the common trees of a network:

$$\Delta = W(Y) = \sum \pm (\text{tree products of the common trees of a network})$$

The addition of active elements to the graph tends to complicate the tree-finding procedure, since the determination of the common trees and the associated signs can be difficult as topological problems.

FORMATION OF THE CIRCUIT MATRIX

One of our objectives is to highlight the importance of keeping the computer in mind when developing the theory on which to base circuit-analysis programs. Since matrix notation is an excellent tool for describing the network problem in a form suitable for programming, we shall discuss the matrix approach involving the various aspects of dc, ac, and transient analysis of circuits on a computer. It is easy to demonstrate the superior organizational powers of the matrix-tensor notation. There is not only a conceptual elegance to this notation, but it also presents a more automatic way of handling the many bookkeeping chores in circuit analysis. It provides us with many of the logical and procedural foundations necessary for programs to analyze circuits. We can use these techniques both to compile and to solve the network equations in a procedural manner.

The matrix formation can provide an algebraic-topological explanation of the network. This type of formulation has been used in a number of programs for circuit analysis as well as for the analysis of networks in electrical power systems.

From a very basic point of view, we are concerned with predicting the behavior of a system of interconnected elements in terms of the element characteristics and the manner in which these elements are interconnected. From a mathematical viewpoint we are concerned with the properties of an underlying topological structure which can be shown by a linear graph, over which we superimpose an algebraic structure consisting of the quantities associated with the nodes, branches, and meshes of the graph. The interconnecting of the network elements introduces certain constraints on the physical variables of the network problem, and this gives us a part of the bookkeeping task.

In order to account for the constraints on the branch voltages e and branch currents i due to the interconnections, we employ Kirchhoffs voltage and current laws. In their basic form, these laws produce the matrix relations

$$C^t e = O$$
$$A^t i = O$$

Here the topological matrix C^t is an operator that sums all the branch voltages around each basic mesh, and the matrix A^t sums all the branch currents leaving each node.

Two alternative and mathematically equivalent forms of Kirchhoff's voltage and current laws occur when we state that the branch voltages are a linear combination of the node voltages and the branch currents are a linear combination of the mesh currents. These two forms produce the matrix equations,

$$e = Ae'$$
$$i = Ci'$$

Here e' is the vector of node-to-datum voltages and i' is the vector of mesh currents. The topological matrices tend to do the bookkeeping, and the basic relations between the network variables and the topological matrix can be shown as a transformation diagram (Figure 5-19). This diagram characterizes the algebraic structure associated with the linear graph. The additional relations needed are

$$C'E = E'$$

which defines the equivalent mesh emfs E' and

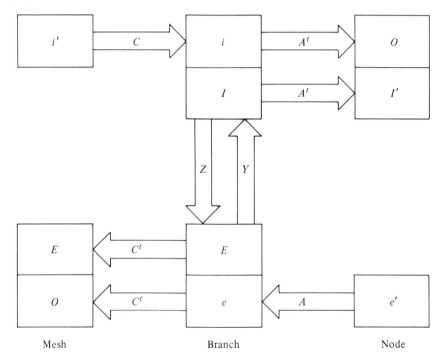

Figure 5-19 The relationships between the network variables and the topological matrix.

$$A'I = I'$$

which defines the equivalent nodal current sources I'.

This algebraic structure can be used for that wide variety of nonelectrical systems including mechanical and structural systems. These also fit this pattern and thus they can be treated as network problems. We can also extend this algebraic structure to characterize topological structures with surface and volumn elements as well as points and lines.

A direct correspondence to the operational structure of the vector calculus is also possible, and a wide class of partial differential equations including Maxwell's equations can be solved. The exploitation of the broader aspects of circuit theory include the simulation and analysis of many engineering and manufacturing problems.

Electrical Network Formulations

The electrical network formulation involves a network given by topological matrices, usually A and C, and the impedance matrix Z or the admittance matrix Y. Then, by knowing the voltage-source vectors E and the current-source vectors I, we can find the branch voltages (e) and branch currents (i). There are four basic ways of approaching the problem. In each case it is necessary to introduce some form of auxiliary variables, such as the node voltages e' or mesh currents i' shown earlier. It is also necessary to use Kirchhoff's law in its two equivalent forms.

In the mesh method we start with the impedance form of Ohm's law. We introduce and rearrange to obtain

$$(E\, i - ZI) + e = ZI$$

Now, if we multiply by C^t and use Kirchhoff's voltage law, we obtain

$$C^t(E - ZI) = C'Zi$$

We then use Kirchhoff's current law and obtain the matrix equivalent of the mesh equations

$$C^t(E - ZI) = C'ZCi'$$

Here $C'ZC$ is the mesh-impedance matrix.

We can solve this system of equations for the mesh currents i':

$$i' = (C'ZC)^{-1}C^t(\, - ZI)$$

Here $(C'ZC)^{-1}$ is the mesh solution matrix. We can then find the branch currents and then obtain the branch voltages.

In the node method we start with the admittance form of Ohm's law, and we treat the network problem following steps similar to those described for the mesh method. The corresponding equations take on the following dual format:

$$
\begin{aligned}
(I - YE) + i &= Ye \\
A'(I - YE) &= A'Ye \\
A'(I - YE) &= A'YAe' \\
e' &= (A'YA)^{-1} A' (I - YE)
\end{aligned}
$$

Here $A'YA$ is the nodal admittance matrix and $(A'YA)^{-1}$ is the nodal solution matrix. The desired branch variable may also be computed as disussed above.

In both of these methods of analysis, the auxiliary variables i' and e' form a basis for all the branch currents or branch voltages. This basis is the linearly independent set of voltages in terms of which all the branch voltages are computed. Another basis besides the node-to-reference-datum voltages can also be used. We can use the set of tree-branch voltages e_T, which are linearly independent, and then the branch voltages can be computed from

$$
e = De_T
$$

Here D is the cutset matrix. This is a form of Kirchhoff's voltage law; the counterpart for Kirchhoff's current law is

$$
D'i = 0
$$

The steps involved in the cutset method take on the following form:

$$
\begin{aligned}
(I = YE) + i &= Ye \\
D'(I - YE) &= D'Ye \\
D'(I - YE) &= D'YDe_T \\
e_T &= (D'YD)^{-1}D'(I - YE)
\end{aligned}
$$

Here $D'YD$ is the cutset admittance matrix and $(D'YD)^{-1}$ is the cutset solution matrix. The branch variables may be evaluated as noted above.

The hybrid method provides an addition to these three traditional methods of analysis. It is beginning to be widely used. The hybrid or mixed method is based in part on the state-variable approach to transient analysis.

The main idea in the hybrid method is that Ohm's law can be expressed in a hybrid form involving the admittance matrix for certain branches of the network and the impedance matrix for the rest of the branches. Thus, Ohm's law takes the form:

$$
\begin{bmatrix} J_y \\ V_z \end{bmatrix} = \begin{bmatrix} V_y & 0 \\ 0 & Z_z \end{bmatrix} \begin{bmatrix} V_y \\ J_z \end{bmatrix}
$$

Here the subscripts y and z are the branches which are treated as admittances or as impedances. Starting with the following equation

$$
\begin{bmatrix} I_y + i_y \\ E_z + e_z \end{bmatrix} = \begin{bmatrix} Y_y & 0 \\ 0 & Z_z \end{bmatrix} \begin{bmatrix} E_y + e_y \\ I_z + i_z \end{bmatrix}
$$

we can analyze the admittance branches using the cutset method and the impedance branches using the mesh method. We consider the two sets of branches as separate subnetworks. We then couple the resulting two sets of equations together by topological matrix.

First, we take all the y-branches of admittances, and a tree-link sort is performed. The y-links which are identified will define basic meshes which contain only y-tree branches, since the z-branches of impedances have yet to be considered. The paths-in-tree for these y-meshes are noted by the submatrix C_{Tyy}. The tree-link sort is continued for the z-branches. The z-links now define basic meshes with paths-in-tree that may involve both y-tree branches and z-tree branches, noted by the submatrices C_{Tyz} and C_{Tzz}. The C_T matrix for the entire network becomes

$$
C_T = \begin{bmatrix} C_{Tyy} & C_{Tyz} \\ 0 & C_{Tzz} \end{bmatrix}
$$

To express the y-branch voltages e_y in terms of the y-tree branch voltages e_{Ty}, we use

$$
e_y = \begin{bmatrix} e_{Ty} \\ e_{Ly} \end{bmatrix} = \begin{bmatrix} U_{Ty} \\ -C^t_{Tyy} \end{bmatrix} e_{Ty} = D_y e_{Ty}
$$

Here D_y is the cutset matrix for the y-branches with the z-branches open-circuited. For the complete network we have

$$
\begin{matrix} e_{Ty} \\ e_{Tz} \\ e_{Ly} \\ e_{Lz} \end{matrix} = \begin{bmatrix} U_{Ty} & 0 \\ 0 & U_{Tz} \\ -C^t_{Tyy} & 0 \\ -C^t_{Tyz} & -C^t_{Tzz} \end{bmatrix} \begin{bmatrix} e_{Ty} \\ e_{Tz} \end{bmatrix}
$$

Here the Dmatrix for all the y- and z-branches is used.

The z-branch currents i_z can also be formed as a linear combination of the z-link currents i_{Lz}. These have a similar form to the mesh currents, as shown below:

$$i_z = \begin{bmatrix} i_{Tz} \\ i_{Lz} \end{bmatrix} = \begin{bmatrix} C_{Tzz} \\ U_{Lz} \end{bmatrix} i_{Lz} = C_z i_{Lz}$$

Here, C_z is the circuit matrix for the z-branches with the y-branches short-circuited. For the complete network, we have

$$\begin{matrix} i_{Ty} \\ i_{Tz} \\ i_{Ly} \\ i_{Lz} \end{matrix} = \begin{matrix} C_{Tyy} & CT_{yz} \\ 0 & C_{Tzz} \\ U_{Ly} & 0 \\ 0 & U_{Lz} \end{matrix} \begin{bmatrix} i_{Ly} \\ i_{Lz} \end{bmatrix}$$

Here the C matrix for all the y- and z-branches is used.

For the complete network

$$D^t i = 0$$

and

$$C^t e = 0$$

Thus we can show

$$D_y^t i_y = [U_{Ty} - C_{Tyy}] \begin{bmatrix} i_{Ty} \\ i_{Ly} \end{bmatrix} = C_{Tyz} i_{Lz}$$

and

$$C_z^t e_z = [C_{Tzz}^t \quad U_{Lz}] \begin{bmatrix} e_{Tz} \\ e_{Lz} \end{bmatrix} = -C_{Tyz}^t e_{Ty}$$

Returning to our basic equation for the hybrid method, we can now write

$$\begin{bmatrix} (I_y - Y_y E_y) \\ (E_z - Z_z I_z) \end{bmatrix} = \begin{bmatrix} Y_y & 0 \\ 0 & Z_z \end{bmatrix} \begin{bmatrix} e_y \\ i_z \end{bmatrix} - \begin{bmatrix} i_y \\ e_z \end{bmatrix}$$

Next we multiply the first row of this equation by D_y^t and the second row by C_z^t and replace e_y and i_z by the expressions previously obtained. Thus,

$$
\begin{bmatrix} D_y^t & (I_y - Y_y E_y) \\ C_z^t & (E_z - Z_z I_z) \end{bmatrix} = \begin{bmatrix} D_y^t Y_y D_y & 0 \\ 0 & C_z^t Z_z C_z \end{bmatrix} \begin{bmatrix} e_{Ty} \\ i_{Lz} \end{bmatrix} - \begin{bmatrix} D_y^t & i_y \\ C_z^t & e_z \end{bmatrix}
$$

This is the same, except for the second term on the right-hand side, as what we would get by using the cutset method of analysis of the y-branches, with the z-branches open-circuited, and the mesh method on the z-branches, with the y-branches short-circuited. Next we replace the terms involving i_y and e_z, using the expressions developed above. Finally we obtain

$$
\begin{bmatrix} D_y^t & (I_y - Y_y E_y) \\ C_z^t & (E_z - Z_z I_z) \end{bmatrix} = \begin{bmatrix} D_y^t Y_y D_y & -C_{Tyz} \\ C_{Tyz}^t & C_z^t Z_z C_z \end{bmatrix} \begin{bmatrix} e_{Ty} \\ i_{Lz} \end{bmatrix}
$$

Here the topological matrix C_{Tyz} couples the two sets of the cutset and mesh equations.

We have seen how the circuit-analysis bookkeeping tasks can be systematized in terms of matrices which describe the connectivity properties of a linear graph. Here is where the graph topology is used to relate the physical variables of the network. These correspond to the quantities which enter into the algebraic structure referred to earlier. The matrix approach correlates these and also identifies the separate roles of the element characteristics and the interconnections which determine the overall behavior of the network.

GENERAL MATRIX CIRCUIT-ANALYSIS TECHNIQUES

The development of a general circuit-analysis computer program must be based on a framework of the general loop and node equations. Otherwise the program might be reduced to solving only special cases and would be of limited usefulness. The form of the computer program can be divided into two phases:

1. Obtain a set of simultaneous ordinary differential equations that describe a network.

2. Define numerical procedure to solve the network equations. We will consider these two phases and how they relate to the details of a general analysis.

The usual starting point is to formulate the necessary loop and node equations in a generalized network-analysis format using state variables. Kirchhoff's current and voltage laws then have the following form:

$$AI(t) = 0$$
$$BI(t) = 0$$

where A is called the reduced incidence matrix and B is the fundamental-loop matrix.

Kirchhoff's laws are used to obtain the branch voltages and currents and express the topology of the network. We must specify the nature of the branch elements (resistors, capacitors, inductors and sources) and the linearity of the branch elements. Each branch of an electrical network may include three distinct electrical devices:

1. A passive element.
2. An ideal voltage source in series with the passive element.
3. An ideal current source in parallel with the passive element.

The relative orientation of these elements can be shown using the notation of the topological graph approach. The analysis of linear active networks is treated in the presentation with reference to passive networks, which are then extended to the active case by the two-element technique. The details of this approach were discussed earlier.

The physical elements of the network can then be represented by a model consisting of passive and active elements. The passive elements are considered to be lumped, linear, and finite. The active elements may be ideal, controlled, or independent sources. This representation can lead to a useful equivalence in the electrical network. Such a representation may use the equations defining the models as derived from the physical properties of the elements, as discussed in Chapter 4.

We have also seen, earlier in this chapter, how Ohm's law will give us a system of ordinary integral-differential equations with constant coefficients which can be solved by the Laplace transform method. A common procedure in solving such a system of simultaneous ordinary integral-differential equations is to first express the system as a higher-order set of differential equations by removing the integrals through differentiation. Then this system of higher-order differential equations is reduced to a set of first-order equations by a change of variable.

Another method involves initially choosing a set of network variables which will produce a set of first-order differential equations. This minimal set of branch currents and voltages will have instantaneous values that are sufficient to determine the instantaneous state of the network. This is the set of dynamically independent network variables or the state-variable set. In order to arrive at such a set we must form the branch equations in a special way. First we can classify the network branches into the following groups:

Capacitive links

Resistive links

Inductive links

Capacitive branches

Resistive branches

Inductive branches

This group classification can be used to partition the network vectors and matrices into link and branch vectors and matrices. Each of these is then partitioned according to the six groups. The voltages across capacitors and the currents through inductors form a minimal set of state variables for electrical networks. This pair then can be used to completely describe the state of a network, and, as dependent variables, they can also describe the network behavior using a system of first-order differential equations. In a similar way, the incidence matrix and the fundamental-loop matrix can be partitioned.

Besides these matrices, an additional matrix that we have used is the cutset matrix. It may be constructed from either of these matrices and is defined as the system of cutsets in which each cutset includes exactly one branch of a tree.

A *cutset* is a set of edges of a connected network. The removal of these edges from the network increases the number of connected parts of the network by one, provided that there is no subset of this set to reduce the number of connected parts by one when it is removed from the network. There is a fundamental cutset matrix associated with each choice of a tree. The cutset provides us with a general method of finding an appropriate set of network equations, giving those with a sufficient number of independent equations. These cutset matrix equations are analogous to the circuit loops, since the rows of the incidence matrix can be expressed as linear combinations of rows of the cutset matrix. Each fundamental cutset contains a tree branch that has no other cutset, and this makes the Kirchhoff current-law equations in the cutset linearly independent.

Thus, the cutset matrix appears more attractive to use than the incidence matrix, since linearly independent equations are ensured, but in the incidence matrix they are not.

From the cutset matrix, Kirchhoff's current law can be expanded, and if the columns of the matrices are ordered according to branches and links as previously discussed, then the cutset matrix can be partitioned to allow us to construct a combined matrix equation that describes the network equations. To do this, we use Ohm's law, Kirchhoff's voltage law, and Kirchhoff's current law in terms of the cutset matrix. This single matrix equation may also be written in an expanded form using the six classes for network branches given earlier.

Using the network equations, we can eliminate variables until an independent set is obtained. To accomplish this we must formulate the branch equations in a certain format. We can do so by classifying the network branches into the groups shown earlier. Then we have twelve groups for the branch voltages and currents. In the elimination step, we express ten of these in algebraic terms of the remaining two. The branch equations that we use can be formed from a particular tree.

The preceding discussion relates to a general computer method of network analysis. We have been mainly concerned with the separation of the network problem into its constituent parts or elements. We now discuss the methods which are primarily used for solving the network problems under the three main conditions: dc, ac, and transient.

As we have seen, the most straightforward way of solving linear dc network problems is by Gaussian elimination of the variables in the mesh or node equations. For a circuit of n equations in n unknowns having a full matrix of coefficients, the amount of computation required to carry out this elimination process is about $n^3/3$ multiplication and addition operations. In general a system of linear algebraic equations cannot be solved in fewer operations than are required by Gaussian elimination. For systems of equations with sparse coefficient matrices, as is the case in many networks, an improvement in computations can be gained using this sparsity.

If several solutions are required for a circuit with a system of equations with different voltage and/or current sources, the usual method is to compute the mesh or nodal solution matrix by finding the inverse matrix and then multiplying it by each source vector. A full matrix inversion will require approximately n^3 operations, and each matrix-vector multiplication requires n^2 operations. Another way to accomplish this is to use LU decomposition. Here we find

a lower triangular matrix L
and an upper triangular matrix U

with a product LU that is equal to the coefficient matrix A in the general system of equations $Ax = b$. In the Gaussian elimination method we produce the upper triangular matrix U with all its diagonal elements equal to 1. But at the same time, the elements of the lower triangular matrix L are implicitly generated, and these need to be used now instead of being discarded. The required elements of the L matrix can be stored on the diagonal, in place of the diagonal 1s of the upper triangular matrix U. These will be below the diagonal in place of the zeros which are generated during the elimination process. This can be done efficiently, since the LU decomposition requires $n^3/3$ operations, which is one-third that required for matrix inversion. Since

$$LU = A$$

the system of equations

$$Ax = b$$

can be replaced by the two triangular systems

$$Ly = b$$

and

$$Ux = y$$

which can both be solved in n^2 operations. This is equal to the efforts required for matrix-vector multiplication. Thus, overall the LU method can save much computer time compared to conventional matrix inversion.

A number of refinements can improve the accuracy of the LU method. These include scaling and interchanging rows and columns (pivoting). We can also take advantage of the sparsity of most circuits by storing and processing only the nonzero elements. The order in which the Gaussian elimination takes place also has an impact on the computation time. One rule is to eliminate the variable which has the fewest nonzero elements; this can produce savings of the order of 4 to 1.

The tensor method provides some tools which can be useful in certain applications. If we desire to study the effect of varying a single parameter by letting it take on a succession of values, this method provides a more efficient way than solving the equations for each case. This method is used for the MODIFY feature of ECAP. Here it permits the nodal solution matrix for the original network to be updated for a change in one of the branch resistances. The amount of computation involved is very small compared to that required for solving the nodal equations or inverting the nodal admittance matrix, unless a sparse-matrix version of the LU decomposition method is used. But the tensor method can also be used with sparse-matrix techniques.

To understand the use of the tensor method, consider the circuit configuration shown in Figure 5-20. This is a single link connected from node p to node q of a tree with branches that are connected to a reference node. The path-in-tree for the single mesh in this network is given by the C_T matrix shown:

$$
C_T =
\begin{bmatrix}
0 \\
0 \\
\cdot \\
\cdot \\
\cdot \\
-1 \\
\cdot \\
\cdot \\
\cdot \\
1 \\
\cdot \\
\cdot \\
\cdot \\
0
\end{bmatrix}
\quad
\begin{matrix}
\\ \\ \\ \\ \\
p\text{th row} \\ \\ \\ \\
q\text{th row} \\ \\ \\ \\
\end{matrix}
$$

The mesh-impedance matrix is

$$C^t ZC = C_T^t I_T C_T + Z_L$$

Here Z_T is the impedance matrix for the tree, and Z_L represents the impedance of the single link being added to the tree. From our earlier work with the mesh solution it can be shown that

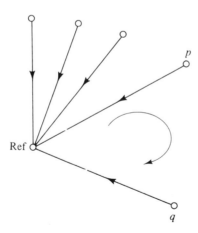

Figure 5-20   The tensor method.

$$e = [Z - ZC(C'ZC)^{-1}C'Z](I - YE)$$

Next we partition this equation into the submatrices and subvectors relating to the trees and links:

$$e_T = [Z_T - Z_T C_T (C'ZC)^{-1} C_T^t Z_T] D^t (I - YE)$$

Finally, by comparing this to the cutset admittance matrix and the above mesh-impedance matrix, we get

$$(D'YD)^{-1} = Z_T - Z_T C_T (C_T^t Z_T C_T + Z_L)^{-1} C'T^Z T$$

Thus, from the mesh method we have an expression for updating the cutset solution matrix for any tree to which a single link has been added. We note that for a tree the impedance matrix Z_T is identical to the cutset solution matrix

$$(D'YD)^{-1}$$

since $D = D_T$ is a unit matrix.

We can also extend this for updating the nodal solution matrix

$$(A'YA)^{-1} = Z_1 - Z_1 A'L(A'LZ_1 A_L + Z_L)^{-1} A_L Z_1$$

Here

$$Z_1 = B_T^t Z_T B_T$$

Now, to update the nodal solution matrix when a single branch resistance between nodes p and q is changed, we can assume that this is done by adding resistance in parallel. If the nodal solution matrix for the network has been computed, this matrix can be interpreted as the impedance matrix Z_T of a tree having the configuration shown in Figure 5-20. B_T for this tree is a unit matrix, so we can substitute Z_T for Z_1 above and thus update the nodal solution matrix one link at a time. We can also use the above equation recursively by adding several links, one after the other. However, as we step through several different values, roundoff errors will accumulate from one step to the next.

We will now consider some techniques that can be used to reduce these roundoff errors. A straight line is one of the most basic functions in a class of functions called *orthogonal polynomials*. These functions can serve as an approximation to help reduce the number of calculations and errors due to roundoff. Other functions can be used, but then the calculations become more complex.

In the general case, the orthogonal polynomial fitting of data seeks to find coefficients a_1, a_2, a_3, ... for the polynomial values $P_1(x)$, $P_2(x)$, $P_3(x)$, ... for the equation

$$y = a_1 P_1(x) + a_2 P_2(x) + \ldots + a_n P_n(x)$$

when

$$x = 0, 1, 2, \ldots, (N - 1)$$

allows a good fit using the least-squares test. The first-order polynomial, a straight line, is also called a *regression line*. Consider the following steps in a computer solution:

1. Set $P_1 = 1$.
2. Set $P_2 = X - C$ and find

$$C = \frac{\sum\limits_{i=1}^{M} x_i W(x_i)}{\sum\limits_{i=1}^{M} W(x_i)}$$

Here $W(x_i)$ is the weighting factor for x_i.

3. Calculate each succeeding polynomial, using

$$P_{N+1} = (X - B)P_N + GP_{N-1}$$

$$B = \frac{\sum\limits_{i=1}^{M} x_i (P_N)^2 W(x_i)}{\sum\limits_{i=1}^{M} (P_N)^2 W(x_i)}$$

$$G = \frac{\sum\limits_{i=1}^{M} x_i P_N P_{N-1} W(x_i)}{\sum\limits_{i=1}^{M} (P_{N-1})^2 W(x_i)}$$

4. Calculate the coefficients a_N, where

$$a_N = \frac{\sum\limits_{i=1}^{M} Y_i P_N}{\sum\limits_{i=1}^{M} (P_N)^2}$$

5. Group the corresponding coefficients of similar terms to obtain the coefficients of each power of X for the polynomial fit.

As an example, assume we wish to write a program that will accept a number of values of two variables as well as the weighting values to fit the input value to a curve that may range from a minimum to a maximum ordered value specified curve. Let us use the following names for the curve-fitting program:

X	First variable
Y	Second variable
NLOP	Order of lowest-order polynomial that fits data
NHOP	Order of highest-order polynomial that fits data
M	Total number of X or Y data values
K	An indicator specifying whether the X values are weighted. If $K \neq 0$, the X values are not weighted. If $K = 0$, the weighted values are read with X and Y.
W	Weighting factor
P	Polynomials
XSUM	Sum of X values
YSUM	Sum of Y values
A	Coefficients of polynomials

The flow chart is shown in Figure 5-21.

We have seen that a best-fit line through a set of points is called a regression line, and the determination of the equation of this line is called *regression analysis*. Since it is difficult to predict the curve fit of even a straight line of the form $y = a + bx$ to a set of data points involving two variables, we determine mathematically the values of a and b from the paired values (x_1, y_1), $(x_2, y_2), \ldots, (x_n, y_n)$. We can also plot the points to determine if the data seems to cluster about a straight line in a linear trend and if the clustering is normally distributed.

Regression analysis can also give us a set of numerical values which measure the confidence or reliability that can be placed on the fit obtained. This confidence level is similar to making a statement such as, "We are 60 percent confident that the system will last an average of 10,000 hours."

The steps discussed above can be summarized as follows:

1. Given a set of data relating factor y to factor x, we assume a linear relationship.

2. We check this assumption by data analysis or plotting.

3. We compute the coefficients of $y = a + b(x - \bar{x})$, where $\bar{x}$ is the average of the x observations.

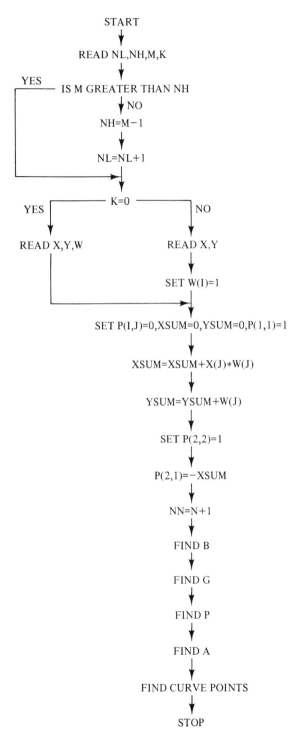

Figure 5-21 Curve-fitting program.

249

4. We compute the confidence figures for the fit and for the projections made using this fit.

For a system with n pairs of data points $(x_1, y_1), (x_2, y_2), \ldots, (x_n, y_n)$, the major quantities are

$$\bar{x} = \frac{1}{n} \sum_{i=1}^{n} x_i$$

$$\bar{y} = \frac{1}{n} \sum_{i=1}^{n} y_i$$

$$a = \bar{y}$$

and

$$b = \frac{\displaystyle\sum_{i=1}^{n} (x_i - \bar{x}) y_i}{\displaystyle\sum_{i=1}^{n} (x_i - \bar{x})^2}$$

As an example, suppose we wish a linear regression analysis for the following data:

x	y
1.0	3.0
2.0	5.8
3.0	9.2

The data is tested to ensure that a linear trend exists. A plot shows that the data points appear to follow a linear trend. From the data the following quantities are computed:

x_i	y_i	$x_i - \bar{x}$	$(x_i - \bar{x})^2$	$y_i - \bar{y}$	$(y_i - \bar{y})^2$	$(x_i - \bar{x})/y_i$
1.0	3.0	−1.0	1.0	−3.0	9.0	−3.0
2.0	5.8	0.0	0	−0.2	0.04	0
3.0	9.2	1.0	1.0	3.2	10.24	9.2
6.0	18.0	0	2.0	0	19.28	6.2

From these we compute

$$\bar{x} = 2.0$$
$$\bar{y} = 6.0$$

and for the regression coefficients

$$a = 6.0$$
$$b = 3.1$$

The equation of the line is then

$$y = -0.2 + 3.1x$$

We note that the original x, y pairs do not satisfy this equation exactly, so the residual errors are computed from

$$e_i = y_i - [6.0 + 3.1(x - 2.0)]$$

Thus

$$e_1 = 0.1$$
$$e_2 = -0.2$$
$$e_3 = 0.1$$

We note that the sum of the residual errors is zero.

Suppose we wish to write a program which determines the best linear fit for this data. We compute using the form:

$$b = \frac{\sum_{i=1}^{n} x_i y_i - n\bar{x}\bar{y}}{\sum_{i=1}^{n} x_i^2 - n\bar{x}^2}$$

We assign the following names for this linear regression program:

X	Variable
Y	Variable
XMEAN	Mean of X values
YMEAN	Mean of Y values
A,B	Coefficients of linear fit
N,P	Number of paired values
XSUM	Sum of X values
YSUM	Sum of Y values
XXSUM	Sum of X^2 values
XYSUM	Sum of X times Y values

XEST   Value of X used for prediction

YEST   Predicted value of Y

The flow chart is shown in Figure 5-22.

There are two areas of concern about the computed regression line:

1. How good or reliable is the straight-line fit?
2. What confidence can we have in the prediction using this straight-line fit?

The first concern can be answered using a measure of the adequacy of the fit, r^2, which is called the *coefficient of determination*. This can be found from

$$r^2 = \frac{\left[\sum_{i=1}^{n} (x_i - \bar{x})(y_i - \bar{y})\right]^2}{\sum_{i=1}^{n} (x_i - \bar{x})^2 \sum_{i=1}^{n} (y_i - \bar{y})^2}$$

In the case where all the points lie on the line, $r^2 = 1.0$, and 100% of the variation of y is taken by the fit. If $r^2 = 0.6$, then 60% of the variation is accounted for and the other 40% is the residual error or variation about the line.

The value of r also has a statistical meaning, where it is called the *correlation coefficient*. We can compute r or r^2 independently of the regression

Figure 5-22   Linear regression program.

coefficients and use this as a preliminary test to determine the degree of the relationship in a paired data set. The correlation coefficient may range from $+1$ to -1. A $+1$ value shows 100% correlation, a -1 value shows an inverse correlation of 100%, and a 0 value shows no correlation at all of the paired data-set values. For computational purposes we can write the correlation coefficient as

$$ r = \frac{n \sum_{i=1}^{n} x_i y_i - \sum_{i=1}^{n} x_i \sum_{i=1}^{n} y_i}{\sqrt{\left[n \sum_{i=1}^{n} x_i^2 - \left(\sum_{i=1}^{n} x_i \right)^2 \right] \left[n \sum_{i=1}^{n} y_i^2 - \left(\sum_{i=1}^{n} y_i \right)^2 \right]}} $$

Suppose we wish to write a program to calculate the correlation coefficient. We assign the following names for this correlation coefficient program:

NP	Number of paired values
XSUM	Sum of X values
YSUM	Sum of Y values
XYSUM	Sum of X times Y values
XXSUM	Sum of X times X values
YYSUM	Sum of Y times Y values
X	Variable
Y	Variable
D	Value of denominator
R	Correlation coefficient

The flow chart for this program is shown in Figure 5-23.

When $r^2 < 1.0$, there is a range over which the regression coefficients a and b may vary. This range or confidence bound can be determined by

$$ a - t \sqrt{\frac{s^2}{n}} \le \text{range of } a \le a + t \sqrt{\frac{s^2}{n}} $$

$$ b - t \sqrt{\frac{s^2}{\sum_{i=1}^{n} (x_i - \bar{x})^2}} \le \text{range of } b \le b + t \sqrt{\frac{s^2}{\sum_{i=1}^{n} (x_i - \bar{x})^2}} $$

where

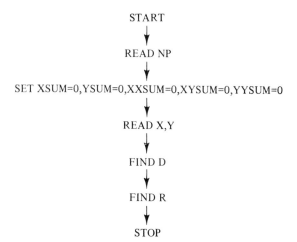

Figure 5-23 Correlation-coefficient program.

$$s^2 = \frac{1}{n-2} \left[\sum_{i=1}^{n} (y_i - \bar{y})^2 - b^2 \sum_{i=1}^{n} (x_i - \bar{x})^2 \right]$$

The true value of a and b lies between these confidence bounds. The value of t can be found from a student's t table. These tables, which can be found in most books on statistics, are available for the purpose of computing the confidence intervals for regression equations with finite sample pairs. Several entries from such a table are shown below:

Confidence levels (student's t table)

$n - 2$	50%	90%	95%	99%
1	1.000	6.314	12.706	63.657
10	0.700	1.812	2.228	3.169
20	0.687	1.725	2.086	2.845

Suppose we wish to be 90% confident of the value of a; from the table, we find that $t = 6.314$ for $n = 3$. For the above example

$$s^2 = \frac{1}{1}(19.28 - 19.22) = 0.06$$

Thus we are 90% confident the true value of a lies within the range from 5.107 to 6.893, as computed from the above equations.

The fit is generally accepted as reliable if the computed range of a and b is small with respect to the value of a and b. If $a = 8 \pm 5$, the results cannot be too reliable regardless of the value of r^2. It is always important to know the ranges or confidence bounds on a and b. In the example given above, the range is quite small.

Our other concern has to do with the confidence we can have in the prediction that is made using regression analysis. We have discussed the confidence bounds on a and b but, there are also confidence bounds that can be determined for y:

$$a + b(x - \bar{x}) - p \leq \text{range of } y \leq a + b(x - \bar{x}) + p$$

Here

$$p = ts \sqrt{1 + \frac{1}{n} + \frac{(x - \bar{x})^2}{\sum_{i=1}^{n} (x_i - \bar{x})^2}}$$

and t is taken from a table, as discussed above.

AC Circuits

All our work up to this point applies to complex as well as to real numbers, so steady-state ac circuit problems can be handled using any of the basic methods of analysis described. By programming the Gaussian elimination procedure for complex arithmetic, the mesh or nodal equations for an ac problem can be solved at a computational cost of about four times that for real numbers. But now the coefficient matrix is frequency-dependent, so the equations must be solved at each frequency. This approach is common, but it may produce some reduced numerical accuracy in the vicinity of a resonant frequency.

Another technique, which is based on the hybrid method of analysis, approaches the task of matrix inversion by first solving the more difficult problem of computing the eigenvalues and eigenvectors of the matrix. Solving the eigenvalue problem seems to be the wrong approach, since the computational effort required is about an order of magnitude greater than that for inverting a matrix. This is true if only a single inverse matrix is needed. But since we are calculating the frequency response, a new inverse with a new solution vector is needed for each frequency. Thus, using the eigenvalues and eigenvectors reduces the problem to one of inverting a diagonal matrix for each frequency.

We can derive the differential equations for an *RLC* network of first-order form as follows. All capacitors can be treated as admittance branches, and these may have a nonzero conductance in parallel. The admittance matrix is

$$Y_y = pK + G$$

Here

$$p = \frac{d}{dt}$$

and K is used for the capacitance. Inductors are regarded as impedance branches with resistance in series; thus the impedance matrix is

$$Z_z = pL + R$$

Using these equations, we can write the differential equations for a constant K and L as

$$
\begin{bmatrix} D_y^t K D_y & 0 \\ 0 & C_z^t L C_z \end{bmatrix} \begin{bmatrix} pe_{Ty} \\ pi_{LZ} \end{bmatrix} + \begin{bmatrix} D_y^t G D_y & -C_{Tyz} \\ C_{Tyz}^t & C_z^t R C_z \end{bmatrix} \begin{bmatrix} e_{Ty} \\ i_{Lz} \end{bmatrix} = \begin{bmatrix} I_T \\ E_L \end{bmatrix}
$$

Here I_T and E_L designate the driving currents and voltages. Using the more compact form, we can write

$$P\dot{x} + Qx = f(t)$$

Here

$$\dot{x} = \frac{dx}{dt}$$

x is the state-variable vector of the capacitive tree-branch voltages and inductive link currents. Inverting P, we can write the last equation as

$$\dot{x} = Ax + g(t)$$

where

$$g = P^{-1}f$$
$$A = -p^{-1}Q$$

This A matrix should not be confused with the branch-node matrix A, which will not be referred to here.

Under steady-state ac conditions, the driving function becomes

$$g(t) = g_0 e^{st}$$

where s is a complex number. The steady-state response is

$$x(t) = x_0 e^{st}$$

Combining these relations we obtain a linear system of equations defined by

$$(sU - A)x_0 = g_0$$

Here g_0 is a known vector and x_0 is the vector to be determined. The solution for x_0 is

$$x_0 = (sU - A)^{-1}g_0$$

An effective way of computing $(sU - A)^{-1}$ uses the eigenvalues λ_i and the eigenvectors x_i of the A-matrix. Assume that the λ_i are distinct; then let $\bar{A}$ be the diagonal matrix of eigenvalues and X be the matrix with columns and of the corresponding eigenvectors. The eigenproblem, then, becomes

$$AX = X\bar{A}$$

or

$$X^{-1}AX = \bar{A}$$

This defines a similarity transformation which diagonalizes the matrix A. The same transformation can also diagonalize $(sU - A)$, resulting in

$$X^{-1}(sU - A)X = sU - A$$

If we solve this expression for $(sU - A)$ and then invert, we obtain

$$(sU - A)^{-1} = X(sU - \bar{A})^{-1}X^{-1}g_0$$

so the solution for x_0 becomes

$$x_0 = X(sU - \bar{A})^{-1}X^{-1}$$

This is the basic technique of this method, which requires the inversion of the diagonal matrix $(sU - \bar{A})$ for each frequency. If we let $d = X^{-1}g_0$, then the ith element of the x_0 vector may be found from

$$x_i = \sum_{j=1}^{n} \frac{x_{ij}d_j}{s - \lambda_j}$$

This partial-fraction expansion of the state variable x_i requires an evaluated number of computations proportional to n operations for each frequency instead of $n^{3/3}$ operations if Gaussian elimination were used. Solving the eigenproblem is equivalent to using the elimination method for ten frequencies. Thus, this method would not be used if solutions were required at only a few frequencies, but for a complete frequency-response calculation it can be very effective. The method is better suited for computerized problems than Laplace transform techniques using ratios of polynomials and poles and zeros. The task of computing the coefficients of the polynomials in a network is not only time-consuming but also prone to serious numerical problems, especially when the polynomials are of high degree. The topological formula approach to computing these network functions involves finding all the trees of a network and then computing the sum of the corresponding tree-admittance products. But the number of trees may be very large, even in a circuit with only 20 or so nodes. The computation of the roots of the polynomials can also be a problem because the roots may be sensitive to errors in the coefficients. The polynomial approach is not always matched well to the analysis which the computer is called to undertake.

The eigenvalue approach may be better suited, and it gives all the information that the Laplace transform methods provide. The eigenvalues are identical with the poles of the network functions, and the network sensitivity can be obtained, either with respect to frequency or some other network parameter including the pole sensitivities.

The eigenvalue method may also present some difficulties. It is possible that large numerical errors may occur when circuits having a very large ratio of greatest to smallest eigenvalue are analyzed. The difficulty is that, although the large eigenvalues can be computed accurately, the small ones cannot, and it is the small eigenvalues which principally determine the behavior of the circuit.

A possible cure for this situation is to solve the eigenvalue problem for the inverse matrix A^{-1}. Then the situation is reversed and the large eigenvalues of A^{-1}, which will be obtained accurately, are the reciprocals of the small eigenvalues of A. Computing A^{-1} may cause some errors or problems because of the large ratio of eigenvalues. But if the Q matrix is nonsingular, then we use

$$A^{-1} = -Q^{-1}P$$

which should compute a more accurate inverse for A.

Even if we are to compute the eigenvalues accurately, then the corresponding eigenvectors must be accurately determined if they exist, and they may not in some cases. It may be required to disturb the matrix A slightly to remove the multiplicities and yield distinct eigenvalues and eigenvectors.

If we use the corresponding expression for $f(t)$, then

$$x_0 = [X(sU - \bar{A})^{-1}X^{-1}P^{-1}]f_0 = Tf_0$$

The new matrix T has elements which we can call the *basic response functions* of the network, since they relate the elements of x_0, the basic response vector, to the elements of f_0, the basic excitation vector.

The diagonal elements T_{ii} are driving-point impedances if they relate an element of e_{Ty} to the corresponding element of I_T. They become driving-point admittances if they relate an element of i_{Lz} to the corresponding element of E_1.

The off-diagonal elements T_{ij} are transfer impedances, admittances, or functions, depending on which elements of the subvectors e_{Ty}, i_{Lz}, I_T, and E_L they are involved with. Note that I_T and E_L will account for the voltage of current sources in every branch, and since every branch voltage and/or branch current can be computed in terms of e_{Ty} and i_z, the elements of the matrix T will completely determine the driving-point and transfer functions of the circuit. This occurs when the basic response function matrix T has been appropriately partitioned as shown below:

$$\begin{bmatrix} e_y \\ i_z \end{bmatrix} = \begin{bmatrix} D_y T_{yy} D'_y & D_y T_{yz} C'_z \\ C_z T_{zy} D'_y & C_z T_{zz} C'_z \end{bmatrix} \begin{bmatrix} I_y \\ E_z \end{bmatrix}$$

This equation defines most of the driving-point and transfer functions explicitly. For example, the elements of $D_y T_{yy} D'_y$ will correspond to the driving-point and transfer impedances of the capacitive branches. The elements $D_y T_{yz} C'_z$ will correspond to the transfer functions relating the voltage excitations in each inductive branch to the response voltages in each capacitive branch.

Using

$$W = X^{-1}P^{-1}$$

which needs to be computed only once, the desired response function may be found using the following partial fraction expansion:

$$T_{ij} = \sum_{k=1}^{n} \frac{x_{ik} w_{kj}}{\lambda - 2_k}$$

The computations are again proportional to n operations for each frequency. Because the eigenvalues have already been computed, the poles of T_{ij} are known. The zeros could be found using a root-finding procedure.

Transient Circuit Problems

Among the types of circuit problems under discussion, transient problems present the greatest computational difficulty. The numerical integration of the differential equations can be complex for nonlinear networks and time-consuming when the network has a wide spread of eigenvalues. The eigenvalue problem has been discussed earlier in this chapter.

Consider the analytical solution of the state-variable equations for a linear network with constant parameters. If we assume a solution of the form:

$$x(t) = e^{At}v(t)$$

then $v(t)$ is a vector function of time and e^{At} is defined by the matrix function

$$e^{At} = U + At + \frac{(At)^2}{2!} + \frac{(At)^3}{3!} + \cdots$$

Once a time history of the circuit response is obtained, the network equations which contain the initial state variables can be solved using matrix operations that produce state-variable derivatives, which can be numerically integrated to produce new state variables for the evaluation at the next time step. Thus, the state variable S at time $i + 1$ can be evaluated from

$$S(i + 1) = S(i) + \Delta t \dot{S}_{(i)}$$

Here Δt is the time step between the evaluations. After we compute the derivatives of the state variables by numerical integration, the variable elements and sources are updated and the system of network equations is then evaluated at the next time step. The value of each element voltage and current is available at each time step. This procedure is shown in Figure 5-24. The repetitive evaluation of the transient solution and the integration of the state-variable derivatives produces a time history of the network response. The solution of the circuit equations depends on integrating the differential equations describing the state variables at each time step. The rate at which the solution proceeds depends on the method of performing this integration. The two basic methods used are:

1. Single-step methods which do not depend on the past history of the solution. The most common of these is the Runge-Kutta method.

2. Multistep methods in which the next solution point is obtained from previous solutions. Methods of this type fall into the predictor-corrector category.

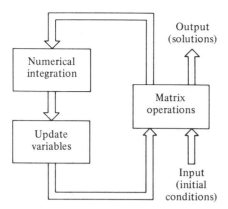

Figure 5-24   The basic numerical integration procedure as it is used in transient analysis.

The general process takes place as follows:

1. Choose a starting point.
2. Compute the slope and move in that direction for a short distance.
3. Select the next point.
4. Repeat steps 1 and 2.
5. Continue on to additional points.

Control of the errors between the true solution and the computed solution is difficult with this simplified method, so usually a slightly different procedure is used. In this method the solution to the first-order differential equation

$$\frac{dx}{dt} = f(x, t)$$

effectively replaces the result of truncating a Taylor-series expansion of the form

$$x_{n+1} = x_n + hx_n + \frac{h^2}{2!} x_n + \frac{h^3}{3!} x_n + \cdots$$

using an approximation in which x_{n+1} is calculated from a formula of the type

$$x_{n+1} = x_{n-p} + h(a_{-1}\dot{x}_{n-1} + a_0\dot{x}_n + a_1\dot{x}_{n-1} + \cdots + a_r\dot{x}_{n-r})$$

In the special case where $f(x, t) = Ax$, where A is a constant, the formula becomes

$$(1 - a_{-1}Ah)x_{n+1} = x_{n-p} + Ah(a_0x_n + a_1x_{n-1} + \cdots + a_rx_{n-r})$$

Here at least one of the coefficients of a_r is nonzero. The general solution for this equation is

$$x_n = c_0p_0^n + c_1p_1^n + \cdots + c_rp_r^n$$

The c coefficients are determined by the initial values of $x_1, \ldots, x_{r-1}$, and $p_1, p_2, \ldots, p_r$ are the roots of the characteristic equation expansion obtained by substituting the particular solution $x_n = p^nx_0$ into that formula, as discussed before.

We have also noted that the principal solution is generated by one of the roots, while the other $r - 1$ roots represent parasitic solutions. The parasitic solutions result since the order of the difference equation exceeds the order of the approximated differential equation by r. When any one of the parasitic roots is greater than unity, the corresponding term in the general solution increases without limits as n increases. This condition, which we have discussed before, is called numerical instability, and it occurs when the integration interval h is too large.

The following two formulas which can be used for numerical integration employ Milne's method:

1. Predictor-based:

$$x_{n+1} = x_{n-3} + \frac{4h}{3}(2\dot{x}_n - \dot{x}_{n-1} + 2\dot{x}_{n-2}) + \frac{14}{45}h^5x^{(5)}(\mu)$$

2. Corrector-based:

$$x_{n+1} = x_{n-1} + \frac{h}{3}(\dot{x}_{n+1} + 4\dot{x}_n + \dot{x}_{n-1}) - \frac{h^5}{90}x^{(5)}(\mu)$$

Here the values of μ lie between the largest and smallest argument involved in the formulas, and in general these are not equal.

In order to avoid numerical instability with the above integration formulas the solution is expressed as

$$\dot{x} = -ax + b$$

Then the integration step h must satisfy

$$ha \le 0.83$$

In the network equations a will be a matrix, so the above restriction on the integration step size requires that h be less than the smallest natural time constant of the network. These roots contribute least to the solution, but they force the numerical integration to be dependent on them and thus contain the allowable error in the solution. Thus, in designing a system for solving the set of differential equations, it is desirable to use as large a value for h as possible.

Also, we can consider a transformation of variables such as

$$y = T^{-1}x$$

Then

$$T\dot{y} = ATy + g(t)$$

or

$$\dot{y} = T^{-1}ATy + T^{-1}g(t)$$

The solution is

$$y(t + h) = e^{\bar{D}h}y(t) + \int_0^h e^{\bar{D}(h-\tau)}[\bar{B}y(t + \tau) + w(t + \tau)] \, d\tau$$

where $w(t) = T^{-1}g(t)$.

This allows us to solve the original problem by transforming to the domain of the new variable y before integrating. From the solution and the relation

$$x = Ty$$

we can find a solution to

$$\dot{x} = Ax + g(t)$$

If T is chosen to reduce $\lambda_{max}(\bar{B})$ sufficiently, a larger integration step h may be used without risking numerical instability. This is discussed in the following example.

An RC network is shown in Figure 5-25. If all resistances and all capacitances are equal, the maximum integration step is approximately equal to the time constant, RC. If we modify the circuit, dividing C_3 in half and adding resistor r, which has a small value compared to R, the integration step will be limited by the time constant rC. The state-variable vector used for both networks could consist of all capacitor voltages. But if a different combination of voltages is used in the second network—for example, the voltages across capacitors C_1, C_2, C_4, and C_5 and the sum and difference of the voltages

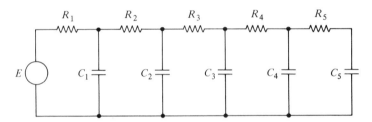

Figure 5-25 Illustrative network.

across the two split capacitors—it is possible to increase the integration step size until it is equal to that used in the first circuit. This change of variables produced a transformation which reduced the maximum eigenvalue of $\bar{B}$.

What we have done to affect the minimum time-constant problem is operate on the coefficient matrix A in a meaningful way. If the A matrix is left intact, then we must accept the limitations on the integration step size.

The simplest type of operation on the A matrix is to extract its diagonal terms. The next more difficult operation is to transform the matrix, and the next is to solve the eigenproblem.

There are also some guidelines to follow in the integration problem in nonlinear systems, where the Jacobian matrix now plays the role of the A matrix. Solving the eigenproblem repeatedly is inappropriate, since the Jacobian matrix changes during the course of the solution.

Finding a transformation for T seems plausible. It is not necessary to update T at each integration step, since a transformation could be used for many integrations before becoming degraded. The feasibility of this approach depends not only on minimizing the frequency of updating T but also on developing an algorithm for computing the transformation.

If the average computational time per integration step can be made proportional to the square of the number of equations, then the minimum time-constant problem can be handled for nonlinear problems as well as for linear. Besides the formulas for integrating each step, it may be required in order to prevent numerical instability to use formulas for the integration interval. The criteria for when to use these are based on comparing the predicted and corrected values.

In contrast to the predictor-corrector methods, Runge-Kutta methods do not use information from previously calculated points and thus are self-starting. They are generally used in starting the methods that do require previous solution points.

In both the predictor-corrector and Runge-Kutta integration methods automatic control of the step size is possible. Predictor-corrector methods may require two derivative evaluations per time step instead of four for the Runge-Kutta method.

The extra derivative evaluations for the Runge-Kutta method are not as serious a drawback if one estimates the local truncation error in the Taylor-series expansion of the solution and, using this error, defines smaller steps in the transient region and larger steps in the steady-state region. The solution can then progress at a rate that depends on the numerical integration errors.

Most integration methods are linear in the sense that the value of the function at a point is expressed as a linear combination of function values and derivative values at this point and at previous points. A modification of this linear method uses an exponential term in the integration routine to provide better stability and allow a larger integration step to be taken. Exponential integration methods have been used in a number of general-purpose network-analysis programs. The exponential method reduces the computing time for a large system of ordinary differential equations in which there is a large spread of time constants.

SENSITIVITY AND WORST-CASE ANALYSIS

The sensitivity of system performance to changes in a system parameter is an important design parameter. There are several ways of obtaining sensitivity information:

1. Matrix inversion.
2. Varying the system parameter slightly and noting changes in the performance criterion (the perturbational method).
3. Symbolic manipulation.

This last method can be handled within the framework of the tree approach to the network problem or by signal-flow graphs. The procedures in these two cases are similar.

Sensitivity criteria relate to two parameters:

P, the system performance criterion.

Q, the system parameter.

G_Q is called the *large-signal sensitivity coefficient*. If P is the voltage at the output of an amplifier and Q is the input voltage to the same amplifier, G_Q indicates how sensitive the output voltage is to the input voltage. This is commonly call the gain:

$$G_Q = \frac{P}{Q}$$

B_Q is called the *small-signal sensitivity coefficient*. If P is the small-signal voltage from the base to the emitter of a transistor and Q is the collector-to-emitter small-signal voltage, then B_Q represents the reverse voltage amplification factor h:

$$B_Q = \frac{dp}{dQ}$$

S_Q is known as the *systematic-variation sensitivity*. This coefficient is the reciprocal of the classical or Bode sensitivity. This sensitivity coefficient relates a relative change in parameter variation to the relative change in system performance:

$$S_Q = \frac{d(\ln P)}{d(\ln Q)}$$

There are other sensitivity criteria, including the *zero-sensitivity*, which shows the ratio of the change in a zero location in the s plane to the fractional change in a parameter.

To determine the classical sensitivity, we note that

$$S_Q = \frac{d(\ln P)}{d(\ln Q)} = \frac{B_Q}{G_Q}$$

Once the sensitivity coefficients are found, a worst-case evaluation or analysis can be performed. Basically this amounts to the determination of whether to let a particular parameter take on the upper or lower limit of its tolerance. The tolerance-limit choice depends upon whether a worst-case maximum or minimum of the performance criteria is to be determined.

If the worst-case maximum is to be found, then all the partial derivatives of the form

$$\frac{\partial P}{\partial Q_i}$$

are found. If this derivative for a particular Q is positive, then set Q_i to

$$Q_i + \Delta Q$$

If it is negative, set Q_i to

$$Q_i - \Delta Q_i$$

The performance criteria can now be calculated for the new Q_i and the sign of

$$\frac{\partial p}{\partial (Q_n \pm \Delta Q)}$$

rechecked for each

$$Q_i \pm \Delta Q_i$$

If the signs do not change, then the worst-case maximum has been found. If some of the signs have changed, then the problem becomes more difficult and we revert to a Monte Carlo technique. Similar techniques are used to obtain the worst-case minimum. The necessary steps in the basic algorithm are shown in Figure 5-26.

We have noted that if the range of circuit variation is large enough and many integration steps are taken, the errors may eventually become serious enough to affect the results. A better technique, but one requiring more memory space, is to update only the original nodal solution matrix each time.

By extending the idea of updating the nodal solution matrix to take into account changes of a single value, differential changes can be dealt with. So

Model the physical problem with ideal elements. (This becomes the equivalent network or system.)
Describe the functional V-I relationships for each element.
Describe how the elements are interconnected.
Choose the elements which are to be tree branches.
Find the nonredundant part of the cutset and circuit matrix.
Develop the signal-flow graph.
Insert the dependencies into the graph.
Close the signal-flow graph with the reciprocal of the system performance criteria which is desired.
Search the feedback loops for those which contain the system performance criteria.
Search for the loops where S_Q is not an explicit function of P.
Find S_Q.

Figure 5-26   Signal-flow graph sensitivity determination.

that the partial derivative or sensitivity of the nodal solution matrix with respect to any change can be computed explicitly, we can show this relation by differentiating the nodal equations. We obtain

$$A^t(dI - Y\, dE - dY\, E) = A^t\, dY\, Ae' + A^tYA\, de'$$

or

$$\mathrm{de}' = (A^tYA)^{-1}\, A^t[dI - Y\, dE - dY(E + e)]$$

This expression gives the variation in node voltages as a function not only of the changes in resistance as specified by dY but also of changes in the I and E vectors. This equation is used in some general circuit-analysis programs for computing sensitivities.

NONLINEAR NETWORKS

A basic method for solving nonlinear problems is the Newton-Raphson iteration method. This method will be described in terms of the nodal equations. Assume that the nonlinearities are voltage-dependent. Then we can write the admittance matrix as

$$Y(V)$$

The network problem requires that we solve the following system of equations:

$$f(e) \equiv A^t[Y(V)(Ae' + E) - I] = 0$$

Here $f(e')$ is a nonlinear vector function of the vector variable e'.

For a given vector e', the function $f(e')$ may not be exactly zero, and f is the error vector. A change de' will cause a corresponding change df, as shown below:

$$df = \left(\frac{\partial f}{\partial e'}\right) de'$$

Here $(\partial f / \partial e')$ is the Jacobian matrix with jk elements defined by

$$\left(\frac{\partial f}{\partial e'}\right)_{jk} = \frac{\partial f_j}{\partial e'_k}$$

Here f_j is the jth element of the vector $f(e')$ and e'_k is the kth element of the vector e'.

Now we will need some iterative scheme to solve the network equations. If the ith approximation $e'_{(i)}$ to the solution vector, $f_{(i)} = f(e'_{(i)})$, is not zero, then from the above equation the approximate change in $e'_{(i)}$ required to reduce $f_{(i)}$ to zero can be found from

$$df_{(i)} = -f_{(i)} \left(\frac{\partial f}{\partial e'} \right)_{(i)} de'_{(i)}$$

Then the $(i + 1)$th approximation to the solution vector e' is

$$e'_{(i'+1)} = e'_{(i)} - \left(\frac{\partial f}{\partial e'} \right)^{-1}_{(i)} f_{(i)}$$

This is known as the *Newton-Raphson recursion formula*. For a well-behaved system, this method converges quadratically. In other cases it may diverge or oscillate from a solution. This formula also requires the inverse of the Jacobian matrix of the system at each iteration, which can present some computational-time problems. There are modifications of the basic Newton-Raphson technique which avoid these major drawbacks. Some of these methods cannot diverge, since they never allow the length of vector f_i to increase. They may also provide a way to update the inverse Jacobian matrix at each iteration, starting with an approximation to this inverse. As indicated above, the Newton-Raphson formula states that a certain correction vector shall be applied to the ith approximation to the desired solution vector. Without the parentheses around the iteration indices, we define this correction vector as

$$p_i = -\left(\frac{\partial f}{\partial e'} \right)^{-1}_i f_i$$

Now the Newton-Raphson formula becomes

$$e'_i + 1 = e'_i + p_i$$

Suppose we do not use this full correction, but use only a part of it, as shown below:

$$e'_{i+1} = e'_i + t_i p_i$$

Here the scalar t_i is chosen so as to minimize or reduce the length of the error vector f_{i+1} relative to that of f_i. Thus, divergence of the iteration is prevented, but convergence may not necessarily occur. But suppose we had an algorithm for computing an approximation to the inverse Jacobian matrix, an approximation which improved as the iteration scheme converged to a solution.

Consider the vector e' above as a continuous function of the scalar variable t in the expression; then we can write

$$e'(t) = e_i' + tp_i$$

This tends to imply that the error vector $f(e')$ is also a function of t. Then the Jacobian matrix becomes that

$$\frac{df}{dt} = \left(\frac{\partial f}{\partial e'}\right)\frac{de'}{dt} = \left(\frac{\partial f}{\partial e'}\right)p_i$$

where

$$\frac{de'}{dt} = p_i$$

Now let H_i be an approximation to the negative of the inverse Jacobian matrix; then we can write

$$p_i = -H_i\frac{df}{dt}$$

We know we can compute df/dt by differencing, so define f_{i+1} as $f(t_i)$, and then we can expand $f(t_i - s)$ as a Taylor series about t_i and retain only the first term in the expansion. Thus we obtain an approximation

$$\frac{df}{dt} \approx \frac{f_{i+1} - f(t_i - s_i)}{s_i} = \frac{y_i}{s_i}$$

Here s_i is chosen to be a small increment in the scalar variable t, and y_i is the corresponding increment in the error vector f.

Since no information is obtained when there is a change in the error vector f due to changes in e' in any direction other than p_i, there is no change in f due to changes of e' in any direction orthogonal to p_i. This results in the following recursion formula:

$$H_{i+1} = H_i - \frac{(s_i p_i + H_i y_i)p_i^t H_i}{p_i^t H_i y_i}$$

We can use this to update the inverse Jacobian matrix without computing the Jacobian itself or inverting it.

We can let $t = 0.1, 0.2, 0.3, \ldots$ and evaluate the magnitude of each corresponding error vector until a minimum is reached. The value of s_i can then be chosen as 0.1, and y_i then is the difference between the minimum f and the f corresponding to the next smaller value of t. The above technique can be used to study the $|f^2|$ versus t curve, but it tends to be inefficient. For more general use, we can let $s_i = t_i$, regardless of how t_i is determined. We can view this as the full-step method, and the above technique as the incremental method. For a single or nominal solution the incremental method is best, but for a statistical analysis the following adaptation of the full-step method is effective. The algorithm in Figure 5-27 can be used for solving nonlinear dc circuits.

Here ε is the convergency criterion. Since the inverse Jacobian matrix is full, no special programming techniques are needed in the first step of the iteration. This step requires a matrix-vector multiplication with N^2 operations of multiplying and adding, where N is the number of nodal equations. The test for convergency occurs when the length of the correction vector p_i relative to that of the solution vector e_i' is negligible. Here we could use a Fibonacci search technique for determining the optimum value of t_i.

The Fibonacci search is based on subdividing the interval $t = (0, 1)$ into successively smaller subintervals and directing the next search above or below the current value of t according to the outcome of the evaluation of the system equations.

To start this process, we set $t = 1$, and if the corresponding value of

$$|f^2_{i+1}|$$

is less than

$$|f^2_i|$$

then we use the value $t_i = 1$ as the optimum. This permits the detection of the Newtonian mode which characterizes the iteration close to the point of convergence. When the choice $t = 1$ results in $|f^2_{i+1}|$ being larger than $|f^2_i|$, a multistep Fibonacci search can be used. Three or four steps are usually adequate, since we can reduce the length of the error vector f_{i+1} and pass on to the next iteration. A more refined Fibonacci search will not greatly decrease the total number of iterations required. If the Fibonacci search does not result in a reduction in length of the error vector, this indicates that the minimum error vector corresponds to $t = 0$, and the iteration cannot proceed.

This result may be due to a poor approximation to the inverse Jacobian. We can restart the procedure by computing $(A'\tilde{Y}A)^{-1}$, where $\tilde{Y} = \partial J/\partial V$. If

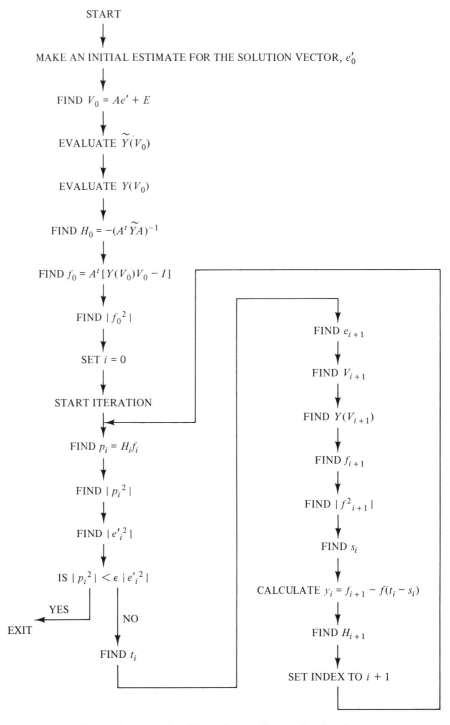

Figure 5-27 Algorithm for nonlinear dc circuits.

this fails, then we must choose a new starting vector e_0'. S_i is set to equal the last increment in t when the Fibonacci search is used; otherwise we choose $s_i = t_i = 1$. In either case, the approximate inverse Jacobian is updated. This requires the computation of two matrix-vector products, $H_i y_i$ and $p_i' H_i$, which take $2N^2$ operations of multiplying and adding, where N is the number of nodal equations. We also require an additional N^2 operations for the postmultiplication of the column vector $(s_i p_i + H_i y_i)$ by the row vector $p_i' H_i$. The updating of H_{i+1} then requires about $3N^2$ operations.

Although this method avoids computing and inverting the Jacobian matrix, that matrix, like the nodal admittance matrix, for most circuits is very sparse. If we invert the matrix $A'\tilde{Y}A$ for each iteration, then to update the inverse we may gain some processing time. We do not need to compute both $Y(V)$ and $\tilde{Y}(V)$. Only $\tilde{Y}(V)$ is needed, as we can see by referring to Figure 5-28. The tangent line at the point $(V_0 J_0)$ is the better approximation to the curve over a small range than the secant line through the origin. The tangent line defines the differential or dynamic admittance $\tilde{Y}(V)$, while the secant line is the static admittance $Y(V)$.

If the tangent line is used in place of the V-J curve, then the intercept $\tilde{I}$ must be used along with the slope $\tilde{Y}$ to define this line. If the V-J curve is represented by a differentiable function, then the formulas for both $\tilde{Y}(V)$ and

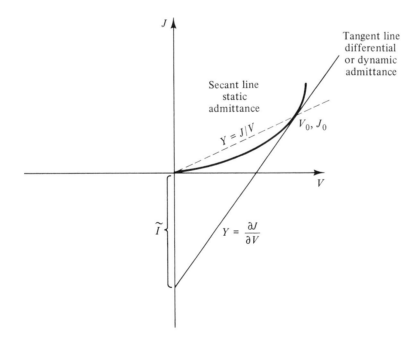

Figure 5-28 The differential and static admittance functions of nonlinear elements.

$\tilde{I}(V)$ can be coded. If a table is used to represent the V-J characteristic, then this table can be coded by a corresponding table of values of $\tilde{Y}(V)$ and $\tilde{I}(V)$. An algorithm for using the sparse-matrix technique is shown in Figure 5-29. For a multivalued nonlinear network (one that may contain tunnel diodes, for example) a different approach is needed, since there is more than one solution. One approach is to use piecewise techniques.

The Iterative Piecewise-Linear Technique

In this approach, the nonlinear resistive elements are characterized by piecewise-linear v-i curves. Each segment k of resistor R_j is specified by three parameters, as shown in Figure 5-30. These include:

1. The conductance kg_j, or the resistance kr_j.
2. The current intercept kI_j or voltage intercept kE_j.
3. A current interval of definition kI_j^-, kI_j^+, or voltage interval of kE_j^-, kE_j^+.

Owing to the piecewise-linear nature of the resistor v-i curves, each resistor k can be replaced by its Norton equivalent circuit or by its Thevenin equivalent circuit. The values of the parameters depend on the particular segment of the curve.

In a multivalued resistive network, we are interested in three major characteristics:

1. The operating point.
2. The driving-point characteristic (DP plot).
3. The transfer-characteristic (TC plot).

The operating point is the solution of interest. The DP plot is the locus of voltage and current operating points across a pair of terminals, as the terminal voltage or current takes on all values. It is the analog of the driving-point impedance for linear networks.

The TC plot is the locus of voltage or current operating points across one pair of terminals, as the voltage or current across another terminal pair takes on all values. It is the analog of the transfer function for linear networks. There is only one type of DP plot, but there are four different TC plots. For multivalued networks, both the DP plot and the TC plot can be multivalued.

In order to find the operating points, the iterative piecewise-linear method starts by assuming a segment combination for a linear network. This network can then be solved by some standard techniques, and the solution is tested to see if it agrees with the assumption. If it does, the answer is accepted

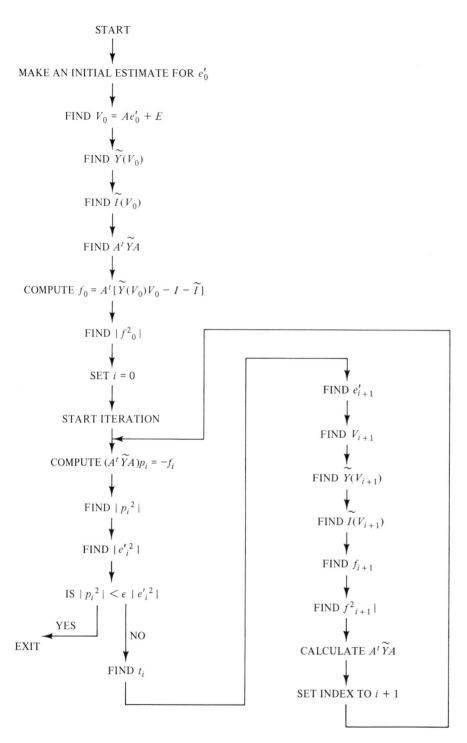

Figure 5-29 Nonlinear circuit algorithm that uses the sparse-matrix method.

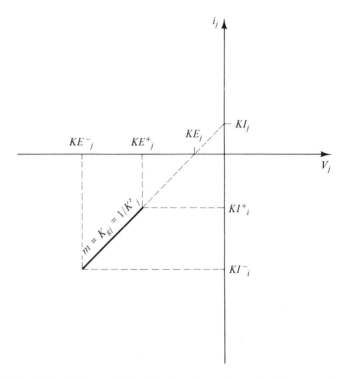

Figure 5-30 The *V-I* graph in the iterative piecewise-linear method. Each segment of the graph is equivalent to a Norton or Thevenin circuit.

as a solution. If it disagrees, the answer is rejected. In either case, the procedure is iterated by assuming another segment combination. This process is continued until all segment combinations have been exhausted. At the end of the iteration all operating points of the network should be found.

This method always converges, since only a finite number of iterations is involved, but the computer time required to run all the iterations can be large if there are many nonlinear resistors. It is desirable, therefore, to use an algorithm such that not all the iterations will be required. A simplified flow chart for such an algorithm is shown in Figure 5-31.

Depending on the requirements, a program of this type may solve only the approximate problem and exit when a suitable function has been obtained, or it may perform the realization only, from a given transfer characteristic, or, finally, it may carry out the whole task, obtaining the circuit parameters from the input specifications. The basic flow chart that can be used for these three cases is shown in Figure 5-32. The partial procedures described by the flow chart for the first two cases require that the rest of the design solution be carried out via a more exact synthesis.

In general, any part of the procedure which does not require the use of

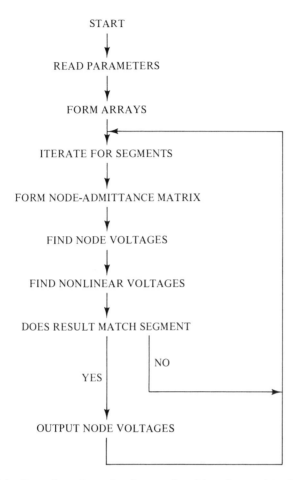

START

READ PARAMETERS

FORM ARRAYS

ITERATE FOR SEGMENTS

FORM NODE-ADMITTANCE MATRIX

FIND NODE VOLTAGES

FIND NONLINEAR VOLTAGES

DOES RESULT MATCH SEGMENT

NO

YES

OUTPUT NODE VOLTAGES

Figure 5-31 Iterative piecewise-linear algorithm for multivalued circuits.

iterative techniques should be done in a noniterative way. This is because all iterative procedures are slow, and the required computer time can be one or two orders of magnitude longer than for a comparable noniterative one.

The iterative technique may not converge at all, or the convergency may be only a local optimum, while most classical synthesis procedures will lead to a global optimum.

An iterative method should, ideally, have the following requirements:

1. Fast execution.
2. Ease of programming.
3. Ease of feeding input data and configuration parameters into the program.

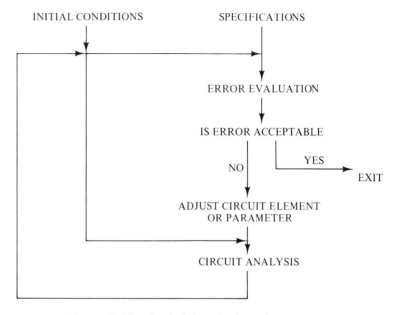

Figure 5-32   Optimizing the iterative process.

4. A readily interpreted output.

5. An assured convergence to a global optimum.

6. The flexibility to accept a wide variety of inputs and constraints.

7. Accuracy of output.

8. Insensitivity to roundoff errors and ill-conditioned inputs.

Some of these properties are contradictory, and a compromise, based on the application and use of the program, must be found. For a program that is widely and often used, for example, requirements 1, 3, and 4 outweigh requirement 2, which becomes less important as the program is used more and more, while some of the other requirements become more important.

Phase-Plane Analysis

The iterative piecewise-linear method may be used to solve all the equilibrium states of any multivalued network. The behavior of the trajectories in the vicinity of each equilibrium state can be found by a computer solution of the initial-value problems. Here the initial conditions are chosen near the equilibrium states. For a second-order large-signal system or circuit, the *phase-plane method* is usually better. Consider the circuit shown in Figure 5-33.

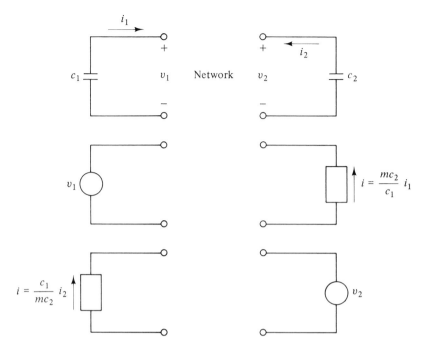

Figure 5-33 Circuit illustrating the phase-plane method. The isocline network is obtained by replacing the capacitive elements by an independent voltage source and a current-controlled source.

Let the capacitors be linear, and the 2-port network be a voltage-controlled resistive network. Then we can write

$$\frac{dv_1}{dt} = f_1(v_1, v_2)$$

$$\frac{dv_2}{dt} = f_2(v_1, v_2)$$

Dividing, we obtain

$$dv_2\, dv_1 = \frac{f_2(v_1, v_2)}{f_1(v_1, v_2)}$$

This equation represents the slope of the trajectories in the v_1-v_2 plane, which is the phase plane. Equating this to a constant m, we obtain

$$f_2(v_1, v_2) = mf_1(v_1, v_2)$$

This is the equation of an isocline with slope m. If we draw a short segment with slope m, called a *director*, through each point of this isocline, then any trajectory intersecting the isocline at a point P must be tangent to the director at P. As more isoclines and associated directors are added, we obtain the phase portrait. If the solution is unique, then no isoclines can intersect one another except at the equilibrium points, where the isocline is indeterminate. Thus, the intersections of the isoclines give the locations of the equilibrium states.

If we are given any initial state, a trajectory can be drawn tangent to the directors. Then the behavior of the trajectories in the vicinity of each equilibrium state can be observed. In this way, the phase portrait gives us a picture of the behavior of the circuit.

In general it is difficult to write the normal-form equations analytically. Thus, in order to obtain the isocline equations, a means must be found which is independent of the normal-form equations.

One way to do this is to construct a new resistive network by replacing the capacitors c_1 and c_2 of the circuit under consideration by an independent source and a current-controlled source. This is called an *isocline network*. The isocline-network theorem states that the isocline (with slope m) of the second-order capacitor network is identical to the v_2 vs. v_1 TC plot of the isocline network which was constructed. To use this technique we:

1. Draw the isocline network for each value of m.
2. Solve the v_2 vs. v_1 TC plot.
3. Repeat steps 1 and 2 to obtain the phase portrait.

Monte Carlo Analysis

A statistical analysis using the Monte Carlo method may involve solving several thousand cases of a given circuit problem, with its parameters chosen at random over the specified tolerance ranges. For this technique to be practical, a rapid method of solving each case must be used. Starting with the nominal solution as the initial estimate e_0' for each case, we require an algorithm that converges in a few iterations. To provide an economical method for statistical analysis, each solution must lie within a relatively small neighborhood of the nominal solution to allow the rapid convergency of this algorithm. The inverse Jacobian matrix H_0 corresponding to the nominal solution should not differ greatly from the successive iterations. We can modify our previous algorithm, Figure 5-27, so as to reduce the operation count to N^2 instead of the $4N^2$ operations required by this algorithm.

This technique applies the correction to H_0 but does not update H_0. Since we use the updated H_{i+1} matrix to produce a new p_{i+1} vector according to $p_{i+1} = H_{i+1} f_{i+1}$, we can multiply by f_{i+1} directly without having to go through the updating process. The correction is thus obtained without the actual updating of H_i.

If we use the full-step technique for establishing s_i, for $s_i = t_i$, then

$$y_i = f_{i+1} - f(0) = f_{i+1} - f_i$$

Using this and making the assumption that $H_i = H_0$, we define $q_{i+1} = H_0 f_{i+1}$. Then we can write

$$p_{i+1} = \frac{(p_i^t p_i) q_{i+1} + (p_i^t q_{i+1})(t_i - 1) p_i}{p_i^t p_i - p_i^t q_{i+1}}$$

The bulk of the computation involved here is the N^2 operations required to calculate q_{i+1}. On this basis an algorithm for Monte Carlo statistical analysis is shown in Figure 5-34.

Now on the very first pass in finding the optimum t_i the first and largest correction $(t_0 p_0)$ is made to the initial approximate solution vector e_0'. There is no approximation involved in setting $H_i = H_0$, since $i = 0$. Thus p_i is evaluated to the full accuracy. The second and the next-to-largest correction $(t_i p_i)$ to e' also is made to full accuracy. Beyond this point the assumption $H_i = H_0$ can begin to degrade the accuracy of the algorithm. In cases where only three or four iterations are needed for convergence, a solution can be reached before this degradation begins. When five or six iterations are required for convergence, one might favor updating the H matrix as in the algorithm of Figure 5-27. For a sparse-matrix circuit the algorithm of Figure 5-29 would be preferred.

MULTITERMINAL NETWORK CHARACTERIZATION

A number of matrices can be used to characterize a multiterminal network. Some examples are impedance matrices, hybrid matrices, and scattering matrices. Because of its simplicity when handling interconnected black boxes, the indefinite admittance matrix (IAM) is one of the most useful characterizing matrices. The IAM is the short-circuit admittance matrix of a multinode network in which ports are formed between each terminal and a reference node, which is left floating.

For a circuit with two-terminal loads to a multiterminal network, we can characterize it as a multiport, with the ports defined at each terminal pair to which a load is connected. If an n-terminal network is then interconnected with other multiterminal networks, we must characterize the network at a set of $n - 1$ ports which correspond to a complete and independent set of terminal pairs. A condition for the voltages of the $n - 1$ ports to be independent is that a graph made of edges representing the port voltages forms a tree.

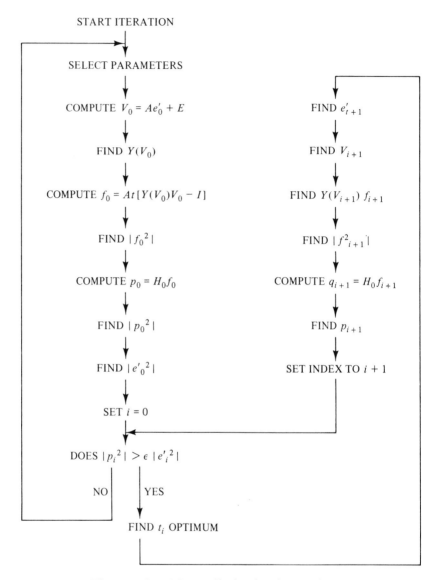

START ITERATION

SELECT PARAMETERS

COMPUTE $V_0 = Ae'_0 + E$

FIND $Y(V_0)$

COMPUTE $f_0 = At[Y(V_0)V_0 - I]$

FIND $|f_0^2|$

COMPUTE $p_0 = H_0f_0$

FIND $|p_0^2|$

FIND $|e'_0{}^2|$

SET $i = 0$

DOES $|p_i^2| > \epsilon |e'_i{}^2|$

NO YES

FIND t_i OPTIMUM

FIND e'_{t+1}

FIND V_{i+1}

FIND $Y(V_{i+1})\, f_{i+1}$

FIND $|f^2{}_{i+1}|$

COMPUTE $q_{i+1} = H_0f_{i+1}$

FIND p_{i+1}

SET INDEX TO $i + 1$

Figure 5-34 Monte Carlo circuit algorithm.

One can easily move back and forth between the indefinite admittance matrix and the definite short-circuit admittance matrix when all the ports have a common node which is connected to the circuit (this is usually ground). If all the ports do not have a common ground, however, the IAM is not obtained so simply. Thus we would like to have a method of going from a given set of ports to a second set with a common node. We can accomplish this by the following:

$$Y = C^T \tilde{Y} C$$

Here Y is the admittance matrix with ports having a common node, $\tilde{Y}$ is the original admittance matrix whose ports form a tree, C is the transpose of the reduced incidence matrix of the graph with edges that represent the ports of Y, and C^T is the transpose of C.

Consider the following example for the circuit of Figure 5-35 with mutually coupled coils. Port 1 is defined by node 1 as the positive terminal and node 2 as the negative one, and port 2 has node 3 positive and node 4 negative. The open-circuit impedance matrix of this two-port network is

$$\tilde{Z}_1 = S \begin{bmatrix} L_{11} & L_{12} \\ L_{12} & L_{22} \end{bmatrix}$$

The inverse of $\tilde{Z}_1$ is the admittance matrix with ports 1 and 2 as defined above:

$$\tilde{Y}_1 = \tilde{Z}_1^{-1} = \frac{1}{S(L_{11}L_{22} - L^2_{12})} \begin{bmatrix} L_{22} & -L_{12} \\ -L_{12} & L_{11} \end{bmatrix} = \begin{bmatrix} y_{11} & y_{12} \\ y_{12} & y_{22} \end{bmatrix}$$

To obtain the indefinite admittance matrix of this circuit it is necessary to obtain the short-circuit admittance matrix of the circuit with ports that go from each terminal to a floating ground. To characterize the circuit we add two additional ports. Let the third port be from nodes 3 to 1 and the fourth port from node 3 to the floating node. The admittance matrix of the circuit with these four ports is

$$\tilde{Y} = \begin{bmatrix} y_{11} & y_{12} & 0 & 0 \\ y_{12} & y_{12} & 0 & 0 \\ 0 & 0 & 0 & 0 \\ 0 & 0 & 0 & 0 \end{bmatrix}$$

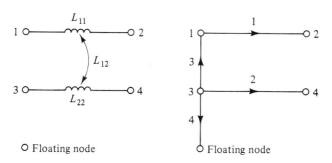

Figure 5-35   A two-port network and its graph.

Now we form the transpose of the reduced incidence matrix C of the graph defining the ports. This is

$$C = \begin{bmatrix} 1 & -1 & 0 & 0 \\ 0 & 0 & 1 & -1 \\ -1 & 0 & 1 & 0 \\ 0 & 0 & 1 & 0 \end{bmatrix}$$

Thus

$$Y = C^T \tilde{Y} C = \begin{bmatrix} 1 & 0 & -1 & 0 \\ -1 & 0 & 0 & 0 \\ 0 & 1 & 1 & 1 \\ 0 & -1 & 0 & 0 \end{bmatrix} \begin{bmatrix} y_{11} & y_{12} & 0 & 0 \\ y_{12} & y_{22} & 0 & 0 \\ 0 & 0 & 0 & 0 \\ 0 & 0 & 0 & 0 \end{bmatrix} \begin{bmatrix} 1 & -1 & 0 & 0 \\ 0 & 0 & 1 & -1 \\ -1 & 0 & 1 & 0 \\ 0 & 0 & 1 & 0 \end{bmatrix}$$

or

$$Y = \begin{bmatrix} y_{11} & -y_{11} & y_{12} & -y_{12} \\ -y_{11} & y_{11} & -y_{12} & y_{12} \\ y_{12} & -y_{12} & y_{22} & -y_{22} \\ -y_{12} & y_{12} & -y_{22} & y_{22} \end{bmatrix}$$

In a similar way the indefinite admittance matrix of other components found in electronic circuits may be obtained. The total indefinite admittance matrix of a large circuit is obtained by adding, in the proper positions, the contributions of each of the devices. This avoids manipulating topological matrices, since the indefinite admittance matrix can usually be obtained by inspection.

The Analysis of Black-Box Circuits
Using the Indefinite Admittance Matrix

We have seen that the indefinite admittance matrix (IAM) is the n-port short-circuit admittance matrix in which the ports are formed between each terminal and an unconnected node, which is floating. The current going into each terminal can always be considered to come out of the floating node for any type of connection, and the condition of having a proper port will not be lost.

Now consider the system of Figure 5-36. The networks N1, N2, and N3 are five-terminal networks, since each has one node not connected and each has its IAM. The IAM of the whole system is the sum of the indefinite admittance matrices of all the networks. All that we need to know is the

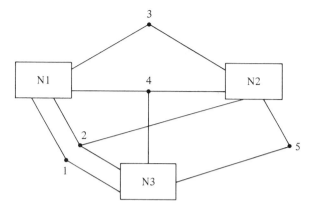

Figure 5-36   A system of networks.

contribution of each network. The network may range from a single resistor to a complex integrated circuit or combinations of these.

The main characteristics of the indefinite admittance matrix are:

1. The sum of entries in each row is zero and the sum of entries in each column is zero.

2. If the floating node is connected to the kth terminal of the circuit, the definite nodal matrix of the circuit with the kth terminal as reference is the indefinite admittance matrix with the kth row and the kth column deleted.

3. If the first p terminals of an n-terminal network are connected together, the new indefinite admittance matrix of the resultant $(n - p + 1)$-terminal network is an $(n - p + 1) \times (n - p + 1)$ matrix.

This matrix is obtained as follows:

1. Form an intermediate matrix Q by substituting for the first p columns of the indefinite admittance matrix Y a column whose entries are the sums of the first p columns of Y.

2. Substitute for the first p rows of Q one row whose entries are the sums of the entries of the first p rows of Q.

The resultant matrix is the new indefinite admittance matrix of the $(n - p + 1)$-terminal network. In forming the indefinite admittance matrix of a circuit we may not wish to use all the nodes for forming ports. Some ports can be defined to simplify the connections to other networks to form a larger network. These nodes where ports are not defined can be considered as internal nodes and suppressed. We can partition the IAM as follows:

$$\begin{bmatrix} I_1 \\ I_2 \end{bmatrix} = \begin{bmatrix} Y_{11} & Y_{12} \\ Y_{21} & Y_{22} \end{bmatrix} \begin{bmatrix} V_1 \\ V_2 \end{bmatrix}$$

where

I_1, V_1 are p-vectors
I_2, V_2 are $(n - p)$-vectors
Y_{11} is a $p \times p$ matrix
Y_{12} is a $p \times (n - p)$ matrix
Y_{21} is an $(n - p) \times p$ matrix
Y_{22} is an $(n - p) \times (n - p)$ matrix

If the first p terminals are the external terminals, $I_2 = 0$, since nothing is connected to these terminals. With $I_2 = 0$ we can solve for V_2 in terms of V_1:

$$V_2 = -Y_{22}^{-1} Y_{21} V_1$$

Then if we substitute back we get

$$I_1 = (Y_{11} = Y_{12} Y_{22}^{-1} Y_{21}) V_1$$

So the suppressed admittance matrix Y_S is

$$Y_S = Y_{11} - Y_{12}^{-1} Y_{21}$$

The external node voltages can be solved by using Y_S, which is smaller than Y. Once the voltages V_1 of the external terminals are found, the voltages of the internal terminals V_2 can be calculated. In the case where the internal nodes are connected to independent current sources, the I_2 is not zero when suppressing the internal nodes but it has entries equal to the currents injected into each terminal by the independent current sources. So

$$V_2 = -Y_{22}^{-1} Y_{21} V_1 + Y_{22}^{-1} I_2$$

gives

$$I_1 = (Y_{11} - Y_{12} Y_{22}^{-1} Y_{21}) V_1 + Y_{12} Y_{22}^{-1} I_2$$

or we can write

$$\bar{I} = (Y_{11} - Y_{12} Y_{22}^{-1} Y_{21}) V_1$$

where $\bar{I}$ is defined as

$$\bar{I} = I_1 - Y_{12}Y_{22}^{-1}I_2$$

These equations show that the internal current sources of I_2 may be replaced by external currents $-Y_{12}Y_{22}^{-1}I_2$ and added to the original external currents I_1 to form an equivalent external current vector.

In order to analyze large circuits, one can divide the circuit into segments with functional divisions. The IAM of each segment can be obtained and the internal nodes suppressed. All the black boxes are then connected, and a larger IAM with only external nodes is used to solve for the external terminal voltages. Then the internal voltages can be obtained. A significant saving occurs from the fact that the internal nodes are not all in memory at once. This technique is similar to the method of tearing tensors. It can include active devices as well as distributed elements.

A common problem in practice is the analysis of a circuit in which a number of subcircuits recur. For example, a circuit may contain a number of identical operational amplifiers. One way of analyzing these circuits is the following:

1. Analyze each subcircuit separately and find its indefinite admittance matrix at several frequencies, suppressing the internal terminals, which are not connected to the rest of the network.

2. Model the subcircuits with polynomials fitting the frequency behavior of the real and imaginary parts of each entry in the admittance matrix.

3. Connect the subcircuits to form a larger indefinite admittance matrix, again suppressing the internal terminals.

4. Repeat the process until the complete network is analyzed and the desired terminals are the only external terminals.

This method is essentially the same as the bottom-up method in designing large systems, where each subsystem is designed separately and then the different subsystems are connected.

Several levels of subsystems may be used, and a whole network which may have been analyzed in several levels may still be modeled with polynomials or other interpolation methods, regardless of how complicated the internal structure of the network is. One works with standard models, which may have the classical R, L, C controlled-source schematics.

Network designers may not be accustomed to handling circuits with admittance matrices, and certain degeneracies may occur for segments of the network even though the whole circuit has a nondegenerate admittance matrix. In many cases these problems can be avoided with the following techniques. The indefinite admittance method is biased toward embedded independent current sources rather than voltage sources. If the voltage source has an impedance in series, a Norton-equivalent current source can replace the voltage source. If there is no impedance in series with the voltage source, one can add a positive and negative impedance of equal value in series and associate the voltage source with either one to produce a Norton-equivalent current source. This creates an additional node. Similar techniques can be used for handling voltage-controlled voltage sources.

Some multiterminal elements will not have an indefinite admittance matrix, since infinite elements in the matrix are created from essentially producing short circuits between some of the terminals. We can avoid this degeneracy by the adding and subtracting of elements in series. Ideal transformers will have no admittance matrix, but if we add positive and negative resistance in series with each winding and consider the positive resistances as though they were associated with the windings and the negative resistances as elements apart from the device, the degeneracy will disappear. This procedure may also be used for many other devices.

Definite Matrices and their Terminal Characteristics

After the suppressed IAM of a circuit is found, the matrix can be made definite by connecting one of the nodes which made ground to the floating node and then deleting the corresponding row and column. Thus we obtain the node-to-ground definite admittance matrix Y_{SG}. The node-to-ground matrix can then be inverted to obtain the node-to-ground impedance matrix Z_{SG}.

Since we may wish to form ports other than node-to-ground, a transformation from node-to-ground ports to other ports like the following can be used:

$$Z = D Z_{SG} D^T$$

Here Z is the impedance matrix for the desired ports, D is the transpose of the reduced incidence matrix of the graph corresponding to these ports, D^T is the transpose of D, and Z_{SG} is the impedance matrix with ports defined from nodes to ground. If the Z matrix above has elements Z_{ij}, then the voltage ratios become

$$\frac{V_i}{V_j} = \frac{Z_{ii}}{Z_{jj}}$$

Often we will wish to consider the loads as part of the network, so Z becomes the impedance matrix with the loads connected.

We may also wish to find the driving-point impedance of the loaded network without the generator impedance at this port. We then connect to this port an additional impedance equal to the negative of the generator impedance.

Let Z_{ii_l} be the load impedance of the generator at port i, then the driving-point impedance z_i at port i is

$$z_i = \cfrac{1}{\left(\cfrac{1}{Z_{ii}}\right) - \left(\cfrac{1}{Z_{ii_l}}\right)}$$

Here Z_{ii} is the ith element on the main diagonal of the Z matrix.

The return loss RL_{ii} at port i in dB is

$$RL_{ii} = 20 \log \frac{z_i + Z_{ii_l}}{z_i - Z_{ii_l}}$$

and the insertion voltage gain IG_{ij} between ports i and j in dB is

$$IG_{ij} = 20 \log \cfrac{\dfrac{V_j}{V_i}\left(\dfrac{z_i}{z_i + Z_{ii_l}}\right)}{\dfrac{Z_{jj_l}}{Z_{jj_l} + Z_{ii_l}}}$$

The Indefinite Transfer Matrix

The indefinite transfer matrix E is useful in cascaded systems. It is defined by the following equations for a $2n$-terminal network:

$$\begin{bmatrix} V_1 \\ \hline I_1 \end{bmatrix} = \begin{bmatrix} A & B \\ \hline C & D \end{bmatrix} \begin{bmatrix} V_2 \\ \hline -I_2 \end{bmatrix}$$

where

$$E = \begin{bmatrix} A & B \\ \hline C & D \end{bmatrix}$$

Here V_1, I_1, V_2 are the n columns corresponding to the currents and voltages of the ports. The matrices A, B, C, D are $n \times n$ matrices. They are the extensions to $2n$ ports of the A, B, C, D parameters of two-port networks. As in the indefinite admittance matrix, all ports are defined with a common floating terminal. Thus the port condition is not lost owing to arbitrary interconnections, and we can go from the indefinite admittance matrix to the indefinite transfer matrix and vice versa.

If we partition the indefinite admittance matrix of a $2n$-terminal network as shown:

$$Y = \left[\begin{array}{c|c} Y_{11} & Y_{12} \\ \hline Y_{21} & Y_{22} \end{array} \right]$$

then the matrices $Y_{11}, Y_{12}, Y_{21}, Y_{22}$ are $n \times n$ matrices. The equations relating Y with A, B, C, D are

$$Y_{11} = DB^{-1}, \qquad Y_{21} = C - DB^{-1}A, \qquad Y_{21} = -B^{-1}, \qquad Y_{22} = B^{-1}A$$

$$A = -Y_{21}^{-1}Y_{22}, \quad B = -Y_{21}^{-1}, \quad C = Y_{12} - Y_{11}Y_{21}^{-1}Y_{22}, \quad D = -Y_{11}Y_{21}^{-1}$$

If several $2n$-terminal networks are connected in cascade, the E matrix becomes the product of the individual E matrices of the cascaded sections. Since all the ports have a common terminal, the port condition is never lost.

In the analysis of circuits with a computer, one can sacrifice computational efficiency to gain generality when using one of the general-purpose analysis programs. When analysis and optimization studies are coupled, one may need to employ the statistical variability to use the analysis routine many times to complete the design. The computational efficiency then becomes increasingly important. For maximum computational efficiency it may be necessary to use specific programs for each type of circuit to be analyzed. Each program would be tailored to the circuit so as to avoid any unnecessary operations. If many units of a particular IC or PCB are to be manufactured, then the writing of special programs for these circuits may be justified.

If many circuits which are members of a particular family are to be manufactured, then it may be better to use a more general program, which could still be more efficient than a packaged general-purpose analysis program.

Suppose we had a group of similar transmission circuits for which Monte Carlo statistical variability studies were required. We could analyze these circuits using the indefinite transfer matrix and gain a computational advantage over other methods, such as the indefinite admittance matrix, which require matrix inversion.

Many of the topics discussed in this chapter indicate the trends and techniques available in the future which can upgrade the network-analysis programs currently available. Along with the incorporation of new and improved techniques, the programs will need to provide more facilities for statistical analysis of circuits and for treating much larger problems. Better graphical presentations of output variables in a variety of forms will be essential along with a much closer degree of machine interaction. A great deal of development is needed to handle more integrated circuits. This technology will place strong demands on our analytical, numerical, and programming techniques, but it will inevitably force the development of more powerful methods. This, in turn, is likely to stimulate the exploration and exploitation of newer techniques of interconnecting solutions and the use of higher-dimensional network models. Beyond these more powerful and effective network-analysis programs will be the development of improved optimization techniques, in which the actual analysis tasks will be subroutines.

Automatic network synthesis will also be much improved, and a majority of computer-aided circuit design will be based primarily on analysis and optimization techniques, with the engineer not only playing an essential role in the design inputs, but also controlling the entire process of design. As the computer takes over the more routine computational circuit tasks, the engineer's more critical creative abilities will tend to be enhanced.

EXERCISES

1. Show how a linear $2n$-variable system can be described by a set of matrix equations.

2. Show that if a root is a parasitic root and if it lies outside the unit circle, the solution eventually diverges. Why is this situation called numerical instability?

3. The solution of the state equations can be found recursively. Diagram an algorithm to accomplish this.

4. An RF transformer has two mutually coupled inductors. Draw the graph of this four-port network.

5. What are the most effective methods for the solution of the eigenvalue problem?

6. A linear electric circuit is under consideration. If its mesh currents are taken as independent quantities, define the open-circuit-impedance matrix.

7. In spite of its utility, few second-order large-signal electronic circuits are analyzed by the phase-plane method. What reasons can be traced to the difficulty in deriving the isocline equation or network?

8. It can be quite effective to use the piecewise fitting of curves for different frequency intervals. Diagram how discrete points may be fed into the computer and how different curves may be fitted for different intervals. Show how one might fit a quadratic polynomial through the first three points and subsequently fit other quadratics through each additional point, matching the previous curve both in value and derivative at the last common point.

9. Describe how a signal-flow graph can result from a formulation based upon the topology of a network.

10. Transient circuit-analysis computer programs are developed to predict the network response in terms of element values and externally measurable device parameters. Should the programs be circuit- and not device-oriented, since the object is not to describe the physical processes of device operation, but to compute the circuit response? Discuss your answer.

11. Many four-port network communication systems fall into a class which may be shown schematically as black boxes labeled N_1, $N_2, \ldots, N_n$ which represent four-terminal circuits plus a ground. Show how a port can be made from each terminal to ground and each four-port characterized by a 4×4 transmission matrix E, each of which is partitioned into A, B, C, D matrices which are 2×2. All matrices may have entries which are complex numbers and depend on frequency. Discuss how a computer program would be used to solve the network solution.

12. In a series of interconnected black boxes, the indefinite admittance matrix (IAM) is to be used as the characterizing matrix. Discuss how the IAM is found as the short-circuit admittance matrix in a multinode network. Show which ports are formed between each terminal and a node which is unconnected to the circuit.

13. Derive the indefinite admittance matrices of some typical devices when they are connected to the lowest-numbered nodes in a circuit (1, 2, 3). Show that if a device is connected to nodes $i, j, k, \ldots$ instead of to $1, 2, 3, \ldots$, then replacement of indices i for 1, j for 2, and k for 3 gives the location of the entries to the corresponding indefinite admittance matrix.

14. Show how the indefinite matrices are used in a system of multi-terminal black-box circuits which are arbitrarily interconnected.

ELECTRONIC
APPLICATIONS

6

The electronics industry was one of the first to make wide use of interactive computer graphics. By the late 60s, circuit complexity and the demand for circuits had increased dramatically. In response, the electronics industry turned to computers to meet the demand for new circuit designs. Graphics systems proved to be very useful in speeding up the circuit-design process.

In the design of integrated circuits and printed-circuit boards, one could now move the components and conductors much more quickly than with the older manual cut-and-paste methods. Since the computer could keep track of the details such as component types and conductor spacing, sign changes could be made easily by modifying the computer database.

During the 60s and 70s, the complexity of circuits doubled every year, and computers became more a necessity than an aid. Today CAD is used in virtually every facet of electronic design. (See Plate 17.) Manual design of highly complex circuits is just not practical, since an integrated-circuit chip with 100,000 devices would then take some 60 years to develop.

TYPICAL CAD SYSTEMS

In a typical system the graphical data in the computer are stored as files. The records in the files consist of data on the graphical elements, which may be electrical symbols. The element names, types, and locations are all included. The information is numerical in form, and all changes are made numerically. Only when the information is displayed or printed is it converted to pictorial form.

The graphical software is formulated with the following objectives in mind. The user at the console should deal with completely graphical information. In drawing a circuit the user should not have to label resistors or specify that R_1 is connected between nodes number 1 and 3. The user need only pick a resistor and connect it to the appropriate nodes and give the resistor a value. The computer has the tasks of:

1. Assigning node numbers internally; the user need not even be aware of these node assignments.

2. Keeping lists of the elements and their values as they are connected to the nodes.

3. Assisting the user in composing the schematic in a step-by-step fashion.

In a typical circuit-analysis program the computer calculates the requested frequency and transient response and then outputs the data, which are translated into pictorial form. The engineer views the graphical output and makes changes in the original schematic. The process is repeated until a satisfactory design is achieved. The process can be likened to an engineer's making changes in a breadboard circuit and viewing the results with an oscilloscope. When the final circuit design is achieved on the computer, the engineer can call up a program that will place the components within the constraints of a grid to reduce the total length of all connections. The final design can then be stored in mass memory for reference.

It is apparent that graphics are very valuable tools in computer-aided electronic design. In order to consider the software and hardware features of a typical graphics system, let us ask the following question: How does the designer draw the schematic on the face of the display? This is done by using a lightpen and programmed control buttons.

The scope face can be divided into two areas: a display area at the center of the screen, usually 9×9 inches or larger, and a control area at the bottom. On this control surface are displayed light buttons. These buttons are actually preprogrammed controls or special graphical entities in a menu format. The light buttons form a special-purpose command language. This language is used for composing the schematic on the computer. The designer need not have a knowledge of programming, since each light button is a preprogrammed subroutine. The programming of the light buttons need not be done by the designer. The input devices can consist of the lightpen and a control keyboard which is made up of fixed and variable function buttons. The lightpen is a light-sensing device consisting of a fiber-optics light pipe with a high-gain photomultiplier. The two main functions of the lightpen are picking and tracking. Tracking is used to define points and to draw curves. Picking is used to select previously defined and currently displayed light buttons to initiate a process.

In addition to the light buttons displayed on the CRT control surface, there are a number of fixed or variable function control buttons on the input keyboard. These buttons are also preprogrammed to initiate specific actions, which are generally distinct from those provided by the light buttons.

The computer must handle two kinds of stored information: display and nondisplay. Display information is that concerned with the display of the actual schematic. These are the nodes, the elements, and their interconnections. The nondisplay information consists of the bookkeeping functions associated with the use of the schematic as input data for the circuit-analysis program. The nondisplay information includes a node table, a listing for the interconnections of elements, and a listing of the element values.

A summary of the applications of computer-aided design in electronic circuits includes many different phases of the design problem:

1. The modeling and automated testing of devices and circuits to determine parameter values.

2. The specification of device designs to meet specific performance objectives.

3. The determination of how devices will be connected together in a circuit to perform the desired functions.

4. The evaluation of the performance of a system using simulation and analysis.

5. The determination of parts lists, wiring diagrams, and patterns as well as other manufacturing information.

6. The determination of the optimum grouping of circuits and functions prior to integration.

7. The generation of test, maintenance, and fault-detection procedures for the completed systems.

The computer-aided design programs for solving these individual problems are generally separate entities. But we must give serious thought to the design of the data structures that these individual programs work with, so the linking of programs together either directly or by interaction can be readily achieved. The linking together of programs should be much more than the patching together of the individual pieces. It must be done on a sound basis, taking into account the detailed methods used in each part and changing these where necessary to give a more effective overall design. One difficulty in the use of circuit-analysis programs is that each program has had a different input language for describing the topology and the element types and values of the circuit.

There are two basic ways to handle the interface problem between the graphics system and the analysis program. One method requires that the nondisplay data associated with the graphics input be tailored for the analysis program. The second method leaves the graphic input system unchanged by devising an interface language for the analysis program. The common interface language is a more efficient approach, since it enables the engineer to use several programs without learning the details of the input language for each one.

This common input language is the first step in establishing a supervisory program. Such a program creates an opaque interface between the engineer and the computer. The engineer need not know the capabilities, input requirements, and output options of the individual programs that might be used in the course of the design. One places the schematic on the graphics display; the supervisory program then asks a series of questions and selects the appropriate programs for use in the analysis. After a number of iterations, if the responses fail to converge quickly, an optimize function could be picked. Control then is given to an optimization program to reduce the solution time.

In a circuit-analysis program the mathematical equations used can be nearly any function of known voltages or currents, as long as certain conditions are satisfied. Among these conditions are continuity of both the function and the first derivative of the function. A continuous function is necessary to avoid any ambiguity in defining a dependent variable. For any value of an independent variable, there must be one, and only one, value for a function of that variable. This constraint may seem obvious, but it is sometimes violated in defining a model. The condition of a continuous first derivative prohibits the use of piecewise-linear models. However, piecewise-nonlinear models can be used as long as equality of the first derivatives, as well as equality of the functions, is preserved at the boundary.

The justification for requiring the continuity of the first derivative can be found in the methods used by the various programs for internally formulating the network equations. In most large general-purpose programs, the state-variable formulation technique is used. The state equations are found from a linear graph of the network. If the network contains a circuit of voltage sources and capacitors or a cutset of current sources and inductors, then a tree and cotree from which the state equations can be formulated may not exist, unless the first derivatives of current and voltage sources are known.

Another constraint on the mathematical equations is that they must have the same form as the network equations used in the general program. For example, in finding a steady-state solution in some programs a current source cannot be a function of the voltage across it, except in the special case of a diode. This constraint means that when using a model in a general analysis program, one must be aware of the unique features of that program.

After the topology and equations have been formulated, it is necessary to find the model parameters. Ideally, these can be read directly or extracted from the device specification sheet. This cannot always be done, since most data sheets do not contain sufficient information to define the entire model. Specifying the capacitance of a diode at one reverse voltage is not sufficient to define complete transient operation of the diode. The information given on specification sheets also differs among manufacturers. The natural tendency is to use data which makes the device performance appear best, even if it is not pertinent to typical applications. Until standardized models are provided by manufacturers, we can expect to expend time and money to provide the data which might be needed for a model. If a designer needs a new model or parameters for an existing model, then measurements are required. Some examples of finding different parameters will be used by way of illustration.

GENERAL DESIGN EXAMPLES

This section will include discussions of some representative problems in transformer design and electromechanical energy conversion. The engineering design methods will be examined, and we will discuss the general design procedure.

Transducers and Speakers

The electromagnetic loudspeaker is typical of a general class of electromagnetic transducers involving both electrical and mechanical parts. The problem of a speaker is more complex that that of a transducer, since it involves acoustical mechanical coupling as well as electromechanical coupling. An electromagnetic loudspeaker might have the following components that must be considered in the model:

1. Infinitely large baffle.
2. Flexible edge suspension.
3. Flexible center suspension.
4. Voice coil.
5. Electrical connection parameters.
6. Holes for air release.
7. Cone (diaphragm).
8. Permanent magnet.
9. Open-web supporting structure.

The speaker is mounted in an infinitely large baffle in order that there be no acoustic power fed from the front of the speaker to the back. This condition is ordinarily found in most speaker enclosures for high-fidelity applications. The cone, which transmits its mechanical power of motion to the air, will be assumed to behave as a rigid piston. This assumption is useful in high-fidelity applications at frequencies to 300 Hz. At much higher frequencies the cone does not necessarily move as a rigid body, and the direct-radiator loudspeaker mounted in an infinite baffle might support higher modes. This can cause complex deformations and destroy fidelity. Figure 6-1 gives a representation of this situation.

The varying signal represented by the generator produces a changing current in the voice coil. The diaphragm, which is rigidly coupled to the voice coil, vibrates, and the resulting mechanical displacements are translated into sound waves. Three different effects must be accounted for: electrical, mechanical, and acoustic. The diaphragm mechanical displacement is equivalent to the motion of the mass M with an elastic restoring force that is represented by the spring k. The damping due to the diaphragm suspension is represented by a resistor R_D, and f is the air density. The lumped constant elements that approximate the load are unlike the mechanical elements, since they have no physical reality but they characterize the behavior of the air load.

Let S be the diaphragm's effective area, which is approximately its

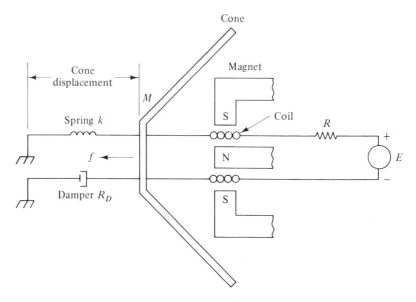

Figure 6-1   Speaker model.

planar area. The coupling coefficient between the diaphragm and the air is assumed to be unity, and no power is lost. The relation between the mechanical elements and the acoustic elements can be represented by a transformer characteristic

$$p = \frac{1}{S} f$$

Then the constant-power requirement gives

$$u = Sv$$

Here u is the air flow, the volume per unit time of air moved by the diaphragm. The acoustical elements are represented by an acoustic mass M_a, two acoustic responsiveness elements G_1 and G_2, and an acoustical compliance P, which are connected as shown in Figure 6-2.

The list that follows is a summary of parameter definitions, some of which are peculiar to the class of problems involving acoustic elements:

1. Open-circuit voltage of audio amplifier, in volts.

2. Internal resistance of amplifier, in ohms.

3. Inductance of voice coil, measured with free motion of voice coil, in henrys.

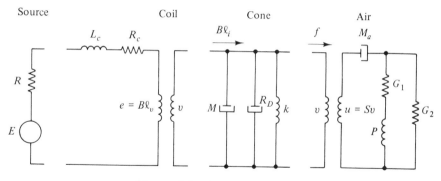

Figure 6-2   Speaker network.

4. Resistance of voice coil, measured with motion of voice coil blocked, in ohms.
5. Mass of voice coil plus diaphragm.
6. Mechanical responsiveness (conductance) (reciprocal damping) of diaphragm suspension.
7. Mechanical compliance of diaphragm suspension.
8. Acoustic mass of air load.
9. Acoustic responsiveness of air load.
10. Acoustic of air load.
11. Current through voice coil, in amperes.
12. Voltage across voice coil, in volts.
13. Force produced by voice coil due to i.
14. Velocity of voice coil and diaphragm.
15. Magnetic flux density.
16. Length of wire on voice coil.
17. Force applied by diaphragm to move air load.
18. Pressure in air at the diaphragm.
19. Flow of air.
20. Effective area of diaphragm.

There is an electrical analog corresponding to the acoustical elements. The analogous circuit has the same topology. Since it is convenient to refer to all quantities in an equivalent electric circuit, we transform the acoustic elements into the mechanical circuit and then transform the mechanical and acoustic elements into the electric circuit. The result is shown in Figure 6-3.

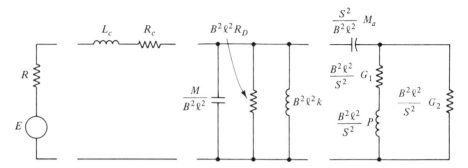

Figure 6-3   Equivalent electrical network.

Transformers

Now we consider a particular electromagnetic component, the transformer. Typically the values of the elements of a transformer together with the transformed electrical parameters can have a large number of variables. Insofar as the analysis of the transformer is concerned, the computer provides a direct solution. Some of these variables include the shape of the core and the wire and insulation to be used. The normal procedure is to select a core first, considering the weight and core-loss requirements. The core characteristics and the electrical transformer and thermal requirements then set the wiring. We then check that the operating characteristics, such as heat loss, hot spots, and pulse response, are satisfied. In some applications in transformer design a computer is used as a calculating device to compute values of a large number of parameters.

These would include the determination of the magnetic flux pattern for various types of cores or calculations of heat losses and temperature rises. In other cases the computer might be used to make a complete analysis of the transformer's performance under various conditions. In these, an initial design is specified in detail, and the computer is used to perform a number of evaluations. Then, based on the results of some of these, one can select the values of the parameters.

In other applications the computer is used both to calculate and to make logical decisions. The transformer requirements are stated as desired operating characteristics. The computer then selects the initial values and, by using a process of analysis of the response characteristics, evaluation, and further selection, it completes several iterations to synthesize a final design. The computer can also be used to prepare the documentation required, including the drawings, parts lists, and construction and production tickets needed for manufacture. The design of transformers is particularly suitable to digital computation. The devices may be custom designed, but the procedures are standard.

Early use was made of computers in the design of transformers. At first the computer was essentially used to mechanize the various stages of the analysis. Now design parameters are changed by the computer in order to achieve more optimum designs. The computer can develop the optimum transformer design for a set of specified performance requirements. A transformer design is a natural application for a computer, since most of the design steps are relatively straightforward and involve the selection of data from a tabular format. We now consider a typical algorithm for the general design process. The process involves the following:

1. The selection of the design parameters.
2. The evaluation of functions for the performance characteristics.
3. The comparison of calculated performance with specifications.
4. The making of changes in the design parameters which produce a design that meets the specifications.

Design techniques and the programs used to implement them vary in the amount of data that is specified initially and the mathematical models. In designing and analyzing the various parts of a transformer, these differences tend to reflect different available materials, or they may be the result of different application requirements. There may also be differences in the models used to describe the transformer.

The problem of transformer design can be reduced to the requirement to solve a series of simultaneous equations that relate the performance characteristics of the transformer, such as core loss and temperature rise, to the design parameters, such as core material, wire size, and winding configuration. Mathematically we can state this as shown below.

Core loss = f(core material, core shape, lamination thickness, flux, volt-amperes, ...)

Wire loss = f(wire size, number of turns, core size, temperature, currents, ...)

Temperature = f(winding, configuration, ...)

The forms of these functions will vary depending on the models used. They are generally complex mathematical functions and may have many nonlinearities. This makes them difficult to solve directly. So it is usual to select a set of design parameters, and these are analyzed and modified until the desired performance is obtained. Thus, we use an iterative solution to the simultaneous equations.

The equivalent network of the transformer permits an analysis of the electrical behavior. But this analysis does not include the interaction between the physical characteristics. These include the dimensions, the material, and the electrical behavior. As we have discussed, the electrical network considerations are not sufficient for design.

The basic algorithm can be illustrated with a sample problem. As we carry out a particular design, we can see how we could arrive at an initial design algorithm. We can also study the sensitivity of the design algorithm to variations in the specifications.

We will follow a simplified synthesis procedure for a small power transformer. We will assume the following characteristics:

1. There is one primary and one secondary coil, and the secondary coil is wound around the primary. There are no center taps.

2. The core is made of standard *E-I* shell-type laminations.

If the operating voltage or regulation is out of specification, another wire size is selected, and if this is sufficient to allow the design within specifications, a larger core is then chosen and the process repeated.

The steps of the calculations are described below:

1. From the secondary voltage and current specifications, calculate the volt-ampere rating and use this rating to select a core from a table. We desire a volt-ampere rating equal to or greater than the calculated rating.

2. The allowable copper loss is found by the difference between the transformer loss and the core loss when the transformer is operating at the volt-ampere rating.

3. The volt-ampere rating will be a fraction of the maximum volt-ampere rating for the selected core. This fraction is used to prorate the maximum copper loss and obtain an estimate of the actual copper loss.

4. The primary volt-ampere rating is found from the sum of the secondary volt-ampere rating and the estimated copper and core losses.

5. The primary current is calculated by dividing the primary volt-ampere rating by the primary voltage.

6. The regulation is estimated by dividing the core loss by a multiple of 2.6 times the secondary volt-ampere rating.

7. The primary turns are found from the induction formula:

$$N = \frac{3.49 \times 10^6}{16,000} \left[\frac{\text{volts, primary}}{(\text{frequency})(\text{core area, inches}^2)} \right]$$

8. The secondary turns are calculated by multiplying the primary turns

by the ratio of the secondary voltage to the primary voltage and then multiplied by another factor given by the estimated regulation.

9. Using the volt-amperes for the primary and secondary, the maximum circular mils per ampere is calculated. This figure is then used to select a wire size.

10. From the wiring diameter the number of turns in each winding and the number of layers and height for each winding are calculated.

11. The average winding lengths of a turn in the primary and secondary windings are estimated, using the circumference of a circle in the middle of the windings.

12. The winding resistances for the primary and secondary are found from the average winding length and the number of turns. We calculate the total lengths of the winding and then multiply this by the resistance of the wire.

13. The voltage drops in the primary and secondary are calculated from the resistance and current of the windings.

14. The copper loss is found from the voltage drop for each coil and the current through that coil. The copper loss is added to the core loss.

15. The temperature rise is found by multiplying this total loss by the per-watt loss for the core. If this exceeds the allowable limit, a larger core is selected and the process repeated.

16. The primary induced voltage is calculated from the difference between the impressed voltage and the *IR* drop. Prorating this by the ratio of the secondary to primary turns gives the secondary terminal voltage. If this is different from the specified secondary voltage by more than a specified allowance, the primary windings are changed and the process is repeated, starting at step 6.

17. The secondary no-load voltage is found from multiplying the primary voltage by the ratio of secondary turns to primary turns.

18. The regulation is found from the difference between the no-load and the load secondary voltages, which is expressed as a fraction of the loaded voltage. If this exceeds a specified allowance, a larger core is selected and the process repeated.

The design procedure as described above is shown to be a combination of analysis and synthesis, since at several points the design is compared with the specifications and if it is not found to be feasible, different variables are reselected and a part of the procedure is repeated.

Check points occur in measuring the winding height so that it will fit in the core, the maximum temperature rise, the tolerance of the secondary voltage, and the maximum regulation. If any of these last three are outside specifications, a larger wire size is selected. If the winding height becomes too large so that the required number of turns will not fit on the selected core, a larger core is selected and the entire process is repeated, starting with the initial wire size. Using successive iterations, a design that meets all design specification is synthesized.

To illustrate the design technique just described, let us consider a design problem. The design specification will include the following:

1. Primary voltage.
2. Secondary voltage.
3. Secondary current.
4. Secondary tolerance.
5. Maximum temperature rise.
6. Maximum regulation.

The design parameters which will either be specified or calculated are:

1. Core type.
2. Primary turns.
3. Secondary turns.
4. Iron loss.
5. Copper loss.
6. Total loss.
7. Secondary tolerance in volts.
8. Temperature rise.
9. Regulation.

These specifications and parameters are fairly standard for step-down power transformers. To ultimately obtain the design, a number of intermediate iterations are required.

First, a core having an adequate voltampere rating is selected based on the secondary requirements. From the estimate of the total loss of the core and the expected iron loss, an estimate of the total copper loss is found. This gives a figure for the primary current and an estimate of the regulation. From the volt-ampere ratings of the primary and secondary windings a limit on the circular mils per ampere is determined. This leads to the selection of a wire size.

Now, since the wire size is known, the total winding height can be found. If it is found to be less than the allowable limit for the core, the length of winding and the winding resistance are calculated next. This resistance and the currents give the total copper losses. We add this to the iron loss for the core to obtain the total loss for the transformer. Using a temperature rise of deg/watt for the core, the total temperature rise is estimated. If this is greater than the allowable rise, the design does not meet the required specifications and we must improve it with a larger wire size. This will give a lower winding resistance and a lower total loss, leading to a lower temperature rise. By selecting a larger wire size, it may be found that an excessive winding height results, so the required number of turns for this size wire will not fit on the core. To overcome this, a larger core must be selected, and the computations are repeated.

Finally it is found that all the test points—winding height, secondary tolerance, temperature rise, and regulation—are within the allowable limits. An iteration map for this design is given in Figure 6-4. This illustrates the types of calculations that are involved in the transformer design algorithm.

Operation	Iteration			
	1	2	3	4
Select core	Start			Start
Estimate maximum total losses				
Estimate copper losses				
Calculate primary current				
Estimate regulation				
Calculate primary turns				
Calculate secondary turns				
Select wire size		Start	Start	
Calculate winding height				
Calculate winding resistance			End	
Calculate cubic losses				
Calculate total losses				
Calculate temperature rise	End	End		
Calculate secondary terminal voltage				
Calculate regulation				End

Figure 6-4 Iteration map used in transformer design problem.

Electric Machinery

In the design of electric machinery the problems are different, since one must design a device in which rotational motions exist between the stationary and the rotating members. From the electrical point of view a motor or generator consists of an electric current in an armature, which is moving within a magnetic field produced by the currents in the field winding. The rotational torque or the emf generated is a result of the interaction between this current and the field. The problems we face in machinery design are concerned with this interaction and require a determination of the currents and magnetic fields created by the field and armature.

Computer applications in electrical machinery designs usually begin with an equivalent circuit involving the field and armature iron forms. These provide an idealized representation of the machine. Most designs begin with a configuration that establishes initial values for many of the variables, instead of using the performance requirements for the machine. The initial values are needed because the design involves a large number of parameters, and there are many combinations and design types that will satisfy these. Thus, a starting design is given or selected from a set of possibilities. From these starting values the process continues to an analysis of the operating characteristics and the determination of the detailed parameters.

The armature design may specify the general size, the metal to be used, and the coil formations. This is the starting point. The size of the laminations making up the armature are based on an analysis of the field and torque. The other characteristics that we may be interested in include the magnetic fluxes, efficiencies, resistances, heat losses, and iron losses. Transient and stability characteristics dealing with the starting and stopping conditions may also be of interest. This usually requires sets of simultaneous differential equations with variable coefficients.

Based on the results of this analysis, the design may be adjusted in various ways and the analysis repeated. After a number of iterations a design that satisfies the performance requirements is achieved. A computer can develop an optimum design from a number of feasible designs. These are analyzed to determine those which are optimum with respect to some property, such as cost or torque.

We will illustrate the use of digital computers for some aspects of motor design. The procedure is based on classical methods, but it tends to be realistic and suggests the nature of the problems in the design of electric motors.

Figure 6-5 shows the major stages in the design process. First we analyze all the information on the required motor, considering the customer specifications, industry specifications or standards, and our own specifications which relate to the parts and materials available. We consider the overall design constraints on the performance characteristics required by the design and the standardized manufacturing practices of the industry.

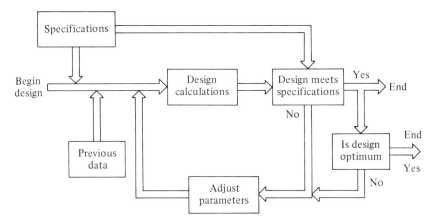

Figure 6-5 The design process.

Next we select an initial set of parameters for the machine design. Some of these, such as the winding type, stator form, and mounting, are relatively fixed. Others, such as the punching design in the stator or armature, may be changed in seeking the optimum design. As an aid in selecting the initial parameters, one may use the characteristics of the design of a motor similar to that which is required. This provides a starting point. If we know how certain characteristics of the motor change with respect to changes in the parameters, we can use the parameters of a previous design as a starting point and then use the difference or the ratio between the characteristics of the new design and the other design. Thus we apply this factor to the old parameter to obtain an estimate of the new parameter. Next, we use this analysis with the parameters selected initially as the basis of computations for the performance characteristics.

A number of models can be used to describe the behavior of a motor. In many respects these models may be similar or equivalent but not necessarily identical. The choice is generally based on experience with the types of models that have in the past most closely corresponded to the application. The models may also reflect differences in manufacturing techniques, using different materials and tolerances, even though these factors are included explicitly.

The calculated performance characteristics are compared with the design requirements and, if the design requirements are satisfied, the design then appears to be feasible. This does not always mean that the design is satisfactory. By changing some parameters, another design will be obtained that has additional desirable characteristics. If the design is not feasible, the parameters must also be changed. Then the analysis is repeated. In any case, the process of selecting and changing parameters is normally repeated several times. Finally a design is obtained that is regarded as optimum in that it is the best that can be obtained within the time allocated.

The computations in motor design are generally straightforward, since they involve mostly rational and trigonometric functions. The principal difficulty lies in evaluating the large number of characteristics of a motor and the need for repeated analysis. The great variety of materials, such as the different types of wires and cores, that can be used in the design of a small single-phase induction motor produce a variety of physical arrangements which add a dimension to an already complex problem.

We will use a model that is based on the cross-field theory. The motor model is shown in Figure 6-6. The direct axis is modeled by the single-phase stator excitation winding field axis. The squirrel-cage rotor is modeled as two windings, one in the direct axis (d) and the second in the quadrature axis (q), which is normal to the direct axis. The equations are:

$$\begin{bmatrix} vd^s \\ vd^r \\ vq^r \end{bmatrix} = \begin{bmatrix} R^s + L^s p & M_p & 0 \\ M_p & R^r + L^r p & -L^r w \\ M\omega & L^r \omega & R^r + L^r p \end{bmatrix} \begin{bmatrix} id^s \\ id^r \\ iq^r \end{bmatrix}$$

where P is the time derivative operator d/dt. From these equations we obtain an expression for the motor and generator torques in terms of their respective flux components. Then, using the relationships between the fluxes and the motor currents, we can relate the design parameters to the design specifications. The motor slip is defined as

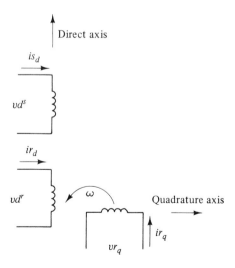

Figure 6-6 Induction-motor model.

$$\frac{\omega_s - n\omega_m}{\omega_s}$$

where n is the number of poles.

Another way to view slip is to consider it as the ratio of the actual speed to the synchronous speed.

A typical computer program would start with the basic motor data along with the desired core losses and a range and incremental value for the slip. The program calculates the actual losses, currents, and torque as well as other output parameters such as the RPM, efficiency, and power factor based on the initial value of slip. It will then increment the slip value and recalculate the parameters until the maximum slip value is obtained.

Control Systems

The models representing a control system can take on a number of forms. In Chapter 5 we saw that when a linear system is modeled, the equilibrium equations describing the system can lead to a set of linear differential equations. In the general case there may be various types of nonlinear functions.

The control system may also involve nonlinear operations due to noise, delays, limiters and bilateral devices. The models may be expressed in terms of the time-domain or linear frequency-domain transforms. The analysis can be carried out in either domain if the system is linear.

The frequency-domain analysis of a linear system reduces many of the operations to simple algebraic functions. But we must transform back to the time domain. This process can be the difficult part. A number of specialized techniques are available to help us perform such analysis.

One approach for the analysis of a control system is to simulate it with a computer. The linear elements can be simulated by using the analogs that exist among the electrical elements and the other physical disciplines. The nonlinear elements are more difficult to simulate, since the functional requirements may be complicated.

Once the system has been simulated on the computer, the system performance can be studied under a variety of different conditions. The immediate contact between the designer and the machine allows the investigation of the system under many easily altered conditions.

Simulation languages have been developed for the study of such system problems using a digital computer. Among the languages for control systems analysis are CSMP. The CSMP language accepts FORTRAN statements. It is problem-oriented and simplifies the use of digital computers in the analysis of block-oriented problems. As a tool for the time-domain analysis of control systems and related problems, it allows the engineer to work directly with the digital computer in setting parameters and changing configurations. One can specify any input, any steady-state errors, stability (due to any wild oscillation of the system when making corrections), sensitivity, and the effects of noise. Other performance characteristics are also possible. Many of these can be done without having to determine the complete solution of the system equations.

Clearly it is more than helpful to know if a system is stable or not; it is, in fact, necessary in control system design to know even more, such as:

1. The degree of instability.

2. What can be done to stabilize the system if it is unstable.

The Routh-Hurwitz stability test is generally not useful in many real situations in which the coefficients of the linear differential equation cannot be found. The situation is particularly true for many closed-loop systems.

The Nyquist test uses a different approach for testing the stability of a linear system. It tests the roots of the equation

$$1 + L(s) = 0$$

Here $L(s)$ is a linear function of the complex variable s.

The total gain of a closed-loop feedback system is

$$T(s) = \frac{G(s)}{1 + G(s)H(s)}$$

Here $G(s)$ is the forward system function and $H(s)$ is the feedback system function.

The total system function of the combined forward and feedback paths, but with the feedback connection open, is $G(s)H(s)$. The presence of any right half-plane poles in the denominator of the total equation gain indicates an unstable system. The right half-plane poles are the poles of $G(s)H(s)$, so the stability of the closed-loop system can be inferred from the open-loop characteristics of the system. In the Nyquist test we map the $G(s)H(s)$ function for a path in the s plane along the imaginary or frequency axis from $-j\infty + j\infty$. As we complete the closed path by an infinite semicircle in the clockwise direction, we note that:

1. Enclosed zeros, which are the right half-plane zeros, cause clockwise encirclements of the origin in the $G(h\omega)H(j\omega)$ plane for the specified clockwise path in the s plane.

2. Enclosed poles, which are the right half-plane poles, result in counter-clockwise encirclements of the origin in the $G(j\omega)H(j\omega)$ plane for the specified clockwise path in the s plane.

3. The net encirclements depend on the difference between the number of right half-plane poles and zeros.

4. The system is unstable if

$$G(s)H(s) = -1$$

Thus, the Nyquist stability test states that a closed-loop feedback system is stable if, and only if, its open-loop transfer locus does not enclose the point $(-1, 0)$ and if the number of counterclockwise encirclements about $(-1, 0)$ equals the number of poles of $G(s)H(s)$ with positive real parts. The following data are required in the Nyquist test procedure:

1. The magnitude and phase angle of $G(j\omega)H(j\omega)$ for ω from $-\infty$ to $-\infty$.

2. The behavior of $G(s)H(s)$ at the poles that lie on the imaginary axis or at the origin of the s plane.

3. The number of $G(s)H(s)$ right half-plane poles.

Note that the Nyquist plot provides a qualitative measure of the sensitivity to changes in system parameters. Because of this, the test is of particular importance in control-system design.

Stability using the method of Liapunov starts from the state-equation formulation. Consider a bounded system's response to a sudden disturbance or input. If the system is disturbed and displaced slightly from the equilibrium state, several different behavior patterns are possible. If the system remains near an equilibrium state, the system is stable. If the system returns to the equilibrium state, it is asymptotically stable. An equilibrium state is asymptotically stable in the large if it is asymptotically stable for any initial-state vector such that every motion converges to the equilibrium state as time approaches infinity.

The Liapunov second method, which is also called the Liapunov direct method, allows a more precise stability test for a system. This method, like Routh-Hurwitz and the Nyquist tests, permits a study of the stability of the dynamic system without requiring the solution of the differential equations of state.

The direct method of Liapunov can be stated essentially as follows:

Suppose that within a neighborhood $S(R)$ of the origin, where R is the radius of a spherical shell in the state space about the point $x(0) = 0$, a scalar function $V(x)$ in the state $x(t)$ can be constructed such that $V(x)$ has a continuous first partial derivative such that $V(x) = 0$ when x is equal to the equilibrium state. Let $V(x) > 0$ for all x other than the equilibrium state and let the time derivative of $V(x)$ be negative. Then the system represented by $V(x)$ will be asymptotically stable.

The Liapunov stability theorem can be stated in more precise terms:

We are given

$$\dot{x} = X(x)$$

where $\dot{x}_1$ is continuous in the state variable x_j for all $i, j = 1, 2, \ldots, n$. If there exists a $V(x)$ such that

$V(x)$ has continuous first partial derivatives with respect to x_i
$V(x)$ is positive definite for all $x_i > 0$
$V(x) \longrightarrow \infty$ for $x \longrightarrow \infty$

then the system is stable with respect to x_i.

If there is a region $S(R)$ defined by $0 < \|x_i\| < S(R)$, where $S(R)$ is some real positive constant, such that in this region $-\dot{V}(x)$ is positive-semidefinite or

$$-\dot{V} = \sum_{i=1}^{n} \frac{\partial V}{\partial x_i} \dot{x}_i \geq 0 \qquad \text{for all } x_i, \ t > 0$$

then the system is asymptotically stable with respect to x_i if in $S(R)$, $-\dot{V} > 0$, $x \neq 0$, thus $-\dot{V}$ is positive-definite.

The system is asymptotically stable in the large if the asymptotic condition is satisfied and if $S(R)$ is the whole of state space.

Since we have a set of sufficient conditions for stability, if we can find a positive-definite function that is nonincreasing, the system is proved to be stable. But if some selected positive-definite function $V(x)$ is increasing for some motion of the state vector, no conclusions may be reached. If the proposed Liapunov function fails to satisfy the requirements of the stability theorem, no conclusions are possible, since another choice of Liapunov function may satisfy the stability requirement.

The main difficulty in the use of the Liapunov theorem is in the construction of a suitable $V(x)$ for a given system. A number of methods exist for generating Liapunov functions for linear systems, and certain types of nonlinear systems lend themselves to these procedures in finding suitable functions, but generating suitable functions for the general nonlinear case can be difficult.

Adaptive control system design techniques for systems with slowly time-varying gains and parameters are available using Liapunov's direct method. An advantage of this technique lies in the inherent stability of the resulting system.

This type of adaptive control system design reduces the effort required to perform the stability analysis in order to demonstrate satisfactory system performance. Many problems can be avoided using this technique, since the examination of the Liapunov function and its time derivative provides the basis for the design, in contrast to the heuristic type of approach. The disadvantage of generally requiring $n - 1$ error derivatives for an nth-order system to implement the controller can be a problem. But in the case of a system with positive real transfer functions and a time-varying gain only, Kalman's lemma can be used to eliminate this, and we can implement the controller using the error signal alone.

The choice of Liapunov functions is important to the design, since it affects the type of stability obtained. For a first- or second-order system with unknown parameters a more heavily damped error response can be obtained by using another feedback loop. This technique follows the Liapunov approach for a linear system. This approach can be extended to include systems with general time-varying gains by making modifications to the Liapunov function.

The technique which we will discuss reduces the required number of derivative networks in an adaptive controller design for systems that do not have positive real transfer functions. The technique is based on a version of Kalman's lemma. It results in an asymptotically stable design if the unknown system gain remains essentially constant. To illustrate the technique, we start a controller with a design that uses no derivative networks in a second-order system. The second-order system can be simulated with the aid of a program that uses Runge-Kutta and Adams-Moulton numerical integration techniques.

We start with the adaptive system of Figure 6-7. $K_v > 0$ is assumed to be a slowly varying or essentially constant but unknown gain,

$$N(s) = B_{n-1}S^{n-1} + B_{n-2}S^{n-2} + \cdots B_0$$

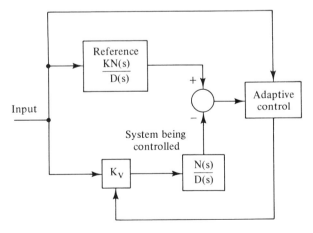

Figure 6-7   An adaptive control system.

and

$$D(s) = s^n + a_{n-1}S^{n-1} + \cdots + a_0$$

The B_i and a_j are known constants, and the roots of $D(s)$ are assumed to have negative real parts. We can write a similar nth-order differential equation for the error signal and from this equation define an equivalent set of n first-order differential equations. We put these in matrix format and then select a potential Liapunov function, which actually begins the design procedure. Using this function for the adaptive controller, we can test the controllability using the Kalman-Meyer lemma and modify the potential function as required by obtaining a numerical solution of these equations with the help of Runge-Kutta and Adams-Moulton techniques. Runge-Kutta methods are used to start the solution technique. The Adams-Moulton, also known as the modified Adams method, is one of the closed types of predictor-corrector formulas.

An Elevator Speed Control

As a general example of a more basic control-system problem, consider now an elevator speed control. Here we wish to control the cable winding at a constant rate. We use a tachometer to sense the cable reel and control the voltage to the motor. The motor can be modeled as a device that produces a torque which is a function of the input voltage. The control system must produce a control signal which is equal to the difference between the desired speed and the measured speed. The basic task is to analyze the system and determine the stability and other performance characteristics. A tentative control system design must be based on the following data:

System Characteristics

Reel dimensions
    Diameter (full)
    Diameter (empty)
    Width
    Moment of inertia of empty reel

Cable dimensions
    Diameter
    Turns/layer

Desired cable speed

Time constants
    Motor
    Tachometer

Torque constant of motor

The analysis requires the calculation of several critical quantities, including the instantaneous moment of inertia and the effect of the time constants. First we assign labels to the necessary quantities, as shown below:

r_0 Initial radius of cable on reel

d Cable diameter

w Width of reel

r_1 Radius of reel without cable

I_{r_1} Moment of inertia of empty reel

p Mass density of cable from turns/layer

To compute the instantaneous radius we know that for a reel of width w and wire diameter d there are w/d windings per layer. This can be written as $2w/d$ radian/layer. Now one layer reduces the radius by d, so the instantaneous reduction in radius of the reel can be expressed as

$$\text{radius drop/radian} = \frac{d}{2\pi\omega/d} = \frac{d^2}{2\pi\omega}$$

The total drop in radius of the reel for an unwinding of θ radians is $(d^2/2\pi\omega)\theta$. If the initial radius is r_0, then the radius of the reel after θ radians have been unwound is

$$R = r_0 - \frac{d^2}{2\pi\omega}\theta$$

To find the moment of inertia of a partially unwound reel, we note that for a cylinder about its axis the moment of inertia is

$$I = \int_0^R r^2\, dm$$

The mass of a cylindrical wheel of radius dr is

$$dm = p\omega(2\pi r)\, dr$$

where p is the mass density of the material. When the cable is partially unwound,

$$I = I_{r_1} + \int_{r_1}^R 2\pi p\omega r^3\, dr$$

or

$$I = I_{r_1} + \frac{\pi p\omega}{2}(R^4 - r_1^4)$$

There are two time constants in the system—the tachometer and the motor. In general this means that the variable of interest which is undergoing change must be expressed as the difference between the two time constants, and the variable is expressed as a differential equation with respect to time. The other equations we will need include Newton's second law for angular motion, in which we will use both the torque and the inertia. We also need to equate the instantaneous velocity of the cable to the angular velocity of the reel. Then the control system voltage is expressed as the difference between the desired speed and the measured speed. From these expressions a series of equations can be written which simulate the system. These we can operate on to study the stability and system parameters, such as the cable strength or speed.

Another technique is to use one of the simulation languages to model the complete system. First we prepare a functional block diagram of the system, using all the relationships discussed above. The block diagram shows all the operations required, as well as the feedback relationships. We then translate the elements of the block diagram into components of the simulation language. Then we enter the initial conditions and parameter output requirements. The program will perform all the integrations required and produce plots of the requested output parameters. These can then be analyzed per the specifications and modifications can be made to improve the stability or meet the specifications.

THE COMPUTER-AIDED DESIGN
OF ELECTRONIC CIRCUITS

In each of these examples, using the available technology, design techniques, and experience, the design engineer formulates a possible design to meet the specifications. The design is then analyzed to determine if the proposed design is reasonable.

In the case of an electronic circuit design it is a logical step to construct a breadboard model and test the design. In the analysis and experimental stages much feedback will occur, and it may even involve the specifications until the design is completed.

In recent years, engineers have turned more attention to the use of computers in electronic circuit design. The central tools are the electronic circuit simulator programs, which can perform dc, ac, transient, sensitivity, and statistical analysis. These programs are used in the design process to perform repeated analysis of the circuit.

The analysis programs include the equation compilers, which generate the necessary network equations from the node and element description of the network. The circuit description input is user-oriented and allows considerable freedom in the description of the numerical values, the order of inputs, and the numbering of nodes. Some examples of these user-oriented analysis programs include SCEPTRE and ECAP. In this section we will examine some of the common features of these types of programs and discuss their use in circuit design. We have already discussed transistor modeling and a number of transistor equivalent circuits. We have also shown how the results may easily be extended to include other active devices.

We have also considered the general network-analysis problem in terms of the state-variable and other approaches and the computer solution procedure. The salient features were presented for the circuit-analysis and solution procedure. Now we will examine the requirements on the operating environment for the effective use of the analysis programs in circuit design. In particular, we discuss the implications for circuit design and the impact of graphic consoles in on-line design. Later in this chapter we will examine the features of some representative circuit-layout programs.

We will stress the need for a design supervisory capability where an opaque interface is created between the user and the computer. The user does not need to know the capabilities, input requirements, and output options of the individual programs that might be used in the course of the design. One merely inputs the schematic on the graphic console. The program then asks a series of questions through a menu and selects the appropriate routines and data for use in the design.

To obtain meaningful results from a network analysis we know that the passive and active linear and nonlinear devices must all be represented to an acceptable degree of approximation. The model used should also be simple enough to present a readily interpretable equivalent circuit, yet it must be accurate in describing the physical devices so as to predict the circuit performance properly.

The language used should have relatively few grammatical rules and otherwise place few demands on the user's knowledge of other computer languages. The specification of a language for any engineering discipline should be determined by the following factors:

1. Since most engineering disciplines deal with a relatively small number of distinct computational processes, most applications should be formulated as special logical groupings of these processes.

2. Most of these logical groupings of computational processes have known names within the discipline. These names should be used in the input language to facilitate their use by the problem-oriented user.

3. There should be an open-endedness to the problem-oriented language with respect to its basic processes. It should be relatively easy to add applications to the basic program.

A number of problem-oriented languages are available. Some language translators, called processors, produce machine-language programs that can carry out the solution directly. Others operate interpretively by executing procedures to implement the problem statements. Still others produce symbolic source programs in assembly or a procedure-oriented language, which are then translated to machine language using an assembler or compiler for execution. This latter implementation is particularly useful if subsystem computations are to be implemented as subroutines.

In a circuit-analysis program such an individual subroutine might exist for transducers or motors. In this case the processor produces a calling program to call the subroutines. Then, as new component types are developed, one can extend this library of subroutines.

In these problem-oriented languages the need for flow-charting algorithms is almost eliminated, since the essential algorithms needed to solve a particular problem are written by the processor. The processor synthesizes the problem-oriented input statements, and the system can be designed to allow individual statements to be entered in almost an arbitrary manner. Since considerable detail is required in the preparation of such translators, a large amount of programming time is necessary for writing them. Much of the translation involves the manipulation and interpretation of symbol strings. One program for the IBM360 is a decision-table translator. It converts decision tables into FORTRAN programs, thus eliminating the need to write program statements for solving a problem. The source or input language is a FORTRAN-oriented decision-table language. It is designed for user flexibility when writing decision tables and requires some knowledge of FORTRAN. It is FORTRAN-oriented so that the translator can effectively produce source programs without being overburdened with chores of decoding and editing.

A problem-oriented program for the solution of network problems is of particular interest to us. Some of the features that are considered desirable in network-analysis programs can serve as a guide from which to measure any program. Any general network-analysis program should be capable of steady-state dc and ac analysis. The more useful features of a network-analysis program include:

1. It should have a convenient, simple input language to describe the topology of the circuit, the element types, and associated values.

2. The language should be able to provide a description of the circuit excitations, the analysis options desired, and the ranges of time or frequencies for which the analysis is to be performed.

3. The language should allow one with no engineering or programming knowledge to prepare the input information from a schematic.

4. The program should be able to handle a wide variety of models. One should be able to change not only the device parameters but also the topological properties.

5. In order to deal with active circuits the program must be able to handle nonlinearities. A linear analysis program cannot obtain a quiescent solution for a transistor with a nonlinear load line. The program can deal with nonlinearities using a piecewise-linear or tabular methods or by using mathematical subroutines.

6. There should be a number of output options, which could be in the form of driving-point or transfer functions, poles and zeros, magnitude and phase response, or transient response.

7. The program should include a parameter-modification facility to allow sensitivity, tolerance, and worst-case studies to be performed.

8. The program should contain error checking to allow the user to examine the reliability of the analysis.

A number of programs that have been written approach the ideal case listed above.

One goal in this chapter is to give the user an idea of which types of programs are best for a given problem, and under what conditions a specific program should or should not be used. The casual user of these programs could well believe that the final solution to the circuit analysis problem has been found. But this, of course, is not true, and a greater understanding of the limitations and applications of the various approaches to the network-analysis problem is still needed. Since most user manuals ignore these limitations, this section points out some of them. An attempt is made to prevent the disillusionment that comes to a potential user of computer analysis programs when encountering the limitations. This disillusionment often obscures the real value of the computer analysis approach.

If we consider the system aspects of computer-based analysis programs, then the decision of which program to use depends on:

1. The purpose of the analysis.

2. The machine to be used.

3. The user's experience with computers.

4. The programming support available.

Many of the comments regarding circuit-analysis programs in this chapter reflect their present status. The techniques used in both the numerical and programming formulations of the programs are constantly improving, and the programs themselves are still being developed to take advantage of these improvements. This chapter reflects, then, the programs as they exist today. Many of the restrictions mentioned will be eliminated or at least lessened in revised and new programs.

There are a number of linear analysis programs, such as ECAP, and large-signal programs, such as SCEPTRE. The general features of each are similar, and the reasons for choosing one program rather than another are usually based on individual analysis needs and computer facilities.

The programs that are representative of the available linear network analysis programs present two types of network-analysis schemes:

1. Those that obtain the network function as a ratio of polynomials.

2. Those that, like ECAP, use a numerical determination of the network function.

Differences can also exist between programs in the mathematical formulation used to find the network function as the ratio of polynomials. Some programs use a topological approach to obtain the network function, while others may use the state-variable technique.

The topological methods used are the techniques described in Chapter 5 for a passive network. The basic problem of solving the node equations by matrix methods is transformed, using the Binet-Cauchy theorem, to the topological and combinatorial problem of finding the trees and associated n-tree products of the linear graph. For an active network the n-tree products now are signed. Some programs use a two-graph approach to determine the sign of the tree products.

The topological approach has advantages and disadvantages. The primary advantage is that the network function, when calculated, will be essentially without roundoff error. The disadvantage occurs in the time required to find all the trees in a large network. In the state-variable approach, computation time depends not on the size of the network but on the number of state variables. This can make a difference of two or three orders of magnitude in computation time. The main disadvantage is the roundoff error in computing the inverse matrix.

Using Analysis Programs in Circuit Design

In a typical analysis program the user determines the output quantities. In some programs, when the describing equations for the network response are being set up, the rows and columns of the incidence matrix are scanned and a reduced incidence matrix is formed. This decreases the computation time during the solution process. The user might also specify whether either a Runge-Kutta or a modified trapezoidal method is to be used.

Subroutines can be inserted into some programs for expanded program flexibility. A section of the program allows the user to define and solve systems of linear or nonlinear first-order differential equations. By allowing elements and sources to be represented in the form of constants, tables, and analytic expressions, as well as expressions which combine these forms, a powerful simulation program can be achieved.

Communication between the user and the circuit-analysis program takes place through statements in a program-oriented language. Input formats may differ in several respects, but many steps in the preparation are common to all programs. In general, the following rules apply:

1. The network is composed of resistors, capacitors, inductors (which may include mutual inductance), and voltage and current sources. Active devices are represented by equivalent circuits using the above elements.

2. All the network nodes must be labeled.

3. The network topology must be described.

4. The control statements indicating the kind of analysis and the time-frequency parameters must be given.

In the preparation of the control statements the user must define the steps used to obtain a transient analysis and the dc initial conditions required for the first step. The network description takes the form of a set of statements, one for each component. These give the labels for node connections.

One of the available programs to which we will give some attention is ECAP (Electronic Circuit Analysis Program), which was developed by IBM and the Norden Division of United Aircraft. We will discuss ECAP as an illustration of a program for ac, dc, and transient analysis. Sensitivity, statistical, and worst-case studies can be performed for the dc case. In ac analysis, magnitude and phase information is available. Steady-state solutions can be obtained by letting a transient analysis go to equilibrium, but these are more directly obtained. As in any program, there are a number of restrictions. These depend on the computer system that is used, and they can affect the following parameters:

1. Nodes.

2. Branches.

3. Dependent sources.

4. Switches.

5. Parameter changes.

Resistors and switches can be combined to form approximate nonlinear resistances using the piecewise-linear method, and this allows diodes and transistors to be modeled in the program.

Other programs may use circuits made up of fixed $RLCM$ elements, junction transistors, and diodes. Transistors and diodes may be referred to by their $1N$ and $2N$ numbers, which are stored in a library file. Parameter data in the library of diodes and transistors may be represented by nonlinear equivalent circuits of the Ebers-Moll type, which may operate in the cutoff, active, or saturated modes.

These canned programs are relatively simple to use. But it is important to appreciate their limitations in order to avoid over-confidence, since there is much that they do poorly or not at all.

ECAP uses the piecewise-linear approach for the analysis of nonlinear circuits. Current-sensitive switches are employed in synthesizing the piecewise-linear functions. Switching depends upon the direction of current in the branches and thus is amplitude-dependent. If $i > 0$, then one value results, and if $i \leq 0$, the other value occurs. The element being controlled can have only one of two values. The control can be remote as well as direct. If more than one current controls the element, then its value alternates each time a current changes direction.

Time-variant elements may be synthesized by using a time-varying current source as a controlling current. One can simulate elements having more than two values using networks of two-valued elements. This allows complicated functional dependencies of multidimensional variables. But the simulation of the functions with two-valued elements can often be difficult.

ECAP is an integrated analysis system that consists of four related programs: the input language, dc analysis, ac analysis, and transient analysis. The *input-language program* is the communication link between the user and the three analysis programs. It provides the means for describing the circuit arrangement of components. It also provides for controlling the type and extent of the analysis as well as the form and amount of output. An important feature of an input language is the use of an English-language style and a simple format for the input. Six input statements are used to define the circuit topology, the circuit-element values, the type of analysis desired, the circuit excitation, and the desired outputs in ECAP.

The *dc analysis program* allows the steady-state solution of linear networks and can provide the partial derivatives and sensitivity coefficients of the network voltages with respect to input parameters. Worst-case analysis and a standard-deviation analysis can also be done for the parameter tolerances.

The *ac analysis program* gives a time-independent solution for linear networks with sinusoidal excitation at a fixed frequency. Automatic modification of the frequency on a logarithmic scale permits a frequency-response analysis to be conducted.

The *transient analysis program* allows one to obtain the time response to one or more driving forces. One can handle circuits with nonlinearities by switching the parameter values, using a switching technique.

The types of circuit elements used in the programs are summarized below:

Circuit	Analysis		
Element	DC	AC	Transient
Resistor	+	+	+
Capacitor		+	+
Inductor		+	+
Mutual inductor		+	
Voltage source, fixed	+	+	+
Voltage source, time-dependent			+
Current source, fixed	+	+	+
Current source, time-dependent			+
Switch			+

The typical branch configurations are shown in Figure 6-8. The reference-polarity and reference-current directions are required parts of the circuit branch. A circuit branch need not be restricted to a single dependent current source, and additional ones may appear in the same circuit branch.

Let us look now at the basic procedure for conducting a circuit analysis using ECAP.

1. The initial step is the preparation of a preliminary circuit schematic that is expected to perform a desired function. The purpose of the analysis is to ensure that the circuit will perform as desired.

2. Next we replace the physical components by their models. Figure 6-9(a) shows a simple series RLC circuit that will be used for illustration. Since there are no active devices in this circuit, no models are used.

3. Next the nodes are identified by circled numbers, while the branch numbers are enclosed in squares.

4. Defining the topology of the circuit is done next, and the component values are specified using the data statements:

   $L = 0.15$
   $R = 100, E = 10$
   $R = 10$
   $C = 0.1E-6$

These are written after the appropriate branch as shown below:

   B1.N = (0, 1), L = 0.15: Branch 1 is bounded by node 0 and node 1 and contains an inductor L of nominal value 0.15 H.

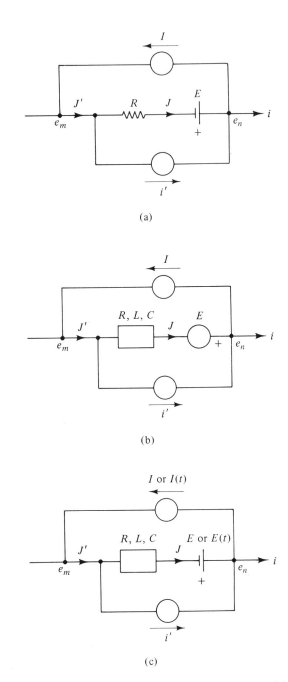

Figure 6-8 ECAP branch configurations: (a) dc analysis, (b) ac analysis, (c) transient analysis.

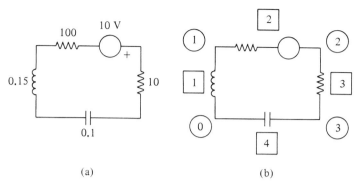

(a)   (b)

Figure 6-9 (a) Illustrative circuit. (b) Circuit with nodes and branches labeled for ECAP.

B2.N = (1, 2), R = 100, E = 10: Branch 2 is bounded by node 1 and node 2 and contains a resistor of nominal value 100 ohms and a voltage source of 10 V with a phase angle of 0 degrees.

B3.N = (2, 3), R = 10: Branch 3 is bounded by node 2 and node 3 and contains a resistor of nominal value 10 ohms.

B4.N = (3, 0), C = 0.1E−6: Branch 4 is bounded by node 3 and node 0 and contains a capacitor with nominal value 0.1×10^{-6} F or 0.1 µF.

Frequency = 1000; the frequency of the ac source is set to 1000 Hz.

5. The control statements define the type of analysis that is to be performed. In this case we could perform an ac analysis followed by a sensitivity analysis, which would show us the effects of the tolerances of the components. The sensitivity analysis is performed on each of the components in the circuit.

When the data and control statements have been fed into the computer, the program will use the data to set up the circuit equations and will determine which solutions of the equations to perform. When the output is available for evaluation, a decision can be made concerning the adequacy of the initial design. Should the analysis indicate the need for changes, these can be made and the altered circuit again analyzed. When the design proves adequate, the circuit construction can begin.

In any ECAP analysis the network must be marked and numbered. The nodes and the branches are numbered, and the reference or ground node is usually assigned the number 0. The current directions are selected. Then the input data, output specification, and command are given.

The available ECAP outputs are as follows:

1. Node voltage.

2. Element current.

3. Element voltage.

4. Branch voltage.

5. Branch current.

6. Element power loss.

We now describe systems for the graphical input for the design of electronic circuits. The two major parts of the design are the display and the analysis. The display portion involves the use of graphical input-output console, and the analysis involves the use of the circuit-analysis programs. Although most users will concentrate on details of the display system, it is well to also have a good understanding of the capabilities of the analysis programs.

There are many powerful circuit-analysis programs which can analyze sizable electronic circuits. These circuits can contain nonlinear transistor models such as Ebers-Moll. The major factor that has limited their use in electronic design has been the input-output formats.

The user may be hampered by an inconvenient and bulky input language and large amounts of tabular output data. In circuit design the natural language of the engineer is schematic. Thus the communications medium between the engineer and computer should be graphic. Ideally the designer should present the computer with a circuit schematic, and the computer, in turn, should return a set of graphic response curves.

Graphical Design Techniques

The principal means of on-line graphic communications is the computer-controlled cathode-ray tube (CRT) display. A popular graphic input device which is used with the CRT is the lightpen, which produces a response as it detects a point of light on the CRT display. A typical console might have a raster of 1024 by 1024 directly addressable locations. The display is tied to the computer, whose memory unit may be shared with the display.

The graphic entities called *glyphs* are software-generated, and the display functions such as points, lines, and characters and the control functions such as focus, intensity, and position are all software-controlled. The language used to create the display list, which is then decoded to form the displayed graphics, should be a simple set of instructions.

The engineer enters the schematic into the computer using the lightpen and a set of preprogrammed graphic subroutines. The CRT face might be divided into two areas: a display area and a control area. On the control area are displayed the functions that allow the user to initiate actions, such as ROTATE, COPY, or CONNECT the circuit elements.

The user initiates the selection by pointing the lightpen, an action known as *picking*. Once a circuit element is picked, the designer can move this element to the display surface using a tracking cross. This allows the designer to compose the schematic in a step-by-step manner.

When the circuit schematic is complete, the designer requests an analysis of the circuit. The data representing the schematic can then be stripped from the display, which is converted into a form acceptable to the analysis. The circuit-analysis program may calculate the frequency response and produce data which is translated into pictorial form. The engineer then views the graphic output and makes changes in the original schematic. The process is repeated until a satisfactory design is achieved. It is somewhat like an engineer making changes on a breadboard circuit and viewing the results on a CRT. Using this procedure, a circuit can be designed in a minimum amount of time, and it still makes use of the engineer's experience.

The process of creating the network in the display area might be as follows. Suppose NODE is displayed at high intensity while all other options are at normal intensity. The lightpen causes a program response when it detects NODE. When the lightpen is placed on the word NODE, a node in the display area comes on. Next we pick this node, which causes a tracking cross to appear in the center of the display area and the option POSITION to become bright in the menu area. Then, using the lightpen, we move the tracking cross to the proper position on the work area of the CRT. Then, as the lightpen picks POSITION, the node is positioned at the tracking cross, and the cross disappears. After two nodes are displayed, a BRANCH can be made.

Once the BRANCH is ready, we:

1. Select an element.
2. Position it on the CRT, using the tracking cross.
3. Connect the element to the two different nodes.
4. Assign a value to the element.

The user then adds the next node or element.

The BRANCH option is active only after two nodes are displayed. Thus one cannot select BRANCH when there are no nodes to which to connect it. If DELETE is chosen, the user picks a particular node or branch. The selected item disappears from the screen, and its memory space is released for use as the data arrays are adjusted.

We note that in the development of the schematic, a number of methods can be used in directing the user. One is intensity control, as the options are displayed at high intensity; this directs the user to the proper choice and can also indicate what is to follow.

Data Structure and Process

The purpose of the circuit analysis is to provide insights into the circuit operation and to verify the design objectives. When the output response is observed, the user may return to the schematic of the network and add, delete, or change the topology and element values.

The data structure is normally divided into two arrays or sections: display and nondisplay. The display section holds the data used to create, maintain, and change the graphic display. The nondisplay data structure may have some similar data, except that it is entered during the analysis phase into the analysis program itself. The data structure has arrays for the node numbers, the branch numbers and types, the element connections, and the element values.

When the display data is changed by using DELETE, this option sets the selected member of the arrays equal to zero and removes the element or node from the display list. Both the display and analysis arrays must be properly dimensioned to accommodate the elements and nodes which will represent the network.

The challenge in many analysis programs is that we have to work with the circuit a part at a time. The interaction between these parts necessitates the iterative process. Processes exist for a limited class of problems for which we can synthesize topologies while simultaneously determining the parameter values.

Optimization

The mathematical optimization techniques which have been developed allow excellent practical results to be obtained for complex systems. To use these techniques, we specify the equations governing the system: the state-variable equations. These equations may have been derived from a given topology or devised to yield a given transformation. In either case there must exist a corresponding topology which is physically realizable. If not, we have nothing to optimize.

We can investigate the adaptation of optimization techniques in the automation of the circuit-design process. We assume first that a topology is given. Also, let the optimization techniques allow inequality constraints to be imposed. These constraints may be necessary to further ensure realizability. Now, if the optimal solution requires some unconstrained parameters to become zero or infinite, the topology will be changed to effect this. With a completely automated system, the circuit designer must enter the following into the computer: the topology, the constraints and tolerances on the devices, the constraints derived from the system in which the circuit must work, and the analysis objective.

The computer then selects the component values which optimize the analysis objective within the limits of the prescribed constraints. Using this facility, the designer can direct complete attention to the selection of a topology and the derivation of meaningful constraints upon the circuit. In order to facilitate this automation, circuit design problems must be defined into two categories: stationary and dynamic.

The *stationary problem* is one in which the criteria, including the objectives and constraints, do not change explicitly with time. Static or dc solutions fall into this class, as do some time-periodic or steady-state problems which can be described in terms of S-plane parameters.

Since many nonlinear and transient design problems can be formulated so as to eliminate time from their criteria, these are also stationary. The circuits which are not stationary are defined as *dynamic*. Whether time can be eliminated from the criteria will depend on what is critical for the particular application. A switching circuit may be formulated as stationary if the switching speeds are implicitly satisfied. One could impose dc constraints on the impedance and junction voltages so as to ensure operation within certain time ranges.

A properly formulated stationary circuit-design problem represents a special type of analysis problem. We can allow for fixed or variable tolerances and the constraints among tolerances as they occur when variations are due to a common cause such as temperature. This is all based on a definition of worst-case design. This is the type of design considered most useful when the designer is concerned about circuit reliability. The dynamic design problem is a type of optimal control problem in which constraints are placed on the state variables.

In the general case of a worst-case design, we assume that a circuit has been completely designed and all nominal values of component parameters have been specified, along with the tolerance ranges. This circuit then represents a worst-case design for some particular systems criterion. If we build the circuit with a physically realizable combination of component values within their specified ranges, it will satisfy this systems criterion in the expected environments.

This definition of worst-case design means that statistical data is used to determine the limits of the tolerances. System reliability may be determined in terms of the probabilities of finding components within these tolerance ranges. This approach is used for several reasons:

1. Limit data is sufficient for most circuit designs and it is available from most manufacturers.

2. Accurate distribution data on most semiconductor devices is difficult to obtain and it is likely to change when variations in the processes are used to produce the same device.

3. The approach also tends to yield more insight into the design process.

If it is assumed that the system criteria is expressed in terms of analytic constraints, and that a circuit topology is selected that provides the required function, then it is also assumed that the designer knows the tolerances and limitations on the devices. In particular, we must know the ranges of parameter values, from production to end of life, and their variation with temperature. Without this information, a true worst-case design could not be performed.

From the circuit topology, using Kirchhoff's and Ohm's laws, a system of equations is obtained, and from the criteria and component constraints, a system of inequalities is obtained. A solution which satisfies both systems is not unique, but it is a feasible solution rather than an optimal solution. Generally, if one feasible solution exists, then there are many. A solution can be chosen which is optimal according to some criterion, such as minimum power dissipation or minimum delay, or some combination.

The variables may be grouped into two types—those for which nominal values are known and those for which they are to be determined. An example of the first type might be the voltage across a diode which has been chosen. An example of the second type might be a resistor whose value is to be chosen. If we call these variables p and x types (predetermined and unknown) and write them in vector form, then:

$$P = \begin{bmatrix} p_1 \\ \cdot \\ \cdot \\ \cdot \\ p_m \end{bmatrix}, \quad X = \begin{bmatrix} x_1 \\ \cdot \\ \cdot \\ \cdot \\ x_n \end{bmatrix}$$

Now, the nominal value of any variable of the system is a component of either the P or X vectors. Associated with each of the nominal values of these components is the tolerance parameter t, which can vary between two limits:

$$t_d \leq t \leq t_u$$

Here

$$t_d \leq 0$$

and

$$t_u \geq 0$$

The tolerance limits will generally be functions of the nominal value of the variable. In the case of an x-type variable

$$t_{d_1} = t_{d_1}(x_1)$$
$$t_{u_1} = t_{u_1}(x_1)$$

and the actual value of the variable $\bar{x}_1$ could exist anywhere in the range

$$(x_1 + t_{d_1}) \leq \bar{x}_1 \leq (x_1 + t_{u_1})$$

These same relations exist for the p variables.

If we associate tolerance vectors T_p and T_x with the P and X vectors, then we call a particular choice of the x variables the *design*, and the n-dimensional space associated with it the *design space*. The variables $p_1, \ldots, p_m, x_1, \ldots, x_n$ then form an $(m + n)$-dimensional space which we can call *parameter space*. Now let

$$\tilde{V} = V + T$$

be a vector with elements which are the actual values of the circuit elements, where

$$T = \begin{bmatrix} T_p \\ T_x \end{bmatrix}$$

Then we can show that Figure 6-10 holds. This problem of choosing an optimum set of variables for the tolerances is a compound optimization problem. There are $(m + 1)$ standard optimization problems, where m is the number of constraint functions. The first m optimization problem gives solutions which allow the constraints to be transformed and put the overall problem in the standard form in parameter space.

We now sketch a method that can be used in solving the optimization problem. First we find a solution for the nominal design satisfying all constraints. The design variables allowed will depend on the circuit, and some problems may have design variable ranges of several orders of magnitude. Under these conditions the feasible region can be a small region in vast high-dimension space.

One characteristic of these problems is that the constraint functions are highly nonlinear over the hypercube of allowed design variables. But in the

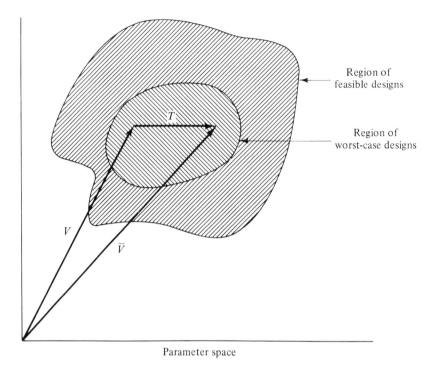

Region of
feasible designs

Region of
worst-case designs

Parameter space

Figure 6-10   Design ranges. A design is feasible when the region of worst-case designs due to the different component values remains within the region of feasible designs.

feasible neighborhood the constraint functions may to some approximation be linear or quadratic.

These problems can be approached in two steps:

1. Perform a random search to find a solution near the feasible region.
2. Having obtained a solution, use an appropriate derivative technique to obtain a feasible solution.

In many problems, obtaining an initial solution can be the most difficult part of the procedure, since constraints can be postulated for which no feasible solution exists. The existence of a feasible region does not guarantee its discovery. When using mathematical functions which measure the nearness of the solution to the feasible region, one must be careful to avoid mathematical traps. Even the simple measures, like the least-squares method for unsatisfied constraints, can be misleading. At this point the increased knowledge about the circuit can be reflected in tighter restrictions on the variable ranges, for faster solutions.

Next we must search for a center of the feasible region. To properly define the center of a feasible region may require a detailed mathematical analysis of the constraint variations with respect to the tolerance variables. Consider the center of the feasible region as the center of mass under a uniform density. There are two basic reasons for locating the center of the feasible region before going on to constraint transformation:

1. The center solution may be considered representative for the constraint transformations throughout the feasible region. We can then proceed to the optimal solution with reasonable confidence without updating the constraint transformations.

2. If a properly defined center solution can be found, it can be a feasible solution to the transformed problem, if a solution exists. In any case, the computational effort should be reduced as the solution approaches the center. A derivative method may be used to locate the center.

Using these numerical values as nominal values for the design variable, we can find the sets of random variables which transform each constraint. A sensitivity analysis can be used here, since the smallness of the tolerance range yields an approximately linear tolerance variation. If interior maxima occur, a grid technique can be used.

Next we obtain a feasible solution to the transformed problem. We might use the same derivative technique as used initially to find a solution near the feasible region. Some iterations may be required in which some constraints are relaxed or even the circuit topology is adjusted. The optimum solution may lie on the boundary, and a boundary-following technique might be needed. Since the constraints have not been updated, the optimum solution will not be precise, and rather than update the constraints at this point, and iterate, one could perform a Monte Carlo analysis.

NONLINEAR ANALYSIS

A number of concepts are fundamental to nonlinear analysis programs. We will briefly describe these concepts. Much of this is basic to system theory.

Systems consist of three elemental parts. In the basic system there are a set of inputs, a set of outputs, and an operation on the set of inputs. The input set, defined by the vector $x(t)$, is independent of the system and is considered in this case to be dependent on time only. The output set, defined by $y(t)$, depends upon the input and the system operator H. Performing the operation of H on $x(t)$ yields $y(t)$—or

$$y(t) = H[x(t)]$$

The model of an electrical circuit consists of electrical elements and voltages and currents. We assume that these quantities will be in the real-number system; then we can use the calculus of real numbers for the representation of the system operation, as shown in the typical cases below:

1. $y(t) = 4x^2(t)$

2. $y(t) = \displaystyle\int_{t-t_0}^{t} x(t)\ dt$

3. $y(t) = \dfrac{d}{dt}\ [x(t)]$

A system which relates only to the present input is an *instantaneous* system. A system which requires knowledge of past or future inputs will have memory and is a *dynamic* system. In the three cases above, the first is an instantaneous system, since a knowledge of $x(t)$ is adequate to determine $y(t)$. The others are dynamic systems, since the second system requires a memory of length t_0 and the third needs a small memory which can be either positive or negative depending on the derivative definition used in the computation.

Systems for which the operation is not affected by time are known as *stationary* or *time-invariant* systems. A system is otherwise known as *time-variant*. The systems illustrated above are all stationary. Two time-variant systems are given below:

$$y(t) = t\ x(t)$$

$$y(t) = \begin{cases} x(t) & \text{for } t \le 0 \\ 2x(t) & \text{otherwise} \end{cases}$$

If we have a system for which a knowledge of the input for the memory-length requirements and time (if time-variant) is adequate for determining a unique output, this system is called *deterministic*. The system is otherwise *nondeterministic*. The systems illustrated thus far are all deterministic, since a knowledge of the input for the memory length and time allows one to compute a unique output. The following system, however, is nondeterministic:

$$y(t) = [x(t)]^{1/2}$$

Note that for each positive $x(t)$, the output may assume one of two possible values. If $x(t) = 4$, then $y(t) = 2$, or $y(t) = -2$. Also, for a solution to exist, $x(t)$ cannot be negative. Deterministic systems which are also instantaneous have an output which is single-valued and completely specified in relation to the input.

A system is *linear* if and only if the following is true:

$$H[ax_1(t)] + \beta x_2(t) = \alpha H[x_1(t)] + \beta H[x_2(t)]$$

Here α and β are two arbitrary scalar constants. Note in Figure 6-11 that

$$y_1(t) = H[\alpha x_1(t) + \beta x_2(t)]$$

and

$$y_2(t) = H[\alpha x_1(t)] + \beta H[x_2(t)]$$

The operation H is linear if and only if $y_1(t) = y_2(t)$ for all t. Both the superposition and the complex frequency domain do not apply to nonlinear systems.

Circuit elements obey the same general form indicated for systems. Thus, we can regard an element as a subsystem. The potential family of subsystems vastly exceeds the conventional circuit elements, such as resistors and inductors. To make use of integrated-circuit modeling techniques, we must be able to extend the domain of conventional circuit elements, and this is where the system concepts become helpful.

It is in the interest of programming ease to consider an element as having a single output which is instantaneously dependent on the circuit electrical quantities. These elements are not restricted to the instantaneous category, since a capacitor has an instantaneous relation between charge and voltage, but its current-voltage relationship constitutes a dynamic system.

The general form of operation of a circuit element can be shown as a vector x composed of components such as voltage, current, charge, or carrier density; then the output $y = f(x)$ can also be one of these quantities.

For the previous example, the operation given by case 1 is nonlinear, since

$$4[\alpha x_1(t) + \beta x_2(t)]^2 \neq 4\alpha x_1^2(t) + 4\beta x_2^2(t)$$

The operation given by case 2 is linear, since

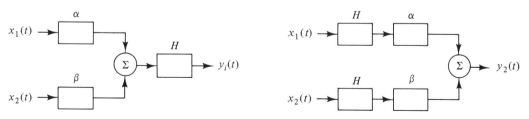

Figure 6-11   An illustration of linearity.

$$\int_{t-t_0}^{t} [\alpha x_1(t) + \beta x_2(t) \, dt] = \alpha \int_{t-t_0}^{t} x_1(t) \, dt + \beta \int_{t-t_0}^{t} x_2(t) \, dt$$

The operation given by case 3 is also linear, since

$$\frac{d}{dt} [\alpha x_1(t) + \beta x_2(t)] = \alpha \frac{dx_1(t)}{dt} + \beta \frac{dx_2(t)}{dt}$$

The two time-invariant systems are linear, and systems that multiply by constants, differentiate, and integrate are linear.

The computer simulates a circuit by a difference equation which approximates integration. A higher-order approximation is normally used for more accurate results. State equations are normally used for linear circuits, and they also can be applied to piecewise-linear analysis.

The order of complexity of a circuit is the smallest order of differential equations required to describe the circuit. If a problem example requires a second-order differential equation, its order of complexity is 2. The order of complexity is an indication of the number of states and the initial conditions needed. For a linear circuit this number corresponds to the degree of the characteristic equation. The number of reactive elements can equal or exceed the order of circuit complexity, since we can have a larger number of states. In a linear circuit an excess of state variables will produce dependent equations, and matrix inversion becomes a problem, since we have inconsistent state-vector components. This situation of an excess of state equations may arise if there exist loops consisting of independent voltage sources and capacitors, or if there exist inductors which are in cutsets with other inductors and independent current sources. Parallel capacitors or series inductors are examples of these two situations.

Linear and piecewise-linear programs are designed to handle this problem. Programs which do not utilize the state equations directly avoid this problem. If a general nonlinear analysis program determines and uses state equations, then the user may have to modify those circuits which lead to excessive state equations.

Noise and Filters

A basic requirement for a signal-processing system is the separation of the low-power signal from miscellaneous noise that inevitably becomes mixed with the desired signal and may be of relatively high power. In these circuit problems the magnitude of the noise interference may lie between two extremes:

1. The noise is of such small magnitude relative to the signal that it is considered negligible.
2. The noise is of such great magnitude that the signal may be unrecognizable.

Another problem is that neither the signal nor the noise may be completely specified. It is necessary then to consider descriptions of signal and of noise:

1. Let the signal be a well-defined mathematical function, such as a single-frequency sinusoid or a finite band of sinusoids.
2. Let the noise be a signal whose amplitude or frequency is of a random nature or an unwanted signal that interferes with a desired signal.

Random noise is usually the type that is of concern in communications systems, while the other type is mainly an interference problem and can be suppressed using tuning and discrimination techniques.

The basic approach of separating signals from noise requires that we exploit the difference in the statistical pattern of the signal and the noise. We can do this by a reduction in bandwidth of the signal-carrying channel so that the unwanted noise is attenuated while the signal is passed without significant modification. In AM and FM reception this is done using tuned bandpass filters that pass the signal from one station while discriminating against the signals from other stations as well as against much of the noise. Similar techniques are used in radar and sonar systems in which the weak return signals are masked by noise. There are also problems from ground clutter in radar and from surface reflections in sonar. It is important to extract the proper signal return and to reject the returns from other sources. There is also noise in the electronic components themselves, including thermal and shot. Filters play an important part in such applications, and we shall discuss this now.

In many noise studies it has been found that frequency-domain analysis is usually the most effective but time-domain techniques tend to be more convenient. Thus, we use transforms often to move between the time and frequency domains.

In the study of a signal-detection system, suppose we know that all the noise in a particular channel lies above some ω_1, which is the signal frequency. The spectrums then are

SIGNAL SPECTRUM: $\qquad F(\omega) = F_1 \quad$ at ω_1
$\qquad\qquad\qquad\qquad\qquad = 0 \quad$ elsewhere

NOISE SPECTRUM: $\qquad N(\omega) = 1 \quad$ for $\omega > \omega_1$
$\qquad\qquad\qquad\qquad\qquad = 0 \quad$ elsewhere

For optimum filtering, then, we would use a low-pass filter with the response of Figure 6-12. Physically realizable filters do not have the sharp cutoff characteristics shown; the characteristics of a simple low-pass filter are more like the dashed line.

Knowing the noise and signal spectrums and the characteristics of the realizable low-pass filter, we can express the output of the filter, from convolution techniques, as

$$f_0 = t*f \qquad \text{DESIRED SIGNAL}$$
$$n_0 = t*n \qquad \text{NOISE}$$

These are the time-domain versions of the functions in the frequency domain; t is used for the time-domain characteristics of the filter and $t*f$ for the convolution of t and f.

The reduction in power of the desired signal is

$$K_f = 1 - \frac{\displaystyle\int_0^\infty F_{0_s}(\omega)\,d\omega}{\displaystyle\int_0^\infty F_s(\omega)\,d\omega}$$

Here

$$F_{0_s} = 2\pi\,|F_0(\omega)|^2$$
$$F_s = 2\pi\,|F(\omega)|^2$$

are the power-spectrum expressions. The reduction in noise power as a result of the filtering action is then

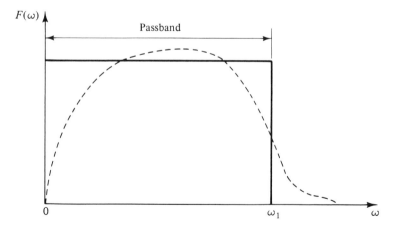

Figure 6-12 Low-pass filter.

$$K_n = 1 - \frac{\displaystyle\int_0^\infty N_{0_s}(\omega)\, d\omega}{\displaystyle\int_0^\infty N_s(\omega)\, d\omega}$$

Here

$$N_{0_s}(\omega) = 2\pi\, |N_0(\omega)|^2$$
$$N(\omega) = 2\pi\, |N(\omega)|^2$$

The functions F, F_0, N, and N_0 are the Fourier transforms of the input and output signals and the noise. If the filter is to be effective in reducing the noise, we require that

$$\frac{K_f}{K_n} < 1$$

Besides the reduction of noise power, there are other criteria in the design of filters. If the unwanted noise lies below the signal frequency, a high-pass filter must be used. In most signal-processing situations the unwanted noise lies on both sides of the signal frequency as well as in it, so a bandpass filter must be used.

In the bandpass filter almost all of the signal is accepted, but only that portion of the noise with frequencies in the passband is accepted. So although the noise may have a high total power, most of this power is rejected, improving the signal-to-noise ratio (SNR). Other schemes can be used to enhance the signal that is embedded in a noise background, and some of these can be shown to be equivalent to a bandpass filter. In any case the bandpass filter is one of the most popular methods for separating a signal from noise.

The analysis of a bandpass filter consists of two main parts:

1. The filter is analyzed for its ac response.
2. The output of the filter must be found when the sinusoidal signal is mixed with colored Gaussian noise.

The analysis can be greatly aided with a program like ECAP. It will consist of plots of the input and output voltages with time. This data can be used in several ways. It can show how the filter rejects noise and still allows deviations from the desired output. The analysis can use a generated random time series from the computer.

The computer analysis of the problem offers several advantages. It is not necessary to build the circuit in order to test it, and a great deal of flexibility in the design analysis is allowed. Besides using a sinusoidal signal, we could modulate the signal in any of a large number of ways; AM, FM, PM, or modulation schemes could be used. Each of these would require special equipment if physical tests were to be used initially in the design phase. We can obtain predictions for any signal frequency with few of the tedious calculations that are often associated with this work.

High-Frequency Amplifiers

Several circuit-analysis programs can be used for high-frequency circuit analysis. One may also wish to write a circuit-analysis program for a computer. One may not be able to use one of the existing programs owing to limited capacity or language incompatibility. We will not rank the various commercial programs. We will point out some of the advantages of the generic approaches in regard to particular problems.

Most circuit analysis begins with the formulation of the node-analysis problem. For circuit analysis, we are taught the two classical methods: loop equations and node equations. We are also taught that for plane-mappable networks these two methods are the duals to each other.

The mesh (or loop) method is generally stressed, since the use of the mesh currents in a plane-mapped network is straightforward and unambiguous. We can then use the results to find the input and transfer impedances and T-equivalent circuits for two-port networks. Since admittance is less familiar than impedance, and the duality principle allows analogous conclusions for the nodal analysis, the nodal approach is not stressed, and its advantages for computer use are often discovered later.

A circuit such as Figure 6-13 can be analyzed using a node-to-ground voltage set of equations. Once the ground node is specified and the nodes numbered this is physically meaningful and can be measured. The equations can be easily constructed since each of the equations is an expression of Kirchhoff's current law at one of the numbered nodes of the network. Each equation gives the algebraic sum of all currents leaving the node through the admittances connected to it, and equates this to the current entering the node due to the current sources which may be present. If we write the equation, which describes node 2,

$$-Y_2 V_1 + Y_2 + Y_3 + Y_4 V_2 - Y_4 V_3 = 0$$

The coefficient of V_1 is the negative of the admittance connected between nodes 1 and 2, and the coefficient of V_3 is the negative of the admittance connected between nodes 2 and 3. Each term represents the current which leaves algebraically, node 2 due to 1 volt existing at nodes 1 or 3. The

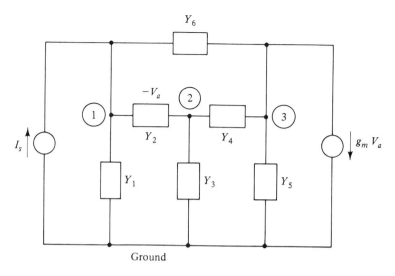

Figure 6-13   A nodal circuit.

coefficient of V_2 is the algebraic sum of all admittances connected to the node.

We can write the equations with the corresponding node voltage expressions on the left side of the equation in order to systematically keep the node voltages on one side and the independent current source terms on the other.

We can see how directly the equations are related to the circuit. In a loop or mesh analysis, the user has to specify how to fix the meshes used to write Kirchoff's voltage law.

In the nodal analysis, the only specification needed is the choice of the ground node and the numbering of the other nodes, which is easier to implement on a computer. This also gives a set of unambiguous equations even for circuits which cannot be drawn on a plane without branches crossing.

A disadvantage of the nodal analysis is that the independent sources must all be current sources and the active elements must be represented as transconductances. For circuits which contain voltage sources in series with an admittance, a Thevenin-Norton transformation of each such pair into an equivalent parallel current source and admittance may be used, provided that the current and voltage of the original Norton admittance are not among the output quantities, and provided that the controlled sources are controlled by voltages in the network. The latter requirement can be accomplished for current-controlled sources in some cases by substituting the product of the controlling branch admittance and voltage in place of the current.

An important network form is the *ladder*. In its set of loop equations the matrix of coefficients of the current terms will contain terms removed from the diagonal which are zero. The general matrix of impedance coefficients for a ladder network will have only three or less terms in a row. This occurs since no more than two adjacent loop currents can contribute mutual-impedance voltage terms to a loop equation. Controlled sources can produce terms which are in arbitrary locations. Because of this simple form of the equations (and this also occurs when node equations are used), solution by such methods as Gaussian elimination tends to be simple and straightforward.

The use of loop equations makes the transimpedance the preferred form of active element along with some use of Norton-Thevenin transformations to obtain the current-controlled voltage sources.

A thin-film UHF amplifier circuit with three transistors for the three stages of gain is shown in Figure 6-14. Resistance-inductance feedback loops are used around the first and third stages.

The schematic diagram of the circuit has a ladder-like form with the transistor model of Figure 6-15. The circuits shown can be used more directly for computer analysis of the gain or impedance of the amplifier, since the various series and/or parallel groups of elements can be reduced to equivalent impedances and then substituted into the generic form of the basic ladder for solution. Many cascade amplifiers fall into this class.

Impedance and Phase-Velocity Calculations

In order to investigate the characteristic impedance and phase velocity of transmission-line configurations, Laplace's equation is to be solved. The mode of propagation is usually assumed to be TEM, so the axial electric or magnetic components can be neglected, and the Laplace equation is solved for points of the cross section only.

The Laplace equation can be reduced to a form suitable for machine computation using finite-difference techniques. Here, the area between the conductors is divided into squares, making a net of rows and columns. The infinite number of domain points is replaced by a finite number of points at the intersections of the rows and columns. In the transmission line of Figure 6-16 the boundaries are parallel to the net lines, which makes it easy to define the problem for machine computation. If we restrict the problem to Cartesian coordinates, then, the differential equation for the potential function $U(x, y)$ is the Laplace equation:

$$\frac{\partial^2 U}{\partial x^2} + \frac{\partial^2 U}{\partial y^2} = 0$$

The boundary conditions are

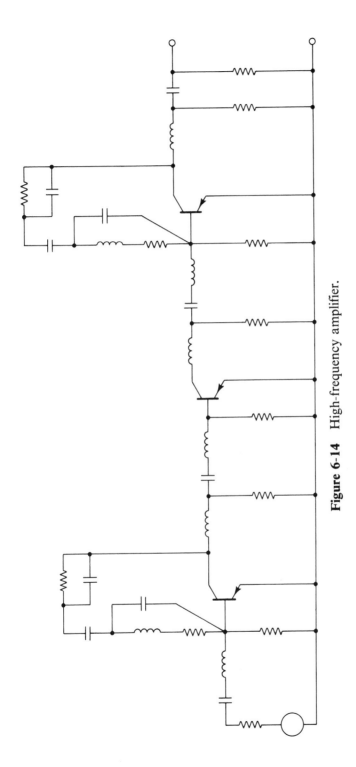

Figure 6-14 High-frequency amplifier.

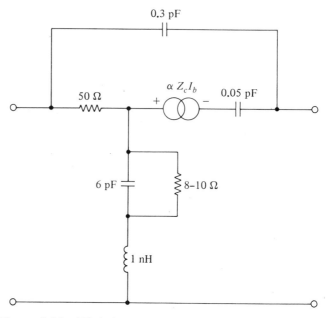

Figure 6-15 High-frequency transistor-equivalent circuit.

$U(x, y) = U_1$ along boundary 1

$U(x, y) = U_2$ along boundary 2

When the cross section has a line of symmetry, then the solution can be reduced for the case of the subdomain only and an additional boundary condition $\partial U/\partial n = 0$ on the line of symmetry. Using the indices i and j, the function of $U(x, y)$ is replaced by the function $U_{i,j}$, which is defined for the discrete mesh points only. This function must also satisfy the Laplace equation.

Suppose now we consider the potential $U_{i,j}$ of the mesh point P in relation to the potential of its four immediate squares only. If we assume a homogeneous medium and a square width a, then, by applying Taylor's theorem in the x direction, we obtain

$$U_{i,j+1} - U_{i,j} = a\,\frac{\partial U}{\partial x} + \frac{a^2}{2!}\frac{\partial^2 U}{\partial x^2} + \frac{a^3}{3!}\frac{\partial^3 U}{\partial x^3} + \frac{a^4}{4!}\frac{\partial^4 U}{\partial x^4} + \cdots$$

$$U_{i,j-1} - U_{i,j} = -a\,\frac{\partial U}{\partial x} + \frac{a^2}{2!}\frac{\partial^2 U}{\partial x^2} - \frac{a^3}{3!}\frac{\partial^3 U}{\partial x^3} + \frac{a^4}{4!}\frac{\partial^4 U}{\partial x^4}$$

Adding these expressions gives

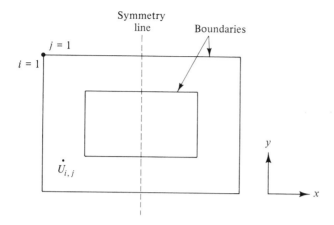

Figure 6-16 The transmission-line problem.

$$\frac{\partial^2 U}{\partial x^2} = \frac{U_{i,j-1} + U_{i,j+1} - 2U_{i,j}}{a^2} - \frac{a^2}{12}\frac{\partial^4 U}{\partial x^4} \cdots$$

$$\simeq \frac{U_{i,j-1} + U_{i,j+1} - 2U_{i,j}}{a^2}$$

This approximation holds within the limits of a^2, which controls the accuracy of the results.

If we apply Taylor's theorem in the y direction, and again combine, the Laplace equation can be shown to be

$$U_{i,j} = \tfrac{1}{4}\,(U_{i,j-1} + U_{i,j+1} + U_{i-1,j} + U_{i+1,j}{}^n)$$

This relates the potential of each mesh point to that of its immediate neighbors. The node potential along the conducting boundaries is defined by the boundary conditions. This equation can be used as an iteration formula. First,

$$U_{i,j}{}^0$$

values of an initial potential distribution for the interior points have to be assumed. Successive approximations can be obtained using the Rich equation:

$$U_{i,j}{}^{n+1} = \tfrac{1}{4}\,(U_{i,j-1}{}^n + U_{i,j+1}{}^n + U_{i-1,j}{}^n + U_{i+1,j}{}^n)$$

Here $U_{i,j}{}^{n+1}$ is the potential of the point P after $n + 1$ iterations, and we relate it to the potential values of the neighboring points after the nth iteration. We would like to have the series of values $U_{i,j}{}^n$ converge into a value $U_{i,j}$ from scanning the lattice along its successive rows and columns. The use of this method for digital computation has the disadvantage that any two successive values $U_{i,j}{}^n$ and $U_{i,j}{}^{n+1}$ for all mesh points have to be retained in the memory at the same time. If, during the scanning process, we refresh the old potential values at each point by the new ones, we get the following iteration formula:

$$U_{i,j}{}^{n+1} = \tfrac{1}{4}\left(U_{i,j-1}{}^{n+1} + U_{i,j+1}{}^n + U_{i-1,j}{}^{n+1} + U_{i+1,j}{}^n\right)$$

For faster convergence, an acceleration factor can be used; then the iteration formula becomes

$$U_{i,j}{}^{n+1} = (1 - \omega)\,U_{i,j}{}^n + \frac{\omega}{4}\left(U_{i,j-1}{}^{n+1} + U_{i,j+1}{}^n + U_{i-1,j}{}^{n+1} + U_{i+1,j}{}^n\right)$$

The simpler problem without finding the optimum acceleration factor will be treated here. In the following discussion only the case of $\omega = 1$ will be considered.

We have assumed that the medium was homogeneous. If the transmission line is partially filled with some dielectric, it can no longer support a pure TEM mode, and the characteristic impedance of the line cannot be defined in the normal way. But if the line dimensions are much smaller than half a wavelength, higher modes cannot propagate, and the TEM approximation gives good results. We will restrict the following discussions to this case.

To solve the Laplace equation for a problem involving an inhomogeneous medium, we apply the iteration formula to the whole area except for the points located on the intersection of the two regions $\varepsilon_r \neq 1$ and $\varepsilon_r = 1$ and on the lines of symmetry and on the angles. The difference equations for these points can be found using a Taylor expansion, as in the homogeneous case, but we must apply additional requirements that the normal components of the electrical displacement be continuous at the interface and that the potential of a point on the one side of a line of symmetry be identical to that of its image on the other side.

The results for all possible cases can be decreased by subdividing the lattice. The potential values for the new mesh points can be obtained by averaging the potentials of the neighboring points. The potential at a fixed point P is a function of the number of iterations for each successive subdivision. The potential has a different asymptotic value after each subdivision which is in agreement with the error associated with a certain mesh width. From the solutions obtained from increasingly fine nets, a more accurate solution can be extrapolated. In the homogeneous case, the characteristic impedance is

$$Z = \sqrt{\frac{L}{C}}$$

For a TEM line the phase velocity is

$$V = \frac{1}{\sqrt{LC}}$$

Let us define the effective dielectric constant of the medium as the ratio of the line capacitances for the medium that is inhomogeneous as C and that of air as C_0. Then, the characteristic impedance of the transmission line with an inhomogeneous medium can be expressed as

$$Z = \frac{1}{v_0 \sqrt{CC_0}}$$

Here

$$v_{\text{eff}} = v_0 \sqrt{\frac{C_0}{C}}$$

With this in mind, we can solve Laplace's equation for any TEM transmission line and determine the characteristic impedance and phase velocity.

A program for this might consist of three parts: a main program and two subroutines. The main program defines the boundary and initial conditions, calls the subroutines, and computes the final results and the convergence factor of the results for increasingly fine nets. One subroutine scans the net and computes the capacitance per unit length. The second subroutine provides the step to a finer mesh.

After setting up the initial conditions, the main program stores the results for the capacitances obtained by integrating around the inner and the outer conductors. Then a finer net may be done. After the results from several increasingly fine nets are obtained, their convergence is checked and a better result is found by extrapolation. The procedure can be done with and without dielectric material in the line.

INTEGRATED CIRCUIT DESIGN

CAD has been widely applied in the design of integrated circuits. The first integrated-circuit CAD systems were primarily drafting aids. Chip topology was created manually by designers who drew chip geometrical features on Mylar sheets. These were drawn thousands of times larger than they would actually appear on the finished chip.

The features laid out on Mylar were digitized and entered into computer memory. A CAD system could then check geometrical features on each layer. Features that usually were checked included the allowable spacing between lines (the design rules) and verification of interconnections. A small amount of logic verification and chip circuit simulation might also be used.

More recent CAD software for IC design aids in designing the chip logic and also provides advanced features for defining chip geometry. One system provides a split-screen display of chip layout. One side of the screen shows in detail the part of the circuit being designed; the other half shows a global view of where the circuit section fits into the chip layout.

Other systems provide symbolic representations of circuit elements which allow designers to design chip circuits by manipulating schematic symbols for gates or registers, rather than layout squares. Other features now being provided include the automatic compacting of layout features for maximum density and route checking.

More advanced software provides logic building blocks or cells that can be called up from a CRT terminal and combined by the user. These programs then generate a layout of the chip from a library of predefined geometries. The user interacts with the software in an attempt to optimize the electrical characteristics.

Since the processing of integrated circuits involves selective diffusion into a semiconductor wafer and the etching of metal patterns upon the wafer, these processing steps are controlled by lithographic techniques using photographic masks. The mask is a high-resolution glass photographic plate used for direct contact exposure on a semiconductor wafer. It determines the size and location of patterns diffused into or etched on the wafer. Since many integrated circuits are fabricated in each semiconductor wafer, each wafer mask is a matrix of identical chip patterns generated by repetitively stepping the appropriate mask master.

The mask stepping is handled by automated equipment, and the generation of the mask masters had been done by manual procedures. Manual mask making goes back to transistor masks. These first masks were cut out of an opaque material with a straight edge and a knife and then reduced to actual size. With the advent of the first integrated circuits, this technique was no longer satisfactory, since the increased complexity required a higher precision to get satisfactory results.

The IC manual procedures started with the layout being done by a layout draftsman from a set of layout rules and the circuit schematic. In this method, a dimensioned, detailed drawing for each device type is used to make geometrical models of the devices, and then various configurations are tried to determine the optimum placements and metal interconnection patterns.

The entire circuit is then drawn to scale, with each layer of the circuit shown using an established line code. When the drawing is complete, it is taken to a coordinatograph, where the mask masters for the various layers are cut on rubylith strip film. This is a material composed of two parts: a hard stabilene base and a soft rubylith overcoat. When the mask is cut, only enough pressure is applied to cut the softer overcoat. Then, portions of the opaque material are removed, and only the clear stabilene remains. The process is known as *stripping*. Now we have a solid-contrast master of opaque and clear areas, or ultimately the diffused and nondiffused areas.

The number of masks required depends on the number of processing steps. There is usually one mask per diffusion and two or more per metal layer. The entire process from circuit schematic to mask set depends on the complexity of the circuit. At each step of the preparation, it is necessary to wait for the preceding step, so the turn-around time from conception to mask set is not shortened by having more personnel; this just helps to eliminate the backlog.

Initially a process had to be developed to reduce the preparation time by automating portions of the manual design process. The availability of automatic drafting equipment made this feasible. An automatic drafting machine can be used to make mask masters by directly exposing photographic material with a moving light source.

The goals of cost and performance have always been keenly felt in the semiconductor industry. The drive for better integrated circuits at lower costs motivated the development of the improved procedures through automation.

The incentive to automate integrated-circuit layout and mask making was amplified by the advent of *large-scale integration* (LSI). LSI is the technology which brought forth a new generation of semiconductor products. The history of the semiconductor industry can be traced through several generations of products. Single components, simple integrated circuits, and multifunction integrated circuits were early milestones in the history of semiconductors.

The overall goal of any approach in a computer-aided implementation is to realize low costs. Set-up costs can include the costs of product specifications, design, and engineering. Production costs include all the phases of material processing and testing. With the use of simplified computer-assisted procedures for design, lower set-up costs can be achieved. The set-up costs are distributed across the production run, and their contribution depends upon the production volume. The costs of fabrication and testing are of a prime significance to low product cost. Over the years, low semiconductor costs have been tied to the batch fabrication of identical items. It is the economics of batch fabrication that brought the cost of early devices below that of the least expensive vacuum tubes.

It is also the economics of batch fabrication that keeps the cost of integrated circuits below that of circuits made up of smaller interconnected devices. The low costs result from the high volume. This should not be interpreted to mean that little can be done through automation to reduce the cost of low-volume integrated systems, but it does mean that low-volume items can never be priced competitively, per function, with high-volume items. Production costs are a function of the quantity of material processed. Thus, the attainment of satisfactory processing yields is essential.

Considerations

Semiconductor fabrication involves a high number of sequential operations. The semiconductor material must repetitively pass through such processing steps as the photo-resist development, etching, diffusion, passivation, and metal deposition. Each of these operations is conducted with great care in a tightly controlled environment; nonetheless, imperfections can result from each processing step.

The percentage of starting material which is still useful following each operation is the supposed yield. If there are 50 processing operations, the yield is the product of all 50 operations. If the average yield per operation were 98%, the resulting yield for the process of 50 operations would be 36%. The yield level that is satisfactory depends upon the total processing cost and the value of the parts.

The process imperfections which affect the yield are almost uniformly distributed over the entire semiconductor wafer. For a given number of imperfections, the chance that one will occur in an individual chip depends upon the area of the chip. If the number of chips per wafer exceeds the total number of imperfections, the yield is better than if the number of imperfections exceeds the number of chips.

VLSI involves the processing of complex chips. The two ways of increasing complexity are to increase the chip size or decrease the size of the elements. Speed is also gained through decreasing the element size.

VLSI designs have both smaller components and larger chip sizes. Although increasing the chip size reduces yield, satisfactory yields for the larger chips can be achieved with improved control through CAM on all processing steps. Total yield is one of the major problems in VLSI technology.

VLSI involves stringent techniques for the minimization of yield loss. Two basic things are done to maximize yield:

1. Improve the control in the processing steps.
2. Improve the element-area minimization.

Another more recent technique, known as *discretionary wiring*, also can enhance yields.

The rationale for discretionary wiring is that an array will not function unless all its circuits are good, and this requires a high yield if a fixed mask pattern is used. The yield of arrays fabricated with a fixed interconnection pattern will be compared to that for a more flexible or discretionary wiring scheme, which also offers lower final test costs.

The testing cost per device is the same regardless of how it is done, but the number of devices subjected to the final test may be lower with discretionary wiring. The yield of discretionary-wired devices will be higher, since the circuits were known to be good before the metallization step.

For discretionary wiring we start with a silicon wafer containing a number of diffused components connected into circuits. The circuits are of the type required in the final array, but the number of each type is in excess of the requirements. Each circuit on the wafer is then tested individually and the results retained as a record of the particular wafer. On the basis of these test results, the interconnection patterns are generated to include only those circuits that are shown to be good. The interconnection patterns are then used to apply the multilayer metallization to the wafer. After metallization, the array is ready for packaging and final testing.

Several features of the discretionary approach are important. Each interconnection mask is unique, and so is each wafer. Since the inter-connection of a complex chip represents a substantial portion of the total design effort, this unique mask is expensive. Even if the design is fully automated, there is a considerable amount of expense for a mask that can be used on only one wafer. Like the other steps in integrated-circuit fabrication, the metallization yields are not 100 percent.

The other drawback is tied to the economics of batch fabrication. Converting the surface of the silicon wafer to salable product requires that a great deal of value be added in the processing. But only a certain number of wafers can be processed in a given furnace at one time, and the mask registration is performed on a wafer-by-wafer basis. These costs are incurred on a wafer basis.

Discretionary wiring assumes that a portion of the wafer will be wasted. This tends to limit the complexity of a device (or the number of devices on a wafer). An additional drawback is that it also reduces the ultimate operating speed by introducing interconnections that are longer than necessary. There is also a need for test pads on each circuit. An even more basic drawback in discretionary wiring is the loss of the advantages of the batch-fabrication process. From the time the individual circuits are tested, each wafer has a unique identity and must be handled individually.

CAD Alternatives to Yield Enhancement

If discretionary wiring is rejected to enhance yield, the solution may be found in the yield problem itself. With a better understanding of semiconductor failure mechanisms, a better design can be done, and with an adequate computer-aided design facility, design optimization becomes a reality.

Computer-aided procedures allow a design flexibility in which exactly the number and type of components needed can be used. The circuit types used can allow optimization of both speed and power. Both circuit and logic techniques can be used to implement the desired result.

The design can be optimized with the best tradeoff between component density and the number of layers of interconnecting tracks. The design optimization resulting from this flexibility allows a product with maximum producibility using batch-processing techniques.

The number of components per device has increased with time. Taking advantage of the greater component density made possible with design optimization allows a larger number of circuits to occupy a space that can be relatively free of imperfections. The chip yield can still be high in spite of the increased complexity. Thus, complex devices can be producible, since the combined effect of increasing component densities and increasing processing yields has been demonstrated.

There are a number of approaches for device implementation. Each approach attempts to attack the dual problems of turn-around time and set-up costs without using discretionary wiring.

The *master-slice* approach attempts to get multiple usage out of a set of diffusion masks. Turn-around time is reduced by stockpiling master-slice wafers and applying custom metal to create unique parts. The concept is the same as used in the discretionary-wiring approach, but the difference is that without the cell testing the probe pads are not needed and the metal masks need not be unique for each wafer.

The master-slice approach has some inflexibility and makes inefficient use of the wafer area. The circuits on the master wafer are all that are available to the designer, and there may not be an appropriate mix of circuit types. The size of the chip is bigger than is essential, owing to the unused elements. The rapid turn-around time is the most significant advantage. The use of a computer-aided design system for generating or modifying the custom metal masks improves this important advantage.

The *cell* approach does not use any part of the discretionary-wiring technique to enhance yield. It does provide the capability for expediting the design through computer-aided techniques. It can allow a high-quality design which is optimized for the minimum chip size and the maximum processing yield. It is the concept of the cell that makes rapid but efficient design by computer practical.

The cell is some logic entity such as a gate, flip-flop, or a complex function. The data structures for these cells are stored in a library. For the design of a particular chip the designer simply specifies the desired configuration of polycells. The computer translates the specific configuration into instructions for an automatic drafting machine, which prepares a complete set of mask masters.

Although the cell approach cannot match the turn-around time of the master-slice approach, it allows lower costs through higher yields. Another advantage of the cell approach is the ease of modifying an existing design.

The master-slice and the cell approach both have their place in the semiconductor technology, and they both depend upon computer-aided design systems. There are additional problems that are being solved in the development of CAD/CAM LSI technology. The following problem areas have not been discussed to this point, although solutions to these problems are being developed.

Program Capabilities

One program that could be viewed as typical of advanced CAD design allows IC schematics to be drawn on the CRT screen with a lightpen. Each schematic symbol corresponds to a layout pattern in computer memory, and the actual spacing between the chip features is automatically determined by the program. The program can shrink the area used by the circuit until it reaches the minimum spacing allowed by the design rules.

IC design programs may manipulate the geometries in different ways. One way is to adjust the circuit cells by stretching or contracting the geometric features to make the interconnections match those of the neighboring cells. The resulting cell geometry might be larger than originally desired, but the chip area required for the wire-routing can often be greatly reduced.

When one uses a library of cells, they can all have the same height. This height uniformity allows the cells to be interconnected using standard interconnection points along the vertical sides of the cells. The cell width can be a function of the cell content. The use of standardized cells allows the cells to be routed automatically. Standard cells also allow the chip logic to be more easily verified.

Some programs can be used to simulate the chip electrical character-istics. The general approach is to combine several circuit blocks, which are defined and stored in the computer. These programs can provide the sample logic-function simulations which take into account operational factors such as timing and the synchronization between circuits.

A simulation program may accept descriptions of the circuit architecture (the routing and processing of the signals) and produce a list of standard circuit elements and the interconnections that will produce the design. Another approach is to generate the circuit layouts from the circuit descriptions in Boolean equation form. These programs usually plan the interconnections for programmable logic arrays. The programs can also provide information such as the amount of silicon area that will be occupied, the aspect ratio, speed, power dissipation, and connectivity factors.

An important feature found in integrated-circuit CAD systems is design-rule checking. The conductor pattern as shown in Figure 6-17 is checked by the computer for conformance to design standards. If the conductor is too close, the system issues an error message. The program may automatically modify the layout and then display the modified pattern.

A number of procedures can be used to reduce the amount of time required to run IC simulation programs. We can reduce the computer time by emulating only those portions of the circuit that are active. We can also mix simulations at the circuit level with simulations at the gate, register, and block level. The objective here is to allow detailed interactions between parts of the chip design before other parts are defined in detail.

There are also programs that assist in defining the interconnections for master-slice chips. Here, predefined circuits on a chip are produced with no interconnections, and the designer specifies the interconnections to synthesize the functions that each individual chip is to perform.

One first develops a logic diagram of the required functions, and this information serves as a database for the circuit-simulation routines. The computer then produces a physical layout, which is automatically checked to ensure that the electrical parameters such as timing and power constraints have not been exceeded. Finally the test patterns are generated to verify the completed chip.

Test Problems

VLSI breaks down the conventional boundary between device and system design and involves both circuit and logic design. With the complexity

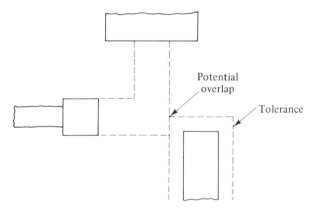

Figure 6-17 Design-rule checking.

of VLSI parts, the logic structure is inseparably linked to the system structure. This changes the manner in which the circuits must be specified.

The specifications still include the circuit parameters, but structure must also be completely defined. To specify the function for such a unit requires detailed system structure data, in the form of logic schematics and also logic equations. Much of this data is proprietary.

The use of a computer-aided design system in the device-system interface may both help and complicate the requirement for protecting proprietary rights. Because of the increased complexity in a VLSI part, its desired system functions cannot always be clearly implied by the specifications. To assure that the VLSI parts will function as desired, it is important that the specifications include detailed functional data which can be verified using a standard testing procedure.

Along with increasing complexity there is an increasing concern that, although the end product may satisfy the specifications, it may fail to function properly in the system. Such problems can entail a great deal of cost and time for the redesign and reprocessing that are needed. A comprehensive design-verification system can include the capability for circuit analysis, and from the results of the circuit analysis the parameters for a model of each circuit can be generated. The parameters and the logic structure of the design can then be used for a system simulation. The simulation allows the behavior of the design to be predicted and compared against the functional requirements.

In a digital system the functional simulation in its simplest form is the logical simulation for the combinatorial networks. The simulation of sequential digital logic is also feasible, but it requires more sophisticated techniques. First, a dynamic model of the logic elements is established. Then, with the initial conditions set, the logic equations for the internal functions can be iteratively solved until the network is stable. Next, the input transitions are applied in sequence. If this type of digital simulation is to be successful, the time increment must be as small as or smaller than the transition time for the model.

The testing of VLSI presents problems not encountered in other integrated circuits. The requirement for parameter testing is complicated by the lack of input and output pins. Functional testing of VLSI devices requires the application of techniques which have been uncommon in testing integrated circuits. The functional operation of many simple digital integrated circuits can be exhaustively tested by monitoring the outputs while sequencing through the possible input and internal state combinations. In larger devices the number of inputs and internal states is so large that the number of possible states is too high, even for very fast automatic testers. Exhaustive testing is impractical, and some other test sequence must be generated.

There are two separate requirements for testing sequences. Until a design is in production, it is desirable to diagnose failure so that the design imperfections can be eliminated and the process procedures optimized. Thus tests which isolate individual failure are desired. When the device is in production, more efficient testing sequences are needed to detect faults using a minimum of tests. Minimizing the test complexity is required here, since this testing cost contributes directly to the final cost of the device.

There are a number of philosophies for testing. Most of these are concerned with the problem of production testing. Here, one must assure a certain probability that parts are good using a minimum of tests. One approach is *comparative testing*. A good unit or an appropriate physical mode is exercised in parallel with a unit under test and the outputs compared. The sequence of input changes during the tests could be random or generated by algorithms from the test criteria. Test by comparison has some merits, but it cannot be used until a good unit is found or built.

There is also a variety of test equipment that does not depend on comparison techniques. These testers require *test sequences* to be generated for the control of their operation. The techniques used for generating these test sequences may involve a large amount of development. The more successful procedures use pseudolanguages. These languages work much like a compiler in that they translate statements of the test criteria into the testing sequences with the correct data format for controlling the test equipment. Automatic test-sequence generation can also be achieved by computer-simulated techniques.

Circuit complexity will increase, since the processing ability and the demand for more powerful integrated circuits exists. Components with greater density, larger packages, and more input-output pins will be in demand. As devices get larger and more complex, the need for automation in layout and mask making grows, as does the need for computer aids in the other design and implementation functions.

PRINTED-CIRCUIT BOARD LAYOUT

Once the circuit is designed, the next step is building the physical circuit. If the circuit is to be built on a printed-circuit board, the computer can play a significant role. The computer's primary function is graphical. It can be used for electronic drafting, as shown in Figure 6-18. It can also assist in laying out the components on a board and in determining an optimum routing for the interconnections, as shown in Plates 18 and 19.

Computers have been used in the design of printed-circuit boards (PCBs) for years, but their role is changing rapidly. Originally, computers were used only to produce precision PCB artwork after a designer had manually determined the component placement and routed the conductors. Now, computers are used to optimize the component placement and conductor routing on the circuit boards.

This change is due to a trend toward more crowded PCBs with many more components. A two-layer circuit board several years ago may have had one square inch of board area for each 14-pin integrated circuit; now the density is less than one-half square inch per IC.

Boards with only a few components can be designed manually. But for boards that may contain upward of 150 chips, a computerized routine may be the only practical method (Plate 20).

The circuit boundaries and packaging considerations affect the topology of the circuit board. Some of the more important considerations are:

1. The pin spacing and the number of pins in the connectors.

2. The board dimensions and the aspect ratio relative to the connector.

3. The number of surfaces on the board. Is it single-sided, double-sided, or multilayer?

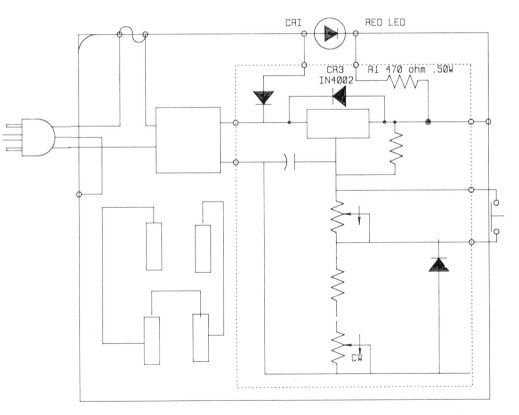

Figure 6-18 A CAD drafting system can be used to create and edit schematics such as shown here. (Courtesy: T&W Systems, Versa CAD Division.)

4. The power distribution and filtering requirements as well as the need for a ground plane.

A number of techniques are available for the etching of printed-circuit cards. The choice of technique ranges from the relatively crude prototype method, using the direct application of an etch-resistant tape or paint to the printed-circuit laminated stock, to using a photo-resist with silk-screening techniques for larger production quantities.

The loading of the boards with components is simpler if placement is systematic. Thus it may be desirable to align resistors and capacitors in arrays with the integrated circuits in some systematic pattern. In high-frequency circuits, the design considerations may require the placement of the components in positions and orientations determined by functional performance characteristics of the circuit.

The highly variable nature of these considerations suggests that a general system which deals with all the known variables in printed-circuit board design may be a formidable unit. Another problem is that innovations in circuitry and packaging can introduce new variables. The complexity of the problem suggests that, in order to rely entirely on a computer program, either the program must be exceptionally detailed, with complex involutions in its algorithms, or the variables must be handled by different programs for particular classes of circuits. In either case the programs could be difficult to modify to keep up with the changing technology.

The answer to the problem of handling the variables in printed-circuit card design while keeping up with the art may lie in systems that rely heavily on human-machine interactions. Thus, the designer can retain control over certain decisions, while the computer solves the topological problems and furnishes a high-quality graphic output for the printed-circuit board production.

The printed-circuit board designer might describe the circuit to the computer by making a sketch on the CRT with a lightpen, tablet, or some other form of input. The computer then presents a display of the circuit tracks to the designer, and the process should be repeated until a final solution is produced. Then the computer can produce a high-quality graphical output.

Our aim in the design of printed-circuit artwork should be the production of printed-circuit boards of acceptable quality at a low cost. Elegant systems that produce topological solutions at a high expense are self-defeating.

Routing Logic

After the schematic has been sketched (Figure 6-19) and the components chosen, we can begin to design the board. Some methods employed to handle this phase may be manual; others are automated. The procedures required by

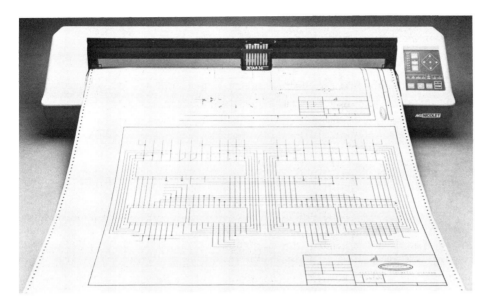

Figure 6-19 A plotter that can generate an electronic schematic. (Courtesy: Nicolet Computer Graphics Division)

the manual and automated approaches differ in many respects, but there are some common characteristics. After a board size is chosen, it is necessary to position the required components. The placement will be influenced by a number of considerations:

1. Interconnecting components should be close together.
2. Components should have the proper orientation to the connector tabs near their respective edges.
3. Components should be spaced in order to evenly distribute the board density and heat.

If we permit modification of the placement during the routing, the time and the amount of modification allowable depend on the routing philosophy used to develop the software.

One of the most practical considerations is to avoid short circuits. The lines that cross each other must be on different layers of the board or be rerouted. The use of parallel lines on opposite sides of the board, which tend to be superimposed over one another and separated by the dielectric material of the board, should be avoided because they would create a large capacitance between them. It is also desirable to minimize the overall wire length, which minimizes the inductance and optimizes the use of board space. The number of holes should also be minimized to reduce feedthrough costs.

In the manual design of a printed board there may be some distinct advantages over a computer-aided system. The primary advantage is the more flexible variety of procedures, since one is not confined to a predetermined set of rules.

One might first establish a rough layout of the components, then route the more obvious connections, keeping the lead length as short as possible while avoiding crossing through the board and all the while planning ahead so as to leave enough area for the other paths.

The more difficult connections may require some shifting of components or connection lines. The more difficult connections may require that some liberties be taken for this particular circuit. The capacitance effect may not be of importance for the pair of lines involved, or one may wish to extend the leads on a particular component in such a way that its terminal spacing allows an additional path to cross below it.

One is not restricted to a particular grid; various curved lines may be used. With a free space to work with, the capability of this visual image can constantly cause one to alter the ground rules. The disadvantages are the increased time and cost. After routing a connection, one may later have to reroute portions of it or the entire connection. To shift large blocks of the routing is a slow and tedious procedure and can be very costly. There is also the problem of errors. No system can be completely error-free, but with automated systems it can be minimal. Humans can also tire and resort to jumpers sooner than necessary.

Automated Systems

Two different philosophies can be used to effect an automated system for printed-circuit design. A three-dimensional model is used by the topological approach, while other systems may use a two-dimensional model.

In the topological approach, first we set up a three-dimensional model with peaks, slopes, plains, and valleys based on the component pin locations. Then, to locate the components, a grid is set up with weighting factors which represent the board's terrain or features. This establishment of a fixed grid is one of the disadvantages of the automated systems. But if the grid is made fine enough, it can closely approximate the optimal connection pattern. The weighting factors may be influenced by voltage or other considerations. As the paths are routed and new paths are created the topography of the model changes. The valleys are chosen as the preferred paths, while the ridges and peaks are the unavailable areas. An incremental process is used to route the path from its origin to its destination.

For any system to be useful, a working framework must be established first. The ground rules may take considerable discussion and experimentation. These rules will be centered around factors such as component placement, board size, dimensions, line spacing, and scaling factors for the graphical output. Most of the rules may come from the following considerations:

1. What size boards are actually needed?
2. What components are available and currently being used?
3. What effects would photographic reduction have on pad size and line width?
4. What line widths are necessary with the current fabrication techniques to insure reliable circuitry?

There are also considerations imposed by both the hardware and software. These include the size of the plotting surface, the grid, pen widths, and increments used in plotting. The software will be influenced by the programming difficulty of the algorithms. It is convenient to use 0.1-inch spacing for lines and pads, because IC component leads and pins are usually fabricated for use on 0.1-inch centers. A double-sided board could have all horizontals on one side and all verticals on the other.

The working area is blocked into squares, and any rectangle within the array can be used. The circular configuration used for some parts must also fit the grid pattern in some convenient and workable way. A centered position can then be chosen for these packages, with rotation provided for alignment. The choice of positioning is a convenience for the user, not a restriction.

A facility must also be provided for specifying discrete points within the grid area. This allows the user to use variable-length resistors and inductors and to shift packages. These various considerations are then used as the framework to build a system.

The coordinate system that is devised should facilitate easy definition of the points to be connected. Each point of the board might be specified by some combination of codes:

1. The type of component.
2. The square boundaries the component is in.
3. The pin being specified with the component.

The points that are to be interconnected together must also be accepted by the program. There will be as many of these inputs as are necessary to describe the circuit.

The additional information which may be necessary to complete a board includes the board dimensions, the location of connector tabs, and such information as the scale to be used for the graphic output.

Experience shows that unnecessary failures can occur when data points are improperly coded. The system should have provisions which examine the data and reject any data that cannot be interpreted. A message is then sent to indicate to the user what data has been rejected. These error messages may warn of errors in the board outline, scale factors, or the interconnection list.

The error messages might include:

1. Component code not valid.
2. Pin code does not agree with component code.
3. Connection called from nonexistent square.
4. Connector cannot be mapped for this board.
5. Connector number greater than allowed for this board.
6. Size specification.
7. Error in board specifications; outline cannot be drawn.
8. Data point exceeds board dimensions.
9. Paths could not be found for the following connections.

Producing the Board Artwork

Manufacturers who do not need computerized routing may still use computers to prepare the board artwork for production. Here the operators enter the board features into a computer database by digitizing the manually designed layout patterns. Computer software then produces the finished pattern by refining the input layout.

The software performs such functions as squaring off and aligning the conductor patterns and verifying that the board features comply with the minimum spacings and the other design rules. The final layout data may be transformed by software known as a *postprocessor* into the proper format to drive a photoplotter.

The photoplotter produces the film masters for each layer of the artwork (Figure 6-20). It uses the information in the database to produce the artwork for the board, the silk screen, assembly drawing, solder-resist mask, and drilling template.

The files that define the circuit-board layouts can also contain data other than what is needed by the photoplotter. Some of the information in the files can be used by a postprocessor to produce paper tapes for operating NC drills that are used to make the boards. Other data could be used to develop the control instructions for automatic component-insertion machines. The postprocessor also allows such tasks as optimizing the drill-head paths to minimize the drill-head travel and drill time.

The software that automatically routes circuit-board conductors works best on boards consisting of all digital circuits. The software can typically route all but 1% to 10% of conductors on these boards. The rest of the conductors are routed manually with some assistance from the computer.

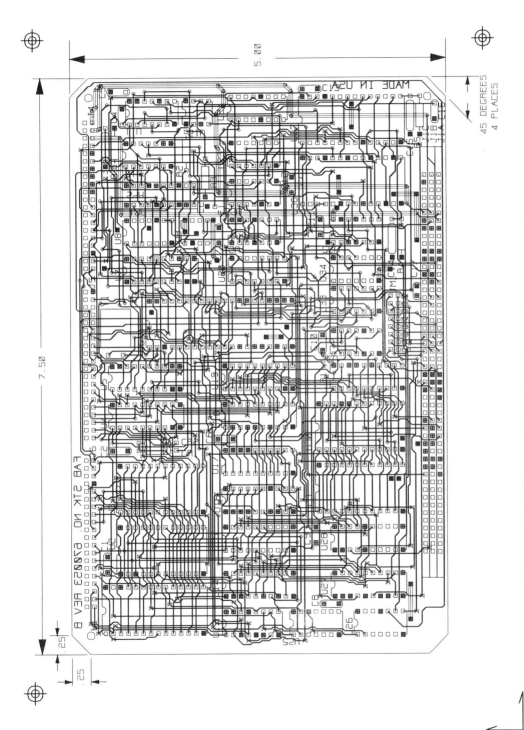

Figure 6-20 PCB artwork produced on a CAD system. (Produced by Vectron Graphic Systems. Courtesy: Nicolet Computer Graphics Division)

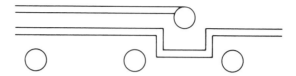

Figure 6-21 Effect of contour following on a digital board. The tendency is to pack the track density around feed-through holes.

Circuit boards that contain many analog components are generally harder to route automatically. The analog components on these boards usually have irregular features, making it difficult for the computer to plan the conductor routes. Digital circuits with their uniform packages can be more easily partitioned into grids. The regular, repetitive locations of the chip pins on a digital board fall neatly within the grid cells, while the irregularly shaped analog component leads do not. If only contour following is used, the regular digital patterns can produce the problem shown in Figure 6-21.

The computer uses grids in calculating the path placements for the conductors and packages in an effort to minimize such problems as track packing. Most routing routines are interactive, so the designers can modify or change the program actions as they occur. The percentage of route completions generally depends on the board density, size, and the design criteria such as the track and pad sizes.

The routing software may use a variety of routines to minimize conductor paths. One routine swaps each IC with the adjacent ICs in both the x-direction and the y-direction to determine if the connection paths can be decreased. Other routines compare the board conductors to the allowable dimensional tolerances to determine if the spacing criterion has been met.

As the software begins moving chips around on the board to minimize conductor lengths, this optimization process may be shown on the screen, so that the user can view the process as it takes place. The software may also provide indicators of how the component placement is progressing. The system, for example, might read out the total length of board connections at a given time. The user may monitor this number and watch it decrease as the optimization progresses.

The first attempt at changing the component placement may be followed by other routines which attempt to shorten the length of each connection on the board by finding the shortest distance between points. This process might use a routine which swaps the chips to see if the connection lengths will decrease. Once these routines are complete, the user may change the layout by using a lightpen to obtain some additional economies.

Special routines may be used to treat the irregularly shaped analog components. The software might place the analog components near the chips they connect to. Other systems may use direct associativity between the

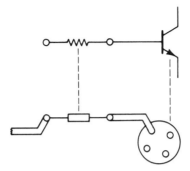

Figure 6-22 An example of associativity.

schematic and the PCB layout, as shown in Figure 6-22; then the various minimization routines may be used.

COMPUTER-AIDED ELECTRONIC DRAFTING

The first step in automatic routing is to prepare lists of components and connections between components from the schematic diagram which may be generated using electronic drafting software.* Using a library of predefined part types, a graphics display, and a mouse for cursor movement and entering the schematic connections, the system provides a method of computer-aided drafting. Some automatic routing systems are hampered by the slowness of entering schematics. To speed up the process, an electronic drafting package can be used to create and edit the schematics (Figure 6-23). The pin list created can be uploaded to a routing computer for placing and routing. All the information needed to place and route a printed circuit board is in the pin list.

The library of symbols of parts will handle most schematic designers' needs. The symbols range from discrete resistors, capacitors, and switches to complex parts like microprocessors and peripheral chips. DeMorgan equivalents are available for most of the logic gates. If a part is not in the library, one can create a symbol for it by using symbol-definition commands.

The insertion of symbols can take about a second for a 16-bit microprocessor, but for some systems it can take as long as a minute during busy periods. Moving and copying components or sections of a schematic can be done in about two seconds for a small section. This speed occurs because one can view the schematic in only two sizes—COMPRESSED, where the

*This section contains copyrighted material supplied by the Future Net Corporation, used with permission.

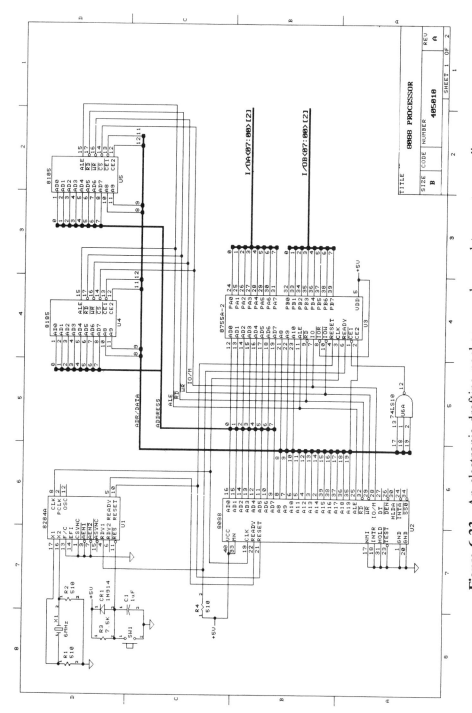

Figure 6-23 An electronic drafting package can be used to create an edit schematics such as this. (Courtesy: Future Net Corporation)

entire drawing is viewed no matter what size has been selected; and FULL, where a section is viewed in legible size.

Systems that allow one to select any size of display, using zoom commands, tend to be slower, since they have to calculate new dimensions each time the screen is changed. If the dimensions are fixed, changing between FULL and COMPRESSED displays can be done quickly.

Since there are three different sizes of characters for labeling and four different types of lines (normal, thick bus lines, dotted, dashed), the choices are enough for most work. Again, with fewer variables for the computer to have to recalculate frequently, the system can respond quickly.

Dots around a component designate the symbol's boundaries. The center of the screen is used for the graphics area. Along the top and bottom of the screen are numbers, and along the sides are letters; these numbers and letters are used for sectioning reference.

On the right side of the screen is the status column for the 12 different status fields. These include FULL, COMPRESSED, ALPHA, and SYM. ALPHA mode is used when text is being entered for the pin names, signal names, pin numbers, and references. The SYM mode is for the symbol definitions.

LINE, CHAR, and ATTR status indicators are used for line width, character height, and attribute status. The attribute status indicates to the program if the next text being entered is a pin number, circuit designation, part number, component value, signal name, drawing title, drawing number, drawing revision, drawing page, drawing date, nonprinting ground or power connection, or any other attribute that is defined. Zero is used as the default attribute, to represent extraneous text for labeling data that is not to go in the pin list.

Six fields are used for position and size status indicators. XLOC and YLOC show the current position of the graphics cursor with respect to the top left corner.

SYMW and SYMH show the symbol width and height of the symbol currently pointed to by the graphics cursor. The size of the drawing selected is shown by DWGW and DWGH. The size and location indicators are based on a square unit. Another status field shows which attribute is assigned to the text that the graphics cursor is presently pointing to, and another status indicator is used to show how much RAM is left in the system.

An area near the bottom is used for the command cursor. This area is the command line where the user enters instructions to create and edit the schematics.

Command Structure

The eight major command groups are Executive, Cursor Movement, Symbol Editing, Line Editing, Alphanumeric Editing, Area Editing, Mouse, and Symbol Definition. The editing command groups are similar except for the prefix notation that selects what the command operates on. For example:

1. The T command means to Target an item for copying or moving.
2. With a "." in front of the T, the command targets a symbol.
3. /T targets a line.
4. 'T targets alphanumeric text.
5. [T targets a schematic area.

The executive command group is used to LOAD, SAVE, and PRINT the schematic drawings. The "C" (COMPRESSED) selection causes the schematic to be printed half the normal size. One can also select which strip of the schematic to print. Each strip corresponds to an 11-inch-wide section of the schematic. This means that with a wide-carriage printer, you can print A and B size drawings in one strip, C and D size drawings in two strips, and an E size drawing in three strips. One can tape these strips together to make a complete drawing or use multiple-page schematics of B size or smaller. The SIZE command selects the size of the drawing. You can also select your own dimensions up to 50 by 50 inches. The drawing sizes and their equivalent display units are shown below:

	Inches		Display Units	
Size	Width	Height	Width	Height
A	11	8.5	198	170
B	17	11	306	220
C	22	17	396	340
D	34	22	612	440
E	44	34	792	680

The display units are about 0.05 inch square, such that the drawing has the proper dimensions.

The PgUp and PgDn keys are used to switch from FULL to COMPRESSED mode. To clear the screen and start a schematic over, the ERASE command is used. The MOUSE command activates and deactivates the mouse hand control for cursor movement and line insertion and editing. The WRITE command creates an ASCII formatted file that contains all the connections, signal names, pin numbers, component values and numbers, and other drawing information, to upload to another system for automatic routing.

There are three ways to move the graphics cursor around the drawing: the mouse, the cursor direction keys, and "GOTO" references. The mouse is a small mechanical/electrical device, as discussed in Chapter 3. When you move the mouse in any direction, electrical signals are sent to the processor, depending on which way the mouse is moving. The system then updates the screen accordingly.

The second way to move the cursor is to use the Up, Down, Left, and Right arrow keys. The cursor moves one display unit at a time in the direction selected. You can move any number of units at a time if you enter that number on the command line first and then press an arrow key.

The other method of cursor movement is the reference mode. You enter "A1" through "D8" at the keyboard and move to the position on the screen corresponding to the reference letters and numbers on the sides of the screen. You can also move a component in the schematic by entering an "N" and the component's reference number. Each symbol entered into the drawing is assigned a reference number in sequence. The twelfth symbol entered is assigned the number 12, and the cursor can jump to that part by entering "N12".

You can also keep track of the last ten cursor positions by using Tab and Shift-Tab. You can then move forward and backward through the last ten positions.

An electronic design system should be able to insert and modify schematic components easily and quickly. It should also have a comprehensive library of parts as well as the ability to add parts. A good library should include most of the discrete components and the more popular integrated circuits. Many of the different types of components are thus already included in the system library.

To list the parts in a library, one enters a command. Other symbol editing commands allow you to:

1. Insert or load a part from a library.

2. Target a component, cancel the current symbol target, move (.M).

3. Copy a component.

4. Erase a component from the drawing.

A component is targeted before it can be moved, copied, or erased.

Symbol Editing commands can provide an easy way to create a rectangular component. A ".B w,h" command creates a block symbol that can be edited to be the diagram of an IC. The width and height of the symbol boundary are defined by "w" and "h". The actual IC block is inside the symbol boundary to leave room for the "pin stubs" and the pin numbering and symbol text. The symbol must be slightly larger than the actual component outline to allow for the extra lettering and numbering.

The new symbols representing ICs not supplied in the symbol library are created using these Symbol Editing commands. Starting with the blank outline of the IC, short lines are added to represent the chip's pin stubs. Four types of pin stubs used are normal, inverted, clock, and inverted clock.

The .D command can be used to erase any pin stubs you do not want. Rectangular IC symbols and other more difficult components can be created by using the Symbol Definition commands.

After you have inserted some components, you need to connect them together. The Line Editing commands provide this capability. Using function keys, one can select normal-sized line segments, thick line segments for bus lines, dotted lines, and dashed lines. The Line commands operate where the graphics cursor is before the command is entered.

These Line Editing commands are used to draw a line connecting the points in a schematic diagram. Suppose the graphics cursor is at pin 8 of chip U2. This location is marked by entering /L, and the graphics cursor is moved over to the other end of the connection. After this destination is marked with the /L command, the complete line appears.

The Line commands can be used to make all interconnections, but the mouse can do this faster. Instead of entering the Line commands at the keyboard, you just press one of three buttons on the mouse for the same result. Pressing one button is the same as entering a /L command. Another button inserts or deletes interconnecting dots, and it also repositions the screen display if it is pressed when the graphics cursor is located at the edge of the screen. The other button is the command for erasing line segments.

To insert the line from pin 8 of U2 as discussed above, you position the cursor at pin 8, press the button on the mouse, move the cursor to the designation, and press the button again. No commands are entered at the keyboard, so the line insertion and editing are quicker with the mouse, and, after a few hours of practice, one can create a schematic much faster.

After you have inserted the components and made the interconnects, the next step is to label these using Alphanumeric Editing commands. As with Symbol Editing, there are commands to target move, copy, and erase alpha fields.

The alpha fields are the areas of text labeling that define the pin numbers, IC reference designations, component part numbers and values, and the signal and pin names. A small boundary is used around the alpha fields similar to the boundary around the symbol blocks. The boundaries cannot overlap, and they must touch the line segment to be associated with the line. The boundary for the pin number must have its boundary touch the pin stub to correctly identify the pin number with the pin stub. Normally the alpha field boundaries are not displayed, but entering a command toggles the alpha boundary display on or off. Another command enables the display of the alpha attribute display.

Each alpha field entered must have an attribute assigned to it to show what the text being entered is to represent:

1. Pin number.
2. Component number.
3. Component reference.
4. Component value.
5. Signal name.
6. Drawing number.
7. Drawing revision.
8. Drawing date.

These attributes enable an automatic routing system to route a printed-circuit board. A command is used to assign the correct attribute to the alpha text that is entered next.

For components that must be added in a section of the schematic where there isn't any room, you use the Area Editing commands. You target an area of the schematic for the move command to make room for the other part. You can also even copy sections of the schematic and then move them.

To target an area for moving or saving, we place the graphics cursor in the corner of the area wanted, enter the target command, then place the cursor in the opposite corner and press the Return key. A dashed block will appear around the area targeted to show what has been selected.

After an area move, there are usually some line segments that need to be reconnected, since the move affects only items that are completely inside the targeted area. To use the moved section again on other schematics, we can SAVE that area on disk.

The Symbol Definition commands must be sufficient to create any schematic symbol needed that is not included in the system's library. When creating a new symbol or editing an old one, the split-screen format is useful. The screen is split up into two sections. One side is the symbol display area; the other side displays the commands entered to create the symbol. The symbol elements can be used to create more complicated symbols, such as arrows, triangles, and circles. The graphics elements may include gates, coils, resistors, and capacitors that can be used to build other parts.

For speeding up schematic entry, a pin-list capability is an important aspect of the system. The pin list gives the details of each connection, pin number, signals tied to each pin, component reference, component part number, and component value. This information could be sent through a communications link to another computer for materials control, purchasing information, or other screening functions.

EXERCISES

1. Discuss the use of the ECAP circuit branches.

2. Discuss how a circuit-analysis program can take advantage of a designer's experience while offering freedom from iterative computations and bookkeeping chores.

3. Model a single-phase squirrel-cage induction motor and discuss a possible computer program for computer-aided analysis.

4. Discuss how the following motor curves could be obtained from a computer-aided analysis.

   a. Speed torque.

   b. Power-factor torque.

   c. Output torque.

   d. Input torque.

   e. Efficiency torque.

5. An important feature of a circuit-analysis program, if it is to be successfully processed and executed, is that the algorithm must be without errors; then the solution will probably be correct. What program checks can be used to ensure that this occurs?

6. In a transformer analysis, details of the cores and wires that may be used are important in selecting the desired materials. Show how the maximum circular mils per ampere for either the primary or secondary design is used in selecting the proper wire size. Draw a flow diagram for this algorithm.

7. Show how an adaptive controller design can lead to analysis problems for a simple system as well as possible instability. What are the problems in writing a computer program of this type?

8. In an interactive circuit-analysis program each option displayed is a light button on the screen with a unique value associated with it. Through programming, the value of the light button is repeatedly checked until the correct one is selected. This prevents the user from selecting an option from which a recovery cannot be achieved. Discuss the advantages and disadvantages of this scheme.

9. Show how the characteristic impedance and the phase velocity can be determined for nonuniform transmission lines.

10. In some engineering problems, when there does not seem to be a unique way of ascertaining the accuracy of the obtained results, one possibility is to find a problem which resembles the problem as closely as possible and which has a known analytical solution. By solving both problems numerically under comparable conditions,

the accuracy found for the standard problem should also apply to the problem under consideration. Discuss how this approach can be applied in a CAD program for transmission lines.

11. Once a circuit board has been completely routed, a number of checking routines are generally used to verify the design. Discuss the checks that could be used for a digital board.

GEOMETRIC
MODELING

7

In many design instances it is far easier, cheaper, and safer to experiment with a model than with a real entity. In many engineering situations, such as commercial pilot training and nuclear-reactor studies, modeling and simulation provide the only feasible method for teaching or designing the system. Thus, computer modeling is replacing the more traditional techniques, such as the building of scale models for wind-tunnel testing or other feasibility studies.

Examples of a model system are the macroeconomic models used to compute the net income produced by a price increase and to compute how advertising would have to be increased to produce an increase in sales volume. As another example, simulated car crashes using computer modeling techniques are much less costly than those involving real cars, occupied by dummies and instrumentation, which are actually crashed into barriers and destroyed. In the process much of the required data may be lost owing to instrument malfunction. Weather forecasting, too, is done by feeding real-time measurements into a model of the local weather system, which is then used to compute the probabilities of the various weather conditions. Modeling techniques also allow astronauts to practice navigation for space missions, and pilots to learn to fly in animated simulators. Safety designers can also test the integrity of the passenger compartment with simulated crashes for a wide variety of aircraft and space vehicles in the air and on the ground.

A major concern in modeling is to design and implement a model which, by using suitably precise quantities, adequately reflects the properties of the system. If possible, the model should be checked against the real system, and if they differ, the designer will try to adjust the model to improve its accuracy and utility.

HOW MODELS ARE CONSTRUCTED

Models are often represented as systems of equations, with input and output variables and adjustable parameters such as coefficients and exponents. In addition, special functions can be defined by the user, thereby allowing the model to take on characteristics oriented to a particular special purpose. In a continuous-system simulation the input and output may be facilitated by means of user-oriented control statements for the preparation of a data set at selected increments of the independent variables. Convenient means must be available for terminating a simulation run with a sequence of computations or logical tests. These can be used to test-run responses and define run-control conditions for accomplishing iterative simulations of the type required in parameter-optimization studies.

The parameter data, run-control data, and connection statements can be prepared in any order for automatic sequencing by the program. This feature permits the user to concentrate on the phenomenon being simulated rather than on the mechanism for implementing the simulation.

Today's microcomputers bring the power of a modern large-scale computer directly to the desk of the engineer and scientist. Multiple terminals connected to a remote computer have become familiar, day-to-day tools in the professional life of engineers. A significant feature of such systems is their conversational ability. Conversational computing, a mode of operation created by a combination of operating systems and data-processing equipment, actually permits the user and the computer to communicate in a conversational manner—giving and requesting new information, correcting each other, and making suggestions.

The user and the computer thus carry on question-and-answer conversations statement by statement. The computer immediately notifies the user if it does not understand or cannot accept a statement. At the same time the user has the ability to interrupt the computer while it is running its program, modify his position, and then resume the job. If so desired, the program can be stopped in the middle, what has been done can be saved, and the computer can go on to something else.

There are many design problems today that cannot be solved with only one answer. After structuring the problem mathematically, one must be able to analyze the data in a sequence of iterations. In order to achieve the best possible result, the problem is solved for one set of conditions, the results are observed, then the conditions are changed, and the results are again observed. This process may be repeated many times before an acceptable solution is obtained. There are three categories of models to which this conversational processing is uniquely suited:

1. Organizational models, including institutional bureaucracies and taxonomies such as library classification schemes and biological taxonomies.

2. Quantitative models, which may include econometric, financial, demographic, climatic, chemical, physical, and mathematical problems.

3. Geometric models, including parts engineering and architectural features, chemical structures, and physical plants.

Models need not be computerized. Because of the usefulness of computer models as computer-based representations of objects and processes, however, we are most interested in those models which lend themselves to graphic interpretation. Among the common types of models for which computer graphics is most useful are those which have intrinsically geometric data associated with them. Abstractions such as organizational models are not spatially oriented, but most such models can be represented geometrically.

An organizational model can be depicted by an organization chart. It may contain geometric information, but the particular graphical representation of the geometry is not dictated. We can change the viewpoint in the chart. A number of projections could be used in addition to the standard viewing options. There might be hidden-line removal, cross-hatching or shading, and various color effects used. The pictorial presentation may be enriched with a number of nongeometric techniques.

Modeling Characteristics

One of our main purposes is to determine how geometrical information is encoded in the model. Among the information that may be present in the model is:

1. Basic data elements and their relationships.
2. The spatial layout and the shape of components. This is their geometry and other information related to their appearance, such as color and shading.
3. The connectivity of components. This is the structure or topology of the system.
4. The data values such as the electrical or mechanical parameters or descriptive text.
5. The actual processing algorithms such as used for a linear-circuit analysis or a finite-element analysis for mechanical structures.

The model is a description of the components and the processes which together specify the structure and the behavior of the system. In some cases it is useful to show either or both of these pictorially.

We might wish to want to see both a circuit's physical layout on a circuit board and its output as a function of the inputs and time. Determining what structural and parameter information is to be encoded in the model can involve many compromises between the simplicity and tractability of the model and the degree of realism required. The computational resources available are another part of the tradeoff.

There are also a number of time-vs.-space tradeoffs. Choices must be made with respect to the schemes that allow fast analysis or fast display. There must be enough information in the model to allow both analysis and display, but the exact choices of techniques are dependent on the application and hardware tradeoffs. In the earlier years of computers the modeling activity was integrated with the display and input handling; now modeling is primarily an activity of the application software. There is a clear distinction now between the building and modifying of models and the using of them.

Modeling applications can be totally designed without involving any graphics. But the use of modern modeling software packages depends on the presence of graphics to make the picture and allow the user interaction. In most modeling application programs the major portion of the program deals with entities, and only about 20% with the picture of them. Thus most application software tends to be data- and processing-intensive and not picture-intensive. There are many applications in which the picture is critical, such as sketching, painting, film animation, and the animating of scenes for flight simulators. However, in computer-aided design we treat the pictorial models as a means to an end in the analysis and construction activities that we are concerned with. In this chapter we deal with models that involve a nontrivial amount of processing.

These models will consist of the application data structure plus a collection of application program procedures that define this structure. Figure 7-1 shows the interrelation between the model, the application program, and the graphical system. The application programs can be grouped into four classes:

1. Programs which build, modify, and maintain the model by adding, deleting, and replacing information in it.

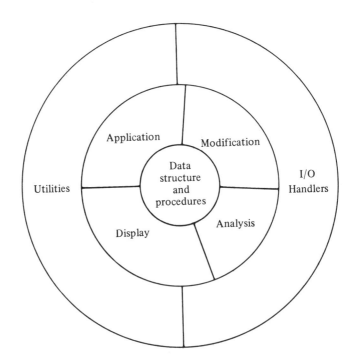

Figure 7-1   The model structure.

2. Programs which test the model in order to extract information from it for display or analysis purposes.

3. Programs which are used in common by the above programs to display information from the model. This may be the output of the analysis program, prompts, and menus. These programs will also handle the user-generated inputs that drive the interaction dialogue.

4. There will also be a collection of routines which are not part of the interactive dialogue but do the housekeeping and postprocessing. These may be distributed throughout the program rather than being in a separate program module.

Figure 7-1 is a conceptual division of logical components. The procedures that modify, analyze, or display the model are not a part of the model itself, although it is not always clear what part of an application program is part of the model or is external to it and manipulates it. One could argue that a circuit-analysis module is a part of the model's definition because it describes the way the circuit behaves. This is not true if one thinks of the model as primarily data. The mixture of data and procedures which make up a model is further explored in the remainder of this chapter.

Model Hierarchy

Geometric or *graphical models* describe parts or systems with inherent geometries and lend themselves naturally to graphical representation. They often have a hierarchical structure, which is built using a bottom-up construction process. Components are used to create blocks, which create higher-level units, which in turn may be used in building still higher-level units. Object hierarchies are common, because most systems can be decomposed into parts.

In an engineering design, a common hierarchy is the assembly-sub-assembly relationship. It is common to use standard components as basic building blocks. These are often drawn using templates of standard symbolic shapes.

Flowcharts and digital logic symbols are common examples of 2D models. In 3D, shapes such as cylinders, parallelepipeds, spheres, and pyramids can be used as basic building blocks.

The standard components can be defined in their own coordinates and may have not only geometrical data but also associated application data. The model must show not only which components are present, but also how they are connected. The hierarchy that is created may have a variety of purposes:

1. A complex object may be constructed employing modular techniques with the repetitive use of standard components.

2. A certain storage economy is gained, since for objects which are repeatedly used we can store only references to those objects rather than redefining them each time.

3. It allows a modification of the basis of the component structure. If we change the definition of one component, that change is propagated to all higher-level components which make use of it to achieve the updated version.

An example of a pictorial representation of an object hierarchy is a tree diagram. Figure 7-2 shows several examples from the large group of 2D block diagrams and 3D mechanical systems. Most of these consist of components connected to form a network.

The hierarchical composition has a number of alternatives. A vehicle could be decomposed into a two-level hierarchy containing at the first level the rear end, the frame, the engine, and the wheels, with the rear end containing the axle for the second level. We could also model it directly as a one-level hierarchy of wheels, axle, frame, body, seats, and engine.

In a circuit one might define the resistors, diodes, and transistor to be the lowest-level components. One could also decompose the circuit in terms of the lowest-level logical block. In the other direction each circuit symbol, such as a transistor, can be decomposed into lower-level drawing components. These hierarchies should have the expected graphical properties in each case. These objects function as user-defined primitives, and one should pick the lowest-level objects which are meaningful and logical for the application.

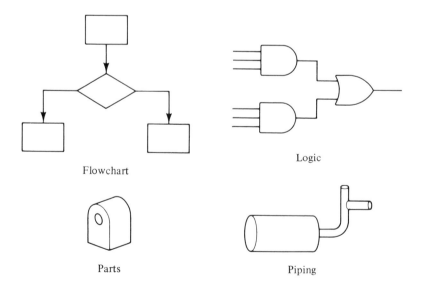

Flowchart

Logic

Parts

Piping

Figure 7-2 2D and 3D models.

3D Representations

Many applications of computer-aided design involve the representation or reconstruction of solids from cross-sectional views. The need to represent 3D shapes occurs in many types of design situations. We may want to represent an existing object, such as the model of a part. In general, we wish the existing object to be precisely matched by its representation. In the worst case, an infinity of coordinate points are needed, one for each point on the object's surface. In the ideal case the object can be exactly defined by combinations of geometrical entities such as planes or spheres. In the typical case, we pick out a set of points on the surface and require that the representation be exact only at those points, and we make the distances between the points and thus the geometrical representation small. Representing the surfaces thus can satisfy most requirements.

There are many cases in which 3D representations are needed in design. There may be no preexisting model of the object, so, working from a sketch, we interactively develop a 3D shape of the object. The representation used should allow the user to manipulate the model easily, so that it can be formed into the desired shape and detail.

We can display a 3D object once it is reduced to lines in world coordinates and traversed in a hierarchical data structure where the lowest-level parts are lines. Representing a 3D object in this way allows us to create a line display of the object, but it does not allow us to obtain accurate surfaces from the display or calculate the weight or volume. The collection of lines alone do not define surfaces, and it is the surfaces that are needed for surface and volume calculations. Figure 7-3 shows how a collection of lines can represent 3D shapes. Thus we can see that a higher-level primitive, a surface, is generally needed to represent 3D shapes.

This chapter is concerned with geometric modeling, which is also called *shape modeling*. This area is expanding quickly, but in general three main methods are used to define computer models of parts. The simplest method uses wire-frame outlines as shown in Figure 7-4. This method requires relatively little computer memory to define the part models. Thus, wire-frame models are often used on inexpensive computers such as desktop units. Many automated drafting systems also use wire-frame models for this reason.

Wire-Frame Models

A fundamental difficulty in depicting spatial relationships is that all practical display devices are 2D. Thus 3D objects must be projected into two dimensions, which entails a considerable loss of information and can sometimes create ambiguities in the image. A number of techniques are used to

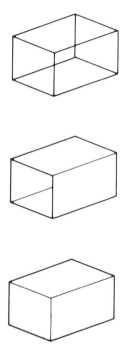

Figure 7-3   Representation of a number of shapes by line drawings.

add back the information so that the human depth-perception mechanism will properly resolve these ambiguities. Consider Figure 7-5, a 2D projection of a cube. There is an ambiguity as to whether the cube in (a) represents the cube in (b) or in (c). This was first observed by Necker in 1832. The mind will imagine that either (b) or (c) will exist, and there is a need for interpretation. One can easily make a reversal between the two, because there simply is not enough information for an unambiguous choice.

The more the viewers know about the object being displayed, the more they form what is called an *object hypothesis*. In Figure 7-6 we see a staircase. But it can be a view we see either looking down upon a staircase or looking up

Figure 7-4   The wire-frame model.

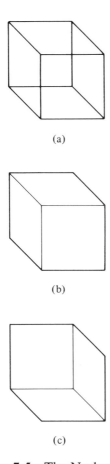

(a)

(b)

(c)

Figure 7-5   The Necker cube.

from below the staircase. We might choose the view looking down, because we frequently see staircases this way. But we can also visualize the alternative of looking up. After we have been staring at the figure, a reversal may occur, and the stairway appears to be viewed from the opposite perspective.

Thus, one goal in display is to show 3D depth relationships unambiguously on a 2D surface. This goal can be served by one of the planar geometric projections, either parallel or perspective.

The easiest projection is the *parallel orthographic* type. To compensate for a lack of depth information, the top, front, and side views are shown together, as in Figure 7-7. It is not difficult to understand simple drawings, but drawings of complicated manufactured parts may require much study in order to be understood. Training and experience will sharpen one's interpretive powers, and a familiarity with the types of objects being represented is also helpful.

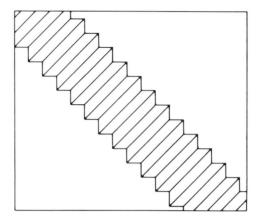

Figure 7-6 A staircase which seems to have a dual perspective.

The *perspective* projection is unlike the parallel orthographic in that it uses depth information. Here, the size of the object is scaled in proportion to its distance from the viewer. The perspective projection of the cube shown in Figure 7-8 shows this scaling. But there can still be ambiguity. The wire-frame projection could be viewed as a picture frame or as the projection of a rectangular parallelepiped with two equal sides. One might also view it as a truncated pyramid with the smaller side closer to the viewer. In the case of a cube or a rectangular parallelepiped, the smaller square represents the face further away from the viewer in this wire-frame model.

Our interpretation of perspective projections is often based on the fact that a smaller object appears further away. A larger house may appear nearer to the viewer. The house may actually be more distant than the other one which is smaller, especially if there are no other cues, such as windows.

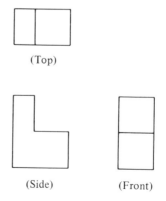

Figure 7-7 Orthographic projection.

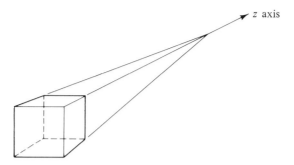

Figure 7-8   A cube projected to z infinity.

Projected objects can convey depth when the parallel lines seem to converge to vanishing points. This convergence can be a stronger depth cue then the decreasing-size method. Perspective projections of some representations are less convincing than parallel projections when there is a lack of converging parallel lines in the structure.

The depth or distance of an object can also be represented by varying the intensity. Objects appear closer when displayed at higher intensity. In intensity depth cueing, depth coordinate line intensity must be adjusted by the processor.

In a vector display, the vector generation provides a way to start and end the coordinates to change the intensity. In a raster display a scan-conversion algorithm is used for this function. The eye's intensity resolution is lower than its spatial resolution, so intensity cueing cannot be used to depict small differences in distance, but it is useful for depicting large differences. Depth cueing has some parallels in real vision; distant objects appear dimmer than closer objects on a hazy day, and the viewer's response to depth cueing may be learned rather than intuitive.

Hidden-surface removal must always be done in a 3D environment prior to the projection into 2D, since this destroys the depth information needed for depth comparisons. This depth comparison can be reduced to the following: Given

$$P = (x_1, y_1, z_1)$$

and

$$P_2 = (x_2, y_2, z_2)$$

does either point obscure the other? This is the same as having P_1 and P_2 on the same projector line, as in Figure 7-9. If this occurs, then comparing z_1 and z_2 will show which point is closer to the viewer. If the points are not on the same projector line, then neither point can obscure the other.

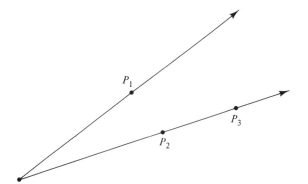

Figure 7-9 Obscuring of one point by another when both are on the same projector line.

Depth comparisons are usually made after a normalizing transformation is made. This sets all parallel-projection projectors parallel to the z-axis and ensures that perspective-projection projectors start from the origin. Then, for a parallel projection, the points are on the same projector line if $x_1 = x_2$ and $y_1 = y_2$. For a perspective projection, one must determine if

$$\frac{x_1}{z_1} = \frac{x_2}{z_2}$$

and

$$\frac{y_1}{z_1} = \frac{y_2}{z_2}$$

to test if the points are on the same projector line.

Some of the divisions can be avoided by transforming the 3D object such that the parallel projection of the transformed object is the same as the perspective projection of the untransformed object. Then test for one point obscuring the other as in a parallel projection. The transformation moves the center of projection to infinity on the negative z-axis, making the projector lines parallel. Figure 7-8 shows how a cube is distorted by the transformation. The transformation tends to preserve the relative depth as well as the straight lines and planes while it performs the perspective task.

As we have seen, wire-frame models do not provide a complete part description. Designers want a model description that can, for example, be fed automatically to an NC machine tool, providing enough information to guide machining. Since wire-frame models can be interpreted in different ways, they are inadequate for these purposes. Surface models are used in more advanced modeling software.

Surface Models

Surface models describe part surfaces but not the interiors. Surface model generation is analogous to stretching a thin fabric over wire-frame models. Two commonly 3D representations of 3D surfaces are polygon meshes and parametric bicubic patches. A *polygon mesh* is a set of connected polygons which form bounded planar surfaces. The exterior of most structures can be represented by a polygon mesh, as can many parts and assemblies. Polygon meshes can also be used to represent objects with curved surfaces. The main disadvantage is that the representation is only approximate. Figure 7-10 shows the cross section of a curved object and the polygon mesh used to represent it. The errors can be made small by using more and more polygons to create a better piecewise-linear approximation, but this increases the memory requirements and the execution time of the algorithms used to process the model representation.

A polygon mesh is a collection of edges, vertices, and polygons as shown in Figure 7-11. The vertices are connected by edges, and the polygons can be thought of as sequences of edges or vertices. A mesh can be represented in different ways. Each has its advantages and disadvantages:

1. The polygon can be represented by its vertex coordinates

$$P = (x_1, y_1, z_1), (x_2, y_2, z_2), \ldots, (x_n, y_n, z_n)$$

2. The polygon can be defined by pointing into a vertex list.
3. The polygon can be defined by pointing into an edge list.

The edge technique is the best for consistency testing, since it contains the most information. The edges are shared in many structural models.

Parametric bicubic patches define the coordinates of points on a curved surface using three equations, one for each x, y, and z. Each equation has two

Figure 7-10   A curved section with a polygon approximation.

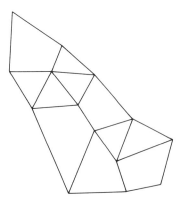

Figure 7-11 Polygon mesh.

variables or parameters, and the terms for all powers of the parameters up to their cube. Thus, they are called bicubic. The boundaries of the patch are parametric cubic curves.

Fewer bicubic patches than polygonal patches are needed to represent a curved surface for fixed accuracy. However, the algorithms for cubics are more complex than those for polygons.

Parametric cubic equations can represent curved surfaces. First, we will discuss representing a 3D curve; then we can generalize from curves to curved surfaces.

The two basic ways to represent curves are:

1. Functions of the variables x, y, and z.

2. Functions of some parameter such as t.

In the first case, the functions take the form

$$x = x, \qquad y = f(x), \qquad z = g(x)$$

and these define points (x, y, z) on a curve.

This representation has some difficulties:

1. An infinite slope may be required at some point on the curve, so we need a way to represent this slope.

2. A curve segment is bounded by a starting and ending point, but testing if a point is on the bounded segment is difficult, especially if the curve loops.

3. Plotting the curve as a smooth line requires that the slope of the curve always be considered.

The parametric representation of a 3D curve greatly reduces these difficulties. It allows closed and multiple-valued functions to be more easily defined and replaces the slopes which can be infinite with tangent vectors which never need to be infinite. A parametric cubic curve uses x, y, and z to represent a third-order or cubic polynomial in some parameter t. For finite segments of a curve, we must limit the range of the parameter. Then

$$\left. \begin{array}{l} x(t) = a_x t^3 + b_x t^2 + c_x t + d_x \\ y(t) = a_y t^3 + b_y t^2 + c_y t + d_y \\ z(t) = a_z t^3 + b_z t^2 + c_z t + d_z \end{array} \right\} \quad 0 \le t \le 1,$$

The derivatives of $x(t)$, $y(t)$, and $z(t)$ with respect to t all take on the same form. The form is

$$\frac{dx}{dt} = 3a_x t^2 + 2b_x t + c_x$$

$$\frac{dy}{dt} = 3a_y t^2 + 2b_y t + c_y$$

$$\frac{dz}{dt} = 3a_z t^2 + 2b_z t + c_z$$

These three derivatives form the tangent vector, and the slopes of the curve are the ratios of the tangent vector components, whatever they may be:

$$\frac{dy}{dx} = \frac{\dfrac{dy}{dt}}{\dfrac{dx}{dt}}, \quad \frac{dx}{dz} = \frac{\dfrac{dx}{dt}}{\dfrac{dz}{dt}}, \quad \frac{dy}{dz} = \frac{\dfrac{dy}{dt}}{\dfrac{dz}{dt}}$$

The slopes are independent of the length of the tangent vector.
Note that

$$\frac{\dfrac{dy}{dt}}{\dfrac{dx}{dt}} = \frac{dy}{dx}$$

We use cubic curves, because no lower-order equations will represent the curve segments and provide the continuity of position and slope at the point where the segments meet and at the same time ensure that the ends of the

Figure 7-12   Joined curve segments.

curve meet at specified points. Then we can build a curve using a series of curve segments like those in Figure 7-12. At the connecting point, the curve segments and their tangent vectors must be equal. This continuity is important to the model, since we cannot have a representation of the cross section of a structure with position discontinuities. Curves are said to be continuous if they have no discontinuities and if also their tangents are continuous. In general, this continuity means that the function and its first i derivatives are continuous.

The parametric cubic, with its four coefficients, is the lowest-order parametric curve that can be forced to meet all four conditions for the position and tangent vectors at each end of the segment. Higher-order parametrics can be used, but these tend to add undesirable curves. The cubic is also the lowest order parametric which can describe a nonplanar curve for 3D representations.

There are three major ways to define a cubic parametric curve:

1. *The Hermite method*, which defines the positions and tangents at the endpoints as discussed.
2. *The Bezier technique*, which defines the positions of the endpoints and uses two other points, which are generally not on the curve, to define the tangents at the curve's endpoints.
3. *The B-spline method*, which approximates the endpoints rather than matching them by allowing both the first and second derivatives to be continuous at the segment's endpoints.

Each has certain advantages and disadvantages.

The Hermite technique uses a Hermite matrix which contains the endpoint conditions. A blending function is then used to match the points. There are two variables of interest:

1. The length of the tangent vector can cause the effect seen in Figure 7-13.
2. The direction of the tangent produces the effect seen in Figure 7-14.

The Bezier technique is similar, except that it differs in the definition of the tangent vectors. The tangent vectors are determined from the line

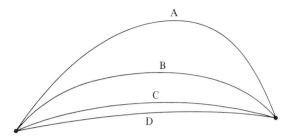

Figure 7-13   Hermite parametric cubic curves with variable lengths.

segments defined by the points. Four control points are used, as shown in Figure 7-15. The Bezier technique is more widely used for two reasons:

1. Its geometric matrix can be easily adjusted by a pointing device to change the shape of the curve.
2. The four points define a convex polygon which acts like a rubber surface stretched around the points. This property turns out to be very useful in defining surface models.

   The B-spline technique does not use any control points, and its first and second derivative are continuous at the endpoints; thus it tends to be smoother

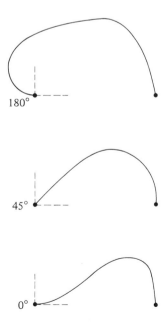

Figure 7-14   Hermite parametric cubic curves wih variable tangent angles.

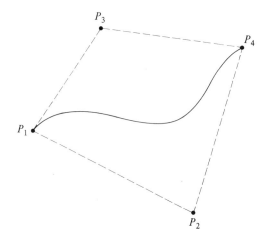

Figure 7-15 A Bezier curve and its control points.

than the other techniques. The name goes back to the flexible strips of metal used to lay out the surfaces of airplanes and ships.

We can approximate the control points $P_1, P_2, \ldots, P_n$ by a series of B-splines, using a different geometry matrix between each pair of adjacent points. The approximation from near P_1 to P_{i+1} takes the form:

$$G_s^i = \begin{bmatrix} P_{i-1} \\ P_i \\ P_{i+1} \\ P_{i+2} \end{bmatrix}, \qquad 2 \le i \le n - 2$$

To show the first- and second-derivative continuity at point P_{i+1} we evaluate the B-spline formulation

$$x(t) = \frac{T}{6} \begin{bmatrix} -1 & 3 & -3 & 1 \\ 3 & -6 & 3 & 0 \\ -3 & 0 & 3 & 0 \\ -1 & 4 & 1 & 0 \end{bmatrix} G_{s_x}$$

with $G_{s_x} = G_{s_x}^i$ and $t = 1$, and we get

$$x^i(1) = \frac{x_i + 4x_{i+1} + x_{i+2}}{6}$$

Now differentiating the same formulation and evaluating at $t = 1$, we get

$$\frac{dx}{dt}\bigg|_{t=1} = \frac{-x_i + x_{i+2}}{2}$$

Differentiating a second time and evaluating again,

$$\frac{d^2x^i}{dt^2}\bigg|_{t=1} = x_i - 2x_{i+1} + x_{i+2}$$

Repeating the process for $G_{s_x} = G_{s_x}^{i+1}$ and evaluating at $t = 0$, we get

$$x^{i+1}(0) = \frac{x_i + 4x_{i+1} + x_{i+2}}{6}$$

$$\frac{dx^{i+1}}{dt}\bigg|_{t=0} = \frac{-x_i + x_{i+2}}{2}$$

$$\frac{d^2x^{i+1}}{dt^2}\bigg|_{t=0} = x_i - 2x_{i+1} + x_{i+2}$$

Note that the expressions for the x coordinates of the two curve segments and for their first two derivatives are identical where they meet, at $x^i(1) = x^{i+1}(0)$. Note also that the joining points and their derivatives are weighted sums of the three adjacent points. Thus, we have a B-spline approximation to these points.

The convex property of Bezier curves holds for B-spline curves also. The convex part of the curve from near P_i to near P_{i+1} is that of the four control points used to generate the curve in the approximation.

A comparison of the Hermite, Bezier, and B-spline techniques will show each of them to be useful in different situations. The Hermite technique is useful for approximating existing surfaces when a combination of point matching and tangent vector matching is needed, while the B-spline method is suitable for approximating points and providing second-derivative continuity. Both the Bezier and B-spline types can be used for interactive design, since their geometry vectors contain only points. Both forms have the convex property, which is useful in displaying the curve. A curve defined in one form can be converted into another form by finding the one form's geometry vector in terms of one of the other's. Even though the Hermite method does not have the convex property, it can be converted to the Bezier or B-spline which does. Parametric cubic surfaces can be generalized from cubic curves. These bicubic surfaces are defined by cubic equations of two parameters, s and t. Varying both parameters from 0 to 1 will define all points on a surface patch. If one

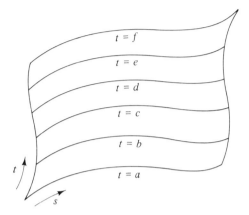

Figure 7-16   Hermite bicubic surface.

parameter is constant and the other parameter is varied from 0 to 1, a cubic curve results.

If a surface is defined by the Hermite technique, the result is similar to that shown in Figure 7-16. When the interior lines are straight, a ruled surface is planar and the surface patch becomes a four-sided polygon. When there is continuity between the patches, there will be a common edge, as shown in Figure 7-17.

The Bezier surface patch is defined in a similar way, but it is more useful, since the controls can be more easily adjusted to change the shape of the patch. A Bezier patch is shown in Figure 7-18. The convex property which we discussed for a Bezier curve also holds for a Bezier surface. Continuity is obtained by making the four control points on the edges equal; this makes the patches line up. To have continuous tangent vectors, we must also have the

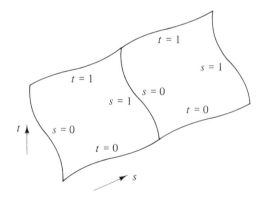

Figure 7-17   Joined Hermite patches.

Figure 7-18   A Bezier patch.

two sets of our control points on either side of the edge collinear with the points on the edge, and the ratios of the lengths of the collinear line segments must be constant.

To define a model using any of these techniques, basically we draw a piecewise-linear approximation to the parametric curves on the surface of the patch. We trace out a curve of constant s by varying t, and we repeat this to obtain all the curves of constant s. This entire process is repeated for curves of constant t, which we obtain by varying s. This tends to generate many equations with many multiplications and divisions. The multiplications can be reduced by using Horner's rule, or we can evaluate the bicubic using the method of forward differences.

Computers can remove the hidden lines from surface models for display. These lines normally would be visible on the display of wire-frame models. Hidden-line removal is relatively simple, because the computer normally keeps track of the order of the surfaces for each particular viewing angle.

It is still important to organize the hidden-surface algorithms to make the removal as efficient as possible. Earlier sections of this chapter have described some general ways to do so, and there are specific algorithms for removing the hidden surfaces from the display of 3D objects defined with polygonal faces. Some of these algorithms can also be adapted for use as hidden-edge removal algorithms.

In the methods mentioned previously, a 3D solid is modeled as a closed surface. Solid modeling, on the other hand, deals directly with solid objects and may use primitive solids, such as cubes, cones, spheres, and cylinders, which are added and subtracted to form various shapes.

The surface models do have some advantages over solid models. Surface models do not require as much computer memory, since solid models store information about edges and surfaces within the model, whereas this data does not need to be stored in surface models because it may be inferred from the position of the surface vertices.

One can calculate the volume of a surface model. To do so, the computer will note the direction of the front face of the object, then proceed inside the

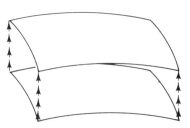

Figure 7-19   Volume calculation from surface model.

object until it hits the back face. The distance between the two faces is then used to calculate the volume based on the surface area of the faces (Figure 7-19). Since the algorithms for storing surfaces are less complex than for storing solids, surface models also use less computer time.

A major drawback of surface modeling is that it provides no inherent information about mass properties. Thus, a surface model cannot serve as a basis for engineering analysis programs, such as finite-element programs, which require information about part material, moments of inertia, centroid, and other properties that affect how the part responds to loads.

Surface models have other disadvantages. Curved surfaces are approximated by combining planes, which produces faceted surfaces. The number of facets is increased to provide a smoother curved surface, and the computing time required for the model increases.

Another drawback of surface models concerns their incompatibility programs that are used to design and machine parts. Parts defined as surface models cannot be easily fed to finite-element or modal analysis programs for stress/strain predictions.

The main problem here lies in the surface definition itself. The surface models contain no information describing the part's interior. Thus, mass properties such as moments of inertia are difficult to calculate using the surface model alone.

Surface models lack the data which are needed for NC machining programs. Solid models generally contain enough information for the definition of part programs for NC machines. NC programming systems can take the data that is needed from the part model and develop the NC commands without other instructions.

Surface models do not contain enough information for automatic NC programming, since these models provide ambiguous descriptions of part interiors. This can be illustrated by considering a slice from the center of a cube-shaped part model. The slice from the solid model would be a solid piece. The slice from the surface model would be a vacant area surrounded by four sides. If this description were used by an NC machine, the model could be interpreted as a thin-walled structure with four sides, not as a solid part.

Solid Modeling

Solid modeling overcomes the drawback of both the wire-frame and surface models by defining parts as solid objects. Solid models require more processing time and memory than wire-frame and surface models. But solid models provide a part. They also describe what can be used as a basis for machining and they can provide the model for other analysis programs, including modal analysis and finite-element programs.

Two basic approaches are used to construct solid models; one is based on primitive solids and the other on topology. The primitive method constructs models by combining simple shapes such as cubes, cylinders, and cones. The boundary method starts with a two-dimensional area and translates or sweeps the shape into a third dimension to obtain a thickness.

Primitive models are constructed from Boolean or logical operators such as union, intersection, or difference. In this method, one positions the primitive parts as desired, then invokes the proper logical operator to obtain a shape.

Boundary models are constructed from definitions of the topology, or boundary shape, and the operations are then performed on the topology to provide the proper geometry.

These two broad categories are also known as *constructive solid geometry* (*CSG*) and *boundary representation* (*B-rep*). The CSG programs, which construct models in building-block fashion, may combine the primitives which are also known as *natural quadrics*, such as a block, cylinder, cone, and sphere. Most commercial programs contain menus of eight to ten other complex shapes to aid the user in the construction of detailed models.

The primitives are combined using Boolean logic operations.

1. The *union* operation combines two primitives.
2. The *difference* operation subtracts one from the other.
3. The *intersection* operation defines a volume common to both primitives.

The user sizes and positions the primitives and then enters the proper operator to produce the resulting shape. A round hole might be produced in a part by subtracting a cylinder from the geometry. Using successive operations such as these, the user can construct a complex model.

Boundary programs build models by piecing together surfaces that enclose the spatial surface boundary of the object. Automated drafting techniques generally are used to produce the various views of the object to define its faces, edges, and vertices. Aiding the user in the construction are sweep operations in which a two-dimensional surface can be translated, rotated, and moved through space to trace out a solid volume.

1. A surface moved with a linear sweep produces an extruded shape with constant thickness.

2. A surface revolved about an axis creates a turned part with an axial symmetry.

3. Variations of these techniques give a surface which is swept through a specified curve to generate a complex solid.

Another boundary-construction technique called *gluing* joins two previously created solids at a common surface, and a method known as *tweaking* can be used to make local changes and minor refinements such as adding fillets to the overall shape. The analytical modeling approach usually has construction techniques similar to these, but the data is organized to use less memory in storing and manipulating the model.

Both CSG and boundary models have certain advantages in representing geometries. CSG systems use the basic shapes common in general industry. These are the flat, rounded, or regularly contoured surfaces typically produced by rolling, milling, turning, cutting, drilling, and other machining operations. As a result, the CSG approach easily models most industrial parts. Also, fewer parameters are needed to represent the solid with CSG. A simple cube may be represented in CSG with 12 parameters (the x, y, z coordinates of the four diagonal corners). A boundary model defines a cube with six faces, 12 edges, and eight vertices.

Solid modeling is considered to be one of the most significant recent developments in computer graphics and the key to the integration of CAD and CAM. It is important because of the new dimension it brings to CAD.

In contrast to the wire-frame and surface models that depict only edges and envelopes of geometry, solid models will define interior material. A brick and a box, for example, are clearly separated with solid models. The solid representation eliminates ambiguities in interpreting the model, and the database, being more complete, can more easily be used in a variety of other computer-aided operations.

This wide range of activities in which the database can be applied is what makes solid modeling significant in CAD/CAM. For example, cross sections can be cut in the model to expose the internal details of a complex part. The action of moving parts can be studied for interference in three dimensions, and the mass properties can be directly computed, including weight, center of gravity, and moment of inertia. Engineering drawings and technical illustrations can be produced with an automated drafting system linked to the model. Finite-element models and NC instructions can be produced from the solid-model database, and photographlike color-shaded images of the parts can also be created.

Primitive Modeling

We have seen that one of the most common solid-modeling techniques is primitive or CSG building-block modeling. It is based on the principle that any part, no matter how complex, can be designed by adding or subtracting simple shapes, such as cubes or cones, and putting these primitive shapes in the proper order. Each primitive shape is a solid model itself, having the mass properties. The finished parts that are composed of these primitives also are solid parts.

The primitive parts can be combined using mathematical set operators like union, intersection, and complement; these are called Boolean operators. Two primitives could be added together at some point with a union operation. A hole can be produced in a part by intersecting the part with a negative cylinder.

Primitive modeling programs work best on parts that do not have intricate surfaces. The modeling systems based on primitives are able to create complex sculptured surfaces but only with some help from the user. The computer has difficulty finding the points at which the primitives intersect to produce complex surfaces, since the potential number of intersection curves for such surfaces is very large. A great deal of time is required to find the exact equations of the intersections.

The primitive modeling programs are designed to allow the user to build parts with a few standard primitive solids, but some programs provide a dozen or more primitives.

Only four surfaces—plane, cylinder, cone, and sphere—are really necessary to define most parts. These four solids are sometimes called the *natural quadrics*. They are the most common surfaces in mechanical design. Planar surfaces are produced from rolling, chamfering, and milling. Cylindrical surfaces are produced by turning or filleting, and spherical surfaces result from cutting with an all-nose cutter. Conical surfaces are produced from countersinking and turning. The torus may also be a primitive, since it occurs in surfaces around the edge of a cylindrical hole or boss.

Primitives can model most engineering parts, since simple shapes are the ones most commonly used in industry. They are easy to form and machine, cost less than complex forms, and usually perform as well. Even when stress/weight ratios are critical, natural quadric shapes may outperform parts with more complex shapes. Studies show that 80% to 85% of all parts can be modeled with planes and cylinders, and 90% to 95% of all parts can be modeled with planes, cylinders, and cones.

A number of functions are used in solid-modeling programs to simplify the model building. Most software includes commands which allow the model to shift, rotate, or be translated. Scaling is also common, so that a geometric structure, once defined, can be duplicated in a number of sizes. If certain combinations of primitives occur repeatedly, the program can define a macrosolids for a group of primitives which collectively can be used the same as a single primitive.

Solid-modeling programs also can provide cutaway views, by positioning a block so that one of its faces forms a sectioning plane, then subtracting the block from the solid to form the sectioned solid. Crosshatching can be added by generating hatch lines in the sectioning plane, then removing everything except the segments of the lines that lie on the sectioned solid surface.

Boundary Models

Boundary models can be used for parts that cannot be conveniently modeled with primitives. These include parts with complicated forms, such as exhaust manifolds, which can be difficult to model if only primitives are used. Complex shapes of this type can be modeled more easily by boundary models.

This approach to modeling begins with the construction of an outline drawing of the part, similar to the outline drawing used in orthographic views. This view is then given a linear sweep to produce a part with the desired thickness (Figure 7-20).

Boundary modeling is based on the philosophy that the part topology and part geometry can be defined separately. Once a given topology has been defined, many different operations can be performed on the part to adjust the geometry without changing the basic topology.

Parts that have a great deal of inherent symmetry, such as axially symmetric parts, can be modeled quickly by this technique. Parts that have

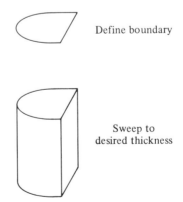

Define boundary

Sweep to
desired thickness

Figure 7-20 Boundary-model sweep.

complex shapes and that would require the use of many different primitive shapes, if modeled with a primitive modeling program, can often be defined simply by a boundary model.

To produce the different parts of the modeled component, different portions of the part may be given various degrees of linear sweep. Holes can be made by defining a circle, then raising it through the part to the top surface. This translation is called a *lift* operation, since it lifts the contour up to form a new surface. Another operation, called a *spin*, rotates a contour about an axis to produce parts, such as those produced on a lathe that have axial symmetry.

Boundary modeling concludes that part geometry is different from part topology. The topology of the part describes how the surfaces are connected, such as what faces share edges and how many faces intersect at a given point.

The object geometry fixes these items in space. Thus, the topology describes how these are connected, but not the dimensions of the items or their connections. Cubes and other parallelepipeds may be identical topologically, but adding dimensions defines the geometry of each.

In boundary modeling, the user adds the object geometry to the topological structure in the model, and the geometry is treated as a set of properties which are associated with the topology. This separation of topology and geometry simplifies the adding of new geometries to the modeling software. The definition of new geometries can take place with the addition of subroutines that do not change the main body of the modeling program, which defines the topology.

Boundary modeling programs define shapes using Euler relationships, which state:

Vertices + Faces − Edges = 2

When the bodies contain holes and passages, the relationship becomes:

Vertices + Faces − Edges − Holes − 2 × Bodies + 2 × Passages = 0

Here an *edge* is the boundary between adjacent faces and a *face* is a bounded surface.

A cube has six faces and 12 Euler edges. An Euler vertex is at each end of a Euler edge. Edges joining at one position form an Euler vertex. The cube has eight Euler vertices, as illustrated in Figure 7-21.

In most programs the topological and geometrical information is held in the boundary models as nodes. The body structure is modeled as links between nodes. Surfaces, points, and tracks are then defined to establish the geometry of a specific structure.

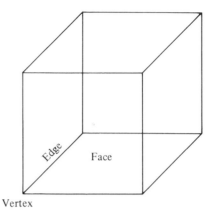

Figure 7-21 Euler geometric relationships.

A *surface node* is associated with one or more face nodes and gives a face its geometry. A *point node* is associated with one or more vertices, producing a fixed coordinate in three dimensions. A *track* is associated with one or more curve nodes, giving them the geometry of a straight line, a circle, or an ellipse.

Every time the user modifies a section in the model, the program maintains the Euler-law relationship between the number of faces, vertices, and edges. In maintaining the Euler relationships the program assures that the resulting model remains unambiguous.

Typical commands in a boundary modeling system would be:

1. Form a face and vertex.

2. Form an edge and vertex.

3. Form an edge and face.

4. Delete edge and vertex.

5. Translate.

6. Rotate.

7. Remove hidden lines.

8. Calculate surface area, volume, or moments of inertia.

The main advantage of boundary modeling is the wider range of geometries that can be depicted. Since they are not restricted to primitive shapes, the software packages are useful in modeling geometries with sculptured surfaces and other complex contours. If constructed with primitive modeling systems, these complex contours can require extensive user interaction and consume large amounts of processor time. In this category of surfaces are parts such as camera cases, appliance housings, exhaust manifolds, and aircraft flight surfaces.

Another advantage of boundary-modeling systems is that the surface boundary of the solid is stored explicitly in the computer and thus does not have to be extracted from the model, as it must be with primitive modelers. As a result, boundary models are more readily converted to wire frames, and transferring wire-frame data to a boundary system is simplified.

The inherent strengths and weaknesses of the two types of model have led to the use of hybrid packages that combine the features of both. The differences between the two categories is becoming less distinct as the technology continues to evolve.

Many commercial systems have features of both types. Some CSG systems have sweep techniques to generate user-defined primitives, and most boundary packages have Boolean operations for combining parts of the model. In addition, many primitive modeling programs convert the primitive-constructed model to a boundary representation for storage and manipulation.

This trend has created considerable confusion in solid modeling. The colorful, three-dimensional displays are usually the most striking feature of most solids packages, and many users perceive the technology as a means of producing more realistic graphic images. But wire frames with hidden lines removed, and shaded-surface models with coloring, can also provide similar displays, and many potential users are unsure of just what constitutes a quality solid-modeling system.

Color-shaded images are produced by most commercial solid modelers, and all can be expected to have this capability. Color-shaded displays can be created with solids through the use of raster graphics. Using an imaginary light source and a specified viewing plane as a basis for the display, the program scans the model to determine the color and intensity of each pixel on the screen. This scan-conversion process determines the visible portion of the model, and the shading is derived from the surface properties, viewing angles, and lighting.

GRAPHICAL CAPABILITY

A striking feature of solid-modeling technology is its ability to create color-shaded images of photographlike quality. Shaded-image solid models can show objects like water pumps and fuselage braces in realistic detail, allowing designers to visualize and refine products before they are built. We now consider some of the ramifications of these visual effects.

A fundamental difficulty in achieving visual realism is the complexity of real images. There are many surface textures, color gradations, shadows, reflections, and slight irregularities. These all combine in our mind to create the visual experience.

A number of techniques have been developed to simulate some of these visual effects with a computer. In many cases the computational costs can be high and the creation of high-quality pictures can take a great deal of processing time.

One goal has been to provide enough information in the model to allow the viewer to understand the 3D spatial relationships. This can be achieved at a lower cost than complete realism and is a basic requirement in computer-aided design.

Highly realistic images can convey the 3D spatial relationships, but they can convey much more as well. A simple line drawing can show that one building is behind the other. There is no need for the building surfaces to have shingles and bricks, or for shadows.

Some of the same techniques that are used for line drawings are applicable to the more realistic shaded images shown on solids. The first step toward realism in these cases is hidden-surface removal. The value of hidden-surface removal is apparent when comparing different presentations with and without hidden surfaces. Objects whose hidden surfaces are to be removed must be modeled either as solids or as collections of surfaces. When viewed from a fixed location, some of the surfaces will be obscured by others, some will be partially obscured, and some will be completely visible. Algorithms for hidden-surface removal are a part of most modeling packages.

A major step toward realism is the shading of the visible surfaces. The appearance of a surface depends on:

1. The types of light sources illuminating the object.
2. The properties of the surface, such as the color, texture, and reflectance.
3. The position and orientation of the surface with respect to the light sources and other surfaces.

The light source might be a point source (a single light) or a distributed source (a bank of lights).

In many environments there may be a considerable amount of ambient light impinging from all directions. This is one of the easiest light sources to model, since it produces a constant illumination on all surfaces, regardless of their orientation. Ambient light by itself will also produce unrealistic images, since real environments are not illuminated solely by ambient light. In an ambient-light environment, two adjacent faces of a cube would appear to be shaded the same, and their common edge would be impossible to distinguish.

More complex to model, but more realistic, is a light source in which the illumination on the surface depends on its orientation to the incident light rays. The surfaces that face the light rays are brightly illuminated. This variation is a powerful cue to the 3D structure of the object.

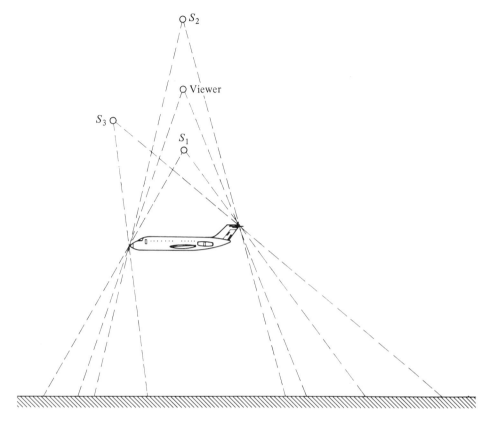

Figure 7-22 Shadows with multiple sources.

Realism is also introduced by reproducing the shadows created by a point source. There may be a number of light sources, some of which produce shadows; these shadows will enhance realism and provide additional depth. Figure 7-22 shows an object and several light sources, S_1, S_2, and S_3. S_2 casts a shadow outside the viewpoint because the shadow is obscured by the object. A light source at the viewpoint or anywhere on the straight line through S_2 and beyond tends to produce a shadow invisible to the viewer. Light sources S_1 and S_3 produce shadows which are visible to the viewer.

Objects illuminated with only a point source tend to look harsh. The effect is similar to that seen when pointing a spotlight at an object in an otherwise black room. This is because in most real environments there is some other light.

There may be some light of a uniform brightness caused by the multiple reflections of light from the many surfaces. An object shielded from the rays coming directly from a point light source is still visible owing to this ambient light. Realistic shading will include a term to account for this ambient light and a term to indicate how much of the ambient light is reflected from the object's surfaces.

If the point source of light is assumed to be coincident with the viewer's eye, then no shadows are cast. This also means that light rays striking the surface will all be parallel for perspective projections. If two surfaces of the same color are parallel and one overlaps the other in the image, their surface normals are the same, so the shading on the surfaces will be equal and the surfaces will be indistinguishable. This can be corrected by recognizing that the light energy drops off as the inverse square of the distance from the source to the surface and back to the eye.

Now, let the light be at infinity for a parallel projection; then the distance is also infinite. For a perspective projection, $1/r^2$ can have a wide range of values, since the viewpoint may be relatively close to the object. This gives different shades to surfaces that have the same angle. More realistic effects are achieved by replacing the $1/r^2$ light source with $1/(r + k)$, where k is a constant and r is the distance from the perspective viewpoint to the surface.

The diffuse reflection of light from colored surfaces can be treated using reflection equations for cyan, magenta, and yellow light with the reflection constants for each color. These subtractive primaries are used because the reflection of light is a subtractive process. For a yellow surface, all the yellow light is reflected, while all the magenta and cyan light is absorbed. If the illuminating light is colored, its three subtractive primary components are reflected in proportion to the reflection constants of the surface.

Specular reflection can be observed on any shiny surface. Illuminate a marble with a bright light; the highlight is caused by specular reflection, and the light from the rest of the marble is caused by diffuse reflection. The highlight will also appear to be white, which is the color of the incident light. If the viewer moves, the highlight also moves. The shiny surfaces tend to reflect light unequally in different directions. A perfectly flat face, such as a perfect mirror, will reflect only in the direction for which angles of incidence and reflection are equal. For a round surface, such as a marble, the intensity of the reflected light falls off as this angle increases.

The shading model developed by Phong Bui-Tuong approximates this fall-off with cos n. The value of n varies from 1 to 200 depending on the surface. For a perfect reflector, n is infinite. The Phong model for specular reflection is based on empirical observations, not on a fundamental model of the specular reflected light.

The Torrance-Sparrow model is a theoretical model which assumes the surface to be a collection of microscopic facets, with each facet being a perfect reflector. The orientation of each facet is determined by the Gaussian probability function. Many experiments show this model to have reflection characteristics very close to those of actual objects.

For polygon mesh shading, three basic techniques are used:

1. *Constant shading*, in which a single intensity value is used for the entire polygon.

2. *Intensity-interpolation shading*, or *Gouraud shading*, which uses a linear interpolation of the vertex intensities along each edge and then between edges along the scan lines. The vertex intensities are found from the vertex normals, which in turn are found by averaging the polygon normals on each side of an edge.

3. Normal-vector shading interpolates the surface normal vector between starting and ending normals, which are found from the vertex normals.

The normal-vector technique can provide improved highlights over intensity interpolation shading. The results are superior to intensity interpolation, since an approximation to the normal is used at each point. This technique reduces Mach-band problems, as shown in Figure 7-23, but increases the cost of applying the shading model. To shade bicubic surface patches, the surface normal is calculated for each pixel from the surface equations. This can also be an expensive process.

Any of the shading models can be used to calculate the intensity, but before a shading model can be applied to a planar or bicubic surface, we must know which light sources illuminate a point, and this means that shadows must be considered. There is a technique for shadowing, called *ray tracing*. It deals with surfaces which transmit as well as reflect light.

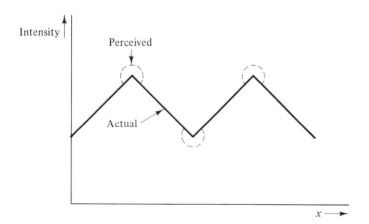

Figure 7-23 The Mach-band effect—an exaggeration of the intensity change at a discontinuity.

Surfaces that have specular and diffuse reflection properties can also have specular and diffuse transmittance properties. The specular transmission of light occurs through transparent materials, such as glass or polished lucite. We can see through transparent material, although the rays may be bent.

Diffuse transmission occurs in translucent materials like frosted glass. The rays passing through these materials are reflected internally by irregularities. Objects seen through translucent material appear to us as blurred. Little work has been done with the diffused transmission of light, but specular transmission can be explained in several ways. The simplest technique ignores refraction, so that light rays are not bent as they pass through the surface; whatever is visible on the line of sight passing through a transparent object is geometrically located on that line of sight. With refraction, the geometrical and optical lines of sight are different. If refraction is considered, then looking through the transparent object along the line of sight can cause a different shading of an object to appear.

In general a ray of light striking a surface breaks up into three parts:

1. Diffused reflected.
2. Specularly reflected.
3. Transmitted (refracted).

Light leaving the surface of an object is the sum of contributions from three sources. Thus each time a ray leaves an object, three new rays might be traced. But, diffuse reflection will generate an infinite number of rays, so only specular reflection and refraction can actually be traced.

If the display resolution is $N \times M$ pixels, then $(N + 1)(M + 1)$ rays are traced. Each ray must be tested for the intersection with each object in the scene. When an intersection is found, the surface properties are tested to determine if the ray is to be split. Each resulting ray is traced by growing a tree. Ray tracing is a slow process, but as it is developed further, speed increases may be achieved by the application of coherence or other properties of the objects being considered. Parallel processing can also be used, because the rays can be traced independently of each other.

Another way to enhance realism is to reproduce the surface properties. Some surfaces are dull and disperse reflected light in many directions, while others reflect light only in certain directions. Surfaces can also be transmitting and refracting some light, while also reflecting some other wavelengths. Most texturing is done with fractal surfaces, which are irregular shapes that are recursively divided to build objects.

Shadow algorithms for point light sources are almost identical to hidden-surface algorithms. Hidden-surface algorithms determine which surfaces can be seen by the viewer, and shadow algorithms determine which surfaces will be hit by the light rays.

The surfaces that are visible both to the viewer and to the light source are not shaded. Those that are visible to the viewer but not to the light source are shaded. This can be extended to multiple light sources. In this approach, shadows from distributed light sources are not included, since both the umbra and penumbra of the shadow must then be calculated.

Since the shadow and hidden-surface algorithms are the same, we can process the object description using the same algorithm, once for the viewpoint, and once for each light source. The results can then be combined to determine the parts that are visible to the viewer and to the light sources, and then the view can be shaded. By organizing the computations, one need perform the shadow calculation only once for a series of scenes of the same objects seen from several different viewpoints, provided that the light sources are fixed with respect to the objects. This is because shadows are not directly dependent on the viewpoint.

There are several ways to generate shadows for polygonal objects. In one approach a polygon which is completely or partially visible to the light source has a second coplanar polygon added to it. The second polygon is a surface-detail polygon and is not used for hidden-surface removal, but for shading.

A part of the object polygon that is visible to the viewer is covered by one of these polygons and shaded to account for the diffuse and specular reflections from the light source and the ambient light. The part of the object polygon that is not covered by the surface-detail polygon is shaded only for ambient light.

The Use of Color

The shading algorithms tend to provide very smooth and uniform surfaces, unlike many actual surfaces we see and feel. The two types of surface detail are color and texture. As color is applied to a smooth surface, it does not appear to change the geometry of the surface, but adding texture detail produces a coarser or rougher surface.

Color can be used to show features on a base polygon. Here the surface-detail polygons are flagged in the data structure and given priority over the base polygon. The surface-detail polygons that are used for shadows are flagged separately.

As the use of color becomes finer and more intricate, this type of explicit modeling with polygons becomes less practical. Then the mapping of a digitized picture of the detail onto a surface can be used. Here, a pattern array that represents the digitized image is mapped to either a planar or a curved surface, as described in Chapter 3. The values in the pattern array are used to scale the color intensity.

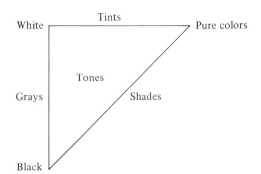

Figure 7-24 Specification of color in terms of tints, shades, and tones.

Generating the color-shaded image can require the computation of color and intensity for millions of pixels. Producing the solid display can consume large amounts of computer time and can be expensive for high-resolution and complex models. As a result, some model systems produce color shading as a final output, and construction is done with wire frame.

The visual sensations that we get from color are much greater than we get from achromatic light. Color descriptions generally include the properties of hue, saturation, and brightness. *Hue* is used to distinguish between the different colors, such as red, green, or blue. *Saturation* is the purity of the color, which is a measure of its freedom from dilution by white light. The more the color appears to have a pastel nature, the lower is its saturation. *Brightness* refers to the intensity of the color and is independent of the hue and saturation.

There are a number of color specification systems that use a standard set of color samples. The Munsell system is organized as a three-dimensional space of hue, brightness, and saturation. There are also the Ostwald system and the newer Coloroid system. Artists use this approach of specifying color in terms of different tints, shades, and tones. The basic relationships are shown in Figure 7-24.

The Munsell and similar pigment-mixing techniques depend on the user's judgment. If we represent the spectral distribution of color as shown in Figure 7-25, then we have a more precise definition of color in terms of the dominant wavelength, purity, and luminance. We can also relate the spectral character-istics of the eye to various colors as shown in Figure 7-26. This curve is known as the *luminosity curve*, since it shows the eye's response to light of constant luminance as the dominant wavelength is varied. We can also separate the response as shown in the dashed lines. Other approaches used to explain color vision characteristics include the opponent-color theory and the zone theory. The theory behind the separated response curves suggests that colors can be specified by weighted sums of red, green, and blue. Some colors require the

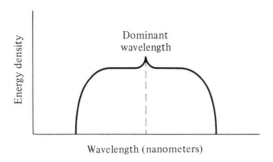

Figure 7-25   Color in terms of dominant wavelength, purity, and luminance.

addition of a primary component before they can be matched by adding two other primaries. This addition produces a negative weight on the sensitivity axis.

Although some colors cannot be matched, the mixing of red, green, and blue to obtain other colors is valid, and there is a large range of colors which can be matched using red, green, and blue. This is what allows color TV to work. Since the human eye is less sensitive to blue light than to green light, less blue light is required in the matching process. The eye can distinguish almost 360,000 different colors, based on experiments in which pairs of colors are judged side by side.

About 130 hues are distinguishable. If the colors differ only in saturation, there are from 16 levels for yellow to 23 levels for red and violet.

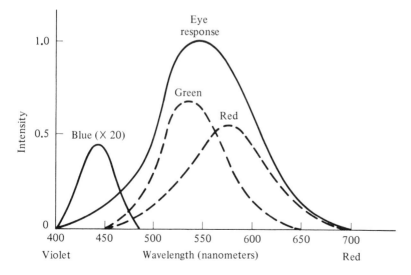

Figure 7-26   The eye's luminosity response and its separate color responses.

The CIE chromaticity diagram can be used for matching and defining a colored light as a mixture of three fixed primaries. The concept was simplified in 1931, when the Commission Internationale L'Eclairage (CIE) defined three primary colors (X, Y, Z) that can be combined, with positive weights, to define all light sensations we can experience.

The CIE primaries are not visible, but they form an international standard for specifying colors. The primaries are defined as three spectral-energy distributions. The Y primary is defined with an energy distribution which matches the luminosity response of the human eye.

X, Y, and Z are the weights of the CIE primaries required to match a color. The chromaticity values depend only on wavelength and saturation, since they are independent of the amount of luminous energy. They can be defined as follows:

$$x = \frac{X}{X + Y + Z}, \quad y = \frac{Y}{X + Y + Z}, \quad z = \frac{Z}{X + Y + Z}$$

Note that $x + y + z = 1$.

Now we plot x and y for the visible colors, obtaining the CIE chromaticity diagram shown in Figure 7-27. The interior and boundary of the enclosed region represent all of the visible chromaticities. All perceivable colors with the same chromaticity but different luminances will map into the same point within this region. The 100% pure colors of the spectrum fall on the curved part of the boundary, as shown by the wavelengths which are indicated. White light, which is like sunlight, is marked by the center dot. It is close to the point where

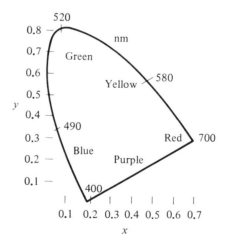

Figure 7-27 The CIE chromaticity diagram.

$x = y = z = \frac{1}{3}$

The CIE chromaticity diagram can be used in several ways. We could measure the wavelength and purity of any color by matching the color to a mixture of the three CIE primaries. There are specialized units for this. When two colors are added together, the new color lies somewhere on a straight line in the chromaticity diagram connecting the two colors being added.

Because the diagram factors out luminance, color sensations which are luminance-related are excluded. Therefore brown, which is an orange-red chromaticity at very low luminance, is not shown.

Complementary colors are those that can be mixed to produce white light. The chromaticity in the mixture is the ratio of line lengths. Colors which are close to the flat part of the boundary cannot be defined by a dominant wavelength. These are called *nonspectral*. In these cases, the dominant wavelength is found by projecting the mixture line up to the curve marked in nanometers. The purity is still defined from the ratio of distances. The colors that must be expressed this way include the purples that occur in the lower part of the CIE diagram.

Another use of the CIE chromaticity diagram is to define color ranges. Any two colors can be added to produce any color on the connecting line by varying the relative luminances of the two colors.

A third color can be used with various mixtures of the other two to produce the range of all colors in the triangle formed by the three colors. Visible red, green, and blue cannot be additively mixed to match all colors, since no triangle whose vertices are within the visible area will completely cover the visible area. A fully saturated color, which contains no white light, can be specified as a mixture of just two primary colors.

In 1943, K. L. Kelly of the National Bureau of Standards used color names to describe the color characteristics in the CIE chromaticity diagram. This scheme, revised in 1955, is known as the Kelly chart (Figure 7-28).

In 1976 the CIE adapted an improved chromaticity scale which used a translated coordinate system, as shown in Figure 7-29. This is now the official recommended system of the CIE. The color boundaries were translated from the revised Kelly chart of 1955.

We can also use a chromaticity diagram of this type to define and compare the color display and hard copy devices. The smaller range of the print devices requires that images originally created on a color CRT must use a reduced range of colors to ensure accurate reproduction. If the goal is other than an exact reproduction, small differences in the color ranges will make little difference.

Color models are a convenient way to define specifications within some color gamut. A major interest is the range for color CRTs, which are defined by the RGB (red, green, blue) primaries. We are also interested in the color range for hard-copy devices.

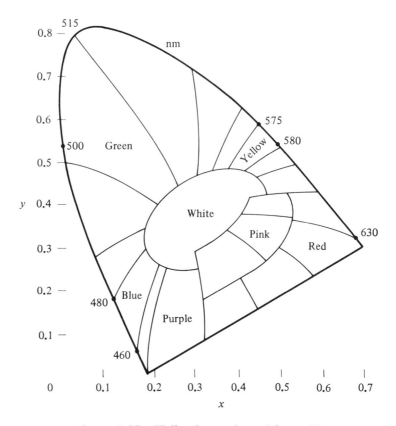

Figure 7-28   Kelly chart adapted from CIE.

A color model is a specification of a 3D coordinate system. In this coordinate system each displayable color is represented by a point. Most color models are based on the RGB primaries, although any three primaries could be used. The models specify only colors in the RGB gamut.

The three major hardware-oriented color models are:

1. The RGB model used for color television.
2. The YIQ model used for broadcast color television systems.
3. The CMY (cyan, magenta, and yellow) model used for color printing devices.

These models do not relate to our intuitive color notions of hue, saturation, and brightness. Other models have been developed which are easier to use. These include the HSV and HLS models.

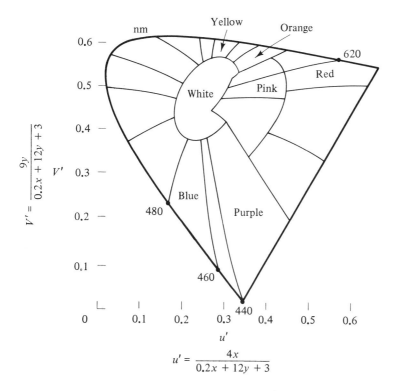

Figure 7-29   1976 CIE Uniform Chromaticity Scale.

The RGB color model is a red, green, and blue model that uses a Cartesian coordinate system. The model space is the unit cube, as shown in Figure 7-30. The RGB cube allows the individual contributions of each primary to be added. The main diagonal of the cube has equal amounts of each primary, and it represents the gray levels. The RGB model is used in color TV monitors and raster displays. Much work has been done in the area of the eye's response and sensitivity to colors as specified by RGB triples.

The YIQ color model is used in raster color graphics. The model is a recoding of the RGB model for transmission efficiency and compatibility with black-and-white television. The CMY model is based on the subtractive primaries of cyan, magenta, and yellow, which are the complements of red, green, and blue. The space in the coordinate system is the same for CMY as RGB, except that white light is at the origin instead of black light.

The colors are specified as subtracted from white light rather than adding to black light. CMY is useful in hard-copy devices which deposit colored inks or pigmentation onto paper. This includes the ink jet plotters.

The RGB, YIQ, and CMY color models tend to be hardware-based; in contrast, the HSV model is more user-oriented and tends to allow a little more

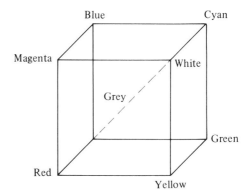

Figure 7-30   RGB cube.

creativity. The model is defined as a six-sided cone as shown in Figure 7-31. Saturation is measured relative to the range of the model, not the CIE chart. The top of the cone is the same as viewed along the principal diagonal of the RGB model from white to black. The RGB model has internal subcubes, and each plane of constant V of the HSV model corresponds to a view of a subcube in the RCB model, so we can convert between the two relatively easily.

The HLS color model is named for hue, lightness, and saturation. It is based on the Ostwald color system and is modeled as a double hexcone, as shown in Figure 7-32. Conversion to RGB is also possible for this model.

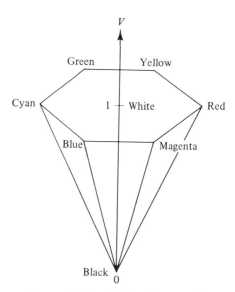

Figure 7-31   HSV color model.

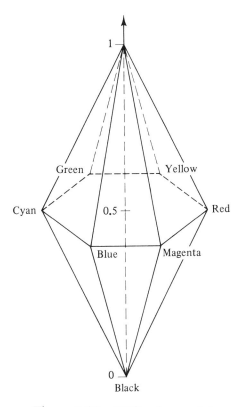

Figure 7-32   HLS color model.

A Solid-Modeling System

We will now consider a packaged hardware and firmware system with local hidden-surface removal and visible-surface shading capabilities.* The system displays incremental construction of solid objects without repainting the entire screen in scan line order. The technique for hidden-surface removal is based on the image space depth-buffer (or Z-buffer) algorithm.

A problem confronting shaded-image generation is the time-consuming process of hidden-surface removal and visible-surface shading. Usually, the host computer must transform and clip the object into a viewing volume, remove hidden surfaces, and calculate intensities for every pixel on each visible surface before pixel data can be sent to the display processor. We can, however, provide a local image space along with hidden-surface removal and

*This section contains copyrighted material supplied by the Lexidata Corporation, used with permission.

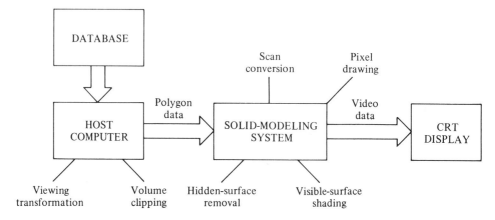

Figure 7-33 Solid-modeling tasks.

visible-surface shading capabilities by overlapping the two most time-consuming tasks necessary to generate a shaded image, as shown in Figure 7-33. The host concurrently performs geometry transformation with pixel data processing within the system. Instead of individual pixels, three-dimensional polygonal data passes from the host to the system so there is no need to duplicate the display image at the host. Once the host has transformed and clipped one polygon, it can be sent to the system and displayed. This not only eliminates response-time delay but also allows the image to be constructed incrementally instead of in scan-line order. This approach is shown in Figure 7-34.

In addition to standard 2D data types, the system can accept:

1. 3D polygons.

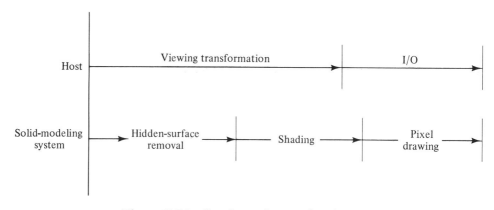

Figure 7-34 Overlapped operational sequence.

2. Vectors.

3. Horizontal segments and points with color and normal attributes.

A user-supplied output data-conversion routine is required at the host computer to convert the internal data representation.

A key element is the depth buffer. For each pixel on the display screen, we record the depth of the object within the pixel that lies closest to the observer. By making this extra information available to the display processor, an interactive 3D display system can have the following capabilities:

1. Hidden surfaces can be removed by comparing the depth of individual pixels in the new polygon with the existing image.

2. We can display polygons in their sequence of arrival from the host. The host computer can easily structure the data such that an object can be constructed incrementally in any desirable sequence.

3. A cutting plane parallel to the screen can be defined such that any subsequent objects sent in front of the cutting plane are removed.

4. Piercing objects are automatically handled by the system, so there is no need for the host to calculate their intersections.

5. By reading back depth or intensity values of a visible surface pixel, the host can determine which surface within the object has been picked. It is also possible to pick any three noncollinear visible points such that the host can generate a new viewing plane intersecting the object.

6. By displaying the intersection line of a displayed object and a virtual invisible object (such as a plane), contouring can be achieved.

The system can provide intensity-variation or spatial-variation shading. Intensity-variation shading may be approached in one of three ways:

1. Constant (polyhedron) shading.

2. Intensity-interpolation (Gouraud) shading.

3. Normal-vector-interpolation (Phong) shading.

In constant shading the host provides one intensity value for shading an entire polygon. Each visible polygonal facet of the approximated surface is distinguishable. This requires less computation for both the host and the solid modeling system.

For intensity-interpolation shading the host provides intensity values at each vertex of a polygon. The system shades each polygon by linearly interpolating between the vertices of the polygon.

In normal-vector-interpolation shading the host provides surface-normal values for each vertex of a polygon. The system shades each polygon by linearly interpolating two surface-normal components independently and combining the result into a single value. Each component is interpolated as described above. This type of shading allows the host to choose different light and shading models by manipulating the color look-up table.

The two spatial-variation techniques are the opaque and the translucent methods. In the opaque technique every pixel along a visible scan is drawn, such that hidden surfaces are completely removed. In the translucent method only selected pixels along a visible span are drawn, such that hidden surfaces are not completely removed. This allows some of the back pixels to show through, producing a screen-door effect.

The program does all the repetitive, primitive work for rendering three-dimensional objects. There is still much work that must be done by the host, however. The program requires transformed, clipped, convex, planar polygons in memory (screen) coordinates. The host must make these transformations, determine the proper shades for the polygons, and load the look-up table appropriately.

Shading Techniques

If only constant-shade drawing is done, the shades of polygons can be encoded in whatever way the user desires. If, however, smooth-shade drawing is done, a specific allocation of look-up table values is required. In designing the system two basic schemes were considered.

The first basic method for specifying shades and loading look-up tables is the creation of a linear range of look-up table entries for each main color in the scene. The high-order bits of the shade could then be the main color, such as red, green, or yellow, and the low-order bits the intensity of that color.

The other basic shading method involves encoding the normal vector to a surface and the main color of the object into the shade. The shade would then have the main color in the high-order bits, followed by one component of the normal, and then a second component in the low-order bits. Normal-vector-interpolation mode would be set via a command, and this encoded normal vector would be determined for each polygon (constant shading) or vertex (smooth shading). Also, the look-up table would have to be loaded with the correct transformation to red, green, and blue values.

As discussed earlier, there are three methods of shading a polygon: constant, intensity interpolation (Gourand), and normal-vector interpolation (Phong). They differ in the number of variables that are linearly interpolated across the face of the polygon. Constant shading has zero variables that are interpolated, as each pixel comprising a polygon has the same value. Gourand or intensity interpolation varies the pixel values of a polygon as a single whole unit. Phong, or normal-vector interpolation, breaks the pixel value into two parts, each of which is linearly interpolated across the face of the polygon. How the bits of each pixel are divided is determined by a call.

Constant shading is the fastest of the three, as there is no interpolation across the face of the polygon. However, because there is no smoothing (interpolation), the polygons that approximate a surface are easily distinguishable.

Gourand shading smooths out the polygons so that they appear as a part of the surface. The disadvantages of this type of shading are that it takes about 10% longer than constant shading and requires more planes of memory to get the smooth shading for each color.

Phong shading interpolates two variables, which may be the x and y components of the normal of the polygon. This allows for smoothing of the polygons and some light-source manipulation. The light-source manipulation can be done by loading the look-up table to interpret the encoded x and y normals to different shades. The disadvantages of this technique are that it takes about 10% longer than the Gourand shading and requires many extra planes for the x and y normal encoding. The requirement for more planes is such that, even for a 12-bit look-up table, tradeoffs must be made between the number of colors and the number of shades per color that are to be used.

Consider the way Gourand shading can be used in the system. Suppose we decided that to achieve a smooth three-dimensional effect, 64 shades would be needed for each of the colors. The look-up table used was a 12 by 8, which has 2^{12} or 4096 simultaneous colors. Dividing 4096 by 64 shades yields the 64 possible gross colors. However, only 63 colors were possible, as one of the 64-word-wide blocks in the table was used for the background. A map of the table is shown in Figure 7-35. The choice of 64 shades of 64 colors forced the bits of each pixel to be essentially divided in half, with six bits denoting the color and six bits the shade.

The Gourand shading technique linearly interpolates the whole 12-bit intensity (pixel) value. However, the desired result was to change only the shade when interpolating across an object of one color. This means that the six least significant bits (lsb's) of each pixel must correspond to the shade and the six most significant bits (msb's) to the color, so that when the interpolation is complete only the six lsb's change and the six msb's remain the same (see Figure 7-36).

The six bits that corresponded to the shade were encoded to be the angle between the normal of the surface at the vertex and the normal to the light-source unit direction vector. The reason is that it is the angle that determines the shade.

If the light source is placed at the viewer, or in the positive z direction as shown in Figure 7-37, the angle between the vector ranges from $0°$ to $90°$, and is broken up into 64 different parts, each $90° \div 64° = 1.4°$ wide. The look-up table has the responsibility of decoding the six color bits and six shade bits of

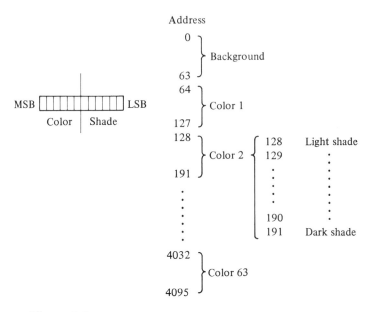

Figure 7-35   Look-up table map for Gourand shading.

each pixel into a particular mix of red, green, and blue to create the selected color and the correct shade.

We have described how data can be encoded in the bit map and how the look-up table is used to decode each pixel and give it the correct color and shade. We now consider how the look-up table is loaded to produce the shaded pictures.

As noted earlier, each pixel is broken in half, with six bits describing the color and six bits describing the angle between the pixel normal and the light-source normal. The table is thus divided into 64 sections, each with 64 entries. An algorithm used to calculate a table entry is:

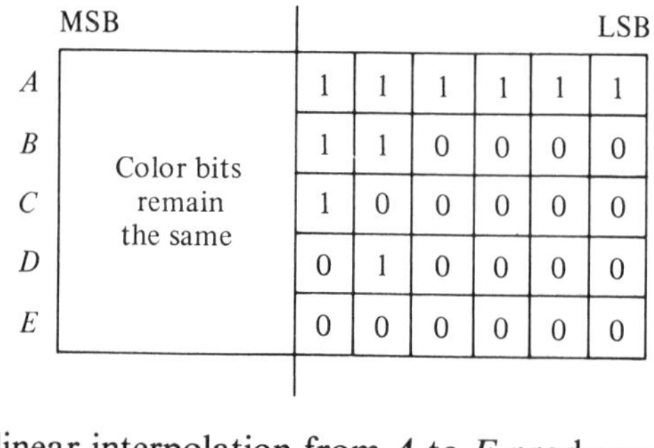

	MSB						LSB
A		1	1	1	1	1	1
B		1	1	0	0	0	0
C	Color bits remain the same	1	0	0	0	0	0
D		0	1	0	0	0	0
E		0	0	0	0	0	0

Figure 7-36   A linear interpolation from *A* to *E* produces three intermediate points.

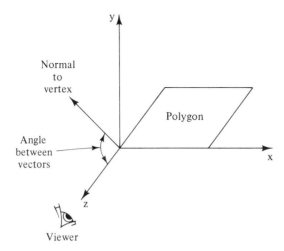

Figure 7-37 Light source angle.

RED = (cosθ) (BRIGHT)[KR + SAT + (cosθ)^N (SPECULAR)]
GREEN = (cosθ) (BRIGHT)[KG + SAT + (cosθ)^N (SPECULAR)]
BLUE = (cosθ) (BRIGHT) [KB + SAT + (cosθ)^N (SPECULAR)]

Here:

RED, GREEN, BLUE are the actual LUT entries.

KG, KR, KB are the amounts of red, green, and blue in the color. The ratio of these variables determines the hue.

BRIGHT is the intensity of the color.

SAT is the 1/saturation, or the amount of white in a color.

SPECULAR is the amount of white specular light added to the color.

N is the amount of highlighting or shine in the specular light.

cosθ is the cosine of the angle between the normal of the pixel and the normal to the light source.

After setting the values for KG, KR, KB, BRIGHT, SAT, SPECULAR, and N, the angle θ is varied from 0° to 90° in 90 ÷ 64 = 1.4-degree steps to produce the table loading for each color. Figure 7-38 shows plots of the different color variables.

Suppose the highest level of data the system accepts is polygon data; then each polygon is described by its set of vertices, and there may be no restrictions on the number of vertices in a polygon or polygons in a picture as long as each polygon is convex and planar. Adding an object to a picture already on the screen does not require that the whole picture be redrawn.

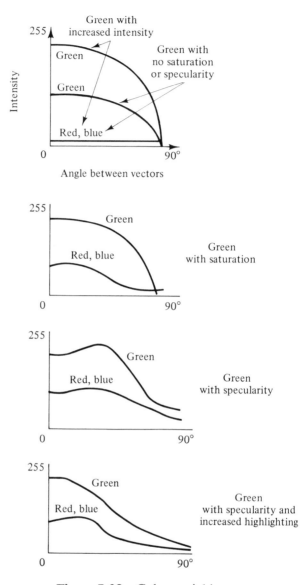

Figure 7-38   Color variables.

However, any change in orientation of objects, sectioning, or making an object translucent requires that the whole picture be redrawn. This occurs because the system keeps only the visible surfaces, and the rest of an object is erased. Changing the orientation, sectioning, or making an object translucent allows the possibility that an object or part of an object that was discarded could be required to become visible.

Computing the Vertex and Surface Normals

In order to do shading of a three-dimensional polygon, it is necessary to determine the surface normal of the polygon for constant shading and the polygon vertex normals for either Gourand or Phong shading. A *polygon surface normal* is a vector perpendicular to the surface of a planar polygon. For convenience the normal can be a unit vector.

A *polygon vertex normal* is a vector perpendicular to the surface of the polygon at that vertex. The polygon vertex normals can be different from the surface normals, as occurs in the case of approximating the surface of a sphere with polygons. Each polygon will have some surface which is normal, and each vertex polygon should have the true normal of the sphere at that point. Thus, the true vertex normals can be approximated by averaging all the surface normals of the polygons containing the vertex.

Two vectors in the plane of a polygon (x_1, y_1, z_1) and (x_2, y_2, z_2) can be obtained by subtracting two adjacent vertices of the polygon, providing that the points chosen are not all collinear. We have

$$(x_1, y_1, z_1) = (p_{x_1} - p_{x_2}, p_{y_1} - p_{y_2}, p_{z_1} - p_{z_2})$$

and

$$(x_2, y_2, z_2) = (p_x - p_{x_3}, p_{y_2} - p_{y_3}, p_{z_2} - p_{z_3}).$$

The ordering of the vertices of the polygon determines the signs of the components of the vectors (x_1, y_1, z_1) and (x_2, y_2, z_2), which in turn determine the signs of the components of the unit normal vector (x'_n, y'_n, z'_n). The signs of the vector components indicate the front- or back-facing surfaces and the different lighting values if the light source is not parallel to the z axis. Here we assume a counterclockwise polygon order with positive z normal components facing outward. If clockwise order is used, either the subtraction for the original vectors or the order of subtraction in the cross-product formula must be reversed.

Given the two previously calculated vectors within a polygon (x_1, y_1, z_1) and (x_2, y_2, z_2) as shown in Figure 7-39, the normal for that polygon can be computed using the following cross-product formula:

$$x_n = (y_1 - z_2) * (y_2 - z_1)$$
$$y_n = (z_1 - x_2) * (z_2 - x_1)$$
$$z_n = (x_1 - y_2) * (x_2 - y_1)$$

The vector is then normalized by dividing by the length of the vector:

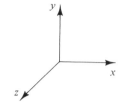

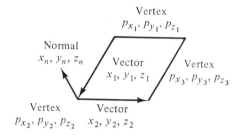

Figure 7-39   The polygon normal.

$$x'_n = \frac{x_n}{(x_n^2 + y_n^2 + z_n^2)^{1/2}}$$

$$y'_n = \frac{y_n}{(x_n^2 + y_n^2 + z_n^2)^{1/2}}$$

$$z'_n = \frac{z_n}{(x_n^2 + y_n^2 + z_n^2)^{1/2}}$$

In this example, the vertex polygon normal for the sphere was approximated by averaging the surface normals for all polygons containing that vertex. This provided a smoothing effect on the approximated sphere. Suppose that a cylinder is approximated by polygons. The cylinder should have sharp distinguishable edges at the top and bottom but have a smooth rounded side. If all polygons were averaged to compute the vertex normals, the sharp edges for the top and bottom would be rounded.

We can avoid this problem by averaging only those polygons that belong to a surface. Thus, the angle between the polygons could be used to determine whether polygons sharing a vertex also lie in the same surface. The dot product between the surface normals can be used to yield a cosine value which can be compared to a test cosine value. If the magnitude of the cosine is less than the test value, we average the surface normal.

Because the normals are unit normals, the cosine between the normals is

$$x_{n_1} * x_{n_2} + y_{n_1} * y_{n_2} + z_{n_1} * z_{n_2}$$

where $(x_{n_1}, y_{n_1}, z_{n_1})$ and $(x_{n_2}, y_{n_2}, z_{n_2})$ are the respective unit normals of the two polygons. For the cylinder, if the arbitrary cosine value was 0, for 90°, the top and bottom polygon normals would not be averaged with the side normals, and the resulting shaded figure would have a smooth shaded side with sharply defined edges at the top and bottom.

3D Cursor and Picking

A 3D cursor may be either a wire-frame object or a single 3D polygon. If it is not too large or complicated, it can be smoothly moved around the screen using some interactive device.

Unlike a 2D cursor, the 3D cursor has a depth or z value associated with it. This means that any portion of the cursor that is behind or inside an object will not be visible. It can be used for defining viewing points and cutting planes.

A 3D cursor can be implemented by drawing a small grid with coplanar 3D constant shaded vectors in an overlay plane. Drawing the cursor by complementing the contents of the frame buffer to produce a new table index is possible, but it produces color variations as the cursor is moved across the displayed objects.

The cursor must be nondestructive so that it can move through 3D polygonal objects. It can be nondestructive if we disable writes to the depth buffer. Conditional writes to the frame buffer based on the z value can still be done, but if the current object is in front of the object already there, it is drawn only in the image buffer, and no update is done to the depth buffer. In this way a cursor can move through an object and not destroy any of the original depth information.

For speed reasons, a mesh rather than a 3D polygon should be used. If the system does not do any transformations, then it is the host's responsibility to:

1. Poll an input device.
2. Interpret the device data as a cursor movement.
3. Erase the previous cursor and draw the new one.

The fewer points that must be transformed, the quicker the cursor can move.

After polling the input device for the change in position, we can update a

Figure 7-40 Using a number line to indicate depth.

transformation matrix with the new translation or rotation and do scaling as well. Then we disable writes to the depth buffer greater than or equal to the z modes and disable all planes but the overlay. We can then draw the old cursor again with color 0 to erase it, which is quicker than clearing the whole plane. Then we apply the transformation matrix to the list of x, y, z vertices that describe the cursor and send 3D vector commands to the program to draw the new cursor, enable all the planes again for writing, and enable all writes to the depth buffer. The correct write modes and the correct planes must be enabled before any drawing or erasing commands are sent.

Although we can see where the cursor is in a relative x, y position, it is difficult to judge the depth of it without some type of depth cueing. Since depth cueing or perspective will take additional computation time, the cursor can use a number line to indicate the depth. A notch in the form of a 2D vector is drawn on the line to indicate the approximate z location of the cursor, as shown in Figure 7-40. The notch above the horizontal line indicates that the current z is between 2048 and 3072 device coordinate units. Another method is to use perspective to indicate the depth.

There are two ways to implement picking with minimal host computation. In this context, *picking* means the ability to select a 3D object out of the host database by picking an x,y point on the screen. We assume that any object in the host database that can be picked is unique.

The first method is the fastest; it involves giving every pixel a code unique to the object to which it belongs. We have seen how the bits in each pixel can be used to describe a pixel's color and shade. If the number of possible colors is greater than the number of objects, a unique color can be assigned to each of the objects. In this way the color bits of the pixel, at the picked x,y location, not only point into a section of the look-up table to determine the object's color, but also into the database to determine which object has been selected.

The second method is slower, and it does not rely on using a unique color code for each object. Instead, the image and z-buffer data at the selected x,y point is erased. The whole picture is then retransmitted, an object at a time. After each individual object is sent, the image and z-buffer values for the picked x,y point are read. If they are the same as the image and z-buffer values that were erased, the object that was just sent was the object that had been picked.

Contouring and Sectioning

Contouring can be done with a write-on-equal command. When a polygon is being drawn in this mode, the system checks the value in the depth buffer for a particular pixel to see if it is the same z as the one already there. If the depth values are equal, then the image buffer is updated with the new color. This capability can be used to achieve two different types of contouring.

The first type of contouring sends down a plane or several polygons which are the same color as the background. This updates the depth buffer but does not change the image. The contouring bit is then set and the 3D polygons describing the object to be contoured are sent. For example: sending a plane parallel to the screen, setting the contouring bit, and then sending the polygons describing a sphere results in a circle. The circle will be at the z value of the plane sent previously. The application program can send any type of object before setting the contouring bit, not only a plane.

The second way to use contouring is to send the displayed picture as usual, set the contouring bit, then send planes or polygons of a contrasting color. If the polygons describe a sphere, then the contouring command, and then a plane parallel to the screen (a 3D constant-shaded polygon), a circle will appear on the surface of the sphere. Sending several planes will result in concentric circles. This technique can be used to display the intersection of groups of objects.

An effect similar to the first type of contouring can be achieved by displaying the z buffer rather than the image buffer. If the depth buffer is displayed, only zs that have a nonzero entry in the look-up table will be displayed. The application program can load colors in the look-up table for those depth values it wishes to display and load the background color in the other entries.

To interactively look at the contours, the look-up table can be changed without retransmitting the picture. This displays only contours of planes parallel to the screen, but using the contouring command allows the display of intersections of all polygons.

We may also have a command that will section a three-dimensional picture in a plane parallel to the screen. This z-clipping is enabled by setting a bit in a command and setting a limit word with the z to be clipped to. The system will then draw only objects that appear behind that z value. We can let $z = 0$ be the furthest point from the viewer and 4095 the closest. A z-bit in the command can be used to disable this clipping. Hidden lines and surfaces are still removed in the usual manner.

The polygons that represent solid objects actually form a hollow shell surrounding the area taken up by the object. A host would normally not send back-facing polygons, as they are always obscured by front-facing polygons if the object is closed. The host can detect back-facing polygons, as they will have a negative *z* normal, while a front-facing polygon will have a positive one. If an object is sectioned, all polygons, front or back, should be sent. This is because at the place an object is sectioned, the inside or the back-facing polygons will be visible.

Depending on the type of shading given to the back-facing polygons, different effects can be created. If the back faces are made a constant shade, cut objects appear solid. If the back faces are smoothly shaded, they look hollow, as they appear to be the curved backside of the object. Doing smooth shading with the same color as the front faces results in ambiguous-looking objects, but smooth shading with another color separates the front and back surfaces and is especially effective when looking at nonclosed surfaces.

FINITE-ELEMENT MODELING

Finite-element modeling provides a method of determining mechanical characteristics such as the deflections and stresses of structures under load. The technique reduces the structure into a network of simple geometrical elements such as rods, shells, or cubes. Each of these elements has stress and deflection characteristics that can be obtained using classical methods. The behavior of the complete structure can then be predicted by having the computer solve the resulting set of simultaneous equations for all elements.

The element model is referred to as a *network* or *grid* and the connection points of the elements are called *nodes*. The simultaneous equations that describe the mathematical model of a large structure can number in the hundreds or thousands.

In constructing the model, the node points are defined on the geometry of the structure and then connected with elements to make up the mesh to be analyzed. Models can contain thousands of nodes. Each node has its own set of coordinates, which are determined and stored in the computer. Data on the connecting elements is also tabulated and stored.

Constructing a finite-element model can involve a great amount of data. In a large problem, the analyst must be strong in visualization to avoid errors.

In the 60s, when finite-element analysis was first introduced, the mesh generation was done by hand. The user would draw an array of node points and connecting elements on an overlay drawing of the part. The coordinates for each node point were measured and transcribed by hand along with the element data on input sheets. This information was keypunched into cards for batch processing of the equations. Writing line after line of numerical data produced frequent errors. Incorrect node coordinates were entered, improperly representing the part geometry and missing elements. To correct these

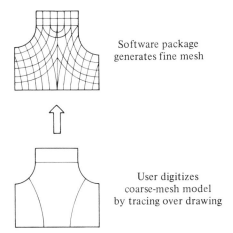

Software package
generates fine mesh

User digitizes
coarse-mesh model
by tracing over drawing

Figure 7-41   Finite-element generation for 2D model.

mistakes, the operator had to check each line of a numerical printout and change a card. The corrected model was then submitted for batch processing again. Then another printout had to be studied to evaluate the results of the new analysis.

Generating a finite-element model this way often took months. The first model typically did not provide satisfactory results, since it did not have enough nodes clustered in critical areas. Thus, several iterations were required for the analysis to be sufficiently accurate in the areas with high stress concentrations or large deformations.

In the mid 70s, the introduction of finite-element modeling packages using interactive computer graphics made mesh generation much easier. Preprocessing routines allowed the user to digitize the node points on a part drawing using an electronic cursor and digitizing tablet (Figure 7-41). The user entered each point by pressing a button on the pointing device, and the node appeared on the CRT screen. These systems would then automatically determine the node coordinates and element connectivity and display the resulting mesh on the screen as it was being constructed.

This interactive approach allowed finite-element models to be created and edited much faster. Since the modeling packages contained post-processing routines for displaying results graphically, the user could quickly evaluate the analysis visually rather than by handling numerical printouts.

In the late 70s, the preprocessors included the capability of generating a mesh by interactively copying nodes and elements. In this approach, as shown in Figure 7-42, the user would digitize the part boundary and a single element in the corner of that boundary. The computer would then replicate the element across one side of the boundary and sweep the row of elements across the entire area. This technique was useful in covering large areas of a model with

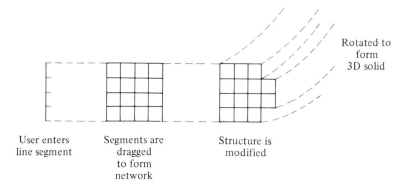

User enters line segment   Segments are dragged to form network   Structure is modified   Rotated to form 3D solid

Figure 7-42   Automatic mesh generation.

straight or smoothly curving boundaries. Irregularly shaped areas still had to be digitized manually.

Most finite-element modeling systems now use a mapped or edged-descriptor generation approach that is a step beyond the drag-mesh technique. Here the part is segmented into areas and the user specifies the mesh density. The system then generates the right nodes and elements for that area.

A program might generate elements in one, two, or three dimensions. The program may also be used to view existing finite-element models. The software reads the bulk data and prompts the user for viewing angles, portions of the model to be shown, and labels.

Special generation features can also convert a constant- or variable-thickness plate into a 3D solid element or automatically generate a 2D or 3D mesh. The software can also convert 2D planar models into 3D solid elements by rotating the grid about an axis or translating it through space.

One of the most important features in interactive finite-element modeling programs is the ability to minimize the cost of computer time by generating the models quickly. One approach is to make sure of symmetry. Here, as shown in Figure 7-42, the user defines the line segments, which the computer drags to generate quadrilateral elements. The user can then manipulate these elements by deleting or adding lines. The computer then adds mid-side nodes.

The user can then command the computer to rotate the elements about one of the axes to generate a mesh of 3D solid elements. The user modifies the resulting structure by adding or deleting solid elements to refine the mesh. For plotting, the computer can remove lines to show hidden faces.

Finite-element software packages can display the model in various ways to aid in the mesh generation. As the models are developed, these capabilities allow the user to manipulate the model graphically for better visualization and easier construction.

Hidden-line removal provides a display of elements only on the viewable forward surfaces of the part to simplify the model. As the hidden-line removal erases the background elements from the display, this capability simplifies the model by allowing the user to see the mesh network more clearly on the forward part surfaces.

Windowing displays the model at any orientation, and up to 16 views can be shown simultaneously on some systems. This allows the user to view the mesh at various angles to verify that the part geometry is properly represented. A zoom capability magnifies portions of the model for closer examination, and a shrink option separates the elements to expose holes in the mesh.

In most modeling packages the mesh density is specified by defining the number of node points required on each segment of the mapped area. Generally, the number of nodes must be the same on opposite sides of the segment. The mesh routine connects the corresponding nodes on opposite sides, creating the network of lines that define the nodes and elements. The final result is a uniform mesh across the segment.

Finite-element models are generally constructed with the smallest number of elements that will provide accurate results. The normal technique is to use an iterative procedure, where the first attempt at a model consists of coarse grids containing a few elements. Increasing the meshes in areas that seem to be critical is done next.

Instead of representing the actual geometry of the structure being modeled, these coarse models represent only how the structure reacts to loads. A rib might be described by a single beam element placed at the centroid of the member in a coarse model. Details such as flanges, holes, and projections might be ignored. These coarse models can ignore details smaller than two or three times the thickness of the basic structure.

The gross values that one gets from a coarse model are useful in making decisions regarding materials and structural shapes. We could use a coarse model in the analysis of the effect of a support rib for stiffness, or for vibration modes that might result from reducing the thickness of a vessel wall. A quick study of the stability of a structure modification might also be done this way. The use of coarse grids and a minimum number of nodes keeps the computer time lower.

The computer-time costs grow exponentially as the number of elements increases. So tripling the number of elements in the model can increase the modeling costs by a factor of ten.

A complex model may prove to be only slightly more accurate than a coarse version. This occurs because accuracy levels off as the grid density increases beyond a certain level.

To minimize the modeling costs, most finite-element programs use algorithms that are able to take advantage of the part symmetries. With this method the results calculated for one area will also apply to any other portions that have an identical or mirror-image geometry. This feature is useful, since many parts have symmetrical sections in at least a single direction.

Rotating equipment such as gears, wheels or turbines often have even greater symmetry. If each section has the same loading, then only one section needs to be modeled.

Antisymmetry in some cases can also be used to minimize calculations. Antisymmetrical parts include many S- or Z-shaped components.

Many curved models can greatly increase the cost of analysis. The complexity of curved models can be reduced through the use of isoparametric elements. These elements are allowed to have curved sides and nodes at mid-wall.

One isoparametric element can replace several straight-sided segments in curved models; thus a 75% reduction in the number of elements required for curved surfaces is possible. Libraries of isoparametric elements are available. Plane elements can represent flat thin-walled structures, and shell elements can represent thin curved surfaces. Thick-shell and bricklike solid elements represent regions with appreciable thickness.

Another time-saving technique in some preprocessor programs is automatic mesh generation. This technique allows element meshes for simple geometric shapes to be defined automatically by computer routines. As discussed earlier, the user lays out a row of elements, and the computer sweeps the row to create a mesh.

This technique can be used on simple parts having regular geometries. Many parts have at least some areas that can benefit from automatic mesh generation.

Even with automatic mesh generation, a model of a complex part such as a housing can require extensive operator interaction to define and blend the mesh network on the many irregular surfaces. In contrast, a symmetrical regular part might be modeled easily in one-tenth the time. On this type of part the user is able to employ the mirroring features in the routine to copy elements on the symmetric areas of the model.

The way that automatic mesh generators organize nodes and elements on the model can expend more computer processing time than necessary to actually analyze the model. As a result, optimization routines are used to rearrange the mesh.

Simple models are often run unoptimized, since more computer time is expended in optimizing than is saved. However, complex models may be too costly to analyze without optimization.

Optimization is performed by the software according to specific features selected by the user. These features operate on the mesh using terms of:

1. Compression.
2. Compaction.
3. Connectivity.

Compression deletes the stray nodes created during the mesh generation that are not connected to any elements. *Compaction* remembers the nodes and creates a contiguous set of nodal identifiers.

Connectivity optimization reorders the nodal numbering pattern so that the computer can analyze the model in the most efficient sequence, according to either the mesh profile or the bandwidth. Profile or RMS wavefront optimization minimizes the amount of processing time required, while bandwidth or maximum wavefront optimization minimizes the computer memory requirements.

Using a single design variable, such as the cross section of a rod, optimization programs can determine the shape which gives an ideal solution. Complex geometries require more effort, and the optimization program may not be effective.

The resulting geometries may also be difficult to manufacture. In a tunnel section, there are five design variables. The task is to guide the optimization routine to feasible solutions. Engineering intuition is required for the final selection of variables.

The goal of iterative modeling is to automate the design process by minimizing designer intervention. A subgoal is for the user to be unaware of the program used in the analysis.

Ideally, only the constraints and simple geometry need to be entered. The exact flow through a specific iterative package is variable, but most iterative systems will contain routines for database management, automeshing, optimization, and probability. Completely automated systems can lead to infeasible designs, and the use of an automated system must still be given a critical engineering review that is unbiased.

EXERCISES

1. What are the advantages and disadvantages of a computer model?

2. What four types of software are involved with modeling?

3. Explain the concept of object hypothesis. How does this apply to model-building software?

4. Discuss the basis of polygon meshes and parametric bicubic patches. Why use only a cubic equation in a patch? Would higher-order equations be more effective?

5. In many model hierarchies, objects are placed in specified locations with connections either interactively by the user or automatically by the application program. Discuss how logic symbols can be placed

by the user without having to define them and by having the application program do simple geometrical transformations.

6. Draw a wire-frame model that is a collection of 12 lines. Show how:

  a. The 12 lines can define a four-sided object open at both ends.

  b. The same 12 lines can define an open box.

  c. The same 12 lines can define a cube.

7. Draw a figure which shows the polygons created on two surfaces of a cube when they are partially shadowed by a triangle. The polygons cover those parts of the cube which are visible from the light source.

8. A number of finite-element modeling programs are available for use on various mainframe computers and even for many smaller computers. However, the modeling capabilities of the software may be limited by the smaller memory size of these computers. Discuss what effect this may have on the finite-element model.

9. What is a shading model and how is it used?

10. Discuss the most common color-specification systems.

11. The production of realistic graphics is often used as sole criterion for determining whether or not a program is a good solid-modeler. Is this criterion appropriate, since most modelers can also produce shaded-image displays? Discuss your answer.

12. One of the most time-consuming facets of finite-element analysis has been the development of models using manual techniques. Show how element meshes are now generated automatically using routines built into the finite-element modeling software.

MECHANICAL
DESIGN
APPLICATIONS

8

The success of computer graphics in the electronics industry prompted its use in other applications. Like circuit design, some of these applications involve two-dimensional layouts. Mechanical and electronic applications make up the largest portion of CAD/CAM applications. The concept of computer-aided design engineering is broader, encompassing such applications as mapping, piping, geography, and architecture. These areas also take advantage of interactive graphics systems to manipulate data and present information pictorially for ready evaluation.

MECHANICAL DESIGN EVOLUTION

One of the key concepts in CAD/CAM is that the individual functions in design and manufacturing not only are computerized, but are tied together using a shared database. This allows the engineer to:

1. Define the design configuration.
2. Analyze the structure and its mechanical parameters.
3. Enter test data and observe the result.
4. Produce engineering drawings. This is done on the same graphics terminal, and the geometric description provided can be used:
   a. As a starting point to create NC tapes.
   b. To determine processing plans.
   c. To instruct robots.
   d. To manage the plant operations.

The evolution of CAD/CAM technology has resulted in the integration of many diverse technical areas that have developed separately over the past thirty years. Initially, CAD systems started as automated drafting stations in which computer-controlled plotters produced engineering drawings. The systems were then linked to graphic display terminals, where geometric models were created, and the resulting database in the computer was used to produce drawings.

Interactive graphics systems now have analytical capabilities that allow parts to be evaluated with data to create an overall model called a *system model*. This model can predict the behavior of the entire structure over its service life. Computer simulation is used to determine the precise loads, so that components can be designed accordingly.

In the traditional build-and-test approach, by contrast, component designs are initially based on load estimates and refined with prototype testing. We can now cycle through design iterations in the computer rather than using hardware prototypes.

Computer simulation reduces the time and cost associated with product design. The computer-aided designs are also closer to optimum, because the engineering effort tends to be oriented toward the evaluation of alternative designs and optimizing rather than emphasizing the physical tests of the design configuration.

With computer simulation, designers can evaluate the overall product considerations such as weight distribution, vibration, stability, and stress concentrations without building a physical model.

Some common mechanical components can be tested less expensively and more accurately than they can be modeled. These parts include those that have low rigidity, such as shock absorbers or engine mounts. These components are generally tested rather than modeled for determination of structural characteristics such as bending modes. Empirical data gathered from these tests can then be combined with finite-element models of the other components in the system.

A critical part of the design process is the system model; this is the mathematical representation of the entire structure which is stored in the computer. The model is created by combining data on the individual components and subassemblies. This data can come from finite-element analysis, modal testing, or other data banks, depending on which data is readily available. Some automotive components such as tires, shock absorbers, and engine mounts can be tested less expensively and more accurately than they can be modeled with finite elements, so test data is normally used in the system model.

The system model is exercised and refined using an iterative process until a detailed, optimum configuration is created. The first simulation may be coarse and not necessarily intended to yield precise results. Successive simulations suggest the changes that produce an increasingly refined model.

The mode shapes may indicate large structural deformations at frequencies near the operational frequency of the structure. So the design is changed through additions or rearrangements of the structural members until the vibration is damped sufficiently.

The next step is to apply the loads determined from the coarse modeling to the models of individual components. The stresses on the components can then be determined and evaluated and the component designs changed as required to withstand the loads indicated by the system model.

The refined design may alter the overall performance of the system, so the refined component models are inserted back into the system model and exercised once again, as shown in Figure 8-1. The design iterations thus transform the coarse component models into increasingly optimal finite-element models.

A prototype can then be built and tested using modal-analysis and stress-testing techniques. The results of these tests may indicate that further changes to the system model and individual components are necessary.

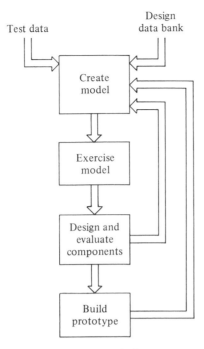

Figure 8-1   The design process.

Prototype testing provides the data for refinement of the system model, and the model guides the redesign by helping the designer understand the prototype behavior. When the prototype is refined, the final design can be released to manufacturing.

The automotive industry has been applying this product design and development process to reduce product lead times and vehicle weight while improving the ride and handling. Aircraft companies simulate airplanes before metal fabrication. In the design of earthmovers and agricultural equipment one can check the handling qualities and other characteristics such as the view from the cab before prototype production. Computer simulation is also used in the design of large rotating equipment such as fans, turbines, electric motors, and pumps.

Finite-Element Analysis

In the past it was impractical to blend empirical test results and conventional analysis to create the computer models. The two types of data were hard to combine, owing to problems in data correlation and integration. When two structures are joined together by flexible mounts to provide some

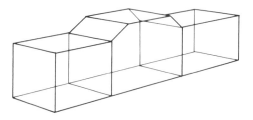

Figure 8-2 A coarse finite-element model which may closely resemble the mechanical structure of the part.

cushioning, the combined structure often exhibits dependent dynamics which can be hard to predict through analysis. To handle the dynamics of these structures we can divide the data into submatrices. Each of these represents some major part of the assembly.

A finite-element program combines the matrices in order to characterize the entire structure. In constructing the finite-element model, nodes are placed at each change of cross section in the structure, as shown in Figure 8-2. Adjacent nodes can be connected through the use of beam elements assigned with the material properties such as Young's modulus as well as stiffness properties such as the moment of inertia, torsional constant, or shear-area ratio. Using these, the computer calculates the node deflections in three-dimensional space. The structural deformations and internal force distributions can then be obtained from these deflections.

In a coarse analysis, the nodes are placed only at points where loads or forces are applied, or at the boundaries on the structure. A beam supported at both ends with a weight near the center, as shown in Figure 8-3, requires three nodes: one at each end and one at the point of applied force.

Large structures can also be modeled with a limited number of nodes. Solid panels can be modeled by rectangular elements. A major consideration

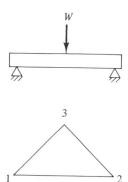

Figure 8-3 Coarse finite-element model of a simple loaded beam.

in node placement is the aspect ratio—the length-to-width ratio for the quadrilateral plate elements. Square elements have an aspect ratio of 1.0 and are often preferred because they yield higher accuracy. Square elements are also a convenient starting point for building finite-element networks in localized stress areas.

The aspect-ratio limitation will depend on the software used. In general the aspect ratios should be under 10 for deformation predictions and under 5 for stress analysis.

Sometimes the coarse finite-element network is accurate enough and there is no need for further analysis. The error in coarse analysis generally does not exceed 20%.

A fine mesh is used in the local areas where the stress and deflection must be more precise. The fine meshes are used in areas of the coarse model which are predicted to produce large deflections. The grid density can be increased until the resulting model predicts the deflections and stresses with a sufficient accuracy as determined by verification algorithms.

The preferred fine-mesh technique is to use simple plate or beam elements as in the coarse models, unless modeling potentially high-stress areas. In these areas, more sophisticated elements such as higher-order isopara-metrics can provide high accuracy at the cost of computer time.

The early finite-element programs used only elements with straight sides. Models of curved surfaces had to be constructed using many small, straight segments to approximate the curved surfaces. The large number of elements required for this procedure limited the models to simple shapes.

This led to more advanced features in finite-element software such as the ability to generate curved elements. A double-curved structure, for example, can be modeled through the use of parabolic general shell elements. The parabolic general shells can be converted automatically into solid elements or rotated to provide three-dimensional parabolic shell elements. Some programs can create a variable-density mesh with automatic transitioning that allows the user to specify different numbers of nodes or elements.

Only a small amount of finite-element modeling is done manually. In these cases the users may be just beginning finite-element analysis—or, if the models are extremely simple or infrequently constructed, the modeling software may not be economically justifiable.

A majority of those who build models use automatic mesh generators, and most analysts use an interactive modeling strategy in which only the topological details and the relative location of holes are specified. For example, the diameter of the holes in a bracket, as well as the spacing between holes, is fixed, while the part shape is free to change in the unrestricted areas.

Modifications to the geometric inputs must be made using engineering judgment. In a pressure vessel, for example, the rules that govern modification of the geometry may need only to control the thickness. But in specifying an I-beam, the thickness of the beam and the critical dimensions such as flange height could be subject to controls. A knowledge of the failure modes, which requires engineering judgment, also plays a vital role.

There are several reasons for choosing the geometry as simply as possible. The most important is the requirement that the model be able to use automatic mesh generation, which eases most of the laborious procedures in model creation. If the geometry is redefined at each iteration, the mesh must also be redefined.

Since the inputs to the program are primarily geometric, any iterative program must modify the initial geometry, so these inputs must be flexible. One approach to the flexible definition of the geometry is to use a parametric description of design elements. A shape is defined by its thickness, a series of straight lines, and a radius. Defining a fillet would smooth out the shape and also reduce the point stress concentrations in corners.

Mechanism Design

A number of computer programs have been developed for the design of mechanisms and linkages. These programs fall into two classes:

1. *Kinematic synthesis* programs create a linkage as the user provides the information about the kind of motion desired.
2. *Kinematic analysis* programs are used to simulate the motion produced by a specified mechanism configuration.

The types of problems that these kinematic programs will solve can be classified into three areas:

1. Kinematic design.
2. Dynamic performance.
3. Structural integrity or statics.

Programs will solve from one to all three kinds of problems.

Mechanism design may be categorized as being either planar or spatial. *Planar* motion is that in which the components move in curves that lie in parallel planes. Planar mechanisms do not necessarily lie in a single plane. *Spatial* mechanisms trace out paths that do not lie in parallel planes.

Most kinematic programs can solve planar mechanism problems, but not all programs can handle spatial mechanisms. Most mechanisms execute only planar motions. The mechanism programs generally are provided with linkage geometry. Geometric properties such as acceleration, velocity, and position are determined in the analysis.

Programs that perform dynamic analysis produce information about characteristics such as moments, time response, and the natural frequencies of systems responding to time-varying loads. The analysis determines the forces applied to the mechanism and is useful in the sizing of actuators and other power devices.

Static or structural analysis determines the forces acting on the mechanism either at rest or moving with a uniform velocity. The analysis can determine if the physical design is strong and durable. It can also act as a check for overdesign as well as underdesign in the linkages.

Finite-element analysis has become firmly established as a credible method for predicting stresses and deflection in mechanical parts and structures. The finite-element process, however, requires that the imposed loads be known. Analytical methods for predicting loads present major difficulties if the design involves dynamic motion. We can test prototypes to get an estimate of service loads. But if prototypes are not available for tests, a gross estimate must be used.

Another part of the design, the stress analysis, has matured from a more basic load analysis in the form of programs for simulating the mechanical behavior.

At the heart of this growth in computer-aided engineering for product design and development is the system model. This model is created in the computer from test, analysis, and stored data.

The *system model* simulates the product performance in the computer, rather than relying on prototype testing as do traditional build-and-test methods. As the system model is exercised to determine the modes of vibration and the natural frequencies, the individual component designs are refined and evaluated based on the loads. Then a prototype is built to verify the computer design. In each of these steps, the system model is refined in an iterative procedure which uses the increasingly precise design information. In this way, an optimum design can be released to manufacturing.

The various types of software that are available for simulating mechanical behavior include kinematic programs that analyze the movement of cams, gears, links, and other mechanisms. The analysis is geometric in nature, determining motion paths and reaction forces for relatively large displacements.

The solutions generally neglect inertia and assume that the mechanism moves in accordance with the input movements. The types of mechanical assemblies analyzed are generally restricted to specific devices such as four-bar linkages and other classical mechanisms that use cyclic, repetitive movements.

The dynamic analysis programs can analyze displacements and forces in more complex mechanical systems, such as automobiles and machines. These packages can be used to determine the vibration characteristics of an entire vehicle for wheel oscillations. These programs are generally limited, in that they operate only with small displacements with linear relationships.

Another class of software can be used for complex systems undergoing large-displacement dynamics. This software can be used to determine the deflection of an automobile suspension system as it makes a turn and to determine the force on the chassis as the wheel hits an object. The simulation of these events is the key to analytically determining loads for many complex systems.

Large displacements can drive the analysis into nonlinear regions and create discontinuities. Techniques for handling these problems include sparse-matrix methods and stiff-system numerical-integration algorithms. These provide a way to control the operations required to deal with linear events.

This sparse-matrix approach provides a mathematical system with a large but sparse set of first-order differential equations. Of the numerous equations that are used to describe the structure, only a few finite terms occur in each. The time required for processing these equations is much less than would ordinarily be involved to solve large dynamic-simulation problems.

The programs are run interactively and when used with the proper terminals can display the linkage motions in real time, so that the user can see how the different parts of mechanisms move. The user enters commands or data by typing in the mnemonics on a keyboard or through a digitizing pen and tablet.

The models are constructed by combining data that defines the geometry and mass properties of the structure with the applied forces. The parts and forces that describe the mechanical system are chosen from a library of elements and linked together in the computer. These are entered using part, joint, marker, force, and generator statements. The input is freeform, using mnemonic keyword descriptors to define the parts and forces.

The part statements define the geometry, mass, and moment of inertia of each rigid part in the structure. Joint statements describe contacts between moving parts that hold the assembly together.

The joints can be specified as providing translational and rotation movement including revolute, spherical, screw, universal, cylindrical, and translational joints, as well as rack-and-pinion motion. The marker statements provide a point on the coordinate system fixed on each part, orienting it to the other parts and in this way defining the overall configuration of the entire mechanical system.

The internal reaction forces in the system are selected from a library of standard elements such as dampers and springs. User-written routines can be used to define nonstandard forces which may be a function of displacement, velocity, and time. The external forces which act on the system are defined by generator statements selected from a library.

A Finite-Element Program, MSC/NASTRAN*

In this section we consider more closely the use of finite-element analysis in a wide variety of mechanical design problems.

The problems that can be solved using MSC/NASTRAN can be grouped into the following general classes:

1. Static structures.
2. Structural stability.
3. Dynamic structures.
4. Heat transfer.
5. Aeroelasticity.
6. General matrix operations.

Each general problem class can be further subdivided into different case types that differ as to:

1. The type of information desired.
2. The environmental factors considered.
3. The method of analysis.

Each case type requires a distinct sequence of functional module calls that are scheduled by the executive system.

A basic static analysis solves for the response of complex structures to static loads. It yields grid-point displacements and forces, constraint forces, element forces, stresses, and strain energy, as well as weight and balance data. A static analysis with inertia relief solves the quasi-static responses to static loads and to balancing inertia loads resulting from steady accelerations.

Stability and Dynamic Analysis

A *normal-mode analysis* solves for the natural frequencies and vibration modes. It yields the generalized masses, normalized modal grid-point displacements, constraint forces, and normalized model element forces and stresses. *Buckling analysis* performs a differential stiffness analysis of a structure and then performs a real eigenvalue analysis based on the linear

---

*MSC/NASTRAN is an advanced proprietary program of the MacNeal-Schwendler Corporation. NASTRAN® is a registered trademark of the National Aeronautics and Space Administration.

combination of the linear stiffness and differential stiffness matrices. This will determine the magnitude of the load distribution which would cause buckling and resulting deformations. It yields normalized displacement, force, and stress information at the threshold load for buckling.

A *direct complex eigenvalue analysis* solves for the frequencies and mode shapes of structures in which the damping may be both viscous and structural. The complex eigenvalue extraction is performed on the matrices, which are formulated directly from the grid-point degrees of freedom. It yields the normalized complex eigenvectors of grid-point displacements and grid-point constraint forces, as well as the complex element forces and stresses.

A direct-frequency and random-response analysis solves two problems in the frequency domain, operating on matrices which are formulated directly in terms of the grid-point degrees of freedom. First, it can solve for the response of a structure having both viscous and structural damping to a spectrum of steady sinusoidal forcing functions. It yields the real and imaginary parts of displacements, velocities, accelerations, and constant-point forces at the grid points and the real and imaginary parts of forces and stresses in the elements. These output quantities can be normalized to a unit forcing amplitude to form transfer functions.

The second problem it can solve is the response of the structure, as characterized by the above transfer functions, to a stationary random loading expressed in terms of its cross-power spectral density. It yields the auto-power spectral density of the quantity used in the transfer functions, which may be:

1. Displacement.
2. Acceleration.
3. Constraint forces.
4. Stress.

It can also integrate the auto-power spectra to obtain the root-mean-square values of the response.

A *direct transient-response analysis* solves for the response of structures to time-varying loads in which the damping may be both viscous and structural. The numerical integration is performed on the coupled differential equations as formulated directly in terms of grid-point degrees of freedom. This yields the time-varying displacements, velocities, accelerations, and constraint forces and stresses in the elements.

A *modal complex eigenvalue analysis* solves for the frequencies and mode shapes of structures, as does the direct complex eigenvalue analysis discussed above. In the modal method, however, a real eigenvalue analysis, which neglects the damping, is performed on the matrices with grid-point degrees of freedom. This sets up smaller matrices in modal coordinates before extracting the complex eigenvalues. The damping is applied in the reduced system. It yields the normalized complex eigenvectors of grid-point displacements and grid-point constraint forces, and the complex element forces and stresses.

A *modal frequency and random-response analysis* can be used to solve the same two problems in the frequency domain as the direct frequency-response analysis discussed earlier. In this technique the problem size is reduced by performing a real eigenvalue analysis, which applies damping in the reduced system, using the matrices with grid-point degrees of freedom to set up smaller matrices in modal coordinates. The output data from this analysis are the same as from the direct frequency-response analysis.

In a *modal transient-response analysis*, the direct transient-response problem formulation is reduced in size by the modal transformation as is done in the modal complex eigenvalue and modal frequency-response analysis. The damping can be approximated by modal damping, using the modal coordinates in an uncoupled set, or by fully coupled damping in the reduced system. Numerical integration of these reduced equations results in the same output data that are obtained in the direct transient-response analysis.

Time-Saving Techniques

Cyclic symmetry is a technique that allows the analysis of only one substructure for a set of equivalent but symmetric substructures. There are two types of cyclic symmetry:

1. *Simple rotational symmetry*, in which the segments do not have planes of reflective symmetry and the boundaries between segments may be general double-curved surfaces.
2. *Dihedral symmetry,* in which each segment has a plane of reflective symmetry and the boundaries between segments are planar.

Taking advantage of symmetry results in a large saving of computer time for most finite-element problems.

Superelements are an automated form of multilevel substructuring. Superelements are mathematically equivalent to *substructures*, but they allow a more complete, convenient implementation.

An analysis that uses substructuring offers a number of advantages:

1. Simpler problem preparation.
2. Computational efficiency.
3. Reduced computer storage requirements.

Superelements provide other capabilities such as automated partitioning of connectivity and load data, identical and mirror-image components, and a larger number of partitions than is convenient using earlier substructuring techniques.

The net effect of these improvements allows the substructuring of a larger class of problems. Models with a higher degree of partitioning may be constructed, as well as models of very large structures where substructuring is the only possible method of solution.

Component-mode synthesis for external superelements is a method of analysis that solves dynamics problems by combining the uncoupled vibration characteristics of a number of structural components. The stiffness, mass, damping, and applied static load matrices are derived from experimental or calculated data for each structural component subjected to vibratory or static excitations.

The method uses degrees of freedom consisting of uncoupled vibration modes and boundary attachment points which exist before the structure is assembled by combining its components. The influence of truncated higher modes can be supplied by static flexibility or stiffness data to generate residual flexibility effects for the boundary degrees-of-freedom. Once assembled, the structural system vibration characteristics and forced responses can be determined.

A *response-spectrum analysis*, also known as a *shock-spectrum analysis*, provides an alternative to dynamic analysis by transient-response methods. It represents the excitations sustained by extensions or components that are mounted upon the primary structural components in a format required by the design codes, such as for seismic problems.

The response of the extension is determined as some combination of maximum responses in each mode of the primary structure as prescribed in the design code. The combinatorial options can include the SRSS method, the absolute method, and the NRL method.

Nonlinear Analysis

A geometric nonlinear static analysis includes all the capabilities of a linear static analysis, plus a nonlinear strain-displacement law and follower forces. Material nonlinear-analysis solution techniques can be used to analyze problems in static analysis, where the stress-strain relationship of the material is nonlinear. These problems can occur in metal plasticity, or in materials such as soils and concrete which involve plasticity analysis, or in materials where the stress-strain relationship becomes nonlinear elastic. All of these come under the category of material nonlinear analysis and can be analyzed using these methods. Plasticity theories such as the von Mises or Tresca for metals and the Mohr-Coulomb or Drucker-Prager for frictional materials such as soils or concrete can be applied by the user. There are three choices for the definition of the yield surfaces:

1. Isotropic hardening.
2. Kinematic hardening.
3. Combined isotropic and kinematic hardening.

The behavior of most materials for plasticity, with or without the Bauschinger effect, can be modeled. Gaps can also be used to model structural separations and sliding effects.

A nonlinear transient-response analysis solves for the response of a structure in which the stress-strain relationship of the material is nonlinear or the strain-displacement relationship is nonlinear. The structure may be subjected to arbitrarily time-varying loads, and damping can be either viscous or structural.

Heat Transfer

Steady linear heat transfer involves the temperature distribution in a structure where the thermal loads and boundary conditions are known. We can plot the grid-point temperatures which are suitable for structural response, the heat of constraint, and the element temperature gradients. A selection of different input parameters can provide the user with options for controlling the heat-transfer analysis. One can define the model for variable boundary conditions, material properties, and initial conditions. Among the control parameters are the following variable loading and boundary conditions:

1. Time-dependent and static conditions.
2. Conductive and convective heat flow.
3. Prescribed heat flux and radiant heat flux from distant sources.
4. Radiative exchange between surfaces.
5. Volume heat additions.

The initial conditions can be homogeneous or varying and include initial temperatures. The material properties include:

1. Isotropic and anisotropic materials.
2. Film heat-transfer coefficients.
3. Absorptivity and emissivity factors.
4. Perfect conductors.

The engineer may build a single model for both thermal and stress analysis, using the same grid points, coordinate systems, property cards, and sequencing for heat-transfer and thermal-stress problems. Since each thermal element has a corresponding structural element, the elements in the structural model are compatible with elements in the heat-transfer model.

Nonlinear steady heat transfer includes all the capabilities of linear steady heat transfer, plus nonlinear radiation as a function of the fourth-power law and temperature dependent thermal conductivity. Transient nonlinear heat transfer solves for the transient temperature response due to time-varying loads and boundary conditions. The nonlinearity may be due to radiation or to temperature-dependent emissivity and absorptivity properties. Variable specific heats can be accounted for by special modeling techniques.

One can also calculate the view factors for radiation heat transfer between surfaces. In this case a module automatically accounts for shading from intermediate surfaces.

Fluid Interactions and Aeroelasticity

In fluid interactions one considers a variety of fluid problems with structural interfaces, compressibility, and gravity effects. The fluid finite-element technique is applicable for fluids contained in an axisymmetric structure and can include the effects of compressibility and gravity. The virtual-mass technique can be used for arbitrary geometry with internal or external incompressible fluids. The standard normal modes of analysis including transient analysis and frequency response are possible with some minor restrictions.

One can also tailor a sequence of instructions to solve similar problems concerning:

1. Electrostatics.
2. Corrosion.
3. Seepage.
4. Mass transfer.
5. Diffusion phenomena.

Aerodynamic flutter analysis is concerned with the dynamic stability of an aeroelastic system. It may involve subsonic or supersonic flows.

A series of complex eigenvalue solutions are determined for the linear equations of motion. A modal approach is used to reduce the problem size. Several methods of stability analysis may be used. These include versions of the American method (or K method) and the British method (or PK method).

The output data can include the damping, frequency, and mode shape of each flutter mode as a function of the airstream velocity.

An aerodynamic-response analysis involves the calculation of the response to either a discrete or random two-dimensional gust field at subsonic speeds. The pertinent output data include displacements, stresses, or constraint forces. The accelerations can be obtained from the response to a double differential with respect to time of the gust profile. A random-gust analysis can be used to produce the response power spectral density, the root-mean-square response, and the mean frequency of zero crossings. An acoustic-resonance analysis has a similar basis but it determines the natural frequencies and pressure modes of an acoustic cavity.

Numerical Analysis Techniques

Numerical analysis techniques can allow the solution of very large problems with a program that has no inherent problem-size limitations. In static analysis the solution procedure can use an active/passive column technique, which allows the same kind of reduction in multiplications as obtained by substructuring techniques. The spill logic which is used in decomposition can remove size restrictions created by the amount of main memory available.

The grid-point sequencing procedure can operate without special inputs from the user. The sequencer may operate on the complete problem or on the interior points of individual superelements. Much of the efficiency in the solution procedure is created by the coding of the inner loops for decomposition and forward/backward substitution.

Most methods of eigenvalue extraction fall into one of two groups—the transformation methods and the tracking methods. In a *transformation method* the matrix of coefficients is first transformed, while preserving its eigenvalues, into a form such as diagonal, tridiagonal, or upper Hessenberg, from which the eigenvalues can be more easily extracted.

In a *tracking method* the roots are extracted, one at a time, using iterative procedures which are applied to the original dynamic matrix. Some methods are better for extracting the eigenvalues of real matrices, and other methods are more suitable for complex matrices. No single method has been found to be completely satisfactory with respect to efficiency and reliability for the generality of applications in all situations. For real matrices there is the Givens/Householder method and the tracking inverse-power method.

For complex matrices there is the QR-transformation of Francis, the tracking determinant method, and the inverse-power method can be used here also.

For integration in transient-response analysis, one can use the Newmark method, which is an unconditionally stable algorithm for linear systems. This method needs no special starting values other than the usual initial conditions on displacement and velocity.

Many of the numerical integration methods, when applied to harmonic problems, produce errors in period elongation and in amplitude. The Newmark method has only a small error in period elongation and no error in amplitude. If, in a modal formulation, there is no direct matrix input or any nonlinear terms, the equations of motion for the individual modal coordinates are uncoupled and the equations may be integrated analytically.

For transient-response analysis with aerodynamic loads that are known only in the frequency domain, we can use Fourier transform methods to obtain the response-time histories. First, the loads as functions of time are transformed into the frequency domain. Then the responses are computed in the frequency domain. Next, the responses in the frequency domain are transformed back into the time domain. If the loads or a gust-field profile are provided as tabular functions of time, the Fourier transforms can be found by assuming a piecewise linearity between tabular values. An inverse Fourier transform method is then used to obtain the time history of the response.

There are a number of optional approaches to decreasing the size of a dynamics problem. These include:

1. Guyan reduction.
2. Generalized dynamic reduction.
3. The modal method.
4. Component mode synthesis.
5. Cyclic symmetry.

Each of these reduces the size of the problem and results in a minimum-size problem for a required accuracy. Cyclic symmetry allows significant reductions in computer time for the analysis of linear systems that possess rotation or reflective planes of symmetry. There can also be a considerable reduction in the tasks of problem preparation, since the entire system can be generated through reflections or rotations of the fundamental region.

Database management and optimization theory can help automate many of the time-consuming tasks in iterative finite-element analysis. The trend in program development and system design is to view the analysis as a part of the design process, and this may go so far as to treat it like a subroutine in the design cycle.

Finite-element analysis may assume a different role because of the increasing multidisciplinary approach in design synthesis. Database techniques, probability theory, and optimization are taking on more important roles in the design process. Much of this is due to the decrease in computational costs. Another factor in this design automation is the increasing cost of engineering labor. All these factors are moving the future programs into more iterative design, driven by a set of simple geometric constraints.

Optimization Techniques

Both the stress analysis and optimization codes may be subroutines in the optimization scheme. In any scheme, there is a supervisory program that calls the subroutines and facilitates the transfer of the data.

A part will be given a parametric description and a set of constraints. The finite-element portion of the program will create the mesh and then analyze it. The results will be compared to the constraints. Then, based on these results, the initial geometry will be modified.

The direction and magnitude of the changes are controlled by an optimization program running in parallel with the finite-element analysis. As a final check, the results can be subjected to a probabilistic analysis.

Many programs such as NASTRAN* versions implement inputs to an optimization code in a finite-element package. These inputs are calculated at the same time the matrix equations are solved, and they represent a gradient. Geometric changes are imposed on the initial model, based on the value of this gradient. The direction chosen is a function of the behavior of the function.

In the case of a static loaded beam, a method often used is based on finite differences. In this method the structure is varied a small amount, and the extent of the variation from the displacement is used. A disadvantage of this method is that it rapidly grows in complexity. The finite difference must be taken for each variable, changed one at a time. For N variables, $N + 1$ runs must be made.

An alternative to the finite-difference method is *analytical sensitivity*. In this method, a gradient function is taken for a unit displacement, and the calculation is a single step. NASTRAN uses this technique. Though it is well suited to linear problems, more complex dynamic problems may cause this method to break down.

In a driven simple harmonic motion, resonance is a discontinuous function. The amplitude peaks at infinity, and just as the part leaves resonance, the phase angle changes sign. Near the area of resonance, there may be no derivative and the gradient will not exist. So there may be no analytical solution. There are, however, algorithmic methods of finding an optimum.

There is a continuum of optimization problems. At one end are the linear, static problems with a single constraint variable, such as the cross-sectional area. At the other end we have the nonlinear, dynamic problems with

*NASTRAN is a registered trademark of the National Aeronautics and Space Administration.

variable geometry. A high-end problem that can be solved is a shaft that goes through resonance. This type of dynamic analysis should become common.

No matter what the problem is, there is a necessary separation of optimization from analysis, since the optimization routines can ignore the relationship's simple physics.

The problem-specific physics are in the analysis routines. The same optimization program can then be used for both aerodynamic-flow and stress-analysis problems.

The goal of the optimization is to generate an optimum design. At each step in the iterative process, the program chooses which direction will better satisfy the constraints. The shape of the initial part geometry is changed according to certain design rules, usually to minimize stress concentrations. The design rules may specify that if a section is below a certain stress level, the critical dimensions are to be decreased. The program may also incorporate a minimum value for all dimensions.

In a typical application a brace may not be eliminated from the design because of the initial geometric definition. The problem with a program that could eliminate a redundant part is that the resulting design might not be adequate. If the initial problem statement ignored a torsional force, elimination of the brace could result in a critical design error.

The problem of optimization is to use the proper links to connect the analysis, optimization, and geometric modification data sets. Each phase of the optimization process tends to have different requirements. The binding of the parts of the analysis procedure with a supervisory program allows the individual analysis programs to be used as subroutines.

The earliest uses of finite elements in the U.S. space program relied on probability theory. The structures were so highly loaded that the stresses approached a significant percentage of the ultimate strength. These high stresses required the use of probability theory to aid in failure prediction. As models reach optimal configurations, indicated by a percentage of ultimate strength, probability plays a greater role in determining the suitability of the design.

One method of applying probability would be in the computation of an overall stress integral. This can be a convenient method to perform comparisons. The sum of the elemental stresses is divided by the sum of the elemental volumes. This number can then be related back to experimental life-stress curves. Weibull curves, which are used in determining product life, represent a volume.

A major difficulty in some analysis is interpreting the results. The sheer volume of data can be overwhelming. In most cases, the results are shown graphically.

Contour plots can turn the lines of data into color-coded plots. But there are situations in which a graphic analysis is not sufficient.

To obtain more rigorous yet not overwhelming answers, *database management* (*DBM*) can be used. These techniques allow one to extract selected information from large data sets. An analysis requires three data sets—input, output, and analysis—and any of the adaptive philosophies consist of using DBM techniques to sort and select this data. These techniques are also useful as tools for postprocessing. The conversational mode of most systems can ease the task of analysis.

In the case of a frame for a building, many different load cases may be run. The analyst must then sift through the data to study the effects of these loads. DBM allows the data to be sorted by groups, and a selection criteria may be exercised to choose all beams that have been stressed to within 50% of their rated load. By using these truncated lists, the comparison becomes quicker.

Another benefit of DBM can be in limiting the amount of data that must be transmitted between systems. File transfers can be a major time factor. Using search-and-sort routines, the size of the file that is transmitted can be made much smaller. Because an analysis file can be several megabytes long, compaction is very desirable.

Another important use of DBM is in determining the actual iteration process. Most geometry modification is rule-based and a function of the output, so we need to connect the input files to the output files.

A pressure-vessel rule might be: if the critical stress level is below a certain level, decrease the thickness by 20%. We would find all the points affected by this rule and apply the change.

The linking of postprocessing and preprocessing is one of the keys to iterative analysis. The program must be able to modify the geometry based on the results of the analysis. Only with the linking of geometry to the results can there be iterative design synthesis.

Pre- and Postprocessing

The use of pre- and postprocessors for finite-element analysis has dramatically reduced the costs associated with structural analysis. For many companies the ramifications of this friendly software go beyond these savings. The added advantages result from the fact that these processors save so much analysis time that several design iterations can be made before any metal is cut. As a result, few if any structural corrections are necessary after the initial product is built.

The product is brought to the certification process more rapidly and is far more refined than it could be by the prior art. Thus, the product can be marketed earlier than before, with the usual benefits in terms of return on investment and competitive position. There are also direct cost savings through a substantial reduction in the need for changes in production fixtures, work procedures, and engineering drawings.

The net result is that what appears to be a local improvement—the implementation of some friendly software in the front and back ends of the stress-analysis software—actually has subtle but substantial effects that reach throughout the project.

The advent of pre- and postprocessors is the latest in a series of developments that have brought less costly and more powerful computer graphics to the once labor-intensive task of structural analysis. These developments have made possible a highly interactive engineering process that brings the designer and computer closer together during the iterations necessary to develop optimum structures. Computer input and output in the form of massive tabulations of numbers have been replaced by three-dimensional images on a video screen, under the direct control of the terminal operator.

These pre- and postprocessing capabilities have largely come about through the specialized development of pre- and postprocessors by users, consistent with the overall goals of a more general-purpose system. Finite-element preprocessors provide for model generation and the interactive display of the model as represented by the data.

The model-generation preprocessor might reside in the preface of the finite-element program and its use invoked through a single command. This preprocessor may generate the finite-element models of the structures from analyst-supplied descriptions of one-, two-, or three-dimensional regions and the associated interconnection specifications. These regions may be bounded by curved lines or surfaces, and the grid spacing in the regions may be even or uneven.

Large models can be generated in several computer executions. The results of each computer execution are stored for later execution or for use in editing and modifying previously generated regions. The analyst can display the generated model at any time and interactively utilize rotation, clip, and zoom commands to assist in the model validation. These functions can be incorporated into the design to provide a complete model-generation capability.

A total pre- or postprocessing capability can include other activities that are sometimes defined as preprocessing tasks, such as:

1. Sequencing to optimize solution times.
2. Generation of time- or frequency-dependent loads or enforced displacements, velocities, and accelerations.
3. The specifications of boundary conditions that are automatically handled internally with a minimal amount of analyst input.

A postprocessor module might also generate a summation of the stress distributions over two-dimensional fields and cross sections of three-dimensional fields. It could also provide:

1. Values of the stress components and stress invariants at the grid points.
2. Maxima and minima of the stress components and stress invariants.
3. Contour plots of the stress components and stress invariants.

These capabilities could be incorporated into the other postprocessing capabilities which are provided.

Some additional postprocessing capabilities can be very useful:

1. View the deformed or dynamic response of the model.
2. Find areas of peak stress or displacement through contour plots on the model surfaces.
3. Create animated sequences that simulate the transient response of the structural model.
4. Selectively scan large volumes of output.
5. Create plots of selected results.

The graphics software can generate simple to complex finite-element models. A preprocessing function builds primitive element-based models as well as models composed of advanced surfaces requiring higher-order Coon and Bezier patches. One can

1. Blend surfaces with user-defined control points.
2. Interactively mesh the surfaces.
3. Use automatic geometric equivalencing to construct a finite-element model from patches and surfaces.

One can display the model and save the data to resume model construction later. Larger models can be divided into a number of super-elements to ease the model manipulation.

The software can also provide the following capability for generating plots:

1. Undeformed geometric projections of the structural model.
2. Static or model deformations of the structural model by either displaying the deformed shape, which can be superimposed on the undeformed shape, or displaying the displacement vectors at the grid points, which can be superimposed on either the deformed or undeformed shape.
3. Modal deformations yielded by real or complex eigenvalue analysis, and plotting of the complex modes for flutter analysis for a user-selected phase lag.

4. Deformations of the structural model for transient response or frequency response by displaying either vectors or the deformed shape for specified times or frequencies.

5. X-Y graphs of transient response or frequency response and V-F and V-G graphs for flutter analysis.

6. Contour plots of displacements, temperature, and stress on the structure.

An output scanning capability can give maximum flexibility for textual output presentation. The data hierarchy can be user-specified. Compact format tables of selected solution results can scan different outputs such as displacements with accelerations and constant forces. A printed copy of the solution results may be formatted by the user. Another powerful post-processing capability is the ability to generate x-y plots of user-defined variables.

Internal Program Organization

The design concepts underlying the system are important to the overall effectiveness of the design process. Most systems consist of a set of modules which communicate with an executive system via external data blocks. The modules are organized into useful blocks by a problem-oriented language. The modules call upon the executive system for all of their I/O and the amount of working storage to use. They may also call upon matrix processing routines and utility routines to further the problem solution.

I/O may be supported with a collection of subroutines that perform the input/output except for such tasks as reading and writing data on the resident system files. The system routines are thus isolated from the actual physical hardware and such concerns as blocking factors and device characteristics.

These I/O subroutines can also enhance the normal unformatted binary I/O by providing end-of-file and end-of-record returns as well as partial record reads and writes. The physical records can be blocked to a constant size with the potential for multiple logical records per block or multiple blocks per record. The data blocks may be written sequentially but read both sequentially (forward and backward) and with a keyed form of direct access. If main memory is used as a scratch pad, then no module can leave values in main memory, and formatted data blocks can make up the bulk of intermodule communications. A set of instructions expresses the interrelationship among data blocks.

An important type of data block is a matrix. The matrices may be stored by column in a packed form, since they must be packed to conserve space. A 10,000-order, double-precision matrix can require 2×10^8 words to store in its full form. Most structural matrices of this size have a density of 1% or less, so even a packed form can require about 3×10^6 words, depending on the location of the nonzero terms. Even this number of terms means that the per-term access time for unpacking must be kept small.

The packing routines may provide access by column, by term, and by strings of nonzero terms. Strings of nonzero terms can be accessed directly in a buffer to save memory move cycles.

Other time-saving techniques involve using memory. One concept of memory management is sometimes called *open core*. Here, the main memory is treated by all the modules as a large single-dimensional scratch-pad array. The length is communicated dynamically to the module by the executive system. A module writer then allocates portions of this array to the various data types according to a set of rules. The buffers are also allocated to this array by the module program.

Finite-Element Evolution

The finite-element approach allows the analyst to represent a distributed physical problem by a discrete number of idealized elements that are interconnected at a finite number of grid points. A library of finite elements in an analysis program can include more than 50 types. This variety of finite elements enables the analyst to solve structural problems ranging from simple trusses to complicated thick-walled shells. Initial finite-element libraries used a total of ten finite structural elements, and many of these were of a much simpler nature than the advanced elements in present libraries.

The available types of analysis have also grown substantially beyond the original structural analysis with the addition of nonstructural elements.

Descriptions of these structural elements are given in Table 8-1. The evolution of these elements and their features are discussed below.

The Bar, Rod, and Tube elements are original elements. One improvement in the utility of the Bar element provides the user with the capability to apply arbitrary static loads along the length of the element, which can be concentrated, uniformly distributed, or linearly vary. Other variations of the Rod element allow a simplified input format that combines the connection and property data.

A Beam element can include the capabilities of a Bar element with the following additional features:

1. The neutral axis, the axis of shear centers, and the axis of nonstructural mass centroid may be different.

2. The cross-section area properties and nonstructural mass may vary along the length.

Table 8-1   Structural elements

Category and class	Element description
Elastic Line	
Rod ⎱ Tube ⎰	Uniaxial members with axial and torsion stiffnesses
Bar	Prismatic beam with axial, bending, shear, and torsion stiffnesses
Beam	Tapered, unsymmetrical beam with axial, bending, shear, and torsion stiffnesses
Bend	Uniform curved beam or pipe elbow with constant radius of curvature and axial, bending, shear, and torsion stiffnesses
Elastic Surface	
Tri Plate	Flat triangular plate with optional coupling between bending and membrane stiffnesses. Includes transverse shear stiffness.
Tri Shell	Curved triangular shell with optional coupling between bending and membrane stiffnesses. Includes transverse shear stiffness.
Shear	Quadrilateral shear panel that resists only tangential edge forces. Membrane stress correction optional.
Quad Plate	Flat quadrilateral plate with optional coupling between bending and membrane action. Includes transverse shear stiffness.
Quad Shell	Curved quadrilateral shell with optional coupling between bending and membrane action. Includes transverse shear stiffness.
Tri Lam	Triangular laminated plate which includes transverse shear stiffness.
Quad Lam	Quadrilateral laminated plate which includes transverse shear stiffness.
Elastic Axisymmetric	
Con Shell	Conical shell with bending and membrane stiffnesses.
Tri ⎱ Tra ⎰	Triangular and trapezoidal thick-walled shells which require axisymmetric loading.
Elastic Solid	
Tetra	Tetrahedron.
Penta	Pentahedron.
Hexa	Hexahedron.

Table 8-1 *(continued)*

Category and class	Element description
Elastic Scalar	
Elast	Spring connecting two selected degrees of freedom which may connect one degree of freedom to ground.
Gen	General element with properties defined by flexibility influence coefficients or stiffness matrices.
Rigid	
Rbar Rrod Rspline }	Multipoint constraint elements used to represent extremely stiff elements.
Geometric Nonlinear Line	
Rod Tube }	Uniaxial member with axial and torsion stiffnesses.
Beam	Tapered, unsymmetrical beam with axial, bending, shear, and torsion stiffnesses.
Geometric Nonlinear Surface	
Tri Plate	Triangular plate
Quad Shell	Quadrilateral shell
Geometric Nonlinear Solid	
Penta Hexa }	Polyhedra
Material Nonlinear Line	
Rod Tube }	Uniaxial members with axial and torsion stiffnesses.
Beam	Tapered, unsymmetrical beam with axial, bending, shear, and torsion stiffnesses.
Material Nonlinear Surface	
Tri Plate	Plastic flat triangular plate.
Quad Plate	Plastic flat quadrilateral plate.
Interface	
Gap	Interface which may maintain or break physical contact and permits sliding contact.

3. The effect of cross-section warping on torsional stiffness may be included.

4. The shear relief due to taper may be included.

5. The distribution of mass polar moment of inertia can be specified.

There are one-dimensional bending elements with a constant radius of curvature that can be used to analyze either curved beams or pipe elbows. The element's cross-section properties are assumed to be constant along its length. It can be used for distributed loading. An optional stiffening due to internal pressure can also be applied.

Two-dimensional structural elements can resist the action of tangential forces applied to their edges. This is in addition to the action of other forces that may be necessary to preserve equilibrium. The action of normal forces may be accounted for by defining an effective extension area. This element is representative of the thin shear webs used in aircraft construction.

The quadrilateral and triangular plate elements can be used as membrane elements, bending elements, or as combined membrane-bending elements. In the latter case, the user may account for coupling between the membrane and bending properties. These newer elements provide an improvement in accuracy and a reduction in the matrix-generation and data-recovery times. These elements can also be used as layered composite-material elements.

There are also quadrilateral and triangular shell elements that allow optional midside nodes to account for double curvature. They offer the same options for the analysis of membrane-bending interactions as the plate element.

A conical shell element can cover the range from cylinders to cones to discs with its straight-line generators and support membrane, bending, and transverse shear loads.

There are constant-strain triangular and trapezoidal axisymmetric ring elements that can be used to model solids of revolution. These elements include a linear strain triangular axisymmetric ring element. They are generally restricted to axisymmetrical loadings.

Constant-strain isotropic tetrahedron elements and modified isoparametric solid elements have replaced the earlier hexagonal and pentagonal elements, which caused inaccuracies. The isoparametric hexagonal elements allow substantial improvements in accuracy and efficiency. However, these elements were found to be deficient in that they could not be used in heat-transfer analysis and they did not provide for anisotropic material properties or yield satisfactory results when used to model curved shells. Other elements were developed to remedy these deficiencies and to supply an accurate formulation for nearly incompressible materials. The differential stiffness formulation, the element stress output, and the performance of these elements in curved-shell analysis have all been improved. Some of the isoparametric hexagonal elements have been retained because of a special utility in crack-propagation analysis of isotropic materials.

A general element can be used if the flexibility or stiffness data for a structure are known partly or entirely without reference to any element classification, so that the data can be input in the form in which they exist. For example, if the flexibility influence coefficient matrix for a structural component were obtained experimentally, it could be input with the general element. A stiffness matrix for a restrained component can be an input using this element.

Several rigid elements can be used which will introduce constraints for certain applications. One is a pin-ended rod which is rigid in extension. There is also a rigid bending element with six degrees of freedom at each end. Another is a rigid triangular plate with six degrees of freedom at each vertex. There are also rigid bodies connected to arbitrary numbers of grid points that can be used to interpolate motions. One can also define multipoint constraints using another element for interpolation of displacements at the grid points. Uses of the rigid elements include the distribution of loads to grid points or the interconnection of elements that may be otherwise incompatible.

There is also an element to model the contact between two surfaces. The two grid points of the gap are placed on opposite sides of the opening, and the direction of the contact surface is specified. The gap may have compression but not tension, and a tangential shear force may be used, but it cannot exceed the product of the coefficient of friction and the compression force.

Nonstructural Elements

Nonstructural elements are scalar elements that are connected between pairs of degrees of freedom using either scalar or geometric grid points, or between one degree of freedom and ground. Scalar springs are useful for representing elastic properties that cannot be easily modeled using structural elements. Scalar masses are useful for the selective representation of inertial properties, such as occurs when a concentrated mass is isolated for a motion in a single direction. The scalar damper is a linear viscous damper. Concentrated masses can also be represented to provide the sixth-order symmetric matrix of inertial properties at a geometric grid point.

Boundary elements for heat-transfer analysis can be used for heat flux, thermal vector flux, and convection radiation. Acoustical-cavity elements allow one to model an axisymmetric central fluid cavity as triangular or quadrilateral regions of the cross-sectional area. There are also elements to model radially slotted extensions of the central cavity as triangular or quadrilateral regions of the cross section. These slots exist in a typical solid-fuel rocket motor.

A fluid element can represent a hydrodynamic theory for use in fluid/

structure interaction analysis. Some elements can represent a compressible or incompressible fluid element in an axisymmetric container. Others can be used to represent a fluid as it is constrained by a free surface. Incompressible fluids can also be represented as constrained externally or internally by an arbitrarily shaped container.

Aerodynamic elements may represent one of several aerodynamic methods used to describe aeroelastic phenomena. One aerodynamic method is the doublet-lattice method for lifting surfaces oscillating in a subsonic flow. Another aerodynamic method considers lifting surfaces by the doublet-lattice method and includes wing/body interference by the slender-body theory and the method of images. A third method is the strip theory that includes corrections for sweep, finite span, and compressibility for subsonic and supersonic speeds. Others include the Mach box method for lifting surfaces oscillating in supersonic flow and the piston theory for surfaces oscillating at high supersonic or hypersonic speeds.

The implementation of each theory in flutter analysis requires different methods. Gust-response analysis is restricted to the first two aerodynamic methods.

Inelastic Analysis

A finite-element analysis can be used to model the deformation of complex structures strained well into the elastic range. The analysis involves inelastic action along with many degrees of freedom.

A typical structure is a protective cab for use on off-road vehicles. The analysis can simulate the structural response of the cab during vehicle rollover.

Models involving many degrees of freedom are not uncommon in elastic finite-element analysis. Some models for offshore drilling platforms, for example, can get very complex. An inelastic analysis of this structure is even more complicated. These large problems are difficult for various reasons, but they are especially difficult when taken into the inelastic range because of the iterative steps the computer must make to arrive at a solution. One must carefully select the size of each step so that the iteration drives the analysis closer to a reasonable solution.

When a material behaving in nonlinear fashion is analyzed by the finite-element method, we are concerned how large the steps should be up the stress-strain curve as the analysis progresses. Each step in the nonlinear range requires a number of iterations, or trial solutions, which attempt to drive the trials toward the correct value.

If the steps are small, the iterations tend to converge to the correct values quickly. Larger steps tend to increase the number of iterations needed before convergence. Using sufficiently large steps, the solution may not converge at

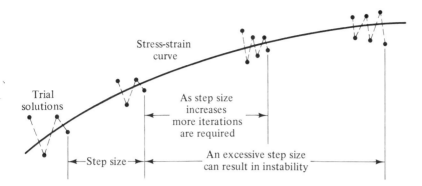

Figure 8-4   The importance of the step size along the stress-strain curve.

all, leading to instability. Smaller steps call for more solution points, which consume more computer time.

The analyst must make a tradeoff involving the size of steps up the stress-strain curve such that the steps are large enough to avoid extra use of the computer while not being so large that they lead to excessive iterations or instabilities. These considerations are sketched in Figure 8-4.

The steps, if not properly sized, can allow the analysis to wander repeatedly above and below the correct values, leading to an instability. If the analysis floats into this state, time and money are wasted searching for a solution.

Another area of difficulty, until a way of handling the problem was found, was the necessity to analytically turn the corner on the stress-strain curve. This step is required to calculate the deformation as loads are removed when the structure relaxes to an unloaded but plastically deformed state.

As a material is loaded into the plastic range, and the load is then released, the stress-strain curve begins to describe a hysteresis loop (Figure 8-5). The point where the curve begins to retreat downward is called the *corner*. If a structure loaded into the plastic range is being analyzed by the finite-element method, the determination of stress immediately after load relaxation is termed *turning the corner*.

Because of the numerical instabilities that can arise the corner has proved to be difficult to analyze. These instabilities can be avoided by ignoring the region near the corner and proceeding some length down the curve before a new condition is calculated.

The structure to be analyzed may be tested in prototype form before the analysis. The analysis may be used to establish an analytical procedure that could then be followed for subsequent new designs. The existence of a tested prototype provides data against which the analytical results can be checked.

The basic objective of the analysis may be to find an alternative to physical testing to meet some performance criteria.

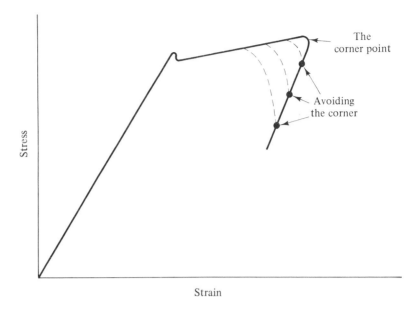

The
corner point

Avoiding
the corner

Stress

Strain

Figure 8-5 Hysteresis in the plastic range.

The test may require that an entire unit be destructively tested—which can be expensive. Another shortcoming of the test is that, although it provides pass-or-fail data, it often gives little indication of how good the design is.

Major inducements for finding an alternative method are cost and time. The prototyping of a structure can take months, and if that prototype fails, the entire design cycle may have to be restarted. Analytical tests in many cases can be conducted for about half to three-quarters of the direct cost of prototyping.

Another major cost in a test program is that of the test facility itself. Testing a number of large structures can involve a large amount of floor space. A significant expense is the thick concrete base for the test platform, which must withstand the loads. There is also the cost of test equipment and personnel to run the tests.

A better choice is to model analytically, since computer time is less costly, the turnaround is quicker, and funds are not tied up in the manufacturing of a prototype that might fail the test.

One cost saving that can be made in the analysis is that of substructing. It is possible to run the analysis series on sections of the model. The difficulty lies in determining which sections will deform inelastically. Unless this is known, misleading results can be generated. When the model is run as a whole, this problem is avoided. The complete approach, though, can create computational difficulties because of the increased problem size.

When a material behaves in a linear elastic fashion, the basic finite-element equation has a simple form, because all the displacement x terms can be put in a single matrix on one side of the equation. When the material is strained beyond the yield point, the behavior becomes plastic or nonlinear. The stiffness K becomes a function of displacement, so x terms appear on both sides of the equation, preventing a closed-form solution and requiring iterative techniques. Thus, for the elastic case,

$$[X] = [K]^{-1}[F]$$

This linear equation has a closed form and can be solved by methods such as the Gauss-Jordan elimination. For the inelastic case

$$[X] = [K_0 + K_1(x)]^{-1}[F]$$

This nonlinear equation must be solved iteratively, because the displacement terms appear on both sides.

The size of the problem can also make it difficult to verify input data. One way to avoid this is to give the analysis a short time limit. If the run is successful, the correctness of the input data will have been confirmed. If the run is not, the input errors can be flagged.

Deflections may also not show clearly in a large, complex structure. A plot of all the elements can be confusing, the deflections often being only fractions of an inch. One way to make the displacements easier to study is to plot only the exterior lines of the structure. These lines are then shown with a scaling factor that exaggerates true deflection, so that the small displacements can be seen.

Some models may also contain so many elements that the stress-intensity plots may be confusing. One way of improving this involves translucent plots.

The conventional methods of plotting stress intensity by means of color are not always easy to interpret with complex models. Newer methods, employing color-coded, nested, shrunken elements, overcome some of these drawbacks. A method of this kind not only allows stress intensity to be shown by simple color-plotting routines, it also gives a translucent character to the model, so that normally hidden surfaces can be seen. In this way, both the interior and exterior stresses can be viewed with a single plot. The colors can also provide different shades for denoting the intensity.

The technique involves representing the shrunken elements by a series of rectangles nested within one another, with the color combinations being selected to represent various stress intensities. The net effect gives the overall model a translucent appearance, with rear surfaces being visible behind the solid frontal surfaces. This allows interior and exterior stress levels to be seen on one plot.

Numerical Considerations

Two different types of nonlinearity can occur in a structural problem, and either can lead to numerical instability. One type is a *geometric nonlinearity*, which occurs when deflections are so large that the geometry of the problem changes during its solution. The solution algorithm must also change to reach this target.

The other type, *material nonlinearity*, occurs when the slope of the stress-strain curve changes constantly after going into the plastic range. If the deflections are relatively small, they do not produce any significant geometric nonlinearity. The nonlinearity of concern then may involve that of the stress-strain curve as the material is taken into the plastic range.

This nonlinearity introduces a problem in the solution of the strain equation. The nonlinearity makes it impossible to separate the stress from the strain, since the two terms cannot be put on separate sides of the equation to allow a direct solution.

The essence of a stress analysis is the solution of an equation involving stress, strain, and the stress-strain response of the material, which, in the elastic range, is the modulus of elasticity. Normally, stress and strain can be separated and placed on separate sides of the equation. In a finite-element solution, the stress or the point load and the material response are known, and strain is the unknown for which the equation must be solved.

In the inelastic range, the material response becomes a function of the strain, and the strain appears on both sides of the equation, making a closed-form solution impossible. This is what creates the need for an iterative solution in the elastic range. To complete the analysis, solutions must be found for a succession of load steps along the stress-strain curve as the structure undergoes loading and relaxation. Each load step requires iterations, so that a solution can be found for that point.

At some given load step, the finite-element program makes successive solutions that come increasingly closer to balancing the stress equation. These solutions may first undershoot and then overshoot as they attempt to converge on a sufficient solution.

The steeper the curve, the fewer iterations are required for convergence. Larger steps tend to carry the analysis to flatter regions of the curve and to require more iterations for convergence. If the curve becomes too flat, the solution may not converge at all. This causes an endless series of iterations in an attempt to drive the solution toward convergence. This is referred to as an *instability*. To complete the analysis, therefore, we must choose the load steps properly. If the steps are too close together, the iterations are performed more often than necessary, causing excessive computer time and solution delays. If the steps are too far apart, the computer must iterate at each load, and this may cause it to step excessively, which can result in an instability.

In terms of the matrix mathematics, the basic finite-element equation is $\{F\} = [K]\{X\}$. The object of the solution is to solve for $\{X\}$. In the inelastic range, however, we have seen that the K matrix also contains x, so an iterative solution is required. Since the value of K changes with each step up the curve, this matrix must be recalculated with each step. We have noted that a flat stress-strain curve can cause numerical instability in the solution process. A way to bypass this difficulty is to arbitrarily assign some small positive stress-strain slope which does not significantly reduce the accuracy of the analysis.

ARCHITECTURAL DESIGN

Most of the design in architectural, engineering, and construction (AEC) projects is closely related, and information from one task is often used as a foundation for another. The functions in various areas are closely tied together. These include:

1. Planning.
2. Layout.
3. Drafting.
4. Material control.
5. Project management.

What happens in one area usually affects others. Piping and heating diagrams, for example, are based on the building layout (Figure 8-6). Changes in one design discipline are likely to affect others. The interrelationships are especially important in complex projects such as power plants, ships, and petrochemical and processing plants.

The typical starting point in a plant design is the generation of 2D *process and instrumentation diagrams* (*P&IDs*). These diagrams functionally show the major pieces of equipment, instrumentation, and the connecting pipes. The P&ID software contains a library of standard symbols, as shown in Figure 8-7.

The equipment arrangement software contains a library of generic components (Figure 8-8), from which the user selects items to create a 3D equipment model. The operator digitizes a reference point, indicating equipment position. Once placed in the plant model, the equipment symbol can be rotated or translated to another orientation.

Primitive shapes such as spheres and cylinders are also provided to create user-defined equipment not contained in the standard library.

Using this set of basic shapes, called primitives, the operator may create custom symbols for specialized equipment.

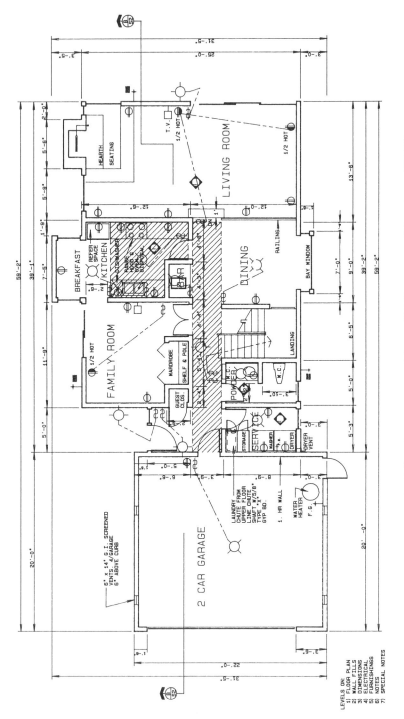

Figure 8-6 A building layout created by a CAD system. (Courtesy: T&W Systems, Versa CAD Division)

476

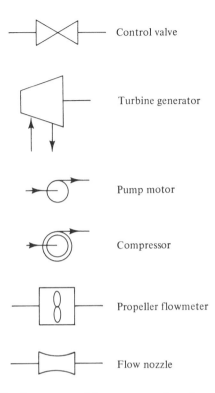

Figure 8-7 Process and instrumentation library symbols.

Another 2D package used early in design is the *electrical schematics program.* The library of symbols in this package represents the electrical components such as switches and motors which the user connects using the plant wiring. The software can be used to configure simple power and switching circuits as well as complex ladder diagrams and logic circuits.

With these 2D functional diagrams used as the basic elements, a detailed component model of the plant can be constructed with a set of 3D design programs. An equipment arrangement package physically positions the various pieces of machinery and other items in the plant, and a piping layout and design program routes the pipes connecting the equipment.

A pipe support package selects and positions the associated hangers, racks, and other support fixtures. A steel layout and design program places the beams and other members for the structure, and a steel detailing program specifies the seats, end plates, splices, and other connectors.

The 3D design programs contain libraries of components for standard equipment, piping, and structural steel components. Primitives are also provided for creating custom items. Using these programs, the user creates the 3D model interactively.

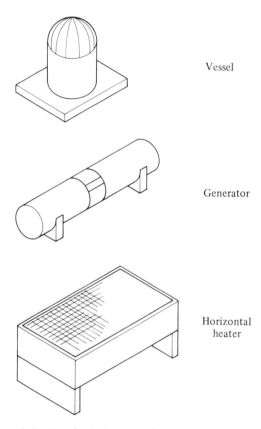

Figure 8-8   Typical plant equipment library components.

The modeling process is done with interactive graphics, usually with a digitizing tablet and two displays. The operator views the model as it is being constructed on one display, while the input and output are shown on the other.

Since the data is compatible for all aspects of the model, the operators who are designing equipment layout, piping systems, and steel structures can readily pass data back and forth to check for design compatibility and interferences. An automatic discrepancy-check feature compares the 3D piping against the P&IDs to ensure that the placement of all valves and other components is in agreement.

An equipment-layout designer could build a model of a storage vessel and pass the data to a pipe designer, who would use the data to route the piping. At the same time, a structural steel designer at another workstation could design the vessel support structure.

Shaded-image models can show steel in yellow, piping in blue, and equipment in red, allowing operators to readily visualize and evaluate the

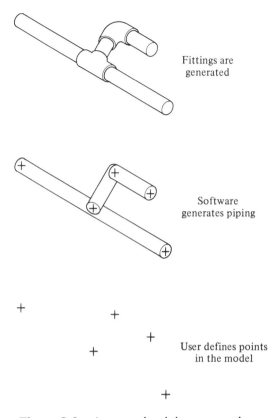

Fittings are
generated

Software
generates piping

User defines points
in the model

Figure 8-9   Automatic piping generation.

position of components in the early stages of design. These models also may
be used later for training purposes.

The 3D model is more than a picture of the proposed plant, since each
graphic symbol has associated data stored in the computer as part of the
model database. The data for each building component might include
information such as size, weight, manufacturer, drawing number, price,
specification, and part number. All of this data can later be used to produce
detailed parts lists, drawings, and specifications.

One of the more productive features of an AEC system is automatic part
placement. In developing the piping program, this feature is used to
automatically place tees, elbows, and other fittings into the pipe sections
specified by the operator, as shown in Figure 8-9. Upon command from the
operator, the program:

1. Detects pipe-connection orientation.
2. Selects the proper fittings from the parts library.

3. Cuts the pipes to the correct length.

4. Inserts fittings into the system.

A similar parts-placement feature in the steel detailing program places the angle seats, plates, bearing pads, and column splices on the steel beams.

During the design, the model is used to check for interferences and stress. Design deficiencies are corrected and the new model analyzed in an iterative procedure until a satisfactory design is reached.

Interferences such as a pipe routed through a structural member may be indicated visually by a highlight color or blinking. A printout showing interferences in tabular form may also be provided.

Finite-element stress analysis can also be performed on piping through using interface codes. Structural stresses are analyzed through interfaces to ANSYS or NASTRAN.

Since the 3D model contains much of the data required for stress analysis, the finite-element models are created quickly. Typically, these finite-element codes require so much processing that it is done on a dedicated computer. The stress-analysis output data is available in both graphic and tabular form.

When the analysis is done and the design is satisfactory, the support-function software is used to produce engineering drawings. Sectioning and hidden-line removal allow one to cut the 3D model and create the required views.

Support documentation can then be created from the model, including bills of material in which the software generates groups of like parts.

There are also 3D application programs for general mapping, civil site preparation, and subterranean modeling. The general mapping program uses survey data to create a gridded digital terrain model of the surface topology. The civil site preparation program is used to modify the terrain model, and it interactively shows how the earth will be cut, filled, and exacavated for the plant foundation, roadways, and landscaping.

The gridded terrain model can show the placement of the plant on the contour of the ground surface, which is interactively cut and filled with the civil site preparation routine.

The subterranean modeling program is used to model the subsurface geological structure. This is useful for the identification and analysis of underground energy resources.

The Distributed-Workstation Concept

Many of the original AEC programs used a central mainframe computer that housed much of the software. Other programs may have resided in separate minicomputers, desktop microcomputers, and even hand-held calculators, so not everyone working on the same job had access to the central database.

The designers often experienced slow response as the computer performed some of the more intensive modeling and analysis. The more costly CAD systems required under this type of system frequently could be afforded only by the larger AEC firms.

Distributed systems now offer an alternative to this centralized approach. These systems are comprised of interconnected workstations with their own 32-bit processors, which have been made available by VLSI technology.

These workstations have enough computing power and memory so that tasks such as model building and drafting can be performed locally. These tasks can be highly interactive when performed on the workstations, providing the operator with quick response to system commands.

The handling of slower tasks such as plotting, analysis, and database management is transferred to a processor in the network which is dedicated to these functions.

The communication capabilities of the workstations allow large data files to be transferred at rates which can exceed 10 million bits per second.

The rapid transmission of data gives different operators broad access to the same information in the network, which can include workstations connected with modems.

A network of this type allows a common database to be used in the system, with one model combining the three-dimensional designs created by the different project disciplines such as piping, equipment, and structures. Also in the model are data such as the layout geometry and specifications.

Lower cost is another benefit of distributed processing. Lower-cost, non-CAD stations allow access to the design database and word-processing capabilities.

The flexibility of being able to build a network in modular fashion lets one configure and change the system as desired, adding stations incrementally to upgrade the capacity in gradual steps. In some cases, hundreds of workstations may be added without system degradation as needs increase.

A variety of network configurations are possible to fit facilities and engineering requirements (Figure 8-10). Computer networks are an extension of the distributed-processing concept. The difference between a distributed-processing system and a computer network is a matter of degree. Computer networks consist of two or more computer systems which are separate. The distance between them may be a few feet within a plant or many miles connected by common-carrier lines. Computer networks are organized in a number of ways. The computers are loosely coupled and are capable of stand-alone operation.

Network configurations can be classed as master-slave, hierarchical, or peer-connected. The configuration determines how control responsibilities are assigned among the processing units.

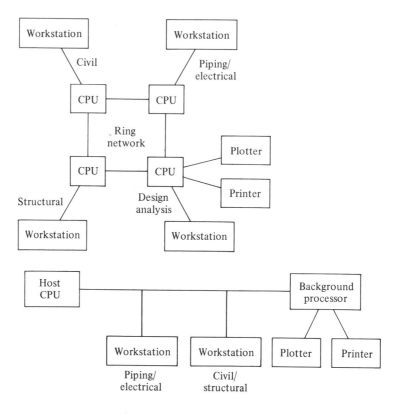

Figure 8-10   AEC networks.

The master-slave configuration is used primarily to provide load sharing. Hierarchical networks use a multilevel master-slave configuration. Various levels in the hierarchy have assigned responsibilities for certain functions. The highest level makes all major decisions, and the lower levels have the responsibilities for specific operations.

In a typical distributed system the host processor is connected by one line to a satellite or workstation processor. The line between the processors is referred to as a *link*. A link may be any communications channel, such as a coaxial cable or telephone line. A device in a network is referred to as a *node*.

In a master-slave network a single program has control and determines which slave computer shall operate on a task. Communication between slave computers is under control of the master. After it is assigned a task, the slave proceeds asynchronously with respect to the master until it completes the task, or until it requires services from the master.

Distributed systems are able to operate in a standard office environment, unlike some large centralized systems, which require an environmentally controlled computer room. Because of these advantages, an increasing number of AEC systems will be arranged in distributed networks. Most of these systems will use interconnected workstations to form the network. Typically, each workstation in the network will contain software for specific tasks in the AEC design. This software is provided in the form of separate application packages. These programs are provided ready-to-use on the workstation, but the source code may also be provided for users who want to customize the software.

One of the more important aspects of the software is that not only must the application programs be compatible, but the resulting database model must also be totally integrated, so that a variety of design disciplines are able to extract information from the same model.

Aiding the user are those routines that tend to automate much of the modeling. For example, the repetitive placement of beams can be done by specifying the part type and required spacing. Steel beams connected to columns are automatically cut and offset so that they fit. Components are specified so that all beams used by the operator are of the same type. Standard components in the parts library are configured automatically to conform to American, Canadian, British, and Australian standards.

The Importance of Standards

In addition to the standards that are necessary for putting together a set of plans that will be easily understood by the wide range of people expected to use them, AEC CAD requires hardware and software compatibility for the transfer of information from one system to another. The Initial Graphics Exchange Specification Committee (IGES) within the National Bureau of Standards has been establishing neutral file requirements that can be used to transfer information between systems.

Information from a particular vendor's graphic database may be translated into a neutral file of the vendor's design, and then transferred into the IGES format where it is available for transfer into another vendor's software format. This can be a cumbersome way to share information between differing hardware, especially since the translation process can reduce the quantity and quality of the information. The vendors, however, consider this procedure essential to protect their software interests.

To write software capable of transferring information directly from one hardware system to another, one would need a thorough understanding of the content and mechanics of the software for each manufacturer. These buffers are used by the vendors to protect themselves.

Each vendor's structuring approach also varies considerably, so we face additional problems in establishing standards to maintain compatibility with the CAD systems.

It is entirely possible that AEC firms will no longer find hard copies of drawings adequate for their files when users can supply an entire electronic file on tape. Electronic files can be manipulated more easily, combined with notes and files throughout construction, and updated into as-built conditions. They can carry over the intelligent aspects of the drawings, such as detailed design considerations, bills of materials, and facility management considerations.

The problems of a neutral file translator are compounded by the differences in the information that can be transferred. Nearly all systems can draw lines, circles, ellipses, and arcs, but some may not be able to draw a spiral or a helix.

Some smaller systems may not have enough storage to hold a 35 × 42 inch complex architectural floor plan as a complete drawing. Other systems may be capable of storing many of these drawings and keeping complex, detailed databases.

In down-loading information from one system, a less sophisticated system may not be able to accept certain types or quantities of information. In the other direction, there may be difficulties also. A sophisticated system may lack one or more of the capabilities of a smaller system.

The data considerations for intersystem transfer include:

1. Lines.
2. Line weights.
3. Circles.
4. Shapes.
5. Parabolas.
6. Helixes.
7. Text.
8. Data levels.
9. Cells.
10. Whole drawings.
11. Colors.
12. Nongraphic databases.
13. Graphic to nongraphic linkages.

Different classes of information can be stored on specific levels as a method of organizing the drawing and the associated databases. Architectural data might be stored on levels 0–9, electrical power data on levels 10–19, and lighting on levels 20–29.

When the architectural background and the electrical power-distribution information are combined to form a complete drawing and transferred through a neutral file to another system, the level locations are lost. The nongraphic data used to define the drawing may also be lost. All of this information can be transferred between identical systems.

If a firm develops its drawings in a particular way, and a file is transferred for review on an identical system, where the reviewer's in-house standard for developing drawings is different, one of two things can occur. All of the drawings and nongraphics data will have to be converted to the reviewer's standards, or all of the internal backup within the reviewer's system will have to be manipulated to fit the new file.

Details, symbols, standard notes, and nongraphic databases may have to be relocated before the reviewer can use the file.

Project Coordination

For overseeing the entire plant-design process a design management and control system program can:

1. Track all drawings and approvals.
2. Flag work to be done on drawings.
3. Monitor the status of various projects.
4. Notify operators of design changes.

This type of system is of great benefit, since many critical requirements must be anticipated well over a month in advance.

A pressing and recurrent problem in architectural production is the coordination of information among all members involved. This is even more critical with large, complex projects, owing to their fast-track nature and the large number of drawings required.

The information in a typical CAD drawing, including those being produced for buildings, is built up in various discipline-specific layers and usually contains information shared among several drawings. Columns or exterior wall assemblies may appear identically on different levels.

The layers describing that information can be shared among several drawings, so that changes made on one drawing will automatically be updated on another.

The layered information is also shared among the various disciplines. Heating, plumbing, and electrical drawings may use a base plane, which is overlaid with the discipline-specific information such as duct layout and lighting plan. One can load an up-to-date structural framing plan and check for conflicts with duct layouts.

This is a key advantage in a multidiscipline CAD system. One can automatically provide up-to-date architectural information to the engineering disciplines for their design work and allow immediate coordination between all disciplines at any time.

One consideration that is especially crucial to the efficient production of working drawings in a multidiscipline environment is deciding which portions of the building description belong to the layers. This should be done before the drawings are actually begun.

Some software imposes no layering conventions on the user, so they may be tailored for each individual project. Making changes efficiently depends on the way in which the information in each layer is created. In a highly modular building plan, extensive use can be made of the system's symbol capability. Not only can individual items such as desks and doors be kept in symbols libraries, but also repetitive sections of the building itself. If the symbols are updated, then the correct version is displayed each time a symbol is referenced. This makes the process of changing items drawn as symbols move quickly, speeds loading of drawing information, and saves storage space.

Successful coordination can result in a ceiling plan that is drawn only once, by the architect, instead of being drawn a second time by the electrical engineer. The symbol used on an electrical plan is different from that shown on an architectural sheet, so the architect draws the location of each fixture symbol on the base drawing and uses the proper architectural symbol; the electrical engineer then uses the same base drawing but uses a different symbol library to create the electrical drawing. Both drawings accurately show the location of the light fixtures, but only one person had to produce the drawing. When a change is made to any of the shared layers, a memo can be sent via the electronic mail facility of the computer system to all affected users of the drawings to avoid conflicts.

Using a language-based command structure, which emulates simple English, the commands are entered as text. Changes can be made from nongraphics terminals or even from batch-mode files. This frees the CAD terminals and their users for the graphics-intensive, interactive work.

To facilitate communications between users, biweekly technical sessions are recommended for all CAD users on the project, the technical coordinators, and the computer staff, to discuss the overall project coordination and suggest improvements in the drawing production.

A 2D DRAFTING SYSTEM

In this section we will consider a packaged 2D drafting system* which allows the user to create a drawing (such as Figure 8-6 or 8-11) using basic building blocks called *objects*. These basic, primitive objects may consist of

---

*This section contains copyrighted material supplied by T & W Systems, Versa CAD Division, used with permission.

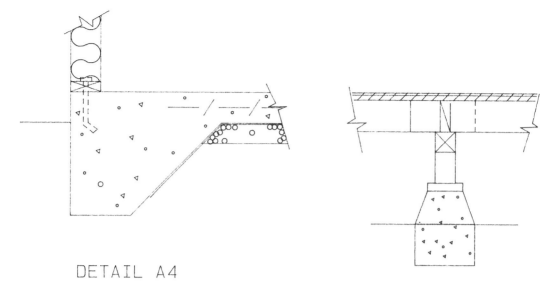

DETAIL A4

Figure 8-11   A detail drawing created by a CAD system. (Courtesy: T&W Systems, Versa CAD Division)

lines, rectangles, polygons, circles, ellipses, user-definable symbols, circular arcs, Bezier curves, and text.

The program allows the user to manipulate a number of different levels. A *level* can be thought of as one sheet of a clear overlay. All objects with the same level number are on the same sheet. Using one level is like viewing only one sheet, and adding a second level is like placing a second sheet on top of the first—you now see the objects on both sheets or levels.

Levels are useful if related objects are grouped together in a common level. If you are doing a floor plan, you might want to put the basic floor plan on level 1, all chairs on level 2, and all fixtures on level 3. One can then work with any combination of the items at the same time.

The program can also allow the user to manipulate objects in groups. A *group* is a user-defined collection of objects. The only relationship that objects in a group have to one another is that they share the same group name. Groups provide a convenient way of manipulating large components of a complex drawing. They allow one to move, copy, and otherwise manipulate large numbers of objects at one time.

Levels and groups are completely independent of one another. Removing a particular level could affect objects in several different groups, and moving a group could move objects in several different levels.

A 2D program will receive most of its input from the *digitizer table*, sometimes called the *graphics tablet*. The *stylus* is the pencillike lightpen shown in Figure 8-12 that the designer moves across the digitizer table. The

Figure 8-12   A packaged 2D drafting system, in which the stylus takes the form of a lightpen which is used with a digitizer table. (Courtesy: T & W Systems, Versa CAD Division)

stylus position on the digitizer is represented on the screen by small cross-hairs. As the designer moves the stylus across the digitizer, the cross-hairs will also move across the screen. The *cursor* refers to the cross-hairs on the screen. The designer may also use a thumb wheel and the arrows located on the keyboard to simulate the stylus.

The stylus is used to create the various graphic objects, such as lines, circles, and rectangles. It is also used to graphically manipulate the entire picture or parts of it. These actions may be performed by:

1. Selecting the appropriate 2D function.
2. Positioning the stylus.
3. Pressing down on the stylus.

The program will acknowledge this action. The pressing down of the stylus means that the user accepts the position being pointed to.

A 2D program can be organized around a collection of *menus*, with each menu being a list of the possible options available. Each menu will have a specific purpose. A FILE menu will allow one to enter commands that will manipulate the graphic files, and an OUTPUT menu will allow the copy of a graphics drawing to be provided by an output device, such as a plotter or a graphics printer.

All menus are displayed in one area of the screen. They may begin with a capitalized title, possibly ending in a number:

ADD1

MODIFY

FILE

Following the title, there is a list of the available choices. To select a choice listed on the menu, one types the letter that is capitalized. There is no need to type the ENTER key after typing the letter.

Most of the menus in the program have many options from which to choose. Sometimes, not all of the choices can be shown on the screen at once. Menus that have a number at the end of their titles have more choices available.

The program may provide the designer with a continuous readout of the cursor's location. This readout may be located in the upper right-hand portion of the screen. The x,y coordinates that are displayed are real-world coordinates. The display could be either in decimal format to four decimal places or in feet and inches to $\frac{1}{64}$ inch.

The program could use several different coordinate systems. One example is the real-world coordinate system of the drawing. This is the coordinate system that is shown on the screen.

Normally, the origin (0, 0) of this coordinate system is located in the lower left-hand corner of the screen. The x and y coordinates grow as one moves up and to the right. It is possible to shift the origin of the drawing coordinate system. When the origin is shifted, the digitizer and numeric coordinates are then in terms of the shifted coordinate system.

It can sometimes be difficult to precisely position an object using the cursor. This is due to the visual problem of placing the cursor exactly on the desired x,y location. Even if you do move the cursor so that it appears to be at the desired location, the limitations of the screen resolution are such that you may not exactly be there. To get the exact location, one could type it in from the keyboard; another way to solve this problem is to use the *snap* feature. The snap feature pulls or snaps the cursor to the precise x,y location that is really wanted.

There are two different types of snap:

The *increment snap* pulls the cursor to the nearest user-definable increment. When the increment snap is used, the coordinates dial always displays the snapped cursor value. The values displayed are multiples of the smallest increment.

The *grid snap* pulls the cursor to the nearest grid intersection point. When a grid snap is used, the coordinate dial displays the snapped cursor value. The values displayed are grid intersection points.

Image manipulation is done using rubberbanding. The objects change size and orientation on the screen as one moves the stylus across the digitizer. This provides visual feedback. This is called *object tracking*, since the graphics objects track or follow each movement. This tracking does have a price: the constant redrawing of an object can slow down the response of the program. So the program allows you to turn off the tracking mode in the ADD and MODIFY menus. These are the two places where one really notices the slowdown.

The normal cursor that appears on the screen looks like a small cross. The program may provide an alternate, long cursor. The long cursor has large cross-hairs extending across the entire screen. It is equivalent in function to the shorter cursor, but it provides a means for more exact visual alignment of graphics objects.

Data Entry

To use the digitizer to place an object, one moves the cursor to the desired location on the screen by moving the stylus across the digitizer tablet. To fix the location, one presses the stylus to signal the computer.

Many objects have more than one characteristic point; for example, to enter a line, one must indicate the location of both ends of the line. If object tracking is used, once the first characteristic point of an object has been placed, the program repeatedly draws rubberband images of the object from the first point to the current cursor position.

The program may provide messages to guide in placing the points. The object is fixed when the final characteristic point associated with that object is placed. Options on a menu may cause the program to draw the object as the cursor is moved.

Options may also allow one to add more than one copy of a particular object without having to select that option each time. For example, when you select a line option, the program may allow you to add lines until you tell it that you want to stop.

The program allows the user to view the drawing through a user-defined *viewing window*. One can imagine that the screen is a movable window through which to view the drawing. The program allows one to move this viewing window and thus look at different portions of the drawing. We can shrink the window to view only a small detail of the drawing, or we can expand the window and look at a larger, overall view of the drawing.

As the primitive objects are created, they are given attributes or properties that determine, in part, what they will look like. An example of a *property* is the linestyle that is used to plot the object. The user can change these property values to allow control over the appearance of the final drawing.

Each drawing is created using the appropriate real-world units. Whether the drawing consists of a small machine part or a large facilities layout, the designer can create and position each object in its actual dimensions on the drawing. Grids and windows are defined using the *x,y* coordinates that are appropriate for the drawing.

Input Modes

The designer has two modes of input: the free mode and the coordinate entry mode. Each of these modes has three methods of specifying *x,y* coordinates while creating or manipulating a drawing. Switching from one method to another requires only one keystroke.

The *free mode* uses one of three devices for specifying the *x,y* coordinate input:

1. Digitizer.
2. Plotter.
3. Knob wheel.

The knob wheel is located in the upper left corner of the keyboard. These three devices are used to position the cursor on the screen. Moving the stylus on the digitizer tablet, moving the pen holder on the plotter, or turning the knob wheel on the keyboard will move the cursor on the screen.

The designer's physical movements are thus translated into cursor movements on the screen (Figure 8-13). As the particular input device is moved, objects can be made to follow the cursor on the screen. This makes the free mode a visual form of input, because one can always see, and immediately change, the relationships between the various pieces of drawing. The free mode uses the snap feature to ensure the precise placement of the cursor.

The *coordinate entry mode* uses three types of coordinate entry:

1. Absolute.
2. Relative.
3. Polar.

These three modes allow one to type in the actual coordinates using the keyboard. The coordinate entry mode does not use the snap feature.

Figure 8-13   In a 2D drafting system the designer's physical movements may be translated by a number of methods into cursor movements on the screen. (Courtesy: T & W Systems, Versa CAD Division)

Absolute coordinate entry is the easiest of the three to use. In this mode, one types in the absolute real-world x and y coordinates. *Relative* coordinate entry is a little more complex. In this mode, one types in the relative x and y coordinates. The x and y coordinates may be relative to different things, depending upon which option is being used. If you are working in the GROUP menu, the coordinates are relative to the last x,y coordinates that were defined. Relative coordinates work differently in the MODIFY menu. As you select an option from the MODIFY menu, the coordinate entries become relative to the object's initial point. The initial point is the first point that was defined when the object was created. A line's initial point is its first endpoint, and a circle's initial point is its center. *Polar* coordinate entry allows one to use a polar coordinate system to specify x,y points. One enters the angle and the line length. Both the angle and length are relative to the predefined point used in relative coordinate entries.

Drawing Options

The line option allows one to create one or more lines. A line is defined by two characteristic points:

1. The first endpoint of the line.

2. The second endpoint of the line.

The program will not draw a line until the first endpoint has been defined. The first endpoint is defined by moving the cursor to the desired location on the screen and then pressing down on the stylus. If object tracking is used, the program will repeatedly draw a rubberband line from the first endpoint to the present cursor location. Moving the cursor changes the line's length and rotation. When satisfied with the line's configuration, we accept it by pressing down on the stylus. One next positions the cursor on a point on the minor axis of the previously created line to the present cursor location. This process will continue until we command a stop.

The keyboard options available while creating a line include:

1. Cause an arrowhead to appear on one end of the line.

2. Remove the arrowhead.

3. Cause a line to become a template line.

4. Remove the template.

5. Cause a marker to be displayed at the center of the line.

6. Remove the marker.

7. Cause the line to maintain a rotation of 0 degrees, which makes the line grow only along the x (horizontal) axis.

8. Cause the line to maintain a rotation of 90 degrees, which makes the line grow only along the y (vertical) axis.

9. Cause the line to follow the movements of the cursor.

10. Detach the current line from the last endpoint entered and enter the new starting point of the line.

11. Cause the last line drawn to be erased and re-enter that line.

A circle option allows one to create a circle. A circle can be defined in two different ways:

1. Center and radius.

2. Diameter.

To draw a circle by the first method, one moves the cursor to the desired location on the screen for the center of the circle, then presses down on the stylus. If object tracking is used, the program will repeatedly draw a circle whose radius grows larger as you move the cursor away from the center, and smaller as you move toward it. One accepts the desired circle by pressing down on the stylus.

The two characteristic points for creating a circle by the second method are the endpoints or the diameter. To draw a circle by the second method, one presses the diameter key and then locates the cursor on the edge of the circle and accepts it by pressing down on the stylus. If object tracking is used, as the cursor is moved away from the first point, the program will repeatedly draw a circle whose diameter is the distance from the cursor to the first point. When the desired size of the circle is reached, it is accepted by pressing down on the stylus.

The keyboard options available while creating a circle include:

1. Cause an arrowhead to appear on the circle.
2. Remove the arrowhead.
3. Cause the circle to become a template circle.
4. Remove the template.
5. Cause a marker to be displayed at the center of the circle.
6. Remove the marker.

The ellipse option allows one to create an ellipse. An ellipse may be defined in two different ways:

1. Three endpoints on the major and minor axes.
2. The center and two endpoints.

The three characteristic points for creating an ellipse by the first method are:

1. One endpoint of the minor axis.
2. The other endpoint of the minor axis.
3. The endpoint of the major axis.

To create an ellipse with this method, one moves the cursor to one endpoint of the minor axis and presses down on the stylus. Then one moves the cursor to the other endpoint of the minor axis and presses down on the stylus. If object tracking is used, the program will repeatedly draw an ellipse whose major axis is located at the position of the cursor. The stylus is pressed again when the desired shape and rotation of the ellipse are achieved.

The three characteristic points for creating an ellipse by the second method are:

1. The center of the ellipse.
2. One endpoint of the minor axis.
3. One endpoint of the major axis.

To create an ellipse using this method, first one types in C (for center) on the keyboard, then one places the cursor at the center of the ellipse and presses down on the stylus. One next positions the cursor on a point on the minor axis and presses down on the stylus. If object tracking is done, the program will repeatedly draw the ellipse. The cursor is used to locate the endpoint of the major axis, and the stylus is pressed when the desired shape and rotation of the ellipse have been obtained. The program will not draw an ellipse until the first two points have been defined.

The arc option allows one to create a circular arc. An arc may be defined in two different ways:

1. Three points on the arc.
2. Center and two endpoints of the arc.

In the first method the three characteristic points are:

1. One endpoint of the arc.
2. The second endpoint of the arc.
3. A third arbitrary point on the arc.

To use this method, one positions the cursor and sets the two endpoints of the arc. If object tracking is used, the program will repeatedly draw an arc through the cursor. The cursor is moved until one is satisfied with the shape of the arc and presses down on the stylus to accept it. If the radius of the arc is known, then the radius option can help position the third point.

Using the radius option, you enter the desired radius of the arc, and, as you move the cursor near the arc, the program will display the four possible arcs that may be drawn with those endpoints and radius. When satisfied with the arc displayed, one presses down on the stylus to accept it. If the arc radius entered is too small, the program will display an error message and give the smallest possible radius.

In the second method the three characteristic points are:

1. The center of the arc.
2. One endpoint of the arc.
3. The other endpoint of the arc.

To use this method, one selects the center option using the keyboard before defining the first characteristic point. Then the cursor is positioned and the stylus is pressed to enter the center of the arc. Next, one positions the cursor and enters the first endpoint of the arc. If object tracking is used, the program will repeatedly draw an arc. By moving the cursor to locate the other endpoint of the arc and pressing down on the stylus to accept it, the arc is completed.

The program will not draw an arc until the first two characteristic points have been accepted.

A symbol option allows one to add one or more complex symbols to the drawing. A symbol is defined as a collection of primitive objects, such as lines, circles, and even other previously defined symbols, that might make up a complex device. Once defined, the symbol is treated as a primitive object within the program, and the operations that are valid for other primitive objects such as lines and circles are valid for symbols.

Typically, a symbol is specific to a particular application and may be used over and over again. For example, the figure for a relay is used frequently in electrical schematics and is therefore a candidate for representation as a symbol.

The components of a symbol cannot be modified individually. A symbol is always treated as an indivisible unit. Even though a symbol may look complicated, the program treats it just like a line or any other primitive object. A group, on the other hand, is also a collection of primitive objects, but all the objects in the group can be individually modified.

A symbol is defined by two characteristic points:

1. The first point entered selects the symbol to add.

2. The second point is the other endpoint on the item that is being

A symbol can be selected in one of two ways:

1. The symbol can be selected by placing the stylus over the desired picture on a symbolic overlay and pressing down on the stylus.

2. The symbol can be selected by typing in a number from a symbol library list.

If object tracking is used, the program will repeatedly display that symbol. Moving the cursor will move the symbol, changing its location on the screen.

A Bezier option allows one to create one or more Bezier curves. A Bezier curve is defined by the following characteristic points:

1. The first endpoint of the curve.

2. The second endpoint of the curve.

3. The first and second curve control points. These two points determine the shape of the curve.

The program will not draw a Bezier curve until the two endpoints have been defined. These points are defined by moving the cursor to the desired locations on the screen and then pressing down on the stylus. If object tracking is used, the program will repeatedly draw a Bezier curve whose shape is dependent upon the location of the two control points. Moving the cursor will now move both control points. One can move just the first or the second control point by selecting the appropriate key. The program always draws from the first endpoint to the first control point, to the second control point, and then to the second endpoint. By moving the two control points separately, one can create various shapes.

After defining the first Bezier curve, the program will wait for the second curve. The first endpoint of the second curve is automatically defined to be the second endpoint of the first curve. The next point to be defined will be the second endpoint of the new curve. Then one must define the two control points. The program will continue creating Bezier curves until keyed to stop.

Bezier curves can be linked together to appear as if they formed one continuous curve with many inflection points. This can be done as follows:

1. Create a Bezier curve. When creating the curve, use the line option to draw a guide line. The dotted guide line will go through the second control point and the second endpoint.

2. Create a second Bezier. Set the beginning point of the second Bezier to the ending point of the first Bezier. This is automatic if you create the curves one after another. The second endpoint of the second Bezier can be placed where desired.

3. Position the first control point of the second Bezier in such a way that it lies on the dotted guide line.

4. Position the second control point of the second Bezier where desired.

The resulting Bezier curves will appear to be continuous.

The keyboard options available while creating a Bezier include:

1. Cause an arrowhead to appear on the end of the Bezier.

2. Remove the arrowhead.

3. Cause the Bezier to become a template Bezier.

4. Cause a marker to be displayed at all four characteristic points of the Bezier.

5. Remove the markers.

6. Draw a guide line that can be used to create continuous Bezier curves.

7. Cause the first control point to follow the cursor and fix the second control point at its current location.

8. Cause the second control point to follow the cursor and fix the first control point at its current location.

9. Cause both control points to follow the cursor.

10. Fix the location of both the control points and allow the cursor to be moved around freely without changing the shape of the curve.

A fillet option allows one to create fillets or rounds between lines, circles, and arcs. A fillet is created by defining two objects bounding the fillet and then defining the radius of the fillet.

To create a fillet on the corners of a rectangle or polygon, we first explode the rectangle or polygon. This creates the necessary starting lines for the fillet.

When the fillet option is selected, the program will display the following prompt:

DEFINE THE FIRST OBJECT BOUNDING THE FILLET.

The digitizer stylus is then placed on the first line, circle, or arc that bounds the intersection to be filleted, and one presses down on the stylus. This tells the program to use the object nearest the point selected. Once the first object has been defined, the program will display the following prompt:

DEFINE THE SECOND OBJECT BOUNDING THE FILLET.

The digitizer stylus is then placed on the second line, circle, or arc that bounds the intersection to be filleted, and one presses down on the stylus. This tells the program to use the object nearest the point selected. Once both of the objects have been defined, the program will produce a fillet between the two objects. Depending on the state of the keyboard, several actions may be taken.

If no object was found near the area that was picked, then the program will display the following error message:

ERROR: CANNOT FIND AN ARC, CIRCLE, OR LINE NEAR THE POINT DEFINED.

If the trim/extend keyboard option is selected, then the program will perform either an automatic or a manual trim/extend on the objects selected. If the automatic trim/extend key is selected, then the program will automatically trim or extend the selected objects such that they will be tangent to the new fillet. If the manual trim/extend key is selected, then the program will ask the user to select which part of the object is to be trimmed or extended. Figure 8-14 shows two methods of creating fillets.

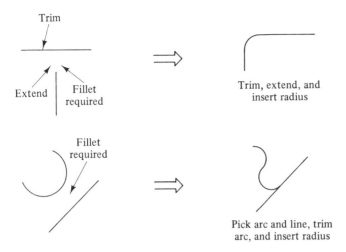

Figure 8-14 Methods of creating fillets.

The dimension option creates dimension lines and measures the distance between any two points on the screen. A dimension line is defined by three characteristic points:

1. The first point is one endpoint on the item that is being dimensioned.
2. The second point is the other endpoint on the item that is is being dimensioned.
3. The third point defines the height (depth) of the dimension; this is the length of the leader lines of the dimension.

To use the dimension option, one places the cursor at one endpoint of the item to be dimensioned and then presses down on the stylus. Then the cursor is moved to the other end of the item, and one presses down on the stylus. If object tracking is used, the program will repeatedly draw a set of dimension lines between the two endpoints. Now the cursor is moved to establish the length of the leader lines. These can be flipped by moving the cursor to the other side of the item being dimensioned. The two endpoints are fixed and cannot be changed. The length of the leader lines is set by pressing down on the stylus.

The set of dimension lines produced has some characteristics that are predefined and are not changeable. When the dimension is plotted, the length of the arrowhead will be $\frac{5}{32}$ inch. If the length of the dimension line is calculated to be less than this amount, the program will not plot the arrowhead at all. The included angle of the arrowhead is 15 degrees.

The keyboard options available while creating a dimension line include:

1. Cause the dimension to be a projection along the x (horizontal) axis.

2. Cause the dimension to be a projection along the y (vertical) axis.

3. Cause the dimension to be at the true angle as it is entered. The dimension leader lines will be perpendicular to the item that is being dimensioned.

4. Delete either or both of the leader lines.

The explode option allows one to break apart an object into its basic components. All objects, with the exception of text and dimensions, can be exploded into their components. The components of a symbol are those primitive objects that make up the symbol. The components of a primitive object are the line segments that make up that object.

When this option is used, the program will explode the object into its basic components. Each of these components is added to the end of the workfile as an ordinary object. Thus, once an object has been exploded into its components, each component can be individually modified. After exploding an object, the program will always delete the original, unexploded object from the drawing.

If a five-sided polygon is exploded, the original polygon will be deleted from the workfile. In its place, five line segments will be added to the end of the workfile. The program may then begin blinking the first of the five lines, anticipating that a modification is needed.

As another example, suppose that a symbol that has a circle inside a rectangle is exploded. The program will delete the original symbol and then add a circle and a rectangle in its place. Either one of these primitive objects can further be exploded into their components. The circle can be exploded into a set of lines just as the rectangle.

Even a line can be exploded. An exploded line can be broken at its midpoint into two identical lines, each half the size of the original. The initial point of each new line is defined as the corresponding endpoint of the original line. This feature allows you to trim lines and then insert other objects.

EXERCISES

1. How is a coarse finite-element analysis used? What must be considered for this technique to be successful?

2. Why is the aspect ratio important?

3. What is a marker statement?

4. Write a flowchart for automatic pipeline generation in which the coordinate data is entered by a mouse to define the points of the piping model.

5. Finite-element modeling can be a costly technique, since large amounts of explicit geometric data and material properties must be entered. Discuss some way to reduce computational costs.

6. Duplicating a finite-element model with the required changes can take almost as long as generating the original model. What are some ways of reducing this time?

7. How can database techniques help in handling analysis of shapes more irregular than symmetric joints and similar parts?

8. Define cyclic symmetry and superelements. How are these used in a structural analysis?

9. When the design and analysis are complete, discuss how software can perform tasks such as hidden-line removal and preparation of engineering drawings from the model geometry. How can the computer also use the model database to generate bills of material automatically?

10. Discuss how temperature distributions can be calculated by a heat-transfer analysis which is input as the temperature load in a structural analysis.

11. What optimization techniques could be used for modeling and analysis with MSC/NASTRAN?

12. Without graphic standards, design tasks will take longer and operations will tend to be error-prone. The need for system standardization is paramount in large, complex AEC projects. Discuss how standards can be successfully implemented while maintaining an efficient and effective computer graphics capability.

13. As a result of the need to share information, integrated CAD systems for AEC need to possess some special qualities. Discuss the characteristics most relative to large, complex projects.

14. Distributed processing systems are made by interconnecting various workstation CPUs into networks, the size and configuration of which depend on the needs of the user. Discuss how relatively small projects can be handled through a simple ring network in which several workstations are connected. Show why a cluster network may be required for larger projects with several rings and a background processor for time-consuming functions.

15. What is the difference between a master-slave and hierarchical network? How can they be compatible?

16. A peculiarity of inelastic analysis is an instability associated with load relaxation, or the retreat back down the stress-strain curve. How can this problem be minimized?

COMPUTER-
AIDED
MANUFACTURING

9

The use of computers in manufacturing operations has been growing rapidly. Computer applications include inventory control, scheduling, machine monitoring, management information systems, and other information applications. These are primarily applications for transferring, interpreting, and keeping track of manufacturing data. The computers make important contributions to the manufacturing operations primarily as data managers.

Another area of computer applications in manufacturing is that of controlling the physical manufacturing process. This area is typically referred to as *computer-aided manufacturing* (*CAM*). This technology presents great economic benefits in improving manufacturing productivity. It also presents a number of technical challenges which are inherent to computer control of a physical process. One effect of this technology is to accelerate the incentive for businesses to modernize plant and equipment, an undertaking in which CAM will play a major role.

CAD/CAM POTENTIAL

The average age of much industrial equipment is over 20 years; in some mature industries, such as steel, paper, and foundries, the equipment can be 50 years old. By contrast, the average age of industrial equipment of some competitors is about 10 to 14 years. If an industry is to compete, it must use the most efficient tools available. The new equipment for computer-aided design (CAD) and computer-aided manufacturing will encourage businesses to update their equipment. This also applies to equipment used in research and development, an important component of productivity growth. Over the long term, only R&D will enable one to maintain a technological leadership and to reverse declines in productivity growth.

A CAD/CAM program is a comprehensive contribution toward improving productivity, but it is only one factor in success. Management has the obligation to contribute in a number of important ways. Management must, for example, take full advantage of the incentives offered by the program. Industry now has an opportunity to get rid of obsolete equipment that deters productivity growth.

To make such investment decisions, managers must begin to take a long-term view of their firm's prospects, and not be concerned only with the short-term gains.

Many managers believe that the key to the future lies with computer-aided design and computer-aided manufacturing. The successful application of these technologies means building better products easier and faster.

During the 80s and beyond, CAD will play a major role in the use of advanced materials in many designs, particularly composites. These composite components are made up of hundreds of layers of graphite epoxy.

Computer techniques will be used to keep track of the shape, endpoints, and direction of the plys. CAD will also provide the means to automate the equipment to produce these fabrications, decreasing the costs while enhancing the structural integrity.

The reasons for the expected growth in the number of components to be produced by CAD reflect the technology's contributions in quality and reliability engineering as well as in the improved communications possible between the design and manufacturing functions.

Improved tolerances can play a major role in reducing fabrication costs. Assembly quality and time is reduced.

It is now possible to produce complex aircraft structures without using a single shim. This is something quite uncommon in the pre-CAD era.

The new technology enables drilling over 23,000 holes and applying the rivets that hold skins to stringers without a single production problem. In this production system the data is directed to the riveting machines to control their operation.

The aircraft industry's use of CAD is better understood when considered in this context; widebody commercial airlines can have as many as 100,000 structural components. The engineering description of these parts may take place in an integrated process that embodies a complete flow of computerized data from the preliminary design to completed drawings and the equivalent sets of stored data that describe the drawings mathematically.

The process can produce assembly and fabrication drawings, tooling information, and interior layouts. It can also provide design aids that make such activities as analysis easier and includes data to detail the stringers and fittings. This technique allows more accurate parts to be manufactured. Correcting errors is always costly, but by using computer accuracy to eliminate these expensive errors during the design stage, manufacturers stand to benefit a great deal.

Computer-aided design also provides increased manpower productivity as one of its prime benefits to industry. Other important achievements include improved engineering quality and the ability for engineering data to interface directly with factory machine tools. Individual manpower productivity gains of up to five-to-one can be achieved in some applications, with some going higher, but gains of two-to-one are average.

The keystone of CAD/CAM is interactive computer graphics (ICG). This technology allows the engineer or drafter to interact with the computer to create, view, and control.

Many control processes are likely to undergo substantial changes and be significantly automated. Scanning devices will be able to compare the physical part shapes with the engineering computerized database and detect defects.

Computer techniques are also being used in scheduling and estimating processes. Statistics for designing components are being used to provide manufacturing departments with data, and, through the use of this computerized data, the manufacturing operation is able to reduce overall costs significantly.

The advent of CAD also makes the increased use of robots more feasible. Integrated CAM (ICAM) is aimed at automated manufacturing, emphasizing robotics.

The use of CAD and CAM can have some serious impacts on corporations themselves and how they operate. Engineering and manufacturing organizations may merge into a single design factory. Under this scheme, the design and manufacturing personnel work together to produce the best possible design for efficient fabrication. Less highly trained people may be able to design many parts satisfactorily, overcoming the shortages of more highly skilled personnel while more stringent quality is accomplished.

The implementation of CAD/CAM will not be easy for many segments of industry. Owing to the complexity and size of many manufacturing operations, any venture to improve significantly the engineering and manufacturing process requires a major capital investment and restructuring.

Once the systems have been adopted, new challenges must also be overcome. Entire engineering departments may have to be retrained to use the systems.

The two technologies are now being combined into unified CAD/CAM systems (Figure 9-1), where a design is developed and the manufacturing process controlled from start to finish with a single system. Such capabilities

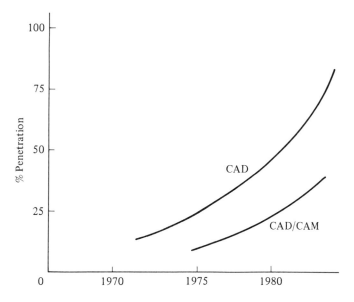

Figure 9-1 Estimated CAD and CAD/CAM manufacturing-task penetration.

are presently available using CAD/CAM systems in a few large manufacturing operations. But more and more plants are gaining these capabilities in an effort to modernize and streamline their operations.

NUMERICAL CONTROL

The most mature of the CAM technologies is *numerical control* (*NC*). This is the technique of controlling machine tools with prerecorded, coded information.

Automated NC machines drill, grind, cut, punch, mill, and turn raw material into finished parts. The technique was first developed in the 50s to make contoured aircraft parts, and since then it has spread into other industries, making machine tool systems much more refined.

In the most basic NC system the programmed instructions are stored on punched paper tapes and interpreted by electromechanical tape readers connected to the machine tool. More advanced systems use *computer numerical control* (*CNC*), in which the machine is controlled by a dedicated computer with the NC instructions stored in its memory. This allows the instructions to be stored, handled, and changed more efficiently. Diagnostic and other intelligent functions beyond simple machine control can be performed by the computer.

More sophisticated systems may use *direct numerical control* (*DNC*), which may also be referred to as *distributed numerical control* when the machine control is distributed among a network of computers. In these systems the individual manufacturing units are connected through communication lines to a central computer that is in command.

The communications lines also provide for the feedback of production and machine-tool status from the shop floor. Some systems use a hierarchical arrangement of computers connected to the central computer, while other systems have eliminated the intervening minicomputers and have direct interfaces between the mainframe and machine tools.

The two basic techniques of distributed control are the loop approach and the unit approach.

The *loop approach* uses satellite processors to perform a fixed number of functions. A processor might perform a function such as required for a single machining operation.

A single processor could also perform a single function in a number of different loops. Normally, a processor is dedicated to a single loop, so a single failure will cause the loss of only one loop.

The *unit approach* has a separate control system for each unit in the system, and a plant processor is assigned to each unit. As an example, a processor might be assigned to the structural function.

Some advantages of distributed control can be had by either approach, but others can be realized only by the unit approach. A major advantage of distributed control is the increase in efficiency. Since the processor's I/O equipment is located in a nearby area, most wires must be run only a short distance. This provides a savings, and, since the runs are shorter, there are fewer problems from interference on the low-level signals. With distributed control there is no need for a large control panel. The unit is inherently modular. Computer control can be added to the units in a plant one at a time, without disrupting control of those units already on computer control. This is attractive to a plant that is operating without computer control. A study can identify the most likely machines for computer control. The unit may be a bottleneck, a large energy-user, or one which is difficult to operate.

The instructions for these NC systems can be prepared either manually or with computer assistance. In manual programming the tool-path coordinates are calculated from the part dimensions.

The program is then prepared in an alphanumeric format suitable for entry into the machine control unit. Manual programming provides the most direct user control over NC instructions; however, it requires numerous calculations and is tedious and prone to errors. The programmer must be familiar with the control language so that the instructions are entered in the proper format.

Extensive measuring of the part is required to define the program sufficiently so that it produces a properly machined part. Manual part programming is used in small machine shops.

In more sophisticated systems, those that are computer-assisted, the programming language enables the user to develop the NC instructions more quickly and with fewer errors. The instructions generally are written either with the APT or the Compact language. These instructions relieve the programmer from manually entering any geometric data.

In a typical computer-assisted system, when the NC program is selected, a menu appears on the screen, and the user designates the machine which is to cut the part. When the machine is selected, another menu appears, allowing selection of:

1. Cutter size.
2. Type of material.
3. Feeds and speeds.
4. Material thickness.
5. Clearance above which the tool must rise when not cutting.

Then the screen displays a geometric model of the part, on which the programmer defines the machining operations using various types of lines. For example, a solid line might indicate a rough cut and a dashed line a finish cut. From these inputs the system automatically generates an NC tape to machine the part.

APT is the original and more universal language. It has become the standard of the NC industry. The language allows the user to produce NC instructions from English-type statements. Working from an engineering drawing, the part programmer enters statements identifying the machine parameters, the part shape, and the tool type. The computer then makes the calculations defining the tool path to produce the shape. For complex curved surfaces the user defines the control points and surface equations.

Most of the NC programming packages also simulate the tool paths so that the program can be checked. The tool motion can be animated to allow the programmer to observe the tool as it moves on the part. The motion shown on the screen can be slowed, and one can zoom in on a specific area for clarifying of details and increased accuracy.

These features allow a verification that the program properly guides the cutter.

After the programming is completed, the computer translates or postprocesses the tool-path description into coded instructions tailored to a specific machine. These instructions are stored on punched paper tape or magnetic tape for input to the machine tool. The instructions may also be transferred directly to a memory in the machine-tool control system.

When NC instructions are written manually, the process tends to be error-prone, because a large number of calculations are required to define the tool paths. Lengthy trial machining may also be required to refine the program—for example, for the tool motion required to machine a three-axis composite surface of slanted planes and cylinders. This can be simulated on a computer unit. Then, after the operator verifies the tool path, the system will automatically generate the APT language instructions for producing the part on the NC machine.

The motion of a five-axis machine tool can also be simulated. The front, top, side, and isometric views of the path are displayed for program verification and editing before the NC instructions are produced.

The computer-assisted systems perform many activities automatically. Some advanced systems use the geometric mode created by computer-aided design techniques as a basis for producing the NC instructions which determine machining parameters, such as:

1. Feed rates and spindle speeds.

2. The proper sequence of work elements.

3. The optimum tool paths to fabricate the part.

After the processor develops the NC instructions, the process can be simulated as an animated color solid model on the screen of an interactive graphics terminal. Using this display, the programmer can check the validity of the machining process and then use the terminal to make any necessary changes.

Beyond computer-assisted programming, the software may use the geometric model created in computer-aided design as a basis for producing the NC instructions. The geometric information is accessed through a shared database in the computer; thus the programmer does not have to enter data manually. The computer may also prompt the programmer to respond to questions displayed on a terminal screen.

These NC programming packages can also display the simulated tool paths so that the programmer can check the program. The system allows the programmer to create the NC instructions graphically, without requiring a detailed knowledge of programming languages.

An advantage of computer-based programming systems is the speed with which they can generate the NC programs. The programmers need not be familiar with the intricacies of the tool-path generation. The engineers designing the parts can do their own NC programming to produce the parts with only a minimal knowledge of machining. The CAD drawing must be modified so that only those lines which have meaning in the manufacturing process remain. If a die or mold is to be made, the inverse image of the original model must be generated. All the construction lines must be eliminated, and the lines that define the edges must be consistent.

There is also the task of defining each surface that is to be formed. The draft angles, relief areas, and any other expansions must be allowed for.

There is also the task of defining each surface that is to be formed. The draft angles, relief areas, and any other expansions must be allowed for.

The mechanics of the various cutting operations must also be determined, including the sequence of the cuts, the type and size of tool, feed rates, and tool-path centerlines.

In some systems, many of the machining parameters such as cutter types and feed rates remain constant, so that the programmer input beyond the geometric mode is minimal for simple part shapes.

In a fully integrated CAD/CAM system with a common database the processor can extract virtually all the information required for generating NC instructions. The part descriptions can be obtained from the geometric-modeling portion of the database, and the appropriate machining parameters can be taken from process-planning data.

Using this generative programming scheme, the processor can:

1. Automatically recognize the solid model of the part.

2. Identify the material to be removed from the raw stock to develop the part.

3. Select the tools required to produce the part.

SELECTING NC SOFTWARE

The CAM programs available for NC programming have a variety of strengths, weaknesses, and prices. Some have their origins as CAD programs, intended to be used in specific design areas such as circuit-board development or civil engineering. They may have shortcomings in some applications when used as the basis for NC commands.

These CAD-based programs may be unable to execute certain commands or carry them out effectively. There is also the possibility that the program, even if it is specifically developed for CAM, will not fit the specific task.

Resolution is one important program capability to consider. The surface finish a program should be able to provide is determined by many cost-influencing factors such as part volume, amount of hand labor, and NC programming and machining time.

One should also consider if there is a single application that dominates the operation. If there is, one can calculate how much would be saved if productivity were increased by a reasonable factor. One can balance this savings against the cost of the CAM system. Normally, if one only does 2D machining, there is no need to buy a system capable of cutting shapes for turbine blades.

Rather than using a list of all the capabilities you would like to have and selecting a package that promises the greatest number of capabilities at the lowest price, the system should be keyed to the most dominant production needs. Two basic tests can be used to determine if a CAM program is suitable in a particular application:

1. One basic test is to generate a tool cutting path for a complex part that is similar to the component that will be manufactured.

2. A more complete test is to carry out a series of tests called *benchmarks*.

Each of these benchmarks measures one or several specific program capabilities. The test results are then evaluated to give a more complete picture of a program's abilities and limitations. Listed below are typical tasks adapted from actual manufacturing needs (Figure 9-2). Each one illustrates a particular shape or machining maneuver which may present some difficulty to the program.

1. *Normal cutting*. Cut a hemisphere with a radius while keeping the cutter axis tangent to the shape's surface. This tests the program's ability to maneuver the cutting tool in five axes and produce normal

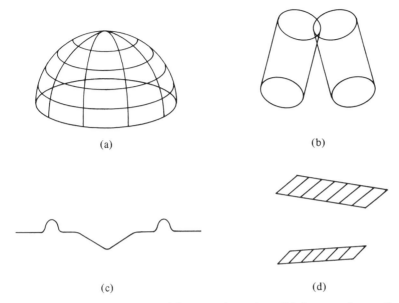

(a)

(b)

(c)

(d)

Figure 9-2 NC benchmarks: (a) normal cutting, (b) intersecting cylinders, (c) complex shape, (d) coordinate translation.

vectors as opposed to cutting with a fixed tool axis. It is considered a simple test compared to others.

2. *Tapered slot*. Cut a tapered slot with a flat bottom in a block. The taper is the difficult task, since it requires five-axis capability. Some programs are limited to 2½D machining (x,y, and only vertical z motion).

3. *Intersecting cylinders*. Cut two cylinders that intersect at an angle. It is difficult to maintain a fillet along the lines of intersection and perform the cut without cutting into the work surface. It also evaluates the efficiency of the tool cutting program. The sequence in which the faces are cut as well as the path the tool takes are both important in minimizing the total cutting time.

4. *Raised patch*. Cut a cylinder with a raised patch. The patch is faired into the cylinder's surface. This requires the ability to modify a basic geometric shape. The blending of the two diameters is difficult. There must be a smooth transition around the patch without cutting into the cylinder.

5. *Leading-edge transition*. Make a transition from a chamfer to a radius and back to a chamfer. This simulates a section on a wing's leading edge. The transition is difficult, since it is not a basic geometric shape. The program must be able to generate a sculptured surface to maintain the required smooth fairing.

6. *Complex shape.* Develop a 2D shape and sweep it through a complex path, creating a channel in three dimensions. This is a difficult control problem, particularly in consistently maintaining the complex 2D cross section.

7. *Trailing edge.* Cut two large planes that intersect to form a small-diameter fillet. The shape is similar to the trailing edge of a wing. The key problem is a clear definition of the fillet. There is a transition from milling a broad flat section to cutting a small radius.

8. *Coordinate translation.* Profile a part with data from different coordinate systems. Each element of a complex system is normally dimensioned in its own coordinate system. When these elements are combined, the separate coordinate systems must be combined into one system. This is a data-handling problem, and the program must be able to transpose images and data.

9. *Tangent planes.* Two planes are tangent to a circle. Several cylinders intersect the planes and the circle. Mill out a section of constant depth with a boundary defined by the centers of the cylinder. This requires establishing a cutting path based on a number of tangent points, maintaining the consistent cut depth in multiple planes, and maintaining the hole wall perpendicular to its respective planes.

10. *Nongeometric sculpturing.* Cut a sculptured surface that changes from convex to concave. Only the geometry of the ends is defined. Surfaces that are not basic geometric shapes are common on aircraft. The smooth transition needed requires the program to establish boundary conditions at several sections between the defined endpoints.

SCULPTURED SURFACES

Sculptured surfaces are made up of arbitrary, nonanalytical contours that may not obey mathematical laws and have been considered to be impractical to machine with NC. These surfaces are found in a wide range of components, including those used for aircraft, automobiles, construction and agricultural equipment, machine tools, and appliances. They are typical of office-machine and computer-terminal enclosures or of products which depend on free-flowing surface contours for performance or aesthetic appeal. These surfaces traditionally have been defined by subjective curve-fitting techniques and manufactured with expensive operations. Part shapes that can be defined by mathematical equations, such as planes, cones, spheres, and paraboloids, can be readily programmed for NC machining, but considerable computer power may be required for the more complex parts.

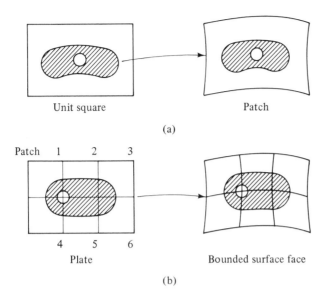

Figure 9-3 Sculptured surface: (a) creating a patch, (b) composites of patches become bounded surface faces.

There is no simple way to create an NC part program for machining the contour of a sculptured surface, since the surface cannot be defined mathematically. NC programming for sculptured surfaces is one of the most challenging areas in NC technology. The complex contours can be represented by a network of patches. Each of these may have a mathematical contour that serves as a close approximation to a corresponding surface element of the surface to be machined. The sculptured surfaces are made up of these parametric patches. Each patch is a stretched image of a unit square in parametric space [Figure 9-3(a)]. A surface can be bounded by constructing a plate in the 2D parameter space and considering a portion of the surface to be the image of the unit square which lies within the plate. By extending 2D plate geometry software to surfaces described as composites of patches, we have the basis for bounded-face geometry. This allows a face to be implicitly bounded in case the natural parametric boundaries of the surface coincide with the boundaries of the part [Figure 9-3(b)]. As the composites are derived from unit squares, they are twisted and stretched by the computer to conform as closely as possible to the sculptured surface and blended together smoothly. They describe a nonanalytical surface that cannot be defined mathematically. There are two basic ways of constructing these patches:

1. A mesh-of-points.
2. Synthetic curves.

In the mesh-of-points approach, the user defines the patches which represent the sculptured surface using a mesh of coordinate points. The computer then runs smooth splines through or near these points in two directions. Each of the input points is assigned a weight to indicate its importance in defining the surface. This allows the computer to shift the splines away from the less important points to maintain the slope continuity across the patch boundaries for a smooth surface.

The maximum deviation of the splines from any point is also specified to maintain a reasonable representation of the sculptured surface. The interconnecting splines form parabolic patch shapes.

In the synthetic-curves approach, the user synthesizes complex curves using simple curve segments, such as straight lines, circles, and conics, which can all be represented mathematically. Once the synthetic curves have been produced, they can be manipulated to generate representations of a variety of surfaces.

The problem of developing NC sculptured surfaces has been attacked by companies in the automotive and aerospace industries. Many of the programs which have been developed have difficulty in guiding a cutter to machine the generalized contours, and the software typically is customized to operate only on large in-house computer systems.

There have been efforts to develop common programs for generalized shapes that can be easily implemented on a wide range of computer systems. Some programs can define arbitrary shapes and manufacture them on NC machine tools. Various versions are being used in industry. Many manufacturers have tailored the program to suit their own particular requirements and use it as a production tool. Some vendors also market modified versions as part of their overall commercial software packages. Here the complex surfaces are represented by a network of interconnected patches in the sculptured-surfaces program. After the surface is modeled, the program output can generate NC machining instructions for a contoured part.

Before the NC program can be produced to machine a sculptured surface, a mathematical representation of the surface must be created. The synthetic-curves approach begins with the user synthesizing complex curves from simple curve segments that can be represented mathematically. These synthetic curves are then swept through space to create the mathematical representation of the sculptured surface. A tabulated cylinder is formed by projecting a free-form curve into the third dimension. It represents a curved plane between two arbitrary but identical parallel curves, as shown in Figure 9-4(a).

A ruled surface is formed by sweeping a straight line through space with its endpoints always in contact with, and at right angles to, two arbitrary and nonidentical curves. This is shown in Figure 9-4(b).

A surface of revolution is formed by revolving an arbitrary curve about an axis—that is, by sweeping an arbitrary curve along a circle, with the two

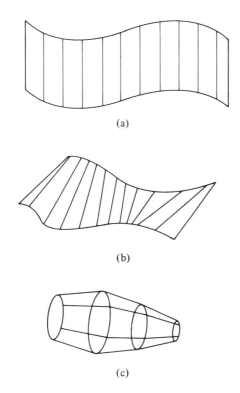

(a)

(b)

(c)

Figure 9-4 Synthetic curves: (a) tabulated cylinder, (b) ruled surface, (c) surface of revolution.

always intersecting at right angles, as shown in Figure 9-4(c). A sweep surface is formed by sweeping an arbitrary curve along another arbitrary curve, with the two curves always intersecting at right angles.

A general-curves surface consists of families of synthetic curves which can define complex contours. It is formed by connecting families of synthetic curves together in such a manner that their curvatures match at the points of intersection, producing a smooth, continuous surface definition.

The Use of Laser Machine Tools

Since about 1965, lasers have interfaced with materials-handling and numerical-control systems to provide viable manufacturing processes in welding, cutting, drilling, and heat-treating applications.

Laser machine tools offer a number of design advantages. The noncontact tools operate continuously, eliminate wear and breakage, and are more energy-efficient. They are compatible with most manufacturers' CAD/

CAM systems and may be configured as a stand-alone system with integrated workstations.

Recent innovations provide increased cut quality and laser speed for cutting and drilling applications. Lasers can solve a variety of complex problems in the fabrication of products made of metal, plastics, rubber, ceramics, glass, paper, and wood. Laser metal-cutting systems can have many benefits. They can be combined with punch presses, moving coordinate tables, and numerical-control systems. The laser excels in cutting lines at an angle and other contours, including complex outside shapes.

Narrow slots, angled slots, and cutouts with acute angles are appropriate for laser cutting. Where small quantities of special-shape cuts are involved, a laser can eliminate the cost and delay of special tooling. Many high-tensile-strength materials that are difficult to punch can be operated on with laser cutting. The edge finish produced in the laser cutting of sheet metal is superior to that obtained by contour nibbling or plasma cutting. The edge is relatively smooth and square, the kerf width is narrow, and the dross is minimal. The heat-affected zone next to the cut is very small, which facilitates the finishing, forming, and joining operations.

CO^2 laser welding can be performed on such materials as cold-rolled steel, titanium, stainless steel, and alloy steels. Aluminum, copper, and similar metals along with their alloys are usually unsuitable. Laser welding often can be the only practical method for bonding dissimilar metals.

Laser welding is superior to plasma arc welding, since it is stable and controllable. Its energy can be focused into one-tenth the diameter with minimal heat damage to adjacent material or devices. The costly vacuum chambers required for electron-beam welding are not required. An inert-gas shield must be provided to prevent oxidation of the material being welded.

Ferrous alloys can be laser-welded to 0.08 inch (2 mm) penetration. The advantages include:

1. Minimal heat input to the part.
2. Welding in a jet of inert gas at atmospheric pressure.
3. No filler material.
4. Minimum fixturing, since it is a noncontact process.
5. Minimal distortion area.

An example of the advantages obtained from CO^2 laser use is the hardening of metal by heat-treating. The classical method heats a very small area of the surface so rapidly that the material quenches itself by heat conduction to the cooler interior as the heat moves on.

The laser method produces less distortion of the treated parts and allows machining to the final dimensions before laser heat-treating. The laser also heats only a small area of the metal, so less energy is used.

The electronics industry uses laser technology to drill and cut ceramic and other materials. By using a laser as a scribing tool and coupling it with numerical-control equipment, fired alumina with or without deposits of multiple electronics can be separated accurately into pieces containing individual circuits.

The machining of alumina calls for a high-absorbing wavelength with a fast energy delivery that completely vaporizes the material. The 10-micrometer wavelength of the CO^2 laser is absorptive and has the peak power adequate for complete vaporization. It also provides high repetition rates for a high throughput.

Laser scribing can produce a cost savings in many circuit-manufacturing processes. A multibeam output capability is one important factor. Instead of delivering the entire output in one beam, it is divided into two, three, or four beams, with each directed on the workpiece to increase the throughput.

A scribing laser can be operated in the pulsed mode with an intermittent output of beam power using a scribe width of 0.006 to 0.008 inch. Hole diameters using a defocused beam should be limited to about 0.015 inch to protect the ceramic against thermal shock. Larger holes can be cut using a rotating lens. Lasers are also an aid to design and manufacturing engineers in increasing productivity. As a highly efficient energy source, they are adapted easily to CAD/CAM automation for micromachining control.

Lasers will be designed for lengthened operating times for minimizing downtime. The systems will have a higher energy-conversion efficiency, smaller size, and higher quality with pulse amplitudes to 1000 W or more for ferrous-metal cutting up to 12 mm and penetration welding up to 6 mm.

Shaping and maneuvering a part on a machine is more difficult than creating and moving an image on a CRT in design. Thus, CAM has traditionally lagged behind CAD technology. The development work in many areas of CAM is closing this technical gap. This development work in CAM falls into four main areas:

1. Numerical control.
2. Process control.
3. Robotics.
4. Process planning.
5. Factory management.

PROCESS CONTROL

The use of industrial computers can be grouped into two areas: continuous processing and discrete-parts manufacturing.

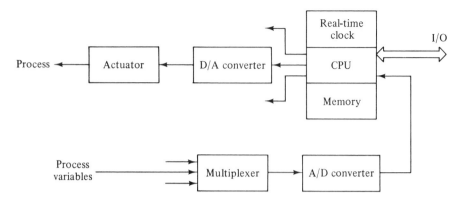

Figure 9-5   Process control.

Continuous processing is concerned with the operation of valves, motors, and other controls in response to measured variables such as temperature, pressures, and flow rates (Figure 9-5).

Discrete-parts manufacturing is concerned with the positioning of machine elements for fabrication purposes such as metal-cutting or metal-forming operations. Computers are used for the positioning of the cutting tools and the controlling of the machine motions as well as for the transfer of parts and materials among workstations. One of the most significant applications of computer technology in discrete-parts manufacturing has been *numerical control*, which provides the means used to position tools and machines along prescribed paths. This technology is also used to control robots in many industrial applications.

In these computer applications, a wide range of computing power is available. At one end are the large mainframe computers used in large refineries and chemical plants to control the petrochemical processes. Large mainframe computers are also used as bases for many CAD/CAM and *direct numerical control* (*DNC*) systems.

At the other end of industrial control are *programmable controllers* (*PCs*). Early PCs were limited to replacing relay panels or timers, but now most PCs are microprocessor-based and they are used for elementary process control.

There are also a wide variety of mini- or microcomputers. The 32-bit superminicomputers that are now available even overlap the domain of the large mainframe computers in many aspects. A simple process-control system like the one shown in Figure 9-5 could maintain the temperature of a process tank which is heated by steam. The analog temperature signal is converted to a digital signal and compared with the commanded temperature, which is also a digital signal. The difference between the two is the error signal. It is converted back to an analog signal, amplified, and applied to the motor. The motor then adjusts the valve to change the flow of steam, forcing the temperature toward the desired value.

In conventional process-control systems we are also concerned with the collection and processing of analog sensor data into digital form for the following purposes:

1. Storage for later use.
2. Transmission to other locations.
3. Processing to obtain additional information.
4. Display for analysis or recording.

The data could be stored in raw or processed form; it might be retained for short or long periods or transmitted over long or short distances, and the display could be on a digital panel meter or a cathode-ray-tube screen.

The data-processing requirements might range from simple value comparisons to complex calculations. One might be interested in collecting information, converting data to a more useful form, using the data for controlling a process, performing calculations, separating signals from noise, or generating information for displays. Many data-acquisition configurations have been used, and a number of considerations are involved in the choice of configuration components, and other elements of the system.

Both process-control and machine-tool (Figure 9-6) servodrive systems are conceptually quite similar, in that they are based on closing the control loop with a feedback signal derived from the function or device being controlled. The closed-loop control system compares the behavior of the device being controlled with the behavior commanded, and, if a difference or error between the two exists, it automatically produces a correction signal which tends to drive the error to zero. If a machine-tool servodrive is commanded to move the machine slide to a certain position, until the slide reaches that position, the position feedback will differ from the input command, and the actuator will continue to drive the slide toward the commanded position.

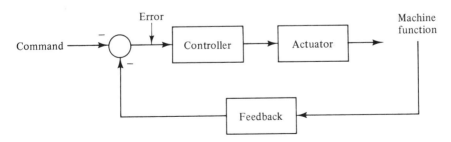

Figure 9-6 Machine control.

Industrial computer-control equipment has evolved from the configuration where a single computer performs all the supervisory control and process monitoring. The computer monitors a process by reading analog or digital data from the input/output equipment. It might change a control set point in performing supervisory control function. The control console can consist of CRT displays, input keyboards, and printers. The peripheral equipment is connected to the I/O channel by the interface circuitry. This hardware performs most of the functions required for the operations between the channel and the peripheral device, such as address detection, decoding, timing, and error detection/correction.

The single-computer configuration has been used in many installations and it has had a major influence on the technical and human aspects of computer control. The central computer has several distinct advantages. More and better software has been available for the large computers than for small systems, and the larger machines have an advantage when a complex problem such as a fast Fourier transform or the solution to a difficult control algorithm must be performed. In process optimization, which can require many calculations and a large memory capacity, the larger computer has been generally more suitable.

Control functions which do not require complex calculations can be handled by small systems. Most of the control tasks in discrete-parts manufacturing involve simple binary inputs and outputs. These tasks can be performed on a microprocessor or programmable controller.

Distributed Processing

It has become increasingly apparent that complex plant control systems often can be divided into smaller and simpler control tasks. Computers then assume the divided responsibility of the complete control system, with one computer controlling the overall flow of the tasks, as shown in Figure 9-7. This is the *distributed-processing* technique. The processors are not always dedicated to any single function but can be assigned tasks by a master processor, which operates the complete network. One advantage of distributed processing is the division of labor, since the remote units off-load the processor to improve the performance of the total system. The improved time response can result in less overhead in the system and improve the execution of functions without waiting for the availability of a central computer. Distributed-processing systems have a modularity which is available in many centralized systems. As sections of a plant are automated, more remote units can be added. In the initial stages there is no need to install a system large enough to meet all anticipated expansions. But still the system must be designed so that any planned expansions can be accomplished.

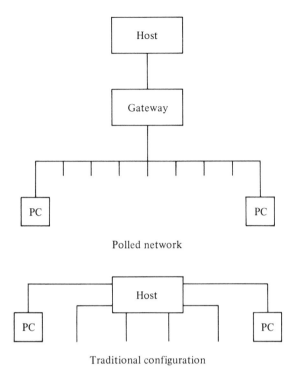

Figure 9-7   Distributed-processing systems with programmable controllers.

Distributed processing also improves the system reliability and failure tolerance. The remote units can allow operation independent of the central computer for short periods of time; thus a short outage in the central computer or a communications link can be tolerated. It is also possible for the central computer to take over control for a limited loss of remote units.

The network can be designed for operation in harsh, noisy, industrial environments, and reliability can be enhanced by:

1. Redundancy options that include fully redundant interfaces and cabling.
2. Fail-safe designs that prevent any single failure in the communication system from bringing the entire system down.
3. Self-repairing mechanisms that automatically disconnect failed devices or add in new devices.

In a *duplexed* configuration the primary or master processor performs the control task. When a failure occurs, the backup processor takes over control. The primary processor can then be taken offline, repaired, and returned to service without interrupting control.

The duplexed processors provide twice the computing capacity, since either processor can control the process. This excess power can often be used for other optional tasks. To guarantee that the higher reliability will be achieved, the system must be analyzed for the effects of each failure classification. The software must also be designed to achieve the higher potential reliability of the duplicated hardware.

Duplexed operation allows the two processors to have special characteristics. One processor could be used to perform fast floating-point calculations, and this would be its function during normal operation of the system. In order for the backup processor to keep up to date with the status of the program, it must have access to the current process status information. If a shared-file system is used, then this information is available by using an access mechanism called *token-passing*. Once a device has gained temporary control of the system, it can communicate with any other device by establishing a virtual circuit with it. These circuits can include different types of devices in a system.

Primary devices are in the token-pass sequence, and they can initiate communications. The secondary devices can only respond when queried, and the demand devices are secondary devices that are allowed to behave like primary devices only if a specific event occurs.

A token-passing system requires that each station on the network have the token before the central computer will talk to the node. The method used to determine which node has the token may be either deterministic or sequential, where the token is passed from node to node in a strict order. The requirement to follow this order can reduce response too severely for some dynamic process applications.

In a system with several processors the tokens or requests from one processor to the others are posted in the shared file. Then a scheduling program periodically checks to determine if a request is waiting. The request can then be scheduled according to the system priority.

The disk files are serial devices which two processors cannot use at the same time. The contention problem must be solved by circuits or another processor (an *arbiter*), which may be part of the file interface.

Some of the sensors in the system might be connected to several process I/O subsystems and others connected to only one. The shared sensors might be those which are critical to the process. If one of the processors becomes inoperable, the other processor still has access to the data in order to maintain control.

Another basic method of connecting processors is a connection through the I/O channels. This could be either a serial or parallel data transfer. The transfer of information then uses the data rate of the slower processor. These systems can use a number of operating modes. The processors could cooperate in solving a problem which requires more computing speed than a single processor provides. Each processor then controls a portion of the process. The necessary coordination can be effected through the interconnections.

In a duplex configuration one must consider when the backup processor should be activated to take over. The primary processor could set a timer in the backup unit on a periodic basis. Failure to set the timer causes the backup unit to assume control and disable the primary unit. This type of timer is known as a *hardware* or *watchdog timer*.

The switchover from the primary to the backup computer must be designed so that it results in only a small control deviation.

The increased use of computer networks in general data-processing applications, along with the increased popularity of remote multiplexing, has resulted in the wider use of distributed control in the process-control industry. *Distributed control* differs from distributed processing, in that it also makes use of remote multiplexing. The processors communicate with field-located multiplexers, and each processor is usually dedicated to performing the same task in an online environment.

In many process industries, such distributed control has been necessary for years. Now the microprocessor-based computer makes distributed control ideal for discrete parts manufacturing, where several separate stand-alone control devices are installed at various points in the production process.

The two basic techniques for distributed control are the loop approach and the unit approach, as we have discussed. The loop appoach has its satellite microprocessors which perform a fixed number of functions. A single programmable controller might perform one function for a number of different loops. If a processor is dedicated to a single loop, then the controllers may be electrically interconnected by data buses, and, depending on the complexity of the system, can operate independently, communicate with each other, or even assume temporary control of each other. This way a failure in the processor will cause the loss of only one loop.

The unit approach uses a separate control system for each unit in the system, with a microprocessor assigned to each unit. For example, one processor might be assigned to the control of a distillation column. Some advantages of distributed control can be realized by either approach, but others can be gained only by using the unit approach.

A major advantage is the reduction in wiring. With the microprocessor's I/O equipment located throughout the system, wires must run only a short distance. This provides a savings in installation, and, since the runs are shorter, there are fewer problems from interference on low-level signals.

Another economy is the ability to share programming units. Ladder logic can be entered step by step at individual PCs. The small display panels usually found on the PC may be difficult to read, so CRT displays can be used to show several rungs of ladder logic at once. In large networks the added convenience can be more easily justified than in a small system.

Distributed systems usually have two communications protocols, one for the local units and another for the high-level devices. A frequently used local protocol is RC232C, but RS422 is gaining popularity because of its immunity to RFI and the low cost of the twisted pair of wires. The high-level, or supervisory, net will more likely use a version of IEEE 802. Also, enough CRT control consoles may be used in the system so that a sufficient number of operators can control the system during critical periods.

With distributed control the reliability and maintainability of a process-control system is improved. The cost of microprocessor hardware is low, so processors in a unit configuration can be backed up with a spare (duplexed processing); then a single processor failure will have no effect on operation. Since most microprocessors are normally on a single printed-circuit board, the system is easily repaired. It is usually a matter of replacing one board.

The unit approach is highly modular, and computer control can be added to the units in the system one at a time, without disrupting control of those units already on computer control. The most likely unit for computer control can be established after a system study is conducted. The unit may be a system or process bottleneck, a large energy user, or one which is difficult to operate without computer control.

Networks

Computer networks are an extension of the distributed-processing concept. The difference between a distributed-processing system and a computer network tends to be a matter of degree. Computer networks consist of two or more computer systems which are separated. The distance between them can be a few feet within the same room or many miles between separate facilities which are connected by common-carrier lines. Some of these networks connect:

1. Programmable controllers (PCs)
2. Computers.
3. CRT terminals.
4. Printers.
5. A/D converters.
6. Badge readers.
7. Robots.
8. I/O devices.
9. Programming panels.

10. Microprocessors.

11. NC equipment.

12. CAD/CAM systems.

13. Time/attendance stations.

14. Production monitoring equipment.

High-speed industrial communications networks, which can link a large variety of programmable controllers, computers, and terminal devices in harsh factory environments, are altering the roles for industrial control devices. These networks permit fast communication between the control devices and also allow them to share peripherals. This reduces the amount of hardware that must be dedicated to single applications and also cuts the cabling costs.

Computer networks may be organized in a number of ways. The computers are normally loosely coupled and capable of stand-alone operation.

The network configuration can be defined as master-slave, hierarchical, or peer-connected. The configuration determines how the control responsibilities are assigned among the processing units.

In the *master-slave* network configuration a host processor is connected to a satellite processor (Figure 9-8). The communication line between the processors is known as a *link*. The link can be any communications channel, such as a coaxial cable or telephone line. Each device in a network is often referred to as a *node*. A master-slave network with multiple slaves is also referred to as a *multipoint* or *multidrop* configuration.

In a master-slave network, a single processor has control and determines which slave computer will operate on a task. Communication between the slave computers is under control of the master. After it is assigned a task by

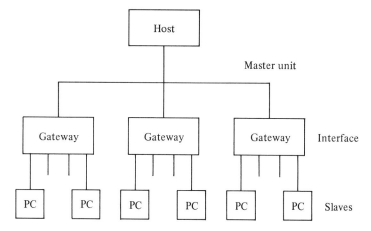

Figure 9-8   Distributed network in a master-slave configuration.

the master, the slave operates asynchronously with respect to the master until completion of the task, or until it requires service from the master. The master-slave configuration is used mainly to provide system load sharing.

A *hierarchical* network uses a multiple-level master-slave scheme. The various levels in the hierarchy are assigned responsibilities for certain functions (Figure 9-9). The highest level in the hierarchy makes the major decisions, and the lower levels have the responsibility for the control of specific operations.

In a *peer* or *peer-to-peer* system, any device can communicate with any other device, and no master or bus-arbitration device is required. This is in contrast to the master-slave and hierarchical networks, which use a top-down control philosophy. The peer network configuration uses mutually cooperating computers in which there are no defined masters or slaves. This type of configuration requires that the operating system of each computer is always aware of the status of the other computers in the network.

A scheduling program can be used to provide the task distribution. When a job is passed to a computer in the network, the originating computer moves on to a new task. A computer which is busy passes the task on to an available computer, which then executes the task. The time response in peer networks can be difficult to predict, since one computer does not know the workload of another and there is no master to impose tasks. Peer networks can provide access to specialized facilities not available on the originating computer, and the processors can share the computing load in a dynamic manner for a more efficient use of the process facility.

In addition to the control configuration, a number of physical connections may be used for a network. The *star* configuration has a host or master processor in the center of the system [Figure 9-10(a)], and each processor

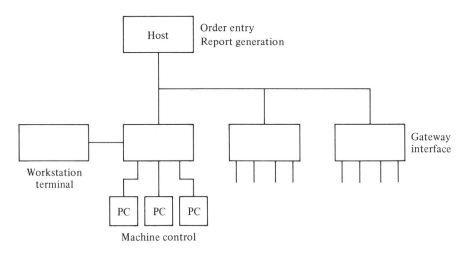

Figure 9-9 Typical network hierarchy.

communicates with the host. Communication between the satellite processors is through the host. This is also known as a *radial* or *centralized* configuration. This configuration is limited by the speed of the host. If more than one satellite is allowed to communicate to the host at the same time, then the host may be burdened with controlling the data flow between satellites.

The *multidrop* configuration [Figure 9-10(b)] is also known as a *data bus, data highway*, or *multipoint* configuration. Here, the host controls the flow of data between any two nodes. Any satellite can communicate with the host or any other satellite at any one time.

The *loop* configuration [Figure 9-10(c)] is normally used in remote multiplexing systems. Here, if a single link breaks, the nodes can still communicate. This is also known as a *ring* configuration. The loop can begin and end at a loop controller, which is a computer that controls the communications. Messages between computers in the loop are handled as a string of words, with some bits or words containing information on the originator and the addresses. When a computer recognizes a message addressed to it, it accepts the message.

As a processor receives and verifies a message, the starting and ending address of that message is passed to the destination processor. This processor then encodes and retransmits the message to the next point in the network. The supervisory processor or controller maintains network information and data-link assignments based on equipment conditions, message load, and the most direct route to the final destination. Loops can be difficult to control, and the way that the messages must pass through the computers requires higher data rates.

In the *point-to-point* network every processor has a direct access to every other processor [Figure 9-10(d)]. For n processors, $n(n-1)/2$ interconnections are required. For a three-processor system, three communication links are required. For five processors the number of links required is 10; for a 10-processor system the number of links becomes 45. This configuration allows a faster response or lower-grade communications lines. The alternate paths allow messages to be forwarded even if some of the links are broken.

In some systems, although they may be based on a complex algorithm, control is relatively simple, in that only two-state commands may need to be issued by the computer. In other cases the commands must be more complex, as in the case when a motor must be operated at varying speeds or a valve must be positioned at an arbitrary point between the full open and closed positions.

Complex commands are required for NC, where up to five or more servodrives must be positioned or moved in synchronism along prescribed paths. Among the simplest types of computer operation are those dealing with logging or reporting functions. Many computers in continuous processing are used for such tasks.

Advancements in microprocessor technology have made programmable

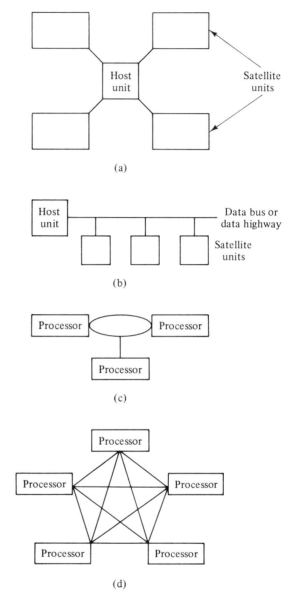

Figure 9-10 Network configurations: (a) star, (b) multidrop, (c) loop, (d) point-to-point.

controllers increasingly attractive for the control of both processes and discrete-parts manufacturing. A key in the growth and acceptance of the early memory-based programmable-logic controllers in replacing relay control systems was their simple ladder-diagram programming. This is still the dominant programming technique for PCs, but many offer English-language programming using functional blocks that are displayed on a CRT.

Many PCs have enough computing power to perform floating-point calculations or to compute trigonometric functions. These PCs can also manipulate relatively large blocks of data. The capability to do square roots and other transcendental functions allows PCs to solve many problems normally left to larger computers.

Programmable controllers were initially developed to replace panels of electromechanical relays. Then they evolved into stand-alone controllers, performing computerlike functions beyond the capability of relay panels. They are now becoming an integral part of factory automation, serving as links between machine tools, processes, and higher-order systems that control entire plants. The role of PCs will become even more important as their capacities and capabilities continue to expand.

Many newer micro-PCs can handle many of the sophisticated functions that even large PCs could not handle earlier. The large PCs can perform functions in process control that formerly required dedicated computers.

PCs are used by pharmaceutical companies to satisfy federal requirements. Each batch of drugs is tracked to ensure that the components of any one batch can be identified. The batch data can be drawn upon even after drugs are shipped. During a recall the batch and lot numbers can be used to track shipments.

Report generation is another aspect of the capabilities of PCs being exploited in factory automation. Many plants are also using PCs for motion control. Even though they may not completely supplant NC equipment, PCs can perform many tasks in motion control such as positioning parts for assembly.

Motor control is another function of PCs. Since PCs can be programmed to deliver specific numbers of pulses, they can easily drive stepper motors, and with the addition of I/O boards some PCs can drive servomotors.

The PC generates the initial command, and a separate processor on the I/O board handles the control function and performs the continuous position corrections.

PCs can also handle simple process equations and correct some process variables in real time. High-level PCs may also be capable of complex machine control. Some microprocessor-based PCs allow closed-loop point-to-point servopositioning. Here, the PC uses an interrupt scheme to divide the services of the microprocessor between a ladder logic scan and the motion-control servo. This allows the PC to service the servoloop frequently enough to provide the precise positioning needed.

The higher-level PCs are not suitable for contouring applications, but they are ideal for point-to-point use on production equipment like grinding machines and transfer devices, where precise positioning is required.

Positioning Control

The more powerful computational aspects of small digital controllers have been accompanied by problems in providing satisfactory dynamic control for inputs which are in the form of discrete signals. Recent trends in the development of distributed systems and the use of microcomputers as control elements has resulted in more freedom in positioning-control system design.

Modern controllers began as programs stored in a time-shared general-purpose medium-sized computer, then evolved to the use of minicomputers, then to special-purpose hard-wired logic, and currently to compact designs which incorporate microcomputers.

A certain amount of commonality can be found in the hardware configurations and computer programs used in the earlier designs. The basic dynamic characteristics of the power drives were usually modeled after a Type 1 servo: a double integration with velocity feedback and velocity and acceleration limiting. Many electrohydraulic power drives generally fall into this class, as do most electrical power drives.

The design approach usually was to make the model of the controlled variable appear to have the same form from the controller's point of view. This was done mainly through the selection of the velocity loop gains. The result was a controller that was applicable to a broad class of power drives. Early controller hardware used a variety of circuit elements. More recent designs are implemented using a microprocessor.

These microprocessor controllers primarily use four types of functional sections or modules:

1. Interface module.
2. Analog output module.
3. Status/text module.
4. Processor module.

The interface module allows many different types of systems to be controlled. These systems may have different characteristics, such as acceleration limits, and unique coefficients for difference equations and the solution of various polynomials may be required. The values of these coefficients are normally stored in ROMs. The signal-interfacing requirements of a particular system and computer are also handled by the interface module.

The analog output module may contain the buffer amplifiers and the D/A converters for the conversion of the digital commands from the controller into analog signals required for control. Each output of the D/A converters is available for connection to a separate summing amplifier, so that it can be summed with the output of the feedback device. Some D/A converters may be used for other functions, such as monitoring position and velocity errors.

The status-test module is used primarily to generate input commands for test purposes. A number of commands, such as steps, ramps, and sinusoids, can be generated. The coefficients for these functions are stored in ROMs.

The processor module provides arithmetic capability, temporary storage for calculations, and the mode select and timing and control functions. All the calculations are usually performed by this module. The use of micro-processors, with their significant space savings, has resulted in the reallocation of some functions which were previously performed in other modules.

In many distributed systems a major goal is to avoid commands from the master computer at an excessively high rate. High update rates can saturate the bus bandwidth. This generally limits the sample rate to about 20 to 30 samples per second.

At a low rate such as this it may be difficult to maintain smooth system operation. A conventional analog system driven at 20 samples per second through a digital-to-synchro converter can produce rough, uneven operation of power drives. This can lead to premature component failure. The usual approach to digital controls of this type is to use an interface that involves some form of data extrapolation for the digital conversion. We can then modify these discrete low-sample-rate commands and send them to the analog loop in the form of a quasi-continuous signal. If the control loop is closed digitally and the digital error signal is used, a sample rate of 20 samples per second can result in acceptable performance with position feedback data from a shaft encoder or similar device.

Stepping and servo motors are used in most applications which require precise motion to reach a digitally defined position. One approach involves an acceleration to the operating speed and then a deceleration to find the programmed position.

Some positioning systems use digital interpolation techniques to generate command pulses for a linear velocity ramp to minimize travel time to the desired position. With this approach the last motion pulse and zero velocity can occur simultaneously. The commands are supplied to a stepper or servo motor in a closed-loop system to reduce the lag between the command and actual positions in order to provide faster positioning.

Another method of controlling position is to use an exponential velocity change for the acceleration and deceleration. A closed-loop system with velocity and position feedback produces the exponential output velocity change from a velocity step-input command. In a stepping motor control this can be achieved with a voltage-controlled oscillator which is coupled to a pulse generator to produce either an exponential rising or falling voltage for the acceleration or deceleration. In a servomotor system, feedback with an exponential characteristic produces a lag between the commanded and actual positions. This lag provides a deceleration to avoid overshooting the commanded position.

In an open-loop system aging and temperature effects in the analog circuits can cause variations in the speed and the exponential time-constant. If the deceleration is started at a fixed distance from the final position, the part being positioned may stop short of the destination or arrive at too high a speed and overshoot the position. Some control schemes force a lower final speed due to creeping to the commanded position, but this consumes excessive time.

Another approach for stepping motor control is to input a linear voltage ramp to the oscillator producing the command pulses. The positioning time is reduced compared to the exponential method, but creeping is still required. This type of system uses the following components: A constant-frequency pulse generator provides an output frequency proportional to the desired velocity. Each pulse represents one increment of motion. An acceleration data store is used to contain a digital number which defines the desired acceleration. The store technique could be ROM thumb-wheel switches or hard-wired registers. Storage is also required for the digital number which represents the distance of motion required. An acceleration pulse generator is used to generate pulses which represent the commanded position increments. The frequency of the pulses increases linearly for an acceleration signal and decreases linearly for a deceleration signal. Finally, a microprocessor system monitors the generated command pulses, determines the acceleration and deceleration phases, and decides when the programmed distance is reached.

Process-Control System Configuration

To accommodate the input or sensor voltage in the process-control system some form of scaling and offsetting may need to be performed by an amplifier. One must also convert the analog information, and, if it is from more than one source, additional converters or a multiplexer will be necessary. To increase the speed at which the information may be accurately converted, a sample-hold may be used, and to compress analog signal information a logarithmic amplifier can be required.

The systems design begins with the choice of sensor. The proper selection of the transducer can go a long way toward easing the system-design task. In the monitoring or controlling of motor shafts, one may have the choice of signals from three different position-sensing approaches:

1. Shaft encoders.
2. Synchros.

3. Potentiometers.

Temperature measurements might be accomplished by thermocouples or thermistors, while force could be measured by strain gauges or obtained by integrating the output from accelerometers. If the transducer signals must be scaled from millivolt levels to an A/D converter's typical ± 10-volt full-scale input, an operational amplifier can be required.

When the system involves a number of sources, each transducer can be provided with a local amplifier, so that the low-level signals are amplified before being transferred. If the analog data is to be transmitted over any distance, the differences in ground potentials between the signal source and the final location can add additional errors to the system.

Low-level signals can be obscured by noise, rfi, ground loops, power-line pickup, and transients coupled into signal lines from machinery. Separating the signals from these effects can become a critical matter.

Most systems can be separated into two basic categories: those suited to favorable environments like laboratories and those required in more hostile environments such as factories, vehicles, and military installations. This latter group includes industrial process-control systems where temperature information may be developed by sensors on tanks, boilers, vats, or pipelines that may be spread over miles of facilities. The data might be sent to a central processor to provide real-time process control. The digital control of steel and petrochemical production, and machine-tool manufacturing, are characterized by this environment. The vulnerability of the data signals here leads to the requirements for isolation and other data-retention techniques. Systems in hostile environments might require components for wide temperature, shielding, common-mode noise reduction, data conversion at an early stage, and redundant circuits for critical measurements.

In a laboratory type of environment application, gas chromatographs, mass spectrometers, and other sophisticated instruments may be used. Here we are more concerned with the performance-sensitive measurements under favorable conditions than with protecting the integrity of the collected data.

Multiplex Configuration

In remote multiplexing, the remote multiplexer units are located throughout the system, and the analog and digital signals are sent to the nearest remote multiplexer. A/D converters in the remote multiplexer convert signals to digital words, which are usually 16 bits long. A control unit signals the remote multiplexer and requests the unit to send a particular block of words or a group of blocks. The remote multiplexer responds by sending the data requested to the control unit. The control unit will scan the data to check that the transmission is complete. After the data is checked, it may be sent to the central computer or displayed.

The installed cost of wiring has been increasing, while at the same time the installed cost of digital systems has been decreasing. The use of remote multiplexing has increased, since it can reduce a large amount of the wiring necessary in a process installation.

Remote multiplexing can also be employed in systems where there is no central computer. A reduction in wiring is still achieved.

In some systems only analog signals are remote multiplexed. Here a less complex multiplexer, which sends analog data, can be used.

Remote multiplexing has been used mainly for process monitoring rather than process control. However, the reliability of remote multiplexing is high enough now so that it can be used for control signals as well. A control system with a remote multiplexing configuration is sometimes called a *total multiplexing system*. This type of system thus allows both analog and digital signals to flow either to or from the computer and the remote multiplexers.

In a flow-control system a flow transmitter can provide the analog signals to the remote multiplexer. The remote multiplexer then converts the analog signals, which are typically currents of 4–20 milliamps, to digital words using an analog-to-digital converter and transmits them back to the computer. A control unit might convert the digital data back to a 4- to 20-milliamp analog signal for use in an analog instrument, such as a flow controller.

Most remote multiplexing equipment transmits data at a rate which allows the update of each analog value at least once every second. In many petrochemical applications, process values which are updated each second act for the most part as continuous signals.

Although the use of electronic instrumentation predominates in most industries, some systems will employ pneumatic instrumentation, especially those which are involved with hazardous materials. Since many of these pneumatic systems must use computers, an interfacing method is required. There are two basic techniques for interfacing the pneumatic instruments to the computer. One technique is to use P/I (pneumatic-to-current) and I/P (current-to-pneumatic) converters. In this type of system the output of the converters is continuous. In the other method a pneumatic multiplexer/ converter is used in either a host or remote multiplexing configuration.

A typical pneumatic multiplexer will handle six pressure inputs per second. Each input of 3 to 15 psi is converted into an analog dc voltage. The computer controls the pneumatic multiplexer as it steps from one input to the next. Another approach is to use a separate control device which accepts the analog signal from the pneumatic multiplexer and controls the stepping. This reduces the software required in the computer. The cost of a single pneumatic multiplexer is less than the cost of individual P/I converters.

ROBOTIC SYSTEMS

Future NC systems will perform functions far beyond the blind execution of machine-control instructions. The next generation of controls is expected to sense and adapt to varying cutting conditions without the intervention of a human operator. Such adaptive control systems may automatically detect and replace damaged cutting tools, or the system might compensate for temperature variations and excessive workpiece vibrations. This level of machine intelligence and independent decision-making capability is planned for extensive use in future automated factories.

Automated manipulator arms or industrial robots can be used to perform a variety of material-handling functions in CAM systems. Robots can select and position tools and workpieces for NC machine tools. Or they can use their hands, which are called *end effectors*, to position and operate tools such as drills and welders.

The instructions for controlling the joints of a typical robot are automatically calculated by a computer to produce straight-line motion. As shown in Figure 9-11, the workpiece orientation is changed through the action of the robot's joints.

Most robots have multiple joints which are manipulated to produce the required robotic motions. Determining each separate joint motion can be a difficult task. Most advanced robot systems use automatic programming to determine the joint command for straight lines and arcs from specified endpoints. Typically the user enters the endpoints on a hand-held pushbutton unit.

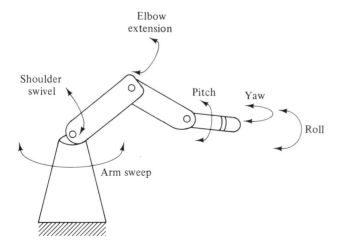

Figure 9-11   Robotic operation.

Robots usually repeat sequences of programmed movements rapidly and with good precision. They are well suited to repetitive tasks such as welding and spray painting in the production of automobiles, appliances, and other high-volume items. This type of consistent performance in mass-production operations increases productivity, and a robot can pay for itself in less than two years.

In a typical automatic system, a vertical-spindle, numerical-control machining center might be adopted to computer control. A set of sensors on the center is used to measure factors such as speed, temperature, and tool position. These feed a small computer system with up to 16 simultaneous channels of information, which is analyzed by fast Fourier transforms to do online dynamic analysis of the machine's performance.

The computer may also use a memory map for the machine's systematic errors, such as errors in the positioning of the tool or table. It then automatically corrects these as the machine operates.

Robot sensor and control systems can put cheap, intelligent robots at the disposal of the machine shop. The more intelligent robots are fitted with innovative vision and control systems. A network of microcomputers in a hierarchical system for high-speed sensory interactions with the environment may control the robot. This type of parallel-processing structure in the control system and real-time decision-processing software with the sensor system allow the sensory data to be introduced at high speed. The robot can then sense changes in its environment, such as sudden shifts in the position of a part, and react to them in an orderly fashion in order to accomplish the desired task.

To be a practical tool in the machine-shop environment an industrial robot must meet some demanding criteria. The control system must interact in near real time with a sensory system capable of assessing the robot's environment, and act on this information in a goal-directed manner. The machine must be able to respond to changes in its tasks and surroundings by adjusting for parts or tools slightly out of position. The control system should be friendly and programmed with a simple, Englishlike command language. This makes it easy to program the robot quickly.

The earliest way to program robots was by manual teaching. In this approach, the user leads the robot through the required motions, which are then recorded in the robot's memory. Typically, only the endpoints of motions are recorded for the part-transfer operations and other point-to-point applications where the motion path and velocity are unimportant. For other applications, such as arc welding and spray painting, the entire path of the robot arm may be recorded.

This type of *teach programming* requires little training and typically can be performed by shop personnel. The cost of teach-mode robots and the associated maintenance required is generally less than that of the more sophisticated robots.

Teach programming has some disadvantages that can cause problems in some applications. Manual teaching is too time-consuming and error-prone for most complex processes. Production facilities usually must be tied up during the programming, and modifying some of the steps in the program to accommodate design changes or new tooling can require the entire program to be retaught.

Many of these disadvantages are overcome with offline programming. In this approach the user described sequences of movements and operations through a computer instead of the robot hardware. Robotic languages allow the user to specify these sequences using a terminal.

Offline programming tends to define and document the robot instructions better than manual teaching. A number of software aids are available with many of the languages to make programming faster and more accurate. Subroutines describing the more frequently repeated steps can be connected together to build a complex program. Programs can be easily modified at the keyboard, using editing routines and symbolic data references. With the programming done offline, production is not held up, and offline programming provides for more flexible use of the sensor data as well as adaptive control.

The offline programming languages can be classified as either explicit or implicit. The *explicit* types include VAL, Emily, Sigla, and Wave. They permit detailed control over the manipulator actions using direct commands such as OPEN, MOVE, and PICK. The *implicit* languages include AL, Robot APT, Autopass, Rapt, and MAL. In these the user describes the tasks to be performed rather than the detailed robot motions.

Using these languages, the programmer enters general task commands such as

PLACE INTERLOCK ON BRACKET SUCH THAT INTERLOCK HOLE IS ALIGNED WITH BRACKET HOLE.

The program then selects the grip points, approach paths, and the motion needed to assemble the parts. For the most part, the control should be as independent of specific databases as possible, since this minimizes the reprogramming necessary to change jobs. It should also be easy to extend the programming language to new commands, since it is likely that new capabilities and sensors will be needed in the future.

A typical approach is to use two parallel hierarchies. One level accepts commands from a higher level, decomposes the commands to simpler subcommands, and then sends them to the next lower level in the hierarchy.

Another approach is based on sensory feedback in which each step in the hierarchy reduces the sensory input data to a form usable in the corresponding step in the control hierarchy. To shorten the response time, decisions are made at the lowest possible level in the hierarchy. In a five-level hierarchy:

1. The lowest level computes the functions for the individual servos in the robot.

2. The second level transforms the coordinates describing the present and desired position of the robot into the coordinates of the robot joint.

3. The third level receives the simple task commands and translates them into the motion commands.

4. The fourth level receives complex task commands and breaks these down into simple task commands.

5. The highest level accepts commands from the programming language and breaks those down into elemental movements.

At each level, the control system can be programmed to act as a state-machine. This means that each level in the hierarchy divides time up into a series of discrete intervals. For each interval it inputs a command such as

MOVE TO A DESIRED LOCATION

based on the sensor data of the robot's present location.

It requires a comparatively simple algorithm to compute where the robot should move in the next interval. The robot must move from one satisfactory state to another satisfactory state. In this system, changes in the task are accommodated at each level of the hierarchy. The system treats the task as a new development during each interval, and it computes the motion of the robot only as far as the next interval. If the intervals are kept short, less than 30 milliseconds, then the feedback data is accepted and acted on as in real time. The system can then become goal-directed.

Such a control system can solve several robotic system problems. The highest-level language can be friendly, and changes to the system, such as the addition of high-level commands or extra sensor systems, need to be made only at the appropriate level in the hierarchy. Only the lowest two levels tend to be machine-specific, so the system is not completely dependent on a particular robot.

This type of hierarchical control technique allows the use of powerful microprocessors that offer increased computing capacity at lower cost.

A robot system can be built with the implementation of the hierarchical control system using a series of individual microprocessors. Here, the various modules in the hierarchy are assigned to separate the microprocessors.

The microprocessors can communicate with each other using a common memory in which the inputs and outputs for each level are defined. This control-system organization can be expanded to include:

1. Robots serving machine tools.

2. A group of cells.

3. The control of an automated factory.

Robots that see must have a flexible, adaptive control system with a well-designed sensor input system. If the machine is to locate parts and tools, it must be able to sense the position and orientation of parts in space.

In a typical vision system the robot uses a light source to flash a plane of light parallel to its arm's axis. The light plane illuminates any object which is the robot's field of vision with a line of light across the object.

The shape and orientation of the object produce identifiable changes in the shape of the line. A cubical shape seen edgewise produces a V shape, and a cylinder produces a curve, as shown in Figure 9-12. A box seen from a face produces a horizontal line. The shape of the line is registered, and the location of the line in the sensor's field of view can be found by triangulation to compute the distance to the object. Reducing the object image to a set of line segments reduces the computational problem; thus the system's reaction time is improved and system cost is reduced.

3D viewing systems are used with robots to carry out welding operations. Sensors are used on either side of the welding hand. A window emits a laser beam which bounces off the work area and reflects into the receiver. The control system evaluates the return beam to determine the weld seam position. Using a look-and-work scheme, the vision system is first moved along the weld seam where it records the exact position of the welds. Then, the welding head operates on the second pass. Using the data from the scanning pass, the weld is accurately completed.

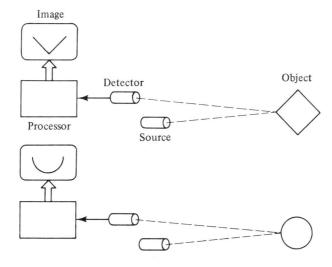

Figure 9-12   Vision sensing.

Giving robots a sensing capability requires a dual effort in developing the sensor hardware and the software needed to translate the sensor output. Vision was the first sense made available in robots, and efforts have concentrated on the following areas:

1. Reducing costs, since vision systems tend to be high-cost.
2. Simplifying lighting, since some systems require special lighting which is not practical in all industrial situations.
3. Increasing the decision speed, since many vision systems generate large amounts of data that take time to reduce.

The more complex the task the robot takes on, the more human-like abilities are required. Initially, robots had success doing simple tasks in ordered environments, such as moving parts from a machine to a bin. The part was always the same size and in a fixed location, and the machine and the bin never changed locations.

Many applications now and in the future require the robot to handle unknown quantities. It must seek and identify several parts or pick a desired part from a number of different parts.

The hands (or end effectors) have always been an essential element of a robot. Early hands were designed for a specific grip force or used a pressure switch to indicate the presence or absence of an object.

More modern hand sensors use feedback loops that allow the handling of delicate parts. There may also be force-pad grids to help identify the shape and texture of an object.

Another possible sense is hearing. Computerized voice recognition is an established technology that has been applied in some robot designs. The robots distinguish and obey a fixed set of vocal commands. As robots become involved in more complex chores or operations in poisonous environments, these and other senses may be required. For robots to become acceptable for more complex tasks, their operating characteristics must be improved. Speed, accuracy, and repeatability can all be increased with better software.

Mechanical changes in the robot design can offer some improvement. Lighter metals in the robot arm can allow greater speed, but this advantage may result in a penalty in rigidity or cost.

Speed can also be increased by reducing the time interval that the robot needs to sense, evaluate, and decide the action to take. The more complex the task is, the slower the robot speed becomes.

Robots must get smarter to do the complex jobs industry expects of them. The robots of the future will include machines with true intelligence. These machines will have the ability to extract information from the environment through sensing techniques and process that information. The machine must then plan a set of actions based on the machine's goal. This differs from technology in which most of the required information is in the machine in advance. The robot's memory will have instructions to cover several possible actions.

The robot's programmer and not the robot is responsible for anticipating the possible events. The workplace must also be designed so that unanticipated events are unlikely to occur.

Future work will be aimed at reducing the need for intelligence in advance to eliminate the problem of unanticipated events from the workplace. Robots must be able to cope with events such as misaligned parts and changes in ambient lighting.

Most industrial robots generally have difficulty operating in the less structured environments of general industry. They cannot readily be taught new tasks, nor can they operate with variable conditions such as parts in random orientations. These robots are considered first-generation machines.

Most efforts to make the robot control system more complex also have the goal of making the robot more simple for the user to operate. This user friendliness is important when a robot is first taught what to do.

Most robots require some degree of interaction with a human to learn a program. The robot may be moved through the program, as is done with most painting robots. The robot may be electrically led through a task by an operator using a control box.

More complex robot systems use offline programming where the programmer creates a program at a console and sends the data to the robot control. In many cases the robot is given a general program, which is then refined on the shop floor.

In the ideal case, the robot is sent general commands; then, using its sensory powers, the robot refines the commands to carry out the task.

Each robot manufacturer has tended to develop its own language to instruct the robot controllers, and it is difficult for robots of different manufacturers to talk to each other. An interface which translates languages must generally be used.

A single programming language for robots and advanced NC machine tools would simplify and speed the development of more complex automated assembly systems. It would also eliminate the need for translators between machines.

The total automated factory will need many different robots. Automated production cells are a step toward total automation. A typical flexible automated production cell consists of a computer-controlled, six-axis industrial robot and two NC turning centers. In this type of system the robot can automatically perform the following operations:

1. Select randomly sized, randomly delivered parts from a stop-station conveyor.

2. Load parts into turning centers.

3. Remove finished parts from the machine.

4. Present finished parts to a laser gauging station.

5. Relay part variations to the machine control for automatic tool compensation.

6. Deliver finished parts to a stacking station.

The accuracy for some robots is in hundredths of an inch for noncritical motions and thousandths of an inch for assembly and machining operations. For most machining operations, accuracies in excess of 0.005 inches are needed.

The mechanics of the robot configuration typically involve an arm extending from a pedestal. This limits payloads to about 10% of the robot's weight. The payload capacity is determined largely by the type of actuation system used, which includes pneumatic, hydraulic, and electrical systems. Pneumatic actuators tend to be lowest in cost. They have an arm with some spring and tend to be used for light loads. Hydraulic actuators can move loads in excess of one ton. They are simple to build and fast in operation. Electric motors are the most accurate and are built for middleweight loads. Increases in payload generated by an actuation system that is strengthened generally experience a corresponding decrease in speed due to the greater mass.

Planning is important if the user is to make full use of the robot's potential. Everything from the simple considerations such as the robot's reach to advanced production plans should be examined. A robot may perform only a simple material-handling task initially; then it may become part of a complex assembly task later. To minimize the costs, the placement of the robot as well as the other production and support equipment should be evaluated. To simplify this procedure, one can use a software package to display a 3D model of the equipment and simulate a variety of work-cell configurations. Using this package, one can compare the efficiency of various system arrangements.

One can use a simple payback formula to determine how much time will be needed to pay for a robot in a specific application:

$$\text{payback} = \frac{C}{W} + I + D - (M + S)$$

where

C = robot station cost, including the robot plus all related equipment, such as sensors

W = yearly salary of worker(s) replaced, including fringe benefits

I = savings because of robot installation (increased productivity and improved product quality)

D = annual robot depreciation rate

M = robot maintenance costs (parts and labor)
S = annual robot staffing costs for operation and maintenance

Other cost savings can include:

1. Reduced energy costs.
2. Less need for safety equipment.
3. Lower supervisory and administrative costs.

Robotics research will result in new robots that are adaptable enough to operate effectively in many general manufacturing applications. Rather than performing as blind slaves, these future robots may serve as active thinking partners in the manufacturing process.

The advanced robots are expected to be critical elements in many integrated CAD/CAM systems. Computer-controlled robots will be teamed with numerically controlled machine tools. These teams may form automated manufacturing centers for building complex products, such as aircraft, from start to finished product. Mating a smart machine tool with a smart robot, however, is far from accomplishing the goal of complete automation. Integration is necessary between the various workstations of the robot-machine tool pairs and the other systems, such as computer-aided design and computer-aided planning, and the support systems, such as safety, material and tool distribution, and scheduling.

The large amount of processing and memory capacity required to manage such an operation would normally require a separate host computer. However, future computers can be expected to be miniaturized to the point where intelligence could be self-contained in the robot.

PROCESS PLANNING

Process planning is the area of CAM technology that determines the sequence of production steps required to make a part (Figure 9-13). The goal is to develop a procedure for making the part as quickly and inexpensively as possible. The process planner must take into account both the state of the workpiece at each workstation and the physical routing of the part along the shop floor. Process planning is an established element of manufacturing, but only recently has the computer been used to develop optimal workflows.

Numerical control is concerned with controlling the operation of a single machine, but process planning considers the sequence of production steps needed to make a part from start to finish, generally using successive operations on several machines. The planning describes the routine of the workpiece through the shop floor and its state at each workstation.

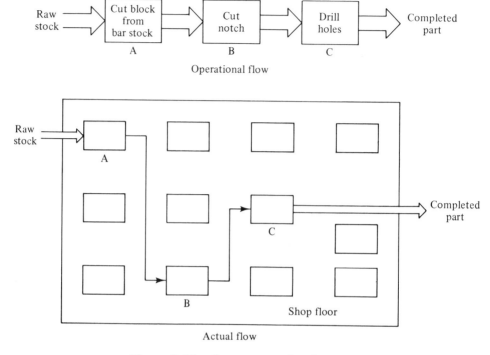

Figure 9-13 Computer-assisted planning.

Flow diagrams and other information such as part specifications, tooling requirements, and machining conditions can be used to develop a production sequence for fabricating the part in the fastest, most economical manner.

Process planning has always been a part of manufacturing, but the computer now is an important part of this activity—largely because of the increase in low-volume manufacturing operations. Many industrial parts are now made in small lots of less than 50 pieces. In contrast to the more rigid operations of mass-production industries, these batch-type shops must change part-routing and machine operations frequently.

In batch-type metalworking shops 95% of the total production time is spent moving workpieces and waiting, 3.5% is spent in secondary operations such as set-up and loading, and only 1.5% is expended in actual metal cutting. Computer-assisted process planning is the desired approach for increasing this productivity.

An important part of process planning is a concept called *group technology*. This is a manufacturing philosophy that takes advantage of the similarities among parts and processes. Instead of treating each part as unique, group technology organizes the parts into families according to either similar shape or common manufacturing operations.

The parts are identified in group technology using alpha-numeric codes to note characteristics as size, shape, material, tolerances, and manufacturing processes. A variety of group-technology coding systems can be used.

In a *monocoded* system, also called a *hierarchical code*, each successive digit identifies increasingly specific subcategories using a hierarchical tree arrangement. A large amount of information can be coded into a short number in this way, but sequentially decoding the digits to determine the part information is time-consuming.

Polycodes, also called *attribute codes*, assign each digit a piece of information, and each digit is independent of the others. Searching these codes is relatively easy.

Mixed coding systems combine these two techniques. Here, a part code is composed of groups of monocodes within a polycode.

Process-planning systems use a retrieval technique based on part families and standard types of tooling and fabrication. Automated process-planning systems group parts in families based on common fabrication methods. Standard plans, which are stored in computer memory, contain the sequential operational codes for fabricating each part family. The process plan for a new part is developed by editing this standard plan. The specific operations required to make the part are selected while the rest are deleted.

This retrieval type of process-planning system uses the computer memory and the operational sequences to replace the human memory. The user provides the missing data.

Industry is entering an era where mass production via hard automation will become less important and where manufacturing systems will be valued for how easily they adapt to a variety of different parts being handled on the same line. The technology for building these types of flexible manufacturing systems is available, but the systems are complicated to design and build. Emphasis must be placed on the technology of modeling these systems by computer.

One aspect of the modeling and simulation of a flexible manufacturing system is that rarely is there only one best design. The class of problems encountered in modeling is complex, and there is no one mathematical method to prove that the solution is an optimum.

Most commercial programs use a heuristic approach to problem solving. Optimal solutions are obtained by incremental improvements in the original models. The general goal involves minimizing costs while maximizing the rate of production. The cost is comprised of factors that include:

1. Direct and indirect labor.
2. Equipment selection.
3. Scheduling.
4. Transportation systems.

    5. Tooling.

The level of detail in the solution depends on the detail of the inputs. A model can give estimates of production to within a few percent. Models can also show the effects of changing the cycle time of a robot by tenths of a second.

The modeling technology can be classified into four categories:

1. The first category is verbal and is used for explaining general system requirements. This type of model is oriented toward people rather than machines.

2. The second type is a design model to answer questions regarding such matters as which machine tools best suit production needs. Models of this type are used for the preliminary selection of tooling.

3. The third and most complex model estimates the actual performance and provides online predictions for the system.

4. The fourth model is used for forecasting the effects of changes in the completed system.

These last two types of models play the greatest role in system selection. The math models of these systems are based on several assumptions. The individual machine-tool performance is used as an input, not an output. Known quantities include the removal times for metal and the cycle times for robots and tooling changes. The models use a black-box approach, and the simulations are based on queuing theory, transportation algorithms, and other math models. The output of these simulations is the total system production. Additional outputs can include queue lengths, percentage utilization of a particular machine, or time lost to tool breakage.

Rules for deciding which part to machine first or which part to pick up next are called *precedence rules* and are vital in system design. Most production problems are similar to the classical types that involve traffic flow, materials flow, or the shortest path between a number of points. In this type of problem the goal might be to visit 48 locations and take the shortest possible path. The number of possible paths in this problem is 47! or 2.5862×10^{59}. Many systems can be more complex than this example. Computational methods cannot evaluate all possible paths in a reasonable time. Instead of having a fast computer do an ordered search, an alternative might be using a better selection algorithm. Although checking each path is not an efficient technique, even a better search technique does not result in a significant reduction in the search time. For the above problem, an algorithm that eliminates 99.99999% of all solutions still leaves over 2.5×10^{52} paths to check.

Mathematical equations have been defined to analyze factory assembly systems. The equations can be interpreted piecemeal to gain an insight into what the symbols mean. Each modeling system has its own symbols, but most are similar.

In the example we will examine, the first equation describes the objective. This equation can be solved to find the minimum of the fixed and variable costs for a specific output. Constraints are then imposed to allow the equations to represent a real situation. Additional constraints on the variables ensure that the integer requirement is met. In these equations,

M = the number of candidate resources
N = the number of tasks
$f_i y_i$ = fixed costs
c_{ijk} = the cost of doing task j on resource i when k is the next step
x_{ijk} = location where the task is to be performed

The subscripts denote such factors as the tool-changing times and precedence. First, we minimize the sum of the fixed and variable costs:

$$\min \sum_{i=1}^{M} \left(f_i y_i + \sum_{j=0}^{N} \sum_{k=j+1}^{N+1} c_{ijk} x_{ijk} \right)$$

A constraint is then imposed to allocate one task to a specific workstation, ensuring that a task is not split between two machines:

$$\sum_{i=1}^{N} \sum_{k=j+1}^{N+1} x_{ijk} = 1, \qquad j = 1, 2, 3, 4, \ldots$$

Another constraint then checks allocations of time at each workstation to ensure that a station is not used more than 100% of the time:

$$\sum_{j=0}^{N} \sum_{k=j+1}^{N+1} t_{ijk} x_{ijk} \leq b_i, \qquad i = 1, 2, 3, 4, \ldots$$

The following group of three equations ensures the continuity of flow and establishes precedence in the order in which the tasks are performed. The continuity of flow prevents the creation or deletion of parts in the model.

$$\sum_{k=j+1}^{N} x_{ijk} - \sum_{l=0}^{j-1} x_{ilj} = 0, \qquad \begin{cases} i = 1, 2, 3, 4, \ldots \\ \\ j = 1, 2, 3, 4, \ldots \end{cases}$$

$$\sum_{k=1}^{N+1} x_{ik} - y_i = 0 \qquad i = 1, 2, 3, 4, \ldots$$

$$\sum_{j=0}^{N} x_{ij, N+1} - y_i = 0, \qquad i = 1, 2, 3, 4, \ldots$$

Then two last constraints determine if a piece of equipment is to be used in a given system. If the value is 0, the station will not be included in the system.

$$x_{ijk}\{0, 1\}, \qquad i = 1, 2, 3, 4, \ldots, \quad 0 \le j < k \le N + 1$$
$$y_i\{0, 1\}, \qquad i = 1, 2, 3, 4, \ldots$$

The change of a precedence rule can affect the final production rate by several percentage points. This effect may be either positive or negative.

In a complex system, more than one strategy can be followed. But many strategies makes the problem formulation more complex. The strategies listed below are typical.

Each strategy may be identified by a mnemonic, using the initial letters of the precedence rule.

1. Each machine uses its optimal loading strategy. This is among the most complex methods.

2. The operations are ordered with the shortest processing time going first.

3. The part with the longest processing time is first.

4. The part with the fewest operations remaining is first.

5. The part with the most operations remaining is first.

6. The part with the shortest remaining processing time is first.

7. The part with the longest remaining processing time is first.

8. The part with the smallest value of operation time times the total processing time for that job is first.

9. The part with the shortest processing time of operation divided by the total processing time for that job is first.

10. The part with the longest processing time of operation times the total processing time for that job is first.

A factory system may not be operating at its peak when all machines are working at 100% of rated capacity. Consider an engineer working on a project. A fourth of the time may be spent on research, a fourth on simulation, another fourth on building a model, and another fourth on writing a report. If the engineer is a better experimenter than writer, the allocation can be changed to allow more time in experimenting. As a consequence of performing the task which is done most effectively, the report completion date could be missed. In this job of report generation, the goal is not efficiency in any one task but in efficient adjusting of the workload to meet the completion date. Thus, a factory system will frequently run at only 80% of rated capacity. The 20% slack time is used to cover delivery lags, breakdowns, tool breakage, and other variables.

In some operations, a piece of machinery may run at only 30% of its rated capacity. Yet, if only a few parts are to be run through this machine, this rate can represent the most effective use of the equipment.

The system shown in Figure 9-14 can be modeled simply if the three 8-spindle vertical lathes are worked at the same rate, if the conveyor is properly synchronized, and if the parts are placed in a strict order on the conveyor.

The robot could go from station to station picking up the parts in order. This situation is ideal, but parts do not have identical machining times, tools break, and parts may be placed at random on the conveyor. Thus, an optimal scheduling strategy cannot be easily done by hand. This system can be modeled with a software program to study the effects of various strategies and breakdown rates.

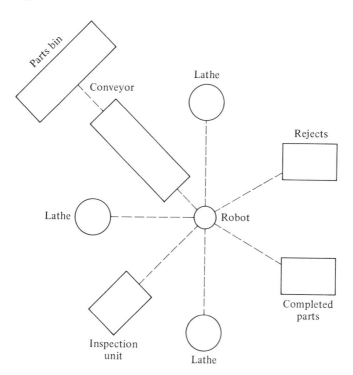

Figure 9-14   Three-lathe system.

Additional difficulties in solving these problems are that they are nonlinear and noninteger. These two constraints present some problems, since equipment can be purchased in only integer quantities. The integer restriction may also hold in the scheduling of both labor and transportation. The integer restriction is often ignored to obtain more answers from a larger solution set. This is known as *relaxation*.

A smaller analytical model requires less data than most simulation programs. These models can be used for modeling long-term trends. This type of model is also a good tool for initial estimates of system performance. The results of a simple model can come to within 3% to 5% of the more complex models. The inputs are:

1. Station names, such as drilling or inspection.
2. Number of stations of each type.
3. Processing data, such as the time spent at each station.

The processing data can be as detailed as needed, with different cycle times for each operation. This type of model is simple in that it ignores materials handling and does not require a layout.

The model can yield results of production rate by part type, machine utilization in percent, queue lengths, and throughput rates. A sensitivity analysis can be used to determine the effects of small changes in the input data. This is critical in finding bottlenecks before the production starts. Some small models can be run on personal computers.

Simulation languages take a different approach to systems modeling. Most general-purpose modeling languages are not complete enough for factory systems, since they do not have provisions for transportation systems.

Factory-management languages incorporate features for simulating robotics, conveyors, monorails, and the other materials-handling features which are found in factories.

There are also complete modeling packages which are menu-driven. The inputs are similar to those of other packages and include the number of operators, the number of machines, cycle times, and transportation methods. The outputs include identification of work in process, parts throughput, bottlenecks, and transportation utilization.

These packages are intended to be front ends for design, since they are planning tools to aid in selecting equipment or in predicting the effects of breakdowns. The complexity and scope can be so great that, even with a simulation, a lot must go into system design.

Systems tend to be sensitive to a number of factors. One of the more subtle of these is the number of pallets in a system. With too few pallets, machines can sit idle. Too many can cause congestion, and machines sit idle, waiting for materials to come or go. The pallets can even go by empty. All of these effects can be determined through simulation.

A large system like an aircraft can have over a million parts. With this many components, there is a high probability that some components will fail (see Appendix A). The model can be used to determine which parts are most likely to fail. Preventive-maintenance schedules can be developed based on this data. In a system with a number of similar parts the statistical failure data may not point to exactly which parts are likely to fail, but it will tell where backup is needed.

When the simulations and planning are complete, a large system may require two to three years to implement. Some of this time is spent in a learning curve, while the rest is required for working out the problems that occur in any large system. The model can also be used during set-up, checking the actual with the expected performance. The model can still be used after the system is running. Changing market conditions may require a change in the product mix. This change can shift the production to parts that may require more machine time. The model can then be used to solve for the sequence of events which generate the highest output.

The model must always include engineering judgments. In the choice of a milling machine, horsepower is a major cost consideration. But if a machine makes only one cut that needs 50 horsepower, then perhaps a 30-horsepower station can be substituted if the less powerful station can make two cuts. These decisions cannot always be modeled so easily, but they can have a great effect on the cost of a system.

Future computer-assisted process-planning systems will have the increased capability to provide more data on fabricating parts and will aid in this decision making.

Ultimately, the computer may generate its own processing plans. In these generative systems the processing plans may be produced directly from the geometric database with little human assistance. In such a system, the planner would review the input from design engineering and then enter this input into the CAM system, which would generate the complete plans automatically.

FACTORY MANAGEMENT

The factory-management area of CAM ties together the coordinate operations of an entire factory, from master scheduling to shipping. Computers perform the various manufacturing management tasks, such as inventory control and production scheduling, in systems that have evolved for *material resources or requirements planning* (*MRP*). These systems determine the batch quantities, release and due dates, and the allocation of finished parts.

Some systems also perform tasks such as processing bills of materials. MRP originally covered only material resources planning, but as more factory processes have become integrated, the initial concept has expanded. This expanded concept, called MRP II, is now used for manufacturing-requirements planning.

The concept now encompasses all phases of plant operation, from scheduling labor and parts assembly to complete order entry and tracking systems, and even includes hourly manpower charges for engineers and manufacturing groups. One result is that the concerns of design engineers, manufacturing engineers, and even accountants have become more closely tied together.

A primary role of an engineer in MRP is the initiation of a bill of materials. This document contains not only the manufacturing data but also scheduling and cost information for the accounting function.

A major change with MRP is an increasing interdependency of job functions. Although there may still be separate manufacturing and design departments, the two groups will work more closely to produce a product at a lower cost and with no defects.

On another level, MRP may be considered as a mathematical model to be optimized. The design and manufacturing functions can be described as an entire plant or a process which can be modeled with computer simulations prior to actual production. The role of the accounting function is to select the optimal combination of labor, machinery, and materials.

The simulation can also be used to spot manufacturing bottlenecks. In this operation accounting can be used to track the time charges.

Many start-up firms use MRP systems. The reason is that, although the plants tend to be small, the managers almost always come from larger firms that used MRP systems. Once managers are accustomed to MRP control, they find it is difficult to do without such systems, especially for short start-up runs.

The role of MRP is expected to grow larger, and the adoption of MRP systems more critical, as product design cycles become shorter. As product lifetimes are reduced, more efficient methods of production are necessary, and MRP can produce these methods.

Some systems have been installed successfully in three months, and there are other systems that are still not running after years, because of inadequate support. There are always problems when changes that are needed are not made. Suppose there is a part coming off the line with some extra flash. If all workers use a file on this flash, then there are no problems. But if a new worker on the job is unaware of past practices, the flash could cause problems later in the production process.

Subtle decisions may have far-reaching effects in an MRP system. Cost-effective decisions in one area, such as assembly, can be costly in other areas, such as labor or inventory costs. Most MRP systems should operate at suboptimal production levels in specific areas in order to maximize total effective output.

Consider the manufacture of spoked wheels. There are many different styles of wheels, and each has its own parts list and assembly procedures. Both automated and hand labor may be necessary to assemble and check each wheel. The parts cost for a wheel with a rim, hub, and spokes is relatively fixed, but the labor cost may be extremely variable.

There are special machines that can assemble wheels automatically, but some can insert one spoke at a time while others can insert 36—the number used in most 20- and 27-inch bicycle wheels. The problem comes in scheduling the production for the various machines that may be used.

To keep the costs down, some wheels must be built on slower machines, while other special wheels must even be built by hand. Another factor is the need to build the different styles. The primary questions involve determining how long a production run should be. Production runs that can optimize the machine usage may not be allowable.

Completed wheels take up more storage space than parts, and holding completed parts adds to the cost of inventory. The completed work has a higher carrying cost than the parts, so the storage becomes more expensive.

The amount of labor spent on inspection also has a significant impact on cost. One might inspect 100% of the wheels, since a bicycle with a faulty wheel will probably be returned, which is a costly procedure. The additional labor to inspect a wheel may be only a small part of the total cost, and thus it is worth this expense to avoid returns. If the same diameter spoke were used in both 20- and 27-inch wheels, the spokes could exhibit vastly different handling characteristics. The spokes for a 20-inch wheel might be three times stiffer than the spokes for a 27-inch wheel. If so, the automatic wheel-building equipment for the assembly of the smaller wheels must be built more sturdily, which produces an additional cost. But if the automatic equipment is used only for building larger wheels, the overall assembly can be slowed down.

Planning is the basis for MRP, but another function of MRP is the documentation. One piece of documentation might be used to serve all departments. It would contain data on routing, parts, labor, and other required information. Having all this information on a single document, however, we violate the basic requirement of good documentation: that it be easily readable and understandable.

Another problem with having a single document for all groups is that the bill of materials is produced by different groups. An assembly with mechanical and hydraulic components can require two different vocabularies. Most design engineers tend to think in terms of parts geometry and not of time or cost considerations. But the functional MRP document includes the detailed cost breakdowns for labor, parts, and machine time.

In many organizations the engineering groups initiate the documentation but may not implement the changes. This can result in a poor product because of poor communications.

The bill of materials is not the only document needed. There are also the bills of labor, which detail the parts movements through the assembly process, and parts explosions, which show a particular assembly. Good support documentation aids in the process planning and helps promote product quality, but it adds to the overhead. If accuracy is critical, quality-control personnel must inspect the tooling, and this inspection produces downtime. Another expense is the maintenance of the databases that hold information such as machine specifications, capacity, and metal removal rates.

Future systems will put more emphasis on actual floor control. Advanced factory-management systems may use closed-loop communications and control for the material flow through the plant as well as for service functions such as maintenance and inspection. These systems will not only control material resources but also monitor and direct the events to make the parts.

In these systems, process definitions and master schedules will be stored in the computer. Data will be received from the manufacturing processes and will include status information on tools, equipment, and manpower.

The system will analyze this data and will determine:

1. The required time and location of all production-related events.
2. The allocation of resources.
3. The actual performance compared with a master production plan.

The output from the analysis will initiate job changes, machine set-ups, job starts, and required adjustments in the production plan.

Trends in Manufacturing-System Design

The present trends in factory management are aimed at developing a unified plant-control system for directing the activities of interconnected manufacturing cells of robots and NC machines. This is expected to pave the way for totally automated factories. *Total automation* does not mean a factory without people, but rather one automated to the fullest practical extent.

Most factory-management systems will be made up of human workers and managers teamed with robots and machine tools. The repetitive tasks that can be programmed are automated, and the functions requiring a higher level of decision-making capability are performed manually. The activities in the factory will be monitored and controlled by an overall computer system that manages the complete production cycle from raw material to finished goods. Individual workcenters of operators and machines will be managed by lower-level control centers. The factory-management system will coordinate the manual as well as automated operations.

This solution has come to be known as *computer-integrated manufacturing (CIM)*. We will explore the current state of the trends of the various components of CIM toward the ultimate goal of integration and then attempt to place CAD in perspective with these developments as it both enforces and competes with them. Manufacturing management has both long- and short-term aspects. The long-term ones are setting objectives, developing strategies, creating organizations, and managing and motivating people. However, all these long-term activities are directed toward managing the factory on a day-to-day or short-term basis. The main objective for a manufacturing-for-profit organization is a return on stockholders' investment. Return on investment can be expressed as:

$$\text{ROI} = \frac{\text{shipments} - \text{factory costs}}{\text{plant} + \text{inventories}}$$

Factory costs include material, labor, and overhead. Both material and labor can be categorized as direct and indirect.

In developing a management system, one must know when to stop expanding the number of categories to be planned and controlled. A point is reached when the cost of acquiring and processing information exceeds the benefits derived. Once we have determined what things need managing, the problem then shifts to how to manage those entities. There are three ways to increase ROI, assuming fixed orders of shipments. They are, in descending order:

1. Inventory reductions.
2. Better utilization of plant.
3. Factory-cost reductions.

Inventory reductions of one-third are possible after the successful implementation of a manufacturing system, while factory-cost reductions of only a few percent can be difficult to achieve. The challenge in making any kind of ROI improvement is that the four variables—shipments, costs, plant, and inventories—interact with each other. Cutting inventories can hurt delivery performance by reducing shipments. It also increases set-up costs and decreases plant utilization. Increasing lot sizes will reduce costs and better utilize the plant. But it increases inventories and limits flexibility in responding to customer demands.

Attempts to maximize or minimize any one of these variables without regard to the effect on the others will at best only produce short-term, apparent improvements. In the long term they may cause perturbations that are counterproductive and morale-destroying. What is needed is a holistic rather than a piecemeal approach. The whole must be optimized by bringing each part to its *optimum* rather than its maximum or minimum. This is the objective of manufacturing management.

Discrete manufacturing, as we have discussed, is a larger portion of the total spectrum of manufacturing. Discrete manufacturing involves production of discrete items, which may be composed of discrete components, with some repetition of the production process, which can be either continuous or intermittent. Discrete manufacturing is bounded on one end by project-oriented manufacturing and on the other end by process control.

The relationships can be divided as follows:

Manufacturing categories

Project	Discrete	Process
Construction	Typewriters	Chemicals
	Televisions	Gasoline
Shipbuilding	Bicycles	Cement
Chemical plants	Automobiles	
R&D	Computers	Food
	Appliances	

Sometimes the boundaries overlap and their planning and control characteristics merge, as in the case of aircraft, some of which is project-oriented and some of which is discrete-oriented. Discrete manufacturing is CAD's greatest arena of application.

Computer-integrated manufacturing (CIM) is emerging as a group of logically related activities which are used to support manufacturing management. These are CAD, CAM, robotics, automated materials handling, and group technology.

During the development of CAD technology, CAM advancements were also being made, mostly in numerical control. Until recently, experienced programmers were required to produce and verify NC instructions. Now, NC programs can be produced automatically by interactive graphics, and tool paths can be verified quickly with computer simulations.

Some systems also have process-planning features for determining sequences of fabrication steps, or they have factory-management capabilities for directing the flow of work and materials through the factory. The newest feature is robotics, which allows automated manipulator arms to handle tools and workpieces.

Most factory-management systems rely heavily on group technology, with families of similar parts being fabricated in individual manufacturing cells. As factories become more automated, these cells will contain increasing numbers of robots and NC machines controlled by computers. Individual manufacturing cells eventually will be linked together and controlled by a unified computer system for the overall automation of a factory.

Factories totally automated by computer will utilize distributed-processing technology. The distributed system will be oriented to the various levels of factory management. At the highest level, a central computer will control the complete production cycle from raw materials to finished goods. This control may be executed by directing the activities of multiple jobs that produce the various components for the end product. Lower-level computers will issue instructions and direct the activities of the smaller workcenters. Within the definitions of manufacturing management, discrete manufacturing and CIM are the basis of the developments in manufacturing-management systems. To place CAD in perspective with those developments toward the goal of complete CIM requires that we reassess the objective of manufacturing management, as previously defined, which is to optimize the relationships of shipments, factory costs, inventories, and plant investments.

The manufacturing system used for this optimization becomes essentially a timing system. It times the receipt of materials, the release of materials to production, the operational steps, and the ultimate delivery of product. It is process-monitored by both cost-control and quality-control subsystems.

The system is a model of an on-going process. The closer the model is to reality, the better the system is. Many systems in plants have grown piecemeal because of changes in computers and programming languages as well as personnel changes in the business. As a result, there may be a number of problems in the system:

1. A lack of integration can occur when subsystems such as sales-order entry, inventory, production, cost, and financials do not communicate properly with each other.

2. Redundant databases can exist when data is in several forms and places within the organization. It may be redundant or not in agreement; there may be varying degrees of accessibility.

3. Some systems lack continuous feedback of results for comparison with plans, and these provide poor control.

4. Most data has a time utility which decreases rapidly with time. The processing of transactions in batches builds in delays and lacks immediate feedback to the operator on the validity of the data entered.

In order to increase the contribution which manufacturing makes to the ROI, we need a system which operates in the same dynamic manner in which the factory should operate. This system would allow us to suboptimize shipments, inventories, investment, and costs. By optimum timing we could reduce inventories and at the same time reduce stock problems by better matching stock to demand. We could reduce the need for additional future investments in plant by a better balancing of load to capacity. We could also reduce set-up costs through better lot sizing.

Besides good employee and customer relations, superior and innovative products, the better manufacturing companies either have, or are quickly moving toward, information systems that have the following characteristics:

1. Online data entry with interactive processing and online inquiry into a single, integrated database.

2. The various factory subsystems are integrated and interactively share data with each other.

3. A closed-loop feedback of results is used for the comparison with expected results to identify the exceptions needing management's attention.

Other important trends are:

1. Decentralized data processing.
2. Automated materials handling.
3. Bar-code data collection.
4. Repetitive manufacturing systems.
5. The integration of CAD systems.

As the use of computers grew, centralized data processing was justified on the basis of economies of scale. Such savings proved to be an illusion, since as these data-processing organizations grew, costs rose and service diminished. With the advent of mini- and microcomputers, processing costs dropped dramatically, and the use of large centralized systems diminished.

There was also a recognition that all data is not alike. Operating data has a high time utility, while accounting data may not. The trend is to put the processing of operating data back in the hands of factory management and leave the accounting to central operations. The manager now has control of the operational system.

Automated materials handling can be used where volume and a continuous flow of material justify it. Robot storekeepers can perform most of the functions of human storekeepers, such as locating and picking, with greater accuracies and speeds. Also, since they are controlled by computers, their actions can be integrated with the manufacturing system. Decisions such as how much material is needed and when to deliver it can be determined by the manufacturing system and then executed by the robot. These decisions can be derived from a master schedule and modified by real-time events.

Repetitive manufacturing systems is today's term for assembly-line or mass production. If production volume and continuity justify it, manufacturers can establish assembly lines with a repetition of product, routing, and operation. Such a scheme provides:

1. Materials-handling efficiency.
2. Lower labor costs.
3. Less inventory.
4. A visible control which tends to be implicit in the line.

The repetition makes it difficult to distinguish between production lots, and control by lot is impractical. However, many manufacturing system packages assume lot integrity. Rather than develop custom systems, some companies use packages based on lot logic and force them to work. A system based on lot or work-order logic does not fit the reality of many operations. Systems based on lot logic usually need major modifications in the areas of:

1. Material issue.
2. Cost control.
3. Production control.

Some basic manufacturing systems accommodate repetitive manufacturing, and a few of these systems function as generalized packages.

A trend within repetitive manufacturing is the growing requirement for *fault-tolerant* computers. As the repetitive plants become ever more dependent on computers, the effects of a computer failure become greater.

There are many cases where a fault-tolerant computer can be justified to avoid small periods of downtime. Typical losses may run from a million dollars a day to $60,000 for one hour or $10,000 for one minute. In these applications a computer which is used for downtime-sensitive operations should be fault-tolerant.

Bar-code data collection has a number of advantages over the other methods of data collection, such as a manual terminal, punched cards, punched badges, and magnetic strips. The main advantage it offers is flexibility. Bar-code labels can be produced by a computer on inexpensive printers anywhere in a plant. They can be attached to raw material, parts, finished goods, and the documents used to control them. The bar codes can be printed using a dot matrix printer with a graphic control option.

The ability to produce the codes where needed and as needed provides a closed loop with the computer. Transcription problems are eliminated, with an improved accuracy of data and lower costs.

If we consider the relationship of CAD to CIM, we might make the following observations.

1. CAD is concerned mainly with the geometry and physical attributes of parts and assemblies.

2. Two derivatives of CAD—CAM and robotics—are also concerned mainly with geometry and physical attributes.

3. Group technology is basically a parts classification and coding scheme which CAD uses as a reference.

4. A manufacturing management system is concerned with the planning and control functions for the movement of material from acquisition to delivery. It is basically a timing system.

5. Automated materials handling is a derivative of the manufacturing management system, since its primary concern is with the movement of material.

Thus, CAD and its derivatives are concerned with geometry and have little to do with timing the movement of material through the production process. Manufacturing management systems generally care little about the geometry of parts. In integrating CAD with manufacturing management to reach the goal of CIM, one obvious step is the sharing of parts from a common file, an item master. As a contributor to increasing the ROI, this integration is not likely to play a major role. The design is normally done offline and is not involved in the dynamics of production. The transfer of parts data between a CAD system and a manufacturing system is normally a minor aspect with some cost and time delay; thus integration may have little cost justification.

The use of workcenters will grow. Each workcenter can be regarded as a manufacturing unit made up of operators, robots, and NC machines controlled by a workcenter computer. Each of these control-system computers can respond to the requirements received from a higher level by issuing more detailed instructions downward and summarizing feedback upward for reports.

Another potential integration is the sharing of the bill of material or product-structure data. We note that an engineering bill of material is not necessarily a manufacturing bill. The more highly engineered or complex a product, the less likely that the two will be identical. The reason is that an engineering bill describes the structural relationship of an assembled product, while a manufacturing bill describes the sequence in which the item is assembled. This sequence is constrained not only by physical properties, but by economics. The fact that an engineering bill differs from a manufacturing bill may not be completely sufficient to prevent integration.

There is also a potential for integration between CAD and the creation and maintenance of shop routings. Some expert systems produce these routings automatically from CAD designs. These systems tend to be limited to product groups that can be more easily defined. They may be extended to freeform parts, but this is similar to CAD's producing designs from freeform instructions.

If we try to draw some conclusions regarding CAM and CIM, we can state that CAD has the potential to produce engineering documentation automatically from designs, but the magnitude of what CAD can produce in design and drafting should not be extrapolated to routings, bills of material, and parts data. Thus, the integration of CAD into CIM may be slowed because of these factors:

1. The cost justification is smaller compared with those derived from integrating the planning and control process with automated materials handling and bar-code data collection. CAD will be competing with these other improvement projects for the available system resources.

2. Changes tend to come slowly in manufacturing operations. In one respect, it is difficult to create islands of integration in an area of nonintegration. Also many milestone changes in manufacturing management, such as statistical inventory control, statistical quality control, and MRP, took almost twenty years to develop to maturity.

3. A major objective is the automation of medium- and short-run production, which requires more sophisticated flexible manufacturing systems. Because such equipment is complicated to design and expensive to build, its complete engineering development will be approached slowly.

EXERCISES

1. What functions can a computer-assisted NC system provide?

2. In generative programming, what functions can be controlled by a processor?

3. Discuss some benchmarks for evaluating an NC CAM program for automobile engine blocks.

4. Discuss how patching is used in defining sculptured surfaces. What is the difference between the mesh-of-points and synthetic-curve techniques?

5. Discuss some ways of improving the reliability of a distributed-processing system in an industrial environment.

6. A hierarchical system uses one master processor and two slave processors in a hierarchical ordered relationship. The master processor can control or supervise the operation of the slave processors in either a tightly or a loosely coupled manner. Which configuration would be best for:

   a. Batch-type metalworking operations?

   b. Electronics assembly?

7. Discuss the use of a watchdog timer in a distributed system.

8. Contrast the loop and unit approaches for continuous-process control. How would these two techniques be used in a discrete-parts manufacturing system?

9. A total manufacturing-control system can be built around a large central computer. Discuss how one could more fully utilize the hardware as used mainly in manufacturing a large assembly, such as done in the automotive industry. The system will handle production scheduling, material flow, machine control, and other tasks as well as the gathering of shop-floor data. Discuss a treatment for each of these areas.

10. The planning, installing, and programming of a computer installation can be complex tasks. A computer failure can cripple communications within the plant or even shut the plant down entirely. Fully redundant systems can ensure the operational integrity of critical applications. These are often found in the continuous-processing industry. Discuss their use in discrete-parts manufacturing and highlight any potential problem areas.

11. In a process-control system samples are separated according to their affinity for a liquid-separating agent, and they emerge from a column separated in time. A detector is then used to define the concentrations of the separated components. Discuss the best way to monitor several columns using the distributed-processing concept.

12. Material control is concerned with the counting, sorting, and identification of raw materials and manufactured parts. Consider some of the characteristics and applications of:

   a. Low-cost microprocessor control systems.

   b. More specialized distributed control systems which may be utilized in the future in a wider range of material-control or information systems.

13. One application of inventory control is the point-of-sale (POS)

system. Show how this same technology can be used in factory management.

14. Show how MRP programs are used in factory-management-system feasibility-paper studies.

15. Discuss how MRP provides a means for controlling raw materials inventory and how it can bring an integrated relationship between design engineering and manufacturing.

16. By going deep into the assembly process itself, show that there is a heavy influence from simple physics, which has a large cost effect on the assembly equipment for a product such as spoked wheels.

17. Discuss how manufacturing changes can be made easily in a special system that is used to make engine blocks for automobiles. The production runs of a particular block might vary from 1000 to 10,000 parts.

18. What factors influence the rate of integration between CAD and CIM?

CAD/CAM TECHNOLOGY UTILIZATION

10

A major milestone in CAD/CAM technology utilization was the combination of CAD features such as geometric modeling, drafting, analysis, and testing into a unified system with the capability for automatic NC tape preparation. This combination of technologies bridged the gap between CAD and CAM, allowing an engineer to go from an initial concept to finished part with one system.

CAD/CAM systems will become widespread throughout industry in the future. CAD/CAM is still in its infancy and must be refined substantially before its full potential is realized. This refinement can be viewed as taking place in two parts. First, the sophistication of individual CAM functions must be improved to mate better with CAD technology. Second, the individual CAD/CAM functions which have developed separately must be combined into truly integrated systems, so that they will be faster and more powerful than systems where the functions are merely interfaced.

TRENDS AND CHALLENGES OF THE 80S AND 90S

Some key trends in numerical control that will affect CAD/CAM directly include:

1. Distributed numerical control (DNC) will be leading the NC technology, and flexible machining systems controlled by computers with mass storage will become a part of plantwide management information systems. This trend will affect the small plant, where it is desired to integrate four or five machines with part program storing and downloading, as well as the large plant with many machines.

2. Computer-controlled systems flexibility will continue to contribute improved productivity. The same control can operate a two-axis lathe or a 16-axis contour mill, so that one does not need to specify a wide variety of controls.

3. Flexible machining systems along with group technology will continue to change manufacturing in several ways. Machining operations are being grouped less by the type of operation than by the type of part. Turning, milling, drilling, and other workpiece operations are performed in one place. One of the major trends is for mass storage capability at the machine level or host-computer level.

4. Improvements will also be made in speeding operations outside the actual cutting activity. The elements of programming, maintenance, tooling, and fixturing both machine and workpieces require improved communications.

5. There is a growing trend toward the availability of machine diagnostics and improved control diagnostics.

A number of other changes are ahead for CAM designers.

1. Systems that recognize voice commands instead of keyboard inputs will be used more.
2. Systems that model the geometry of objects as solids rather than as surfaces will be more productive later in the 80s, and during the 90s designers will be using holographics.
3. Completely synthesized total design systems will leave the designer the task of specifying only general characteristics.

One challenge faced by industry regarding the expanded use of CAD/CAM is getting into step with the way business must now be conducted. Companies will spend large sums of money to train personnel in the needed computer skills. They must face up to the need for modern computing systems if they are to contribute to the development of this fast-paced technology.

In the 80s we face a whole new set of challenges of vital importance to industry. Increased productivity is the goal. But, in the face of rising prices, uncertain supplies of fuel and critical materials, and increased competition, increasing productivity is more than a goal; it is a necessity. Recent advances in high technology—electronics, materials, and computers—offer us the key to increased productivity. But to make use of our technological power, we must keep pace.

One of the most important areas is the automation of small-batch manufacturing, a field where dramatic increases in productivity are likely to occur. It bears directly on the issue of quality control, and improved quality control has been identified as a key factor in the renaissance of industry.

Product Quality

Two fundamental measurement strategies can be used to monitor product quality. The traditional approach in discrete-parts manufacturing is to measure critical product parameters at either the end of the production process or at key points along the way.

This procedure allows rejection of flawed items, and, if the production process is sufficiently well known, it allows the tracing of errors to the particular production step for making the appropriate corrections.

If the production process is well known and completely automated, so that no human element is involved, and if the machines are deterministic in the sense that their behavior is completely known within statistical limits, one will be measuring not the part but the production process itself. If the process is under control, the products will have an acceptable quality.

A chief element in complete automation is to push this concept as far as possible. Smart sensors that feed data to a control system that is sufficiently smart to make the corrections in real time are required.

Consider the case of a vertical spindle machining center. A high-speed rotary postage-stamp-perforating cylinder is the final product. Its manufacture can require the drilling of thousands of 1-mm holes on the surface of a drum, which is only half a meter in diameter and about one meter in length. The hole centers must be located within two micrometers of nominal position over this one-meter length.

One approach to accomplish this task is by using process controls rather than built-in machine accuracy. A number of factors must be considered. One is the static positioning errors. Owing to its three carriages moving in straight lines along three mutually orthogonal axes, the machining center has 21 degrees of freedom. Imperfections in machine construction will cause each of the coordinates to have some built-in positioning errors. These are called *static errors*, since they change very slowly with the wear of the machine.

We can construct maps of these static errors for each degree of freedom using laser interferometers. This data can be stored in the memory of the computer system; then the control system will compensate automatically for the positioning error, using corrections to the machine commands as they pass through the control unit.

Compensating for dynamic errors is more complex. The thermal expansion of the machine base during operation can cause most of these errors. These errors could be corrected by using a laser interferometer to plot error maps as a function of temperature or to measure thermal expansion, then correcting with real-time feedback. These approaches tend to be complex.

A better approach is to use temperature sensors mounted on the machine and linked to a computer that calculates the machine distortions using finite-element analysis techniques. These distortions are then operated on by the postprocessor in the same way as static errors.

Some other sources of dynamic error can include:

1. Tool wear and chatter.
2. Machine vibration.
3. Spindle motion error or runout.

The latter is one of the most important factors in precision machining. One solution is a microprocessor-based system using a position encoder, a high-speed sample-and-hold circuit, and an analog-to-digital converter.

Any displacement transducer used in this system should have a wide bandwidth and dynamic range. It should measure error motions for at least 512 points in an angular resolution at a speed to 10,000 rpm.

The sensing of tool wear is still in early stages of development. A combination of the following techniques can be used:

1. Acoustic emission signals generated by drilling.
2. Power-consumption measurements at the motor head.
3. Measurements of the axial and radial forces transmitted by the workpiece.
4. Pattern recognition.

An automatic tool-setting station machine will determine automatically the length of each new tool and the diameter of the cutting edge as the tool is loaded into the tool changer. We can monitor the machine tool to make sure of its safe functional condition, and thus it must by its nature produce good products. Accurate metrology is essential to making this come true.

We must go beyond simple trying for accurate measurements and view the measurements in the machine shop from a new perspective. It will no longer be enough just to measure finished parts to make sure they conform to specifications or to occasionally check work-in-progress to ensure that the machines are behaving properly. Metrology must be a continuous process in the automated shop—an automatic, online, real-time operation, with results constantly analyzed.

Another problem common to the quest for higher productivity is that of rapid measurement. More and more industries are turning to automated test equipment (ATE). This investment is repaid by higher productivity only if the measurements are reliable, proving that reliability is a major problem.

These ATE systems can range in size from a small rack of instruments controlled by a microprocessor to units that fill most of a room. They can make rapid and complex measurements on products ranging from TVs and automobile engines to missiles and aircraft. The question usually is whether they can be accurately calibrated and tested. Many other technical barriers exist. Measurements can be made at the product test point or for the system as a whole.

The fact that most ATE systems are controlled by microprocessors adds another dimension. These systems do not simply report data; they manipulate raw data according to the software programs and report on the results. Software validation thus becomes another important factor. This may prove to be a series of challenges. The speed requirements and the intrinsic complexity may necessitate built-in or self tests. These may be coupled with onsite tests of the overall system performance, which can be a formidable measurement task.

As materials, particularly the composites, become more complicated, and as the applications become more and more demanding, we have to achieve new heights of sophistication in both measurement and quality control.

Modern requirements push many sophisticated materials to their limits of performance. Under these circumstances, even small imperfections in the microstructures can cause unacceptable losses of performance. Turbine blades for jet engines, for example, are used at such high temperatures that even small changes in the microstructures cause them to fail. This puts a great importance on industrial quality control. Nondestructive examination capable of detecting minute flaws is vital during the manufacturing process of products such as these. Modern rapid-solidification processes combined with powder metallurgy allow a new level of performance which cannot be fully exploited without better methods of quality control for porosity and microstructure. A whole new generation of measurement methods may be required.

The measurements on small-scale systems, such as surfaces, interfaces, precipitates, powders, fibers, and their combinations, will have to be made more accurately and preferably in real time in order to serve the required production-control systems. The measurement technology in this area includes:

1. Nuclear magnetic resonance (NMR) using resolution-enhancing techniques.
2. Scanning transmission electron microscopy (STEM).
3. Small-angle neutron scattering (SANS).
4. Synchrotron radiation.
5. Polarized low-energy electron diffraction (PLEED).

These techniques, together with advances in computer control and numerical processing, can solve the challenges in factory measurement.

COMPUTER-INTEGRATED MANUFACTURING SYSTEMS

The common view of the future factory, as shown in Figure 10-1, shows every research, design, and production area networked and linked in real time to a common database. The advantages to this approach include:

1. Reductions in costs from the elimination of duplicated efforts.
2. Standardized manufacturing and test procedures.
3. Improvements in engineering, manufacturing productivity, and product quality.

Computer-integrated manufacturing (*CIM*) is a technology that uses controls, sensors, computers, and computer networks for the complete control of the manufacturing process. An essential component of this process is the *automated testing equipment* (*ATE*). To show the interrelations of these

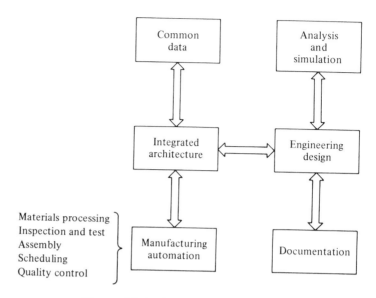

Figure 10-1 Factory of the future.

components, the architecture of CIM is shown in Figure 10-1. It consists of five levels:

1. Factory.
2. Center.
3. Cell.
4. Station.
5. Process.

The lowest level is the *process*. It is the only level without some form of computer control. It is the level of the actual machine without an imbedded computer. Each of the other levels is a computer network, consisting of a computer, a translator to a superior network (except for the factory level in some cases), one or more translators to inferior networks (except for the station level), and one or more interfaces to the processes. Translators to a network at the same level, whether or not they are subordinate to the same network, are not permitted.

The name assigned to a network indicates both its level and function. Some typical names are:

1. Machining Cell.
2. Welding Cell.
3. Milling Station.

4. Fabrication Center.

5. Warehousing Center.

6. Management Information Center.

Each network may also be assigned a numerical name-code to indicate its position in the hierarchical structure. Each connection to the network—computer, translator, or interface—may have a unique address that also indicates its place in the hierarchy. It is also possible to use a single multiple address to direct data simultaneously to several nodes. Because of the specialized manufacturing function provided by each network, the word size of the computer, its language and the protocol of the network are usually different. One function of the translator between two networks is to match these differences, so that two-way data exchange between the networks is possible.

Since this architecture operates in the factory environment, many computations related to the computer control are taking place in real time. Thus, each computer must perform real-time multitasking, and the interlocking systems of networks must handle multicomputers of this type. Constants required for these computations are stored as part of the network where they are used. An exception is provided by parameters utilized by more than one network; these are stored as part of a common superior network. One application of protocol in CIM states that networks do not share a common memory, except in the case of a virtual memory system.

System software falls into three groups:

1. Operating system.

2. Database management.

3. User interface.

The most critical element of the operating system will be its ability to deal with a proliferation of linked workstations and data-acquisition equipment with full support for networking, virtual memory, and multiprocessing. The Aegis operating system might be used, or Unix, if a version that supports virtual memory is readily available.

Among network architectures, the proposed IEEE standard is a candidate. Alternatives include a twin token ring or single token ring. Ethernet has an advantage in that it is a de facto standard in some companies, but its performance in a multistation, heavy-use environment may limit its utility.

The options in database management are clearer. The highly structured CODASYL and hierarchical databases of the 70s have given way to the relational databases of the 80s. The relational approach is a better way to tie together the divergent elements of CIE without major disruption or design database obsolescence each time a new capability comes on line.

An integral part of these systems is the inspection stations required for automated integrated manufacturing. These stations are concerned mainly with the receiving inspection of raw materials and with the final inspection of the finished product. They may also be used to inspect tool wear and to inspect the various subassemblies of the finished product. The equipment used to make the various inspections may be grouped by function.

Stations for inspecting wear in tooling are grouped together under the control of a single computer. Stations for inspecting the performance or characteristics of the subassemblies are controlled by different computers. Other computers and microprocessor-based systems are used for the control of computer-numerical-control (CNC) machines, automated materials handling, assembly, and warehousing. All of these separate forms of computer-controlled equipment are organized into a hierarchical pattern.

A large mainframe computer may be used for overall control, and, depending upon the system complexity, there may be more than one layer of subordinate computer control. In such a system this comprises an automated integrated manufacturing facility.

We are concerned with the selection of equipment that is available and the integration of this equipment into a completely integrated, hierarchical, computer-controlled automated factory. In conceiving this system we may wish to have some portability among instrumentation at the various inspection stations. An instrument used for receiving inspection should work equally well for inspecting the wear of machine tools. This requirement may be imposed even though the same generic instruments come from different manufacturers. We must also pay particular attention to the languages used for communicating to the instruments and the formatting and protocol used.

Communication at the lowest level may be through RS232C, RS422, or some other standard. Typical transactions on such a link might be the downloading of programs or the coordination of instruments, as on a large process line where the actions of one instrument station can affect another. In a plant with a sequential assembly operation, if one machine were to run out of parts, the line must be programmed not to build incomplete, defective assemblies.

High-level communication requires a total factory commitment. Part of industry's reluctance to install high-level systems has been the cost. There is a tremendous front-end expenditure necessary before a complete system can be installed. The entire planning stage, which is of extreme importance, is pure overhead. But once the system is installed, there are benefits such as:

1. Direct control of plant processes.
2. Decreased response time in emergency situations.
3. Higher product quality.

The high-level communications allow the data to be stored as part of one network as it is required by computations performed by a computer of another network. The data must be first copied from the first network and then sent to the second network for temporary storage and subsequent use. Each data item is permanently stored in only one database, assuring easy and positive update of the data as required.

The architecture thus uses an interlocking series of networks to control au automated factory. There are many manufacturing operations requiring the measurement of some physical property. These measurements may be related either to control or to inspection and test.

There are two approaches for using automatic test equipment (ATE) in CIM. One approach is to associate the ATE directly with the machine producing the part that is to be tested. Here we have a small work area, consisting of:

1. One or more of the same types of machine.
2. The ATE.
3. Terminals and temporary storage for input and output.
4. Materials handling equipment.
5. Robotic positioning for the materials.

A translator should be used to connect the ATE to the network.

This method is convenient, but it makes computer control difficult. The programming languages used for most machines and robots are different from those used for instrumentation. Different protocols are also required. In order to accommodate these differences, we must impose severe conditions on the translator that sometimes may not be realized. To avoid these complications we could operate the instrumentation offline without computer control, but this prevents full automation of the work area.

One solution is to have all the instrumentation on a separate network, which may be at the cell or center level. If the instrumentation is grouped at the center level, then specialized groups could be established at the cell level. There might be a cell for:

1. Inspecting the tool wear.
2. Checking for performance of subassemblies.
3. Measuring dimensional characteristics.

This solution allows a choice of computer language, network, and protocol in order to optimize the operation of the instrumentation. Even though the instrumentation is on the network, it is separate from the associated factory machines, but this does not prevent the instrumentation from being as close to the machine as required.

This hierarchical architecture of interlocking networks allows the computers to perform real-time multitasking computations and control operations using individual networks for instrumentation. Some important considerations greatly influence the effectiveness of this architecture.

For high-level communications many are counting on the IEEE 802 standard. This standard was developed for several different applications and it has six versions. One version, which was developed primarily for office automation, will present some difficulties if applied to real-time process control. This version is based on the 802.4 standard. It uses a carrier-sense multiple-access/collision-avoidance scheme, and the data packets may be delayed by several seconds. For time-critical applications, a token-passing should be used to guarantee delivery of a message within a specified time period.

Another problem with high-level networks is that the size of a data packet may be limited. Usually a packet consists of leading data, which specifies the node number and type to ensure signal synchronization, and the data itself. The data packet may have a maximum size of only a few kilobytes, but many real-time processes can require transmission rates of several megabytes per second.

Systems are usually composed of equipment from several different makes. Few plants will have all equipment supplied by only one manufacturer. Since most plants will have a mixture of equipment, this creates a significant burden on the high-level control computer.

The automatic test equipment is a key part of modern computer-controlled manufacturing. The full potential of the ATE is achieved only when it is fully integrated with the other subsystems comprising the computer-controlled factory.

Such a factory contains too many operations to be controlled by a single computer. Thus, we use a hierarchical system of interlocking computer-controlled networks for the manufacturing processes. This is computer-integrated manufacturing (CIM).

The topology of these networks can be in the form of an inverted, unrooted, branched tree as shown in Figure 10-2. Each node of this system may have several branches. The minimum configuration of each node is shown in Figure 10-3. It consists of:

1. One branch to a superior, or controlling, node.
2. One branch to a computer that controls the data transmission through the node.
3. A branch to external memory.
4. Two or more branches to processes controlled by the node or subordinate nodes.

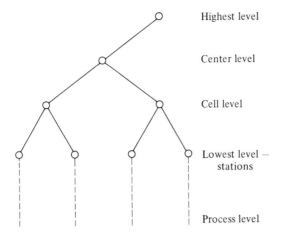

Figure 10-2 Tree network hierarchy.

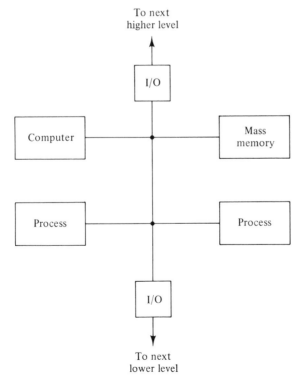

Figure 10-3 Typical minimal node configuration.

If a node has fewer than two subordinate nodes, that node becomes degenerate and serves no purpose. It may be eliminated without any adverse effects. The location of any node is characterized by the number of nodes between it and the trunk. Nodes having the same number of other nodes between them and this trunk are at the same level in the topology.

There are five levels in this topology. The first level is associated with the highest level of computer control; this is the factory level. The lowest level of computer control is the fourth or station level. The fifth level is the process level. The final process at this level is controlled by the computer at the station level.

A single station will control one process or it may control several processes, such as with a direct numerical control (DNC) system. There is no direct connection between branches at the same level, and there is no direct data exchange between nodes at the same level. Exchanges must be routed through a superior node.

The network must operate in real time and be capable of multitasking, where one node can schedule or abort any task in any node, including itself. Only one data exchange is allowed to take place over the same path at any time. Since the system has many different paths, there are many different data exchanges taking place at any one time.

The efficiency of a node is based on the time the node is involved in data exchanges. In a real-time system, it is required that none of the nodes be very busy; otherwise the data becomes queued at that node. When this condition develops, it is desirable to create another branch at a superior node and then divide the subordinate node between these two branches.

The overall efficiency of each node is improved by having it control only similar operations. This is illustrated in Figure 10-4, where the topology is shown by level and by function for a typical factory operation. Many types of operations can exist in such a factory. The technology exists today for automating each of these operations, but as automation spreads throughout the factory, the potential for increased productivity may not be fully realized

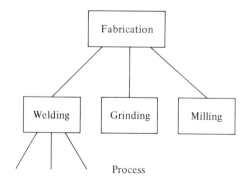

Figure 10-4 Typical operational tree.

unless all the data inputs are automatically acquired and all the data exchanges occur without human intervention. The human operator in these systems is concerned only with monitoring performance, with an occasional intervention if an unforeseen event occurs.

We will consider the requirements for such a network in terms of data exchange and computer language. Emphasis will be placed on the utilization of those methods and procedures that have been standardized by the American National Standardized Institute (ANSI) or are likely to become standards in the future.

In computer-controlled manufacturing, the ATE may be combined with postprocessors, simulators, or other electronic instruments. These form *computer-aided testing* (*CAT*) at the center level of the topology. The primary interface of the CAT system is with the common database of design information found from the computer-aided design efforts. By viewing the present-day automatic test equipment and comparing it to the test equipment of only a few years ago, one can easily see the impact of computerization. Despite this computerization, ATE still exists, in many manufacturing plants, as an island separated from the mainstream of product design and production, and it is primitive in view of what is possible in the integration of test instruments and inspection equipment in the manufacturing plant.

The test and measurement portion of the system becomes more critical as the product reaches the prototype or finished-product stage. In the case of electronic digital circuit boards, logic analyzers may be attached to prototypes and used to run the same stimulus patterns that were used during the earlier logic-simulation phase. The system will then capture the outputs from logic analysis and compare them to the simulation outputs to obtain a comparison. Mixed-mode simulations may be run, using part of the system in hardware and part in software.

Any manual data entry is prone to error. It can easily become the bottleneck, limiting production and productivity for the entire plant. This can be eliminated only if the input data exchange to the ATE is automated.

There are several benefits to such an automatic data exchange. One is the capability to check a circuit design before it is actually placed into production. It is also possible to make some parametric variations to optimize the design.

The level of computer control in CAT allows complete test documentation. This includes the test fixture wire lists, which can be automatically generated. An automated operation similar to that used in process planning can be used to assign the units to be tested.

The effective use of stand-alone ATE requires that circuit designs be complete. Changes in design require the test procedure to be altered, resulting in nonproductive time. Automating the CAT interface allows one to react more quickly to design changes. The use of postprocessors and the appropriate software allows the database to be automatically converted into codes for:

1. Artwork drafting.

2. Numerical-controlled (NC) fabrication.

3. In-circuit functional testing.

This last operation may require some form of simulation in addition to postprocessing. The circuit simulation can also be combined with analog testing procedures to generate circuit test patterns. All these techniques can use automatic high-speed data acquisition and data transmission to make the CAT system fully integrated into computer-controlled manufacturing.

System Considerations

When test systems were first introduced, they normally used a proprietary language and network. The language may have been an extension of a language standardized by ANSI, and sometimes these extensions were the same as those being considered for inclusion in the next revision of the standard. Often a system based on nonstandard language extentions was not much different from a proprietary language, except that it might have been easier to read.

In systems that use a language of the same form as the one that has been standardized, the application software can be compatible with a similar system from a different source, if the hardware and software use standard or proprietary interfaces, algorithms, and protocols.

A disadvantage of the one-vendor approach is that the options are limited by the selection of equipment available from the chosen vendor. Some companies, such as manufacturers of optical readers and graphics CRTs, address only one aspect of the entire factory environment. However, they deal with that aspect so well that many customers choose to integrate these products into an overall factory system.

Because considerable time is required to fully develop application software and because requirements for specific and unusual peripheral equipment may be difficult to forecast, it is cost-effective for such software to be fully portable—that is, for it to be usable on the widest possible range of equipment.

In the selection of a language for application software consideration must also be given to the languages used in the other networks of the CIM system. In order for data to be exchanged between any two networks, not only the language must be the same, but also:

1. The protocol or the rules for data exchange.

2. The word size or the number of bits in a word.

3. The character set or the decimal number assigned to each different alphanumeric character and graphic symbol.

The three most popular character sets are ASCII and EBCDIC for alphanumeric characters and IGES for graphic characters.

The most common languages are:

1. FORTRAN.
2. COBOL.
3. BASIC.
4. PL/I.
5. ADA.
6. APT.
7. PROMPT/COMPACT.
8. ATLAS.

In earlier days problems occurred because the native language of each computer was different, and each needed its own version of the high-level languages to translate programs into machine code. In the absence of standards, a program written in Pascal might run only on a machine compatible with one for which it was designed. The high-level languages have become more and more machine-independent. At first, only logical and mathematical instructions were standardized. Later, input, output, and file handling were added. Program syntax at the command level was prescribed, while the responsibility to reduce that syntax to native machine-language instructions rested with the computer maker.

In some cases, these standards defined new languages. For the automatic test industry, first ATLAS and then ADA were developed for use by the Department of Defense. Eventually, the DoD required that all testers purchased after a certain date be programmed in ADA. Some immediate beneficiaries were the makers of logic simulators for components and assemblies. A model designed by either a vendor or a third party could be used by anyone. This ability becomes more important as the number of different components needing testing increases.

The networks between which data exchange is desired are connected by an I/O translator. The translator section may be passive until specifically addressed by a network. It then buffers the data to be sent to the other network, determines if the data has been correctly received, perhaps by making a cyclic redundancy check, and finally observes the protocol governing the transmission to the other networks.

When there are differences in any of the characteristics of the networks being connected, the translator function takes on a more complicated form. It is then necessary for the translator to harmonize, or eliminate, the differences. This can be done by a programmable read-only memory (PROM). A table look-up is performed using the incoming bit stream as the index. The bit stream required by the other network for the identical meaning is returned from the table. The message is then reconstructed, with the header and trailer which were stripped from the incoming message being placed around the new bit stream.

As a protocol for computer networks, the United Nations Consultive Committee for Telephone and Telegraph (CCITT) has published through the International Standardizing Organization (ISO) a Reference Model of Open Systems Interconnection (OSI) that has been adopted by ANSI. This model has been given the designation X.21. It consists of seven layers. They are, from the lowest (first) to the highest (seventh):

1. Physical.
2. Data link.
3. Network.
4. Transport.
5. Session.
6. Presentation.
7. Application.

Physical communication between the networks occurs only at the physical layer and is managed by the data-link layer, which serves the other upper layers. The RS-232C or RS449 standards implement the first layer. The protocol at the data-link layer is the High Level Data Link Control (HDLC) standard, and it supports the higher layers. The three-layer X.25* standard also implements this layer. The link layer is concerned with the assembly of data, addresses, and acknowledgements into the message frame. The outgoing frames include the destination and source addresses as a header and an error detection/correction code as a trailer. For received messages, it is in this layer that the source address is inspected; if it is not intended for this node, the frame is discarded. Sometimes correction may not be performed until the third layer. The National Bureau of Standards (NBS) has been developing standards for the network, transport, and session (the third, fourth, and fifth) layers.

Those frames whose source address is recognized by the translator are passed to the network layer. NBS has identified the Transport Control Protocol (TCP) and the Internet Protocol (IP). Some other protocols which

---

*X.25 is the packet-switching standard of CCITT. It contains three layers: physical, data link, and network.

are generally accepted as de facto standards in the telecommunication industry include:

1. File Transfer Protocol (FTP).
2. Virtual Terminal Protocol (VTP).
3. Mail Transfer Protocol (MTP).

In general, the user can add to the header or trailer fields of a frame the additional protocol information necessary to insure the proper application of the terminal equipment and the proper processing of the message or data field of the frame. The exact nature of what must be added depends on the different pieces of machines, subsystems, equipment, and instruments that make up a particular system implementation.

Four major types of transmission media and interconnections can be used for a system of networks for computer-controlled manufacturing:

1. RS-232C/RS-449
2. IEEE-488
3. IEEE-802
4. ETHERNET

Another possible interconnection is PROWAY, which is a version of IEEE-802. The first technique, RS-232C or RS-449, is intended only for communications between two specific nodes, and it does not include any method for transferring from one selected node to another.

IEEE-488 was originally developed for instrumentation. There has been some broadening of this range of applications, but it does not have enough of the transmission control features necessary for general control applications. Its main use in CIM is in the CAT center and for the instruments that are used at the cell and station levels of the system.

The use of IEEE-488 can impose severe restrictions on the implementation of the translator I/O between the CAT center level and the factory level. Because of this, the use of either IEEE-802 or ETHERNET is preferred.

There are several important differences between these standards. ETHERNET uses a tightly drawn set of specifications, so that every ETHERNET system is compatible with every other. In the case of IEEE-802, application tailoring is allowed, and compatibility is not insured between two or more nodes of the network unless each node uses exactly the same options.

Both of these network techniques require transceivers at the nodes, but the cables connecting the transceiver I/O to the node are different. There are also differences in addressing conventions, encoding, control fields, and the synchronizing and access methods. Except for the access methods, these differences are mainly physical, and it is always critical which network, ETHERNET, or IEEE-802, is used.

The access method is usually more important. In ETHERNET any node may transmit a message frame when the network is not in use. When two or more nodes are transmitting on the same network at the same time, the message is beyond recognition and a contention problem exists. This contention problem can be resolved by a Carrier Sense Multiple Access (CSMA) algorithm. One form of CSMA is collision detection (CSMA/CD). It requires that before a transmission is made, the node must first monitor the network. Transmission is not allowed unless the network is free for transmission.

When the monitoring of two nodes results in a contention, the procedure is repeated. Because the timing is random, it is unlikely to be repeated. IEEE-802 allows either CSMA/CD or token-passing. These two systems, however, are not compatible and therefore cannot be used interchangeably.

In token-passing, only the node that has the token (which is a particular bit pattern) can transmit. The node can hold the token only for a fixed time before it must be passed on to another node. The nodes of a network can be assigned a priority, so that one or more nodes can have a greater opportunity to transmit than other nodes.

The CSMA/CD technique becomes inefficient when the network traffic exceeds 30% of the channel capacity. Token-passing becomes inefficient when the traffic is even less than this. The main difference between the CSMA/CD technique and token-passing is the method of encoding, and CSMA/CD requires a carrier to operate.

Many CIM systems can use ETHERNET or IEEE-802. Each network can be capable of using either and switching back and forth as determined by the computer controlling network, after measuring the channel efficiency or the percentage of use of the network. This would require a carrier, and under high-traffic conditions it might not eliminate all contentions.

An extension of IEEE-802 could be used for a network of CIM systems. ETHERNET and IEEE-802 can interchange data at 10 Mbits/s, which is 500 times faster than the RS-232 or RS-449, even at the higher data rate of 9600 baud. For this reason, these techniques should only be used at the very lowest levels. A wide variation in machine architectures can make the sharing of information difficult, requiring the development of hardware and software compatibility at the level of the network.

In order to effectively integrate CAT into a manufacturing CIM environment, the CAT network should have the following characteristics:

1. The language should be ADA for the real-time multitasking environment.

2. The protocol should be the CCITT X.21 seven-layer OSI structure with HDLC supporting the data-link layer.

3. The IEEE-802 network techniques can be used to support the physical layer and define the header, data, and trailer fields of the message frame. Other protocol can be developed as required by implementing the FTPV and VTP rules.

4. The access method may use a combined form of CSMA/CD and token-passing by switching between these methods, depending on the network efficiency required.

5. The word size should be at least 16 bits, but processing can be in 32- or 64-bit blocks, depending on the efficiency required.

6. The character set should be ASCII for characters, and graphics support should use the IGES standard.

The cost of implementing these techniques increases as the number of nodes in the network is increased. In very high electrical-noise environments, plastic optical cable should be used.

If proper attention is given to the selection of the instrumentation, it is possible to greatly increase the portability of the instrumentation so that it can be used in a great variety of applications. The following characteristics are important to the portability:

1. The standardization of all functions.

2. A wide selection of ranges.

3. Adjustable addressing in the network.

4. A standardized instruction set.

5. A standardized protocol.

In making the selection, it is also desirable to choose a combination supported by at least two or more suppliers. Of the above characteristics, the first three are normally found to some extent in most instruments.

Many manufacturers use special versions of standardized language and protocols. These versions may consist of the standard version and the manufacturer's additions, or they may be a subset of the standardized version. A special version of a language might not be able to use a standardized compiler. For ATE the standard language has been ATLAS and is now ADA. Other languages such as BASIC, FORTRAN, PL/I, and Pascal may use extensions or enhancements that may be standardized by the Purdue Industrial Control Workshop (PICW) or the Instrumentation Society of America (ISA). Only the extensions to BASIC have been used for instrumentation. Many popular extensions are now in the process of being standardized. In the case of a protocol and network for instrumentation, the standards most frequently used are IEEE 488 and IEEE 802. Others that are rapidly becoming standardized are PROWAY, which is a ruggedized version of IEEE 802, and ETHERNET.

An instrumentation system using one of these languages and protocols is bound to have some portability. This allows the instruments to be utilized for a variety of purposes. If another instrument is required to replace a unit being repaired or to balance changes in the production line, another unit from elsewhere in the factory can easily be used.

Application software acts to hold the centralized factory together. There are basically three kinds of testing software:

1. The self-test.
2. The self-learn.
3. The simulator.

Self-test software can be used at both the component and the board level, with some portion of the board dedicated to the testing of the logic. On some systems almost 30% may be used for that function. The advantage in self-test is that it can be written by the same designer responsible for the board or component. The resultant analysis is usually better than could be achieved in most cases by a generic tester, unless it is particularly well suited architecturally to the task and programmed carefully.

Self-learn software is most often used for shorts and opens detection. The algorithm for shorts measurement is straightforward, and it allows this technique to be practical even on very large boards.

Simulation software can be further divided into two categories:

1. A simulator that takes a given input stimulus and calculates the output response.
2. Automatic program generation (APG), which decides on the input stimuli and estimates the fault coverage for the resultant program.

The single biggest problem in the successful implementation of computerization throughout the factory may be the long software-development cycle. As hardware becomes more powerful and more versatile, the demand for supporting software grows, and there is an inability to keep up with these demands.

The structured programming techniques of the 70s improve the productivity of software development by providing guidelines which facilitate the processes of design, code generation, and maintenance. Languages such as PASCAL and C are far more suited to structuring than, for example, FORTRAN.

Software Design Methods

The last ten years have been marked by a number of new approaches to software design. The cause is partly evolution and partly the increasing complexity of the problems involved. The availability of these many approaches has left many wondering which ones fit their class of problems.

During a design effort designers must think intuitively and procedurally at the same time. As the effort progresses, the emphasis shifts. At the outset the designer initiates the ideas which set the design into motion. One may have an intuitive feel for the solution but suspect that it may be wrong, so one scrutinizes the ideas and makes some conclusions. The process can be characterized as divergence, transformation, and convergence.

The bigger problem is broken down into smaller problems, which is the basis of modular design. As in a modular hardware design, the modules isolate separate functions, making designing, troubleshooting, and debugging easier. The advantages of these program modules are that programming efforts may be distributed among several individuals, the program modules can be run and tested separately before they are tied into the control program, and modules designed with surrounding open locations allow for changes without affecting other parts of the program.

Modular programming uses techniques in which programs are written, tested, and debugged in smaller units that are then combined. Top-down design requires modular programming, but modular programming is older and often is used independently of other techniques. The modules are most often divided along functional lines. In CIM applications this division can be most useful, since the modules can form a library of programs that can be used in later designs.

In top-down design the testing and integration can occur along the way rather than at the end. Incompatibilities can be discovered early. Testing can be done in the actual system environment instead of requiring driver programs. Top-down design tends to combine the design, coding, debugging, and testing stages of software development.

Top-down design sometimes forces the overall system design to take poor advantage of the hardware. It may require the hardware to perform tasks that it does poorly. Top-down design can be difficult when the same task occurs in several different places. The routine that performs the task must interface properly at each of these places. The proper interface stub can be difficult to write. The programs may not have the simple tree structures that mesh easily using the top-down approach. The sharing of data by different routines may also present problems. Errors at the top level may have major effects on the entire project. In some applications, top-down design has improved software design productivity considerably. It should not be followed to such an extreme that it interferes with the development of reliable CIM programs.

The Structured Design Method

This method consists of measures, analysis techniques, and guidelines for following the flow of data through the system to formulate the program design. The data flow is found from each data transformation, the transforming process, and the order of occurrence.

The system specification is used to produce a data-flow diagram, the diagram is used to develop the structure chart, the structure chart is used to develop the data structure, and the results are used to reinterpret the system specification. While the process is iterative, the order of iteration is not rigid.

In structured design the key is the identification of the data flow through the system and the transformations that the input data undergoes in the process of becoming output.

The process seems simple; but as one attempts to use it, difficulties can be encountered. Consistently identifying the transformations of data is not always easy. It is possible to be too detailed in some parts of the data flow and much less so in other parts.

Identifying the incoming and outgoing flow boundaries is important in the definition of the modules and their relationships. The boundaries of the modules can be moved, leading to different system structures.

The structured design method aids in the rapid definition and refinement of the data flows. This has been done for military command and control applications. But the techniques used are not always an integral part of the structured design method. The method and its graphics can also reveal previously unknown properties of some systems, such as the generation of information already contained elsewhere in the system.

The method is well suited to problems where a well-defined data flow can be derived from the specifications. Some of the characteristics that make the data flow well defined are that input and output are clearly distinguished from each other and that transformations of data occur in incremental steps. Single transformations will not produce major changes in the character of the data.

A software design method is a collection of techniques based upon a concept. Some other design methods include:

1. The Jackson method.
2. The logical construction of programs (LCP).
3. The META stepwise refinement (MSR).
4. Higher-order software (HOS).

Each of these methods prescribes a set of activities and techniques intended to ensure a successful software design. The view taken by either the

Jackson method or the logical construction of programs method (also called the Warnier method), is that the identification of the data structure is vital, and the structure of the data can be used to derive the structure and some details of the program.

The *Jackson method* was popularized in England by Michael Jackson. This method views the program as the means by which the input data is transformed into output data and sees the paralleling of the structure of the input data and output report as insuring a good design. Other assumptions are that the resulting data structure will be compatible with a rational program structure, that only serial files will be used, and that the user of the method knows how to structure the data.

Some features of this method include:

1. It is not dependent on the designer's experience or creativity.
2. It uses principles by which each design step can be verified.
3. It is not difficult to learn and use correctly, so two designers working independently should arrive at nearly the same design.

The process appears simple, but difficulties can include the supporting documentation and lack of some required structures for practical implementation. For example, error processing must be fitted in, as erroneous data do not exist in the structural sense. Also, various file accessing and manipulation schemes may not be acceptable. Much data structuring is dictated by the database management system used, so there is not always a causal link between the data structure and the program. If this is the case, some of the basic assumptions of the method may not be valid.

The *logical construction of programs* (*LCP*) method is similar in nature to the Jackson method in that it also assumes data structure as the key to software design. But this method is more procedure-oriented in its approach. LCP uses the following guidelines:

1. Identify and organize the input data in a hierarchical manner (files, records, entries, items).
2. Define and note the number of times each element of the input file occurs and use variable names to note the ratio of occurrences, such as: N custom records.
3. Repeat steps 1 and 2 for the desired output.
4. Obtain the program details by identifying the types of instructions required in the design in a specific order:
   a. Read instructions.
   b. Preparation and execution of branches.
   c. Calculations.

    d. Outputs.

    e. Subroutine calls.

5. Using flow-chart techniques, graph the logical sequence of instructions using Begin Process, End Process, Branch, and Nesting labels.

6. Number the elements of the logical sequence and expand each, using step 4.

There are additional guidelines for data-structure conflicts.

Many of the difficulties in the use of this method are similar to those of the Jackson method. The method forces one to contrive a hierarchical data structure not previously apparent. It does not address issues such as run environment or file-access methods. With the hierarchical data structure we can get a pseudocode statement of the program rapidly, but the resulting program may not be optimum.

The method is well suited to problems where one or only a few modules are involved and the data are tree-structured. This leaves it susceptible to the same kind of problems as the Jackson method.

The *META stepwise refinement (MSR)* method is based on the premise that the more times one does something, the better the final result is. The designer assumes a simple solution to the problem and gradually builds the detail until the final solution is derived. Several refinements at the same level of detail are used by the designer each time the additional detail is required. The best of these is selected, and more detailed versions are proposed. Only the selected solution is refined at each level of detail.

Specific features of this method are that:

1. It uses an exact, fixed problem definition.

2. It is language-independent in the early stages.

3. The design is done by levels.

4. The details are postponed to lower levels.

5. The design is successively refined.

MSR is a combination and refinement of top-down design, the stepwise-refinement concept, and level structuring. It produces a tree-structured program using level-structuring concepts.

By proper program organization it is possible to separate functionally independent levels or layers into programs. The higher levels reflect the problem statement, while the lower ones contain increasing amounts of implementation detail. The modules at a specific level invoke modules at the next lowest level.

In theory the method appears sound, but real applications require constant evaluation and modification. Since the solution at any one level depends on prior higher levels, and changes in the problem affect prior levels, a solution at any level is undermined until the changes are made. If one refuses changes until the design is complete, then the solution and the requirements are not synchronized.

The handling of multiple solutions is another problem. Selecting the best solution can be difficult. Owing to the number of times the problem will be solved, this approach is best on smaller problems. It can be useful where the problem specification is fixed and an elegant solution is required, such as in developing an executive for an operating system.

The *higher-order software* (*HOS*) method was developed on NASA projects as a formal means of defining reliable, large-scale multiprogrammed multi-processor systems. Its basic features include:

1. A set of formal laws.
2. A specification language.
3. An automated analysis of the system interfaces.
4. Layers of system architecture produced from the analyzer output.
5. Transparent hardware.

This method is based on axioms which define a hierarchy of software control, where the control is a specified effect of one software object on another:

1. A module controls the invocation of a set of valid functions on only its immediate, lower level.
2. A module is responsible only for elements of its own output space.
3. A module controls the access rights to a set of variables which define the output space for only each immediate, lower-level function.
4. A module may reject invalid elements of only its own input set.
5. A module controls the ordering of each tree for only the immediate, lower levels.

HOS can be used with an automated analyzer program to check the solution as expressed in the HOS metalanguage. The analyzer is not required, since one can use pseudocode.

HOS seems to be most useful in applications where the accuracy and auditing of the algorithms are major concerns, such as scientific and detailed financial computations. HOS appears to insure reliability consistency by the interface definitions and the attention to detail.

In most software designs the database design is addressed implicitly, since the structure of the code is the major problem. Large systems usually require the design of code and database to be synchronous in nature.

Table 10-1 summarizes some of the characteristics of the concepts discussed.

No single method exists which would apply in every problem. The assumptions made by each method are only assumptions and cannot be proved. Any of these methods can only contribute to the design effort. A problem may be well suited to a particular technique, but it may also be unique. The software design methods only assist in solving some of the routine aspects of the problem. Using a particular method only reveals the issues in a design problem and gives more time to address them.

Problem solving is usually a fundamental, personal issue. Design methods that are imposed may be resisted. The adoption of a method may require a fundamental change in how certain problems are solved. Accomplishing the desired change can be difficult.

All these methods are important, but their successful application can occur only in a supporting environment. The required elements of planning, scheduling, and control must also be effective.

Table 10-1 Software design characteristics

	Graphical method	Procedure used	Compatibility	Application area
Structured design	Structure charts	Iterative framework	Good for any modular technique	Where data flow is graphic
Jackson method	Tree charts	Defined guidelines	Usable with other structured methods	Where data structure is well known
LCP	Warnier charts	Defined procedures	Limited	Where data structure is well known
MSR	Tree diagrams	High-level guidelines	Limited	Where requirements are well known
HOS	Structured flow charts	Theoretical procedures	Limited	High-reliability multiple processors

FACTORY INFORMATION SYSTEMS

Many problems remain when each function in the manufacturing cycle is performed independently, with the consequences of one activity being unknown elsewhere. First, the output data from the various testing functions can be consolidated, and management reports produced which at least give an overall picture of what is going on.

This data-management scheme requires the rudiments of the vast information networks that have appeared. As the factory began to automate, payroll and inventory were also computerized, and MRP (materials resource planning) and similar packages became available which linked the inventory control, order entry, and purchase functions in an attempt to improve delivery schedules and minimize inventory holding costs. Their use created a demand for a more centralized system for handling information both from and for the entire factory.

An information system is a key element for low-cost production. Its potential benefits include automatic data collection, reduced paper flow, and feedback to make decisions about. A general-purpose system can provide these benefits only if it meets the requirements of diverse manufacturing environments. We now consider the features of such a system. The system's objectives, users, boundary, hardware, inputs, and outputs are all important. Emphasis is placed on the critical factors necessary for success.

We will assume the product of interest is electronic circuit boards, but most of the features discussed apply to other types of industrial production.

Over the past two decades circuit-board production has become a large industry. Paralleling this growth has been the introduction of new equipment and techniques to reduce the cost of manufacturing. One important technique is a monitoring system, which can have a dramatic effect on the cost of the boards by providing feedback to solve both short- and long-term problems by eliminating paper-flow problems. First we consider the manufacturing environment and identify the problems in this environment. Then we can propose a monitoring system as a solution to these problems. The objectives, system boundary, potential users, hardware, inputs, and outputs are all among the success factors for a monitoring system in a production environment.

The typical production-flow steps for a circuit board are shown in Figure 10-5. This shows that a board undergoes a number of processing steps or phases. A board is inspected, assembled, and tested in many ways before it is released as a product. For each organization, the particular steps and the order of these steps may be different. Also the production-flow process may be changed to accommodate new technologies and needs.

An important element that is not shown is feedback. Each organization has some feedback loops built into its production flow. Because this feedback is often based on paper forms, many problems result.

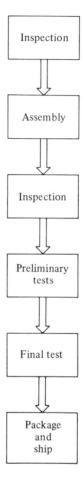

Figure 10-5 Production flow.

Paper flow can lead to a redundant and inconsistent database, since the same data is collected at many points in the production flow. If integrity checks are not performed at each data-entry station, the data may be entered incorrectly. Also the data entry is seen as a burden by factory personnel. The result is expensive and ineffective data collection.

Other problems exist when one examines the management feedback from this paper flow. Feedback on an immediate problem is difficult to obtain; instead, critical problems are often discovered informally. This system is not effective.

Feedback about a problem may require the manual correlation of several forms. The information on the forms may be inconsistent, and the resulting reports are not always credible.

The reporting problems become even more serious when the economics of production are considered. Fault detection and repair costs increase dramatically as a board progresses through the production cycle. The cost of finding a bad IC may be about $0.20 at first inspection, about $2.00 at the first tests, and about $20.00 at final test. There is a great incentive to devise a cost-effective test strategy that will detect the faults early and to closely monitor the actual performance of the testing strategy. The information needed to devise and monitor the strategy are not readily obtainable from a data-collection system based on paper flow.

A solution to these problems is found in an automated information system that monitors a circuit board throughout production. Certain standard aspects of an information system are graphically shown in Figure 10-6. The system boundary shown by the dotted lines defines the scope of the system. The system boundary excludes the external elements, such as users and functions that are performed elsewhere. The input is the information supplied to the system from the external sources, such as users and other systems. The output consists of the reports, queries, and the data sent to users and other systems.

The database is the permanent information which is necessary to produce the outputs. The database content can be derived from the inputs and outputs.

One major purpose is to provide management information in the desired quantity and format. This information should allow one to solve an immediate type of problem, such as detecting a low production yield at a station. Another purpose is to provide an effective data-collection method which tends to be convenient and error-proof. The system should be capable of showing the history of the product—in this case a circuit board—at any stage of production. Another objective is to interface to the other systems such as master scheduling, material requirements planning (MRP), and CAD/CAM.

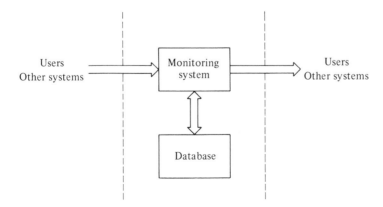

Figure 10-6 Information system characteristics.

These systems may need some of the data collected or may have data to input into the system.

The system will collect data from each point of inspection and test in the production flow. The initial point is usually referred to as incoming inspection. The assembly phase may also have inspection points in between its phases. Test types can include prefunctional, functional, and systems.

There may also be repair steps associated with the inspection and test stations. Each time a board fails a test or inspection, a repair may be made. Data collection from the repair sites is just as important as from the inspection test sites. A boundary separates other manufacturing systems, such as material requirements and master scheduling.

The production model may be very different for each organization, so the monitoring system must be flexible. The system must allow each organization to define the stages of its production model and then to identify the routing of a part through the model.

One technique for accomplishing this is the generation of test-flow diagrams using interactive graphics. This can be an integral part of the test-planning operations. By providing a rapid overview of the test plan, test inadequacies and overtest conditions can be detected and corrected. The extent of test-equipment utilization can also be determined.

Test-Flow Diagrams

One of the biggest problems of all test plans or models is incorrect communication between the designer of the product and the tester. *Test-flow diagrams* are one means of bridging this communication gap. Test-flow diagrams supply graphic illustrations of test events. They can consist of boxes, circles, numbers, and letters and can depict a test philosophy for a specific product test.

The *test philosophy* is the result of planning between design engineering and test engineering. This requires reviewing the detail of the system at the various levels—which, in the case of circuit boards, include components, bare boards, printed wiring assemblies, chassis assemblies, and the completed system.

The detail information, such as the types of board functions (digital, analog, hybrid, and memories), I/O pins, power requirements, and timing information, needs to be gathered during this phase. As it is compiled, the test engineer evaluates these requirements and compares them to the available test equipment for possible utilization.

At this time, the requirements for special-purpose test equipment can be determined for test needs that exceed the capability of the standard facilities test equipment. As this evaluation continues, this data can be transformed into a test-flow diagram. The diagram resembles a reverse pyramidal sequence, beginning with the piece parts such as vendor components and ending with a composite system.

As stated earlier, the test-flow diagrams are the result of an evaluation of the product requirements. Copies of the test-flow diagrams are distributed to various departments so they can perform their function. Test-flow diagrams are prepared on all new products, since it is important to determine the cost, manpower, and test-equipment requirements before committing to full production. Manufacturing can use these test-flow diagrams to develop the recurring cost of testing. Other departments may review the test-flow diagrams to evaluate the cost of the test software and the fixturing hardware required to put these parts online in a production operation. Logistics support can evaluate the required special test equipment that is defined in the test-flow diagram and develop the costs for designing and building each item.

Besides the cost analysis, the test-flow information can be used to determine the facilities needs. By reviewing the test-flow diagrams, one can determine the quantities of different parts and the number of tests performed on each part on a particular piece of test equipment. Once this information is compiled, it can be loaded into a resource-planning system, where it is combined with the other product lines to generate test-equipment loading charts. These charts can be used to forecast where additional test equipment is required.

Test-flow diagrams can be a valuable tool, but a major problem is the time required for them. Since the evaluation phase may not be reduced, improvements must come from the generation phase of the test-flow diagrams. When diagrams are generated manually, they require a considerable amount of time.

The solution to the problem of generating test-flow diagrams lies in the adaptation of interactive graphics drawing systems to the factory operations. The systems used primarily to create printed wiring-board layouts can be implemented to create test-flow diagrams.

These CAD/CAM system workstations consist of a central processing unit (CPU), a disk storage unit, keyboard and graphic devices for data input, and a plotter to make hard copies. The workstation allows one to carry out instructions and review results at the same time. It includes the following equipment: CRT display, lightpen, printer, and graphic tablet.

The system language can be very simple to use, since commands can use a verb-noun combination with modifiers added. To place a circle with a radius of 2 inches on a part, the command might be:

1. INSERT (VERB)

2. CIRCLE (NOUN)

3. RADIUS (MODIFIER)

The system may also have online menu documentation, where you can ask for the commands and the system will list them, or you might ask for the modifier to go with a verb or noun command.

Using the knowledge of what CAD/CAM systems can and cannot do and the experience of generating test-flow diagrams in the past, we can develop a plan. If we view the test-flow diagrams as individual test boxes, the boxes can be standardized. A board may be required to pass through a test to ensure that no shorts or opens are on it before assembly. Instead of each test-flow diagram having its own symbols for the same function, one can standardize the symbols. The system may have the means to do this. But first one must create figures for the symbols. This is done by creating the individual parts and then transforming the part into a subfigure. The command sequence can allow graphical and nongraphical information in one part to be included in another part. We can then build a library of subfigures, and the subfigures can be combined to create even more complex subfigures.

Instead of using three individual test symbols, one for the circuit check, another for the product assembly, and a third for the functional test, we could use one symbol for all of these combined. This decreases the time required to create the test flow. Other features of the CAD/CAM system can be used to obtain even more savings in time.

One of these is the use of the menu. Using the menu almost eliminates the need for the keyboard to type in the commands. Instead, one can use the lightpen.

Another useful technique is the COPY command. This allows the duplication of parts that can be used in other test-flow diagrams with minor changes. Using the library of subfigures and the CAD/CAM system, one can quickly generate the test-flow diagrams.

Better departmental communications can be realized, since all test-flow diagrams are now standardized, using the same style of boxes, circles, numbers, and letters. This eliminates any confusion as to how each product is tested. Readability can also be improved over that of a manually drawn document.

Response time has been decreased, not just in the creation of the test-flow diagrams but in the adaptation of these diagrams to any changing test strategy. As new test strategies are developed, the test flows can be edited easily to reflect the new strategy. Overall time reductions of 3-to-1 on the generation of test flows can be realized. This time reduction not only saves costs in generating a test-flow diagram, but gives departments more time to do the job accurately. This, in turn, tends to avoid the costly mistakes which can affect productivity.

In some organizations quality control may be directed by manufacturing; in others it is scattered under several departments. The managers and supervisors in manufacturing, quality engineering, production test, and product engineering are the primary users of management reports. Manufacturing management is responsible for the assembling and inspecting functions. Quality engineering is responsible for troubleshooting the problems that may occur in manufacturing. The production test group is responsible for the different types of tests, such as prefunctional, functional, and system.

Product engineering may not have any direct line responsibility, but they may be charged with the long-term planning functions, such as devising test strategies.

The final users of the system are the test and inspection operators. These groups interact as input to the system via a test machine or a terminal. They may not be highly skilled, so the data-entry methods must be easy to use.

The hardware requirements (Figure 10-7) should reflect these data-entry concerns. At each test, inspection, and rework station, bar-code readers can be located. A bar-code strip identifies each board, so the data-entry time is reduced. A label maker can generate the label strips at some inspection point. The data generated from the automatic test equipment may be sent to the resource manager computer using a high-speed communication link, so that test results can be immediately available.

Graphics is becoming more cost-effective, and more stations will have to provide a graphic output.

The administration station is the control point for the system. This

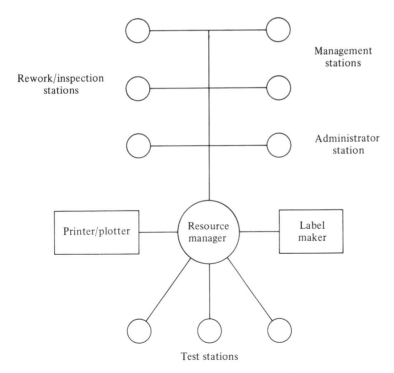

Figure 10-7   Information system hardware.

station has privileges unavailable to others, such as defining the passwords, backing up the database, changing the calendar, and stipulating the user access rights.

Most of the input for the system is related to the test, rework, and inspection stations. An operator may inspect a batch of parts—in this case circuit boards—and then register them by entering the part number, revision level, and serial number. The part number identifies the type of circuit board, while the revision level identifies the change level of a circuit-board type. Each board is uniquely identified by a part and serial number.

After the data is sent to the resource manager, identifying bar codes are printed, and the existence of each board is placed in the central database. Each board is then identified at each test, inspection, and rework station by a bar-code reader.

The data collected at the inspection, test, and repair stations is similar. A scan of a bar-code reader captures the part and serial number, the operator identification, and the station number.

At each inspection station, the operator notes whether the board passed or failed. At each test station, the tester will send all the results to the resource manager, including any diagnostic analysis. The test operator could also enter rework suggestion codes.

At each rework station, the operator enters each repair action performed on the board along with the designation code where the repair was performed. The repair time for each rework action can automatically be computed and stored.

Some of the data will originate from the administrator. This includes the types of miscellaneous changes, such as:

1. Adding and updating part types.
2. Revisions to part types.
3. Rework codes.

The administrator may also supervise all changes to the user privileges, passwords, manufacturing calendar, and system configuration.

One input is the parts list, which originates from a CAD/CAM system. The parts list contains a list of schematic designations for a board type along with the corresponding generic part name for each reference designation. The parts list can be used to provide integrity checks as an additional reporting dimension for a more useful display of test results.

These additional integrity checks occur as an operator enters a schematic designation. If this designation does not exist, an error is displayed. One can also scan the reports for failure rates of the generic part names.

The primary output of the information system is management reports. Many different types of reports are possible, but we will consider only the major types. Several different groups use many of the report types.

Manufacturing managers need information about defects, components, yields, and throughput so that immediate problems can be resolved. Defect and component reports can alert a manufacturing manager to an assembly problem in a certain area of a board. Product and quality engineering can use the same type of reports for solving long-term problems and planning. Product engineers can use data such as the average test and repair times and the most frequently occurring types of defects to develop a cost-effective test strategy. Upper management is more interested in high-level summaries of these report types. Production-test supervisors need information about throughput and yields so that the testing bottlenecks can be resolved. Manufacturing and test management need status information so that operators and equipment can be effectively allocated to upcoming work. Table 10-2 illustrates the typical types of reports to be generated.

A rework code summary can be used to summarize the occurrences of rework actions (defects). A summary of the time lost due to defects could be provided in a related report. A rework location summary can be used to summarize the occurrence of schematic areas for specific rework actions. Another report could provide a breakdown by part names instead of by schematic designations. A throughput summary can be used to show the average time to process a group of boards. It can show the elapsed time from the first test to the time a board passes a test. The test and rework times, which

Table 10-2 Typical types of reports

Report type	Description	User group*
Defect	Summarizes the occurrence of, and lost time due to, defects.	MM, QE, PE, UM
Component	Summarizes the occurrence of part names and schematic designations as related to defects.	MM, QE, PE, UM
Yield statistics	Summarizes the percentage of boards passing on the first and subsequent tests, the percentage of boards that fail at a later step, and the average number of tests performed.	MM, PT, PE, UM
Throughput	Summarizes the number of boards worked in a time period and the test, rework, and total times.	MM, PT, PE, UM
Status	Lists the number of boards awaiting a specified action and shows the history of a particular board.	MM, PT

*Legend: MM: Manufacturing Management
PE: Product Engineering
PT: Production Test
QE: Quality Engineering
UM: Upper Management

are the time spent at a test/inspection or repair station, can also be shown here.

Most of these management reports will tend to have common selection variables. The part number and revision level select the group of boards, the date range selects the time period, and the phase can select the production step. Other variables such as operator and station identification will be in some of the reports.

Some form of user-defined reporting is desirable. This allows standard reports to be changed by adding or deleting report fields and by changing the sort order. Production supervisors should be able to produce a summary of the work performed by their operators. For each operator identification, the report can show the frequency and average time for each type of repair performed.

Other types of outputs include test results and administrator reports. The test results show the output from a failed test. The rework operator views these test results on the CRT screen instead of on a repair tag. The results can also be shown graphically.

For troublesome boards, a supertech operator can view the entire test/rework history of a board. The administrator reports include listings of rework codes, board types, system performance, and employee access privileges. The rework code lists can be distributed to various other groups.

We have taken a broad overview of a monitoring system. Now we consider those features that are most important to the success or failure of a monitoring system in a production environment. These features can be divided into three major categories:

1. Performance.
2. Extensibility.
3. Interfaces to automatic test equipment.

A fast response time at the data-collection points is an important requirement. The inspection, test, and repair stations depend on information from the central database, and the production throughput is adversely affected by a slow response. A slow and inconsistent response can also lower the morale of production operators and thus create resistance to the monitoring system.

High-speed data links at some or all of the data-collection stations can improve productivity. One of the important areas for high-speed links is at the test stations because so much data is sent to the central database and, in some organizations, an assembly is repaired immediately after testing.

Another performance factor is reliability. Because of the reliance on the system, downtimes during production hours can be detrimental. Any unavailability of the system causes a shift to a backup data-collection method or to no collection at all.

Extensibility features allow a user organization to customize the system. An important area is the definition of the production-flow model. Each firm must define the various phases in its production model using its own in-house terminology. This customization allows the monitoring system to closely fit the environment of each organizational user.

Another area of extensibility includes the user-defined codes and reports. Most organizations may already have a set of defect codes in place. The codes may be multileveled, with defect codes pertaining to the various areas such as inspection and burn-in. The monitoring system can provide for both single- and multilevel codes. User-defined reports can provide management with control over the report format and content.

A critical area is the interface to the automatic test equipment. The data from the test equipment often is used by a repair operator and sometimes is used in reports. Automatic links between the testers and the board-monitoring system are highly desirable because of the volume of data from failures.

We have considered the problems associated with the typical feedback loops built into the production cycle and discussed an automated information system to alleviate these problems. A major problem with most feedback loops is the reliance on paper flow. The end result is an ineffective data-collection method and inadequate management reporting. Because of increasing product complexity, feedback is critical for minimizing manufacturing costs. An automated information system can cover the entire production cycle from first inspection to field repairs. These systems can have a great effect on factory productivity.

COMPUTER-AIDED REPAIR

Computer-aided repair (*CAR*) offers another major opportunity for productivity improvement. We will discuss the economic viability of CAR and describe the features for a typical system. We will also consider some of the important issues that must be addressed before CAR is introduced into the manufacturing environment. We will identify problems that exist in circuit-board repair operations as an extension of the preceding section.

In a typical modern manufacturing facility, as we have discussed, the circuit boards proceed from assembly to final test. Every part of the board must be tested. The nodes must be tested for shorts and opens, and mechanical components must be tested for proper assembly and operation. Nodes or components that do not perform as expected may be identified as faulty.

We will take an ideal automatic repair system as a model for discussion. In such a system, the failed boards move directly from test to repair via an automatic conveyor. All repairs are performed shortly after a board reaches the repair area. Within a few minutes, the defects are removed and the board is returned for testing. The repair tag is eliminated and the failure information is stored on the board itself, in a RAM, or on a coded strip.

If an operator is involved, the board tells the operator what problems exist. Shorts and faulty components are indicated, and a voice synthesizer on the board may tell the operator how to perform the repairs.

If the operator is eliminated, then the computer may read the data in the failure memory and produce instructions for the repair robots. A shorts-removal robot may seek out and remove the solder splashes in order to clear the shorts.

A pull-and-replace robot arm removes the defective components and sends instructions to the supply robot, requesting the proper replacement parts. When the pull-and-replace robot arm is ready to insert a replacement component, the correct part is available for insertion.

Each machine in the manufacturing cycle automatically sends reports to a supervisory computer. These reports may include information on:

1. The time taken in performing tasks.
2. The delays between completion of one task and the start of the next.
3. The types and frequency of errors and failures. The supervisory computer analyzes this information and provides corrective feedback as needed, while maintaining a strict automatic control.

Until recently, totally automatic board testers were viewed as financially impractical. The development of robotics for board testers had not yet advanced to the point where the labor saved and the increased throughput would result in a reasonable payback period. However, the developments in robot technology have resulted in fully automatic systems for use in the factory environment.

The most advanced of these automatic board-test systems have robotic circuit-board loading and unloading techniques. In these systems, the boards move in a way similar to the action of the sheet paper-feed system of a printing press.

Through the use of vacuum suction cups, the robot arm picks up the board to be tested from a stacker/feeder or a conveyor and transports it in a straight line to a feed tray. A clamping mechanism on the feed tray grips the circuit board on its edge and moves forward to position it on the test fixture.

We have seen that automation is a tool that can be used to improve manufacturing systems. Computer-aided repair is a form of automation. It is concerned with the repair process, and it can improve the overall manufacturing process. Computer-aided repair may be applied in four main areas:

1. Data transmission.
2. Materials movement.
3. Task scheduling and materials handling.
4. Data analysis and system feedback.

The data needed for repair includes the failure diagnostics that are generated when a board is tested. This information tells which parts have failed and the nature of the failure. Information about the board's history, such as when it was built, when tested, and previous failures, is also relevant. This information is peculiar to an individual board. Other information may apply mainly to boards of the same type; this can include the physical layout and parts list, which are the same for all boards of the same type.

Two types of data may be correlated for use in repairs. The physical location of a fault can be determined by correlating the failure data with the physical board layout. The parts lists may be used to find the part numbers and the locations for replacement components.

Materials movement involves the mechanisms for moving materials from one place to another. In repair these movements include:

1. Moving failed assemblies from test to repair.
2. Bringing components from stock to the repair bench.
3. Sending repaired boards back to the test area.

The mechanisms may include conveyor belts, carts, and robots.

Many manufacturing processes tend to be interlocked. Some must occur sequentially or in parallel for the most efficient operation. Waste exists when machines are not being used, materials are stockpiled, and operators have insufficient work or work that does not utilize the machine's full abilities.

Task scheduling tries to make operations more efficient by minimizing both the idle and delay times. Idle time can result when materials are waiting for work because the previous process is not producing parts quickly enough. Delay time can result when materials are waiting between processes because the previous process is too fast for the next process.

The time it takes for a unit to return from repair depends on the volume of repairs and the speed at which repairs can be made. The volume of repair work depends on the number of assemblies, the rate at which they are assembled, the quality of the assembly, and the speed and number of test stations. Task scheduling tries to optimize the relationships among these factors.

Data analysis extracts data from the sources, identifies relationships in the data, and changes the processes that need adjustment. Information analysis and the related adjustments tend to keep the process running smoothly and minimize waste. Tracking an assembly as history and removing it from the test-and-repair cycle after repeated failures is one example of analysis and feedback. Adjusting an assembly machine because errors occur at the same point repeatedly is another example.

The speed and quality of the repair depend on having:

1. Reliable information that is readily available.
2. Materials and parts that are easily found and quickly accessed.
3. A steady flow of work to be done.
4. Feedback that can show if the repairs are successful or if time is being spent repairing the same problems repeatedly.

Computer-aided repair provides significant benefits due to its superior capabilities of information handling. The failure information is clearly associated with a specific assembly and cannot be lost between test and repair. The information-handling system identifies problems so that they can be quickly corrected. It can also assist in finding the exact locations of problems and in locating replacement parts so that the repairs can be made quickly. It can also instruct the operator on repair techniques. With the proper equipment, the system can control parts dispersal so that the needed parts are always there.

We have noted the problems associated with a paper system. In the elimination of the paper repair tag, each part is assigned a unique serial number which is encoded on a bar code label. The test-repair information associated with a particular unit is saved in a history file stored in the database. This file is updated each time a unit is tested or repaired. One can add notes to the file to facilitate future repairs.

At the time of repair the bar code is read and its serial number is transmitted to the computer that maintains the database. The test-repair history is retrieved and sent to the repair station for review on the display screen. The need for paper is eliminated, and there is no longer the problem of the data being lost or misassigned.

In the case of an electronic circuit board, sometimes a test will indicate that a component on a board is out of tolerance. The component will be replaced, but it will still test out of tolerance on the second pass of what could be an endless test-repair loop. With the common practice of removing the diagnostic tickets at the repair station, these units become difficult to spot. In a CAR system, however, the data associated with a particular assembly is saved until that unit leaves the test-repair system. Since each repair station has access to a complete test-repair history for any board, the repair-station operator can review the test-repair data for a particular unit and pull the difficult cases.

Incorporating CAR in a Manufacturing Facility

A computer-aided repair station is only one node in an automated factory network. The factory floor organization will have a significant effect on the usefulness of the CAR station.

The simplest computer-aided repair system provides a basic data link between test and repair. This link replaces the paper system with an electronic history file. Implementing this arrangement requires the resolution of several technical issues. The type of data-transmission link must be established. Possible choices include a serial RS232 line or a local area network, such as ETHERNET. These choices will be influenced by the particular manufacturing system requirements, as discussed earlier.

With this link in place, the failure data and board identification can be transmitted over the line. All machines in the test-repair system must be able to use this information. This is done by establishing the data formats for the network. The database must be accessible by all testers and repair stations.

In a simple CAR system, the database contains only an identification entry. This is a duplication of the information that would have been carried on a paper repair tag, along with any information that has been manually added. In more advanced systems, the database will contain coded repair data, the history of the board, and a description of the most common problems for this type of board.

The advanced CAR systems can interpret the failure data for the operator. This can include:

1. Instructions on how to repair a particular type of problem.

2. Analysis of the interactions that may cause multiple failures.

3. Mechanisms which identify the physical location of a fault.

The interpretations are primarily a software function of the system, but sophisticated tools can require complex and sophisticated software.

In one type of CAR implementation a director function analyzes and interprets all diagnostics. This type of expert system can be expensive and may even be prohibitive. But as these systems and their software evolve, such tools will become more practical.

The best use of resources is to have the computer perform the tasks that it does best and have humans do what they do best. Computers work with numbers; they can manipulate them and compare them correctly to an expected result very quickly. Humans tend to work well with pictures; they easily discern overall patterns, images, and variations in color. This fact can be exploited in CAR systems by having the computer analyze data and present it visually.

Location aids are an example. The computer is given a description of an assembly. This description includes the part names and types and their physical location.

When the computer receives failure data, it retrieves the part descriptions from memory. The following could be used to present a description of an electrical component location:

R1; 10K; 1/4W carbon resistor; x = 12; y = 24

A text format such as this requires that the operator interpret the information string; since humans work better with pictures, this information could be used to illustrate the fault pictorially, employing graphics or spot projectors.

Spot projection can operate in the following manner. When an assembly is checked in at a repair station, the physical locations of the faulty parts are retrieved, and this information is fed into the spot projector. The light spot then moves and points to the location of interest. Since the repair technicians never have to remove their eyes from the assembly, the probability of replacing the wrong part is very low.

Translation techniques exist that allow the spot to track the board regardless of its orientation. This allows one to rotate the part to the most convenient working position and still have the light spot point to the problem location.

Graphics can be limited to simple outlines and the major components. Graphics can show more detail, but displaying more detail means that more information must be provided to the computer. Displaying a large, complex assembly can require a lot of details, but the areas of interest can be enhanced by highlighting. The most difficult part of the process of illustrating an assembly is getting an adequate description of the assembly into the computer. Once this information exists, calling up the appropriate pieces for display is not difficult.

Three major prerequisites must be satisfied before a picture of an assembly can be drawn on a CRT or a spot projection can be used to highlight certain parts. First, some representation of the assembly must be made. In the case of a circuit board this could be the board itself, the board artwork, or a list of points, connections, and identifiers describing the topology.

There must be a means of describing the board to a computer that can control the spot projection and graphics. This computer could be a remote host or a local workstation computer. The board description could be entered with a keyboard, lightpen, or tablet or received through a network from another computer.

After the computer has this information, it must be able to use it to identify the faults. In a graphics terminal, the computer must be able to tell the terminal how to draw the board and how to modify the picture to show a problem area. The computer must know how to direct a spot projection to this location.

The CAR user must provide the data needed for the representation. The CAR software will supply the means of using the information and the needed translation and display tools.

CAD-generated data can be used to draw a picture on a CRT, but this data has no semantic information that would allow a specific piece of the picture to be modified to illustrate a fault. Many CAD systems do not provide data in a format that is readily usable in CAR. Some advanced systems can provide this capability.

If the CAD input is unavailable or unusable, the board artwork may be digitized. This approach is more time-consuming, and for a short production run more time could be spent in digitization than is spent on repairing the failed boards. For a long production run it may be a reasonable approach.

We have seen how a test-repair facility can be improved with computer-aided repair. The major areas in which CAR can allow improvements are data transmission and interpretation, materials movement, task scheduling, materials flow, data analysis, and system feedback.

CAR can provide many productivity benefits. The major ones include the elimination of the paper system, the ability to trap problem units, and the ability to assist an operator in locating a fault. Other benefits result when the computer is allowed to assist in parts handling or to function as an expert system in the repair operations.

COMPUTER-AIDED SERVICE CENTERS

A typical view of the factory of the future includes the following areas:

1. Computer-aided design.
2. Computer-aided manufacturing (CAM).
3. Computer-aided service (CAS).

We will consider the planning involved in developing the concepts that would integrate the technology with corporate goals to meet the current and future service needs of an organization. The approach needs to be based on long-term commitments rather than being a short-term action that depends on an early return on investment.

The service function is viewed as a new source of revenue, but for the maximum effective performance it must be treated as a separate entity. To bring all the different pieces together into a coherent strategy, various factors and technologies must be considered with respect to their impact on the performance of CAS.

If we again consider computers or computer boards as a product, then as a result of the continued decreases in the price of hardware and the trend toward decentralized computer facilities, the number of computer systems in use today has increased dramatically in the past few years. This phenomenon has been coupled with the increased complexity of electronic systems due to the use of LSI and VLSI components. This has created some problems in providing reliable and timely service to computer-system users at a reasonable cost.

The function of any service organization should be to provide reliable and timely service to the user at a reasonable cost while operating at a profit. Service is now one of the fastest-growing segments of industry. In order for any organization to meet its service-revenue projections, an effective strategy must be formed to provide for the integration of the service function with other parts of the organization. As a part of the repair strategy, we may prefer to treat CAS as a separate entity. Nonetheless, effective communications must exist between all groups of the organization.

Consider again assemblies which use electronic circuit boards. We can assume that the repair philosophy utilized in the field will be board swap, with repairs being done at the CAS center or satellite location. While this approach gets the customer served in the shortest amount of time, it also creates problems in terms of pipeline inventory.

Pipeline inventory of the product lines of some companies can account for up to 5% of the company's total assets. Thus the strengths and weaknesses of this repair approach must be weighed in view of the goals of the company.

When defective boards are swapped, they are usually returned to one of three places: the local field office, the factory, or the repair centers. In most cases the local field office will not have the equipment or personnel to effectively repair the boards. The factory has the equipment and personnel to repair the board, but its main function is to produce enough assemblies in order to meet its quota, rather than to repair them. For this reason the field returns may be given a priority second to the needs of the factory. The repair center then appears to be the only viable alternative.

There may be a number of differences between the repair center and the factory in such areas as expected failure modes, test philosophy, and test volumes. The selection of the ATE between these two environments can be based on a different set of selection criteria.

Factories tend to experience more process failures, but repair centers may experience more functional failures. Factory testing can be more like an automated inspection process, while in repair centers testing is more involved in functional diagnostics.

One strategy is to employ successive screening and repair at different levels of repair facilities. The central part of this strategy is the computer-aided service center (CASC). It can provide a centralized facility for repairs, technical expertise, documentation, and inventory. The complete strategy is to provide satellite repair facilities in addition to a main repair facility in order to meet the total service needs.

The CASC can be treated as a separate profit/loss center within the organization. It can be the focal point for all the satellite repair facilities. Its input into the design of the product, such as testability, reliability, maintainability, and repairability, should be used along with those of engineering and manufacturing. In addition to the need for close cooperation with engineering and manufacturing, there is also a need to establish closer ties with marketing. Then, using quantitative modeling science, one can develop strategies and models which determine the impact of the product on the service function. Pricing, maintenance contracts, and return rates can all be a part of the concept, as shown in Figure 10-8.

Since the framework of this type of system is software-intensive, the different groups using this system should reach a consensus as to the design of the CAD database. The database design should be global enough to encompass all the different user requirements and still be flexible enough to allow each group access to only that information that is needed to meet their needs.

The software needed to obtain that information should be modularized, so that any changes to the database or user requirements can be made without extensive rewriting. The software should be menu-driven, self-correcting, and self-documenting to enable the user to concentrate on the test programming instead of the data entry. The data can be transmitted by high-speed data links to the test stations, simulators, drafting, fixture building, or documentation.

An efficient and timely program development dictates the trend toward more powerful computers capable of performing multiple simulations. The ability to translate the simulation results into different formats is also a prerequisite for effective operations.

Data collection is another benefit gained with the use of computers and a distributed network. Since at each level of the test flow the assembly is tracked

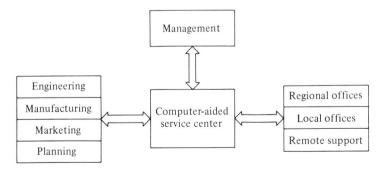

Figure 10-8 The general concept of a computer-aided service center.

and the data collected, the information obtainable from this source is valuable in providing the latest status as well as alerts to potential problems. In this way we can determine in a short period of time the optimal use of machines and personnel. To achieve the maximum repair flow from the defective units returning from the field, the data that must be collected includes the test results and the failure symptoms. From an interpretation of this data we can determine product yields, productivity, and types of faults. The system can also receive from other repair facilities information on failure data and inventory levels that can be used to provide an overview of the total status of the operation at any point in time.

With the increase in the price for transportation, high labor costs, and lack of experienced personnel, there is the need of implementing some form of remote diagnostic capability. Since the implementation of such a remote diagnostic center can require a considerable amount of capital, an alternative is a technical information center.

This type of facility provides technical support to the customer via a telephone hotline and requires the use of technical repair specialists. This operation can be linked to the information system to obtain data which may be used to aid in diagnosing and correcting problems. As the service operation becomes more mature, the development and implementation of remote diagnostics can be phased in over a period of time to avoid high start-up costs and to allow for a build-up of technical expertise.

One approach for implementing remote diagnostics for CAD/CAM equipment is to provide customers with modems, so that the customer's system can be accessed by the CASC. This access to the customer's computer allows system-level diagnostics to isolate the problem. This approach requires that the system be designed and built with the required hardware and firmware to monitor the product while it is in an online mode. The system should have a data-logging file that can be accessible onsite or from a remote location. In this approach the CAD/CAM equipment must have:

1. Built-in diagnostic capability.
2. The ability to operate in a degraded mode.
3. The ability to record the failure data.
4. The ability to run diagnostics while in the operating mode.

This is one of a number of approaches that can be used to implement CAS. In some cases there may be neither the need nor the funds to implement every aspect. While the ideas presented are feasible in most cases, there are problems associated with any approach as well as hidden costs that must be considered.

There are many strong points for the development of the CASC strategy but there are also hidden problems that must be addressed. Strengths and weaknesses of the strategy must be analyzed and their impact on the service organization as well as the total organization must be considered. Both long-term and short-term effects should be considered, and contingency plans should be prepared at each stage. Most of the problems lie in the areas of organization, hardware, software, and communications.

A multilevel service strategy that uses successive levels of screening and repair at different repair facilities is shown in Figure 10-9. The first level is the focal point of the total operation; in this case it is the CASC. The second level would be the regional service centers determined by the geographical distribution of the product base. The third level would be the local field service office. The levels would be linked by global and local communications networks which provide information and data to personnel and equipment at each of the locations.

The third level provides the local support for that particular region. The function of the local field offices is to get the system up and running in the shortest amount of time. This can be accomplished by board swapping with the aid of remote diagnostics, built-in test, and the field-test equipment. The circuit boards are returned to the local field office for repair.

The extent of the board repairs at the third level involves the simple problems which can be detected by the available test equipment.

Updates to both hardware and software at this level should be kept to a

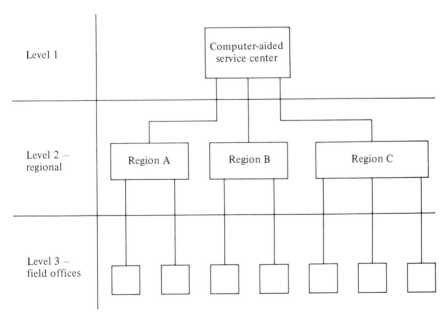

Figure 10-9 A multilevel system.

minimum. Effective operations at this level will allow the volume in the pipeline to be decreased and a lower level of inventory to be maintained.

The second level of regional centers will tend to be larger and capable of more sophisticated operations. The test equipment will be more advanced and capable of detecting problems that were not detectable at the third level. Complete system checks will be able to be performed at the regional level.

In some cases, the second-level facility could also act as the first-level repair facility. The first level would normally be the CAS center. It would serve as the primary point for all returns and provide a central location for equipment, documentation, inventory, and technical experts.

The CAS center would be linked to the other parts of the organization such as engineering and manufacturing, so any information critical to the operation of the service center from these areas could be obtained and distributed. One could distribute information such as engineering changes, diagnostics, data logging, service performance, and cost-control reports.

The communications network is critical to the effective operation of the CAS center and the total repair strategy. A global communications network enables all sites to communicate with the CAS center as well as with each other, while a local area network will provide the intraconnections between systems at the same locations. These networks can serve as a regular means of normal communications, such as an electronic mail system, and also as the basis for the transmittal of test programs and other documentation.

The communication network can also be linked to the service information system to allow the tracking of system-level and board-level information. Field data analysis can also be conducted using the data collected at the different sites. The global network could be in the form of dedicated or leased lines using the X.25 packet-switched network protocol or a similar technique. Transmission rates would range from 1000 to 100,000 bits/sec with an emphasis on error elimination. The issues of security and reliability of the transmission of information should also be addressed.

The local area networks can consist of high-speed data links connecting the different systems at the repair locations. The transfer rates would be in the range of 1 to 30 megabytes/sec to allow for file and data transfers in both ASCII and binary. Errors in transmission, reliability, and security are considerations for these networks. The network should also be capable of being expanded. It should have the capability to accept additional devices without any degradation in performance or extensive modifications to the existing network.

The complete factory of the future may include eight-bit, 16-bit, and 32-bit processors on a variety of computer bus standards and operating systems. To meet both performance and price constraints, a variety of GPIB interfaces will be required, with price/performance needs for each bus structure being met by a high-speed DMA version and a low-cost programmed I/O version of each GPIB interface.

Where possible, the interface software can be provided as an integral part of the operating system to improve system performance. The addition of a software module will permit the exchange of files between any computer on the GPIB. These networks may be configured with a variety of computers, instruments, and peripherals.

The concept of distributed testing allows several testers to be connected to one or more computer systems, which would provide and receive data from the testers during the performance of their tasks. Each tester can be linked to the central computer, which can download the test programs to the testers for execution and receive the test data in return. An extension of this can allow each tester to have several testheads associated with its operation, thereby testing several units at once. In either case the central computer serves as a centralized place for program and data storage, and each field office acts as a subset of the entire operation in terms of organization, function, and equipment.

The development of a major strategy which will automatically treat most of the other factory operations will include additional aids to the CAS operation, such as the use of CAD data, MIS operations, and remote support. By working with the engineering and manufacturing groups the CAD database can be structurally developed to provide useful data to enable the development of programs, test patterns, fixture information, and standardized documentation. Other benefits from the use of the CAD data include:

1. The faster development of test programs.
2. A ready means of archiving.
3. An easier and more efficient installation of engineering changes.

Some problem areas that occur in the implementation of CAS include planning obstacles, equipment selection, software, and communications.

A major planning obstacle is to convince management of the need for an independent service organization and to have the total support of the organization behind all efforts. The establishment of effective communications among all groups of the company is essential.

The CAS organization will be responsible for the total repair operation, with all of its facilities reporting to it. Cost control will be its responsibility, and its value can be judged by its profitability, just like any other functional section.

The selection of equipment will be another major task. The selection is not limited to selecting the types of testers that will meet the requirements of the various levels of the repair facilities; there is also the problem of compatibility. The decision to make or buy some equipment can also be an issue. The choice of the global and local communications hardware is another decision that must be made. Planning and unbiased documentation are two major keys to equipment selection. Reliability and downtime must be addressed and compared to implementation costs and availability.

The hardware issue tends to be more tangible to deal with, but the problem of software must also be approached carefully. Since software is not a tangible object, selecting it becomes a critical task. Operating systems, formats, network software, and database structure are just a few of the issues that must be addressed and resolved.

The software should be transportable as well as compatible with as much equipment as possible. Poor software maintenance and inadequate documentation are two major problem areas that must be considered. The establishment of global and local networks that will operate at high speeds with error-free transmission and that are also secure and reliable can be a major task. Problems include the selection of the appropriate communications protocols, both the hardware and software for the network, access, expandability, and compatibility.

CAD/CAM PRODUCTIVITY IMPROVEMENTS

Computer-aided design and manufacturing applications have been among the most dynamic and rapidly evolving within the industry, allowing graphic information to be processed, stored, accessed, manipulated, and displayed with high accuracy and speed. It is this high speed with which many functions may be carried out that has so greatly increased cost-efficiency during the design and production phases, with the promise of both higher yields and higher quality.

One of the most powerful and distinctive features of CAD/CAM systems compared to manual drafting is their 3D capability, which allows the viewing and analysis of three-dimensional objects. This greatly facilitates spatial planning and reveals potential structural problems early in the design process.

Computer-aided drafting offers many distinct advantages:

1. Faster drawing production.
2. Automatic dimensioning.
3. More extensive visualization through scale control.
4. A broad variety of consistent text and line fonts.
5. Almost instantaneous inputting in the case of repeated symbols or other visual elements.

The most important advantage, however, is the computer's data-management capability. Here the utility of standardization is most apparent. Libraries of symbols can be created, stored, and called up at any time. The more frequently a particular symbol is used, the less the time required, and the greater the cost saving.

The major trends in CAD/CAM technology stem primarily from the advances in the electronics industry that affect the workstation and graphics display, CPU and memory, peripherals and storage devices, and the connections between these components.

The increasing density of microelectronic circuitry, which has been quadrupling every four years, and the advances in microprocessor technology have increased workstation terminal intelligence, enabling the decentralization of CAD/CAM systems.

Because the costs of central processing power, memory, and peripherals all have been coming down, a decentralization has occurred. The integration of central processing power at the local workstation level, along with the evolution of graphics displays, has been most dramatic in the CAD/CAM arena. The power of the CPU has been augmented by reducing the need for frequent CPU access for specific drafting and design functions, such as:

1. Board layout.
2. Process and tool design.
3. Generation of wiring-diagram databases.
4. Numerical control.

With the CPU free to service the peripherals and the storage and output devices and with the cost of memory lower, mass storage makes feasible the storage of tens of thousands of drawings. Remote diagnostics can also be implemented through telecommunications to a central service center, allowing specific problems to be corrected.

The aeronautical and automotive industries were among the first to use CAD/CAM for mechanical drawing (Figure 10-10), and before long the technology enjoyed widespread acceptance within the architectural engineering and construction (AEC) industry. In the late 1960s approximately 200 workstations were in use. By the end of 1979 over 12,000 were in operation. CAD/CAM has been influencing every level of design, manufacturing, and documentation in most industries. According to the National Science Foundation Center for Productivity, CAD/CAM has the potential to increase productivity more than any development since electricity.

In large part, the ability of CAD/CAM to establish new trends in industry has been due to the potential applications of computer-aided drafting and design (CADD), which has the proven ability to transmit 2D and 3D mechanical and structural designs in exploded and assembly views.

The promise of acquiring a competitive edge in the marketplace by increasing production while lowering production costs accounts for much of the growth of CAD/CAM techniques. While the costly hazards of inefficient implementation have not been completely eliminated, the large number of

Figure 10-10 Early use of CAD/CAM methods in the aeronautical industry. (Courtesy: Nicolet Computer Graphics Division)

systems in use speaks well for the capacity to deliver this improved productivity.

Productivity can have at least two separate, yet overlapping, meanings. In macroeconomic terms, productivity is defined as the total output divided by the number of labor hours worked. Any time savings over manual methods due to CAD/CAM application is thus a productivity increase.

The classical cost-justification definition is tied more specifically to financial goals. A faster output can have a theoretical economic impact but no direct financial impact unless it can affect either departmental billings or budgeted labor costs.

Acceptable productivity gains are usually limited to decreases in budgeted labor costs per dollar of income. Using this cost justification, CAD can have an undeniable economic worth, yet fail to show a definable benefit within the organizational budget. One approach to this problem is to use a more qualitative justification. This can include:

1. Quality improvement.
2. Product consistency and reliability.

3. Product technology improvement.

4. Risk reduction.

5. Cost avoidance.

If one chooses to use only financial considerations when making an investment decision, then even for in-place systems, expansion and improvement decisions will hinge on being able to show a cost savings over manual methods. There is a more practical method that we can use for quantifying the cost savings from the projected increases in productivity. Figure 10-11 shows how we can break down the costs associated with a CAD/CAM project.

Some of these associated costs may already have been captured by the accounting system, but the consideration of a CAD/CAM project may result in their identification, yielding a truer picture of the costs. One can even use sampling techniques in which the costs are subject to a detailed audit.

The best measurement depends on the type of project accounting system in use. If the user department is a profit center, the most effective method

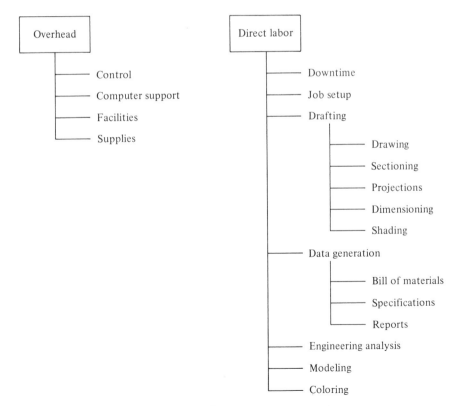

Figure 10-11   CAD/CAM productivity factors.

may be to use costs or labor hours as a percentage of billed charges or hours. Productivity gains will show up as changes in these percentages.

A cost-center arrangement may be more limited in analysis, since there is usually no useful measure of output for comparison. Here, the percentages of the total budget allocated to each cost can be used to estimate the productivity changes.

A common error made when estimating productivity gains occurs from the failure to properly document labor hours spent in tasks that may have no direct relation to output. These include general department overhead and nonbillable downtime for design and drafting personnel. These may have significant associated costs, but they are not considered in the introduction of CAD/CAM, since they have only an indirect impact on output.

The faster job-turnaround time made possible by CAD/CAM may require additional supervisory personnel to keep the work flowing, since any system develops a greater need for information handlers as it is accelerated.

CAD departments often increase overhead and productivity gains by hiring or training their own personnel to be specialists in user training, software development, and hardware maintenance. Additional facility costs and specialized supplies can also act as hidden factors in cost improvements.

The amount of time spent by design personnel in nonbillable tasks can be as high as 50%. This must also be considered as part of the productivity total. The physical design of the CAD workplace can also have an impact. With modularized workstations, gains in efficiency may compromise other efforts, and the facilities need to enforce productive interactions.

Depending on the nature of the work, significant decreases in job set-up time can be realized through the use of CAD/CAM. Two tasks that are reduced are the data gathering and the partial reproduction of existing drawings. With manual methods designers can spend a considerable amount of time searching for drawings which are to be used as models or source documents for a new project. A well-designed database can greatly speed this data search by making the job history and prototype information available through the workstation. This is also one of the factors that differentiates some of the available equipment. The use of an appropriate symbols library and computerized facilities can offer significant time savings. While starting a new project from an existing database produces significant gains in productivity, the initial generation of the data can be a slow process. This is often overlooked. The system allows for quick input, but the verification step remains a tedious process.

In the more specialized tasks that require high precision and detail, CAD/CAM productivity improvements can be great, and often CAD/CAM is the only practical method, since the manual methods are just too time-consuming and error-prone.

A productivity improvement ratio of 5:1 is projected for a well-managed CAD/CAM facility, and as much as a 20:1 improvement can be realized under certain conditions. Statistical documentation of production runs is often difficult to verify, but many long-term users have witnessed these radical improvements of CAD/CAM productivity over a period of time.

THE FUTURE OF CAD/CAM

The computer-aided systems of today put unprecedented power at the user's fingertips. We have seen that one can:

1. Define sculptured surfaces and other complex contours.
2. Construct color-shaded solid models of proposed products.
3. Compute the moment of inertia and other physical properties.
4. Animate and study the action of moving parts with kinematic programs.
5. Evaluate the overall behavior of a system with dynamic simulation.
6. Determine stresses and deflections through finite-element analysis.
7. Prepare numerical-control programs for parts manufacturing.

CAD/CAM has progressed far beyond the scopes and plotters of the early years, and features that seemed exotic just a few years ago may now be common. Even greater changes are envisioned for systems in the future.

We must prepare now to develop products for the computer-oriented world of the twenty-first century. Some of these ideas may seem too futuristic, but only if we limit our thinking according to the economics and technology of today. If we consider how far computers have come and how fast the technology is moving, then we realize that the possibilities for tomorrow's systems are vast.

Since the introduction of ICs in the early 70s, computer size and cost have decreased about 40% a year, while processing speeds and memory have grown in almost the same proportions. Today's microcomputers cost a few thousand dollars and have the same computing power as the early million-dollar mainframes that occupied entire rooms.

This increasing miniaturization and economy in computing power is expected to lead to the development of highly compact, portable CAD/CAM terminals. These devices could have sufficient intelligence to perform the range of design, analysis, and simulation tasks of present systems. They may be connected to a central computer system via a radio link for access to a database shared by the users.

A variety of portable terminals are possible:

1. A pocket-size, hand-held module complete with keyboard, graphic display screen, and alphanumeric readout.
2. A wrist terminal with a flip-up screen.

3. A module with a top-mounted keyboard which is held against the user's face for viewing an internal wide-angle screen.

4. A set of goggles with frames that project images onto the lens.

In any of these systems the user enters data and commands by speaking into a built-in microphone connected to a voice-recognition system.

These portable terminals will likely be used when one is away from a primary workstation. Increasing numbers of individuals may be working at home using such portable devices. The increasing use of a remote computer coupled with advanced telecommunications may make working at home more common in the future than commuting to centralized offices. There may be as many as 10 million workers using this technique by 1990.

The configuration of CAD workstations is expected to evolve from the traditional designs to a more integrated approach. General-purpose stations would serve as a CAD/CAM system as well as a traditional desk area where one can perform clerical and administrative tasks. Keyboards and other input devices would be built-in and slide out of sight in a drawer when not in use. The display screens may double as a desktop, sliding vertically in and out of the workstation, or hang like a blackboard.

CAD workstations may evolve into enclosed booths or even complete

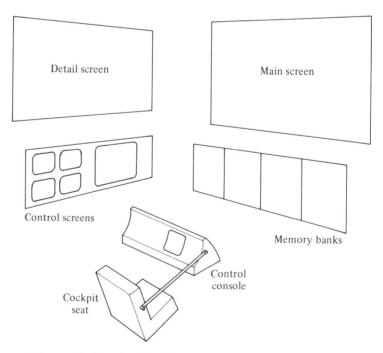

Figure 10-12   A CAD/CAM workstation of the future.

rooms devoted to interactive computer graphics, as shown in Figure 10-12. The user might be surrounded by several large and small screens displaying various types of graphics and numerical data. The system could produce a variety of tactile, audio, and other special effects to realistically show the behavior of proposed designs.

In this type of multiple-media room, displays of different types of data are shown simultaneously on several screens. The largest of these screens could measure 10 feet diagonally and comprise an entire wall. Coupled to the display is a computer-controlled audio system with speakers that surround the operator to provide additional information. Thus, we totally immerse the user in an information space that serves as an interface between the operator and the computer. The audio level in each speaker is individually controlled so that the sound is given a spatial location with respect to the user. Also, the intensity and pitch of the sounds can also be modified, using dropoff and Doppler effects, to make the sound sources appear to be moving toward or away from the operator.

Audio cues can be projected as an aide to the CAD/CAM system operation. Different sounds can be associated with the various types of data stored in the system, which are given locations in the three-dimensional space around the user. Part numbers might be directly forward, drawings above, and geometric models to the right.

To enter any of these regions, the user listens for the sound cue, such as a beep for part numbers. The closer the user is to the data, the louder the sound.

Based on the apparent location of the sound, the user guides the system with the input device. This can include touch-sensitive surfaces positioned on the control chair.

The operations in a room-size interactive graphics system would be controlled from this cockpitlike seat, with armrest angle and length, display tilt, and contour adjusted for operator comfort. Personal screens could display selected numerical data and preview the large-screen display.

The data is displayed on the main screen as the user seeks the proper region. In this manner, the operator can navigate through a complex information system much as a pilot maneuvers in a three-dimensional physical world. The result is a datebase management system based on interactive audio and graphics display technology.

In addition to the graphic input devices, the room can also contain a voice-recognition and gesture-sensing system. With this system, the user can build and modify the database by pointing at the screen and speaking commands. Unlike present voice-input systems that provide responses only to highly specific commands, these systems make the interactions more natural by allowing operators to make the same basic command with several different words. This capability is provided by syntactic- and semantic-analysis software that allows the computer not only to detect verbal commands but also to interpret the intent of the operator. The system may also verbally interrogate the user about parts of commands it does not recognize.

Future product-development teams may operate in CAD pods with multiple display screens and work surfaces. Four to six operators might specialize in areas such as design, electronics, mechanics, production, and human-factors engineering. Engineers may also use dedicated design stations geared specifically to certain tasks. Design cockpits in the form of enclosed booths could be used to realistically show the behavior of complex products. In these systems, auditory, tactile, and visual effects would be used to simulate the products.

This concept could be applied to a vehicle design chamber to let the designer experience the handling characteristics and road noise of a proposed automobile. The chamber would use a system of stereophonic speakers, vibration transducers, and three-dimensional holographic displays.

The display screens for future CAD systems are likely to evolve in two different ways. Large screens will be used with workstations and media rooms to view full-size displays of complex products as well as to view entire engineering drawings.

Miniaturized screens will be developed for the compact, hand-held systems. These would have all controls for the CAD system contained in one compact, portable module. These devices would be wireless, transmitting signals from the input transducer surface to the display screen via the computer.

A number of different display technologies may be used to serve a range of applications. CRT displays are superior to other imaging technologies in terms of cost, reliability, and resolution. They will probably maintain this superior position through most of the 90s. The use of raster terminals will lead most of the increased applications. The main reason for this is the capability of raster displays for color and animated images.

Vector-refresh CRTs may still be used where high resolution and animation are needed, and storage tubes will be used for applications requiring extremely high line densities. As raster terminals continue to improve, however, the factors that impede their use, such as pixel density and memory cost, will be overcome. Pixel density may increase to 5,000 × 5,000, and the trend in lower-cost memory is expected to continue at least into the 90s, driven by further advancements in semiconductors as well as other innovations affecting computer processing and memory.

The magnetic discs and tapes used for mass storage of computer data may be replaced by high-density optical discs on which lasers etch the digital data on thin metal coatings. Because the laser etchings are much more condensed than the polarized areas on magnetic media, optical discs can store thousands of times more data in the same area at a lower cost. A laser disc may have a storage capacity of 100 billion bits at a projected cost of $10. Optical discs are less sensitive to dust and other contamination, making them easier to record, handle, and store. The first discs will be nonerasable. Erasable read-write will follow, and as the technology progresses, coin-sized optical discs eventually may be used in compact CAD/CAM systems for program and data storage.

Flat-panel displays will replace CRTs in the future. These will be based on one of the following technologies:

1. Gas discharge.
2. Plasma.
3. Vacuum fluorescence.
4. Liquid crystals.

Practical 3D displays using holographic imaging may also be a reality. One approach is to use a rotating panel of light-emitting diodes that are selectively illuminated to create a 3D effect. A row of projectors would simultaneously direct various views of an object onto a set of oscillating screens to produce the 3D images.

We have seen how data and commands are entered into CAD/CAM systems through a variety of devices such as keyboards, lightpens, digitizers, pushbuttons, electronic tablets, and touch panels. Many of these input devices are integral parts of graphic terminals while other systems have detached data-entry keyboard and graphic modules connected to the terminals through a cable or fiber-optic or rf link.

These detached systems allow the operator greater freedom to move around and to arrange the workspace individually. Most systems are expected to incorporate wireless keyboards, remote lightpens, and other input devices for operator convenience. Other input devices would not require the user's hands and eyes to be fully occupied with the display-screen operations. One approach to this is voice input, which, as we have seen, is already being used in commercial systems. Most of these systems use a menu from which items are voice-selected from a vocabulary.

The advantage of voice input is increased operator productivity. Operators using voice input have been known to enter data almost 20 percent faster with 60 percent more accuracy. The technical problems in voice recognition systems include:

1. A limited vocabulary.
2. Speech must be patterned with pauses.
3. Voice tone changes can cause errors.

In yet another approach, a bionic ear clip transmits brain-wave signals directly to the computer system. The concept is based on the characteristic of the brain where it generates certain electrical potentials when different symbols or objects are recognized. The operator may be able to carry on a dialog with the computer by producing these potentials at will through learned biofeedback.

Another technique is eye tracking, which allows the computer to sense where the user is looking at the screen. This positional information could be used to:

1. Address data and menu items.
2. Construct lines and other elements.
3. Manipulate symbols on the display.

One technique of eye tracking is to use a low-level infrared or laser lightbeam reflected from the retina to indicate the eye position. Accuracy with this method is not good, and the user must wear special glasses or keep the head in a fixed position.

A more complex approach is to use a television camera coupled with pattern-recognition software to monitor the location of the pupil relative to the face. This approach is more accurate and permits greater freedom of movement. The cost is high, and many limitations must be overcome before eye tracking becomes practical.

Another technique that may be used in the future is gesture detection. Here, specific movements of the limbs, head, shoulders, or other body parts are sensed and used to control the screen or computer.

Future Software

CAD/CAM software in the future will allow the user to perform a wider range of tasks faster and with more ease. Color-shaded solid models will be produced with fewer operations. Modeling programs will be less expensive, and users will be able to move and rotate models interactively with simple commands. The use of solid modeling will eventually replace wire frames for most applications.

Analysis capabilities in future workstations will include routines for:

1. Environmental tests.
2. Heat-flow studies.
3. Drop-and-crash tests.
4. Airflow simulation.

Finite-element models will be easier to create, and preprocessing and postprocessing routines may become automated such that the finite-element analysis becomes almost transparent to the user. The system could move directly from the geometric model to an analysis of stress and deflection with little input or other intervention from the user. Advanced systems will automate the design process itself.

Design-synthesis programs would generate the geometric configuration of a mechanical assembly based only on a description of the intended function or required operating characteristics. The user would only need to describe the key requirements for a product, and the computer would respond by providing a display of the possible design alternatives meeting the specifications. These designs would be new products drawn from the computer's analysis of the functional requirements.

One of the first steps in this area is the kinematic programs that can produce four-bar linkages and other mechanisms from a description of required characteristics. These programs suggest the linkage configurations that produce the required output motion as the user defines the motion on the display.

Computer simulations more extensive than those presently used may be applied to predict product/service behavior. Expert routines, which can provide guidance in making judgment decisions, may aid CAD/CAM users in:

1. Creating new products.
2. Defining designs.
3. Troubleshooting malfunctions.

The computer would then act as an intelligent data bank in providing advice in specialized areas. These expert routines, which run on expert systems, are also known as "knowledge systems." The programs use symbolic reasoning and problem-solving methods from artificial intelligence.

While conventional programs run the algorithmic routines sequentially as required to solve numerical problems, expert systems draw conclusions based on inferences from the observation of human experts as they perform their jobs. With the aid of a symbol-manipulating computer language such as Lisp, one can use heuristic concepts to make formal rules and translate these into representations on the display.

An important part of an expert system is the knowledge base. This is the information drawn from books, papers, and other sources. An expert system manipulates this knowledge base using an inference procedure to reach the conclusions that normally only a human would deduce.

These techniques are employed in some medical analysis software, which may be used when the symptoms are not clear and diagnosis is difficult. One type of program analyzes patient data to identify lung disorders. Another system for medical diagnosis covers most of the diseases known to internal medicine. The program starts with symptoms and determines a diagnosis while separating the effects of multiple simultaneous diseases.

The same inference techniques used in these medical diagnosis systems can be used for expert systems in other areas. An engineering program could assist designers in identifying the best analysis strategies to be used in simulation programs. Other expert systems can be used for:

1. Equipment troubleshooting.
2. Chemical identification.
3. Mineral exploration.
4. Electronic circuit design.

The artificial intelligence that provides the capability for these expert systems is laying the foundation for what could become the second computer age, in which computers will be making increasingly complex decisions.

Future CAD/CAM systems will make greater use of distributed processing. In these systems, small computers will be connected in networks rather than all processing being done on a central computer. The use of distributed processing has increased; it will continue its rapid growth because of lower computer prices. Costs continue to drop at a rate of about 30 percent per year, making smaller computers and distributed networks more attractive.

Distributed CAD systems in the future probably will have a hierarchical structure. Microcomputers in the workstations will be connected to higher-level processors controlled by a host mainframe. In this hierarchical arrangement, system functions as well as physical configuration will be distributed.

Rather than each processor executing programs for a workstation, several middle-level processors may be dedicated to special-purpose functions performed for all workstations. These functions might include:

1. Database management.
2. Graphics.
3. Arithmetic computation.
4. Data communications.

This structure tends to increase processing speed by performing functions in parallel rather than serially as done in most single-processor systems.

A librarian function or data control must be dedicated to continuous service of the distributed users and be capable of quickly changing and updating databases. As new electronic parts are released by industry, the device models must be quickly released to the distributed users in order to employ these parts. This function can be implemented using a dedicated computer with substantial communications capability.

Figure 10-13 shows a distributed architecture for CAD/CAM systems.

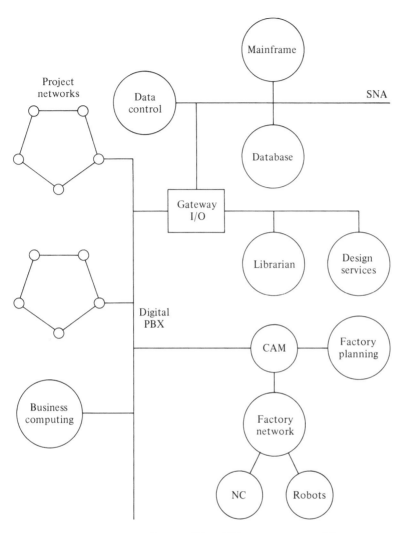

Figure 10-13   A future CAD/CAM system architecture.

Based on the systems network architecture (SNA), this system uses a digital PBX to provide point-to-point communications. The total communications system consists of a corporate network (SNA), the backbone network (digital PBX), and the local area networks that will operate at much faster speeds as discussed earlier.

Data management involves great discipline in engineering work, and as we enter the paperless engineering era, the procedures for maintaining configuration control are not much different from those used during the drawing era. Released masters are stored in an engineering drawing vault to establish the configuration of the product. The process of release and control through the drawing vault for both original designs and changes establishes each configuration even in the paperless engineering era. The equivalent of the engineering drawing vault is the data control system. The same procedures must be used.

In the past the circuit design group released the schematic drawing to the packaging group using the release system and the drawing vault. Now, the schematic dataset must be released to a computer system that will store it and make it available to the packing group. All of these functions are now machine-to-machine transfers.

Many companies in industry have CAD/CAM systems presently in place with many users. As the next generation of systems evolves with distributed CAE workstations, management faces the challenge of keeping the old system in use while moving up to the newer systems. Since these companies' existing CAD/CAM architectures are not the same, their approaches to solving this problem will not be the same. However, two major aspects of the problem solution should apply to most companies:

1. Both management and the system designers must create a phased plan to accommodate these changes.
2. Some elements of existing centralized systems can grow to accommodate parts such as the librarian and engineering data control functions while these older elements can still perform their original functions.

Later, further network integration can tie the CAD/CAM database into management information systems and into the broader corporate data banks. A single integrated computer system would perform the complete range of engineering and administrative tasks including:

1. Design.
2. Analysis.
3. Testing.
4. Manufacturing.
5. Cost estimating.
6. Inventory control.
7. Management of shipping data.

The system could be tied to external data banks to provide the latest information on new materials, technical advances in specialized fields, overall technical summaries on selected topics, and reports on market trends.

The further integration of functions into the CAD/CAM system will expand the capability of the workstation to include office functions such as word processing, electronic mail, message services, and telecommunications. Information and storage-retrieval systems will replace filing cabinets since the electronic storage and transmission of information is much more convenient and economical than the handling of paper.

Thus, the merging of these technologies into integrated systems will make the paperless factory a reality. There will be a communications revolution based on systems in which the technologies of the telephone, computer, and television are combined.

These integrated systems will fuel a new information-based society in the same way that new energy sources fueled the industrial revolution. With such a high level of computer usage, so many functions will be computer-aided that terms such as CAD/CAM may fade gradually from the vocabulary. The integrated approach requires the development of strategies involving great innovation, research and development, and capital investment. The risks are inevitable, but they will quickly pay off in the future.

EXERCISES

1. Discuss five key trends in numerical control. Which two could be expected to have the greatest effect on the factory of the future? Discuss your answer.

2. Discuss the use of smart sensors in the two basic techniques used to measure quality control. What are some ways to compensate for dynamic errors in these measurements?

3. What is the importance of the operating system in the CIM environment? What characteristics must the OS have?

4. Diagram two approaches to using ATE in CIM.

5. Discuss the importance of the size of the data packet in a high-level network in CIM.

6. What are the advantages and disadvantages of ETHERNET?

7. What characteristics are important in a CIM system?

8. Write a structured routine to move a number of elements specified by MAX from memory locations in one array (BLK) to the memory locations in another array (BLK 1).

9. Discuss some aspects of both continuous processing and discrete-parts manufacturing in which a formal method of software development might be advisable for a CIM system. Select a method or methods for both types of manufacturing and discuss your answer.

10. Draw a simple test flow diagram for an eight-cylinder ignition system. What graphic commands would be needed to generate this diagram?

11. What is the importance of the administrator station in a factory information system? What reports would be most important in a factory assembling computer memory boards?

12. Draw a basic overall plan for a CAR system for televisions. Use a spot projection system for locating problems. How would an expert system be used at this facility?

13. Diagram a corporate CASC plan that uses ten regional centers. Discuss the communications systems that would be used.

14. What are the important considerations in justifying a CAD/CAM system? How can these affect the measurement of productivity gains?

15. What features are future CAD/CAM workstations likely to have? What additional capabilities is the software likely to contain?

16. Discuss the use of a librarian function in an integrated electronic assembly plan in the future.

17. Discuss how microprocessors are reducing the risks involved in integrated factory systems by providing operating systems for multiprocessing and multitasking system applications. How are these operating systems expected to increase the use of multi-microprocessor systems in the factory of the future?

BIBLIOGRAPHY

Albus, J. S. Computer integrated manufacturing and robotics. *Automated Manufacturing*, Greenville, S.C., March 19–22, 1984.

Alsberg, P. A., and Day, J. D. A principle for resilient sharing of distributed resources. Urbana, Ill: Center for Advanced Computation, University of Illinois at Urbana-Champaign, 1976.

Armit, A. P., and Forrest, A. P. Interactive surface design. *Computer Graphics, 1970*, Brunel University, Uxbridge, England, April 1970.

————. The interactive languages of multipatch and multiobject design system. *Computer-Aided Design*, 4 (1), Autumn 1971.

Armstrong, J. R. Design of a graphic generator for remote terminal application. *IEEE Transactions on Computers*, C-22 (5), May 1973.

Atherton, P. K., Weiler, K., and Greenberg, D. Polygon shadow generation. SIGGRAPH '78 proceedings, published as *Computer Graphics*, 12 (3), August 1978.

Badler, N. I. Disk generators for a raster display device. *Computer Graphics and Image Processing*, 6(6), December 1977.

Baecker, R. M. Picture-driven animation. SJCC, 1969. Montvale, N.J.: AFIPS Press.

————. A conversational extensible system for the animation of shaded images. SIGGRAPH '76 proceedings, published as *Computer Graphics*, 10 (2), Summer 1976.

Barnhill, R. E., and Riesenfeld, R. F., eds. Computer aided geometric design. New York: Academic Press, 1975.

Barnhill, R. E., Brown, J. H., and Klucewicz, I. M. A new twist in computer aided geometric design. *Computer Graphics and Image Processing*, 8 (1), August 1978.

Barrett, R. Automatic routing of pc boards. *Computer Graphics World,* March 1984.

Baskett, F., and Shustek, L. The design of a low-cost video graphics terminal. SIGGRAPH '76 proceedings, published as *Computer Graphics*, 10 (2), Summer 1976.

Baskin, H. B., and Morse, S. P. A multilevel modeling structure for interactive graphics design. *IBM Systems Journal*, 7 (3/4), 1968.

Batter, J. J., and Brooks, F. P., Jr. GROPE-1: A computer display to the sense of feel. Amsterdam: North-Holland, 1971.

Baumgart, B. G. Geometric modeling for computer vision. Stanford Univ. Computer Science Dept., AIM-249, STAN-CS-74-463, October 1974.

_____. A polyhedron representation for computer vision. NCC, 1975.

Bayer, B. E. An optimum method for two-level rendition of continuous tone pictures. *International Conference on Communications*, 1973.

Bechtolsheim, A., and Baskett, F. High-performance raster graphics for microcomputer systems. SIGGRAPH '80 proceedings, published as *Computer Graphics*, 14 (3), July 1980.

Belser, K. Comment on an improved algorithm for the generation of nonparametric curves. *IEEE Transactions on Computers*, C-25 (1), January 1976.

Bergerson, R. D., Bono, P., and Foley, J. D. Graphics programming using the core system. *Computing Surveys*, 10 (4), December 1978.

Berthod, M., and Maroy, J. Learning in syntactic recognition of symbols drawn on a graphic tablet. *Computer Graphics and Image Processing*, 9 (2), February 1979.

Bezier, P. Numerical control—mathematics and applications. A. R. Forrest (trans.). London: Wiley, 1972.

_____. Mathematical and practical possibilities of UNISURF. In R. E. Barnhill and R. F. Riesenfeld, eds. Computer aided geometric design. New York: Academic, 1974.

Bickart, T. W. Matrix exponential: approximation by truncated power series. *Proc. IEEE (letters)*, May 1968.

Birss, E. E., and Fry, J. P. Generalized software for translating data. *AFIPS National Computer Conference*, 1976.

Blatt, H. Conic display generator using multiplying digital-analog converters. FJCC, 1967. Washington, D.C.: Thompson Books.

Blinn, J. F. Models of light reflection for computer synthesized pictures.

SIGGRAPH '77 proceedings, published as *Computer Graphics*, 11 (2), Summer 1977.

————. A homogeneous formulation for lines in 3-space. SIGGRAPH '77 proceedings, published as *Computer Graphics*, 11 (2), Summer 1977.

————. Simulation of wrinkled surfaces. SIGGRAPH '78 proceedings, published as *Computer Graphics*, 12 (3), August 1978.

————. Computer display of curved surfaces. Ph.D. dissertation, Univ. of Utah, Dept. of Computer Science, December 1978.

Blinn, J. F., Carpenter, L., Lane, J., and Whitted, T. Scan line methods for displaying parametrically defined surfaces. *Communications of the ACM*, 23 (1), January 1980.

Blinn, J. F., and Goodrich, A. C. The internal design of the IG routines: an interactive graphics system for a large timesharing environment. SIGGRAPH '76 proceeedings, published as *Computer Graphics*, 10 (2), Summer 1976.

Blinn, J. F., and Newell, M. E. Texture and reflection in computer generated images. *Communications of the ACM*, 19 (10), October 1976.

————. Clipping using homogeneous coordinates. SIGGRAPH '78 proceedings, published as *Computer Graphics*, 12 (3), August 1978.

Boehm, B. et al. Interactive problem-solving—an experimental study of lock-out effects. SJCC, 1971.

Bolt, Richard A. Spatial data-management. Report to DARPA, MIT architecture machine group, Cambridge, Mass., 1979.

————. Put-that-there: voice and gesture at the graphics interface. SIGGRAPH '80 proceedings, published as *Computer Graphics*, 14 (3), July 1980.

Bond, A. H., Rightnour, J., and Coles, L. S. An interactive display monitor in a batch-processing environment with remote entry. *Communications of the ACM*, 12 (11), November 1969.

Bonice, P. E. How to evaluate raster scan CRT monitors. *Computer Graphics World*, April 1983.

Bouknight, W. J. An improved procedure for generation of half-tone computer graphics representations. Univ. Illinois Coordinate Science Lab, R-432, September 1969.

————. A procedure for generation of three-dimensional half toned computer graphics representations. *Communications of the ACM*, 13 (9), September 1970.

Bouknight, W. J., and Kelly, K. C. An algorithm for producing half-tone computer graphics presentations with shadows and movable light sources. SJCC, 1970. Montvale, N.J.: AFIPS Press.

Bowman, W. J. Graphic communication. New York: Wiley, 1968.

Bracchi, G., and Somalvico, M. An interactive software system for computer aided design: an application to circuit project. *Communications of the ACM*, 13 (9), September 1970.

Braid, I. E. The synthesis of solids bounded by many faces. *Communications of the ACM*, 18 (4), April 1975.

Branin, F. H., Jr. A new method for steady-state A-C analysis of RLC networks. *IEEE International Conv. Rec.*, March 1966.

Brenner, A. E., and de Bruyne, P. A. Sonic pen: a digital stylus system. *IEEE Transactions on Computers*, EC-19 (6), June 1970.

Bresenham, J. E. Algorithm for computer control of digital plotter. *IBM Syst. J.*, 4 (1), 1965.

_____. A linear algorithm for incremental digital display of circular arcs. *Communications of the ACM*, 20 (2), February 1977.

Brown, F. H., and Zayac, M. T. A multi-color plasma panel display. Owens-Illinois, 1971.

Brown, H. G., O'Brien, C. D., Sawchuk, W., and Storey, J. TELIDON: a new approach to videotex system design. *IEEE Transactions on Consumer Electronics*, Special Issue on TELETEXT and VIEWDATA, July 1979.

Bui-Tuong, Phong. Illumination for computer-generated pictures. *Communications of the ACM*, 18 (6), June 1975.

Buttnyk, N., and Wein, M. Interactive skeleton techniques for enhancing motion dynamics in key frame animation. *Communications of the ACM*, 19 (10), October 1976.

Burton, R. P. Real-time measurement of multiple three-dimensional positions. Univ. Utah Computer Science Dept., UTEC-CSc-72-122, 1972, NTIS Ad-262 028.

Burton, R. P., and Sutherland, I. E. Twinkle box: a three dimensional computer input device. NCC, 1974. Montvale, N.J.: AFIPS Press.

Burton, W. Representation of many-sided polygons and polygonal lines for rapid processing. *Communications of the ACM*, 20 (3), March 1977.

Busick, E. L. CAD/CAM workstation trends. *Computer Graphics World*, April 1984.

Butland, J. Surface drawing made simple. *Computer-Aided Design*, 11 (1), January 1979.

BYTE, Special Issue on Smalltalk, 6 (8), August 1981.

Cannara, R. Ergonomics, aesthetics and CAE. *Computer Graphics for Design*, April 15, 1984, Pratt Center, Hawthorne, N.Y.

Capowski, J. J. Matrix transform processor for evans and sutherland LDS-2 graphics system. *IEEE Transactions on Computers*, C-27 (7), July 1976.

Card, S. W., English, W. K., and Burr, B. J. Evaluation of mouse, rate-controlled isometric joystick, step keys, and text keys for text selection on a CRT. *Ergonomics*, 21 (8), August 1978.

Card, S. W., Moran, T., and Newell, A. The keystroke-level model for user performance time with interactive systems. *Communications of the ACM*, 23 (7), July 1980.

Carlbom, I., and Paciorek, J. Geometric projection and viewing transformations. *Computing Surveys*, 1 (4), 1978.

Carlbom, Ingrid B. System architecture for high-performance vector graphics. Ph.D. thesis, Dept. of Computer Science, Brown University, Providence, R.I., 1980.

Carpenter, L., Fournier, A., and Fussell, D. Fractal surfaces. Published in *CACM*, 1981.

Carterette, B. C., and Friedman, M. P., eds. Handbook of perception. Vol V: Seeing. New York: Academic Press, 1975.

Caruthers, L., and van Dam, A. User's tutorial for the general purpose graphics system. Technical Report, Katholieke Universiteit, Nijmegen, The Netherlands, 1975.

Castelman, P. A., et al. The implementation of the PROPHET system. ICC, 1974. Montvale, N.J.: AFIPS Press.

Catmull, E. A subdivision algorithm for computer display of curved surfaces. University Utah Computer Science Dept., UTEC-CSc-74-133, December 1974.

————. Computer display of curved surfaces. *Proc. IEEE Conference on computer graphics, pattern recognition and data structure*, May 1975. Reprinted in: Tutorial and selected readings in interactive computer graphics, H. Freeman, ed., IEEE, 1980.

————. A hidden-surface algorithm with anti-aliasing. SIGGRAPH '78 proceedings, published as *Computer Graphics*, 12 (13), August 1978.

————. The problems of computer-assisted animation, SIGGRAPH '78 proceedings, published as *Computer Graphics*, 12 (3), August 1978.

————. A tutorial on compensation tables. SIGGRAPH '79 proceedings, published as *Computer Graphics*, 13 (2), August 1979.

Catmull, E., and Smith, A. R. 3D transformations of images in scanline order. SIGGRAPH '80 proceedings, published as *Computer Graphics*, 14 (3), July 1980.

Certaine, J. The solution of ordinary differential equations with large (small) time constants. Chapter 11 in: Mathematical methods for digital computers, A. Ralston and H. S. Wolf, eds. New York: Wiley, 1960.

Chapman, O. L. Computer applications in manufacturing. *Automated Manufacturing*, Greenville, N.C., March 19–22, 1984.

Chasen, S. H. Geometric principles and procedures for computer graphics applications. Englewood Cliffs, N.J.: Prentice-Hall, 1978.

Cheek, T. B. A graphic display system using raster-scan monitors and real-time scan conversion, *1973 SID Int. Symp. Dig. Tech. Papers*, May 1973.

Cheriton, D. Man-machine interface design for timesharing systems. *Proceedings ACM 1976 Conference.*

Christ, Richard F. Review and analysis of color coding research for visual displays. *Human Factors*, 17 (6), June 1975.

Christensen, C., and Pinson, E. N. Multi-function graphics for a large computer system. FJCC, 1967. Washington, D.C.: Thompson Books.

Citron, J., and Whitney, J. H. CAMP: computer assisted movie production. FJCC, 1968. Washington, D.C.: Thompson Books.

Clark, J. H. Designing surfaces in 3D. *Communications of the ACM*, 19 (8), August 1976.

————. Hierarchical geometric models for visible surface algorithms. *Communications of the ACM*, 19 (10), October 1976.

————. Parametric curves, surfaces and volumes in computer graphics and computer-aided geometric design. Ames, Iowa: NASA Ames Research Center, 1978.

————. A VLSI geometry processor for graphics. *IEEE Computer*, 12 (7), July 1980.

Cohen, D., and Lee, T. M. P. Fast drawing of curves for computer display. SJCC, 1969. Montvale, N.J.: AFIPS Press.

Cohen, E. R., and Flat, H. P. Numerical solution of quasi-linear equations. *Proc. of Seminar on Codes for Reactor Computations, Vienna, Austria, 1960.*

Comba, P. G. A procedure for detecting intersections of three dimensional objects. *Journal of the ACM*, 15 (3), July 1968.

Computer Aided Design Centre, GINO-F User Manual. Cambridge, England, December 1976.

Cook, R. L., and Torrance, K. A reflectance model for computer graphics. SIGGRAPH '81 Proceedings, published as *Computer Graphics*, 15 (3), August 1981.

Coons, S. A. Computer graphics and innovative engineering design. *Datamation*, May 1966.

————. Surfaces for computer aided design of space forms. MIT Project Mac. TR-41, June 1967.

Cornsweet, T. N . Visual perception. New York: Academic Press, 1970.

Cornwell, B. Computer generated simulation films. *Inf. Disp.*, 8 (1), January 1971.

Cotton, I. Network graphic attention handling. *Online 72 International Conference*, Brunel University, Uxbridge, England.

Crow, F. Shadow algorithms for computer graphics. SIGGRAPH '77 proceedings, published as *Computer Graphics*, 11 (2), Summer 1977.

————. The aliasing problem in computer-generated shaded images. *Communications of the ACM*, 20 (11), November 1977.

————. Shaded computer graphics in the entertainment industry. *Computer*, 11 (3), March 1978.

————. The use of grayscale for improved raster display of vectors and characters. SIGGRAPH '78 proceedings, published as *Computer Graphics*, 12 (3), August 1978.

————. A comparison of antialiasing techniques. *IEEE Computer Graphics and Applications*, 1 (1), January 1981.

Csuri, C. A. Real-time computer animation. IFIP, 1974. Amsterdam: North-Holland, 1974.

Curry, C. K. Electronic CAD innovations. *Computer Graphics World*. March 1984.

Danielsson, P. E. Comments on a circle generator for display devices. *Computer Graphics and Image Processing*, 7 (2), April 1978.

Date, C. An introduction to database systems, 3d ed. Reading, Mass.: Addison-Wesley, 1981.

Dawson, F. CAD in the A/E environment. *CADCON East 84*, Boston, June 12, 1984. New York: Morgan-Grampian.

Day, D. The ATE/CAD interface—what are the benefits? *ATE East*, June 11–14, 1984, Boston, Mass. New York: Morgan-Grampian.

DeFanti, T. A. The digital component of the circle graphics habitat. NCC 1976. Montvale, N.J.: AFIPS Press.

————, ed. SIGGRAPH Video Tape Review, No. 1, 1980.

Denert, E. GRAPHEX68: Graphical language features in algol 68. *Computers and Graphics*, 1, 1975.

Denes, P. R., and Gershkoff, I. K. An interactive system for page layout design. *Proc. ACM National Conference*, 1974.

Denes, P. B. A scan-type graphics system for interactive computing. *Proc. IEEE Conference on Computer Graphics, Pattern Recognition and Data Structure*, May 1975.

Denham, D., and Singer, M. Enhancing color display resolution. *Computer Graphics World*, December, 1983.

Dertouzos, M. L., and Graham, H. L. A parametric graphical display technique for online use. FJCC, 1966. Washington, D.C.: Spartan Books.

Dill, J. D., and Thomas, J. J. On the organization of a remote low cost intelligent graphics terminal. SIGGRAPH '75 proceedings, published as *Computer Graphics*, 9 (2), 1975.

Dionne, M. S., and Mackworth, A. K. ANTICS: a system for animating LISP programs. *Computer Graphics and Image Processing*, 7(1), February 1978.

Donovan, K. Trends in the low-cost CAD market. *Computer Graphics World*, April 1983.

Doros, M. Algorithms for generations of discrete circles, rings, and disks. *Computer Graphics and Image Processing*, 10 (4), August 1979.

Drucker, P. F. The age of discontinuity: guidelines to our changing society. New York: Harper & Row, 1968.

Dube, R., Herron, G. J., Little, F. F., and Riesenfeld, R. F. SURFED: an interactive editor for free-form surfaces. *Computer Aided Design*, 10 (2), March 1978.

Duda, R. D., and Hart, P. E. Experiments in the recognition of hand-printed text, II: context analysis. FJCC, 1968. Washington, D.C.: Thompson Books, 1968.

Dungan, W., Stenger, A., and Sutty, G. Texture tile considerations for raster graphics. SIGGRAPH '78 proceedings, published as *Computer Graphics*, 12 (3), August 1978.

Eastman, C., Lividini, J., and Stoker, D. A database for designing large physical systems. NCC, 1975. Montvale, N.J.: AFIPS Press.

Eastman, C. M., and Henrion, M. GLIDE: a language for design information systems. SIGGRAPH '77 proceedings, published as *Computer Graphics*, 11 (2), 1977.

Embley, D., and Nagy, G. Behavioral aspects of text editors. *Computing Surveys*, 13 (1), March 1981.

Embley, L. Standardizing A/E/C graphics. *Computer Graphics World*, November 1983.

Encarnacao, J., et al. The workstation concept of GKS and the resulting conceptual differences to the GSPC core system. SIGGRAPH '80 proceedings, published as *Computer Graphics*, 14 (3), July 1980.

Engel, S., and Granda, R. Guidelines for man/display interfaces. Technical Report TR 00.2720, 1975, IBM, Poughkeepsie, N.Y.

English, R. E. Systems management of a CAD/CAM instation. *CADCON East 84*, Boston, June 13, 1984. New York: Morgan-Grampian.

Entwisle, J. An image-processing approach to computer graphics. *Computers and Graphics*, 2 (2), 1977.

Estes, V. Robots—the key to the factory with a future. *Automated Manufacturing*, Greenville, N.C., March 19–22, 1984.

Evans & Sutherland Computer Corporation. Picture System 2 User's Manual. Salt Lake City, Utah, May 1977.

_____. Picture System 2/PDP-11 Reference Manual, E&S 901130-001-AL. Salt Lake City, Utah, 1977.

_____. PS300 User's Manual. Salt Lake City, Utah, 1981.

Everline, W. On the evaluation of e^{AT} by power series. *Proc. IEEE (letters)*, March 1967.

Ewald, R. H., and Fryer, R., eds. Final report of the GSPC state-of-the-art subcommittee. *Computer Graphics*, 12 (1/2), June 1978.

Fabrycky, W. J., Ghare, P. M., and Torgersen, P. E. Industrial operations research. Englewood Cliffs, N.J.: Prentice-Hall, 1972.

Faux, I. D., and Pratt, M. J. Computational geometry for design manufacture. New York: Wiley, 1979.

Feiner, S., Nagy, S., and van Dam, A. An integrated system for creating and presenting complex computer-based documents. SIGGRAPH '81 proceedings, published as *Computer Graphics*, 15 (3), August 1981.

Feldmann, R. J. The design of computing systems for molecular modeling. *Ann. Rev. Biophys. Bioeng.*, 5, 1976.

Feng, D. Y., and Riesenfeld, R. F. A symbolic system for computer-aided development of surface interpolants. *Software Pract. Exper.*, 8 (4), July–August 1978.

Fenves, S. J., and Branin, F. H., Jr. A network-topological formulation of structural analysis. *ASCE J. Struct. Div.*, August 1963.

Fields, A., Maisano, R., and Marshall, C. A comparative analysis of methods for tactical data inputting. Army Research Institute, 1977.

Finkel, J. I. Improved software for IC layout. *Computer-aided Engineering*, November–December 1983.

Fisher, M. A., and Nunley, R. E. Raster graphics for spatial applications. *Computer Graphics*, 9 (2), Summer 1975.

Floyd, R. W., and Steinberg, L. An adaptive algorithm for spatial gray scale. *SID 1975 Int. Symp. Dig. Tech. Papers*.

Foley, J. D. Evaluation of small computers and display controls for computer graphics. *Computer Group News*, 3 (1), Jan./Feb. 1970.

_____. An approach to the optimum design of computer graphics systems. *Communications of the ACM*, 14 (6), June 1971.

_____. Managing the design of user-computer interfaces. *Computer Graphics World*, December 1983.

_____. Software for satellite graphics systems. *Proc. of the ACM 1973 Annual Conference*.

_____. A tutorial on satellite graphics systems. *Computer*, 9 (8), August 1976.

_____. User's manual: GWU core system with raster extensions. The George Washington University, Dept. of EE&CS, Technical Report GWU-E/CS-7913, Washington, D.C., 1979.

_____. The structure of interactive command language. In R. A. Guedj, et al., eds., Methodology of interaction. Amsterdam: North-Holland, 1980.

Foley, J. D., and Wallace, V. L. The art of natural graphic man-machine conversation. *Proc. IEEE*, 62 (4), April 1974.

Foley, J. D., Templeman, J., and Dastyar, D. Some raster graphics extensions to the core system. SIGGRAPH '79 proceedings, published as *Computer Graphics*, 13 (2), August 1979.

Foley, J. D., Wallace, V., and Chan, P. The human factors of interaction techniques. The George Washington University, Institute for Information Science and Technology, Technical Report GWU-IIST-81-03, Washington, D.C., 1981.

Foley, J. D., and Wenner, P. A. The George Washington University core system implementation. SIGGRAPH '81 proceedings, published as *Computer Graphics*, 15 (3), August 1981.

Forrest, A. R. Interactive interpolation of approximation by bezier polynomials. *Computer J.*, 15 (1), January 1972.

_____. Mathematical principles for curve and surface representation. In *Curved Surfaces in Engineering*, I. J. Brown, ed. Guildford, Surrey, England: IPC Science and Technology Press Ltd., 1972.

_____. A computer peripheral for making three-dimensional models. *Automatisme*, 16 (6/7), June/July 1974.

Forrest, D. R. On Coons and other methods for the representation of curved surfaces. *Computer Graphics and Image Processing*, (1) 4, December 1972.

Freeman, H. Computer processing of line-drawing images. *Computer Surveys*, 6 (1), March 1974.

Freeman, H., and Loutrel, P. P. An algorithm for the solution of the two-dimensional hidden-line problem. *IEEE Transactions on Computers*, EC-16 (6), December 1967.

Fryer, R. A Fortran windowing technique for simulation and CAD. *Proceedings Vector General User's Group*, 1972.

Fuchs, H. Distributing a visible surface algorithm over multiple processors. *Proceedings 1977 ACM National Conference.*

Fuchs, H., Duran, J., and Johnson, B. A system for automatic acquisition of three-dimensional data. NCC, 1977. Montvale, N.J.: AFIPS Press.

Fuchs, H., Kedem, Z. M., and Uselton, S. P. Optimal surface reconstruction from planar contours. *Communications of the ACM*, 20 (19), October 1977.

Fuchs, H., and Barros, J. Efficient generation of smooth line drawings on video displays, SIGGRAPH '79 proceedings, published as *Computer Graphics*, 13 (2), August 1979.

Futrelle, R. P. GALATEA: interactive graphics for the analysis of moving images. IFIP, 1974. Amsterdam: North-Holland.

Galimberti, R., and Montanari, U. An algorithm for hidden-line elimination. *Communications of the ACM*, 12 (4), April 1969.

Garrett, M. Logical pick device simulation algorithms for the core system. *Computer Graphics*, 13 (4), February 1980.

————. Unified non-procedural environment for designing and implementing graphical interfaces to relational data base management systems. Ph.D. dissertation, The George Washington University, Washington, D.C., 1980.

Germann, J. J. Using special processors to enhance engineering workstations. *CAD/CAM West 84*, San Francisco, February 7–9, 1984. New York: Morgan-Grampian.

Geyer, K. E., and Wilson, K. R. Computing with feeling. *Proc. IEEE Conference on Computer Graphics, Pattern Recognition and Data Structure*, May 1975.

Ghosh, H. N., de la Mondea, F. H., and Dono, N. R. Computer-aided transistor design, characterization and optimization. *Proc. IEEE*, vol. 55, pp. 1897–1912, November 1967.

Giloi, W. Interactive computer graphics—data structures, algorithms, languages. Englewood Cliffs, N.J.: Prentice-Hall, 1978.

Gino-F user manual. Issue 2. Computer-Aided Design Centre, Cambridge, England, December 1976.

Glenn, B. T. Alphabet and text in presentation graphics. *Computer Graphics World*, January 1984.

Goldberg, Adele, and Robson, David. A metaphor for user interface design. Xerox Palo Alto Research Center, 1979.

Gonzalez, M. J., and Ramamoorthy, C. V. Parallel task execution in a decentralized system. *IEEE Transactions on Computers*, December 1972.

Goodwin, N. Cursor positioning on an electronic display using lightpen, lightgun or keyboard for three basic tasks. *Human Factors*, 17 (3), June 1975.

Gordon, W. J., and Riesenfeld, R. F. Bernstein-Bezier methods for the computer-aided design of free-form curves and surfaces. *Journal of the ACM* 21 (2), April 1974.

————. B-spline curves and surfaces. In R. Barnhill and R. F. Riesenfeld, eds., Computer aided geometric design. New York: Academic Press, 1974.

Gouraud, H. Continuous shading of curved surfaces. *IEEE Transactions on Computers*, C-20 (6), June 1971.

Grant, E., and Leavenworth, R. S. Statistical quality control. New York: McGraw-Hill, 1972.

Griffiths, J. G. A surface display algorithm. *Computer Aided Design*, 10 (1), January 1978.

————. A bibliography of hidden-line and hidden-surface algorithms. *Computer Aided Design*, 10 (3), May 1978.

Groff, G. K., and Muth, I. F. Operations management: analysis for decisions. Homewood, Ill.: Irwin, 1972.

Grossman, D. D. Procedural representation of three-dimensional objects. *IBM J. Res. Dev.*, 20 (6), November 1976.

Status report of the graphics standards committee. *Computer Graphics* 13 (3), August 1979.

Guedj, R., et al., eds. Methodology of interaction. Amsterdam: North-Holland, 1980.

Gupta, S., and Sproull, R. Filtering edges for gray-scale displays. SIGGRAPH '81 proceedings, published as *Computer Graphics*, 15 (3), August 1981.

Gupta, S., and Sproull, R. A VLSI architecture for updating raster-scan displays. SIGGRAPH '81 proceedings, published as *Computer Graphics*, 15 (3), August 1981.

Gurwitz, R. F., et al. BUMPS: a program for animating projections. SIGGRAPH '80 proceedings, published as *Computer Graphics*, 14 (3), July 1980.

Gurwitz, R., Fleming, R., and van Dam, A. MIDAS: a microprocessor instructional display and animation system. *IEEE Transactions on Education*, February 1981.

Hamlin, G., and Gear, C. Raster-scan hidden surface algorithm techniques. SIGGRAPH '77 proceedings, published as *Computer Graphics*, 11 (2), Summer 1977.

Hanau, P. R., and Lenorovitz, D. R. Prototyping and simulation tools for user/computer dialogue design. SIGGRAPH '80 proceedings, published as *Computer Graphics*, 14 (2), July 1980.

Hansen, W. User engineering principles for interactive systems. *Proceedings 1971 Fall Joint Computer Conference*.

Harrison, S. Coordinating A/E/C CAD. *Computer Graphics World*, November 1983.

Hartke, D. H., Sterling, W. M., and Shemer, J. E. Design of a raster display processor for office applications. *IEEE Transactions on Computers,* C-27 (4), April 1978.

Hayes, P., Ball, E., and Reddy, R. Breaking the man-machine communication barrier. *Computer*, 14 (3), March 1981.

Heindel, L., and Roberto, J. LANG-PAK—an interactive language design system. New York: Elsevier, 1975.

Helmers, C. T., ed. Robotics age, in the beginning. Rochelle Park, N.J.: Hayden, 1983.

Herot, C. F. Graphical input through machine recognition of sketches. *Computer Graphics*, 10 (2), Summer 1976.

_____ et al. A prototype spatial data base management system. SIGGRAPH '80 proceedings, published as *Computer Graphics*, 14 (2), July 1980.

Hersksowitz, G. J., ed. Computer-aided integrated circuit design. New York: McGraw-Hill, 1968.

Hertz, C. H., and Mansson, A. Color plotter for computer graphics using three electrically controlled ink jets. IFIP, 1974. Amsterdam: North-Holland.

Hoehm, H. J., and Martel, R. A. A 60 line per inch plasma display panel. *IEEE Transactions on Electronic Devices*, ED-18 (9), September 1971.

Hordeski, M. F. Digital control of microprocessors. *Electronic Design*, December 6, 1975.

_____. Digital sensors simplify digital measurements. *Measurements and Data*, May–June, 1976.

_____. When should you use pneumatics, when electronics? *Instruments & Control Systems*, November 1976.

_____. Guide to digital instrumentation for temperature, pressure instruments. *Oil, Gas and Petrochem. Equipment*, November 1976.

_____. Digital instrumentation for pressure, temperature/pressure, readout instruments. *Oil, Gas and Petrochem. Equipment*, December 1976.

_____. Innovative design: microprocessors. *Digital Design*. December 1976.

_____. Passive sensors for temperature measurement. *Instrumentation Technology*, February 1977.

_____. Adapting electric actuators to digital control. *Instrumentation Technology*, March 1977.

————. Fundamentals of digital control loops and factors in choosing pneumatic or electronic instruments. Presentation at the SCMA Instrumentation Short Course, Los Angeles, April 6, 1977.

————. Balancing microprocessor-interface tradeoffs. *Digital Design*, April 1977.

————. Digital position encoders for linear applications. *Measurements and Control*, July–August 1977.

————. Future microprocessor software. *Digital Design*, August 1977.

————. Radiation and stored data. *Digital Design*, September 1977.

————. Microprocessor chips. *Instrumentation Technology*, September 1977.

————. Process controls are evolving fast. *Electronic Design*, November 22, 1977.

————. Fundamentals of digital control loops. *Measurements & Control*, February 1978.

————. Using microprocessors. *Measurements & Control*, June 1978.

————. Illustrated dictionary of micro computer terminology. Blue Ridge Summit, Pa.: Tab, 1978.

————. Microprocessor cookbook. Blue Ridge Summit, Pa.: Tab, 1979.

————. Selecting test strategies for microprocessor systems. *ATE Seminar Proceedings*, Pasadena, Calif., January 1982. New York: Morgan-Grampian.

————. Selection of a test strategy for MPU systems. *Electronics Test*, February 1982.

————. Trends in displacement sensors. *Sensors and Systems Conference Proceedings*, Pasadena, Calif., May 1982. Campbell, Calif.: Network Exhibitions.

————. The impact of 16-bit microprocessors. *Instrumentation Symposium Proceedings*, Las Vegas, May 1982. Research Triangle Park, N.C.: Instrument Society of America.

————. Diagnostic strategies for microprocessor systems. *ATE Seminar Proceedings*, Anaheim, Calif., January 1983. New York: Morgan-Grampian.

————. The human interface in CAD/CAM product design. *CADCON West*, San Francisco, February 7–9, 1984. New York: Morgan-Grampian.

————. Microprocessors in industry. New York: Van Nostrand Reinhold, 1984.

————. The design of microprocessor sensor and control systems. Reston, Va.: Reston, 1984.

Horn, B. K. P. Circle generator for display devices. *Computer Graphics and Image Processing*, 5, 1976.

Hornbuckle, G. D. The computer graphics/user interface. *IEEE Trans*. HFE-8 (1), March 1967.

Hosaka, M., and Kimura, F. An interactive geometrical design system with handwriting input. IFIP, 1977. Amsterdam: North-Holland.

Houtzel, A. The graphics side of group technology. *CADCON East 84*, Boston, June 13, 1984. New York: Morgan-Grampian.

Hubschman, H., and Zucker, S. Frame-to-frame coherence and the hidden surface computation: constraints for a convex world. SIGGRAPH '81 proceedings, published as *Computer Graphics*, 15 (3), August 1981.

Hudry, J. Man-machine interface issues. *Computer Graphics World*, April 1984.

Hunt, R. W. G. The reproduction of color, 3d ed. New York: Wiley, 1975.

Ingalls, D. The smalltalk graphics kernel. Special issue on Smalltalk, *BYTE*, 6 (8), August 1981.

Intel Corp. 8086 user's guide. Santa Clara, Calif.: Intel, 1976.

Irani, K., and Wallace, V. On network linguistics and the conversational design of queueing networks. *Journal of the ACM*, 18, October 1971.

Irby, C. H. Display techniques for interactive text manipulation. NCC, 1974. Montvale, N.J.: AFIPS Press.

Jackson, M. A. Principles of program design. New York: Academic, 1975.

Jarvis, J. F. The line drawing editor: schematic diagram editing using pattern recognition techniques. *Computer Graphics and Image Processing*, 6 (5), October 1977.

Jarvis, J. F., Judice, C. N., and Ninke, W. H. A survey of techniques for the image display of continuous tone pictures on bilevel displays. *Computer Graphics and Image Processing* 5 (1), March 1976.

Jarvis, J. F., and Roberts, C. S. A new technique for displaying continuous tone images on a bilevel display. *IEEE Trans.*, Com-24 (8), August 1976.

Jensen, Kathleen, and Wirth, Niklaus. Pascal user manual and report. 2d ed. New York: Springer-Verlag, 1974.

Jern, M. Color jet plotter. *Computer Graphics*, 11 (1), Spring 1977.

Joblove, G. H., and Greenberg, D. Color spaces for computer graphics. SIGGRAPH '78 proceedings, published as *Computer Graphics*, 12 (3), August 1978.

Johnson, C. Solids modeling. *CADCON East 84*, Boston, June 12, 1984. New York: Morgan-Grampian.

Johnson, S., and Lesk, M. Language development tools. *The Bell System Technical Journal*, 57 (6, 2), July–August 1978.

Jordan, B. W., Jr., and Barrett, R. C. A scan conversion algorithm with reduced storage requirements. *Communications of the ACM*, 16 (11), November 1973.

Jordan, B. W., Lennon, W. J., and Holm, B. C. An improved algorithm for the generation of non-parametric curves. *IEEE Transactions on Computers*, C-22 (12), December 1973.

Jordan, B. W., Jr., and Barrett, R. C. A cell organized raster display for line drawings. *Communications of the ACM*, 17 (2), February 1974.

Judice, J. N., Jarvis, J. F., and Ninke, W. Using ordered dither to display continuous tone pictures on an AC plasma panel. *Proc. SID*, Fourth Quarter 1974.

Kajiya, J. T., Sutherland, I. E., and Cheadle, E. C. A random-access video frame buffer. *Proc. IEEE Conf. on Computer Graphics, Pattern Recogition and Data Structure*, May 1975.

Kaplan, M., and Greenberg, D. Parallel processing techniques for hidden surface algorithms. SIGGRAPH '79 proceedings, published as *Computer Graphics*, August 1979.

Kaprow, A. The designer's workstation. *Computer Graphics for Design*, April 14, 1984, Pratt Center, Hawthorne, New York.

Kay, Alan C. Microelectronics and the personal computer. *Scientific American*, 237 (3), September 1977.

Kay, D., and Greenberg, D. Transparency for computer synthesized images. SIGGRAPH '79 proceedings, published as *Computer Graphics*, 13 (2), August 1979.

Keller, P. Standardizing CRT measurements. *Test & Measurement World*, April 1984.

Kelly, K., and Judd, D. COLOR—Universal language and dictionary of names. National Bureau of Standards Spec. Publ. 440, Government Printing Stock No. 003-003-01705-1, 1976.

Kemper, A. The architectural data base. *Computer Graphics for Design*, Pratt Center, Hawthorne, New York, April 14, 1984.

Kennedy, J. R. A system for timesharing graphic consoles. FJCC, 1966. Washington, D.C.: Spartan Books.

Kilgour, A. C. The evolution of a graphic system for linked computers. *Software—Practice and Experience*, 1, 1971.

_____. A hierarchical model of a graphics system. *Computer Graphics*, 15 (1), April 1981.

Klemmer, E. T. Keyboard entry. *Applied Ergonomics*, March 1971.

Knapp, J. M. The ergonomic millennium. *Computer Graphics World*, June 1983.

Knott, G. D., and Reece, D. K. Modelab: a civilized curved-fitting system. *Proc. ONLINE '72*, Uxbridge, England, September 1972.

Knowlton, K. C. Virtual pushbuttons as a means of person-machine interaction. *Proc. IEEE Conf. on Computer Graphics, Pattern Recognition, and Data Structure*, May 1975.

Knowlton, K. C., and Harmon, L. Computer-produced gray scales. *Computer Graphics and Image Processing*, 1 (1), April 1972.

Knuth, D. E. The art of computer programming. Volume 1: Fundamental algorithms. Reading, Mass.: Addison-Wesley, 1973.

Kriloff, H. Human factor considerations for interactive display systems. In S. Trem, ed. *Proceedings ACM/SIGGRAPH Workshop on User-Oriented Design of Interactive Graphics Systems*. ACM, 1976.

Kroemer, K. H. E. Human engineering the keyboard. *Human Factors*, 14 (1), February 1974.

Kuenning, M. K. Programmable controllers: configuration and programming. *Automated Manufacturing*, Greenville, S.C., March 19–22, 1984.

Kuo, F. F. Network analysis by digital computer. *Proc. IEEE*, June 1966.

Lafue, G. Recognition of three-dimensional objects from orthographic views. SIGGRAPH '76 proceedings, published as *Computer Graphics*, 10 (2), Summer 1976.

Laib, G., Puk, R., and Stowell, G. Integrating solid image capability into a general purpose calligraphic graphics package. SIGGRAPH '80 proceedings, published as *Computer Graphics*, 14 (3), July 1980.

Lampson, Butler W. Bravo manual. In Alto user's handbook. Palo Alto, Calif.: Xerox Palo Alto Research Center, November 1978.

Land, E. H. The retinex theory of color vision. *Scientific American*, December 1977.

Lane, J., and Carpenter, L. A generalized scan line algorithm for the computer display of parametrically defined surfaces. *Computer Graphics and Image Processing*, 11, 1979.

Lawrence, S., and Marcus, L. S. Designing PC boards with a centralized database. *Computer Graphics World*, March 1984.

Leahy, W. Data base management—automated graphics generation. *CADCON East 84*, Boston, June 12, 1984. New York: Morgan-Grampian.

Leininger, M. Present and future developments in robotic applications. *Automated Manufacturing*, Greenville, S.C., March 19–22, 1984.

Levin, J. A parametric algorithm for drawing pictures of solid objects composed of quadric surface. *Communications of the ACM*, 19 (10), October 1976.

————. QUADRIL: a computer language for the description of quadric-surface bodies. SIGGRAPH '80 proceedings, published as *Computer Graphics*, 14 (3), July 1980.

Levoy, M. A color animation system based on the multiplane technique. SIGGRAPH '77 proceedings, published as *Computer Graphics*, 11 (2), Summer 1977.

Lieberman, H. How to color in a coloring book. SIGGRAPH '78 proceedings, published as *Computer Graphics*, 12 (3), August 1978.

Liou, M. L. A novel method of evaluating transient response. *Proc. IEEE*, January 1966.

Lipscomb, J. Three-dimensional cues for a molecular computer graphics system. Ph.D. dissertation, Dept. of Computer Science, University of North Carolina, Chapel Hill, 1979.

Lloyd, G. Managing the CAD transition in the design. *CADCON East 84*, Boston, June 22, 1984. New York: Morgan-Grampian.

Loutrel, P. P. A solution to the hidden-line problem for computer drawn polyhedra. *IEEE Transactions on Computers*, EC-19 (3), March 1970.

Lunden, J. W. Intelligent vision: rapid advances in industrial automation. *Automated Manufacturing*, Greenville, S.C., March 19–22, 1984.

Magnenat-Thalmann, N., and Thalmann, D. A graphical Pascal extension based on graphical types. *Software—Practice and Experience*, 11, 1981.

Mallgren, A., and Shaw, A. C. Graphical transformations and hierarchic picture structures. *Computer Graphics and Image Processing*, 8, October 1978.

Manos, B. Intelligent digital plotters. *Computer Graphics World*, May 1983.

Marcus, A. Computer-assisted chart making from the graphic designer's perspective. SIGGRAPH '80 proceedings, published as *Computer Graphics*, 14 (3), July 1980.

Martin, J. Design of man-computer dialogues. Englewood Cliffs, N.J.: Prentice-Hall, 1973.

Martin, W. A. Computer input/output of mathematical expressions. *Second Symposium Symbolic Algebraic Manipulation, ACM*, March 1971.

Max, N., and Clifford, W., Jr. Computer animation of the sphere eversion. *Computer Graphics*, 9 (1), Spring 1975.

McCool, M. Interfacing CAD/CAM with ATE. *ATE West*, January 10–13, 1983.

McCracken, T. E., Sherman, B. W., Dwyer, S. J., III. An economical tonal display for interactive graphics and image analyst data. *Computers and Graphics*, 1 (1), 1975.

McKay, C. W. An approach to distributing intelligence among a network of cooperative, autonomous, functional computing clusters. *Automated Manufacturing*, Greenville, S.C., March 19–22, 1984.

McLain, D. H. Computer construction of surfaces through arbitrary points. Amsterdam: North-Holland, 1974.

McManigal, D., and Stevenson, D. Architecture of the IBM 3277 graphics attachment. *IBM Systems Journal*, 19 (3), 1980.

Mehr, M. H., and Mehr, E. Manual digital positioning in 2 axes: a comparison of joystick and track ball controls. *Proceedings 16th Annual Meeting, Human Factors Society*, 1972.

Metcalfe, R. M., and Boggs, D. R. ETHERNET: distributed packet switching for local computer networks. *Communications of the ACM*, 19 (7), July 1976.

Meyer, G. W., and Greenberg, D. P. Perceptual color spaces for computer graphics. SIGGRAPH '80 proceedings, published as *Computer Graphics*, 14 (3), July 1980.

Meyer, J. D. Commercial machine vision systems. *Computer Graphics World*, October 1983.

Meyrowitz, N., and Moser, M. BRUWIN: an adaptable design strategy for window manager/virtual terminal systems. *Proceedings of the 8th*

Annual Symposium on Operating Systems Principles (SIGOPS), Pacific Grove, Calif., December 1981.

Michener, J. C., and Carlbom, I. B. Natural and efficient viewing parameters. SIGGRAPH '80 proceedings, published as *Computer Graphics*, 14 (3), July 1980.

Miller, K. Standardizing color CRT measurements for avionics and computers. *Test & Measurement World*, April 1984.

Miller, N. Bus-oriented graphics systems. *Computer Graphics World*, May 1983.

Miller, R. B. Response time in man-computer conversational transactions. FJCC, 1968. Montvale, N.J., AFIPS Press.

Minardi, L. R. CAD/CAM's drawing/model dichotomy. *Computer Graphics World*, January 1983.

Mitchell, W. J. Computer-aided architectural design. New York: Petrocelli-Charter, 1977.

Moran, T. The command language grammar: a representation for the user interface of interactive computer systems. *International Journal of Man-Machine Studies*, 15, 1981.

Mullins, M. Instrument controllers—evaluating cost and function. *Test & Measurement World*, April 1984.

Murch, G. M. Perceptual considerations of color. *Computer Graphics World*, July 1983.

Negroponte, N., ed. Computer aids to design and architecture. New York: Petrocelli/Charter, 1975.

_____. Raster-scan approaches to computer graphics. *Computers and Graphics*, 2 (3), 1977.

Nemeth, W. G. Selecting a graphics terminal. *Computer Graphics World*, March 1984.

Newell, M. E., Newell, R. G., and Sancha, T. L. A new approach to the shaded picture problem. *Proc. ACM Nat. Conf.*, 1972.

_____. The utilization of procedure models in digital image synthesis. University Utah Computer Science Dept., UTEC-CSc-76-218, Summer 1975.

Newgard, W. Putting the design into CADD. *Computer Graphics World*, May 1983.

Newman, W. M., and Sproull, R. F. Principles of interactive computer graphics, 2d ed. New York: McGraw-Hill, 1979.

Ng, N., and Marsland, T. Introducing graphics capabilities to several high-level languages. *Software-Practice and Experience*, 8, 1978.

Norton, F. J. CADD, human relations, and the management process. *CADCON West 84*, San Francisco, February 7–9, 1984. New York: Morgan-Grampian.

Novitsky, M. P. MRP in the process industry. *Automated Manufacturing*, Greenville, S.C., March 19–22, 1984.

Nunn, M. CAE/CAD/CAM Testability—an overview. *CADCON West 84*, San Francisco, February 7–9, 1984. New York: Morgan-Grampian.

O'Brien, Michael T. A network graphical conferencing system. Santa Monica, Calif.: RAND Corporation, 1979 (N-1250-DARPA).

Olmstead, K. The future factory—a first report. *Test & Measurement World*, December 1983.

Ottinger, L. Using robots in flexible manufacturing cells/facilities. *Automated Manufacturing*, Greenville, S.C. March 19–22, 1984.

Parent, R. E. A system for sculpting 3-D data. SIGGRAPH '77 proceedings, published as *Computer Graphics*, 11 (2), Summer 1977.

Park, F. Simulation and expected performance analysis of multiple processor *z*-buffer systems. SIGGRAPH '80 proceedings, published as *Computer Graphics*, 14 (3), July 1980.

Pavlidis, T. Filling algorithms for raster graphics. *Computer Graphics and Image Processing*, 10 (2), June 1979.

————. Contour filling in raster graphics. SIGGRAPH '81 proceedings, published as *Computer Graphics*, 15 (3), August 1981.

Pearson, D. E. Transmission and display of pictorial information. New York: Halstead Press (Wiley), 1975.

Pearson, D. J. Graphics workstation intelligence. *Computer Graphics World*, January 1983.

Peters, G. J. Interactive computer graphics application of the bi-cubic parametric surface to engineering design problems. NCC, 1974. Montvale, N.J.: AFIPS Press.

Pferd, W. A new boost with automated data capture. *Computer Graphics World*, March 1983.

Pfister, G. F. A high level language extension for creating and controlling dynamic pictures. *Computer Graphics*, 10 (1), Spring 1976.

Piller, E. Real-time scan unit with improved picture quality. *Computer Graphics*, 14 (1 & 2), July 1980.

Pinto, J. Artificial intelligence and robotics in the future factory. *Test & Measurement World*, December 1983.

Poiker, T. K. An intelligent cursor. *Computer Graphics World*, October 1983.

Porter, T. Spherical shading. SIGGRAPH '78 proceedings, published as *Computer Graphics*, 12 (3), August 1978.

————. The shaded surface display of large molecules. SIGGRAPH '79 proceedings, published as *Computer Graphics*, 13 (2), August 1979.

Prado, E. Voice input for CAD/CAM. *Computer Graphics World*, June 1983.

Preiss, R. Storage CRT display terminals: evolution and trends. *Computer*, 11 (11), November 1978.

Price, R. F. Applying optical mass memory to CAD storage. *Computer Graphics World*, January 1983.

Ramot, J. Nonparametric curves. *IEEE Transactions on Computers*, C-25 (1), January 1976.

Reisner, P. Formal grammar and human factors design of an interactive graphics system. *IEEE Trans. on Software Engineering*, SE-7 (2), March 1981.

Renfrow, N. Tools for facilities management. *CADCON East 84*, Boston, June 12, 1984. New York: Morgan-Grampian.

Requicha, A. Representations for rigid solids: theory, methods, and systems. *Computing Surveys*, 12 (4), December 1980.

Resch, R. D. Portfolio of shaded computer images. *Proc. IEEE*, 62 (4), April 1974.

Riesenfeld, R. F. Applications of B-spline approximations to geometric problems of computer-aided design. University Utah Computer Science Dept., UTEC-CSc-73-126, March 1973.

_____. Aspects of modeling in computer-aided geometric design. NCC, 1975.

_____. Non-uniform B-spline curves. *Proceedings 2nd USA-Japan Computer Conf.*, 1975.

Riley, J. Process control for a PWB facility. *Automated Manufacturing*, Greenville, S.C., March 19–22, 1984.

Robbins, M. F., and Beyer, J. D. An interactive computer system using graphical flowchart input. *Communications of the ACM*, 13 (2), February 1970.

Roberson, R. E. Automated manufacturing and management decision information. *Automated Manufacturing*, Greenville, S.C. March 19–22, 1984.

Rodden, W. P. Introduction to MSC/NASTRAN. Los Angeles: MacNeal-Schwendler, September 1982.

Rodgers, R. C. Peripherals for programmable controllers. *Computer-aided Engineering*, November/December 1982.

Rogers, D. F., and Adams, J. A. Mathematical elements for computer graphics. New York: McGraw-Hill, 1976.

Rosenfeld, A. Picture processing: 1977. *Computer Graphics and Image Processing*, 7 (2), April 1978.

Ross, C. A. Automation policies, practices and procedures. *Automated Manufacturing*, Greenville, S.C., March 19–22, 1984.

Roth, G. Integrated test functions aid in process control. *Test & Measurement World*, December 1983.

Roth, J. P. An application of algebraic topology to numerical analysis: on the existence of a solution to the network problem. *Proc. National Academy Sciences*, 1955.

Rubin, F. Generation of nonparametric curves. *IEEE Transactions Computers*, C-25 (1), January 1976.

Samit, M. L. Computer and color. *Computer Graphics for Design*. Pratt Center, Hawthorne, New York, April 14, 1984.

Sanders Corporation. The graphic 8 system. Nashua, N.H.: Sanders Corporation, 1980.

Schaeffer, E. J., and Williams, T. J. An analysis of fault detection correction and prevention in industrial computer systems. Purdue Laboratory for Applied Industrial Control, Purdue University, October 1977.

Schmidt, W. C. The promise of automatic digitizing. *Computer Graphics World*, April 1983.

Schrack, G. Design, implementation and experiences with a higher-level graphics language for interactive computer-aided design purposes. Proceedings ACM Symposium on Graphics Languages, *Computer Graphics*, 10 (1), Spring 1976.

Science Accessories Corporation. Graf/Pen Sonic Digitizer, Southport Conn.: Science Accessories Corp., 1970.

Sechrest, S., and Greenberg, D. A visible polygon reconstruction algorithm. SIGGRAPH '81 proceedings, published as *Computer Graphics*, 15 (3), August 1981.

Seybold, J. The Xerox professional workstation. *The Seybold Report*, 10 (16), August 1981.

Sherr, S. Electronic displays. New York: Wiley, 1979.

Shneiderman, B. Human factors experiments in designing interactive systems. *Computer*, 12 (12), December 1979.

Shoup, R. Color table animation. SIGGRAPH '79 proceedings, published as *Computer Graphics*, 13 (2), August 1979.

Sigsbly, B. ATE in the future factory. *Test & Measurement World*, December 1983.

Sloan, K., and Brown, C. Color map techniques. *Computer Graphics Image Processing*, 10 (4), August 1979.

Slottow, H. G. Plasma displays. *IEEE Transactions on Electron Devices*, ED-23(7), July 1976.

Smaby, G. Business graphics. *Computer Graphics World*, December 1983.

Smythe, M. Applications in mechanical CAD. *CADCON East 84*, Boston, June 12, 1984. New York: Morgan-Grampian.

Sneeringer, J. User-interface design for text editing: a case study. *Software-Practice and Experience*, 8, 1978.

Socci, V. Microprocessors in distributed graphics. *Computer Graphics World*, May 1983.

Sproull, R. F. Raster graphics for interactive programming environments. SIGGRAPH '79 proceedings, published as *Computer Graphics*, 13 (2), August 1979.

Sproull, R. F., and Thomas, E. L. A network graphics protocol. *Computer Graphics*, 8 (3), Fall 1974.

Sroczynski, C. 3D modeling in process and power plant design. *CADCON East 84*, Boston, June 12, 1984. New York: Morgan-Grampian.

Stephenson, M. B., and Christiansen, H. N. A polyhedron clipping and capping algorithm and a display system for three-dimensional finite element models. *Computer Graphics*, 9 (3), Fall 1975.

Stone, Harold. Critical load factors in two-processor distributed systems. *IEEE Transactions on Software Engineering*, SE-4 (3), May 1978.

Stover, R. N. Automating database capture for CAD/CAM. *Computer Graphics World*, March 1983.

Suenaga, Y., Kamae, T., and Kobayashi, T. A high-speed algorithm for the generation of straight lines and circular arcs. *IEEE Transactions on Computers*, TC-28 (10), October 1979.

Sutherland, I. E., and Hodgman, G. W. Reentrant polygon clipping. *Communications of the ACM*, 17 (1), January 1974.

Sutherland, I. E., Sproull, R. F., and Schumacker, R. A. A characterization of ten hidden-surface algorithms. *Computing Surveys*, 6 (1), March 1974.

Taylor, A. P. Getting a handle on factory automation. *Computer-aided Engineering*, May–June 1983.

Teicholz, E. Low cost systems for design. *Computer Graphics in Design*, Pratt Center, Hawthorne, New York, April 14, 1984.

Teschler, L. CAD for printed circuit boards. *Computer-aided Engineering*, May/June 1983.

————. Electronic design done right the first time. *Computer-aided Engineering*, September/October 1983.

Thanhouser, N. Intermixing refresh and direct view storage graphics. SIGGRAPH '78 proceedings, published as *Computer Graphics*, 10 (2), Summer 1978.

Thorton, R. W. The number wheel: a tablet based valuator for three-dimensional positioning. SIGGRAPH '79 proceedings, published as *Computer Graphics*, 13 (2), August 1979.

Three Rivers Computing Corp., Graphics display programmer's guide. Pittsburgh, Pa.: Three Rivers Computing Corp., June 1978.

Torrance, K. E., and Sparrow, E. M. Polarization, direction distribution, and off-specular peak phenomena in light reflected from roughened surfaces. *Journal Opt. Society America*, 56 (7), July 1966.

Torrance, K. E., and Sparrow, E. M. Theory for off-specular reflection from roughened surfaces. *Journal Opt. Society America*, 57 (9), September 1967.

Trowbridge, T. S., and Reitz, K. P. Average irregularity representation of roughened surfaces for ray reflection. *Journal Opt. Society America*, 65 (5), May 1975.

van Dam, A. Some implementation issues relating to data structures for interactive graphics. *International Journal of Computer and Information Sciences*, 1 (4), 1972.

Vanderbrouche, L. Selecting CAD/CAM displays. *CADCOM West 84*, San Francisco, February 7–9, 1984. New York: Morgan-Grampian.

van den Bos, J. Definition and use of higher-level graphics input tools.

SIGGRAPH '78 proceedings, published as *Computer Graphics*, 12 (3), August 1978.

van Din, P. A draftsman's interface to solid modeling. *CADCON East 84*, Boston, June 12, 1984. New York: Morgan-Grampian.

Vector General Inc. Graphics display system, model 3404. System Reference Manual, Pub. No. M110700REF. Woodland Hills, CA, 1978.

Vector General Inc. Series 3400 technical manual, Vol. I. Graphics Display System, Pub. No. M110700. Woodland Hills, CA, 1978.

Voelcker, H. B., and Requicha, A. G. Geometric modelling of mechanical parts and processes. *Computer*, December 1977.

Voelcker, H. B., et al. The PADL-1.0/2 system for defining and displaying solid objects. SIGGRAPH '78 proceedings, published as *Computer Graphics*, 12 (3), August 1978.

Wallace, V. L. The semantics of graphic input devices. SIGGRAPH/ SIGPLAN Conference on Graphics Languages, proceedings published as *Computer Graphics*, 10 (1), April 1976.

Warner, J. R. Device-independent tool systems. *Computer Graphics World*, February 1984.

Warnock, J. The display of characters using grey level sample arrays. SIGGRAPH '80 proceedings, published as *Computer Graphics*, 14 (3), July 1980.

Wasserman, G. Color vision: an historical introduction. New York: Wiley, 1978.

Watkins, G. S. A real-time visible surface algorithm. University of Utah Computer Science Dept., UTEC-CSc-70-101, June 1970, NTIS AD-762 004.

Wegner, P. Programming with ada: an introduction by means of graduated examples. Englewood Cliffs, N.J.: Prentice-Hall, 1980.

Weiler, K. Polygon comparison using a graph representation. SIGGRAPH '80 proceedings, published as *Computer Graphics*, 14 (3), July 1980.

Weiler, K., and Atherton, P. Hidden surface removal using polygon area sorting. SIGGRAPH '77 proceedings, published as *Computer Graphics*, 11 (2), Summer 1977.

Weiman, C. Continuous anti-aliased rotation and zoom of raster images. SIGGRAPH '80 proceedings, published as *Computer Graphics*, 14 (3), July 1980.

Weisberg, D. E. Performance and productivity in CAD. *Computer Graphics World*, June 1983.

Weiss, B. Evaluating graph and chart output. *Computer Graphics World*, February 1984.

Weller, D., and Williams, R. Graphic and relational data base support for problem solving. SIGGRAPH '76 proceedings, published as *Computer Graphics*, 10 (2), Summer 1976.

West, J. Emerging importance of engineering workstations in manufacturing.

CADCON East 84, Boston, June 13, 1984. New York: Morgan-Grampian.

Westerhoff, T. Software in the future factory. *Test & Measurement World*, December 1983.

Whitted, T. An improved illumination model for shaded displays. *Communications of the ACM*, 23 (6), June 1980.

Wilde, D. J. Optimum seeking methods. Englewood Cliffs, N.J.: Prentice-Hall, 1964.

Williams, L. Casting curved shadows on curved surfaces. SIGGRAPH '78 proceedings, published as *Computer Graphics*, 12 (3), August 1978.

Williams, R. On the application of relational data structures in computer graphics. *Proceedings 1974 IFIP Congress*. Amsterdam: North-Holland.

Wong, E., and Youssefi, K. Decomposition—a strategy for query processing. *ACM Transactions on Database Systems*, September 1976.

Woodruff, G. Automated inspection of PWB's. *Automated Manufacturing*, Greenville, S.C., March 19–22, 1984.

Woodsford, P. A. The HRD-1 laser display system. SIGGRAPH '76 proceedings, published as *Computer Graphics*, 10 (2), July 1976.

Woon, P. Y., and Freeman, H. A procedure for generating visible-line projections of solids bounded by quadric surfaces. *Proceedings 1971 IFIP Congress*. Amsterdam: North-Holland, 1971.

Wright, J. A two space solution to the hidden line problem for plotting functions of two variables. *IEEE Transactions on Computers*, TC22 (1), January 1973.

Wu, S. C., Abel, J. F., and Greenburg, D. P. An interactive computer graphics approach to surface representation. *Communications of the ACM*, 20 (19), October 1977.

Yamaguchi, F. A new curve fitting method using a CRT computer display. *Computer Graphics and Image Processing*, 7 (3), June 1978.

Zambuto, D. A. Robotic system needs for non-standard components assembly in electronics manufacturing. *Automated Manufacturing*, Greenville, S.C., March 19–22, 1984.

Zeman, P. A CAD service bureau. *Computer Graphics for Design*, Pratt Center, Hawthorne, New York, April 14, 1984.

Zimmerman, H. H., and Sovereign, M. G. Quantitative models for production management. Englewood Cliffs, N.J.: Prentice-Hall, 1974.

APPENDIX A
CAD/CAM EQUIPMENT RELIABILITY

It is impossible to know exactly how a CAD/CAM system or part will react to its operating environment during its active life. But it *is* possible to decide what will probably happen by making statistical statements concerning the operation of the devices in the system.

The reliability of a device is defined as the probability that it will perform its function adequately for the period of time required under the operating environment specified. If sufficient test data of a part type has been performed, the probability of a device shorting, opening, or drifting beyond its specified parameter values can be estimated.

Reliability prediction requires the assignment of numerical probabilities to the occurrence of events and the interpretation of this information into a quantitative description of the likelihood of overall system success. The purpose of this section is to provide some background in the probability theory that is used to perform reliability analysis. Statistical theory treats randomness as an empirical phenomenon since the events that occur randomly do not have absolute predictable outcomes. The only regularity of the outcomes lies in their relative frequencies of occurrence.

Consider the placing of bets at a roulette wheel. The outcome of a single turn of the wheel cannot be predetermined, but there is a regularity in the results. A roulette wheel has 38 slots into which a ball randomly falls. The wheel is designed so that the ball is equally likely to fall in any single slot.

A series of tests should verify that each number is a winner in 1/38 of the trials. The odds against selecting a single winning number on any turn of the wheel are 37 to 1, with an average of 37 losses per 1 win.

Various definitions of probability have been proposed, and some of these definitions can be considered adequate and sufficiently rigorous. Two definitions will be considered here.

If a trial has n different equally likely possible outcomes, and in exactly m of these outcomes an attribute E appears, then on any particular trial, the probability that E appears is m/n and the probability that E does not appear is $n - m/n$. Thus

$$P(E) = \frac{m}{n} = p$$

or

$$P(\text{not } E) = P(\bar{E}) = \frac{n - m}{n} = 1 - \frac{m}{n} = 1 - p$$

This definition agrees with most intuitive concepts of probability, but it becomes weak when the outcomes are not equally likely. The second definition is equivalent, but it requires a different viewpoint. It assumes a stability in the relative frequency of occurrence of the random events.

If the ratio of the number of times the attribute E appears in n trials is m/n and this ratio approaches p as more and more trials are made, then, on any particular trial, the probability that E appears is p.

Thus

$$P(E) = \lim_{n \to \infty} \frac{m}{n} = p$$

This definition gives us a method of measuring the probability of E. It also provides a way to demonstrate probability. Assume we toss a coin: the outcomes of a head appearing and of a tail appearing are equally likely. The only way we can justify this assumption is to actually toss the coin many times. If approximately half the tosses result in heads and half result in tails, we can assume that the outcomes are equally likely. We cannot be certain, however, since if we toss a coin 1000 times, there is a definite probability that all the outcomes will be heads. But if we take the limit as the number of trials approaches infinity we can predict based on statistics that half of the outcomes will be heads and half tails.

If a CAD/CAM unit has a probability p of surviving three years of use, and a probability $q = 1 - p$ of failing before three years, then the probability that, of N units placed in use, F will have failed and $N - F$ survived at the end of three years is shown by the following:

The probability that a specified F will fail and $N - F$ will survive is $p^{N-F}q^F$. There are $N!/(N - F)!\ F!$ different permutations of N devices for the F failures and $N - F$ survivors, and each of these permutations has a probability of occurrence of $p^{N-F}q^F$. Thus the overall probability of F failures in N units is:

$$P(F \mid N, q) = \frac{N!}{(N - F)!\ F!}\ q^F p^{N-F}$$

$$= \frac{N!}{(N - F)!\ F!}\ q^F (1 - q)^{N-F} = b(F; N, q),$$

for $F = 0, 1, 2, \ldots, N$

This is the binomial distribution (b), and variables which are distributed in this manner are known as binomial distributions.

The exponential probability function is one of the basic theories used to explain electronic failures. Suppose we let each atom be acted upon by a force of decay that is constant with time. During a small time interval ΔT, the probability of failure is $\lambda \Delta T$, where λ is constant with time and is a coefficient of failure for each element. There is no warning that decay will occur. This type of event is known as *random decay*.

To calculate the probability of survival of a single element for a length of T, consider the time interval to be composed of $T/\Delta T$ intervals of length ΔT. The probability that the element will survive during this time is the product of surviving each short interval. The probability of failure for each small time interval is $\lambda\Delta T$, and the probability of survival is $1 - \lambda\Delta T$.

$$P(\text{survival to time } T) = (1 - \lambda\Delta T)\frac{T}{\Delta T}$$

$$= \lim_{\Delta T \to 0} (1 - \lambda\Delta T)\frac{T}{\Delta T}$$

$$= C^{-\lambda T}$$

The probability of survival decreases exponentially as the required time of survival increases.

Investigations into the causes and nature of failures of electronic devices show that the rule of random failure applies. The errors incurred by assuming that electronic failures are random are very small, and by assuming random failures, estimates of the reliability of complete CAD/CAM systems can be made by knowing the failure rates of the individual units.

Now consider a CAD/CAM system consisting of n units with failure rates $\lambda 1, \lambda 2, \ldots\ldots, \lambda n$. If the failure of one unit (a failure refers to either complete breakdown of the unit or a degradation of important characteristics; this implies failure of a part or circuit), then the reliability of the system is the product of the reliability of the parts.

Reliability of part $i = e^{-\lambda_i T}$
Reliability of system $= e^{-(\lambda_1 + \lambda_2 + \ldots \lambda_n)T}$

Thus the failure rate of the system is the sum of the failure rates of the parts.

This type of estimate of the reliability of a system is conservative in some ways. If all the components remain within specifications, the system will function properly. It is quite likely that some of the devices can drift beyond specification without causing failure of the system while others may have less design margin and cause failures when they are within specification. We can, however, predict the reliability for circuits and systems with satisfactory results. When electronic parts fail, they are usually discarded. When a circuit or system fails, it can usually be repaired by replacing one or two failed parts.

When discussing the reliability of a complex system, a repair is not only possible but necessary. A large system requiring 25,000 parts each having a three-year reliability of 0.9999 has an overall three-year reliability of less than

0.2. Thus it may not only be necessary to estimate the reliability of a system for the specified operational life, but also to estimate the probability that one, two, or more failures will occur until some system degradation limit is reached.

To determine the probability that a system will fail F times during an operational time T, we can assume that the failed parts are replaced quickly so that it is unnecessary to consider the nonoperational failure rates compared to the operational times. The operational time is divided into $T/\Delta T$ intervals of length T. Since the system's failure rate is λ, the probability of failure during any interval is $\lambda\Delta T$. The problem now reduces to the probability that the system will fail in each of F intervals and survive in $T/\Delta T - F$ intervals. This is a characteristic of a binomially distributed probability.

$$P(F \text{ failures}) = \lim_{\Delta T \to 0} \frac{\left(\dfrac{T}{\Delta T}\right)!}{\left(\dfrac{T}{\Delta T} - F\right)! \, F!} (\lambda\Delta T)^F (1 - \lambda\Delta T)^{\frac{T}{\Delta T} - F}$$

$$= P(F \mid \lambda T) = \frac{(\lambda T)^F}{F!} e^{-\lambda T}, \quad F = 0, 1, 2 \ldots \infty$$

This gives the Poisson distribution of F. Studies of failure trends in electronic equipment show that the Poisson statistics provide a good description of the distribution of failures among the various types of equipment used in CAD/CAM systems.

The expected value, which is also called the expectation or the mean for a random variable, is the value toward which the mean of a random sample of size n would tend as n becomes large. For a discrete distribution, the expected value of the random variable is

$$E(x) = \mu = \sum x_i p(x_i)$$

Here the summation is over all possible values of X.

For a continuous random variable X, the sum is replaced by an integral

$$E(X) = \mu = \int_{-\infty}^{\infty} xf(x)dx$$

The expected value of a random variable is a measure of the center of the distribution and is analogous to the center of mass. The mean of a sample approaches the expected value of the random variable as the sample size becomes infinite, but this provides no information about the spread or dispersion of the distribution. Most of the probability might be close to the mean, or it might be spread over a wide range. A measure of this spread is the variance of the distribution as defined by

$$\sigma^2 = E[(x - u)^2] = E[(x - E(x))^2]$$

This is analogous to the moment of inertia of a body. We note that

$$\sigma^2 = E[(x - E(X))^2] = E(X^2) - [E(x)]^2$$

since

$$\sigma^2 = \int_{-\infty}^{\infty} (x^2 - 2x\mu + \mu^2) f(x) dx$$

$$= \int_{-\infty}^{\infty} x^2 f(x) dx - 2\mu \int_{-\infty}^{\infty} x f(x) dx + \mu^2 \int_{-\infty}^{\infty} f(x) dx$$

$$= E(x^2) - 2\mu E(x) + \mu^2 \cdot 1$$

$$= E(x^2) - 2\mu^2 + \mu^2 = E(x^2) - [E(x)]^2$$

Another common measure of spread is the standard deviation, σ, which is the square root of the variance.

We have noted that the binomial distribution has the form

$$P(F|N, q) = \frac{N!}{(N - F)!F!} q F_p (1 - q)^{N-F}$$

The expected value of F is the number of units that can be expected to fail, of the N placed in service.

$$E(F) = \sum_{F=0}^{N} (F)P(F|N, q)$$

$$= \sum_{F=0}^{N} F \frac{N!}{(N - F)!F!} q^F (1 - q)^{N-F}$$

Since zero is the term corresponding to $F = 0$, the range of summation can be changed to $1, 2, \ldots, N$, which gives

$$\sum_{F=1}^{N} F \frac{N!}{(N - F)!F!} q^F (1 - q)^{N-F}$$

$$= \sum_{F=1}^{N} N_q \frac{(N-1)!}{(N-F)!(F-1)!} q^{F-1}(1-q)^{N-F}$$

$$= N_q \sum_{F=1}^{N} \frac{(N-1)!}{(N-F)!(F-1)!} q^{F-1}(1-q)^{N-F}$$

If we substitute a new variable $H = F - 1$ by replacing F by $1 + H$ in the sum and then summing from 0 to $N - 1$,

$$E(F) = N_q \sum_{H=0}^{N-1} \frac{(N-1)!}{(N-H-1)! \, H!} q^H (1-q)^{N-H-1}$$

$$= Nq(1)^{N-1}$$

$$= Nq$$

Thus, the expected number of failures is the number of units times the probability that a single unit will fail.

The variance of the binomial distribution is

$$\sigma^2 = E(F^2) - [E(F)]^2$$

$$= \sum_{F=0}^{N} F^2 \frac{N!}{(N-F)! \, F!} q^F (1-q)^{N-F} - (Nq)^2$$

We note that

$$F^2 = F \cdot (F - 1 + 1) = F(F - 1) + F$$

and the sum for $E(F^2)$ becomes separated into two sums.

$$\sigma^2 = \sum_{F=0}^{N} F(F-1) \frac{N!}{(N-F)! \, F!} q^F (1-q)^{N-F}$$

$$+ \sum_{F=0}^{N} F \frac{N!}{(N-F)! \, F!} q^F (1-q)^{N-F} - (Nq)^2$$

The first sum will have zero and second terms and so we can change the range of summation to $F = 2$ to $F = N$ without changing the value of the sum. The second sum is the mean of the distribution, Nq. Thus,

$$\sigma^2 = \sum_{F=2}^{N} F(F-1) \frac{N!}{(N-F)! \, F!} q^F (1-q)^{N-F} + Nq - (Nq)^2$$

$$= N(N - 1)q^z \sum_{F=2}^{N} \frac{(N - 2)!}{(N - F)!\,(F - 2)!} q^{F-2}(1 - q)^{N-F} + Nq - (Nq)^2$$

If we set $H = F - 2$, and change the range of summation in this sum to $H = 0, 1, \ldots, N - 2$, then we have the binomial expansion for

$$[q + (1 - q)]^{N-2} = 1^{N-2} = 1$$

Thus

$$\sigma^2 = N(N - 1)q^2 + Nq - (Nq)^2$$
$$= -Nq^2 + Nq$$
$$= Nq(1 - q)$$

The exponential density function is defined as

$$f(t) = \begin{cases} e^{-t}, & t \geq 0 \\ 0, & t < 0 \end{cases}$$

This gives the density of the probability of failure at time t. The expected value of this distribution is the expected life or the mean time between failures (MTBF).

$$E(t) = \int_{-\infty}^{\infty} tf(t)^{dt}$$

$$= \int_{-\infty}^{\infty} t \cdot 0 \, dt + \int_{0}^{\infty} t\lambda e^{-\lambda t} \, dt$$

$$= 0 + \lim_{L \to \infty} \left[\frac{e^{-\lambda t}}{\lambda}(-\lambda t - 1) \right]_{t=0}^{t=L}$$

$$= \lim_{L \to \infty} \left[\frac{e^{-\lambda L}}{\lambda}(-\lambda L - 1) \right] - \left[\frac{e^{-\lambda \cdot 0}}{\lambda}(-\lambda \cdot 0 - 1) \right]$$

$$= 0 + \frac{1}{\lambda} = \frac{1}{\lambda}$$

Thus, the MTBF or the expected life is the reciprocal of the failure rate. The variance of the exponential function is found by

$$\sigma^2 = E(t^2) - [E(t)]^2$$

$$= \int_{-\infty}^{\infty} t^2 f(t) dt - \left(\frac{1}{\lambda}\right)^2$$

$$= \int_{-\infty}^{\infty} t^2(0) \, dt + \int_{0}^{\infty} t^2 \lambda e^{-\lambda t} \, dt - \left(\frac{1}{\lambda^2}\right)$$

$$= 0 + \lim_{L \to \infty} \left[\frac{1}{\lambda^2} e^{-\lambda t}(-\lambda^2 t^2 - 2\lambda t - 2)\right]\Bigg|_{t=0}^{t=L} - \frac{1}{\lambda^2}$$

$$= \frac{2}{\lambda^2} = \frac{1}{\lambda^2}$$

$$= \frac{1}{\lambda^2}$$

The failure rate of an electronic device such as a microprocessor is a function of the following factors:

1. Device maturity.
2. Quality level.
3. Device complexity.
4. Temperature.
5. Ambient environment.
6. Package type.

These factors are well documented in the military standard 217 series.

The failure rates for some typical microprocessors are shown below. The ambient air is 25°C and the failure rates are in failures/10^6 hour

6800	1.0189
8085	.88184

Failure rates such as these can be used to predict the reliability of any electronic system or circuit that is used in CAD/CAM equipment. To select equipment we can use the reliability ratings developed for the various units from the different manufacturers. These are the equipment MTBFs that are based on the individual part-failure rates. These can be calculated from a library of the part-failure rates based on data taken from samples of parts specifically for this purpose. The MTBFs can be used to compare equipment, and the analysis will also show what units or boards are most likely to fail under adverse conditions. All one needs to perform such an analysis is the failure data and the parts list.

These techniques can be used in product reliability/quality programs to determine how specific methods can be devised to ensure that the reliability/quality goals are achieved. Some of the equipment areas to which these techniques have been applied include: microcomputers, energy conversion systems, multiple processor controllers, television, control systems, high voltage systems, multiplexing systems, 1750 and 1862 military standard computers, 1553 military standard interface controllers, automotive computers, manufacturing systems, digital communications systems, digital plotters, video editors, and instrumentation systems.

INDEX